Michael Eichhorn, Tiziano Bellini, and Daniel Mayenberger (Eds.)
Reverse Stress Testing in Banking

The Moorad Choudhry Global Banking Series

Series Editor
Professor Moorad Choudhry

Reverse Stress Testing in Banking

A Comprehensive Guide

Edited by
Michael Eichhorn, Tiziano Bellini,
and Daniel Mayenberger

DE GRUYTER

The views, thoughts and opinions expressed in this book represent those of the authors in their individual private capacities, and should not in any way be attributed to any employing institution, or to the authors as directors, representatives, officers, or employees of any affiliated institution. While every attempt is made to ensure accuracy, the authors or the publisher will not accept any liability for any errors or omissions herein. This book does not constitute investment advice and its contents should not be construed as such. Any opinion expressed does not constitute a recommendation for action to any reader. The contents should not be considered as a recommendation to deal in any financial market or instrument and the authors, the publisher, the editors, any named entity, affiliated body or academic institution will not accept liability for the impact of any actions arising from a reading of any material in this book.

ISBN 978-3-11-064482-1
e-ISBN (PDF) 978-3-11-064790-7
e-ISBN (EPUB) 978-3-11-064495-1
ISSN 2627-8847

Library of Congress Control Number: 2020949254

Bibliographic information published by the Deutsche Nationalbibliothek
The Deutsche Nationalbibliothek lists this publication in the Deutsche Nationalbibliografie; detailed bibliographic data are available on the internet at http://dnb.dnb.de.

© 2021 Walter de Gruyter GmbH, Berlin/Boston
Cover image: Nikada/E+/Getty Images
Typesetting: Integra Software Services Pvt. Ltd.
Printing and binding: CPI books GmbH, Leck

www.degruyter.com

MIX
Papier aus verantwortungsvollen Quellen
FSC® C083411

Acknowledgements

Many people contributed to the successful completion of this book. Key among these are the contributing authors, without whose excellence and hard work this book would not have been possible. Immense gratitude is owed to Nasir Ahmad, Claudio Albanese, Daniel Almehed, Assad Bouayoun, Fabio Caccioli, Jean-Pierre Charmaille, Iulian Cotoi, Stéphane Crépey, Jon Danielsson, Sidhartha Dash, Brandon Davies, Heike Dengler, Morgane Fouché, Philipp Gann, Jérôme Henry, Stefano Iabichino, Evgueni Ivantsov, Magdalena Kolev, Meha Lodha, Robert Macrae, Paolo Mammola, Philippe Mangold, Bahram Mirzai, Ashutosh Nawani, Torsten Pfoh, Aaron Romano, Hyun Song Shin, Robert Stamicar, Thomas Steiner, Andreas Uthemann, Marcela Valenzuela, Konrad Wälder, Olga Wälder, Ilknur Zer and Jean-Pierre Zigrand.

We also want to express our gratitude to all the people who were involved in the process of making this book.

Chapter 2: Philipp Gann would like to thank Melanie Eichhorn-Schurig for her help.

Chapter 7: Fabio Caccioli would like to thank Daniel Grigat for his collaboration on the development of the reverse stress testing model that Chapter 7 stems from.

Chapter 8: The chapter by Jérôme Henry presents his own views and not those of the ECB. The author wishes to thank the editors of the volume for having initiated this research and for their regular support, in particular Tiziano Bellini when fine-tuning the draft. The work benefited from comments by participants in the Central Banking Windsor Series seminars and in the World Finance Banking symposium, in particular from suggestions by the discussant Kangli Li. Thanks also go to Elena Rancoita for exchanges on generating stressed asset prices scenarios.

Chapter 15: Iulian Cotoi would like to thank Microsoft and notably Lindsey Allen, Xiaoyong Zhu, Jim Williams and Andrew Comas for their help on training, setting up computations in Azure ML (see) and the joint presentation at the Ai4 Finance conference.

Chapter 17: The research of Stéphane Crépey benefited from the support of the Chair Stress Test, RISK Management and Financial Steering, led by the French Ecole polytechnique and its Foundation and sponsored by BNP Paribas. The authors are thankful to Alex Miscampbell for discussions.

Chapter 18: Assad Bouayoun would like to thank Andrew Green and Ryan Ferguson, Andy Mason and Alexei Kondratyev for their help and guidance.

Chapter 21: Jon Danielsson, Robert Macrae thank the Economic and Social Research Council (UK) (grant number ES/K002309/1) and the Engineering and Physical Sciences Research Council (UK) (grant number EP/P031730/1) for their support.

Chapter 23: Heike Dengler would like to thank Dirk Brechfeld, Niklas Werner and Leonard Külpp for their help and guidance.

It is a pleasure to thank Jaya Dalal, Stefan Giesen and Natalie Jones for their careful review of earlier versions of the manuscript, their helpful comments and for suggesting several ways in which the book could be improved.

https://doi.org/10.1515/9783110647907-203

Foreword

Most people know what a bank does, and what a bank is for, but the requirement to undertake stress testing as part of a bank's routine risk management processes is less well known. The importance of undertaking reverse stress testing is of lesser familiarity still. One might say that this book, a detailed presentation of the many ins and outs of reverse stress testing (RST), is one that would command a very narrow and focused readership.

Nothing could be further from the truth! RST is a technique that has value in many industries besides banking and finance, as a tool to assist managers to get a better understanding of the risk exposures their business faces and how they should be managing these exposures. As such, contrary to initial perception, this book is actually of genuine value to most practitioners in finance, particularly those involved in any aspect of risk management.

I've learnt much from reading, and re-reading, this book. I do wish it had been around when I was first asked to undertake, and document, an RST. Back in 2013 I was with Group Treasury at the Royal Bank of Scotland and appointed the "IPO Treasurer". I was part of the executive committee responsible for what was intended to be (but never became) a spin-off from RBS, the new bank Williams & Glyn. At one stage, I and a few of my team presented the bank's liquidity adequacy assessment, or "ILAAP", to the UK Prudential Regulation Authority (PRA). During the meeting one of the supervisors asked that we include a "reverse stress test" in the ILAAP submission. I was aware of the concept, but less certain of its precise value.

"Apply a stress test that the bank would not survive," one of the PRA supervisors requested.

My initial thought was, "What about an atom bomb drop in London?" but I kept that thought to myself! My scepticism arose because I could not see the practical value-added of such a stress test; okay, we draft a storyboard that describes a scenario that "tests the balance sheet to destruction", as the parlance goes. But how does that help me as a balance sheet risk manager?

As it happens, RST can help a great deal. RST had a low profile start in bank regulation, which explained partly my unfamiliarity with its processes, but it was not a requirement unique to the UK regulatory authority. It was part of international bank supervision guidelines. But the PRA was one of the earliest regulators to require its adoption by banks as part of the capital and liquidity adequacy assessment processes.

During 2020, banks, as all corporate entities, have had to deal with managing through the market-wide stress event that has been the Covid-19 impact on the global economy. For risk managers, during this time RST came into its own. I myself have been recommending to bank asset-liability management committees (ALCOs) that they should from the start undertake more than one type of RST in order to help them determine how much balance sheet resource, in the form of capital and liquidity reserves, they could utilise in support of the customer franchise and still remain a

https://doi.org/10.1515/9783110647907-204

viable long-term concern once the crisis had passed. In effect, apply the RST and then gradually "work backwards" to a scenario that the bank *does* survive. This is an effective way to discern what level of balance sheet they can commit as they continue to undertake risk-bearing customer business.

This is but one example of the way the RST process and discipline adds value to senior executives. It tells them something that enables them to run the bank better, more efficiently and with greater understanding of risk management.

I could highlight any number of gems in this volume. The editors have done a fine job in assembling a group of high-quality commentators and practitioners in the RST field, and there is much of practical value that can be derived from studying the chapters here. Part IV of the book is dedicated to the use of artificial intelligence (AI) techniques – for instance, Natural Language Processing (NLP), Quantum Computing and Machine Learning (ML) methods for accelerating pricing, as the most advanced methods and a megatrend in the banking industry. And, of course, there is also an update on the Covid-19 stress event and its implications for stress testing.

The book moreover illustrates that RST is a flexible and versatile tool. It offers a spectrum of case studies on RST – qualitative and quantitative – ranging from portfolio and risk type level to individual banks and the entire banking system. At the same time, the book introduces new forms of RST like Reverse Liquidity Stress Testing, macro-prudential RST and Mild RST. In fact, RST can be used for non-extreme risk assessment, and not just "fat tail" risk. Its usage does not need to be restricted to tail risk alone. For example, with Mild RST the editors introduce a less severe form of RST.

Ordinary banking business entails risk. Bank practitioners should embrace any knowledge, tool and technique that assists them in the process of managing such risk. This book belongs in all three categories of usefulness. It's a supreme, and superior effort, and deserves the widest possible readership.

Moorad Choudhry FCSI FLIBF FIoD FRM
Surrey, England
30th September 2020

Contents

Part III: **Qualitative Use Cases**

Part IV: **Application of Artificial Intelligence, Quantum Computing and Technology**

Michael Eichhorn, Tiziano Bellini, Daniel Mayenberger

1 Reverse Stress Testing: A Versatile Thinking Tool

Definitions, Objectives, Challenges, Configurations
and Organisation of the Book

1.1 Motivation

To the best of our knowledge, this book is the first comprehensive collection of contributions dedicated to reverse stress testing (RST).

While we were finishing the book, the following transpired within a few weeks in June 2020:

- The Institute of Chartered Accountants in England and Wales (ICAEW) published an article with the title "Why all businesses should reverse stress test". Together with a webcast from the ICAEW Audit and Assurance Faculty, it encourages entities of all sizes and industries – from a small coffee shop to a large bank – to consider using RST to enhance their going concern assessments and related disclosures. In essence, each business should answer three questions: What would it take for the entity to fail? What event or combination of events might lead to this outcome? What can we do now to prevent this from happening? (https://www.icaew.com/insights/viewpoints-on-the-news/2020/june-2020/why-all-businesses-should-reverse-stress-test).
- On the back of the March Covid-19 market-wide stress, a Core College of regulators asked G-SIB banks to stress their revised 2020 funding plan using a combined scenario. The hypothetical scenario should start with a prolonged market-wide stress (i.e. slow L-shaped recovery from the Covid-19 crisis). It should then add a severe idiosyncratic stress with uncertainty about the survival of the bank. The combined outflows from the hypothetical scenario should push the bank significantly beyond the impacts seen in March 2020 and subsequent stress tests towards the highest severity levels of its contingency funding plan. The bank should land in a territory where it is not only in breach of its regulatory liquidity metrics requirements but is possibly in recovery and resolution. On this basis the bank should assess the remaining management actions, their feasibility, timing and execution risk.
- In a post-mortem of the Covid-19 crisis, a G-SIB bank reportedly conducted individual interviews with members of its Executive Board. The objective of the interviews was to understand how a function of the bank performed prior to, during

https://doi.org/10.1515/9783110647907-001

and after the peak of the Covid-19 crisis in March 2020. One board member suggested to run more table-top simulations to confront the board with concrete stress situations and discuss tangible trade-offs. This, he said, would be more helpful than abstract discussions around risk appetite frameworks and standard updates.

In all of these discussions, RST was repeatedly referenced. This book will help readers to further develop their own thinking and RST frameworks.

We are of the view that RST should be first and foremost considered a versatile thinking tool – an understanding that holds all subsequent individual contributions of this book together. In our opinion, it represents the cornerstone for the next generation of risk management. Indeed, a big step has been accomplished by introducing regulatory stress tests. Nevertheless, RST should provide a more comprehensive view of potential unexpected sources of risks by focusing on each bank's peculiarities. RST should be much more creative and extensively used by setting strategic and other targets. Using a spectrum of different configurations and test designs, the book is dedicated to demonstrating how RST can support deep and deliberate thinking. In fact, the main limitation of RST, in our opinion, is often not the method itself (which will also differ from case to case and be more or less difficult to overcome) but our own thinking.

The book is organised in six parts. Part I introduces RST as a versatile thinking tool with various configurations and test designs. Parts II, III and IV contain quantitative and qualitative case studies as well as applications based on artificial intelligence (AI), machine learning and quantum computing. Part V demonstrates the link between RST and recovery and resolution planning (RRP) by outlining how to best organise the infrastructure and construct the stress testing narrative and mitigating management actions. The book closes with Part VI, which provides an outlook on how the aforementioned objectives, challenges and choices will be covered in the remainder of the book.

1.2 Definition

Reverse stress testing (RST) is a concept that calls for a definition. It is useful to start by breaking down the acronym RST into its individual terms:

- The term *stress* comes originally from materials research where it denotes force over area. If the force is small, we are in the elastic regime: the medium may react linearly to external forces and tend to vibrate and revert to its original configuration. If the force is excessive, the medium may react non-linearly: firstly, it experiences plastic, irreversible deformations and then it fractures. A similar description also applies to finance: a small level of volatility and diffusion processes for risk factors can be hedged with no friction, but when shocks hit a critical threshold, friction develops and ultimately trading strategies undergo an abrupt blow up.

- The term *reverse* relates to the inversion of the cause-effect into an effect-cause relationship in the test design. In finance, traditional stress tests start with defining a (idiosyncratic and/or macro-financial) scenario and then assess its impact on their business, typically in terms of earnings, capital and liquidity. RST starts with defining the outcomes followed by reverse-engineering scenarios that, should they unfold, lead to the specified outcome. In this aspect, RST goes one step further than scenario-based stress testing, which examines synthetic future scenarios that have not already been experienced in the past and determines their financial impact. So scenario-based stress testing is *forward-looking, but it* first defines the cause (scenario) and then determines the effect (loss), while RST reverses this relationship.
- The term *testing* particularly relates to the scenarios being applied to a specific portfolio. In contrast, we know by historical experience what circumstances typically give rise to large trading book losses at financial institutions independently of their specific portfolio positions. RST instead is more specifically aimed at discovering stress scenarios that, when tested against the specific position at hand, give rise to a transient of severe friction and systematic losses or fracture. In RST, scenarios are often designed to be so severe that they "break the bank", i.e. they render the business model unviable or cause the bank to fail.

The idea to reverse a cause-effect to an effect-cause relationship is not new. Comparable resilience tests are long established in material research. They are also common practice elsewhere, e.g. in IT safety management and the military. What is new is the regulatory requirement to apply RST to analyse the failure of a bank or the unviability of its business model.

1.3 Objectives

As a complementary method to sensitivity analysis and risk measures, RST can support a variety of different objectives:
- Capture high-severity events not covered by sensitivity analysis and scenario analysis.
- Back-test the existing scenario inventory for completeness, relevance and severity.
- Complement banks' ICAAPs scenarios which were criticised for not being severe enough.
- Strengthen cross-linkage with other frameworks (ICAAP, ILAAP, recovery and resolution, risk appetite, strategy and financial planning).

- Mitigate cognitive biases such as availability bias, anchoring (to historical stress scenarios) or salience bias of traditional stress tests.
- Improve processes and methods used for regulatory stress testing.
- Support an integrated and holistic stress testing across risk types where traditional stress tests may fail to capture complex aspects from real situations.
- Identify hidden vulnerabilities that may otherwise remain undetected and are not considered during traditional stress tests.
- Identify specific vulnerabilities for individual business lines, geographies and institution size and complexity.
- Facilitate a better understanding of the dynamic interplay of risks over time and their impact on capital and liquidity – for example, between operational, conduct and reputational risk or macroeconomic, credit and structural interest rate risks.
- Understand the dynamic interplay of risks, capital and liquidity over time, including feedback loops and non-linear effects, and allow gathering insights into scenarios that involve combinations of these factors.
- Allow for a more narrative-orientated design to better capture the (inter)dependencies between risk types, financial resources and markets.
- Improve preparedness by enabling a constructive debate on the treatment of risks – decide whether they should they be accepted or managed through a combination of business activity reduction and additional controls. The broader the choice of scenarios and related mitigating actions, the better the response and the lower the actual losses in real stress occurrences.
- Provide an additional metric in risk-adjusted return quantification, comparing revenues of a business against potential losses.
- Overcome the limitation of risk models such as VaR, which break down in periods of crisis. Potentially help managers hedge against hidden scenarios.

Practitioners agree with most of these objectives. For example, a survey by Ernst & Young (2013) quotes an executive as follows:

> *"What does it take to break [a bank]," one executive said, "is a more interesting thing than just taking a random scenario and seeing what happens."*

However, at the same time, there are challenges to the implementation of RST.

1.4 Challenges

At least in parts typically stated, challenges directly relate to the aforementioned objectives:
- The search for scenarios that cause the business model to become unviable may mean that RST is by design constrained to rather remote (high severity, low

probability) scenarios. At the same time, it would be difficult to set the stress scenarios with a plausible magnitude of the stress on the risk parameters, to determine the maximum level of stress the organisation can withstand.

- The infinite number of extreme scenarios that could cause a business model to become unviable or a bank to fail creates a multiplicity challenge which requires solutions to identify the most relevant scenarios.
- The efficient search for RST scenarios that are plausible is difficult for portfolios comprised of nonlinear positions. Search algorithms need to embed a metric for plausibility and the use of AI techniques has been gaining traction to reduce the computational burden.
- Many decisions in test design (e.g. scenario choice) could suffer from the same decision biases that RST was meant to overcome in traditional stress tests.
- Storyboards may be too subjective, rather trivial, not focused on the "right vulnerabilities", or not rich enough to derive management actions.
- The integration and cross-linkage with other frameworks (ICAAP, risk appetite, planning, recovery and resolution planning) may frequently be poor as would be the coherence between the individual components of RST frameworks.
- Integrating RST with VaR platforms would be challenging since VaR models typically do not generate enough hidden scenarios around a given loss level.
- RST would create enormous complexity as it tries to simultaneously consider a vast range of risk factors and their interplay. Operationally, it requires collecting and aggregating the data, information and knowledge, spread across the bank, in a consistent and coherent manner.
- For certain risk types (e.g. Reputational Risk), an adequate quantitative modelling would not be available. However, for a holistic firm-wide RST, their integration would be imperative.
- Its one-sided focus on the downside would miss upside considerations, such as how to profit from uncertainty. Each market-wide crisis could also offer chances, e.g. win clients that in benign economic situations are unwilling to move their business.

As a consequence, practitioners, policy makers and academics consider it challenging to implement RST. The authors of the Financial Stability Institute (2018, p.13) Insights on policy implementation paper No 12, called "Stress-testing banks – a comparative analysis" consider it difficult to interpret for policy purposes:

> While helpful to identify additional vulnerabilities going forward, this approach is challenging to implement and to interpret for policy purposes, due, for example, to the diversity and complexity of interactions across risk types and factors.

1.5 How to Configure Reverse Stress Tests?

The Basel Committee on Banking Supervision (2009) chooses the following (narrow) definition:

> *Reverse stress tests start from a known stress test outcome (such as breaching regulatory capital ratios, illiquidity or insolvency) and then asking <u>what events could lead to such an outcome for the bank</u>.*

This book takes a broader view. We argue that RST does not need to be restricted to a business model scope and a high severity failure, but that it also includes situations of (less) severe frictions.

As in engineering and material research, there are many different ways and design tests, but we are interested in how elastic (linear) response turns into non-linear plasticity and finally leads to fracture and failure. In finance, users could similarly consider different scopes and levels of severity in their test design. These are just two of many configuration dimensions.

Figure 1.1 summarises typical dimensions of RST test designs and configurations, based on a review of use cases, regulatory requirements, as well as discussions with practitioners and academics. The table should be read as a morphological box – under each column, different choices are possible, resulting in a variety of possible configuration sets. The test design may also differ with regard to the sequences of steps that link these elements.

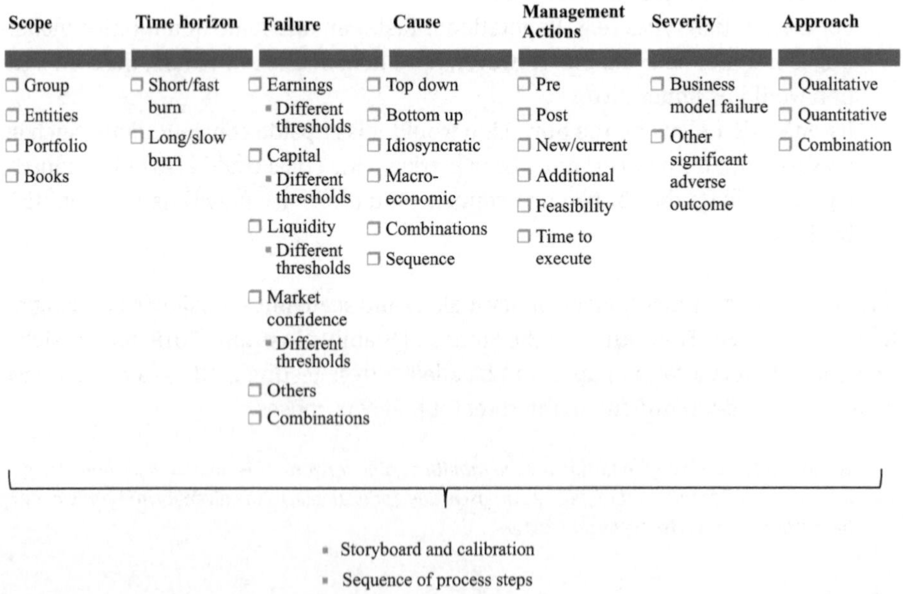

Scope	Time horizon	Failure	Cause	Management Actions	Severity	Approach
☐ Group	☐ Short/fast burn	☐ Earnings	☐ Top down	☐ Pre	☐ Business model failure	☐ Qualitative
☐ Entities		▪ Different thresholds	☐ Bottom up	☐ Post		☐ Quantitative
☐ Portfolio	☐ Long/slow burn	☐ Capital	☐ Idiosyncratic	☐ New/current	☐ Other significant adverse outcome	☐ Combination
☐ Books		▪ Different thresholds	☐ Macro-economic	☐ Additional		
		☐ Liquidity	☐ Combinations	☐ Feasibility		
		▪ Different thresholds	☐ Sequence	☐ Time to execute		
		☐ Market confidence				
		▪ Different thresholds				
		☐ Others				
		☐ Combinations				

- ▪ Storyboard and calibration
- ▪ Sequence of process steps

Figure 1.1: Elements of reverse stress testing.

As shown, the RST users may choose different scopes, ranging from individual books, to portfolios, entities, banking, groups and beyond (e.g. interbank networks). They may consider scenarios which crystallise fast, in a matter of days or weeks, and those that take years to materialise.

Beyond the loss of earnings and/or financial resources (capital, liquidity), an RST users may choose other aspects, such as the loss of operational capabilities and the loss of market confidence. Each of these may be operationalised using different metrics for which different thresholds could qualify the word "failure".

Users may scrutinise the potential cause of failure top-down (for the bank as a whole) or bottom-up, e.g. from the aggregation of risks identified by individual business units. Thereby, they may consider idiosyncratic, macro-economic or a combination of both scenarios (whereby not only the sequence of events may vary).

The test design may operationalise the outcome (e.g. failure) prior to any management actions or after all current management actions have been exhausted. In the latter case, additional actions may be explored. RST users may also challenge whether each management action is relevant in the specific scenario, with regard to feasibility and time to execute.

While RST approaches usually focus on high-severity outcomes such as a business model failure, users may also choose outcomes that do not lead not non-viability but help test the risk acceptance, such as for a particular portfolio ("Mild RST"). Alternatively, they may analyse individual risk factors in reverse. For example, which liquidity risk factors need to change and by how much should the liquidity buffer be reduced below a given amount? Or what size of shock of one currency causes a reduction of the CET1 ratio by, say, 10 bps? And what size of unexpected outflows of non-maturing deposits could result in a loss of US $1 million (e.g. due to the need to unwind hedges that are no longer matched at a loss)?

These tests may use quantitative models, qualitative subject matter expert input or a combination of both. The choice may differ depending on the scope (for example, an individual portfolio versus an entire bank) and type of risk (traded market risks versus difficult to quantify reputational risks).

Over and above these configuration choices, the test design may differ in terms of the number and sequence of steps. RST users may, for example, decide not to include management actions into the test design for a certain business line. They may also vary the sequence by, for example, setting the failure points prior to the scenario generation, and vice versa. Within each step of the chosen test sequence, further design choices are possible.

Overall, the morphological box offers a common classification frame across the different dimensions of RST. Each of the subsequent chapters should lend itself to one or more of these dimensions.

1.6 Organisation of the Book

The book is intentionally set up in a modular way to gather and share a spectrum of ideas and approaches to RST. For better understanding, the editors have grouped the chapters by themes into Part I to Part VI.

- **Part I** introduces RST as a versatile thinking tool with various configurations and test designs. It summarises the regulatory guidance on RST, which is still evolving. While the authors generally confirm the widely held view that regulatory guidance remains often and, in parts, intentionally limited, they refer readers to specific regulatory publications which provide answers to questions frequently asked by industry practitioners. As such, it helps to addresses this problem statement that there would be limited guidance available.

- **Part II** portrays different quantitative approaches to RST and proposes different innovations. An important challenge in designing an effective stress test is to select scenarios sufficiently extreme and plausible to allow understanding of the key weaknesses of a bank. RST pursues the goal to highlight circumstances causing the failure of a business. In this regard, both external conditions as well as bank internal sources of risk need to be considered. A variety of methods is introduced by focusing on alternative RST perspectives.

- **Part III** shares different qualitative approaches to RST. In line with the central message of this book, it encourages users to experiment with different configuration sets and test designs. The chapter introduces a generic process-orientated approach. Using the example of Cognitive Maps and Strategic Management tools, it actively discusses the integration of analytical and management tools into RST designs. Part III closes with an innovative and less severe configuration set called Mild RST. The different ideas may be particularly helpful for risks that are difficult to quantify and for smaller firms and firms that are in an early stage in their RST application. However, Part III can equally provide assistance beyond these segments.

- **Part IV** discusses the implementation of RST in the context of technology, Artificial Intelligence (AI) and Quantum Computing. The applications of AI-based methods range from Natural Language Processing to identify specific vulnerabilities of banks based on alternative data and economic indicators to an increase in computational speed by a factor of up to 40 by learning a pricing profile. It presents an XVA framework that integrates capital, liquidity and wrong way risk, followed by the Quantum Technology required to accelerate the necessary XVA calculation by several orders of magnitude. The crucial choice of the relevant technology will make a further difference of up to 100 in computational speCed, and the most efficient hardware and software choices are explored. It further shows a resilient model setup, from assumptions through flexible implementation to run RST and withstand actual crisis scenarios. The part concludes with

a glimpse into the future by pointing out the advantages and potential risks of AI-based risk management and macro-prudential regulation.
- **Part V** links RST to recovery and resolution planning (RRP). It points out the efficiencies that RST and RRP can gain from each other to design stress testing scenarios, detect a bank's vulnerabilities and conduct ad-hoc scenario tests to make business decisions. The framework is taken further by simulation of RRP scenarios to determine the most relevant and efficient management actions to turn around banks from scenarios threatening its viability.
- **Part VI** closes the book with governance considerations and a summary and outlook.

Given this modular structure, the book can be read in many different ways. Readers may prefer to read it end to end. Other readers may pick and choose individual chapters that are most relevant for their specific needs:
- **Chapter 2** provides a foundation for the rest of the book. It sets RST in the "real world" context of a bank's Risk Management function, including the linkage of RST to strategy, regulatory requirements and other frameworks such as ICAAP. The chapter discusses how a significant reduction in complexity can be achieved by defining "epicentres" and considers different quantitative and qualitative tools to extract scenarios with the highest relevance – for example, simulation-supported procedures, an expert-based iterative process or decision-theory instruments such as Bayesian networks.
- **Chapter 3** addresses the common notion that RST is a new concept with little guidance from regulators. It provides readers with an overview about the available regulatory guidance and answers to frequently asked questions. It further differentiates four phases in the development of the regulatory guidance, derives central development lines and discusses areas for further development.
- **Chapter 4** introduces the key elements for quantitative RST. A first step in building a reverse stress test is to specify a suitable objective function to embrace external and internal potential sources of insolvency. Additionally, one needs to point out that both the long-term as well as the short-term bank's capabilities to face its obligations need to be scrutinised. Furthermore, given that a bank is exposed to many interdependent risk sources, risk integration is introduced as a key element for RST. As a key element for the quantitative RST, specific focus may be addressed on bank specific features (e.g. concentration) investigated through what-if analysis and other expert-driven investigations. External macroeconomic conditions under which a bank fails to meet its obligations constitutes the final step of this comprehensive introduction to quantitative RST.
- **Chapter 5** provides the key requirements for practical reverse stress testing of a banking portfolio. Different metrics are presented to measure the severity of the stress and to identify reverse stress test scenarios that meet specified levels of loss to the portfolio. It turns out that the ability to generate scenarios across a wide

range of macro-financial variables is key to a successful reverse stress test. A comparison of different approaches is performed for scenario generation, including macroeconomic modelling techniques, supervised machine learning and a hybrid approach. Moreover, we discuss how to visualise and analyse the results of a reverse stress test using clustering techniques in order to derive actionable risk management and mitigation information.

- **Chapter 6** introduces the Danger Zone concept for Reverse Liquidity Stress Testing – a concept which, among others, challenges the common notion that RST would raise the requirements on data, project management, infrastructure and governance to a whole new level.
- **Chapter 7** proposes a framework for reverse stress testing networks of direct interbank exposures. It shows how the propagation of shocks between financial institutions can be modelling by means of dynamical processes on networks. The framework is based on the so-called DebtRank algorithm, which assumes that shocks are propagated linearly between interconnected banks. The framework computes the smallest exogenous shock that, given the dynamic of shock propagation, would lead to final losses larger than a given threshold. As a use case, an application is presented to a network of 44 European banks reconstructed from partial information.
- **Chapter 8** presents reflections on why and how a macroprudential RST could be conducted. It argues that supervisors define and frame microprudential RST exercises for individual banks to conduct. By contrast, there would be no such commonly understood approach on the macroprudential side. The chapter aims to define such a macroprudential RST, reflects how a corresponding framework can be set up and discusses how a scenario search exercise can be analytically embedded in a macro set-up.
- **Chapter 9** contributes to a further development of RST, considering methods from reliability analysis and, especially, analysing the hazard rate and thus the type of failures can help understand the causes of failure. From a theoretical point of view the Weibull distribution and the IDB distribution are useful to model all types of failure.
- **Chapter 10** provides a generic process-orientated approach to RST consisting of six steps. The approach inter alia allows for the inclusion of difficult to quantify risks (e.g. reputational risks). As a qualitative approach it may be particularly helpful for smaller banks. For each step references to available regulatory guidance are provided.
- **Chapter 11** investigates the case of the Pension Protection Fund (PPF). This chapter covers the different steps of non-quantitative reverse stress testing, from the definition of failure to the design of scenarios. A series of techniques is explored. Particular emphasis is devoted to cognitive maps for scenario design and a more general understanding of the vulnerabilities of an organisation. Cognitive maps can be used in two ways for reverse stress testing. First, we can use collective maps

to plot the collective knowledge and ideas of a group of subject matter experts. A second use is to map the key relationships of an organisation and the interactions between them.

- **Chapter 12** examines whether strategic management tools are helpful in the process of identifying vulnerabilities of a bank's business model for RST purposes. Together with expert interviews, financial statements and other publicly available information, two strategic management tools – a PESTLE and a SWOT-analysis – are tested to identify the vulnerabilities of FinTech banks. The results are relevant, given the shared focus of RST and strategic management tools on the business model and strategic risks.
- **Chapter 13** offers a milder version of RST to apply the reverse thinking logic to a wider set of practical Risk Management questions. It proposes different techniques to apply this milder version and present the results in practice, including iterative expert interviews to consider the aforementioned cognitive biases.
- **Chapter 14** shows how Natural Language Processing (NLP) methodologies from AI can be used to identify specific weaknesses of banks and in the process mitigate cognitive biases such as availability bias, anchoring (to historical stress scenarios) or salience bias of traditional stress tests. These methodologies range from sentiment analysis and search engine technologies to the most recent word embeddings and their fine-tuning with economic indicators to take into account the context in alternative data to identify the most relevant bank weaknesses.
- For the quantitative search of stress scenarios, **Chapter 15** discusses how the AI approach of Gaussian Process Regression can deliver acceleration by a factor of 35–40, demonstrated on the valuation of derivatives in the widespread Heston stochastic volatility model.
- **Chapter 16** introduces an holistic approach of Funding Value Adjustments (FVA) that takes into account capital impacts through the Regulatory Capital Valuation Adjustments (KVA) and makes the case for the new concept of funding set instead of the traditional netting set that has been used for calculations. This shows also the linkage between capital and liquidity, affecting regulatory liquidity metrics such as RLAP and R2.
- The specifics of the computation for the more integrated approach part to FVA from Chapter 16 are laid out in **Chapter 17**, describing an in-memory architecture for large-scale, holistic and ab-initio nested Monte Carlo simulations for capital and funding requirements. The chapter analyses the impact, evolution, possible mitigation measures and challenges of two exemplary stress scenarios to that end. It provides an additional metric in risk-adjusted return quantification, comparing revenues of a business against potential losses and discusses such metrics and KPIs.
- **Chapter 18** demonstrates the use of Quantum Computing technologies to achieve an acceleration in any funding valuation adjustment (XVA) calculations by several orders of magnitude, made possible as the Quantum Annealing method

has linear complexity with respect to the number of risk factors, whereas the usual exhaustive search has exponential complexity.

- **Chapter 19** discusses technology choices in the context of RST. It shows how the appropriate choice of hardware may accelerate the task of choosing appropriate scenarios from a sheer infinite number of extreme scenarios by a factor of up to 100.
- **Chapter 20** presents a framework that shows how to design a robust modelling framework that will handle RST efficiently and withstand actual crisis scenarios as well. The design builds on conceptually sound models and determines the validity boundaries to use the right model for the right scenario. Crucial for implementation is a flexible infrastructure that embeds these models with the facility to switch models.
- **Chapter 21** describes how Artificial Intelligence may be utilised in risk management of banks as well as in the macro-prudential regulation of the entire financial system. It describes the benefits and efficiencies that can be gained with such a set-up as well as the intrinsic pitfalls that will require human intervention.
- **Chapter 22** highlights the similarities between recovery and resolution planning process and the reverse stress testing process, both from a framework and an implementation perspective. It also demonstrates how the two frameworks can benefit from each other to identify business vulnerabilities, select scenarios and run ad-hoc analysis to make business decisions.
- **Chapter 23** further emphasises that bridging RST, RRP and other contingency frameworks offers the chance to develop one overall more coherent framework. The UK PRA already requires firms to integrate ILAAP into the ICAAP, thereby acknowledging the intrinsic dependency of capital and liquidity. Similarly, the FRB requires that banks include the recovery and resolution planning into the capital planning (CCAR) submission. Consequently, the determination of which path each bank takes – recovery or resolution – provides supervisory authorities with salient information for contingency plans in case of severe stress.
- Similar to the note that social sciences differ from physical sciences and computer technologies in that experiments are not repeatable, **Chapter 24** discusses how finance differs from complex systems in geology and meteorology and what this means for the board-level governance of RST.
- **Chapter 25** exemplifies how recent research work can help to identify hidden vulnerabilities and inform new scenario narratives in the context of RST. Topics covered include biases in risk measurement, cyber risk, political risk, model risk, systemic risk and the endogenous nature of the latter.
- **Chapter 26** analyses why RST's potential remains underused and offers some changes that should make RST much more useful for decision-makers. The analysis suggests that there are four areas of the RST process that banks need to improve if they want to open up the full potential of the RST as an effective risk management tool. The main weaknesses with a use of RST can be divided into the following groups: weaknesses in the scenario development and scenario selection process,

overreliance on stress impact quantification, oversimplification of RST methodology (e.g. ignoring the stress dynamics, interconnectedness and sequencing of events when modelling scenarios), underestimation of the importance of the development of mitigating action plans which leads to relegation of the contingency planning to an ancillary element of RST.

– **Chapter 27** concludes the book with a summary and an outlook.

Each chapter reflects the individual views and experiences of the respective expert. The views are generally meant to complement each other. Where they differ, the editors consider this equally welcome and evidence that there is no established practice and that different ideas may be helpful for different readers.

For the editors it has been a huge privilege to work with this unique group of experts from industry and academia. Different authors are guest speakers from the Masterclasses who were kind enough to also share their views in this book. Others worked with us in Risk Management Think Tanks, on academic projects or we actively approached them due to their insightful publications on the subject.

We hope readers will enjoy the insights of our unique expert panel in equal measure.

Philipp Gann

2 Reverse Stress Testing in Banks

A Multidimensional Approach

2.1 Introduction

In recent years, stress tests have become an integral part of risk management in banks.[1] Stress tests enable the identification and comprehensive assessment of significant risks, as well as an in-depth and future-orientated analysis of a bank's risk potential.[2] The associated increase of transparency of the banks' individual risk profile enables banks to establish well-founded and consistent planning, management and decision-making processes. In the context of value-based corporate management, stress tests can generate control stimuli, which, when implemented, can contribute to positive risk adjusted earnings and thus a sustainable increase in equity value, competitiveness and the overall strength of the bank.[3] Potential positive economic implications by increasing an individual bank's financial stability and thus contributing to the overall stability of the financial markets are the main motivation for banking regulators to create comprehensive regulatory stress testing requirements (micro-prudential regulation).

These regulatory requirements for stress tests – formulated for the first time as part of the implementation of Basel II – have undergone an extremely dynamic and sustainable development in the recent past. This was primarily due to the insights

---

1 In this contribution, the term *stress testing* is used as an umbrella term for various methods utilised by institutions to assess their individual risk potential, including extraordinary but plausible events. This definition includes both sensitivity and scenario analyses. For a potential classification of stress tests, see Section 2.3.
2 See for example the corresponding comments in Basel Committee on Banking Supervision (2018), European Banking Authority (2018a), European Banking Authority (2018b), European Central Bank (2018a) and European Central Bank (2018b). Stress tests can also be used in the identification and measurement of model risks, thus contributing to a deeper understanding of a bank's risk situation.
3 The terms *shareholder value* and *value orientation* are used synonymously in this chapter. According to the shareholder value concept, a sustainable increase in equity value is only possible if the credit institution achieves profits that exceed the cost of capital, which is to be interpreted as the interest claim of the investors. For this to happen, the return on invested capital must exceed the bank's weighted average cost of capital. To achieve this, the bank's net profit must be greater than the risk-adjusted cost of capital calculated with the help of, for example, theoretical capital market modelling approaches such as the Capital Asset Pricing Model (CAPM) or the Arbitrage Pricing Theory (APT).

Note: Edited by Michael Eichhorn

https://doi.org/10.1515/9783110647907-002

gained by the financial industry and regulators in the aftermath of the subprime mortgage crisis and the evident incompleteness and weaknesses in the internal risk management methods and processes predating which were in place prior to this. In order to eliminate or at least to minimise the recognised weaknesses, widespread changes have been made to the international and national banking regulatory frameworks, particularly with regard to stress testing. In particular, the inability of institutes to identify and address previously unknown crisis triggers, correlations, amplifications and feedback effects on the basis of the stress tests carried out historically was recognised as a central problem area in the risk management of credit institutions. In addition to a general expansion of the regulatory requirements addressing the quality, scope and complexity of the institute's internal stress testing programme, the supervisory authorities introduced a completely new category of stress tests, so-called reverse stress tests, for the majority of banking institutions. While a classic or conventional stress test is based on a precisely specified scenario (e.g. macroeconomic downturn) and the effects of this scenario on the credit institution are quantified and analysed, a reverse stress test uses a precisely defined result as a starting point. By using a reversing approach, parameter changes are identified, and the associated scenarios or events which lead to this result are specified.[4] As evident by its name, the process of conventional stress tests is inverted in the case of reverse stress tests. The aim is to reduce the short-sightedness of a crisis ("disaster myopia"), which is a recognised weak point of conventional stress tests, and to reduce any false sense of security for the decision-maker.[5] Reverse stress tests should help to increase the transparency about relevant risk drivers and to better classify the suitability and severity of the scenarios of classic stress tests through back testing them.[6] In addition, reverse stress tests are intended to provide an additional reference point for the susceptibility of a bank towards developments that might jeopardise its existence and thus to facilitate the identification of potential threats for its own business model.

Although, since 2010, European credit institutions have been regularly confronted with the regulatory requirement to perform reverse stress tests, the methods and processes for reverse stress testing are still in a developmental stage. Uniform procedures and methods which are used by the majority of credit institutions are yet to be developed. Instead, existing principle-orientated regulatory requirements for reverse stress tests are currently filled with life in various ways, depending on the size of the institution, the business model, the complexity and the risk content of the business activities, but also the given – often historically grown – bank-specific stress testing philosophy.

---

4 See for example European Banking Authority (2018a), p. 14 and paras 83–96.
5 On this and on the following see European Banking Authority (2018a), Basel Committee on Banking Supervision (2018), European Central Bank (2018a), European Central Bank (2018b) and, additionally, Committee of European Banking Supervisors (2010) and Counterparty Risk Management Policy Group (2008).
6 Se inter alia European Banking Authority (2018a), para 83.

From the range of possible approaches, this chapter outlines a comprehensive, quantitatively orientated, cross-risk angle to reverse stress testing, which is closely defined by the European Banking Authority (EBA) guidelines on institutions' stress testing (EBA/GL/2018/04). Thus, the following chapter is structured as follows: The first section outlines the essential national and international regulatory require- ments. The benefits of reverse to conventional stress tests and their integration into the general classification of stress tests are discussed in Section 2.3. On this basis, Section 2.4 presents a quantitative, cross-risk approach that enables the generation of economic control stimuli within the framework of value-based corporate manage- ment which enables large and complex institutions to fulfil their regulatory require- ments at the same time. Following a summary of the central components of a com- prehensive reverse stress testing framework (Section 2.4.1), Section 2.4.2 provides an explanation of the term "failing or likely to fail" within the meaning of Article 32 of the Bank Recovery and Resolution Directive (BRRD, Directive 2014/59/EU) as well as a discussion of the term "non-continuity of the business model", since accord- ing to the EBA guidelines (EBA/GL/2018/04) previously mentioned, both a failing or likely-to-fail state and the non-continuity of the business model are the starting point when performing reverse stress tests. On this basis, Section 2.4.3 defines the amount of loss or liquidity outflow that jeopardises the institute's existence, which should not be exceeded by any reverse stress event. Section 2.4.4 then discusses potential approaches to identify and extract relevant scenarios which might threaten the sur- vival of the bank. Section 2.5 focusses on the close relationship between reverse stress tests, business model and risk strategy requirements. Section 2.6 concludes with a summary.

2.2 Regulatory Requirements

In June 2004, as part of the International Convergence of Capital Measurement and Capital (Basel II for short), the Basel Committee on Banking Supervision (BCBS) for the first time issued guidelines for carrying out stress tests as an integral part of the Internal Capital Adequacy Assessment Process (ICAAP) and hence the bank's inter- nal risk management.[7] The extensive revision of these recommendations by the Basel Committee with regard to stress testing of credit institutions was induced by the expe- riences gathered during the international financial market crisis, which was triggered by the subprime crisis and culminated in the document "Principles for sound stress testing practices and supervision", eventually published in May 2009. The aim of this publication was to fundamentally strengthen the importance of stress tests within the risk management processes of credit institutions and to create a consistent and

---

[7] On ICAAP, see in detail Gann (2006), Gann (2011) and Gann (2020).

uniform supervisory framework to carry out stress testing in a bank.[8] The BCBS principles emphasised the importance of reverse stress tests for the identification of hidden risks and interdependencies between risks (or risk factors) as well as for the determination and analysis of scenarios that could threaten the survival of the institute (henceforth referred to as "RST scenarios").[9] In addition, the following basic requirements were developed:

– Based on a precisely specified stress result which endangers the going concern of the institute (e.g. the violation of regulatory capital ratios, illiquidity, bankruptcy), the underlying events or risk drivers must be identified.
– Systematically relevant extreme scenarios or events characterised by contagion effects must be explicitly included in the analysis. In principle, all risks identified as essential must be taken into account.

Reverse stress tests are intended to enable senior management to carry out an in-depth assessment of potential weak points and risk concentrations. According to BCBS, particular business areas for which conventional risk models indicate extremely advantageous risk-return ratios or new products which have not yet been exposed to a greater scrutiny benefit from the increased transparency that results from the implementation of reverse stress tests.

In the "Principles for sound stress testing practices and supervision", an international supervisory authority described for the first time the requirement for credit institutions to implement reverse stress tests. These requirements were taken up and further specified at European level by the new version of the document "CEBS Guidelines on Stress Testing (GL32)" of the Committee of European Banking Supervisors (CEBS), published in December 2010.[10] However, here too, there was deliberately no definition of a specific approach to reverse stress testing indicating any regulatory preference.[11] However, CEBS made it clear that reverse stress tests must always start with the identification of an exceptionally negative result, the causes of which must

---

8 In revising the recommendations on stress testing, the Basel Committee also explicitly referred to the financial industry's own acknowledgement to fundamentally expand and strengthen its methods and processes for stress testing in order to reduce both the probability and the extent of a future crisis. See Basel Committee on Banking Supervision (2009), p. 7 and Institute of International Finance (2008). The introduction of reverse stress testing was also recognised by the financial industry as an important element in improving the bank's internal risk management. See for example, Counterparty Risk Management Policy Group (2008).
9 On this and the following, see Basel Committee on Banking Supervision (2009), Principle 9, pp. 14–15.
10 The recommendations of the BCBS and CEBS formed the basis for the binding national requirements for conducting reverse stress tests subsequently formulated by various National Competent Authorities (NCA) (see, for example, the requirements of the German supervision authority as set out in the Minimum Requirements for Risk Management (MaRisk)). On 1 January 2011 CEBS' mandate was transferred to the European Banking Authority (EBA).
11 See Committee of European Banking Supervisors (2010), para 64.

be determined and analysed on the basis of a retrograde procedure.[12] Where possible, first-round and feedback effects as well as non-linear dependencies should be taken into account. Accordingly, reverse stress tests must go far beyond univariate sensitivity analyses. For the identification of risk factor combinations, events and risk concentrations that are not usually considered in the context of conventional stress tests, those scenario results are of essential importance that fundamentally endanger the sustainability of the business model. Other key characteristics of reverse stress tests according to CEBS are summarised as follows:

- As an integral part of risk management, reverse stress tests should reduce the crisis short-sightedness ("disaster myopia") and the associated, and possibly wrong, sense of security of the decision-makers. In order to ensure the acceptance of the results of reverse stress tests, scenarios must be identified which, despite their severity, are relevant for a specific bank.
- Depending on the size and complexity of the institute, both qualitative and quantitative approaches are permitted. On the basis of the explanations, however, it becomes clear that qualitative approaches for larger and more complex institutes can only serve as a starting point and that, in accordance with the principle of proportionality, these institutes are expected to implement further quantitative processes in the medium- to long-term. Here, for instance, a specific loss level or a certain change in the capital ratios may be assumed as the basis for the use of a retrograde, quantitative-orientated procedure to identify the causal risk drivers and the scope of changes required.
- The reverse stress tests which need to be carried out on a regular basis should be viewed as an independent risk management tool that complements the institute's classic stress testing programme.
- The results of reverse stress tests do not result in immediate implications for the level of capital requirements and capital adequacy but are an instrument to increase transparency, both with regard to possible scenarios that threaten the existence of the company and to the dynamics of the underlying risk drivers. However, the results of reverse stress tests can be extremely helpful when it comes to assessing the assumptions of the business model, business strategy and capital plans. To identify weaknesses in the business model and to develop a comprehensive understanding of the importance of self-reinforcing and non-linear effects, the development of a storyline for reverse stress tests is essential.[13]

Since the publication of these documents in 2009 and 2010, the role of stress tests in credit institutions and their importance has enhanced significantly in many countries. Stress tests are now a central element of risk management for credit institutions

---

12 For this and the following see Committee of European Banking Supervisors (2010), paras 63–67.
13 See Committee of European Banking Supervisors (2010), para 67 in connection with para 45d.

and also a core instrument for micro- and macro-prudential regulators. In line with the rapid development of the importance of stress tests, there was a detailed review and extensive revision of the corresponding regulatory requirements for both conventional and reverse stress tests.[14] The EBA Guidelines on institutions' stress testing (EBA/GL/2018/04) in particular clarify and detail the current fundamental expectations of European supervisors regarding the procedural and methodological framework for carrying out reverse stress tests. The requirements set out in other European regulatory documents for carrying out reverse stress tests (e.g. the ECB Guides on ICAAP and ILAAP)[15] refer to the expectations defined in the EBA guidelines and do not generate any additional requirements. Accordingly, the requirements of EBA/GL/2018/04 form the central point of reference for the following presentations of the current essential regulatory requirements and their consideration when defining and implementing the procedural and methodical approach for carrying out reverse stress tests by a credit institution. The essence of the EBA's basic expectations of reverse stress tests can be characterised as follows:[16]

- Reverse stress tests must form an integral part of the institute's entire stress testing programme. Accordingly, reverse stress tests are to be integrated consistently (and thus equally stringently) into the stress testing governance into both the ICAAP and the ILAAP of the institute.
- Reverse stress tests must be based on a precisely specified stress result (that threatens the existence of the firm), which, for example, can lead to a "failing or likely to fail" state or a "non-continuity of the business model", and identify the underlying events or risk drivers through a retrograde approach.[17]
- As a risk management tool that is to be used regularly, reverse stress tests should help to increase transparency for current and future potential weaknesses and

---

14 See Basel Committee on Banking Supervision (2018), p. 1.

15 See European Central Bank (2018a) and European Central Bank (2018b).

16 The stress testing guidelines EBA/GL/2018/04 are aimed entirely at institutions in category 1 (systemically important). In addition, against the background of the proportionality principle, these requirements also provide the relevant framework for conducting reverse stress tests for institutions in category 2 (less or non-systemic) and categories 3 and 4 (small- and medium-sized organisations). See European Banking Authority (2018), p. 7.

17 See European Banking Authority (2018), para 9 (10). "Reverse stress test means an institution stress test that starts from the identification of the pre-defined outcome (e.g., points at which an institution business model becomes unviable, or at which the institution can be considered as failing or likely to fail in the meaning of Article 32 of Directive 2014/59/EU) and then explores scenarios and circumstances that might cause this to occur." See also European Banking Authority (2018), para 88: "institutions should: identify the pre-defined outcome to be tested (e.g., of a business model becoming unviable)" and European Banking Authority (2018), para 94: "Institutions should work backwards in a quantitative manner to identify the risk factors, and the required amplitude of changes, that could cause such a loss or negative impact."

situations that threaten the existence of the institute.[18] This is logically linked to the requirement to take reverse stress tests into account when updating and developing the institute's business strategy.[19]

- In addition to sensitivity analyses,[20] quantitative[21] and qualitative[22] analyses must be carried out by larger and more complex credit institutions.
- Reverse stress tests should generate a supplementary reference point for the evaluation of the severity and probability of occurrence and plausibility of conventional scenarios.[23]

-----

18 See European Banking Authority (2018), para 87: "Institutions should use reverse stress testing as a regular risk management tool in order to improve their awareness of current and potential vulnerabilities, providing added value to institutions' risk management" and European Banking Authority (2018), para 88: "As part of their business planning and risk management, institutions should use reverse stress testing … to identify circumstances where they might be failing or likely to fail within the meaning of Article 32 of Directive 2014/59/EU … . institutions should: … identify possible adverse circumstances that would expose them to severe vulnerabilities and cause the pre-defined outcome."
19 See European Banking Authority (2018), para 88: "Institutions should use reverse stress testing to understand the viability and sustainability of their business models and strategies" and European Banking Authority (2018), para 89 "Institutions should use reverse stress testing … to challenge their business models and strategies in order to identify and analyse what could possibly cause their business models to become unviable."
20 See European Banking Authority (2018), para 87: "Institutions should also consider that the pre-defined outcome of reverse stress testing can be produced by circumstances other than the circumstance analysed in the stress test." and European Banking Authority (2018), para 95: "Institutions should, where appropriate, use sensitivity analyses as a starting point for reverse stress testing, e.g., shifting one or more relevant parameters to some extreme to reach pre-defined outcomes. An institution should consider various reverse sensitivity analyses for credit risk … market risk, liquidity risk … and operational risk, among other risks."
21 See European Banking Authority (2018), para 94: "Institutions should perform quantitative and more sophisticated analyses … in setting out specific loss levels or other negative impacts on its capital, liquidity … or overall financial position. Institutions should work backwards in a quantitative manner to identify the risk factors, and the required amplitude of changes, that could cause such a loss or negative impact (e.g., defining the appropriate loss level or some other measure of interest on the balance sheet of the financial institution such as capital ratios or funding resources)." and European Banking Authority (2018), para 95: "A joint stressing of all relevant risk parameters using statistical aspects (e.g., volatility of risk factors consistent with historical observations supplemented with hypothetical but plausible assumptions) should be developed."
22 See inter alia European Banking Authority (2018), para 93: "Institutions should perform qualitative analyses in developing a well-defined narrative of the reverse stress testing and a clear understanding of its feedback and non-linear effects." and European Banking Authority (2018), para 95: "The qualitative analysis should lead to the identification of the relevant scenario, combining expert judgement from different business areas, as thinking might be the most effective way to prevent a business model failure. … Qualitative analyses and assessments, combining expert judgements from different business areas, should guide the identification of relevant scenarios."
23 See European Banking Authority (2018), para 83: "For assessing the appropriate degree of severity of scenarios, institutions should also compare them with the scenarios outlined in their reverse stress testing, considering specific implications of the reverse stress test design for the scenario's plausibility."

The risks and vulnerabilities identified by reverse stress tests are to be avoided or reduced by preparing or taking suitable measures.[24]

The comparison of the expectations formulated in 2018 by the EBA guidelines EBA/GL/2018/04 with the "Principles for sound stress testing practices and supervision" defined by the BCBS in 2009 and the "CEBS Guidelines on Stress Testing (GL32)" defined by the CEBS in 2010 clarifies that the basic regulatory requirements for the implementation of reverse stress tests are almost unchanged and have only been selectively developed in relation to two subject areas. Thus, adjustments resulted from the increased reference to the need to take appropriate measures to avoid or reduce the risks and vulnerabilities identified by reverse stress tests.[25] This further development in terms of content is consequent against the background of the meanwhile defined requirements of the Bank Recovery and Resolution Directive (BRRD, Directive 2014/59/EU) and the subsequent necessity for the regular and event-related preparation of comprehensive recovery plans and their consistent embedding in the entire risk management framework of the institutes.[26] As reverse stress tests are considered a central risk management tool for the identification of scenarios that can lead to a "failing or likely to fail" state or a "non-continuity of the business model" (consequently, to a state in which remediation options only have a limited effect with regard to averting a fundamental crisis situation), it is only logical that the results of reverse stress tests must be actioned in accordance with the assessed probability of occurrence of the underlying scenarios by taking or preparing management actions in order to avert the occurrence of the restructuring situation.

European Banking Authority (2018), para 85: "Institutions should include scenarios identified through the reverse stress testing to complement the range of stress test scenarios they undertake and, for comparison purposes, in order to assess the overall severity, allowing the identification of severe but still plausible scenarios. Reverse stress testing should be useful for assessing the severity of scenarios for ICAAP and ILAAP stress tests. The severity of reverse stress testing scenarios can also be assessed by comparing it to, inter alia, historical or other supervisory and publicly available scenarios.", European Banking Authority (2018), para 88: "institutions should ... assess ... the likelihood of events included in the scenarios leading to the pre-defined outcome." and European Banking Authority (2018), para 95: "The plausibility of the parameter shifts required to reach the pre-defined outcome gives a first idea about possible vulnerabilities in the institution. To assess the plausibility, historical (multivariate) probability distributions – adjusted, where deemed necessary, according to expert judgements – should, inter alia, be applied."

24 See European Banking Authority (2018), para 88: "institutions should ... adopt effective arrangements, processes, systems or other measures to prevent or mitigate identified risks and vulnerabilities." and European Banking Authority (2018), para 90: "Where reverse stress testing reveals that an institution's risk of business model failure is unacceptably high and inconsistent with its risk appetite, the institution should plan measures to prevent or mitigate such risk."

25 See also European Central Bank (2018a), para 98 and European Central Bank (2018b), para 88.

26 On the necessity of consistently linking an institution's restructuring plan with its ICAAP and ILAAP, see inter alia European Central Bank (2018a), paragraphs 35 and 36 and example 2.1, and European Central Bank (2018b), paragraphs 35 and 36 and example 2.2.

The second major development of the requirements within the EBA guidelines EBA/GL/2018/04 compared to the expectations formulated by the BCBS and CEBS in 2009 and 2010, respectively, places greater emphasis on the need to consistently embed reverse stress tests in the overall governance and the ICAAP and ILAAP of the institute. The reason for this is the dynamic further development of the fundamental requirements of the supervisory authorities with regard to the governance of the institutes that can be observed in recent years and the associated linking of internal processes to ensure capital and liquidity adequacy. This development stemmed from the supervisory authorities' observations that there are significant weaknesses within the internal governance of numerous credit institutions, despite the fact that solid governance is the central prerequisite for effectively managing risks during serious events and to ensure sufficient capital and liquidity resources.[27] In connection with this, the supervisory authority emphasises that in the supervisory assessment of the quality of the ICAAP and ILAAP, the actual control relevance of these processes will play a central role against the background of ensuring stringent and consistent overall bank management.[28] The fundamental prerequisite for ensuring the control relevance of ICAAP and ILAAP is the non-contradictory linkage and extensive embedding of these processes in the governance of the institute. In addition to the high level of consistency in the content of the requirements documented in the ECB guidelines on ICAAP and ILAAP, other recent supervisory publications also indicate that supervisory authorities aim to create an integrated overall banking management steering process within the sense of an Internal Capital and Liquidity Adequacy Assessment Process (ICLAAP). ICLAAP comprehensively and consistently interlinks the economic and normative capital and liquidity dimensions of risk management in an institution and connects them stringently with the other strategic processes. An institute's stress testing programme is a central component of both ICAAP and ILAAP. Accordingly, these fundamental developments are also reflected in the requirement of EBA/GL/2018/04, requiring institutions to integrate reverse stress tests consistently in the stress testing governance and thus equally stringent in both the ICAAP and the ILAAP.[29]

---

27 See inter alia Basel Committee on Banking Supervision (2015), European Banking Authority (2017), European Banking Authority (2018c) and European Central Bank (2016). For the embedding of reverse stress tests in an institution's ICAAP and ILAAP see, for example, European Central Bank (2018a) and European Central Bank (2018b), in each case Principle 7.

28 Thus, due to the great importance for a bank's management, the ECB attaches identical importance to the evaluation and continuous improvement of ILAAP and ICAAP and defines both processes as a central supervisory priority within the framework of SREP in 2019 and 2020, analogous to 2018. See European Central Bank (2017), European Central Bank (2018c) and European Central Bank (2019).

29 The individual requirements of all supervisory documents with a micro-prudential perspective can be classified with regard to the two central objectives of ensuring capital adequacy and solvency at all times. In addition to the micro-prudential national and international supervisory authorities, the European Systemic Risk Board (ESRB), as part of the European System of Financial Supervision

2.3 Use and Classification of Reverse Stress Tests

As specified in the regulatory requirements, reverse stress tests should complement an institution's stress testing programme in order to reduce the weaknesses of conventional approaches or, if possible, eliminate them. The main limitation of classic stress tests lies in the nature of their approach: assumptions about the nature of identified relevant risk factors are being made on the basis of a historical, hypothetical or hybrid scenario. The changes in the parameters considered in the scenario are normally theoretically justified and, in the best-case scenario, take into account empirically observable data between the individual parameters or – in the case of hypothetical and hybrid scenarios – the potentially possible interdependencies and dependencies. The impact on key performance and risk indicators under assessment (KPI, e.g. risk capital requirement, LCR, non-performing loan ratio) is then quantified.[30] The stress situation is then assessed on the basis of the indicators determined in this way. Thus, any defined stress situation only ever leads to one specific result for the set of indicators under consideration. However, a multidimensional dimension of possible parameter variations that induce the same result is not established. By choosing the scenario for a conventional stress test and the associated choice of a specific value vector for the relevant risk parameters, these stress tests represent a closely defined and highly subjective model domain. Interdependencies that contradict an intuitive approach or the historical "experience" with regard to common parameter values are regularly disregarded. The main limitation of conventional stress tests is therefore the ex-ante determination of certain assumptions regarding the markets considered, risk factors, parameter characteristics and impact relationships as the starting point for the classic scenario analysis. The resulting "blinders thinking" results in blindness or "disaster myopia" (CEBS) with regard to possible (albeit empirically not observed) risk-determinant, mutual dependencies and second-round effects. In addition, the recipients of the stress test results often only insufficiently include them in their management-relevant decisions, particularly if the underlying stress assumptions – as is often the case – are considered too strict, too mild, unrealistic or simply impossible and extremely unlikely.

Reverse stress tests have the theoretical potential to reduce specifically these identified limitations of classic stress tests. The retrograde methodology inverts the procedure of classic stress tests (see Figure 2.1) and thus enables a completely new perspective of an institution's risk potential. In contrast to traditional stress tests, risk situations can be interpreted independently from the comparison of the

---

(ESFS), is an institution responsible for macro-prudential supervision in the euro area. The main objective of the ESRB is to issue warnings and recommendations, based on a continuous monitoring of developments within the financial system, that contribute to averting or mitigating systemic risks to financial stability in the Euro area.

30 See on this and the following Gann (2012).

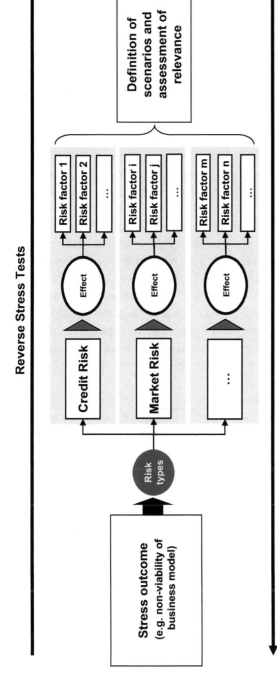

Figure 2.1: Retrograde procedure of reverse stress tests.

scenario-induced value of a considered risk measure (e.g. risk capital requirement) and the volume available to cover it (e.g. risk-bearing capacity). Reverse stress tests identify possible combinations of parameter changes that induce a previously specified value of a deliberated target variable. This spans the institute's actual multidimensional risk domain, which is not limited by an ex-ante definition of the parameter combinations, as is the case with conventional stress tests. On the basis of a previously specified value of a defined target figure (e.g. the free risk bearing capacity not yet utilised by risk positions), a retrograde determination of the maximum multivariate variations of risk parameters can be carried out, which can (just) be carried by the target figure value. Since individual risk factors do not change in isolation from each other, existing (i.e. empirically observable) or conceivable future interdependencies and dependencies between the individual risk factors must be taken into account in the analysis and scenario definition.

As part of the individual risk assessment, the scenarios relevant to the institute with regard to their probability of occurrence are to be extracted on the basis of the parameter combinations considered. These correspond to the retrograde identified stress scenarios or events.[31] If the considered (multivariate) change in the risk parameters – i.e. the occurrence of a (hypothetical) scenario – is assessed as probable, this may have significant implications for the review and, if necessary, revision of the assumptions of the business model, business strategy and capital plans and allocation.[32] If necessary, management measures must also be taken or prepared in order to avert a restructuring or winding up of the organisation that would transpire if the corresponding scenario occurred.

By identifying a genuine multidimensional risk area, new scenarios can be developed that are separate from scenarios based on the past and dependency relationships. These new scenarios can lead to a specific expression of a target value under consideration of scenarios which, for example, were not observable in the past due to the emergence of new markets or products, but are very conceivable for the future. This allows reverse stress tests (potentially) to identify (new) causal relationships that exist but are not recognisable in conventional stress tests and to analyse their effects on the risk profile. Since reverse stress tests contemplate extreme outcomes in the sense of tail events, contagion effects, systemic risk drivers and feedback effects must also be taken into account.

Figure 2.2 illustrates the fundamentally different perspective of reverse stress tests compared to conventional stress tests. In order to maintain the simplicity of the representation in Figure 2.2, it is assumed that the risk potential of the assessed institution is determined by only two risk factors: the default probability *PD* and the

---

31 See Section 4.4 for further details.
32 See Section 5.

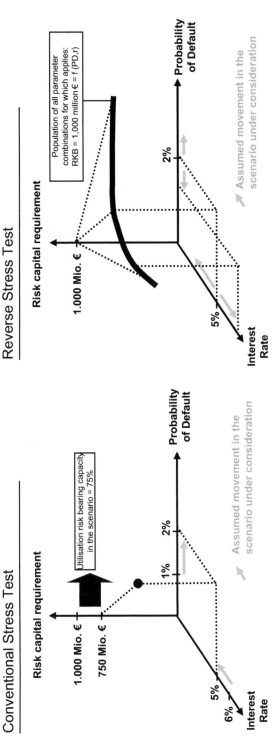

Figure 2.2: Conventional versus reverse stress test.

interest rate r.[33] On the vertical axis, the expression of the considered risk size induced by the combination of the two risk parameters – economic risk capital requirement, in this example – is plotted. If the institute has a total economic risk coverage potential of EUR 1,000 million, a conventional stress test focuses on the determination of its utilisation rate in the event of stress. The experts responsible for stress testing will thus carry out the scenario definition and parameterisation (in this example, reducing the interest rate from $r = 6\%$ to $r = 5\%$ and increasing the probability of default from PD = 1% to PD = 2%) and, on this basis, calculate the risk capital requirement (in this example, EUR 750 million). This results in determining the utilisation rate of the risk coverage potential for a single combination of parameters. In the above example this amounts to 75%, meaning that the risk-bearing capacity would also be ensured in the event of stress. A reverse stress, however, can (at least theoretically) identify an unlimited amount of parameter combinations, which can lead to a utilisation rate of 100% and thus be an acute threat to the institute's continued existence. As a result, there is no ex-ante reduction of the risk area under the consideration of a single scenario.

As the previous explanations and the regulatory requirements demonstrate, reverse stress tests do not fit the classical classification in place for conventional stress tests, i.e. scenario and sensitivity analyses. Quantitative-orientated reverse stress tests build on the sensitivities of the risk factors identified as essential but must go well beyond sensitivity analyses (see Section 2.4 for details). Similarly, with regard to historical or hybrid scenario analyses, reverse stress tests cannot be delineated clearly. For reverse stress tests, the main objective is to change perspective in order to direct the view away from historically existing and empirically observable relationships. Furthermore, since the derivation of a scenario (and the assessment of its relevance) does not represent the starting point – as in classic stress tests – but rather the result of reverse stress tests, these cannot be clearly described as hypothetical or hybrid scenarios in the conventional sense, even if the formation of hypotheses about the change and the interplay of the essential risk factors is a central component of the implementation of reverse stress tests. Rather, as Figure 2.3 shows, reverse stress tests represent an independent class of stress tests that can be classified between sensitivity and conventional scenario analyses and aim to eliminate the "white spots" of classic approaches with regard to the generation of comprehensive transparency of the actual risk potential.

---

33 The example abstracts (risk-dependent) yield curves, maturities, borrower-specific rating assessments, etc.

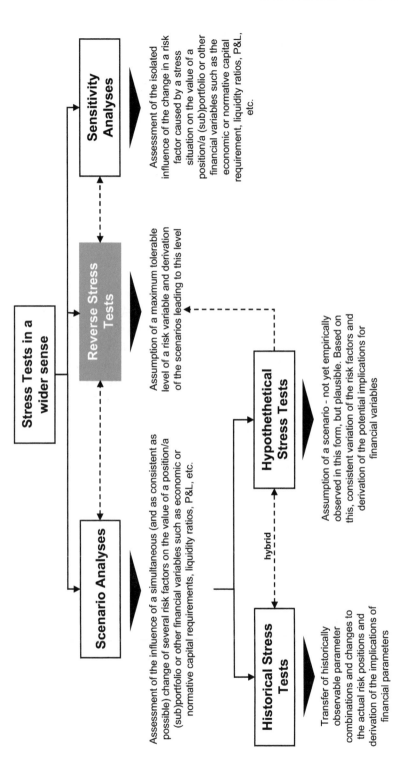

Figure 2.3: Classification of stress tests.

2.4 A Quantitative Approach

2.4.1 Dimensions of a Comprehensive Approach to Reverse Stress Testing

The requirements formulated in the stress testing guidelines EBA/GL/2018/04 make clear that sensitivity tests as well as quantitative and qualitative analyses of larger and complex credit institutions are expected in the context of reverse stress tests (see Section 2.2). Accordingly, a comprehensive approach to reverse stress testing must include the three dimensions shown in Figure 2.4 and as explained in the following section.

2.4.1.1 Sensitivity Analyses

In the context of sensitivity analyses, adverse changes in specific risk factors are considered, which have particularly strong implications for the relevant financial parameters due to the business strategy of the institute. The definition of the most important risk factors for the institution should be based on the risk identification process and the main risk drivers identified there as well as the analyses carried out as part of the restructuring planning and risk type-specific scenarios. Sensitivity analyses enable a deeper understanding of the central weaknesses of the institute and form the basis for a comprehensive discussion of historically observed and hypothetically possible dependencies (including feedback and reinforcement effects) between individual risk factors as part of reverse stress tests. Thus, this is the starting point for quantitatively orientated scenario considerations.

2.4.1.2 Quantitative-Orientated Scenario Analyses

The quantitative scenario analyses must take into account the specifics of the business activities as well as the structure, network and risk profile of the institute. Based on the structure of the on- and off-balance sheet assets and liabilities as well as the political and macroeconomic environment, an in-depth analysis of the risk potential resulting from the business and risk strategy requirements must be carried out as a first step. This analysis forms the basis for the selection of the scenarios included in the reverse stress tests. The most relevant and plausible scenarios are to be identified – the materialisation of which can create a threat to the existence (Near Default) of the institute by taking into account the institute's most significant risks.[34] The scenario identification and

---

34 For an operationalisation of the term *near default* as the starting point for the quantitative scenario considerations, see Section 2.4.2.

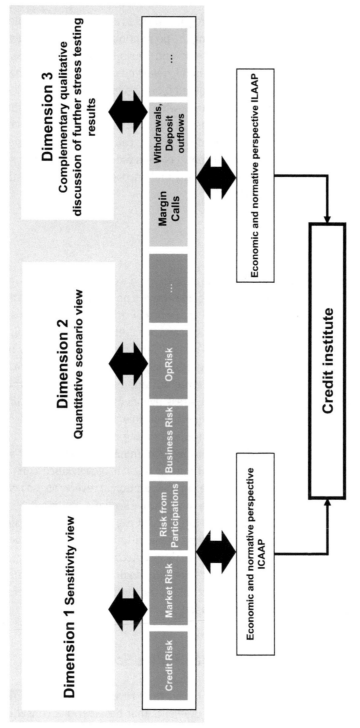

Figure 2.4: The three dimensions of a comprehensive reverse stress testing approach.

definition should be based on a retrograde process using various complexity reduction techniques with the aim of restricting the population of possible or analysed scenarios. This ensures the practical applicability and feasibility of reverse stress tests in terms of regulatory requirements and economic relevance. The quantitative near default scenarios – taking into account the potential reinforcement and feedback effects – must show specific idiosyncratic and market-wide vulnerabilities for the institute which are qualitatively summarised in a consistent storyline. In doing so, they increase transparency regarding those risks that threaten, or are caused by, the implementation of the business strategy. Quantitative scenario considerations also provide a supplementary reference point for assessing the severity and purposefulness of the institute's conventional stress testing programme.

2.4.1.3 Qualitative Analyses

Other idiosyncratic or market-wide crises, which were not explicitly considered in the context of the quantitative analyses, may have a noticeable impact on an institution's capital or liquidity adequacy. The occurrence of such further scenarios could accordingly reduce the capital or liquidity capacity defined as the starting point for the quantitative scenario analyses. As a result, the capacity changed by the occurrence of alternative scenarios would (possibly significantly) influence the reverse stress parameterisations derived from a retrograde approach. Recognising this relationship and potentially further significant stress events and their possible implications on the amount of the capital loss or liquidity outflow that could jeopardise the existence of the company permits a deeper understanding of the restrictions associated with quantitative stress scenarios. Accordingly, an intensive discussion of other potential stress events at management level and in relevant governance committees should always be undertaken as part of the implementation of reverse stress tests (in addition to the qualitative assessment of the quantitative scenario analyses).

Figure 2.5 illustrates the ideal interplay of the individual dimensions of reverse stress tests. The focus of the following explanations is on the implementation of the quantitatively orientated scenario analyses. Accordingly, sensitivity analyses and supplementary qualitative analyses are only dealt with on the basis of their ability to provide an imperative starting point for the derivation and comprehensive assessment of the quantitative scenario analyses.

2.4.2 Starting Point for Quantitative Scenarios

As regulators prescribe, the main objective of reverse stress tests is to identify and analyse events and combinations of events that have serious consequences for the institute. In accordance with the EBA requirements, a failure or likely to fail result and

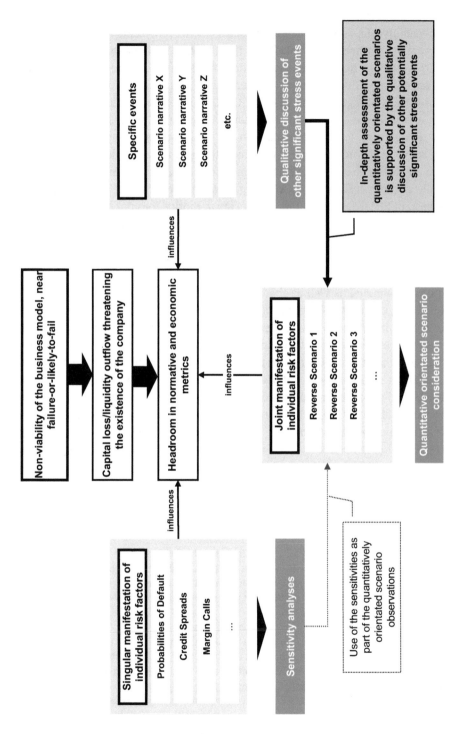

Figure 2.5: Interaction of the individual dimensions of reverse stress tests.

the non-viability/non-continuity of the business model represents the starting point for carrying out reverse stress tests.[35] The term "failure or likely to fail" stems from Article 32 of the Bank Recovery and Resolution Directive (BRRD, Directive 2014/59/EU) and is, according to BRRD, an essential prerequisite for the transition to the winding up regime.[36] The EBA guidelines EBA/GL/2015/07 aim to enable (more) objective criteria for assessing the occurrence of the conditions of a failure or likely to fail condition.[37] By referring to failure or likely to fail in the stress testing guidelines, the EBA makes clear that reverse stress tests have to relate to existential situations that threaten the existence of the institute beyond the possibility of restructuring itself.

While a failing or likely to fail situation is given a certain degree of clarification on the basis of EBA/GL/2015/07, the supervisory authority does not further define the non-viability of the business model. The concrete interpretation and operationalisation is thus left to the individual institutions, with reference to a specific loss amount or the negative change in the capital or liquidity position.[38] The non-viability of the business model is linked to institution's balance sheet.[39] In principle, the viability of the business model as well as the continued existence of a bank is determined by its liquidity, capital and earnings position. If the business model proves to be no longer viable with regard to one of these dimensions, the bank's existence is at risk. Changes in the earnings, capital and liquidity situation are always determined by the materialisation of risks and the related implementation of a non-sustainable business strategy. The strategic misjudgment of environmental developments, business opportunities or legal developments of the management induces the materialisation of the business or strategic risk, which among other things leads to an adverse change in the revenues and costs of the institute and thus a deterioration in the earnings situation (e.g. a reduction of net interest incomes in the event of a strategic mispositioning within the institute's refinancing strategy and framework which does not match

---

35 See European Banking Authority (2018a), p. 14 and para 88.

36 At the same time, pursuant to Article 32 BRRD, for a transition of the institution to the winding up regime, the prospects of success for measures of the private sector or of supervision for a restructuring (e.g., inclusion of institution guarantee, conversion of capital instruments) within a reasonable time frame must be low and the winding up of the institution must be considered to be of public interest.

37 See European Banking Authority (2015).

38 See for example European Banking Authority (2018a), para 94.

39 In general, it seems sensible to base qualitative approaches to reverse stress testing on the bank's figures. If the possibility of an extreme change in the democratic political framework is abstracted from the analysis, then the business model is deemed to be unsustainable primarily if the current business model induces a change in financial parameters that causes a negative reaction from the institute's stakeholders (e.g., supervisory authorities, owners, creditors), which questions its continued viability. Accordingly, any actual threat to the business model's ability to continue as going concern ultimately accumulates and manifests itself in the form of financial parameters. See also the comments in following sections.

the maturity profile of assets and liabilities).[40] Price losses in existing long positions (materialisation of market risk), the default of a debtor (materialisation of credit risk) or claims due to the failure of internal procedures, people and systems (materialisation of operational risk) also have a direct impact on the earnings, capital and liquidity positions. Changes of refinancing conditions or sudden and unexpected liquidity outflows correspond to the materialisation of liquidity risk and directly determine an institution's liquidity.

Determining the conditions under which the business model can no longer be continued or sustained with regard to the risk situation is thus of central importance for reverse stress tests.[41] The business model's viability can generally be assumed to be at risk if the capital or liquidity-related risk-bearing capacity (RBC) is violated in a dynamic perspective (for example, within the planning period of the institution) – that is, if the risk potential is exceeding the corresponding risk coverage potential.[42] Such a situation inevitably implies a reaction from the institute's stakeholders. Depending on the quality (normative versus economic risk-bearing capacity in ICAAP or ILAAP) and the quantity of the failure to meet the target levels, this can have massive implications (insolvency or resolution) or only slight implications for the business model and business strategy (modification of the business strategy). A risk-bearing capacity given in the actual situation will be threatened by events that induce a (potential) capital loss or a (potential) liquidity outflow, which reduces the risk coverage potential or increases the risk potential in such a way that the institution is no longer risk-bearing. If a loss potential or liquidity outflow is realised and jeopardises a company's existence, the existing business model cannot be followed. At the same time, this also fulfills the central requirements for defining a failing or likely to fail state in accordance with EBA/GL/2015/07.[43] This loss potential or liquidity outflow thus represent the appropriate starting point for carrying out reverse stress tests. In this context, the implementation should simultaneously take into account capital and liquidity dimensions. As described in Section 2.2, this is an essential prerequisite for the steering and control-orientated embedding of reverse stress tests in the integrated ICAAP-ILAAP framework of the institute.

---

40 For the quantification of the business and strategic risk of credit institutions, see for example Gann/Igl (2019).

41 The materialisation of risks can take place quickly or slowly, as it is the case, for example, with the realisation of business and strategic risks. Accordingly, reverse stress tests must cover both a short-term and a long-term horizon.

42 This applies to both the normative and economic risk-bearing capacity perspective in ICAAP and ILAAP. Cf. European Central Bank (2018a), European Central Bank (2018b) and the following comments in Section 1.4.3.

43 Cf. European Banking Authority (2015), in particular para 19–25.

2.4.3 Determination of the Amount of Losses or Liquidity Outflow Threatening the Existence of the Company

The non-viability of the business model or a failing or likely to fail situation can be induced by both inadequate capital and liquidity adequacy. Capital and liquidity adequacy comprises a normative and an economic perspective.[44] Within the framework of the normative perspective of ICAAP or ILAAP, the institution has to assess – on the basis of a capital, funding and liquidity planning process consistent with the business strategy – to what extent the existing quantitative regulatory and supervisory capital or liquidity requirements and specifications (such as, among others, the minimum capital requirements according to CRR and SREP, leverage ratio, LCR and NSFR) as well as which other external financial constraints (e.g. minimum dividend requirements) can be fulfilled. The ECB expects this assessment to be based on both a credible baseline scenario and complementary institution-specific adverse scenarios. Within the economic perspective, the institution must identify and assess all material risks which, from a purely economic perspective, could cause losses and substantially reduce internal capital or liquidity resources. On this basis, the institution must ensure that all economically relevant risks are sufficiently backed by internal capital and liquidity resources. The normative perspective and the economic perspective must be integrated into the institution's governance in such a way that they inform and complement each other.[45]

In accordance with the two fundamental dimensions of risk-bearing capacity (capital versus liquidity adequacy) and their two perspectives (normative versus economic), there are various starting points for defining a capital or liquidity capacity. Once the capacity is consumed, the ability to continue as a going concern business is threatened. With regard to ensuring normative capital adequacy, for example, a reference could be made to the maximum amount of free – that is, not allocated with risk positions – shareholder equity or equity classes (tiers), which can be utilised before the specific regulatory thresholds of capital ratios are undercut to such an extent that it could endanger the existence of the bank. For example, the institution could refer to the CET1 capital to define the RST Scenario loss threshold and determine that if the total SREP Capital Requirement (TSCR) is not met without the simultaneous ability of the institution to generate sufficient equity or reduce risk positions to fully comply with the TSCR in the short- to medium-term, the business model is not viable as a going concern or is likely to fail. If, for example, with a total CET1 volume of EUR 10 billion, the sum of the institution's risk positions amounts to EUR 100 billion and the regulatory TSCR is 6%, EUR 4 billion of the CET1 capital is currently not occupied with risk positions. Furthermore, if it is assumed for the sake of simplicity that the institu-

---

44 See European Central Bank (2018a) and European Central Bank (2018b), Principle 3.
45 For further details see Gann (2020).

tion has no feasible restructuring options at its disposal, EUR 4 billion of "free" CET1 capital exists at the TSCR of 6% defined as the reference point for the amount of losses threatening the existence of the institution. The institution can "lose" EUR 4 billion – be it through a (potential) event that directly reduces the capital (e.g. a sharp reduction in the actuarial interest rate for discounting an institution's pension provisions) or an increase in risk positions (e.g. as a result of rating downgrades of numerous exposures) – before normative capital adequacy is breached, in the sense that a situation, defined as non-compliance with the TSCR, occurs and threatens the institution's continued existence. Instead of TSCR the institution may also specify, for example, the Overall Capital Requirement (OCR) or alternative regulatory or supervisory capital requirements (e.g. MREL ratio or leverage ratio) as a starting point for determining the amount of loss. Comparable options are also available if economic capital adequacy is to serve as a reference value for defining the amount of loss. Different conceivable reference values and thresholds also exist with regard to the normative and economic perspective of liquidity adequacy. For example, the ratios usually used in the context of economic liquidity adequacy to measure the survival horizon (Distance-to-Illiquidity measures) are based on different minimum requirements (measured in days) in order to define the amount of the liquidity outflows that could threaten the existence of the institute. The same applies to a definition of the liquidity outflows that endanger the bank's continued existence as a going concern, which can, for example, be aimed at specific LCR thresholds that should not be undercut.

As a result of the different definitions of risk coverage potential and the different approaches and methods for quantifying the risk potential in the normative and economic perspectives of ICAAP and ILAAP, different capital and liquidity capacities appear in the individual risk-bearing capacity perspectives.[46] Accordingly, there are several reference values for defining the amount of the loss or liquidity outflow which threatens the bank's continued existence and which lead the institution from the actual (at best) strong financial situation to the non-viability threshold. The choice of which of the possible capital losses or liquidity outflows should constitute the starting point for carrying out the reverse stress tests ultimately depends on the credit institute's individual assessment. Even if the regulator provides specific indications as to the point at which the business model can no longer be described as a going concern or when a failing or likely to fail condition exists,[47] discretion still remains with regard to the concrete definition of the capital loss or liquidity outflow threatening the existence of the bank. Accordingly, the credit institute must define its individual tolerance limit with regard to a breach of the individual risk-bearing capacity and,

---

46 The perspective in ICAAP and ILAAP requiring the least capital or liquidity capacity depends on the capital or liquid funds included in the corresponding risk coverage potential and the respective methods for determining the risk potential.
47 See European Banking Authority (2015), European Banking Authority (2018b) and Section 2.4.2 of this contribution.

linked to this, the acceptable severity of the resulting implications for the business model, in consistence with its risk appetite. In accordance with this definition, the reference value for the amount of the capital loss or liquidity outflow that threatens the existence of the bank must then be defined. Here it should be noted that the severity of the implications for the ability to continue as a going concern in the event of a breach of risk-bearing capacity is determined not only by the quality (breach of normative versus economic risk-bearing capacity) but also by the quantity (extent and duration of the breach of risk-bearing capacity) of the failure to meet the threshold. In principle, it is therefore not possible to give a blanket answer to the question of the appropriate capital or liquidity scope as to what the starting point of reverse stress tests should be (see Figure 2.6). Rather, the choice is largely determined by the institute's subjective risk appetite and thus, among other things, by management attitude, the expectations of the markets, investors and business partners, the individual business model and the capital market situation.

In general, specific characteristics of certain normative indicators (e.g. TSCR) must always be met to ensure the continued existence of the institution and are thus mandatory for the viability of the business model or the avoidance of a failing-or-likely-to-fail situation. The amount of capital loss or liquidity outflow that could endanger the existence of the company can therefore under no circumstances be greater than the minimum requirements defined by the supervisory authorities. In addition, alternative thresholds for economic and normative ratios can also be defined, depending on the bank's individual interpretation of the concept of the non-viability of the business model or failing-or-likely-to-fail.

The determination of specific ratios and their thresholds as a reference value for the capital loss or liquidity outflow defined for a specific reverse stress test outlines the risk-bearing capacity perspective primarily considered in the reverse stress test. This specification determines the methods for quantifying the risk potential in the event of stress and, indirectly, the maximum univariate and multivariate possible changes of the risk factors identified as relevant – and accordingly also the maximum severity of the scenarios considered – which (precisely) lead to the specified amount of loss or liquidity outflow. For example, management can determine that in a specific capital-related reverse stress testing scenario, the normative perspective should form the primary reference point of the analysis and the amount of loss threatening the existence of the bank should be operationalised using the free CET1 capital determined for the TSCR. The free CET1 capital is thus determined by the CET1 capital, the risk potential in terms of the existing risk positions, and the TSCR as a reference value for determining the minimum CET1 capital. Accordingly, when determining the relevant reverse stress scenarios (see Section 2.4.4), both the effects of risk factor changes on the free CET1 capital and the level of the normatively measured risk potential must be taken into account simultaneously. However, the implications of the identified scenarios should not only be analysed with regard to the primary perspective – in the example mentioned, the normative ICAAP perspective. Rather, they should also

- Choice of the reference value for the loss or outflow of liquidity threatening the existence of the company depends on the individual bank's understanding of when the business model can no longer be described as going concern

- In this respect, the credit institution shall define the tolerance regarding the severity of the implications for the business model in the event of a breach of the various risk-bearing capacity perspectives in ICAAP and ILAAP

- The quality and quantity of the missed targets determines the severity of the implications for the current business model

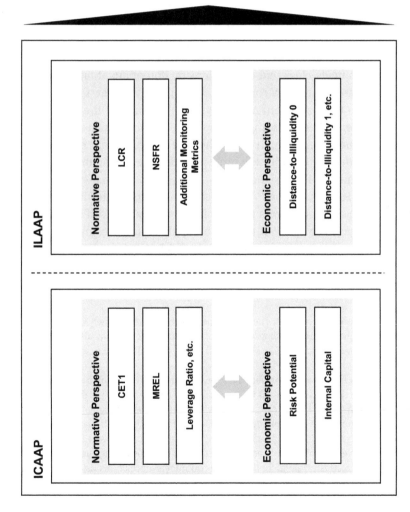

ILAAP

Normative Perspective

LCR

NSFR

Additional Monitoring Metrics

Economic Perspective

Distance-to-Illiquidity 0

Distance-to-Illiquidity 1, etc.

ICAAP

Normative Perspective

CET1

MREL

Leverage Ratio, etc.

Economic Perspective

Risk Potential

Internal Capital

Figure 2.6: Determination of the amount of loss threatening the existence of the company.

be determined for the other perspectives of risk-bearing capacity in the sense of a consistent overall bank management. By simultaneously analysing all perspectives in ICAAP and ILAAP in this way, it is possible to check whether individual scenarios in the perspective primarily considered would lead to such a situation in other risk-bearing capacity perspectives even if the parameters were less strictly defined. Such a situation is possible in principle due to the different approaches to determining the risk potential and the risk coverage potential within the individual perspectives of ICAAP and ILAAP. This approach allows the analysis of capital and liquidity adequacy to be carried out in an integrated manner within the framework of reverse stress testing and thus consistently interlinks ICAAP and ILAAP.[48]

2.4.4 Identification of Scenarios Threatening the Existence of the Company and Scenario Extraction

Previous explanations made clear that the implementation of quantitatively orientated reverse stress tests is extremely complex and requires the integration of different functional areas of the institution. Accordingly, in the course of the operational implementation of reverse stress tests, the relevant business or specialist areas as well as those experts who are essential for a comprehensive and consistent implementation must be identified. Together with the process owner, the individual specialists are to be (formally or informally) assigned to a working group hereinafter referred to as the Reverse Stress Test Committee.[49] The mission of this committee is the operational implementation of reverse stress tests in close coordination with senior management and the management body of the institute, taking into account regulatory requirements.[50] As a result of this institutionalised cross-linking of different types of

---

48 Cf. also the comments in Section 2.4.2. The aim of the article is to introduce a comprehensive quantitative approach to reverse stress testing across risk types. In addition, it may also be useful to perform reverse stress tests at an individual risk type level. This is particularly the case for the risk of insolvency.

49 The experts taking part must also be involved in the development and design of the reverse stress testing approach for which the process owner is responsible. Since reverse stress tests must be carried out at the same level as ICAAP and ILAAP in accordance with regulatory requirements, it is appropriate to define the organisational unit of the institution responsible for the cross-risk type dimension of ICAAP and ILAAP or the senior manage responsible for this unit as the process owner.

50 The comprehensive involvement of the management body and senior management in the performance of reverse stress tests is essential for the factual control relevance of this risk management instrument, and thus ultimately also for a successful assessment of an institution's reverse stress test framework by the supervisory authorities. See European Banking Authority (2018b), para 89 and 93, among others; for a definition of the terms management body and senior management, see Directive 2013/36/EU, Article 3(1), points (7) and (8) and point (9).

risk and specialist areas, the "disaster myopia" of risk management criticised by regulators will be significantly reduced.

The definition of the capital or liquidity capacity as a reference value for the capital loss or liquidity outflow threatening the continued existence of the company (see Section 2.4.3) and the selection of the risk types and factors included in reverse stress testing form the basis for determining the scenarios threatening the continued existence of the bank. The RST scenarios must be assessed by the process owner in close coordination with the experts involved and the management body or senior management, taking into account the aspects of stringency, consistency, plausibility and appropriateness (see Figure 2.7).[51]

As shown in Section 2.2, reverse stress testing governance must be consistently integrated into the institute's overall stress testing governance, including ICAAP and ILAAP. In practice, the process owner will therefore regularly be identical with the organisational unit responsible for the entire stress testing framework and the reverse stress testing committee will have a high – if not complete – overlap with the group of experts responsible for conventional stress testing.

The scenario definition is a very complex and challenging step in the reverse stress testing process. Figure 2.8 provides an overview of the relevant subject areas.

Formally, the determination of a scenario in a quantitative reverse stress test approach corresponds to the identification of a specific vector of changes of all risk factors identified as relevant, which, with regard to the portfolio of all risk positions of the institution on valuation day, induces a (potential) capital loss amount or liquidity outflow which (largely) corresponds to the amount of capital loss or liquidity outflow threatening the institution's continued existence. Knowledge of the value sensitivities of individual risk factors and assumptions or hypotheses about the interdependencies of the risk factors involved are a fundamental prerequisite for a theoretically sound specification of such a vector. In this context, historical dependencies can only serve as a reference point. In order to overcome crisis short-sightedness, the Reverse Stress Test Committee must focus its discussions on purely hypothetical but conceivable relationships.[52] Thus, the performance of sensitivity analysis of the identified risk factors as well as the discussion of possible dependencies are essential for defining

---

51 It is not absolutely necessary to integrate all risk types defined as material in the risk identification process into the reverse stress testing framework. If justifiable, individual risks in specific scenarios can be explicitly disregarded within specific scenarios. With regard to the selection of risk factors, it should be noted that for practical application and internal acceptance of reverse stress tests within the bank, the risk factor universe to be included must be suitably restricted depending on the methodology used for scenario definition.

52 The derivation of scenario-consistent (hypothetical) dependencies between the individual risk factors and thus the scenario-consistent parameterisation of individual risk types involved in the reverse stress test represents an enormous challenge in the process of conducting reverse stress tests, but can contribute fundamentally to a comprehensive reduction of crisis short-sightedness criticised by the supervisory authorities.

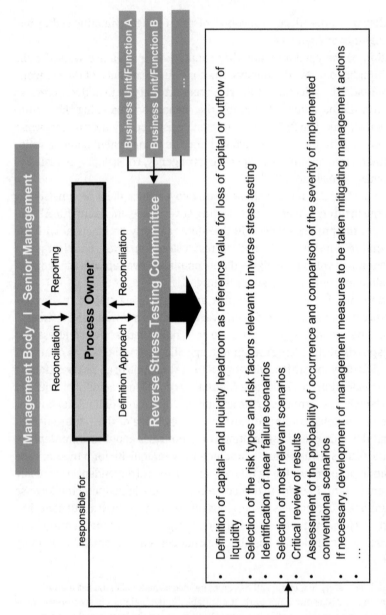

Figure 2.7: Reverse stress testing governance.

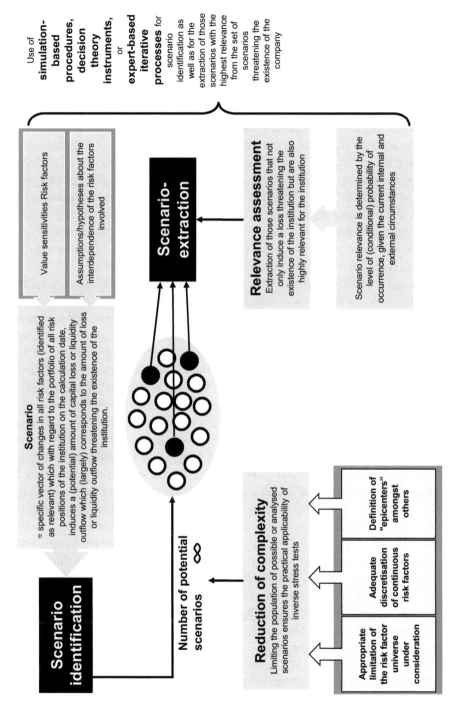

Figure 2.8: Scenario identification and scenario extraction.

scenarios. Sensitivity analyses thus form the basis of quantitatively orientated reverse stress tests (see also Section 2.4.1).

Each identified vector – that is, each possible combination of risk factor changes that could threaten the existence of the company – corresponds to a theoretically conceivable reverse stress scenario. Even with two risk factors (and unlimited constant changeability of these), the number of potential scenarios is basically infinite. From management's point of view, it is therefore essential to extract those scenarios from the matrix of all theoretically possible combinations of risk factor changes which not only induce a severe capital loss or liquidity outflow but are also highly relevant for the institution. The relevance of a scenario threatening the bank's existence is determined by the level of (conditional) probability of occurrence given the underlying internal and external framework. The relevance assessment is a central sub-aspect in the process of scenario definition. The result of this sub-process determines both the internal acceptance of the stress results within the institute and thus the actual relevance of reverse stress tests for management purposes and the actual reduction of crisis short-sightedness.

In this context, it should be noted that, in order to ensure the practical applicability of reverse stress tests with the aim of reducing complexity, irrespective of the methodology used to identify scenarios threatening the bank's continued existence and to extract scenarios, the universe of possible or analysed scenarios must always be restricted. To achieve this, it is beneficial to restrict the considered risk factor universe appropriately and to carry out an adequate "discretisation" of continuous risk factors. A significant reduction in complexity can also be achieved by defining "epicentres". In this context, in accordance with the actual internal and external framework, situations and specific developments with the potential of a capital loss or liquidity outflow that could threaten the existence of the institution must first be identified (e.g. the euro crisis). In the course of defining the scenario, the types and risk factors particularly affected by these developments are then examined and a comprehensive discussion of the crisis-induced (hypothetical) dependency relationships is to take place. An institution with a large portfolio of European government bonds could, for example, consider developments that induce a sharp fall in value or a need for write-downs of these assets as a potential epicentre and, with regard to the scenario definition, concentrate on the changes and interaction of the risk factors that are particularly relevant for their market value.

In principle, both the identification of all factor combinations with severe capital loss or liquidity outflow potential as well as the extraction of those scenarios with the highest relevance can be carried out on the basis of simulation-supported procedures or as an expert-based iterative process. In addition, decision-theory instruments such as Bayesian networks can also be used to assess the relevance.

Simulation-based approaches allow the identification and extraction of relevant existence-imperiling scenarios on the basis of mathematical and statistical methods, which can be retraced by third parties. Furthermore, the results of such approaches are often perceived as highly objective, despite the fact that the selection of the methods applied as well as their parameterisation is subject to a high degree of subjectivity. This may increase the acceptance of reverse stress tests in a bank with a more quantitative management culture. Compared with an expert-based iterative process, using a system-supported scenario identification creates the option of being able to record, evaluate and analyse more complex and multi-layered relationships, a larger population of RST scenarios as well as a larger scope of risk factors which can be varied as the starting point for scenario extraction. However, a major disadvantage of simulation-based approaches for scenario identification and extraction is that these approaches are not easy to communicate and may not be accepted within a bank with a management culture that is more qualitatively orientated. Furthermore, an empirical validation of these approaches is very difficult as they are still at a very early development stage. A further central weakness is the often highly mechanical approach inherent in these methods. This can only be partially remedied by intensive discussion of the methods selection and their parameterisation as well as the scenarios extracted on this basis by experts or specialist departments involved. This entails the danger that reverse stress tests may simply develop into a complex calculation task for the institution's risk control unit and that critical reflection of the (apparently objective) results obtained may be pushed into the background. This severely restricts both the potential for reducing crisis short-sightedness and, where applicable, the management acceptance of reverse stress tests.

This is exactly where the main strength of expert-based iterative processes lies. The identifications of risk factor change combinations and scenario extraction are carried out iteratively by the Reverse Stress Test Committee on the basis of a dynamic control loop process. Expert-based iterative processes are highly complex and require an in-depth examination of the (hypothetical) interrelationships of considered risk factors as well as an intensive discussion between the experts and specialist departments involved. In order to solve the inversion problem and to extract scenarios, these processes require considerably more (technical as well as time) effort compared to the use of simulation-based approaches, but they have the advantage of significantly reducing the regularly encountered "blinders thinking" of individual departments. Thus, these processes can result in a significant reduction of risk management's short-sightedness. This is valid despite the often-required reduction in complexity that may be necessary compared to simulation-based approaches (with regard to an ex ante restriction of the population of scenarios, risk factors and risk factor characteristics). From the point of view of overcoming the "disaster myopia", expert-based iterative processes thus have clear advantages.[53]

---

[53] The assessment of the relevance of the extracted scenarios is, however, more difficult for third parties to understand in expert-based iterative processes than in simulation-based processes, as these are fundamentally based on the subjective expectations of the involved experts. If there is a divergence of expectations between management and the experts involved, this situation may restrict the use of the stress results in risk management and in the review and adjustment of the assumptions of the business strategy and capital planning.

Furthermore, additional qualitative scenario analyses can be easily included into such an approach. The integration of qualitative aspects can be regarded as a fundamental prerequisite for the comprehensive fulfilment of regulatory requirements. Quantitative approaches to scenario building regularly adopt the model risks and weaknesses inherent in the methods of risk measurement. To reduce complexity, it is also necessary to make assumptions that are in some cases highly simplified to ex ante limit the risk factors considered as well as the characteristics of the risk factors and the scenarios that threaten the bank's continued existence. This means that fundamental influencing factors and interrelationships may not be taken into account. Qualitatively orientated scenario observations can usefully supplement quantitative approaches with regard to these weaknesses and can create a deeper awareness of the restrictions associated with these approaches.[54] For example, a qualitative discussion or analysis of the effects of adverse developments impacting major subsidiaries increases transparency with regard to the implications of these developments for the amount of capital losses or liquidity outflows of the parent company. The transparency of the influence of such a scenario on the capital or liquidity scope under consideration allows a more in-depth assessment of the validity of the extracted quantitatively orientated scenarios.

In principle, it is possible to consider a wide range of supplementary qualitative analyses. Corresponding to these explanations, qualitative analyses therefore also allow one to concentrate on a selection of scenarios which are to be assessed as relevant due to the external or internal framework conditions. While quantitatively orientated scenarios are based on the carried out sensitivity analyses and display the interaction of specific factor variations with losses or liquidity outflow potential, the primary task of supplementary qualitatively orientated scenario analyses must therefore be to enable a comprehensive understanding of the validity of the extracted scenarios and to create a deeper awareness of the restrictions associated with the model world of quantitative scenarios. The possibility of a consistent integration of quantitatively and qualitatively orientated scenario observations represents a further advantage of using expert-based iterative processes for the definition of existential scenarios and for scenario extraction.

Within the framework of expert-based iterative processes, decision theory instruments can also be applied in addition to direct expert evaluation during the relevance assessment. For example, the use of Bayesian networks enables a consistent determination of the probability of occurrence associated with a specific scenario under

---

54 Qualitatively orientated scenario analyses inevitably always include quantitative elements in order to be able to make valid assertions regarding the implications of specific scenarios for the institution. Nevertheless, in this context quantitative aspects are of secondary importance. Rather, the core of qualitatively orientated scenarios is the identification and definition of aspects that are helpful for a comprehensive interpretation as well as a deep understanding of the extracted quantitatively orientated scenarios and their restrictions.

consideration of senior management. Using Bayesian networks during stress testing is built on the idea of deriving valid probability models of complex stress scenarios on the basis of (subjective) estimates of conditional likelihoods of occurrence on the basis of the Bayesian theorem resulting from expert interviews.[55] However, the use of Bayesian networks for relevance assessment has proven to be of little practical use in recent years due to their high complexity and the difficulty of communicating them within the institute. Figure 2.9 provides a schematic, highly simplified overview of the basic procedure of using Bayesian networks for the relevance assessment of reverse stress tests.

On the basis of the extracted scenarios, and thus the combinations of factor characteristics selected as relevant, a comparison can be made with the factor parameterisations used as the basis for conventional stress tests in the sense of a gap analysis. This enables a more detailed assessment of the severity and probability of occurrence or plausibility of conventional scenarios in the sense of back testing and, in conjunction with an evaluation of the differences in factor values between conventional and reverse stress tests, also creates an additional point of reference for the institute's susceptibility to developments that threaten its existence. Since gap analysis is a central instrument to supplement conventional stress tests and also provides essential support for a comprehensive critical reflection of the results of reverse stress tests, it should be seen as an important component in fulfilling the intention of the supervisory requirements. On the basis of the knowledge gained from this analysis, the risks and vulnerabilities identified by reverse stress tests must be avoided or reduced at an early stage by preparing or taking suitable measures. Figure 2.10 summarises the basic components of the approach described here for conducting quantitative reverse stress tests.

2.5 The Relationship between Reverse Stress Testing and Business Strategy

Reverse stress tests are used to identify scenarios that endanger the institution's ability to survive. In the sense of overcoming or reducing crisis short-sightedness, this results in increased transparency with regard to the risk factors that are significant

---

55 Bayesian networks have been used as expert systems in various disciplines (e.g. medicine) for quite some time, see for example Koller/Friedman (2009), Heckerman/Horowitz/Nathwani (1992), pp. 106–116 and Pearl (1988). The idea of using these relationships in stress testing of financial services companies goes back essentially to Ricardo Rebonato, see Rebonato (2010).

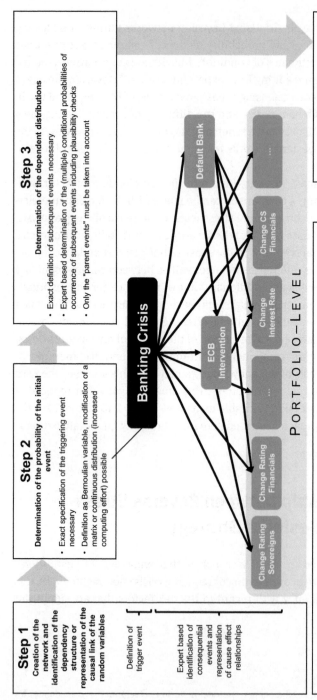

Step 1

Creation of the network and identification of the dependency structure or representation of the causal link of the random variables

Definition of trigger event

Expert based identification of consequential events and representation of cause effect relationships

Step 2

Determination of the probability of the initial event

· Exact specification of the triggering event necessary
· Definition as Bernoulian variable, modification of a matrix or continuous distribution (increased computing effort) possible

Step 3

Determination of the dependent distributions

· Exact definition of subsequent events necessary
· Expert based determination of the (multiple) conditional probabilities of occurrence of subsequent events including plausibility checks
· Only the "parent events" must be taken into account

Step 4

Calculation of joint distribution

· Determination of the joint distribution
· Usage of the conditional probabilities and the Bayesian formula

Banking Crisis

Default Bank

ECB Intervention

Change Rating Sovereigns

Change Rating Financials

Change Interest Rate

Change CS Financials

PORTFOLIO–LEVEL

Step 5

Calculation of profit and loss distribution

· Determination of all combinations of risk factors that could lead to a loss or outflow of liquidity that could threaten the existence of the company (requires determination of the loss for all possible combinations of risk factors)
· Since Bayesian networks make it possible to determine the probability of occurrence of each scenario, the question can be answered as to how likely it is that a scenario will occur that leads to a loss or outflow of liquidity that would threaten the existence of the company. This probability corresponds to the sum of the probabilities of all scenarios that lead to a loss or outflow of liquidity that would threaten the company's existence.

Figure 2.9: Use of Bayesian networks in the context of reverse stress tests.

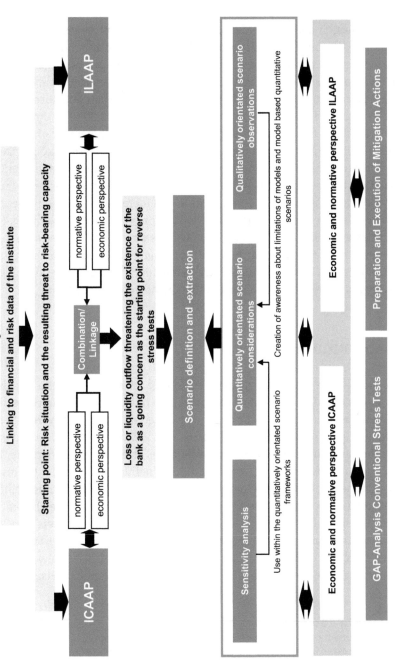

Figure 2.10: Key components in implementing reverse stress tests.

for the institution and its interdependencies.[56] Reverse stress tests thus strengthen the link between business strategy and risk management as required by ICAAP and ILAAP and have important implications for the strategy process. This is because a business strategy, based on the bank's business model and by taking the greatest possible account of future disturbance variables, articulates activities which serve to achieve specific (financial and non-financial) objectives. Reverse stress tests now identify precisely those scenarios that acutely threaten the ability of the business model to continue as a going concern. In other words, reverse stress tests make it possible to increase transparency with regard to those risks that threaten the implementation of the business strategy or are caused by it. Reverse stress tests can thus help to identify inconsistencies, contradictions and vulnerabilities in the business model or business strategy and thus also in capital, funding and liquidity planning.[57] Therefore, when reviewing and adjusting the business strategy, it makes sense to assess its key assumptions regarding the results of reverse stress tests. Such a procedure supports a critical discussion of the key assumptions of the business strategy and, accordingly, the creation of a stable foundation for strategy formation.

2.6 Summary

The main objective of supervisory requirements for reverse stress tests is to reduce the crisis short-sightedness identified as a weakness of conventional stress tests and to reduce the associated false sense of security of decision-makers. Reverse stress tests should help to increase transparency in the bank about key risk drivers and to better assess the suitability and severity of conventional stress tests. Furthermore, reverse stress tests are intended to provide an additional point of reference for the institute's susceptibility to developments that could threaten its existence and thus facilitate the identification of potential threats to its own business model. As the elaborations in this chapter show, the quantitatively oriented approach, which covers all risk types, is a suitable instrument for meeting these objectives. At the same time, however, it has become clear that conducting reverse stress tests is extremely complex and requires the comprehensive involvement and sustained support of various specialist areas and

---

56 In order to ensure the plausibility of the business strategy and the consistency of the risk strategy, supervisory authority requires, in particular, that the risk-bearing capacity is taken into account in ICAAP and ILAAP when defining and adapting the strategies. In addition, the capital and liquidity requirements expected in the future as a result of the business strategy must already be included into today's assessment of capital and liquidity adequacy. Cf. inter alia European Central Bank (2018a) and European Central Bank (2018b). The supervisory authority thus regards the relationship between strategy formation and risk-bearing capacity as interdependent. On the link between ICAAP and strategy, see also Gann (2006).
57 See European Banking Authority (2018), para 88 and 89.

experts. The potentially great benefits of reverse stress testing are therefore met by the considerable effort involved.

Correctly applied, reverse stress tests can make a substantial contribution to improving internal transparency with regard to the bank's own risk situation and vulnerabilities of its business model. Transparency enables well-founded and consistent planning, management and decision-making processes and thus ultimately increases the stability, profitability and competitive strength of the institute. Reverse stress tests can therefore make a fundamental contribution to value-orientated corporate management that is geared to the interests of investors, while ensuring creditors' claims can be met at all times. An elementary prerequisite for this is finding an appropriate balance between the benefits and costs caused by reverse stress tests. It is to be hoped that regulators acting with the objective of safeguarding financial market stability will use this balance as a guideline – both in the interpretation of the current requirements and in further specifications of the supervisory requirements for reverse stress tests that are expected in the foreseeable future.

Bibliography

Basel Committee on Banking Supervision (2015). Guidelines. Corporate governance principles for banks, July 2015.

Basel Committee on Banking Supervision (2018). Stress testing principles, January 2018.

Committee of European Banking Supervisors (2010). CEBS Guidelines on Stress Testing (GL32), 2010.

Counterparty Risk Management Policy Group (CRMPG) (2008). Containing Systemic Risk: The Road to Reform, 2008.

European Banking Authority (2015). Guidelines on the interpretation of the different circumstances when an institution shall be considered as failing or likely to fail under Article 32 (6)of Directive 2014/59/EU (EBA/GL/2015/07).

European Banking Authority (2017). Final Report – Guidelines on internal governance under Directive 2013/36/EU, September 2017.

European Banking Authority (2018a). Final Report – Guidelines on the revised common procedures and methodologies for the supervisory review and evaluation process (SREP) and supervisory stress testing, EBA/GL/2018/03, July 2018.

European Banking Authority (2018b). Guidelines on institutions' stress testing, EBA/GL/2018/04, July 2018.

European Banking Authority (2018c). Guidelines on internal governance, EBA/GL/2017/11, March 2018.

European Central Bank (2016). SSM supervisory statement on governance and risk appetite, June 2016.

European Central Bank (2017). ECB Banking Supervision: SSM supervisory priorities 2018, October 2017.

European Central Bank (2018a). ECB Guide to the internal capital adequacy assessment process (ICAAP), November 2018.

European Central Bank (2018b). ECB Guide to the internal liquidity adequacy assessment process (ILAAP), November 2018.

European Central Bank (2018c). ECB Banking Supervision: SSM supervisory priorities 2019, October 2018.

European Central Bank (2019). ECB Banking Supervision: SSM supervisory priorities 2020, October 2019.

Gann, Philipp (2006). Die Umsetzung der aufsichtsrechtlichen Vorgaben zum Internal Capital Adequacy Assessment Process (ICAAP) in deutschen Kreditinstituten, in: *Finanz Betrieb*, 8. Jg., Nr. 9, S. 529–538.

Gann, Philipp (2011). *Regulatorische und ökonomische Aspekte eines modernen Kreditrisikomanagements*, Bern 2011.

Gann, Philipp (2012). Reverse Stress Tests in Kreditinstituten: Ein quantitativ orientierter Ansatz, in: *Corporate Finance biz*, 3. Jg. (2012), Nr. 6, S. 285–299.

Gann, Philipp (2020). ECB Guide to ICAAP – Mindestanforderungen an solide interne Prozesse zur Beurteilung der Kapitaladäquanz, in: *Handbuch Bankenaufsichtsrecht*, ed. von Binder, Jens-Heinrich et al., Köln 2020.

Gann, Philipp/ Igl, Andreas (2019). Quantifizierung des Geschäftsrisikos in Kreditinstituten, in: *Methodenhandbuch ICAAP*, ed. von Igl, Andreas und Heuter, Henning, Köln 2019, S. 187–214.

Heckerman, David/ Horowitz, Eric J./Nathwani, Bharat N. (1992): Toward normative expert systems I: The Pathfinder Project, in: *Methods of information in medicine*, Vol. 31, Nr. 2, S. 106–116.

Institute of International Finance (2008). Final Report of the IIF Committee on Market Best Practices: Principles of Conduct and Best Practice Recommendations – Financial Services Industry Response to the Market Turmoil of 2007–2008, Washington D.C. 2008.

Koller, Daphne/ Friedman, Nir (2009). *Probabilistic Graphical Models: Principles and Techniques*, Cambridge, Massachusetts, 2009.

Pearl, Judea (1988). *Probabilistic Reasoning in Intelligent Systems*, Waltham, 1988.

Rebonato, Ricardo (2010). *Coherent Stress Testing: A Bayesian Approach to the Analysis of Financial Stress*, Hoboken, 2010.

Michael Eichhorn, Aaron Romano

3 Reverse Stress Testing: An Overview of Regulatory Guidance

Evolution, Development Lines, Frequently asked Questions, Outlook

3.1 Introduction

In 2018, one of the authors chaired a two-day Masterclass in Kuala Lumpur.[1] The pre-course questionnaire asked participants to answer the following question: "What are the major challenges you are facing regarding reverse stress testing?" A Chief Risk Officer who worked for the local subsidiary of a global bank answered as follows:

> New concept with little guidance from our regulator.

During the Masterclass, this view was echoed by participants from banks based in Malaysia, Indonesia, India and other Asian countries. In a different Masterclass held in 2019 in London, the challenge was reiterated by participants from Northern, Central and Western Europe, amongst them delegates from Central Banks.

Typical questions included the following:

- How can I perform RST?
- Which capabilities do I need to demonstrate to regulators?
- How do I know I can demonstrate these capabilities to regulators?
- Which points should my documentation cover?
- How should I structure my documentation?

In particular, users wished for more guidance on how to perform RST. For example, banks frequently acknowledge the major challenge of finding an approach which suits their internal capacity and simultaneously enables them to meet the minimum regulatory requirements. However, regulators generally refrain from providing prescriptive guidance. The European Banking Authority (2018, p. 31) gives at least a recommended sequence of steps. The Basel Committee on Banking Supervision

---

[1] This chapter is an updated and extended version of an earlier contribution published in the *Journal of International Banking Law & Regulation* 34(9), pp. 339–51 (2020). We thank Sweet & Maxwell for the permission to reproduce.

https://doi.org/10.1515/9783110647907-003

(2017, p. 53) provides one of the rare descriptive examples, including a reverse sensitivity analysis:

> To that end, institutions should: a) identify the pre-defined outcome to be tested (e.g. of a business model becoming unviable); b) identify possible adverse circumstances that would expose them to severe vulnerabilities and cause the pre-defined outcome; c) assess (depending on the institution's size, as well as the nature, scale, complexity and riskiness of its business activities) the likelihood of events included in the scenarios leading to the pre-defined outcome; and d) adopt effective arrangements, processes, systems or other measures to prevent or mitigate identified risks and vulnerabilities.

> In practice, a range of banks make use of reverse stress tests to identify those events that would threaten the viability of the bank. One bank starts with an analysis of those risk factor variations that would lead to a breach of the regulatory minimum capital requirements. This reverse sensitivity analysis is performed for each material risk type and represent the starting point for the development of an enterprise-wide reverse stress test. Depending on the importance of the risk factors for the bank's business model, the identified risk factor variations are weighted and combined to parameter set(s) for an enterprise-wide reverse stress test covering all material risk types. This multivariate analysis includes a qualitative and critical evaluation of the events that would lead to such parameter sets.

Users raised other questions related to the (technical) challenges of implementing RST, which are also outlined in Chapter 1 of this book. In parts, these challenges are acknowledged by supervisors, for example, the Financial Stability Institute (2018, p. 13):

> While helpful to identify additional vulnerabilities going forward, this approach [RST] is challenging to implement and to interpret for policy purposes, due, for example, to the diversity and complexity of interactions across risk types and factors.

Against this background, the following chapter seeks to provide readers with an overview about the regulatory guidance available to help develop their own frameworks. Following this introduction, the chapter is organised around three sections: Section 3.2 differentiates four phases in the development of the regulatory guidance to date; Section 3.3 derives central development lines and discusses areas for further development; and Section 3.4 closes the contribution with a summary.

In addition to the following synopsis, readers will find further details on regulatory guidance in various chapters of this book (such as in Part I in Chapter 2, in Part III in Chapter 10 and in Part V in Chapter 22 and Chapter 23).

3.2 Evolution of Regulatory Guidance

The development of the regulation on RST can be broken down into four phases. These are summarised in Figure 3.1 and explained in the following chronology.

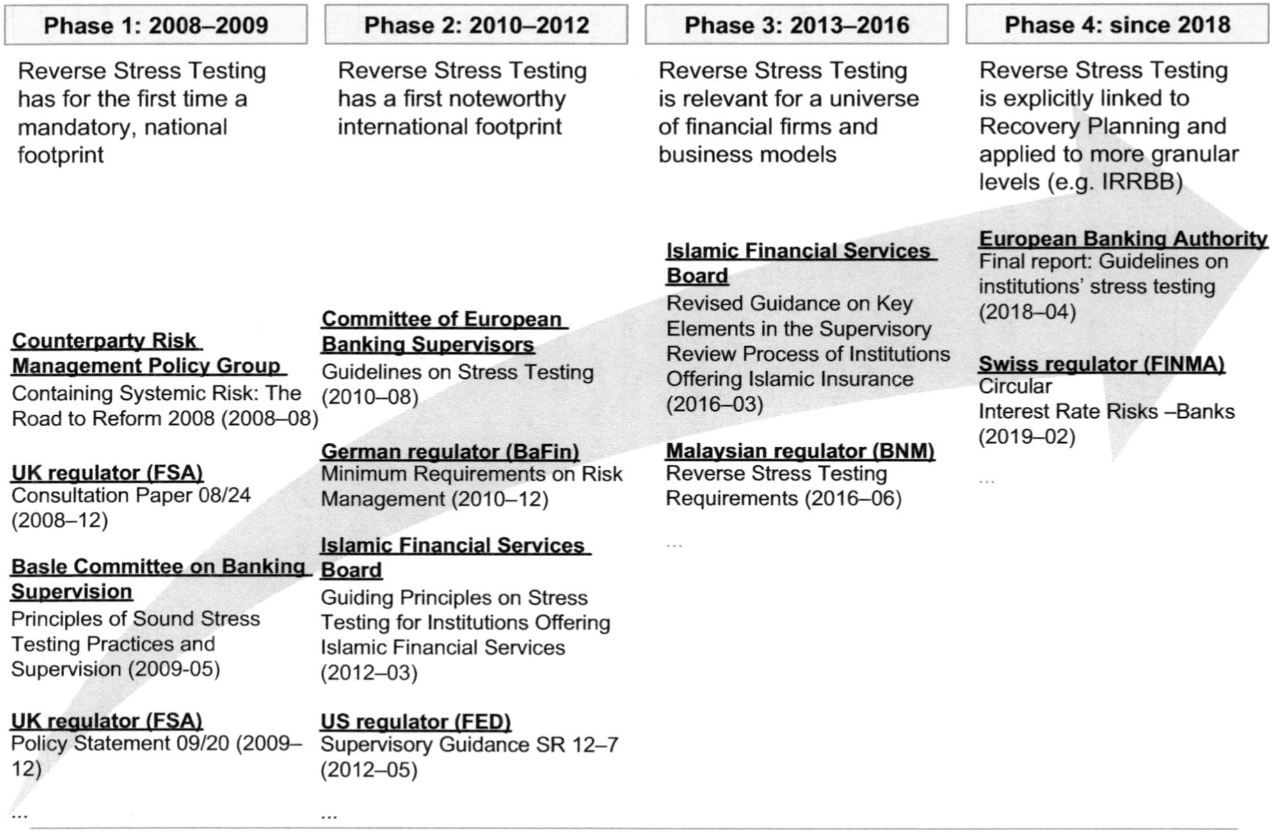

Phase 1: 2008–2009

Reverse Stress Testing has for the first time a mandatory, national footprint

Counterparty Risk Management Policy Group
Containing Systemic Risk: The Road to Reform 2008 (2008–08)

UK regulator (FSA)
Consultation Paper 08/24 (2008–12)

Basle Committee on Banking Supervision
Principles of Sound Stress Testing Practices and Supervision (2009–05)

UK regulator (FSA)
Policy Statement 09/20 (2009–12)

...

Phase 2: 2010–2012

Reverse Stress Testing has a first noteworthy international footprint

Committee of European Banking Supervisors
Guidelines on Stress Testing (2010–08)

German regulator (BaFin)
Minimum Requirements on Risk Management (2010–12)

Islamic Financial Services Board
Guiding Principles on Stress Testing for Institutions Offering Islamic Financial Services (2012–03)

US regulator (FED)
Supervisory Guidance SR 12-7 (2012–05)

...

Phase 3: 2013–2016

Reverse Stress Testing is relevant for a universe of financial firms and business models

Islamic Financial Services Board
Revised Guidance on Key Elements in the Supervisory Review Process of Institutions Offering Islamic Insurance (2016–03)

Malaysian regulator (BNM)
Reverse Stress Testing Requirements (2016–06)

...

Phase 4: since 2018

Reverse Stress Testing is explicitly linked to Recovery Planning and applied to more granular levels (e.g. IRRBB)

European Banking Authority
Final report: Guidelines on institutions' stress testing (2018–04)

Swiss regulator (FINMA)
Circular
Interest Rate Risks –Banks (2019–02)

...

Figure 3.1: Evolution of regulatory requirements.

3.2.1 Phase 1: 2008–2009

> At the end of Phase 1, reverse stress testing had for the first time a mandatory, national footprint.

A decade ago, few, if any, banks worked on RST. After the financial crisis, regulators and de-facto regulatory bodies introduced different requirements and recommendations for banks to perform RST (as a new method, complementary to sensitivity analysis and scenario analysis).

In August 2008, the Counterparty Risk Management Policy Group (CRMPG) issued the paper "Containing Systemic Risk: The Road to Reform 2008". In the paper, CRMPG proposes the use of RST in response to the financial crisis.

In December 2008, the Financial Services Authority published Consultation Paper 08/24 in the United Kingdom. The paper introduced RST as a method. However, the regulator did not prescribe how individual firms should perform it. Instead, the paper left the application at the firm's discretion but advised firms to expect the challenge of their RST assumptions and approaches.

In May 2009, the Bank for International Settlements issued the revised "Principles for sound stress testing practices and supervision". The publication introduced RST in Principle 9 (as one of 14 principles), confirmed the principle of proportionality and identified business lines that may particularly benefit from the use of RST (pp. 14–15):

A stress testing programme should also determine what scenarios could challenge the viability of the bank (reverse stress tests) and thereby uncover hidden risks and interactions among risks. Commensurate with the principle of proportionality, stress tests should feature the most material business areas and events that might be particularly damaging for the firm. This could include not only events that inflict large losses but which subsequently cause damage to the bank's reputation ...

A reverse stress test induces firms to consider scenarios beyond normal business settings and leads to events with contagion and systemic implications. Hence, reverse stress testing has important quantitative and qualitative uses, such as informing senior management's assessment of vulnerabilities. For example, a bank with a large exposure to complex structured credit products could have asked what kind of scenario would have led to widespread losses such as those observed in the financial crisis. Given this scenario, the bank would have then analysed its hedging strategy and assessed whether this strategy would be robust in the stressed market environment characterised by a lack of market liquidity and increased counterparty credit risk.

Given the appropriate judgements, this type of stress test can reveal hidden vulnerabilities and inconsistencies in hedging strategies or other behavioural reactions. ... Areas which benefit in particular from the use of reverse stress testing are business lines where traditional risk management models indicate an exceptionally good risk/return trade-off; new products and new markets which have not experienced severe strains; and exposures where there are no liquid two-way markets.

In December 2009 – following the completion of the consultation phase – the Financial Services Authority issued Policy Statement 09/20. The Policy Statement established RST, for the first time, as a mandatory requirement. Firms were inter alia asked to identify and assess scenarios that were most likely to cause their current business models to become unviable.

3.2.2 Phase 2: 2010–2012

At the end of Phase 2, reverse stress testing had a first noteworthy international footprint. A survey of major international financial institutions points to RST as a "valuable addition" and shows that the importance of RST as a tool for risk measurement and risk management increased (Ernst & Young, 2013, p. 37).

In August 2010, the Committee of European Banking Supervisors published the CEBS Guidelines on Stress Testing (GL32). In Guideline 11, the supranational supervisor states that "institutions should develop RST tests as one of their risk management tools to complement the range of stress tests they undertake". The Committee clarifies that RST is not introduced to determine capital add-ons but rather as a diagnostic tool (applied at same level as ICAAP) with a strong focus on the business model and strategy. It allows firms to start with a more qualitative approach but emphasises the need for clear narratives (pp. 19–20):

64. No single definition of reverse stress testing methodology is provided for the purposes of these guidelines. Reverse stress tests evolve around causes, consequences and impacts, all of which are relevant and any of which can be taken as a starting point. Moreover, qualitative and quantitative approaches are appropriate, depending on the size and complexity of the institution. For example, a reverse stress test for simple and small institutions could be a qualitative discussion of key risk factors and their possible combination in relation to the institution's risk profile at a senior management level. Alternatively, a more sophisticated quantitative approach could be used in identifying a specific loss level, or some other impact on the balance sheet (e.g. movements in capital ratios), and working backwards in a quantitative manner to identify the macro-economic risk drivers, and the required amplitude of movement, that would cause it.

65. .... Reverse stress testing is not expected to result in capital planning and capital add-ons. Instead, its use as a risk management tool is in identifying scenarios, and the underlying dynamism of risk drivers in those scenarios, that could cause an institution's business model to fail. This analysis will be useful in assessing assumptions made about the business model, business strategy and the capital plan. Reverse stress test results may also be used for monitoring and contingency planning.

66. Reverse stress testing should be carried out regularly by all institutions at the same level of application as ICAAP. As a starting point, reverse stress testing may be carried out in a more qualitative manner than other types of stress testing as senior management consider the types of events likely to lead to insolvency.

67. Even for large and complex institutions, reverse stress testing may be undertaken in a more qualitative manner, focusing on the events and materialisation of risk concentrations that could cause their business models to become unviable. As experience is developed, this might then be mapped into more sophisticated qualitative and quantitative approaches developed for other stress testing. Even in a qualitative sense, the impact of macro-economic shocks on an institution's solvency should consider first round and feedback effects as far as possible. Given the importance of a clear narrative running through the reverse stress test to identify business vulnerabilities and to develop an understanding of feedback and non-linear effects, reverse stress testing is more than a simple sensitivity analysis, e.g. simply shifting one relevant parameter to some extreme.

National regulators followed. For example, the German Regulator BaFin integrated reverse stress testing as a new requirement in the Minimum Requirements on Risk Management in December 2010.

In 2012, the proliferation continued with two further milestones. In March 2012, the Islamic Financial Services Board (IFSB) issued "Guiding Principles on Stress Testing for Institutions Offering Islamic Financial Services". It criticised firms for the limited use of RST and demanded that stress test programmes should, among others, support bottom-up and top-down stress testing, including reverse stress testing.

In May 2012, the US Federal Reserve issued "Supervisory Guidance on Stress Testing for Banking Organizations with More Than $10 Billion in Total Consolidated Assets, SR 12–7". The guidance advised firms to consider RST alongside other approaches, such as scenario analysis, sensitivity analysis and enterprise-wide stress testing.

However, most of the guidance remained high-level – that is, it did not go beyond the level of detail shared here, which, as noted, is challenged by industry practitioners. Breaking this mould, the FSA published its final guidance in the so called "Reverse Stress Testing Surgeries" in April 2011. The paper answers 45 frequently asked questions, including many of the questions raised in the introduction of this chapter. As of today, it still represents one of the richest sources of regulatory guidance on RST.

3.2.3 Phase 3: 2012–2017

> At the end of Phase 3, reverse stress testing had relevance for a universe of financial firms and business models.

Phase 3 was characterised by the further rollout across the globe, with national regulators increasingly introducing RST. At the same time, individual supranational bodies advocated the use of RST for supervisory purposes and stressed the linkage of RST to other regulatory initiatives, most notably Recovery Planning.

In March 2014, the IFSB issued its "Revised Guidance on Key Elements in the Supervisory Review Process of Institutions Offering Islamic Insurance (IFSB 16)".

It, amongst others, asked supervisory authorities explicitly to verify the application of RST.

In December 2015, the European Banking Authority published a Comparative Report on Recovery Plan Scenarios. The following extract highlights the linkage of RST to Recovery Planning through the identification of failure points and their related scenarios (pp. 9–14):

> According to the EBA Guidelines on the range of scenarios to be used in recovery plans, 'Reverse stress testing should be considered as a starting point for developing scenarios that should be only "near-default"; i.e. they would lead to an institution's or a group's business model becoming non-viable unless the recovery actions were successfully implemented'. The analysis showed that the use of reverse stress testing was made explicit as a means to identify the highest loss that could bring the institution to its point of non-viability in roughly one-third of the plans and, more generally, to test the severity of the scenarios selected for Recovery Planning purposes. In another case, it was said that reverse stress testing is indeed part of the tools regularly used by the bank, but it is not included within the recovery plan as such a procedure would belong to a resolution plan rather than to a recovery plan. In all the other cases, the link with reverse stress testing was relatively weak, both from a quantitative point of view (i.e. key factors that would drive the institution towards a certain level of loss) and from a qualitative point of view. Indeed, reverse stress testing can be a powerful tool when designing the appropriate recovery scenarios, as it allows the identification of the point of non-viability for the bank and the possible scenarios that would lead to this point.

Following the examples mentioned in Phase 1 and 2, more and more national regulators introduced RST. For example, in June 2016, Bank Negara Malaysia introduced RST requirements for licensed insurers, licensed takaful operators, licensed professional reinsurers and licensed professional retakaful operators. In October 2016, it published a concept paper applicable to licensed banks, licensed investment banks, licensed Islamic banks and licensed International Islamic banks.

At the end of Phase 3, the international footprint of RST became more proliferated. This is evidenced by the Basel Committee on Banking Supervision (2017, p. 9 and p. 53) in its report "Supervisory and bank stress testing: range of practices". Issued in December 2017, the "report primarily draws on the results of two surveys completed during 2016: (i) a survey completed by Basel Committee member authorities (banking supervisors and central banks), which had participation of 31 authorities from 23 countries; and (ii) a survey completed by 54 respondent banks from across 24 countries, including 20 global systemically important banks (G-SIBs). Case studies, and other supervisory findings, are also included to supplement the results of the surveys by providing more detail on specific aspects of stress testing …".

> Reverse stress testing is conducted as a complementary stress test by two-thirds of the institutions. Reverse stress testing is considered a risk management tool that helps banks to assess and understand key risks by identifying scenarios that may put the bank's business model at risk. Solvency stress tests are usually conducted with a time horizon of one to three years, whereas liquidity stress tests cover a much shorter time horizon, ranging for the majority of banks between one and three months …

In reverse stress tests, there is no explicit scenario but instead the objective is to produce a scenario that will cause a specified adverse outcome (such as a breach of capital requirements). Nearly three-quarters of institutions report that they regularly conduct reverse stress tests. This is surprising given that few supervisors conduct or mandate such tests. A capital or liquidity hurdle rate was the most common threshold for the reverse stress tests, with some institutions also modelling a liquidity crisis or breach of risk limits.

Despite this proliferation, most of the regulatory guidance remained at the high level noted for Phase 1 and 2. However, in 2018, the EBA published guidance that went further than most other publications.

3.2.4 Phase 4: Since 2018

In Phase 4, the regulatory guidance seems to evolve towards the application of reverse stress testing to more granular levels (e.g. risk type) and its further linkage to Business Planning, Stress Testing, Recovery Planning and other frameworks, including the better linkage between CFO and CRO departments.

In July 2018, the European Banking Authority (EBA) issued "Final report: Guidelines on institutions' stress testing" (EBA-GL-2018-04). The paper contains a strong call to action for national regulators to progress the usage of the reverse stress tests (beyond Recovery Planning).

The report also offers a wider and more differentiated definition of RST compared to most other publications noted previously. The EBA's definition of RST supports the wider usage of the method by linking it to constituent characteristics as opposed to a rather narrow exhaustive definition. The definition (EBA, 2018, pp. 14–15) also allows for innovative configuration sets like Mild RST, which will be discussed in Part III of this book.

Reverse stress test means an institution stress test that starts from the identification of the pre-defined outcome (e.g. points at which an institution business model becomes unviable, or at which the institution can be considered as failing or likely to fail in the meaning of Article 32 of Directive 2014/59/EU) and then explores scenarios and circumstances that might cause this to occur. Reverse stress testing should have one or more of the following characteristics: (i.) it is used as a risk management tool aimed at increasing the institution's awareness of its vulnerabilities by means of the institution explicitly identifying and assessing the scenarios (or a combination of scenarios) that result in a pre-defined outcome; (ii.) the institution decides on the kind and timing (triggering events) of management or other actions necessary for both (a) rectifying business failures or other problems; and (b) aligning its risk appetite with the actual risks revealed by the reverse stress testing; (iii.) specific reverse stress testing can be also applied in the context of Recovery Planning (e.g. reverse stress tests applied in a wider context can be used to inform a recovery plan stress test by identifying the conditions under which the recovery might need to be planned).

The paper further dedicates an extensive section to RST, structured in three parts. The first part outlines expectations on the implementation such as embeddedness, proportionality and the presence of relevant risks, including systemic risk.

The second part covers the general usage of RST as an analytical tool, a strategy tool, a planning tool, a tool to derive scenarios narratives and general management and a modelling tool. It links RST to topics such as the reliance on models, scenario narratives, backward simulations, the scaling of sensitivities and Asset Liability Management. Beyond the backtesting of traditional stress tests, it pushes for the cross-linkage of RST, for example, to Business Planning, Risk Appetite, ICAAP and ILAAP.

The third part covers the specific usage of RST for Recovery Planning purposes. It explains that banks may use the reverse stress testing process for both regular stress testing and Recovery Planning purposes, e.g. with two complementary reverse stress testing configurations - one to complement ICAAP and ILAAP with the same level of application and a second to complement Recovery Planning.

Finally, the paper offers an Appendix, which responds to challenges received during the consultation process. The relevant parts allow for a deeper understanding of the regulatory views, including guidance on questions raised in the introduction of this book. Together with the RST Surgery paper referenced previously, the guidance addresses concerns raised by industry participants in response to an earlier consultation. The views shared during the consulting process are also shared in the Appendix 2 for the reader's ease of access.

In a separate development, the application of RST at sub-type level emerged. Consistent with the wider RST definition, it implied the usage of RST at the departmental level (as opposed to group-wide approaches often lead by the Enterprise Risk function). For example, based on a translation by KPMG (2018, p. 7), the Swiss regulator FINMA expects institutions to also perform RST at a risk type level for Interest Rate Risk in the Banking Book, whereby "banks shall assume a severe worsening of their capital and earnings in order to reveal vulnerabilities in view of their hedging strategies and the potential behavioural reactions of their customers".

From this chronology, varying development lines and areas for further development can be identified. They are summarised in the following synthesis.

3.3 Synthesis

3.3.1 Development Lines

At least six development lines run through the four phases:
1. RST is visibly growing in importance. It is rolled out across geographies, risk types and business models of financial services firms. As noted, supervisors

themselves are increasingly expected by supranational supervisors to apply the method to individual institutions and to the financial system as a whole (e.g. to assess systemic risk).

2. Regulators (intentionally) do not tell users how to perform RST. Even the few regulatory publications that reference specific practical implementations tend to remain largely descriptive.

3. Regulators seem to recognise the challenges related to the implementation of RST. For example, the Financial Stability Institute (2018, p. 13) references the complexity as a key challenge:

> A scenario can be designed in at least three different ways ... . A third option is reverse stress testing, whereby the scenario is calibrated so as to deliver a given estimated likelihood or an expected capital ratio post-stress. While helpful to identify additional vulnerabilities going forward, this approach is challenging to implement and to interpret for policy purposes, due, for example, to the diversity and complexity of interactions across risk types and factors.

4. The regulatory requirements tend to remain high-level and rather generic. A common key message is the principle of proportionality, according to which the implementation of RST can differ depending on the size, nature and complexity of the business model. This allows for implementations with different degrees of sophistication, including solely qualitative approaches for smaller firms. Some regulators focus on large banks and expect the latter to evolve towards a more quantitative approach over time – for example, the Reserve Bank of India (2013, p. 16, para 4.5.3):

> Reverse stress testing should be carried out regularly by large and complex banks (i.e. Group A banks) to investigate the risk factors that wipe out their capital resources and also make their business unviable. As a starting point, reverse stress testing is likely to be carried out in a more qualitative manner than other types of stress testing. As experience is developed, this should then be mapped into more sophisticated qualitative and quantitative approaches developed for other stress testing.

5. Most regulators still choose a rather narrow definition of RST, linking its application to the business model becoming unviable and a firm's failure. However, as highlighted in Phase 4, the application of different configurations based on a wider definition of RST and narrower settings on individual risk types suggests a more versatile use of the tool.

6. The building of bridges between RST and other crisis management and contingency frameworks seems to deserve further attention.

Individual banks may wish to discuss all of these points further in their ongoing regulatory dialogue.

3.3.2 What to Further Discuss in the Regulatory Dialogue

With regard to the first points, regulators may argue that it should not be their responsibility to tell banks how to perform RST and overcome its challenges. Nevertheless, further publications, like the aforementioned report by the Basel Committee on Banking Supervision (2017) on the range of practices, seem desirable and can form an appropriate reference point. Alternatively, readers can use available qualitative and quantitative use cases (including those presented in Part II and III of this book) to further discuss the expectations of the respective regulator. As an example, in Part III of this book, Eichhorn/Mangold map the regulatory guidance from different supervisory bodies to each step of their generic, process-orientated qualitative approach (see the Appendix in their chapter).

Furthermore, publications, such as the aforementioned Financial Services Authority (2011) RST Surgeries guidance and the consultation paper on the "Guidelines on institutions' stress testing" issued by the European Banking Authority (2018), can be of great help to answer frequently asked questions. Readers may want to review with their respective regulator if the guidance given can be equally applied in their jurisdiction.

Beyond this guidance on current practices and regulatory expectations, point 5 and point 6 seem particularly relevant for the future development of RST as a testing method. The next section discusses them in more detail.

3.3.2.1 Consideration of Different Configuration Sets and Tests Designs

As highlighted in the introduction of this book, similar to the original usage of stress tests in material research, RST can use many different configurations and test designs. This was illustrated in the form of a morphological box which should be read as a "menu table" – that is, under each dimension, different choices are possible, resulting in a variety of potential test designs and potential configurations.

For example, here are some RST calibrations the user may consider:
- Different scopes - ranging from individual books to interbank networks
- Different time horizons - ranging from scenarios that crystallise in a matter of days to those that take months or years to materialise
- Aspects beside the loss of earnings and financial resources – for example, the loss of operational capabilities or market confidence; each of these may be operationalised with different metrics for which different thresholds may qualify the "failure point"
- Risks top-down or bottom-up, i.e. aggregating risk identified by individual business units
- Idiosyncratic, macro-economic or combination scenarios, whereby not only the sequence of events may vary

- The outcome (e.g. failure) prior to or after all current management actions have been exhausted
- Different quantitative models, qualitative techniques or combinations of both

Over and above these choices, the test design may vary in terms of the number and sequence of steps. The different applications should be proactively discussed with regulators.

In creativity techniques literature, one method directed at reverse thinking, is called "headstand". The method includes easier application techniques (e.g. analysis of individual risk factors or sensitivities in reverse) which are relevant in light of the complexity challenge highlighted by FIS at the outset of this chapter. Applying different calibration sets and test designs allows for different and smaller headstands. In Part III of this book, the chapter on Mild RST provides a practical example for such an innovative calibration set.

Another relevant topic for the regulatory dialogue seems to be the cross-linkage of RST. In practice RST seems - with differences between banks and regulators - increasingly linked with planning work, risk appetite, ICAAP/ILAAP and traditional stress testing frameworks, including the use of RST results for backtesting purposes. By contrast the linkage to other management frameworks, in particular neighbouring crisis management and contingency frameworks seems to be covered less expansively, if at all. However, it seems worthwhile to "look over the fence", as the following section illustrates.

3.3.2.2 RST and Crisis Management and Contingency Frameworks

Figure 3.2 provides an overview over neighbouring crisis management and contingency frameworks. On the left-hand side, it shows recovery and resolution planning (RRP) – that is, the preparatory planning work for a near failure (recovery) or actual failure (resolution) alongside the severity continuum. The Point of Non-Viability (PoNV), a pre-calibrated failure point, delineates the business planning for going concern (viable) to gone concern (non-viable). Depending on the position, either the Recovery Plan or the Resolution Plan are executed. As illustrated by the arrows, each of these plans are in turn closely linked to other crisis management and contingency frameworks.

Regulators and banks often treat RST, Recovery and, in particular, resolution planning as separate initiatives. However, as Table 3.1 illustrates, RST and RRP share commonalities, amongst them the focus on stressed financial resources (capital, liquidity), entry points and other building blocks such as management actions (spectrum of actions, feasibility, time to execution, and so on).

At the very minimum, it seems recommendable to build bridges in internal frameworks as well as in the regulatory guidance. Amongst other things, RST can, in the context of Recovery Planning, inform the selection of shocks, "be seen as a starting point for developing scenarios to test the effectiveness of the menu of recovery options"

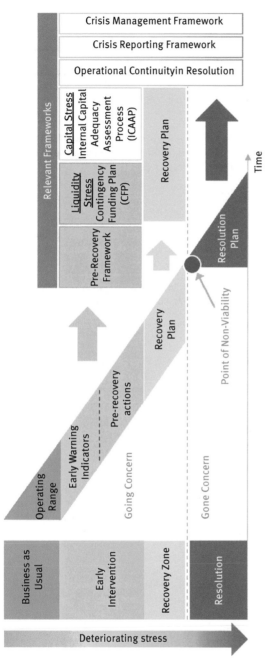

Figure 3.2: Stress continuum and relevant frameworks.

Table 3.1: Comparison of RRP and RST.

	Recovery and Resolution Planning	**Reverse Stress Testing**
Objective	Enable orderly recovery and resolution (e.g. plan for retracting and resolvability, solvent wind-down)	Identify vulnerabilities and scenarios that could lead to failure
Regulatory guidance	Resolution planning spearheaded by Financial Stability Board with focus on large institutions; further guidance – e.g. by the EBA on Recovery Planning and by the US FED on resolution planning	Initially largely spearheaded by the UK Financial Services Authority with focus on all types of institutions.
Owner	Often led by Chief Financial Officer function (e.g. Treasury department)	Often led by Chief Risk Officer function (e.g. Enterprise Risk Management department)
Integration in frameworks	Integrated in Crisis Management framework	Integrated in Enterprise Risk Stress Management framework
Severity	Going concern (recovery) and gone concern (resolution)	Mainly going concern (but dependent on test design)
Target metrics	Financial resources (capital and liquidity)	Financial resources (capital and liquidity) and other (e.g. operational failure)
Building blocks	Failure points, scenario path, narrative, management actions	Failure points, scenario path, narrative, management actions
Scope	Group and entities (different portfolios may be affected at different points in time depending on presumptive path)	Depending on RST configuration, mainly group, entities, portfolios
Documentation	Detailed playbooks to activate crisis management, ensure operational consistency, activate communication plans, monitor financial resources	Frameworks, policies and procedures with lower level of detail
Step width and scenario evolution	Slow continuous scenario evolution in small, incremental steps (e.g. from BAU, to month 1, month 2, etc., to resolution weekend and so forth)	High-level scenario evolution usually in large, discrete steps, no "baby steps", potential "timetable mismatch" to RRP
Capabilities (models and IT infrastructure)	Build-up of new models and infrastructure (Funding in Resolution, Capital in Resolution, Valuation in Resolution)	Usually use existing models and infrastructure (proportionality principle)

(Financial Stability Board, 2013, p. 7) and help to "make contingency plans, or take other steps to mitigate the identified risks" (Islamic Financial Services Board, 2016, p. 49). In turn, RST frameworks can benefit from recovery[2] and resolution planning[3] work.

As previously noted, the European Banking Authority consider Recovery Planning as a special usage of RST. The main requirements are shown in Table 3.2.

The authors have discussed with regulators and subject matter practitioners in Asia, Europe and North America who by and large agreed that more should be done towards one cohesive, joined up framework. For resolution planning, banks are currently working on dedicated programmes to comply with regulatory requirements spearheaded by the Financial Stability Board, including the build of new capabilities and infrastructure, which RST could, in parts, leverage. The topic is further deepened in this book, in particular in Part V of this book.

3.4 Summary

As noted in the introduction of this book, RST is still a relatively new method which has the potential to improve current risk management practices but is not without challenges. One of these challenges, discussed in this chapter, is the request from practitioners to receive further regulatory guidance.

Against this background, Section 3.2 established the evolution and current status of RST regulation in the form of a chronology consisting of four phases. The analysis confirmed six development lines, amongst them the principle of proportionality and the high-level nature of most regulatory guidance. In parts, the latter is intentionally kept at a higher level to provide discretion to institutions on how to customise RST to their business model. Given this rather generic nature of regulatory guidance, there is no "tick box" list against which users can assess the compliance of their practices, and there most likely never will be. However, the authors identified selected regula-

---

2 RST users may also identify weaknesses in their institution's existing RST frameworks by performing a read-across from comparative reports on Recovery Planning implementation practices – for example, the "Recovery Plan Scenarios - Comparative Report" published by the European Banking Authority in 2015.
3 So-called playbooks often describe in detail the specific entry points, governance protocols, tools (e.g. management information and calculations made available) and activities (e.g. management actions). As such, a (scenario agnostic) walkthrough can help RST users to understand what happens along the continuum, who is deciding what, what mitigating actions are planned, and what changes are made if the bank reaches the next severity level - ultimately, in resolution, the handover of decision-making to regulators. Many banks are currently enhancing their RRP capabilities, including new model capabilities (e.g. to support dynamic balance sheet projections, Funding in Resolution, Valuation in Resolution, Capital in Resolution) and infrastructure functionalities (e.g. "dials" which allow to "scale" impacts up and down depending on the individual scenario path). Furthermore, the regulatory requirements for RRP often seem more extensive compared to RST, while equally pertinent for the latter.

tory publications (e.g. FSA Surgeries) that should help readers who are working on the implementation of RST. Key extracts of the guidance provided are shared in the appendices of this chapter. As recommended before, readers may confirm with their respective national supervisor where the latter shares the respective guidance (and where not). Furthermore, reports like the BIS Report on the range of practices offer valuable reference points on how to perform RST. Regulators may consider more of these publications on actual practical implementations in the future.

Section 3.3 deepened two of the six previously identified development lines that, in the views of the authors, future guidance should follow up on. Most importantly, future guidance should consider RST more as a thinking tool that can use different configurations and multiple test designs for different purposes. As such, RST does not need to be restricted to a business model scope and a high severity failure. As noted, the European Banking Authority is using a less narrow definition and at least one national regulator started to apply RST at risk type level for Interest Rate Risk in the Banking Book. The other development line relates to the further linkage of RST with other crisis management and contingency frameworks, beyond the "mere" back-testing of traditional stress tests and work on deliverables related to business strategy, financial planning, risk appetite, ICAAP and ILAAP. Given commonalities and conceptual overlaps, this particularly applies for recovery and resolution planning (RRP) – that is, planning work for a (near or actual) failure. As noted, the European Banking Authority already considers Recovery Planning as a special usage of RST.

Overall, the authors believe that regulators can and should play a key part in the further development of RST.

Table 3.2: Regulatory requirements linking RST and Recovery Planning.

Reverse Stress Testing and Recovery Planning and Contingency Planning		
EBA	Para 97 p. 33/34	Institutions should …. use specific reverse stress testing to develop 'near-default' scenarios (institution close to failure but no further) and as an input to inform and test the efficiency and effectiveness of their recovery actions and their Recovery Planning, and analyse sensitivities around corresponding assumptions. Such 'near-default' scenarios should identify and describe the point that would lead an institution's or a group's business model to become non-viable unless the recovery actions were successfully implemented. The scenarios should allow the estimation of results and the suitability of all the available recovery options. The terminology used in the description of recovery scenarios should help to determine which recovery options were tested under particular stress scenarios. The description should have a sufficient level of detail, through both a set of quantitative assumptions and a qualitative narrative, in order to determine whether or not the scenario is relevant for the institution and how severe it is. The events should be described in a logical sequence and the assumptions underlying the main drivers (e.g. net income, risk-weighted assets (RWAs), capital) should be laid down very clearly. The scenarios should also take into account a possible estimation of the cross-effects of executing different recovery plan options in the same stress scenario. The scenarios should also allow an understanding of how the events unfold by providing an appropriate timeline that makes it clear at which point in time certain actions will be developed (with implications for their credibility and feasibility). The purpose of this exercise is to test the effectiveness of the institution's recovery options in restoring financial strength and viability when the institution comes under such severe stress.
EBA	Para 98 p. 34	Because of the different objectives of the two sets of reverse stress tests, the stress tests for ICAAP and ILAAP purposes and Recovery Planning should not be interlinked but compared with one another.
EBA	Para 99 p. 34	Institutions should use reverse stress testing to assist with the development, assessment and calibration of the 'near-default' scenarios used for Recovery Planning.
EBA	Para 100 p. 34	Institutions should use reverse stress testing to identify the risk factors and further understand and describe the scenarios that would result in 'near default', assessing effective recovery actions that can be credibly implemented, either in advance or as the risk factors or scenarios develop.
EBA	Para 101 p. 34	Reverse stress testing should contribute to the recovery plan scenarios by using a dynamic and quantitative scenario narrative, which should cover: (a) the recovery triggers (i.e. at which point the institution would enact recovery actions in the hypothetical scenario); (b) the recovery actions required and their expected effectiveness, including the method of assessing that effectiveness (i.e. indicators that should be monitored to conclude that no further action is required); (c) the appropriate timing and process required for those recovery actions; and (d) in the case of further stress, points (b) and (c) for the potential additional recovery actions required to address residual risks.

Appendix 3.1: Financial Services Authority: Response to Frequently Asked Questions (Extract from Reverse Stress Testing Surgeries, April 2011)

Category	Question	Response
Scope	1. At what level in my firm are reverse stress tests required?	BIPRU firms (banks, building societies and investment firms) and insurers that fall within the scope of SYSC 20 must carry out reverse stress testing on both a solo and consolidated basis. This will obviously include the overseas branches of UK-regulated firms within that scope.
	2. For which entities should a reverse stress test be carried out?	All solo entities must carry out a reverse stress test and be captured by the reverse stress test carried out for the consolidated group. However, where a solo entity is not material to the risk profile of the group, and its going concern status can be shown to depend primarily on the solvency of the group, a simple qualitative submission from that solo entity pointing to the group reverse stress test will suffice.
	3. How does the requirement apply to firms with non-regulated entities in the group?	The reverse stress test carried out on a consolidated basis must include all entities – both regulated and non-regulated – in the consolidation group falling within the scope of the requirement, but on a solo basis, only regulated entities falling within the scope of the requirement need to be considered.
	4. What if my firm is a UK-regulated subsidiary with an unregulated parent (overseas or otherwise)?	Where the unregulated parent is overseas and there is no UK group in existence, the firm should undertake the reverse stress test on a solo basis. In this case, the potential impact on a subsidiary of an event overseas affecting the parent should be considered and factored in where appropriate. Where the unregulated parent is based in the UK, see the response to question 3.
	5. Are you asking overseas parents of UK-regulated firms to comply with the reverse stress testing requirement?	No, but the relevant UK entity undertaking the reverse stress test should consider the potential for a parent to have a material impact on its subsidiary (e.g. through an event at the parent resulting in significant reputational risk for the UK entity only).
	6. Is a full quantitative analysis of the parent required where it is an overseas group and the UK entity is a material undertaking?	No, but the potential for the state of the parent to affect that of the subsidiary in an adverse manner must be addressed. On the basis of materiality and proportionality this may be undertaken in a largely qualitative manner. (See response to question 5.)

(continued)

Category	Question	Response
	7. How should the reverse stress test be carried out where the UK-regulated firm is a subsidiary of an overseas parent on which it is wholly reliant for its survival?	The failure of the parent may be the most clearly relevant scenarios but the subsidiary should also consider local stresses that give rise to business model failure – for example, an operational risk event affecting just the UK-regulated entity.
	8. How does the requirement apply to groups that have operations outside the UK?	All operations outside the UK that are part of a UK solo entity or its consolidated group should be captured in the reverse stress testing exercise.
	9. How detailed does my exercise have to be at the solo and/ or group levels?	For solo entities, the level of detail should be proportionate, reflecting the materiality of those entities and their dependency on other group entities. The group exercise should include an assessment of interlinkages between entities within the group and the potential for risk contagion to crystallise (e.g. through reputational risk).
	10. Is the reverse stress test requirement being implemented by other countries outside of the UK?	Yes, to differing extents by different international supervisors – for example, for banks through the Basel Committee and the European Banking Authority (EBA). We are also aware that other international authorities are considering implementing this requirement (see response to question 11).
	11. The UK is pursuing a policy that is not being implemented elsewhere. Is there a discussion with other regulators about implementing reverse stress testing? (This is a particular issue with regard to obtaining sign-off at board-level.)	We are keeping other regulators informed of our work in this area and guidelines drawn up by umbrella supervisory organisations recommend that supervisors consider reverse stress testing for their supervised institutions (see response to question 10).

(continued)

Category	Question	Response
Process	12. What has to be done by the implementation date?	Firms to which the requirement applies should be in a position to carry out a reverse stress test for submission with their next Individual Capital Adequacy Assessment Process/Individual Capital Assessment (ICAAP/ICA). (For eligible firms other than BIPRU investment firms the implementation date is 14 December 2010, and for BIPRU investment firms within scope of SYSC 20 it is 28 March 2011.)
	13. What should we do if our strategic planning process is in September every year? Will the FSA simply ask us for the reverse stress test in September 2011?	We require you to have procedures and processes in place to produce a reverse stress testing exercise as of 14 December 2010 (or 28 March 2011 for relevant investment firms). In the future, your reverse stress testing submission should form part of your ICAAP/ICA submission (and we would expect to see it play a role in your planning exercises) – although, if supervisors wish to see it and discuss it with you before that time, they will give you appropriate notice.
	14. In reverse stress testing, will firms be considering the same risks as they do for other stress tests? Doesn't this create overlap?	The reverse stress testing requirement should build on and complement the existing stress testing framework. While the stress tests performed for capital planning purposes will have an adverse impact on the financial situation of the firm, for reverse stress testing purposes, we are asking firms to consider where one or more causes lead to the existing business model of the firm becoming unviable – i.e. crystallising risks cause the market to lose confidence in it, with the consequence that counterparties and other stakeholders are unwilling to transact with it or provide it with capital.
	15. Does the implementation template imply that we need to deploy additional resources/make wholesale changes to IT infrastructure to undertake a reverse stress test?	No, the reverse stress testing framework should complement your existing stress testing framework. (The cost-benefit analysis undertaken in relation to this requirement, published in PS09/201, found that several firms surveyed for the policy statement indicated that incremental IT costs for reverse stress testing would be zero).

(continued)

Category	Question	Response
	16. How should the point at which the business model fails be identified?	Firms may start to develop scenarios that lead to the business model failing by considering the cause, consequence or impact (financial or otherwise) of one or more events that lead to the failure of the firm. Firms should note that 'failure' is not necessarily identified with the point at which the capital and/or liquidity of the firm is exhausted. For example, it may be the point at which: — market participants see that the firm is over-exposed to a particularly risky sector (cause); — market sentiment results in the refusal of market counterparties to deal with the firm or under such onerous conditions that it is economically unviable for the firm to do so (consequence); or — the firm is unable to transact any new business and its revenue streams dry up (impact). Firms might consider any one of these as a starting point from which to develop the scenarios. (This may be contrasted with a real-world failure, where the sequence of cause-consequence impact occurs in that distinct order.)
	17. How do I define a business model failure?	The firm should decide what constitutes business model failure, based on risks crystallising that cause the market to lose confidence in the firm (see response to question 14). It is important to note that it is not solely about inadequate financial resources.
	18. Is it acceptable if my firm starts off only including qualitative analysis in reverse stress-tests and moves on to include more quantitative analysis over time?	We would expect the overall process to be primarily qualitative in nature for smaller firms, given our view on proportionality. In the future, smaller firms may well retain a primarily qualitative focus in their analysis, but we would expect larger, more complex firms to undertake more detailed analysis, incorporating quantitative analysis from the outset.

(continued)

Category	Question	Response
	19. Do management actions need to be signed off by senior management, or is the FSA just looking for agreement in principle to management actions in the reverse stress test?	The firm should consider whether the management actions need to be signed off by senior management – this will depend on the action being considered (and it should be noted that the board or senior management will sign off the exercise in its entirety anyway).
	20. We are asked to submit the results of reverse stress tests after taking account of currently available management actions, but we are asked to then think about mitigating management actions based on the results of the reverse stress tests. How do these two sets of management actions fit together?	The reverse stress tests that cause a firm's business model to fail are those where prospective management actions would not be sufficient to prevent such a failure. Having identified such scenarios, we ask firms to think about ways in which they might strengthen their business models now to mitigate the risks posed by the scenarios. This strengthening may include enhancing the impact that prospective management actions would have or putting in place the necessary conditions for taking new management actions that could avert business model failure.
Scenarios	21. Is the FSA asking firms to produce eight reverse stress tests that cover the extremes of the reverse stress testing 'cube' illustrated in the first round of surgeries?	No, we are asking firms to consider adverse but plausible events or confluences of events that might give rise to their business model failing. However, it is for firms themselves to consider whether events at the extremes are relevant to their own circumstances (see responses to questions 22 and 23).

(continued)

Category	Question	Response
	22. There are any number of scenarios with a range of complexities. Is the FSA going to give more guidance about their expectations in regard to the complexity of the scenario?	No, the reverse stress testing exercise supplements the firm's existing risk appetite statement, which itself is informed by, among other things, 'normal' stress testing. Firms should start by considering a wide number of scenarios that might potentially threaten their business model, despite credible management actions – subject to those scenarios being plausible – and narrow them down to the ones most likely to cause the business model of the firm to fail (see responses to questions 21 and 23).
	23. There are any number of scenarios that may be considered. Are we required to discount scenarios and submit the most likely scenarios?	Yes – the most relevant, severe and plausible scenarios that might give rise to the business model failing, despite credible management actions, should be identified via a process of elimination and submitted (see responses to questions 21 and 22). These should be the most likely scenarios, given that business model failure is a prerequisite for a scenario to be considered, and not necessarily based on an assessment of the absolute probability of the scenario occurring.
	24. Should firms document scenarios that have been considered but dismissed as being deemed too unlikely?	No, but the process undertaken to choose the final scenarios should be documented, and firms may wish to record all scenarios considered, both for internal reference purposes and for future iterations of the reverse stress testing exercises.
	25. What about scenarios that are considered, but after being run show that the firm does not fail?	We expect firms to have considered a range of scenarios and to submit detail on any that significantly threaten the firm's business model to the point of failure, although we are also interested in those where the firm does not fail but material issues are uncovered.
	26. How many scenarios should firms focus on in detail in their submission?	We would generally expect all firms to include a number of relevant scenarios in the submission, and larger, more complex firms to consider and submit more scenarios. Firms should undertake a filtering process, starting with a wide set of potential scenarios and narrowing these down until those that present the greatest threat to the failure of the business model are left for detailed analysis and for inclusion in the submission.

(continued)

Category	Question	Response
	27. At what stage should the management actions be incorporated into an assessment of the impact of events that threaten the business model?	We are asking firms to identify those events (or confluences of events) that would lead to their business model failing after currently available management actions had been taken. This will enable firms to identify those management actions that would not be sufficiently effective in their current state of development and/or would not currently be possible. Given this knowledge, firms should then consider: (i) strengthening currently available management actions to the point that they could prevent failure of the business model and/or (ii) putting in place the conditions necessary for new, credible management actions, with the outcome that the business model subsequently would not fail under the same single event or set of events.
	28. Should firms include scenarios where the management actions prevent business model failure?	These may be useful to illustrate to your supervisors how you have identified relevant scenarios, particularly where the scenario(s) in question may at first have appeared to be relevant and likely to result in the failure of the business model. However, the requirement for the reverse stress testing exercise is that each scenario should result in business model failure after all available existing management actions have been deployed.
	29. What quantitative analysis should be included in the submission?	As a starting point, every scenario should be described in qualitative terms, with quantitative analysis where appropriate and possible. We expect larger, more complex firms to undertake more extensive quantitative analysis in their reverse stress testing as appropriate, relative to smaller, less complex firms.
	30. Do firms need to assess the likelihood of a scenario crystallising in quantitative terms?	No, the likelihood can be expressed by ranking the scenarios, rather than deriving a probability and/or confidence level.
	31. Can we consider reverse stress test scenarios where the firm does not take enough risk? (That is, it is too conservative and therefore loses out to competition.)	Yes, if this leads to potential failure of the business model (e.g. through reduced income).

(continued)

Category	Question	Response
Time horizon	32. Should we incorporate only those events that crystallise over an extended period?	Although firms should consider events that might occur at any time within a time horizon of three to five years, it may be that there is an event (or a set of events) that leads to the firm's business model failing more rapidly – for example, the discovery of a significant internal fraud event with resultant loss of market confidence. Firms must, therefore, consider both slow- and fast-crystallising events that might cause the business model to become unviable.
Governance	33. Who needs to sign off on the reverse stress test?	The board or senior management of the firm must sign off the reverse stress test. However, as generally under our rules in SYSC, both the board and senior management are ultimately responsible for the management of a firm's prudential risks. Sign-off by the board is recommended in any event and may present an opportunity for it to use the reverse stress testing exercise and outputs to inform the firm's risk appetite and business planning.
	34. What degree of engagement is required by the Board for reverse stress testing?	The board or senior management will ultimately sign off the outputs of the exercise on a periodic basis, but we would also expect the board to perform several other tasks, such as: – input into identifying potential events that might result in failure of the business model; – challenge the outputs of the reverse stress testing exercises; and – approve changes to the reverse stress testing framework.
Outputs	35. How will the results of the reverse stress testing exercise be used?	Firms should use the results to inform their own risk mitigation plans that would be enacted should the scenarios occur, as the primary purpose of the exercise is for firms to identify weaknesses in their business model, and associated management actions, under those scenarios. We may discuss the results with each firm in the context of their risk management framework, and we may look across the spectrum of firms to see whether any common themes arise – for example, a common event that might lead to the business model of multiple firms failing (such as the failure of a firm that provides an outsourced service to multiple users). Firms should note that we will not use the results of the exercise to generate additional capital requirements directly, but they might give rise to additional capital requirements where they highlight more general shortcomings in the existing oversight and governance processes in a firm.

(continued)

Category	Question	Response
	36. Does the FSA have a template for submissions?	No, we want firms to develop a format that is appropriate for their own risk framework and makes all relevant components of the exercise clear.
	37. What will supervisors do if they believe that the firm's exercise, including the analysis and outputs, are poor?	Firms should strive to submit the outputs of a good quality reverse stress testing exercise the first time around. Assuming that this has been done, where supervisors find a submission to be wanting, they will adopt a pragmatic approach, and give the firm feedback on its submission and an opportunity to re-visit the exercise. We recognise that, to begin with, the development, review and refinement of the exercise will be an iterative process for both firms and supervisors.
	38. Will the outputs of a firm's reverse stress testing exercise be used to set part of its Individual Capital Guidance and/or Capital Planning Buffer?	No – however, any new risks highlighted during the course of the exercise may feed back into the Pillar 2 assessments in the case that the reverse stress testing exercise highlights potential shortcomings in either the ICAAP/ICA and/or general risk management framework (see the response to question 35). The reverse stress testing exercise is an internal risk management exercise intended to be a complement to the ICAAP/ICA, and will not prompt us to raise the bar in terms of our expectations of those assessments.
	39. What will the FSA use the outputs of reverse stress tests for and why is the FSA asking for it if there is no capital outcome?	We want to understand what firms think about potential weaknesses in their business models and, in particular, how they are integrating the analysis of these into their risk management processes. In doing so, we seek to enhance firms' own risk management, which is not only advantageous to firms but also helps us to meet our regulatory objectives of consumer protection, market confidence and financial stability. See also guidance in SYSC 20.2.7G.
Banks	40. What if my firm is currently applying for a banking licence?	You should liaise with the FSA contact dealing with your application regarding the stage at which you might be required to present the results of your reverse stress testing exercise. We expect you to build in the ability to perform the reverse stress tests alongside the development of your more general risk management framework.
Insurers life	41. How does the requirement apply to a group that includes a bank and an insurer?	In accordance with SYSC 20.2.2R, firms must conduct reverse stress tests in relation to their insurance group or UK consolidation group or non-EEA sub-group. Where one of these groups is part of a broader financial conglomerate the requirement to undertake a reverse stress test must be met at any intermediate level, too.

(continued)

Category	Question	Response
	42. How does reverse stress testing link with Solvency II implementation?	We will clarify the requirements for submitting firms' reverse stress testing exercises when the reporting requirements arising from Solvency II are finalised, but firms will be expected to be able to submit the outputs of their annual reverse stress testing exercise to their supervisor from 14 December 2010.
	43. What are the FSA's expectations about 'unviability' for insurers? Is it insolvency, run-off, etc.?	It is any set of circumstances that, either on a standalone basis or in conjunction, cause the firm to arrive at the point that crystallising risks cause the market to lose confidence in it, with the consequence that counterparties and other stakeholders are unwilling to transact with it or provide it with capital. While financial insolvency might be one reason for reaching this point, other earlier trigger points leading to this state might be the withdrawal of authorisation by the supervisor or an adverse audit opinion. These might not represent the end-point of business model failure, but they may potentially be the start of an inexorable move to such status.
	44. Do we need to calibrate the reverse stress test and does it link with the '1 in 200' stress test?	The reverse stress test will require firms to identify one or more events that cause the failure of the firm's business model, and should therefore be linked to your overall business and strategic planning process. There is no explicit link to the '1 in 200' stress test (that is focused on ensuring the firm has sufficient capital to withstand such a stress) as the intention is that the reverse stress testing requirement will enable firms to identify circumstances that bring about failure of the business model – not necessarily through a shortage of capital – and thereby to strengthen currently available management actions, or to develop new ones, that prevent such failure. (While this may involve some aspects of your ICA, it is not necessarily the case that the two exercises would be closely calibrated.)
Investment firms	45. How does the requirement apply to a group that has an investment firm with a consolidation waiver? (That is, it does not have to submit an ICAAP, but is in scope of the reverse stress test requirement.)	The fact that an investment firm may benefit from a consolidation waiver is irrelevant for reverse stress testing purposes. The requirement will apply both to the consolidated group, including the investment firm(s) to which the waiver applies, and the investment firm(s) on a solo basis, given that a potential failure of other group firms might lead to one or more investment firms failing.

Appendix 3.2: European Banking Authority Response on Industry Comments (Extract from Consultation Paper, EBA/CP/2017/17, 31/10/2017)

Comments	Summary of responses received	EBA analysis	Amendments to the proposals
Para 82 **Reverse stress testing – requirements, general use, and use for recovery actions and planning**	One respondent mentioned that would be clearer to see separate sections on a) recovery plan stress testing (near-default) ideally cross-referring to specifics contained elsewhere in other papers, and b) general guidance on reverse stress testing as a stress testing technique. This in turn would result in definitions for the scope of recovery plan stress testing and reverse stress testing more generally.	The GL mentions that the reverse stress testing should be used in a wider context, not only for recovery and resolution planning. The GLs for reverse stress testing are organised in three sections. The first section presents the requirements more generally. The second section presents the use of this type of institution stress tests also in a more generally way. The third section presents the reverse stress testing and respective specific use for recovery actions and Recovery Planning, that is in a more specific way. The definitions and scope of reverse stress testing are already defined in taxonomy.	No change
Para 83 **Reverse stress testing – use to determine the severity of ICAAP and ILAAP**	Two respondents mentioned that the use of reverse stress tests to determine the severity of ICAAP and ILAAP scenarios does not seem feasible. In the overall context, it is reasonable to use reverse scenarios as plausibility instruments. The determination of the severity, however, should be carried out based on risk appetite, as well as the coherent scenario specification, which is comprehensible for the management.	The GL mentions that institutions should include scenarios identified through the reverse stress tests to complement the range of stress tests scenarios they undertake and for comparison purposes in order to assess the overall severity, allowing the identification of severe but still plausible scenarios. The reverse stress testing should be useful to set the severity of scenarios for ICAAP and ILAAP stress tests. The severity of reverse stress testing scenarios can be also assessed by comparing it inter alia to historical or other supervisory and publicly available scenarios.	Para 83 changed to provide clarification regarding the useful way to assess severity of scenarios

(continued)

Comments	Summary of responses received	EBA analysis	Amendments to the proposals
		The GL mentions that scenarios identified through the reverse stress tests are used as complementary/ additional information to comparison purposes and as useful way to assess the severity of scenarios.	
		The EBA considers that the paragraph could be clarified to mention the useful way of assessment.	
Para 85 **Reverse stress testing – use**	Another respondent welcomed, in principle, linking reverse stress testing and Recovery Planning scenarios. Reverse stress testing is always performed at individual institution level under these guidelines. In the case of Recovery Planning, institutions which belong to an institutional protection scheme are given the option of conducting Recovery Planning at individual institution level or at institutional protection scheme level. It should therefore be ensured that this option for institutions belonging to an institutional protection scheme is not impaired by linking Recovery Planning and reverse stress testing.	The principle of proportionality is recognised and applies to all aspects of these guidelines, including reverse stress testing, ensuring that it is proportional to the nature, size and complexity of their business and risks. The EBA is providing several incentives for the use of reverse stress testing in a wider context, not only for recovery and resolution planning. Institution should consider reverse stress testing not only as part of the stress testing programme but also as a regular risk management tool, carried out regularly by all types of institutions and at the same level of application as ICAAP and ILAAP (e.g. institution-wide and covering all relevant risk types), sharing the same governance and quality standards and to complement other types of stress testing.	No change

(continued)

Comments	Summary of responses received	EBA analysis	Amendments to the proposals
		The EBA considers that the GL provides sufficient degree of discretion when performing stress testing. The degree of freedom that is available when constructing a scenario for reverse stress testing should be seen as an advantage of this type of stress tests. Institutions should include scenarios identified through the reverse stress tests to complement the range of stress tests scenarios they undertake and for comparison purposes in order to assess the overall severity, allowing the identification of severe but still plausible scenarios. As part of regular risk management tool, it is important that institution identify measures that provide alerts when a scenario turns into reality. So the existence of multiple scenarios and the non-linear causal relationships, despite possible difficulties to interpret, should be identified by institutions and taken into account as complementary information.	
Para 86 **Reverse stress testing – use**	Two respondents mentioned that paragraph 86 states that institutions must identify measures which trigger an alarm as soon as a scenario becomes a reality. This potentially too one-dimensional approach is difficult to comprehend, especially since scenarios never unfold exactly as expected. Reference to the recovery indicators to be developed as part of the recovery plans would be more useful.	The GL mentions that as part of their business planning and risk management, institutions should use reverse stress test to understand the viability and sustainability of their business model and strategies, as well as to identifying situations where they might be in the situation considered as failing or likely to fail in the meaning of Article 32 of Directive 2014/59/EU. It is important that institution identify measures that provide alerts when a scenario turns into reality. To that end, institutions should: a) identify the pre-defined outcome to be tested (e.g. of business model becoming unviable); b) identify possible adverse circumstances which would expose them to severe vulnerabilities and cause the pre-defined outcome;	No change

(continued)

Comments	Summary of responses received	EBA analysis	Amendments to the proposals
	Another respondent mentioned that they would appreciate further clarification on what the regulator expects on the reverse stress testing, such as hurdle rates, and so on.	c) assess depending on the institution's size as well as the nature, scale, complexity and riskiness of its business activities the likelihood that events included in the scenarios are leading to the pre-defined outcome; and d) adopt effective arrangements, processes, systems or other measures to prevent or mitigate identified risks and vulnerabilities.

The paragraph is general and not only to Recovery Planning. The EBA considers that the paragraph includes already possible recovery indicators, among other indicators.

The EBA considers that the GL needs to provide sufficient degree of discretion when performing reverse stress testing – for instance, regarding hurdle rates, and so on. | |
| **Para 90**

Reverse stress testing – internal models | One respondent noted that, in a number of paragraphs, the GLs state that stress testing should be used as a risk management tool for revealing the possible inadequacies of internal models. | The GL mentions that institutions using internal models for credit risk, counterparty credit risk, and market risk, when carrying out reverse stress testing in accordance with Articles 290(8) and 368(1) (g) of Regulation (EU) No 575/2013, should endeavour to identify severe, but plausible, scenarios that could result in significant adverse outcomes and potentially challenge institutions overall viability. | Para 90 changed to provide clarification

regarding both CRR and model risk |

(continued)

Comments	Summary of responses received	EBA analysis	Amendments to the proposals
	In severe stress scenarios, the respondent agrees that model risk will increase and may lead to a breakdown in the models' predictability. But this should not be necessarily taken as an indication that the modelling of the inputs into the IRB formula are inadequate. The respondent suggests that the GLs could be re-drafted to reflect this. The EBA in that paragraph also references CRR Article 290 (8) in support of this requirement. The respondent encourages the EBA to review the guidance to ensure that it is aligned with the CRR. Another respondent mentioned that paragraph 90 correctly says that reverse stress tests should be seen as complementing the internal models used to calculate capital requirements. It also says that they are designed to reveal inadequacies of these internal models. We do not understand this.	Institutions should see these reverse stress tests as an essential complement of their internal models for calculation of capital requirements and as a regular risk management tool for revealing the possible inadequacies of these internal models. The EBA agrees that should not be necessarily taken as an indication that the modelling of the inputs into the IRB formula are inadequate. The EBA considers that the paragraph could be clarified to take into account that in severe stress scenarios, even if should not be necessarily taken as an indication that the modelling of the inputs into the IRB formula are inadequate, model risk will increase and may lead to a breakdown in the models' predictability. The EBA considers that also Article 177 of the CRR – Requirements for the IRB approach – stress tests used in the assessment of capital adequacy – could be mentioned to support the requirement.	

(continued)

Comments	Summary of responses received	EBA analysis	Amendments to the proposals
	These models were not normally developed on the assumption of a stress situation, i.e. under fundamentally different environmental conditions. Validation of these internal models on a stress test basis is not possible. The requirement should be deleted.		
Para 92 **Reverse stress testing – quantitative analysis**	Two respondents mentioned that the requirements for the quantitative "reverse engineering" of the specifically required stress parameters sometimes appear to be too theoretical, and do not necessarily add any additional insight. It would, however, be more practical and more comprehensible for the management if a certain number of alternative scenarios is shown, which cover the target loss. It would thus be reasonable to refrain from the requirement for a quantitative calculation.	The GL mentions that institutions should perform a quantitative and more sophisticated analysis, taking into account the institution's size as well as the nature, scale, complexity and riskiness of its business activities, in setting out specific loss levels or other negative impacts on their capital, liquidity (e.g. the access to funding, in particular to increases on funding costs) or overall financial position. Institutions should work backwards in a quantitative manner to identify the risk factors, and the required amplitude of changes, that could cause that loss or negative impact. The EBA considers that the GL provides sufficient degree of discretion when performing reverse stress testing. The GL mentions that institutions should, where appropriate, use sensitivity analysis as a starting point for reverse stress testing – for example, shifting one or more relevant parameters to some extreme to reach pre-defined outcomes.	No change

(continued)

Comments	Summary of responses received	EBA analysis	Amendments to the proposals
		However, institutions should not use sensitivity analysis to find the scenario relevant for the reverse stress test. The qualitative analysis should lead to the scenario, combining expert judgment from different business areas, as thinking might be the most effective way to avoid a business model failure. A joint stressing of all relevant risk parameters using their statistical aspects (e.g. volatility of risk factors consistent with historical observations supplemented with hypothetical but plausible assumptions) should be developed. The plausibility of the required parameter shifts to reach the pre-defined outcome gives a first idea about possible vulnerabilities in the institution. To assess the plausibility historical (multivariate) probability distributions – adjusted, where deemed necessary, according to expert judgements – should, among others, be applied. Qualitative analyses and assessments, combining expert judgements from different business areas, should guide the identification of relevant scenarios. The EBA is providing several incentives for the use of reverse stress testing based on quantitative and qualitative analysis.	
Para 93 **Reverse stress testing – sensitivity analysis**	One respondent mentioned that it is unclear why a sensitivity analysis should be performed as a starting point for reverse stress testing in particular if it should not be used to find the relevant scenario.	The GL mentions that institutions should, where appropriate, use sensitivity analysis as a starting point for reverse stress testing – for example, shifting one or more relevant parameters to some extreme to reach pre-defined outcomes. However, institutions should not use sensitivity analysis to find the scenario relevant for the reverse stress test.	

(continued)

Comments	Summary of responses received	EBA analysis	Amendments to the proposals
		The qualitative analysis should lead to the scenario, combining expert judgment from different business areas, as thinking might be the most effective way to avoid a business model failure. A joint stressing of all relevant risk parameters using their statistical aspects (e.g. volatility of risk factors consistent with historical observations supplemented with hypothetical but plausible assumptions) should be developed. The plausibility of the required parameter shifts to reach the pre-defined outcome gives a first idea about possible vulnerabilities in the institution. To assess the plausibility historical (multivariate) probability distributions – adjusted, where deemed necessary, according to expert judgements – should among others be applied. Qualitative analyses and assessments, combining expert judgements from different business areas, should guide the identification of relevant scenarios.	No change
		The GL mentions the use of sensitivity analysis, only where appropriate, and provides an example, namely to test relevant parameters. This provides a sufficient degree of discretion when performing reverse stress testing. Finding a relevant scenario can be a different part of the process.	

(continued)

Comments	Summary of responses received	EBA analysis	Amendments to the proposals
Para 94 **Reverse stress testing – scenarios that combine solvency and liquidity stress tests**	One respondent mentioned that the GLs should provide more precision on those required scenarios that combine solvency and liquidity stress tests and define with more clarity those situations that can aggravate a liquidity stress event and transform it into a solvency stress event, and vice-versa, and eventually to a business failure.	The GL mentions that institutions should use reverse stress testing as a tool to gather insights into scenarios that involve combinations of solvency and liquidity stresses, where traditional modelling may fail to capture complex aspects from real situations. Where appropriate, institutions should identify and analyse situations that can aggravate a liquidity stress event and transform it into a solvency stress event, and vice-versa, and eventually to a business failure. Institutions should endeavour to apply reverse stress testing in an integrated manner for risks to capital or liquidity with a view to improve the understanding and the management of related risks in extreme situations. The EBA considers that the GL needs to provide sufficient degree of discretion when performing reverse stress testing, for instance regarding the combination between solvency and liquidity stress tests.	No change
Para 95 to 99 **Reverse stress testing – Recovery actions and Recovery Planning (use)**	One respondent mentioned that due to the required severity for the reverse stress test, this approach leads by definition to scenarios with a low probability of occurrence, which may be less credible and less appropriate to test the recovery plan.	The GL mentions that institutions should use reverse stress testing to assist with the development, assessment and calibration of 'near-default' scenarios used for Recovery Planning. Institutions should use reverse stress testing to identify the risk factors and further understand and describe the scenarios that would result in 'near default', assessing effective recovery actions that can be credibly implemented, either in advance or as the risk factors or scenarios develop.	No change

(continued)

Comments	Summary of responses received	EBA analysis	Amendments to the proposals
	Recovery Planning should thus primarily rely on the most relevant "near default" scenarios as they ensure the proper balance between severity, consistency with the institution's strategy and business model and, finally, higher credibility. In addition, it is not clear why reverse stress testing should be required to fulfil the expectations regarding a recovery plan as outlined in paragraph 99. This can fully be achieved in the regular Recovery Planning framework.	Reverse stress testing should contribute to the recovery plan scenarios by using a dynamic and quantitative scenario narrative: a) the recovery triggers – that is, at which point the institution would enact recovery actions in the hypothetical scenario; b) the recovery actions required and their expected effectiveness, including the method of assessing that effectiveness (i.e. indicators that should be monitored to conclude that no further action is required; c) the appropriate timing and process required for those recovery actions; d) in case of further stress, points (b) and (c) for possibly required additional recovery actions to address residual risks.	
	Two respondents mentioned that the overall classification – that is, the relationship between ICAAP stress test (or regular scenarios) versus inverse scenarios versus Recovery Planning scenarios and their interaction during calibration – seems unclear.	The EBA is providing several incentives for the use of reverse stress testing. Institutions should consider reverse stress testing also as a regular risk management tool, carried out regularly by all types of institutions. At the same time, it provides a sufficient degree of discretion when performing reverse stress testing. For instance, as part of regular risk management tool, it is important that institutions identify measures that provide alerts in the context of Recovery Planning and recovery indicators, when a scenario turns into reality.	

(continued)

Comments	Summary of responses received	EBA analysis	Amendments to the proposals
Para 96 **Reverse stress testing – Recovery actions and Recovery Planning – ICAAP/ILAAP**	Two respondents mentioned that according to paragraph 96, stress tests for ICAAP and ILAAP purposes, as well as the Recovery Planning, should not be combined, but should however be comparable. In terms of content, in paragraph 96 there appears to be a contradiction in the requirement that stress scenarios and ICAAP/ILAAP stress tests should not be interlinked, since this is asked for in other parts of the draft guidelines (e.g. paragraph 224). The respondent mentioned that the ban on interlinking should be removed. Another respondent mentioned that given that paragraph 96 implies the necessity of two sets of reverse stress test respectively for ICAAP/ILAAP purposes and for Recovery Planning, more detailed explanations as to how reverse stress tests should be engineered for ICAAP purposes would be welcome.	The GL mentions that due to the different objectives of the two sets of reversed stress tests the stress tests for ICAAP and ILAAP purposes and Recovery Planning should not be interlinked but compared to one another. The GLs also mentions, regarding supervisory stress testing, that competent authorities should also use the scenarios and outcomes of supervisory stress tests as additional sources of information in the assessment of institutions' recovery plans, in particular, when assessing the choice and severity of scenarios and assumptions used by the institution. In this assessment, the supervisory stress tests scenarios should, where appropriate and in particular where they satisfy the conditions set out in the EBA Guidelines on the range of scenarios to be used in recovery plans, be used as a reference point for the assessment of the institution's own scenarios and assumptions. If a competent authority identifies deficiencies in the scenarios or assumptions by the institution for the purposes of Recovery Planning, it should, where appropriate, in addition to requiring the institution to modify their own scenarios, demand that institution uses the supervisory stress testing scenarios and assumptions. When assessing the appropriateness of such a demand, competent authorities should take all relevant factors into account paying particular attention on whether institutions have failed to incorporate system-wide events into their Recovery Planning.	No change

(continued)

Comments	Summary of responses received	EBA analysis	Amendments to the proposals
	What are the pre-defined outcomes that should be targeted/tested?	The EBA considers that there is no contradiction. The GL refers to comparisons, additional sources of information and reference points for assessments. At the same time, the GL needs to provide sufficient degree of discretion when performing reverse stress testing for both purposes.	
Para 99 d) **Recovery actions and Recovery Planning – residual risks**	Two respondents mentioned that the paragraph requires "additional recovery actions to address residual risks". Stress scenarios for Recovery Planning follow the "near-default" criterion – that is, they are severe enough that the institution can only restore capital and liquidity by carrying out all realisable, private recovery measures available. Hence, by definition there will be no further recovery measures available. The respondent therefore suggests withdrawing paragraph 99d.	The EBA considers that reverse stress testing should contribute to the recovery plan scenarios by using a dynamic and quantitative scenario narrative, taking into account the following: the recovery triggers – that is, at which point the institution would enact recovery actions in the hypothetical scenario; the recovery actions required and their expected effectiveness, including the method of assessing that effectiveness (i.e. indicators that should be monitored to conclude that no further action is required; the appropriate timing and process required for those recovery actions; and in case of further stress, points (b) and (c) for possibly required additional recovery actions to address residual risks.) In a dynamic setting, the EBA considers that residual risks may exist and may not be totally covered, so further recovery measures may be available during the process.	No change

Source: European Banking Authority (2017), pp. 84; see also European Banking Authority (2018), pp. 86.

Bibliography

Bank Negara Malaysia (2016a). Stress Testing, 30 June 2016, BNM/RH/PD 029-7; https://www.bnm.gov.my/index.php?ch=57&pg=137&ac=618&bb=file

Bank Negara Malaysia (2016b). Concept Paper on Stress Testing, 14 Oct 2016, https://www.bnm.gov.my/index.php?ch=en_announcement&pg=en_announcement&ac=466

Basel Committee on Banking Supervision (2009). Principles for sound stress testing practices and supervision, May 2009, https://www.bis.org/publ/bcbs155.pdf

Basel Committee on Banking Supervision (2017). Supervisory and bank stress testing: Range of practices, December 2017, https://www.bis.org/bcbs/publ/d427.pdf

Bundesanstalt für Finanzdienstleistungsaufsicht (2010). MaRisk – Veröffentlichung der Endfassung, GZ: BA 54-FR 2210-2010/0003, https://www.bundesbank.de/resource/blob/598696/1f16bc36e7dfbaac51538c450fe77a02/mL/2010-12-15-marisk-veroeffentlichung-der-endfassung-data.pdf

Committee of European Banking Supervisors (2010). CEBS Guidelines on Stress Testing (GL32), 26 August 2010, https://eba.europa.eu/sites/default/documents/files/documents/10180/16094/ee1e7b7b-5b45-4758-bc64-22b159c3f66c/ST_Guidelines.pdf?retry=1

Counterparty Risk Management Policy Group (2008). Containing Systemic Risk – The Road to Reform, 6 August 2008, http://www.crmpolicygroup.org/docs/CRMPG-III.pdf

European Banking Authority (2015). Recovery Planning – Comparative report on the approach taken on recovery plan scenarios, 8 December 2015, https://eba.europa.eu/sites/default/documents/files/documents/10180/950548/432ab246-8c82-4120-bb38-115402a39f2b/Report%20on%20benchmarking%20scenarios%20in%20recovery%20plans.pdf

European Banking Authority (2017). Draft Guidelines on institution's stress testing, https://eba.europa.eu/sites/default/documents/files/documents/10180/2006781/0c4ac326-1330-4799-850c-632510f26ed1/Consultation%20Paper%20on%20Guidelines%20on%20institution%27s%20stress%20testing%20%28EBA-CP-2017-17%29.pdf

European Banking Authority (2018). Final report: Guidelines on institutions' stress testing, July 2018, EBA-GL-2018-04, https://eba.europa.eu/sites/default/documents/files/documents/10180/2282644/2b604bc8-fd08-4b17-ac4a-cdd5e662b802/Guidelines%20on%20institutions%20stress%20testing%20%28EBA-GL-2018-04%29.pdf?retry=1

Federal Reserve (2012). Supervisory Guidance on Stress Testing for Banking Organizations with More Than $10 Billion in Total Consolidated Assets, 14 May 2012, https://www.federalreserve.gov/supervisionreg/srletters/sr1207.htm

Financial Services Authority (2008). Consultation Paper – Stress and scenario testing (CP08/24), 09 December 2008.

Financial Services Authority (2009). Policy Statement 09/20: Stress and Scenario Testing – Feedback on CP08/24 and final rules (PS09/20), December 2009.

Financial Services Authority (2011). Finalised Guidance: Reverse stress-testing surgeries. Frequently Asked Questions (FAQs), April 2011, https://www.fca.org.uk/publication/finalised-guidance/fg11_07.pdf

Financial Stability Board (2013). Recovery and Resolution Planning for Systemically Important Financial Institutions: Guidance on Recovery Triggers and Stress Scenarios, July 2013, https://www.fsb.org/wp-content/uploads/r_130716c.pdf

Financial Stability Institute (2018). FSI Insights on policy implementation No 12 – Stress-testing banks – a comparative analysis, November 2018, https://www.bis.org/fsi/publ/insights12.htm

KPMG (2018). Interest Rate Risks – Banks, Measurement, management, monitoring and control of interest rate risks in the banking book, Translation of FINMA Circular 2019/2, https://assets.kpmg/content/dam/kpmg/ch/pdf/finma-circular-2019-02-en.pdf

Islamic Financial Services Board (2012). Guiding Principles on Stress Testing for Institutions offering Islamic Financial Services, IFSB-13, March 2012, https://ifsb.org/standard/IFSB-16%20 Revised%20Supervisory%20Review%20Process_March%202014%20(final-clean).pdf

Islamic Financial Services Board (2014). Revised Guidance on Key Element in the Supervisory Review Process of Institutions Offering Islamic Insurance (IFSB 16)", March 2014, https://ifsb.org/ standard/IFSB-16%20Revised%20Supervisory%20Review%20Process_March%202014%20 (final-clean).pdf

Islamic Financial Services Board (2016). TN-2, Technical Note on Stress Testing for Institutions Offering Islamic Financial Services, December 2016, https://www.ifsb.org/

Reserve Bank of India (2013). Guidelines on Stress Testing, December 2013, https://rbidocs.rbi.org.in/ rdocs/notification/PDFs/FC021212ST.pdf, RBI/2013-14/390

Part II: **Quantitative Use Cases**

Tiziano Bellini

4 Quantitative Reverse Stress Testing

4.1 Introduction

Regulatory stress testing frameworks are usually highly standardised due to a need to systemically compare financial institutions. As a consequence, they may leave unexplored areas of risk.

As detailed in Section 4.2, a reverse stress test aims to structurally identify the most important risks to which a bank is exposed. This removes much of the arbitrariness of the usual stress test based on historical or hypothetical scenarios. On this, a difference arises between the long-term and short-run solvency. When focusing on the long-term, the attention is on the quantification of a loss big enough to cause a bank to fail. On the contrary, when the focus is driven by a short-term perspective, liquidity mismatching becomes the objective function.

For a bank exposed to multiple risk factors, many different combinations of stress might result in similar losses. Hence, Section 4.3 pinpoints how bank-specific portfolio composition as well as asset and liability balance are relevant items to inspect in attempting to find core weaknesses.

In line with a structural approach, one needs to identify a threshold beyond which a firm collapses. In this regard, Section 4.4 takes into account both long-term as well as short-run boundaries. On the one hand, the regulatory capital may be considered as the last line of defence against unexpected losses. On the other, liquidity buffers are vital to ensure solvency in the day-by-day banking activity.

All in all, macroeconomic adverse conditions are a typical source of bank weakness. On this subject, Section 4.5 wraps up all competences needed for highlighting a surface of macroeconomic conditions that may cause a bank failure.

From a tool-kit perspective, a mix of statistical techniques and expert driven procedures are used throughout this chapter.

4.2 Reverse Stress Testing Objective Function

The definition of a reverse stress test objective is the primary goal of the entire framework. In what follows, a distinction is made between insolvency due to abnormal losses against lack of liquid resources to run the business. Once the scope has been outlined, the focus moves to a function mapping a bank extreme occurrences and external macroeconomic conditions. The goal is to track a link connecting internal ruinous events and external scenarios.

https://doi.org/10.1515/9783110647907-004

4.2.1 Reverse Stress Testing: Economic Capital vs. Liquidity Mismatching

In what follows, a series of alternative objective functions describe how to formally identify conditions leading a bank to fail. Two broad threatening event categories are studied.
On the one hand, internal features are explored as potential sources of bankruptcy. On
the other, external economic conditions are investigated while bank operations are considered as given. As a result, a mix of these causes may end in a bank insolvency.

–   **Internal features (Y).** The set of asset, liabilities and other internal characteris-
    tics representing a bank operational system is denoted with Y. Loss and liquidity
    mismatching (LM) are subsets of Y. Therefore, Y, Loss and LM are jointly consid-
    ered to have a full picture of a bank.
–   **Macroeconomic scenarios (x).** A p-dimensional macroeconomic vector rep-
    resenting external conditions is the additional component to be studied when
    assessing potential sources of a bank's insolvency.

Armed with this framework, let us denote the joint distribution function of Y, Loss,
LM and $x\, f(Y, x, Loss, LM)$. This distribution allows us to conduct a reverse stress test
by pursuing two broad objectives. On the one hand, the aim is to investigate internal
features capable to cause a bank failure. On the other, the research focuses on adverse
macroeconomic conditions causing the collapse. Moreover, for each of these two categories, a distinction is made between long-term and short-run solvency, as detailed
in the following section.

1. **Internal features: Economic capital.** A first way to represent the reverse stress
    testing objective function is to focus on a what-if scenario affecting a bank's eco-
    nomic capital. In this case, the focus is on internal events causing Loss to exceed
    a given threshold ℓ.

$$\Upsilon^*(\ell) = \underset{\Upsilon}{argmax}\ f(\Upsilon|x, Loss \geq \ell, LM) \tag{4.1}$$

In this case, the solution $\Upsilon^*(\ell)$ intercepts internal event originating bank's
unwillingness to face its obligations. Specific areas of interest include high losses
due to single name default, sector concentration, and so on.

2. **Internal features: Liquidity mismatching.** For the liquidity risk, the following
    optimisation problem needs to be solved:

$$\Upsilon^*(lm) = \underset{\Upsilon}{argmax}\ f(\Upsilon|x, Loss, LM \leq lm), \tag{4.2}$$

where the liquidity mismatching threshold lm[1] may be defined by relying on the
liquidity distribution.

---

[1] Note that liquidity mismatching is risky when liabilities exceed assets. Hence, has negative value
and the threshold is such to identify (high) negative value LMs.

3. **Internal features: Economic capital and liquidity mismatching.** When considering both economic capital and liquidity mismatching, the following equation holds:

$$\Upsilon^*(\ell,\mathrm{lm}) = \underset{\Upsilon}{argmax}\ f(\Upsilon|x, Loss \geq \ell, LM \leq \mathrm{lm}) \qquad (4.3)$$

4. **Macroeconomic scenarios: Economic capital.** A reverse stress testing may pursue the goal to identify macroeconomic scenarios causing *Loss* to exceed a given threshold ℓ. In this case, the objective function is written as follows:

$$x^*(\ell) = \underset{x}{argmax}\ f(x|\Upsilon, Loss \geq \ell, LM), \qquad (4.4)$$

where the solution $x^*(\ell)$ is the most likely macroeconomic scenario causing a bank failure due to large economic losses.

5. **Macroeconomic scenarios: Liquidity mismatching.** In the short-term period, liquidity mismatching may trigger a series of events encompassing the potential for a bank failure. The relationship between macroeconomic conditions and internal features is scrutinised and detailed as follows:

$$(x)^*(\mathrm{lm}) = \underset{x}{argmax}\ f(x|\Upsilon, Loss, LM \leq \mathrm{lm}) \qquad (4.5)$$

6. **Macroeconomic scenarios: Economic capital and liquidity mismatching.** When searching for scenarios causing $Loss \geq \ell$ and $LM \leq \mathrm{lm}$, the following applies:

$$(x)^*(\ell,\mathrm{lm}) = \underset{x}{argmax}\ f(x|\Upsilon, Loss \geq \ell, LM \leq \mathrm{lm}) \qquad (4.6)$$

7. **Internal features and macroeconomic scenarios: Economic capital and liquidity mismatching.** In an attempt to merge together these perspectives, the following equation summarises scenarios and bank-specific events that may cause a bank to become insolvent:

$$(\Upsilon,x)^*(\ell,\mathrm{lm}) = \underset{(\Upsilon,x)}{argmax}\ f(\Upsilon,x|Loss \geq \ell, LM \leq \mathrm{lm}) \qquad (4.7)$$

This reverse stress testing mechanism relies on a system supplying information on integrated measures of risk (both for economic capital as well as for liquidity) and macroeconomic scenarios. At the same time, all of these optimisation functions rely on the definition of a vulnerability threshold. Section 4.3 illustrates both these topics. In what follows, the focus is on the techniques one may use to capture the set of events causing a bank to bankrupt (i.e. Υ^* and x^*).

4.2.2 Conditional Mean and Hull Contours

Originating from a market portfolio perspective, Glasserman et al. (2015) investigate how to make inference on the conditional distribution of a trading portfolio losses. Focusing on equation (4.4), the first step of this process is to estimate $\mathbb{E}\,(x|\Upsilon, Loss \geq \ell, LM)$, the conditional mean of the macroeconomic variables given a loss exceeding a given threshold. They rely on observations of past scenarios and their corresponding losses. The combinations characterised by losses exceeding a given threshold ℓ (i.e. $(x_1, Loss_1), \ldots, (x_K, Loss_K)$) are taken into account. Then, once these observations are specified, the problem of estimating a conditional mean reduces to an unconditional mean computation. On this subject, they apply an empirical likelihood method which relies on convex combinations of the observations as candidate estimates of the mean:

$$\mathcal{R}(Y) = \max\left\{ \prod_{k=1}^{K} Kw_k : \sum_{k=1}^{K} w_k x_k = Y \right\}$$

s.t.

$$\sum_{k=1}^{K} w_k = 1,$$

$$w_k \geq 0,$$

(4.8)

where the product inside the braces is the likelihood ratio of the probability vector $(w_1, \ldots, w_K)$ to the uniform distribution $\left(\frac{1}{K}, \ldots, \frac{1}{K}\right)$.

The confidence region for x^* is defined under specific assumptions on the distribution of observations. In particular, Glasserman et al. (2015) suppose that observations are i.i.d. with mean μ_0 and the convex hull contains μ_0 with probability approaching 1 as the number of observations increases. A new maximisation problem is defined as follows

$$\operatorname*{argmax}_{w_1, \ldots, w_K} \sum_{k=1}^{K} \log w_k$$

s.t.

$$\sum_{k=1}^{K} w_k = 1,$$

$$\sum_{k=1}^{K} w_k x_k = Y.$$

(4.9)

For less regular portfolios and when the number of observations causing $Loss \geq \ell$ is small, this framework hardly applies. However, the idea of searching for a suitable contour of scenarios causing banking failure may be followed. On this, one may use bivariate box-plots for identifying contours. Such a technique has recently been used in robust statistics for initialising the so-called forward search Atkinson et al. (2004) in multivariate analysis. Furthermore, Bellini (2012) exploited bivariate box-plots for detecting atypical units in data envelopment analysis.

A natural non-parametric way of finding a central region in two-dimensions is to use convex hull peeling. The output of peeling is a series of nested convex polygons (hulls) which might be fitted through B-spline curves to obtain smooth contours. In order to find a central part of the data, as described in Zani et al. (1998), a robust bivariate centroid is found based on the observations inside the inner region defined by the fitted splines. In this way, both the efficiency property of the arithmetic mean and the natural trimming offered by the hulls are used.

The plots calculated from B-splines are over elaborate to find a central part of the data. Therefore, it can be useful to exploit a simpler method in which ellipses with a robust centroid are fitted to the data as in Riani and Zani (1997). The robust centroid of the ellipse is found as the component wise median of the two variables in the scatterplot. The shape of the contours is based on a covariance matrix in which the univariate medians are used, but which is otherwise calculated in the usual way. The combination of centroid and covariance estimate gives a Mahalanobis distance for each observation and a family of ellipses that need to be scaled.

4.3 Integrated Risk Modelling and Vulnerability Threshold

As detailed in equations from (4.1) to (4.7), one needs to rely on a fully integrated framework to specify the combinations of Υ and x causing $Loss \geq \ell$ and $LM \leq \mathit{lm}$. Additionally, the need to specify ℓ and lm thresholds arise. In what follows, risk integration candidate models as well as vulnerability thresholds are examined.

4.3.1 Long- and Short-Run Risk Integration

The starting point of the analysis is an integrated model willing to capture interconnections and represent a bank behaviour in front of adverse conditions. In what follows, three alternative models are explored.

- **Economic capital: Assets and liabilities.** A first way to represent the *Loss* distribution feeding the objective functions is to rely on the fully integrated loss to use for economic capital purposes, as follows:

$$Loss_{h,g} = -\sum_{i=1}^{N} (PVA_{i,\Delta,g} - PVA_i) + \sum_{j=1}^{M} (PVL_{j,\Delta,g} - PVL_j) +$$

$$- PNI_{h,\Delta,g} - NIR_{h,\Delta,g} + NIE_{h,\Delta,g} + \Delta NPL_{h,\Delta,g} + Tax_{h,\Delta,g} + \Delta NPL_{h,\Delta,g} \quad (4.10)$$

Where *PVA* is the present value of asset, *PVL* is the present value of liability, *PNI* stands for performing net interest, *NIR* is the net interest revenue, *NIE* represents non interest expenses, *Tax* indicates taxes and ΔNPL refers to the increase in non performing loan losses. This function embraces value changes on assets, liabilities and P&L movements due to fluctuations in market, interest rate and credit risks.

- **Economic capital: Assets only.** In line with the hypothesis to consider as given the liability structure Kretzschmar et al. (2010), one may shrink the focus on asset losses and P&L, detailed as follows:

$$Loss_{h,g}^{\Delta A} = -\sum_{i=1}^{N} (PVA_{i,\Delta,g} - PVA_i) - PNI_{h,\Delta,g} - NIR_{h,\Delta,g} +$$

$$+ NIE_{h,\Delta,g} - \Delta NPL_{h,\Delta,g}, \quad (4.11)$$

whereby the superscript ΔA in $Loss_{h,g}^{\Delta A}$ stands for value change in assets only.

- **Economic capital: Credits only.** An additional way to investigate a commercial bank vulnerability is to focus on its credit risk only:

$$Loss_{h,g}^{CR} = -\sum_{i=1}^{N} (A_{i,\Delta,g} - A_i) - \Delta NPL_{h,\Delta,g}, \quad (4.12)$$

where, the superscript *CR* in $Loss_{h,g}^{CR}$ stands for value changes due to credit only. In this equation, all debtors $i = 1,\dots,N$ are taken into account, but $A_{i,\Delta,g}$ is affected by credit risk only and is compared against the initial exposure A_i. The reason behind this simplified representation is to concentrate on the key portfolio risk sources. Other potential combinations of assets and liabilities should be considered. Nonetheless the above proposed scheme captures the major challenges for commercial and retail banks.

- **Liquidity mismatching.** In spite of the long-run economic capital analysis, the analysis may be focused on liquidity. On this subject, the following equation introduced in Chapter 7 is a useful candidate to perform the study:

$$LM_{q,g} = \sum_{t=0}^{q} \left[\sum_{i=1}^{N} 1_{i,liq,t} \, A_{i,cf,t} \left(1 - H_{i,\Delta,g,t}\right) - \sum_{j=1}^{m} 1_{j,liq,\Delta,g,t} \, L_{j,cf,\Delta,g,t}^{nm} + \right.$$

$$\left. - \sum_{j=m+1}^{M} 1_{j,liq,t} \, L_{j,cf,t}^{m} + \tilde{n}_{\Delta,g,t} \, B_{\Delta,g,t} \right]. \quad (4.13)$$

where $A_{i,cf,t}$ represents asset cash flow at time t, $(1 - H_{i,\Delta,g,t})$ is the complement to one of the haircut, L^{nm} indicates non-maturing liabilities (j = 1, . . ., m), L^m stands for liabilities with a defined maturity, and the last term is the product of liquidity shrinkage coefficient (belonging to the interval [0,1]) and interbank market buffer $(B_{\Delta,g,t})$ that allows bans to balance cash outflows and inflows.

It is worth mentioning that LCR and NSFR introduced by Basel III constitute a useful corollary to assess a bank liquidity profile.

The next section aims to investigate the threshold ℓ and $\mathfrak{lm}$, beyond which a bank becomes insolvent.

4.3.2 Vulnerability Thresholds

The overall reverse stress testing framework requires a threshold to identify a bank failure. The following Business Case 1 helps understanding the role of such a boundary and its practical implications.

4.3.2.1 Business Case 1 *Dexia Group*

As a result of Belgian, Luxemburg and French local government finance banks merger, Dexia Group became a major player in European local government finance and retail banking in the early nineties. In the middle of the last financial crisis, its total asset was approximately Euro 650 billion.

During the period between 2007 and 2012, the Group balance sheet was repeatedly damaged through losses due to the US subprime crisis. Dexia was hit by high refinancing costs coupled with low loan margins. The severe annual losses required comprehensive public recapitalisations through the stakeholder governments Belgium, Luxemburg and France in 2008 and 2012. Additionally, in October 2008 and in 2011, Dexia new unsecured bond issues and interbank deposits had to be enrolled into large public guarantee programmes. During this period, major structural measures were adopted, encompassing sale of operational franchises in a number of countries. The 2012 restructuring plan led to the disposal of the Belgian and Luxemburg operations under Dexia Bank Belgium and Dexia Bank Internationale. It left the parent company under an orderly resolution plan with Euro 350 billion in residual assets to be managed and disposed.

From a capital perspective, in 2008, the bank received its first series of capital injections for Euro 6.35 billion. An additional implicit recapitalisation measure was Euro 17 billion in asset guarantees provided in 2008. In light of the Greek crisis, at the end of 2012, another capital injection of Euro 5.5 billion was carried out by national and local governments of the stakeholder countries.

After its first recapitalisation in 2008, Dexia was permitted only to fulfill contractual obligations for coupon payments on hybrid capital and subordinated debt while committing itself to make no early calls. Yet, dividend payments and calls or discretionary payment on any of this debt could be made subject to the condition that the Core Tier 1 ratio would always exceed 10% of risk-weighted assets.

The risk-weighted asset benchmark of the EU decision was a poor metric for the capital risk of the bank, since it entirely ignored sovereign credit risk that ultimately severely hit the bank. Dexia was chronically undercapitalised running leverage ratios in the range of 50.

This business case shows that a loss as well as an unbalanced structure undermine a bank solvency. In this regard, few alternative capital buffer thresholds may be used for reverse stress testing, detailed as follows.

- **Tier 1 core capital.** This is the tightest trigger one can use for reverse stress testing purposes and, to some extent, it does not completely represent the overall funds on which a bank relies to run its business.
- **Tier 1 capital (inclusive of additional Tier 1 capital).** In this case, a more extensive definition of own funds is taken into account. Innovative capital instruments sharing common characteristics with core capital are included as the extended line of defence.
- **Total capital.** A broader definition of capital buffer based on Tier 1 and Tier 2 constitutes an additional alternative vulnerability threshold.

All in all, liquidity issues as well as the overall financing structure needs to be taken into account in addition to these thresholds. This is emphasised through the following Cyprus Popular Bank business case.

4.3.2.2 Business Case 2 Cyprus Popular Bank

In the mid 2000, Cyprus Popular Bank was the second largest bank in Cyprus. In 2006, it was consolidated in a group based in Greece which expanded in Eastern Europe and Russia in 2007 and 2008. Its total asset approximated Euro 43 billion in 2010. In 2011, the headquarter returned in Cyprus as a consequence of the pressure actioned by the Cypriot central bank.

Through parallel downgrades of Greek and Cypriot securities, in 2011, the bank's assets also became increasingly ineligible for European Central Bank repo operations. The result was a steep increase of Central Bank of Cyprus exposure to Cyprus Popular Bank (i.e. Euro 9.8 billion in September 2012).

Cyprus Popular Bank issued a significant amount of hybrid capital in 2009 and 2010 in the form of contingent convertibles. Hybrid instruments classified as Lower Tier 2 were used to boost capital ratios. Core Tier 1 capital was also increased by means of these instruments while the government was investing in the Bank.

During the period from 2010 to 2012, the bank suffered deposit withdrawal for more than Euro 7 billion. Only domestic Cypriot deposits from retail customers remained almost unchanged.

After discussions over the extent of creditor participation, the bank was finally resolved in March 2013 and its good parts were sold to Piraeus Bank (Greece) and Bank of Cyprus.

Cyprus Popular Bank highlights the role of both capital as well as fund raising. This example together with Northern Rock, Lehman Brothers, and so on highlights the importance of an overall asset liability sustainable structure as well as the need of a strong liquidity regime. This example enforces the importance of identifying a vulnerability threshold in terms of liquidity (lm), listed as follows.

- **Liquidity mismatch.** A complete integration with the macroeconomic scenario simulation used for economic capital purposes constitutes the major advantage of this risk measure described in equation (4.13). Different parameter combinations (e.g. haircut) may be used to strengthen or release liquidity burdens.
- **Regulatory ratios.** Liquidity coverage ratio and net stable funding ratio thresholds may be set equal to the regulatory ones or more restrictive limits can be used.

The definition of the framework through which to assess conditions under which a bank may become insolvent is a crucial step of the reverse stress testing process. A Monte Carlo simulation mechanics was used to outline the connection between macroeconomic scenarios, bank's losses and liquidity mismatching. For reverse stress testing, this approach can be additionally enriched through heuristic algorithms. The operative framework used for reverse stress testing becomes crucial to assess the bank's weaknesses, as detailed in the next section.

4.4 Bank-Specific Disastrous Event Fact-Finding

In the previous sections, the reverse stress testing problem has been described in terms of objective function and models to assess a bank's behaviour under adverse conditions. In what follows, a qualitative analysis is conducted to explore a bank's potential weaknesses. This qualitative analysis is reinvigorated by a more sophisticated quantitative investigation based on a what-if framework. The awareness of organisational deficiencies allows a bank to define a safe way of doing its business. An inspection needs to be conducted by focusing on the following main areas: trading book, banking book, liquidity and overall financial structure. The next sections detail how to conduct the study.

4.4.1 Trading Book

Some of the most important failures experienced during recent crises, by including COVID 19 pandemic, pinpoint the influence of joint factors driving insolvency. A qualitative analysis may be conducted in an attempt to uncover trading book shortcomings by focusing on the following key areas.

- **Exposure.** Trading book exposure may be inspected from different angles. A useful starting point is to consider: debtor, sector and risk band (e.g. rating class). More precisely, one of the key questions arising when dealing with trading book is: What does unwillingness to repay imply in terms of portfolio single names or group of names? Consider the example of a massive investment on a specific corporate through bonds with different maturities and coupons. What happens to the bank if this corporate defaults? A what-if process may be conducted by starting from the highest exposures and conjecture the worst scenario. As an example, one may select the name with the greatest outstanding balance in the trading book and hypothesise its failure: Which are the implications for the bank? Is the failure of the counterpart threatening bank solvency?
- **Financial instrument type.** An equity investment is usually characterised by higher volatility than a bond. Hence, one should start from equity exposures when searching for a ruinous path. Nonetheless, bond creditworthiness, market liquidity and other investment specific features need to be further inspected to figure out potential solvency issues.
- **Sector.** Contagion or domino-effect is one of the common sources of risk for investors. Therefore, one may study the impact of a sector failure on a bank.
- **Counterpart rating.** A poor rating is a symptom of risk. Thus, an additional what-if path may be rooted on clustering investments according to their rating class (or probability of default). Assuming the poorest rating investments to collapse allows us to assess the low-quality portfolio impact on a bank proficiency.
- **Instrument trading frequency.** Some portfolios are made up by very liquid instruments, but it is not always the case. Lehman Brother's example highlights the role of opaque investments. Hence, assessing the damage of a low-frequency instrument is a very important exercise on the way of assessing potential causes for a bank to collapse.

Table 4.1 exemplifies some of the elements to take into account to make conjectures on events with the potential to cause a bank failure. Illustrative thresholds are also highlighted to pave the way for an effective recognition of portfolio deficiencies. Each item within the columns may be connected with others in a what-if scheme, as detailed in Example 4.1.

Example 4.1 introduces the idea of a heuristic algorithm to search for events that may cause a bank to become insolvent. This kind of research is deeply rooted in expert

Table 4.1: Trading book reverse stress testing. Illustrative example of qualitative items to be explored.

Outstanding Balance % of Tier 1	Instrument Type	Sector	Counterpart Rating	Instrument Trading Frequency
[0–10%)	Bond	Chemical	[AAA;A–]	Infra-day
[10–20%)	Equity	Finance	[BBB+;BB–]	Daily
[20–30%)	Hybrid	Real estate	[B+;B–]	Weakly
≥ 30%)	Derivative	Telecom	[CCC;C]	Monthly
...	...	...	...	...

assessment and managerial actions will take place according to the bank's sensitivity at reverse stress testing findings.

Example 4.1 Trading book individual (joint) default algorithm

Let us sample from the trading book portfolio and hypothesise an individual or group (i.e. up to p) of debtors' default, as depicted in Figure 4.1. *LGD* is assumed to be 100% and a given *Loss* threshold is defined. The algorithm works as follows.

- Step 1.
    - Select debtor i. The simplifying assumption of the one-debtor, one-financial instrument is followed in order to avoid unnecessary hurdles.
    - If statement. Verify whether debtor the exposure A_i is higher than the bank's bankruptcy threshold. If the answer is *yes*, then the loop stops. Otherwise, see the next step.
- Step 2.
    - Select a couple of debtors i and j.
    - If statement. Verify whether the outstanding balance invested in debtor i and $j \neq i$, $A_i + A_j$ is higher than the bank's bankruptcy threshold. If the answer is *yes*, then the loop stops. Otherwise, see the next step.
- Step 3. Continue the process by considering all sets made up by $p \leq n$ debtors.
- Step 4. All events originating the bank's failure are stored (as detailed in the bank's bankruptcy event box). This set is then scrutinised to assess the relevance of each event. The algorithm does not supply any probability of occurrence – however, expert panels may be involved into the process to assess each event plausibility.
- Step 5. All plausible events constitute the output of the reverse stress testing process: $Y^{*}_{tradingbook}(\ell)$.

A more sophisticated framework may be drawn by introducing conditions in terms of rating, sector, exposure, and so on. Example 4.2 relies on a poor rating threshold and a sector contagion mechanics.

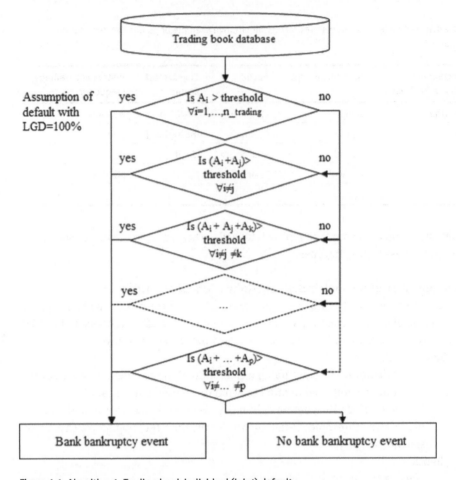

Figure 4.1: Algorithm 1: Trading book individual (joint) default.

Example 4.2 Trading book poor rating sector contagion algorithm

Let us focus on the worst layer of the portfolio in terms of rating by introducing a poor rating threshold BB (i.e. select customers with rating $\leq BB-$). Additionally, assume that a given number (#) of customers in a specific sector (s) default. The maximum number of default per sector is set equal to # (i.e. $\max\left(\sum_{i=1}^{n_s} 1_{(i,s,\leq BB-)}, \# \right)$). In the case where less than # poor rating debtors belong to a given sector, all these (poor rating) debtors are taken into account. Furthermore, hypothesise $LGD=60\%$. A given $Loss$ threshold is defined according to Section 3.2.

The algorithm described in Figure 4.2 can be summarised as follows.

- Step 1.
  - Select debtor i.
  - If statement. Verify whether debtor i rating is worse than BB −. If the answer is *yes*, then see the next step. Otherwise, select another debtor.

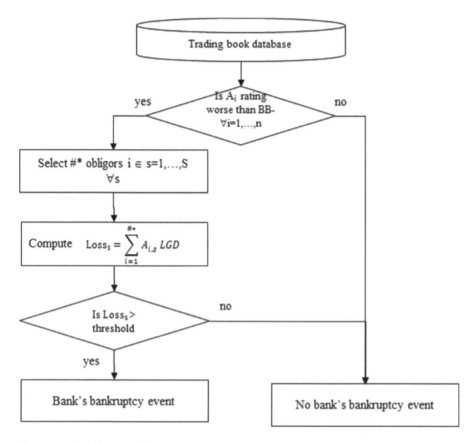

Figure 4.2: Algorithm 2: Trading book poor rating sector contagion.

- Step 2. Select all customers belonging to sector s by aligning with the rule $\max\left(\sum_{i=1}^{n_s} 1_{(i,s,\leq BB-)}, \#\right)$.
- Step 3. Compute $Loss_s$ as $\sum_{i=1}^{n_s} A_{i,s} \times LGD$. A constant $LGD = 60\%$ is assumed.
- Step 4. If $Loss_s \geq threshold$, then a bank failure event is captured.
- Repeat the process for all debtors and all sectors.
- Step 5. All plausible events constitute the output of the reverse stress testing process: $\Upsilon^*_{tradingbook}(\ell)$.

Examples 4.1 and 4.2 can be enriched by including different thresholds and modify parameters. Moreover, combinations of algorithms may be used to capture real dynamics under stressed conditions.

In Step 5 of the Examples 4.1 and 4.2, the set of events causing a bank to fail its obligations is specified according to equation (4.1). In other words, this set of event is $\Upsilon^*(\ell)$ referred to the trading book (i.e. $\Upsilon^*_{tradingbook}(\ell)$).

The next sections enter into the details of banking book and liquidity algorithms.

4.4.2 Banking Book

An accurate asset review is at the very heart of banking book strategies. Thus, an effective diagnose of name and sector concentration may prevent a bank to be dragged into unexpected tumultuousness. For these reasons, a summary of the key risk sources is a useful what-if analysis starting point. For the banking book, exposure class, financial instrument type, sector and counterpart rating play a key role, as detailed in Table 4.2.

Table 4.2: Banking book reverse stress testing illustrative example of qualitative items to be explored.

Outstanding Balance % of Tier 1	Instrument Type	Sector	Counterpart Rating
[0–10%)	Secured loan	Chemical	[AAA;A–]
[10–20%)	Unsecured loan	Finance	[BBB+;BB–]
[10–20%)	Current Account	Real estate	[B+;B–]
≥ 20 %)	Bond	Telecom	[CCC;C]
...	...	...	...

In line with the previous section, a series of combined events may lead to a bank insolvency. In what follows, an algorithm which takes into account exposure, sector and rating is detailed.

Example 4.3 Banking book name and sector concentration
Let us concentrate on both name and sector concentration. A relevant threshold corresponds to 5% of Tier 1 for the single name and 20% for the sector concentration. With regards to sector concentration, customers with rating worse than *BB* − are taken into account. Additionally, assume *LGD* = 60% and a given *Loss* threshold is defined according to Section 3.2.

The following steps summarise the algorithm process represented in Figure 4.3.
- Step 1.
    - Select debtor *i*.
    - If statement. Verify whether the outstanding balance is greater than the 5% Tier 1 threshold. If the answer is *yes*, then compute the (namer concentration, *nc*) loss by applying *LGD* = 60%. Otherwise, see Step 2.
- Step 2. Select all customers in a sector having rating worse than BB −. If the sum of their outstanding balance is greater than 20% of Tier 1, then compute the (sector concentration, *sc*) loss by applying *LGD* = 60%.
- Step 3. Sum name and sector concentration.
- Step 4. If $Loss_s \geq threshold$, then a bank failure event is captured.

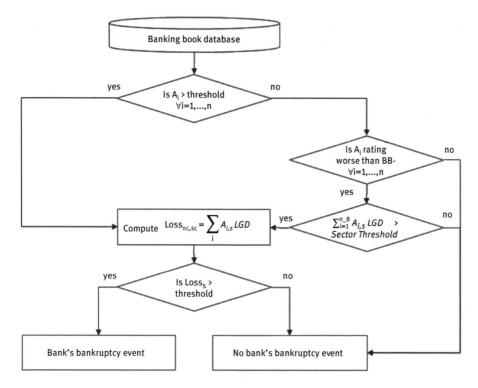

Figure 4.3: Algorithm 3: Banking book name and sector concentration.

- Repeat the process for all debtors, and all sectors.
- Step 5. All plausible events constitute the output of the reverse stress testing process: $\Upsilon^{*}_{bankingbook}(\ell)$.

Example 4.3 combines few elements of name and sector concentration. However, the choice of considering as risky all debtors worse than rating $BB-$ affects a bank's failure event collection. Setting another rating threshold generates a different set of reverse stress testing events. Additionally, combinations of trading and banking book events may enrich the spectrum of bankruptcy plausible sources.

Step 5 of Examples 4.3 depicts the ruinous event set $\Upsilon^{*}(\ell)$ referred to the banking book (i.e. $\Upsilon^{*}_{bankingbook}(\ell)$).

All in all, a broader category of fatal events may be ascribed to structural imbalance between assets and liabilities, as detailed in the next section.

4.4.3 Liquidity and Overall Financial Structure

As for a trading and banking book, a what-if analysis may help understanding a bank major risk sources in terms of liquidity. In this regard, one of the key issues experienced by Cyprus Popular Bank as well as Northern Rock was a deposit run. On this, one needs to bear in mind the distinction between liabilities having a pre-defined cash flow schedule and deposits without a contractual maturity. In the latter case, a distinction is made between stable and non-stable deposits.

Hypothesising volatility in deposits is a first way of thinking about liquidity as principle of a bank insolvency. Likewise, difficulties in arranging a bank's own bond placement is an important source of financial tension which can eventually cause distress. The same occurs when a short-term misalignment between cash outflows and inflows occurs at the same time as unruliness pervades interbank liquidity market. On the contrary, the asset side may be lashed by unwillingness to pay, increase in credit line usage, and so on.

Bank Alpha, as depicted in Table 4.3, is a useful example to investigate liquidity issues causing a bank to become insolvent. Let us focus on Bank Alpha liquidity ladder. Table 4.3 shows that bucket $[0-1M)$ is marked out by a massive negative gap. A question arises: Which are the consequences of a 10% deposit withdrawal? Is bank solvency affected by a 20% cash repay? Under which conditions does a liquidity tension cause Bank Alpha to collapse?

Table 4.3: Bank Alpha's liquidity gap analysis ($ billions).

	[0–1M)	[1M-3M)	[3M-6M)	[6M-12M)	[1Y-2Y)	[2Y-5Y)	[5Y-10Y)	≥ 10 Years	Total
Assets	3.00	8.00	23.50	30.99	13.74	8.91	0.86		89.00
Liabilities	−62.50		−2.50	−16.00	−5.00				−86.00
Gap	−59.50	8.00	21.00	14.99	8.74	8.91	0.86		3.00

From the liability side, a distinction is made between instruments having a pre-defined contractual maturity ($L^m_{j,cf,t}$), and non-maturity facilities ($L^{nm}_{j,cf,t}$). Withdrawals affect the latter that can also be represented as a function of macroeconomic conditions $L^{nm}_{j,cf,t}(x_t)$.

Table 4.3 does not provide all information required to infer Bank Alpha's riskiness from the liquidity perspective. Nonetheless, bucket $[0-1M)$ liability gap is due to $ 62.5 billion deposits. In the case where all deposits are stable, no risk arises. However, a more detailed investigation on deposit stability is needed to check whether the $59.5 billion bucket $[0-1M)$ liability gap is a potential cause of failure. Assuming customers to withdraw a 5% of their deposits, Bank Alpha net outflow is $0.13 billion ($3.13 billion liability outflow minus $3 billion asset inflows). In case of a 10% deposit withdrawal, bucket $[0-1M)$ liability gap becomes $3.25 billion. In both cases, Bank Alpha is required to borrow liquidity from other sources. The most common and quicker way is to turn to the interbank market. In the case of a 5% withdrawal, $0.13 billion may be probably easily raised. However, when $3.25 billion is required in a very short term, Bank Alpha may face some difficulties.

In addition, when adverse conditions are taken into account, the entire liquidity profile may be at risk, as highlighted through the integrated liquidity mismatching equation.

In particular, one needs to consider interbank market buffer (B_t), the credit liquidity line as well as the liquidity shrinkage due to macroeconomic adverse conditions (ϱ_t). Let us assume that Bank Alpha can promptly (within 5 working days) activate credit liquidity lines for a maximum $4 billion. A liquidity shock due to deposit withdraw contagion affecting 5% of overall non-maturity liabilities is a substantial threat. In fact, economic conditions as well as reputation implications may induce the interbank market to shrink liquidity. If this contraction achieves 30% of the upper limit, thus a more complex process is triggered by implying Bank Alpha to re-negotiate its assets. Hence, most liquid assets are due to be sold and a haircut $H_{i,t}(x_t)$ needs to be applied. Given the nature of the trading book, low haircuts may be applied in the case of asset selling. Thus, the hypothesised 5% deposit withdrawal seems not to be harsh enough to cause Bank Alpha collapse. However, a 10% or 20% withdrawal insinuate more doubts about a bank's capability to face liquidity issues. Therefore, these circumstances can be described as a set of events $\Upsilon^*(\mathfrak{lm})$.

All in all, these described mechanics show the importance of a deep inquiry of the bank's liquidity profile. Basel III requirements may hide fragilities implicit in bank-specific business, which can be uncovered through a rigorous reverse stress testing process. Additionally, a combination of economic capital and liquidity mismatching events should be captured in line with equation (4.3) (i.e. $\Upsilon^*(\ell,\mathfrak{lm})$.

The next section focuses on macroeconomic scenarios that may compromise bank solvency.

4.5 Ruinous Macroeconomic Scenarios Exploration

According to CEBS (2010),

> Reverse stress testing consists in identifying a significant negative outcome and then identifying the causes and consequences that could led to such an outcome. In particular, a scenario or combination of scenarios that threaten the viability of the institution's business model is of particular use as a risk management tool in identifying possible combinations of events and risk concentrations within an institution that might not be generally considered in regular stress testing.

Hence, the idea of searching for a scenario or combination of scenarios that may cause a bank to collapse is a leading component of an entire risk management framework. As anticipated in the previous sections, a miscellany of external and bank specific idiosyncrasies may originate insolvency.

As described in the next section, this framework has the earmarks of being the ideal candidate to spot macroeconomic scenarios having a catastrophic impact on a specific bank.

4.5.1 Long- and Short-Run Ruinous Scenarios

Risk integration models constitute an ideal framework to identify ruinous scenarios for a given bank. In this regard, the distinction between long-run and short-term solvency needs to be taken into account. Additionally, alternative default thresholds can be chosen. All in all, a mix of models, thresholds and inference functions may be used to detect macroeconomic scenarios leading a bank to collapse. The following components are the necessary ingredients of this process.

- **Long-run: Model choice of economic capital function.** The definition of economic capital affects the entire analysis. The following three alternatives may be pursued.
- **Fully integrated loss ($Loss_h$).** It is computed by relying on credit risk adjusted (simulated default) present value of both assets and liabilities, net interest income, non-interest revenues, non-interest expenses and non-performing loss variation.
- **Integrated loss, $Loss_h^{\Delta A}$.** In line with equation (4.11), it relies on asset present value and liability face value.
- **Credit portfolio loss ($Loss_h^{CR}$).** This loss is calculated by leaning on equation (4.12).
- **Long-run: Default correlation hypothesis.** Default correlation plays a crucial part as a risk source. Hence, analysis may additionally be enriched by acknowledging on alternative correlation hypothesis such as, for example, historical estimate, extreme scenario and judgemental assessment.
- **Long-run: Economic capital vulnerability threshold.** The choice of the vulnerability threshold is crucial to identify critical scenarios. In this regard, core Tier 1, Tier 1, Total capital are potential candidates, but some other thresholds may be considered in line with the scope of the analysis.
- **Short-term: Liquidity mismatch.** A fully integrated perspective should be followed when aiming at considering a comprehensive spectrum of liquidity risks. On the contrary, regulatory measures such as LCR and NSFR may also provide a suitable alternative.
- **Short-term: Vulnerability threshold.** As per the economic capital, even in the case of liquidity analysis, a line needs to be drawn to ascertain when bank insolvency occurs. On this subject, one may rely on a percentage of total asset book value, regulatory thresholds applied to LCR and NSFR, and so on.

Table 4.4 sketches combinations of elements to consider when defining a long-run solvency framework. One needs to specify a path by choosing a combination of the following items.

Table 4.4: Vulnerability scenario set-up. Economic capital, default correlation and threshold potential combinations.

		Correlation Hypothesis		Vulnerability Threshold		
		b.1 **Historical Corr.**	**b.2** **Hypothetical**	**c.1** **Core Capital**	**c.2** **Tier 1**	**c.3** **Total Capital**
$Loss_h$	a.1					
$Loss_h^{\Delta A}$	a.2					
$Loss_h^{CR}$	a.3					

- **Economic capital definition.** Alternatives are pointed out in terms of rows of Table 4.4.
- **Default correlation hypothesis.** The first two columns of Table 4.4 describe potential options.
- **Vulnerability threshold.** Alternatives are summarised in the last three columns of Table 4.4.

For example, Table 4.5 highlights the mix (a.1, b.1, c.1). This combination leads to identify the scenarios for which $Loss_h$, computed by relying on historical default correlation, exceeds the *Core Capital* threshold. As an alternative (not depicted in the table), one may consider the mix (a.2, b.1, c.3). It highlights catastrophic scenarios deriving from the combination of $Loss_h^{\Delta A}$, computed by relying on historical default correlation, exceeds the *Total Capital* threshold. One can consider other miscellanies, as pinpointed in Table 4.5.

Table 4.5: Vulnerability scenario set-up. Economic capital, default correlation and threshold potential combinations.

		Correlation Hypothesis		Vulnerability Threshold		
		b.1 **Historical Corr.**	**b.2** **Hypothetical**	**c.1** **Core Capital**	**c.2** **Tier 1**	**c.3** **Total Capital**
$Loss_h$	a.1	X		X		
$Loss_h^{\Delta A}$	a.2					
$Loss_h^{CR}$	a.3					

Moving to the liquidity area, a similar path may be followed. In this case, a simpler double entry representation is drawn as listed in Table 4.6.

Table 4.6: Vulnerability scenario set-up. Liquidity mismatching potential combinations.

	Vulnerability Threshold	
	d.1 Total Asset %	**d.2 Reg. Threshold**
LM_h	X	
LCR		X

One needs to bear in mind that alternative objective functions may be used for reverse stress testing purposes. In particular, the following options hold.

- **Macroeconomic set** $(x)^*(\ell)$. Equation (4.4) spotlights scenario causing *Loss* to exceed a given threshold ℓ.
- **Macroeconomic set** $(x)^*(\mathfrak{lm})$. Equation (4.5) focuses on liquidity mismatching lower than a (big) negative threshold $\mathfrak{lm}$.
- **Macroeconomic set** $(x)^*(\ell, \mathfrak{lm})$. Equation (4.6) takes into account both components.

4.6 Summary

Reverse stress testing was introduced as a managerial and regulatory framework through which to explore weakness sources. Few alternative objective functions were investigated by pointing out the difference between internal features and macroeconomic conditions causing a bank to become insolvent. A bunch of integrated risk models were explored in an attempt to uncover all major bank weaknesses. Additionally, vulnerability thresholds were investigated by relying on both a long-term (economic capital) as well a short-term (liquidity) perspective.

What-if analyses were proposed as a qualitative tool for inspecting trading book, banking book and overall liquidity vulnerabilities. Thus, examples of heuristic algorithms were introduced in order to clarify how to proceed in the (quantitative) computational analysis. Finally, macroeconomic scenarios were investigated as a source of potential bank failure. Interactions between external and internal conditions were studied. The relevance of a fully integrated framework was highlighted as a challenge for a renewed risk management process.

Bibliography

Atkinson, A. C., Riani, M., and Cerioli, A. (2004). *Exploring Multivariate Data with the Forward Search*. Springer-Verlag, New York.

Bellini, T. (2012). The forward search outlier detection in data envelopment analysis. *European Journal of Operational Research*, 216, 200–207.

CEBS (2010). CEBS guidelines on stress testing (gl32).

Glasserman, P., Kang, C., and Kang, W. (2015). Stress scenario selection by empirical likelihood. *Quantitative Finance*, 15, 25–41.

Grundke, P. and Pliszka, K. (2015). A macroeconomic reverse stress testing. Discussion Paper, Deutsche Bundesbank, No. 30, 2015.

Kretzschmar, G., McNeil, A., and Kirchner, A. (2010). Integrated models of capital adequacy – why banks are undercapitalised. *Journal of Banking and Finance*, 34(12), 2838–2850.

Riani, M. and Zani, S. (1997). An iterative method for the detection of multivariate outliers. *Metron*, 55, 101–117.

Zani, S., Riani, M., and Corbellini, A. (1998). Robust bivariate boxplots and multiple outlier detection. *Computational Statistics and Data Analysis*, 24, 257–270.

Bibliography

[illegible faded reference text]

Bahram Mirzai

5 Reverse Stress Testing Asset and Liability Portfolios

5.1 The Stress Testing Paradigm

In the aftermath of the global financial crisis (GFC), regulators introduced a new set of metrics to measure the susceptibility of large banking institutions and, with them, a significant part of the financial system to potential future economic stress events. With stress testing and, more generally, with a forward-looking scenario driven analysis of assets and liabilities, a through-the-cycle assessment of balance sheet was introduced. The new paradigm considers an economic cycle unfolding over a period of three to five years according to scenarios specified for a set of macro-financial variables. It requires the financial institution to assess the impact of the scenarios on their capital by evaluating their impact on the assets and liabilities. In retrospect, one may argue whether such metrics could have been introduced earlier to diversify away from pure value-at-risk based measures with their benefits and shortcomings to model stress events.

The necessity for a scenario-driven view can be exemplified by the way credit ratings and probabilities of default change through a cycle. During an economic downturn, the score of a counterparty may change due to the changes in the fundamentals underlying the score. We assume that the new score results in a lower rating – say, a downgrade from A to BBB. During the downturn, not only the ratings are impacted but also the probabilities of default (PD). The rating of a counterparty and the PD assigned to a rating are two related factors but require separate assessments. The through-the-cycle PD for rating class is obtained by averaging historical defaults over decades of data. As a result of the averaging, the through-the-cycle PD reacts slowly to changes in the credit cycle. The point-in-time view, however, provides PD levels that react faster to such changes. S&P Global Rating data (S&P Global Ratings, 2018) shows that for investment grade corporates the PD increases by a factor of 3.5 when comparing the through-the-cycle level with the level prevailing during 2009.

Supervisory stress tests are designed to serve two key goals. First, they provide the ability to assess capital adequacy of large banking institutions through an economic cycle while maintaining the ability to compare and contrast the risk profiles of different banks by using a common set of scenarios and a unified stress test reporting approach. Second, they provide an aggregate view of the economic impact of a crisis on large banking institutions as a critical part of the economy. Although the scope ignores contagious effects on other parts of the financial industry, such as medium- to

Note: Edited by Tiziano Bellini

https://doi.org/10.1515/9783110647907-005

small-sized banks, asset managers or mutual funds, these actors are seen either as not system critical or as providers of liquidity, the impairment of which can be bridged by accommodative monetary policy actions of the central bank.

In contrast to supervisory stress tests, a reverse stress test (RST) attempts to capture the risks of a particular financial institution to macro-financial stress events, which may be of a systemic or idiosyncratic nature. While in a supervisory stress test, a specific scenario is the relevant input.[1] In a reverse stress test, identification of those scenarios that can lead to a depletion of capital in excess of a critical loss is the relevant objective.

RST scenarios depend on several factors that are specific to the bank performing RST. First, the severity of the critical loss determines the severity of RST scenarios. The greater the loss level is, the more severe the scenarios are. Hence, the choice of the critical loss is linked to the risk tolerance level adopted by the bank. Second, independent of the critical loss level, the structure of the assets and liabilities on the balance sheet is a determining factor for the scenarios resulting from RST. The structure of the assets is a reflection of the business decisions made on product types, geographic diversity, asset quality, or portfolio duration, leverage, and diversification. Such choices derive the value of the assets and their sensitivity to the macro-financial variables underlying their valuation which in turn determine the RST scenarios to result.

The practical challenges of RST are twofold. First, as the requirements for a transaction level RST can be demanding, segmentation of balance sheet into portfolios of homogenous risks can significantly facilitate RST process. Second challenge is posed by the ability to generate robust and consistent scenarios for a large set of macro-financial variables required to perform valuation of the portfolios. In the following section, we explore these challenges and propose practical procedures for an implementable RST framework that can be iteratively enhanced by increasing the modelling granularity of the balance sheet.

5.2 A Simple Example

To illustrate the main concepts of RST, we consider a simple example of two bonds with different maturities and ratings but with the same initial value of 100 at time $t = 0$. Table 5.1 provides the description of each bond. Throughout this chapter, we use Standard & Poor's rating scheme, assuming that internal ratings can be mapped to it.

---

1 An example would be when the real GDP drops from 2% growth to −6% within 1.5 years and recovers to its initial level within the consecutive 1.5 years.

Table 5.1: Bond parameters.

	Loan IG	Loan HY
Maturity (years)	5	5
Initial rating (Standard & Poor's)	A	BB
Initial value	100	100

We use the following equation to assess the value of each bond V_t at time $t = 1$, that is after one year, as a function of the relevant macro-financial variables:

$$V_{t=1} = \frac{100 \left(1 - PD_{1,R}\, LGD_{1,R}\right)\left(1 + r_{0,T} + s_{0,T,R}\right)^T}{\left(1 + r_{1,T-1} + s_{1,T-1,R}\right)^{T-1}} \tag{5.1}$$

where $r_{t,T}$ is the risk-free rate at time t for maturity T, $s_{t,T,R}$ is the credit spread at time t for maturity T and rating R, and $PD_{t,R}$ and $LGD_{t,R}$ are the (annual) probability of default and loss given default at time t for rating R, respectively. For simplicity, we ignore the possibility of rating upgrades and downgrades, assuming that at the end of the year, the rating is either the initial one or default D.

The bond valuation is subject to both market and credit risks. The market risk component consists of interest rate risk and credit spread risk. The credit risk component consists of downgrade and default risk. Both risks are correlated with key macro indicators such as inflation, GDP and unemployment rate. For the valuation of the bonds, the following macro-financial variables are required: inflation, risk-free interest rates, credit spreads, default probabilities and loss given default rates. Using US macro-financial data, we construct two scenarios representing baseline and adverse outcomes. The scenario values are provided in Table 5.2. The subindices 0 and 1 refer to $t = 0$ and $t = 1$.

Table 5.2: Macro-financial scenarios for US and the resulting loan values.

Variable	Baseline	Adverse
$r_{0,5}\%$	2.95	2.95
$r_{1,4}\%$	2.74	0.77
$s_{0,5,A}$ bps	57	57
$s_{0,5,BB}$ bps	167	167
$s_{1,4,A}$ bps	57	285
$s_{1,4,BB}$ bps	173	807
$PD_{1,A}\%$	0.06	0.49

Table 5.2 (continued)

Variable	Baseline	Adverse
$PD_{1,BB}$ %	0.51	4.89
$LGD_{1,A}$ %	65	65
$LGD_{1,BB}$ %	85	85
Real GDP Growth %	2.8	−6.7
$V_{1,IG}$	104.3	79.3
$V_{1,HY}$	104.8	66.9

In a supervisory stress test, the baseline and adverse scenarios are considered as given and the values of the bonds are computed subject to the scenarios. In contrast, in a reverse stress test, a critical loss to the portfolio of the bonds is assumed and the scenarios resulting in or exceeding the critical loss are to be identified. Assuming a loss level of 15%, the adverse scenario clearly meets the RST condition. However, there are many other scenarios that meet the loss condition too, which still need to be identified. The purpose of RST is to identify all such scenarios and to classify them.

Our naive example can be used to derive some key implementation considerations for a practical reverse stress testing process and methodology. To that end, we consider the bonds in Table 5.1 as proxy models for portfolios of homogeneous loans asset. As it turns out, this level of abstraction significantly simplifies the RST process.

Let us assume that the assets of a bank consist of mortgage and consumer loan portfolios. To model these loan portfolios, we use bonds as proxy models. In each case, the rating and maturity of the bond is determined as an average rating and mean time to maturity of the loans in the portfolio. The averaging may consider a weighting proportional to the exposures of the portfolio assets. The bonds can be further furnished with a diversity score accounting for the degree of the diversification within each portfolio. The proxy models then replicate the aggregate behaviour of the assets in each portfolio by using appropriate credit cycles. The credit cycle, in turn, is the risk factor representing the credit risk profile of assets in the portfolio, such as migration and default dynamics. Assuming that the loans in the portfolios are funded by cash equivalent deposits, a capital depletion of 15% becomes equivalent to a total devaluation of the proxy bonds by 15%. Hence, the RST scenarios identified for the proxy models can be used as RST scenarios for the mortgage and consumer loans. The naive example together with the proxy modelling analogy suggest the following key steps for a practical RST.

Portfolio Segmentation. The first step for a practical RST is a segmentation of asset portfolios in homogenous asset classes and modelling of each class by a proxy model. The segmentation not only facilitates the RST process but also helps to identify portfolio segments that derive losses. Segmentation can then be applied across different portfolios of business – e.g. mortgage and consumer loans, or within an asset portfolio to obtain more homogenous subsets. For example, the mortgage portfolio may be segmented in prime, subprime and jumbo mortgages. An appropriate segmentation increases the accuracy and transparency of RST and contributes to the simplification of the process.

Loss Measure. The second step is definition of an appropriate loss measure and a critical loss level. The loss measure provides a metric that allows to identify the relevant scenarios in an RST process. The critical loss level is then used to set the severity of the RST scenarios. The choices of loss measure and critical loss level are often linked to risk appetite and incentive schemes within an organisation.

Scenario Generation. The third step is the ability to generate scenarios for macro-financial variables representing the distribution of possible outcomes in a consistent and forward-looking manner. The manifold nature of the variables required to perform valuations of assets and liabilities can encompass a wide range of macro-financial data across several countries and financial markets. A silo approach to RST, scenario generation for individual business units in isolation may be considered a simplification. However, it can result in inconsistencies, particularly when an aggregate view of the bank's balance sheet during a stress period is desired. The generation of consistent scenarios can be a challenging task, as it requires a robust multivariate approach to model hundreds, if not thousands, of variables exhibiting a diverse range of dynamic features.

5.3 Portfolio Segmentation

Banking business activities are usually divided into the banking book and trading book. The banking book comprises primary lending activities of a bank across retail and corporate sectors. Retail business, in turn, can be subdivided into mortgage, car, credit card and other small but high-frequency lending activities. The corporate sector may be subdivided in small- and medium-sized enterprises, large corporate and sovereign lending. The banking book assets are in general held to maturity. The banking book liabilities are essentially the deposits. The trading book consists of financial assets and commodities that are held either for trading purposes or in order to hedge market risk positions across trading and banking books.

A bank-wide RST requires a valuation of all positions in banking and trading books under a large set of scenarios. In practice, this is often a demanding task, requiring an engagement of resources across all relevant business areas. Moreover, the valuation of individual assets may not be readily feasible for a large number of macro-financial scenarios, particularly in the case of structured and bespoke assets such as specialised lending.

Therefore, for practical purposes, a segmentation of portfolio in homogenous classes of assets combined with use of proxy models can significantly simplify the RST process. Homogeneous classes of assets are already used by banks for risk assessment or pricing purposes. An example of creating homogenous classes in the lending business is the grouping of obligors into rating, maturity and sectoral buckets. Within each bucket, the exposure weighted average rating and mean time to maturity of assets are computed to replicate the risk profile of the bucket through a proxy model. In addition to migration and default probabilities, the proxy modelling needs to consider migration and default correlations within and between buckets. Correlations of the credit cycles provide an intrinsic approach to model default and migration correlations of the respective portfolios.

In Figure 5.1, a segmentation of retail lending business in homogenous groups is exhibited. The granularity of the segmentation depends on the business and underwriting policies – for example, the extension of no credit lines to customers with BB or lower ratings.

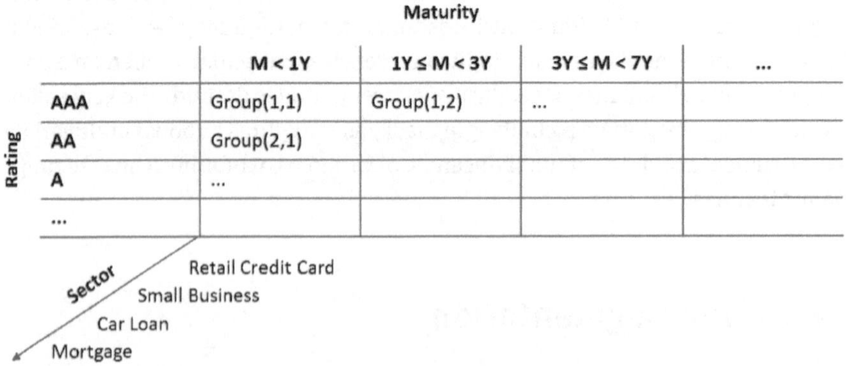

Figure 5.1: Retail lending segmentation in homogenous buckets.

For internationally operating banks, a further dimension arises from the geographic spread of business. To what extent portfolios of different countries can be arranged into homogenous groups will also depend on factors such as legal entity structure, regulatory treatment, or similarities of the macro-financial environments.

Macro-financial scenarios leading to an exceedance of the critical loss are likely to be of systemic nature. The lending business due to its concentration risk is often the main driver of the losses. This is further amplified by the fact that benefits of portfolio diversification diminish during stress periods, as in addition to default probabilities, default correlations increase too. In contrast, severe idiosyncratic losses are often due to either large exposure positions or operational risk losses. Although the banking regulation is designed on the premise that large exposures are managed within certain limits outside the minimum capital requirement framework, there have been rare instances of bank failures in the past due to exposures to individual counterparties. RST can, nevertheless, provide insight to measurement of idiosyncratic risks such as large exposure risks by including the underlying risk factors or proxy drivers as additional variables in the scenario generation process.

The scope of RST usually excludes advisory services such as wealth management and investment banking. The underlying risks of these activities are primarily of operational nature, including events such as fraud, unauthorised activities, cyber risk, or execution and business practice losses. It is argued that some severe operational risk events may be driven by economic downturn. However, strong evidence has not yet been presented, in part due to the low frequency of such events or their idiosyncratic nature. An additional factor is the latency of operational risk events. As a result, it is not clear whether an economic downturn or the business practices prior to it trigger the loss.

In summary, the macro-financial scenarios identified as part of RST are primarily addressing the systemic risks inherent to banking and trading books that arise from stresses to macroeconomic environment and financial markets. RST may enhance the risk measurement of large exposures and help in understanding exposure to high-frequency operational risk losses.

5.4 Loss Measure

The loss measure is required to assess the impact of the macro-financial scenario on the value of the assets and liabilities. It can either be defined at the aggregate balance sheet level or at a more granular portfolio level. It allows to identify those scenarios that exceed a critical loss level. The critical loss level is linked to the objectives of RST. Possible objectives include reverse identification of scenarios for capital adequacy applications such as ICAAP[2] or risk appetite setting.

We will consider two examples of loss measures. The first one is defined at the balance sheet level, where the impact of scenarios on capital is assessed. More specifically, we are interested in those scenarios that can result in a depletion of capital in excess of the critical loss:

$$\Omega = \arg_{S}(A_t(S_t) - L_t(S_t) \geq CL = \lambda E_0) \tag{5.2}$$

where Ω corresponds to the set of scenarios that satisfy the condition in the arg() function at time t. The time t corresponds to the horizon of the RST. The minimum

---

2 Internal capital adequacy assessment process.

time horizon is typically one quarter, which is in line with the reporting frequency of most macro variables.

In Equation (5.2), $A_t(S_t)$ describes the value of the assets at time t subject to the scenario S_t. Similarly, $L_t(S_t)$ describes the value of the liabilities at t subject to S_t. As the structure of assets and liabilities at t is unknown, several portfolio strategies can be considered to specify their structure at the RST time horizon. These strategies include rollover, run-off and static portfolio assumptions. In the case of a roll-over strategy, the assets and liabilities are assumed to be replaced with assets and liabilities of similar structure, thus prior to run-off key portfolio characteristics such as duration, rating and asset allocation are preserved. A run-off strategy means managing assets and liabilities with no rebalancing and with cash settlements at maturity. A static portfolio model assumes assets and liabilities to be constant over time with no maturing and no principal payouts. For the purpose of RST, we adopt the rollover strategy, assuming that while some loans expire, new loans are extended and, hence, the overall portfolio characteristics are preserved.

The critical loss CL in equation (5.2) is expressed as a factor λ applied to the equity funds E_0 at time $t = 0$. As these funds are invested by the treasury in low-risk assets with hedged interest rate and currency risks, we can assume $E_t = E_0$, given no new capital issuance before t.

The second definition of risk measure for RST is based on a risk appetite. Risk appetite is often defined by risk type or by business unit to incentivise or discipline business activities within the risk appetite statement. The firm-wide risk appetite is then obtained by the sum of the individual risk appetites. Therefore, we confine the analysis to portfolio of a business unit, such as retail credit card loans, and use the corresponding risk appetite measure to identify RST scenarios.

To this end, we consider the following approach:

$$\Omega = \arg_S \left(V_0(S_0) - V_t(S_t) \geq C_{V_0} \right) \tag{5.3}$$

where V_0 is the initial value of the portfolio, $V_t(S_t)$ the value of portfolio at time t subject to the scenario S_t, and C_{V_0} is the capital allocated to the business unit owning the portfolio.

Although the two measures exhibit similarities, the resulting RST scenarios can be different. In the first case, the focus is on managing balance sheet risks from a systemic point of view – whereas in the second case, the idiosyncratic risk of a business unit is considered and RST is used to identify the macro-financial scenarios that can breach the risk appetite limits.

In both cases, a modified definition of RST measure may be used by introducing a limit on how much worse the portfolio loss relative to the critical loss should be to avoid inclusion of extreme scenarios. The revised definition, in case of Equation (5.3), is given by:

$$\Omega = \underset{S_t}{\arg}\left(V_0\left(S_0\right) - \left(1+\alpha\right)C_{V_0} \le V_t\left(S_t\right) \le V_0\left(S_0\right) - C_{V_0}\right) \tag{5.4}$$

where the choice of $\alpha > 0$ sets the degree to which extreme scenarios are considered.

5.5 Scenario Generation

5.5.1 Introduction

A prerequisite for an efficient RST is the ability to generate consistent scenarios across a wide range of macro-financial variables. In contrast to supervisory stress tests, where the scenarios paths are explicitly given, RST requires an appropriate representation of the space of possible outcomes to identify the RST scenarios. In Table 5.3, we provide a list of typical macro-financial variables used by banks. This list is not meant to be comprehensive, but it highlights the complexity of the task, which increases further when the dimension of the geographic spread of the business is added.

Table 5.3: Typical macro-financial variables in a reverse stress test.

Type	Variable
Macro	Real GDP
	Unemployment rate, unemployment claims
	Inflation, CPI
	Residential and commercial real estate indices
	Household debt, income and savings
	Government debt, revenue, expenditures
	Current account and capital account
	Import and export of goods and services
	Retail Sales Indices
Financial	Equity Indices
	Treasury, interbank, and swap rates
	Credit spreads, CDS and ABS spreads
	FX spot and forward rates
	Cross currency, FX, and basis swaps
	Commodity prices
	FX, equity, and swaption implied volatilities

The econometric modelling literature offers a wide range of approaches including vector autoregression, moving average, distributed lag and factor models which may in addition come in forms of structural, Bayesian or stochastic dynamic models (Hamilton, 1994). As an example, the popular and widely used vector autoregression model (Hamilton, 1994) is described by:

$$x_t = a + A_1 x_{t-1} + \cdots + A_p x_{t-p} + \varepsilon_t \tag{5.5}$$

where the vector x_t consists of several stationary macro-financial variables, the vector a and the matrices A_i constitute the model parameters to be estimated, and ε_t is a zero-mean white noise corresponding to the residual part that cannot be explained by the selected model variables. As x_t is assumed to be stationary, in the case of variables with trend, their first order difference is used. Another popular approach is given by structural models in the form of:

$$x_t = a_0 + \sum_{i=1}^{p} a_i x_{t-i} + \sum_{k=1}^{q} b_k y_{t,k} + \varepsilon_t \tag{5.6}$$

where x_t is the variable to be predicted, $y_{t,k}$ are the explanatory or exogenous variables that used to explain x_t in addition to its own lagged values, and ε_t is a zero-mean white noise. The model parameters to be estimated are a_0, a_i and b_k.

While these models are based on a set of linear relationships between transformed and lagged values of the data, there is not one standard approach among economists that would be consistently applied to model variables of similar type. In fact, in practice, there is a wide range of the implementations of Equations (5.5) and (5.6) that depend on factors such as available data, views of the economist on structural relations or modelling objectives. In trying to understand the wide range of approaches used among economists, a consideration of the following aspects proves to be helpful:

– Weak model identification
– Applicability to stress testing
– Regularisation

Due to their importance for scenario generation as a key step in a reverse stress test, we elaborate them in the following sections.

5.5.2 Weak Model Identification

By weak model identification, we refer to the characteristic that econometric models assume relations which are not always manifestly observable in the data, no matter how plausible. Hence, the assumed relations may fail to hold in general. One of the reasons for weak model identificatn is the diversity of economic regimes observed between countries – that is, the internal and external constraints within which these economies have to operate. Regime differences arise from social and institutional factors such as wealth distribution, bankruptcy laws, legal environment, regulations or geopolitical consideration

Regime differences can constitute a limiting factor for developing universally applicable macroeconomic models on the basis of a common set of principles. As a result, the macroeconomic modelling lends itself rather to a discipline of engineering and exploitation of empirical economic data. We explore this by considering some examples.

If the growth strategy of a country is such that a larger share of GDP is allocated to the elites than to the labour force, the consumption levels will be inevitably lower and the saving levels higher, as the labour force is the main driver of the consumption. Any increase in consumption will have to be at the cost of increasing household debt burden unless there is a redistribution of GDP. This example highlights how wealth distribution can result in different levels of household savings and consumption.

Financial asset prices are even less forgiving to regime differences. A comparison of credit spreads for corporate bonds of similar ratings and maturities shows that bonds issued by corporations in Greater China have a lower spread than those issued by corporations in Mainland China. The difference in spread is a reflection of different recovery rates perceived by bond traders which in turn can be due to different bankruptcy laws.

Another example of regime difference is obtained by comparing oil and gas exporting and importing countries. While soaring energy prices impact inflation levels of energy importing countries, the energy exporting countries may not opt to pass on in full such price surges to their own economies. To avoid distorting effects of energy prices on inflation, economists have devised different measures of inflation by including and excluding energy prices. In ECB global macro model (ECB, 2017), the need for differentiation goes beyond inflation to the extent that a different modelling approach for the oil exporting countries is considered.

Weak model identification has led economists to use semi-structural approaches where they combine calibration and judgement to circumvent empirical mismatches between model and data – for example, the ECB global macro model (ECB, 2017). To ensure consistency across several economies, the model parameters are determined by applying informed judgement rather than using historical data, highlighting the challenges to reconcile economic intuition with empirical facts. To overcome this, at least in part, a paradigm change is required by employing data-driven approaches that consider the univariate dynamics as well as the multivariate aspects more explicitly in their own right than is practically achievable through standard modelling approaches such as those in Equations (5.5) and (5.6). We refer to Section 5.7 for an alternative approach that provides the flexibility to account for idiosyncratic patterns observed in different regimes while applying a unified set of modelling principles.

5.5.3 Applicability to Stress Testing

One of the features of macroeconomic models is that their design is primarily focused on forecasting expected behaviour of modelling variables. In fact, for macro-econometric models to be useful for policy makers, particular emphasis is made on their long-term equilibrium properties. The dynamic up to the equilibrium, if not modelling explicitly, is a side effect of transition from the current state to the equilibrium. Moreover, techniques required to account for modelling stress events are not part of the modelling tool kit. As a result, model calibration becomes tuned to the average behaviour implied by the data which can lead to underestimating the severity of the stress events. The following examples seek to illustrate this aspect.

The first example we consider is provided by a macroeconomic model (Moody's Analytics, 2014) for the FX rate GBPUSD:

$$\log(\text{GBPUSD}) = a \log(\text{UK PR}/\text{US PR}) + b \log(\text{US CPI}/\text{UK CPI}) + c \quad (5.7)$$

where PR and CPI and refer to policy interest rate and consumer price index, respectively. From a macroeconomic point of view, this model appears to be intuitive and appropriate. The interest rate differential accounts for the interest rate parity modelling the short-term dynamics while the CPI differential accounts for purchasing power parity modelling the mid-term dynamics. A calibration of this model using two different historical periods reveals, however, some of the shortcomings of the approach.

Figure 5.2 depicts the results of the model in Equation (5.7) calibrated with historical FX, PR, and CPI data of the two periods 1994Q2–2005Q4 and 1994Q4–2015Q2, representing the periods prior to GFC and Brexit vote, respectively. For convenience, we refer to them as GFC data and Brexit data. The blue curve shows the historical FX rates. The green and red curves correspond to the results of the model calibrated with the GFC data and the Brexit data, respectively. The in-sample estimates of FX are depicted as dashed curves while the solid curves show the out-of-sample results of the model. By Figure 5.2, both the in-sample and out-of-sample model estimates exhibit modest error rates as long as the historical FX rates remain in the proximity of the sample mean of the data used for calibration. However, the model performance deteriorates during stress periods of the Dot-com bubble, GFC, and post-Brexit vote.

In the next example, we consider three regression models calibrated using the annualised quarterly growths of the US and the UK real GDP during the period of 1990Q1–2019Q4. In each case, the target variable UK GDP is regressed against the explanatory variable US GDP.

Figure 5.3 depicts the regression results for the three models. The dashed grey line represents the unconditional calibration using the entire data sample. The grey line goes through the sample mean depicted in orange colour. The red and blue lines are conditional regressions where the conditions are given by US GDP Growth ≤ 0 and US GDP Growth > 0, respectively. For convenience, we denote the three regression results

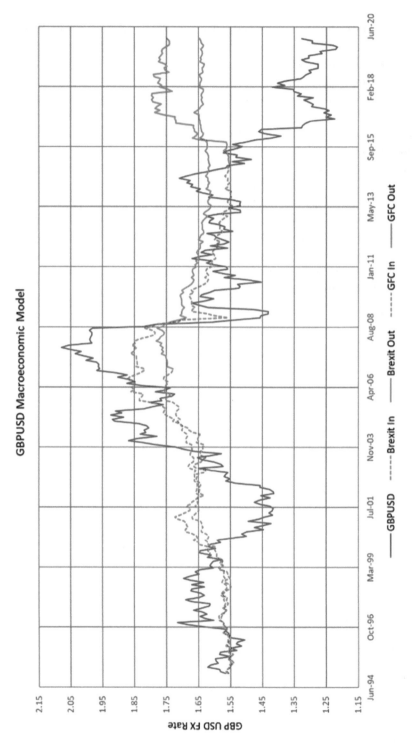

Figure 5.2: Structural macroeconomic model for the FX rate GBPUSD.

as unconditional, recession and boom regressions. By Figure 5.3, the unconditional regression shows, in accordance with the empirical data, stronger spillover effects from the US to the UK compared to sample regression, whereas the boom regression is in line with the unconditional regression.

A different way to look at these results is obtained by comparing the GDP growth correlations for these data sets. The correlation of the annualised quarterly growths for the entire sample is 58%, while for the conditional recession data it is 76%. The increases in correlation level during recession periods suggests a state conditional correlation. In other words, the level of correlation is dependent on the state of the economy. In a macro-financial data context, state conditionality often means higher correlations during stress periods and weak correlations in periods of no stress. A realistic modelling of macro-financial variables during stress periods requires accounting for state conditional correlations to ensure the appropriate propagation of shock signals from scenarios to response variables. State conditional correlations can be modelled using techniques from risk management (Embrechts, Klüppelberg, and Mikosch, 2011; Maugis, 2016).

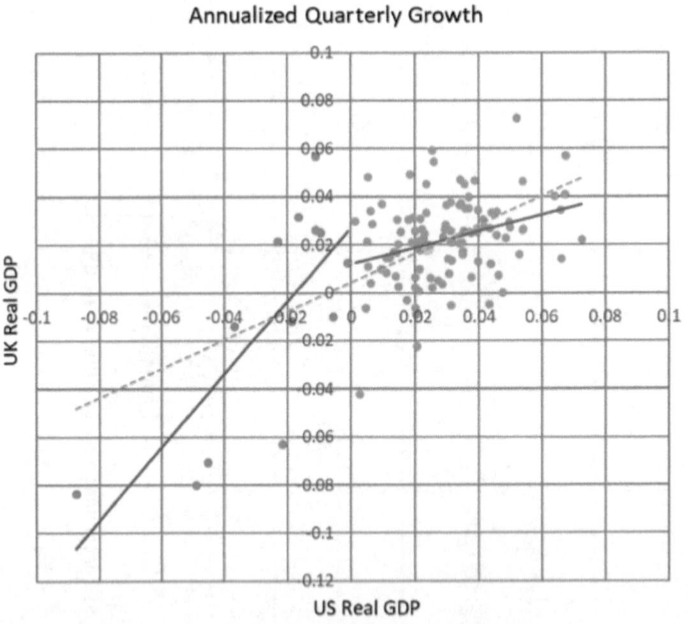

Annualized Quarterly Growth

Figure 5.3: Behaviour of stress events in regression analysis.

In practice, linear regression works well in cases where there is a high level of non-spurious correlation between the variables. Even then, the assumption of linearity can break down in the tails resulting in a weak propagation of a stress shock to the response variables. Non-linear relationships are observed, particularly for financial variables such as interest rate term structure, credit spread, interbank rates or implied volatilities of derivatives. A joint modelling of macro-financial variables with linear and non-linear relationships within a unified framework is a challenge to models similar to Equations (5.5) and (5.6).

We conclude this section by looking at the example Taylor rule, which also illustrates the practical limitations of econometric models during stress periods. In its original form, the Taylor rule was proposed as (Taylor, 1993):

$$i = 2 + \pi + 0.5\,(\pi - \pi^*) + 0.5\,y \qquad (5.8)$$

Broadly speaking, it recommends that a central bank should set its interest policy rate i by considering two factors. First, the deviation of the actual inflation π from the target inflation π^* and, second, the output gap y in real GDP. The output gap measures the deviation of the real GDP from the real potential output – the economy's maximum sustainable output.

We apply the Taylor rule to the data during the period 1990Q1–2019Q3 and estimate the federal funds rate by expressing Equation (5.8) as a linear regression problem:

$$i_t = r_t^* + \pi_t + \alpha\,(\pi_t - \pi^*) + \beta\,y_t \qquad (5.9)$$

where r_t^* is the real interest rate and the output gap is defined by $y_t = log\,(Y_t) - log\,(Y_t^*)$ with Y_t denoting the real GDP and Y_t the potential output. Figure 5.4 depicts the results of the regression analysis for a steady-state real interest rate assumption of $r_t^* = r^* = 0.02$.

As shown in Figure 5.4, in the aftermath of GFC, the model suggests interest policy rates that fall well below zero to unprecedented levels that would imply a bank run if the rate was to be passed on to the depositors. Similarly, given the growth period following the GFC, a higher rate than the actual one is implied. The central bank's decisions on monetary policy stance may follow traditional economic wisdom in normal times, but not necessarily during stress periods or periods following a severe stress. As the former Chair of the Federal Reserve Ben Bernanke remarked (Brookings Institution, 2014): "The problem with quantitative easing is that it works in practice but it doesn't work in theory."

5.5.4 Regularisation

Economists apply expert views and plausibility assumptions to select a small set of variables for modelling. This engineering process, albeit legitimate, may miss some other variables that can prove useful in explaining a target variable. For example, in the case of GBPUSD FX rates, besides the intuitive choices of policy rate and CPI, other macro variables including current account, foreign currency reserves, quantitative

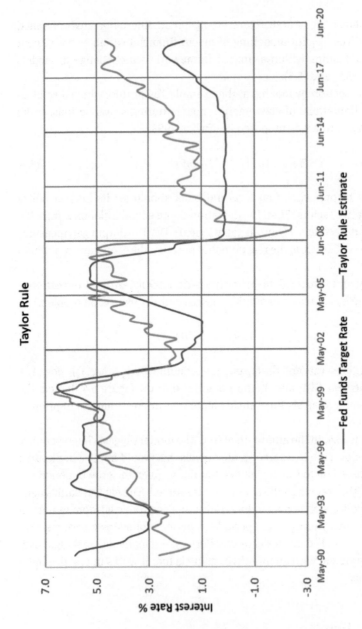

Figure 5.4: In-sample fit of the Taylor rule applied to historical data during the period 1990Q1–2019Q3.

easing measure, tourism activities and Google search term frequencies for GBPUSD may prove helpful in explaining the dynamics of the exchange rate.

There is, however, a trade-off between the complexity of the model due to increasing the number of explanatory variables and the availability of data. In a case of limited macro data, a more complex model may lead to overfitting or low significance levels of the estimated model parameters. This trade-off can be addressed by applying regularisation techniques. Regularisation provides a statistical framework to identify the principal model variables while suppressing the redundant ones.

In the following, we demonstrate the use of regularisation techniques for solving linear regression problems. A similar approach can be applied to general optimisation problems. For the regression model, we assume input x_t, target y_t, and regression parameter a. One of the widely used regularisation methods is the Tikhonov regularisation (Alexander and Smola, 2002). For a linear regression, the Tikhonov regularisation is given by:

$$E(a) = \sum_t (y_t - ax_t^T)^2 + \lambda aa^T \tag{5.10}$$

where λ is the regularisation factor and $E(a)$ the loss function to be minimised. The last term in the equation is the regularisation term, which leads to suppressing the weights a_i of insignificant variables with irregular behaviour. The case $\lambda = 0$ corresponds to the standard linear regression. The additional parameter λ is estimated empirically by using the method of validation (Alexander and Smola, 2002).

5.6 Machine Learning

Machine learning techniques have gained significant interest in recent years due to the availability of big data, improved performance of the learning algorithms, and distributed computational power on clouds. The improvement of the learning rates has been to the extent that in some applications, machine learning algorithms have surpassed human performance. It is, therefore, tempting to consider their potential use in stress testing applications. Machine learning utilises either supervised or unsupervised learning methods. Examples of supervised learning are linear regression and prediction problems. In the case of supervised learning, labelled data – i.e. pairs of input-output that correspond to each other – is used to learn. Unsupervised learning is learning without labels – i.e. only with input data. Clustering is an example of unsupervised learning where similarities in data are explored to classify the data.

There are several caveats concerning the application of machine learning to macro-financial data. First, the amount of data, particularly in the case of macro variables, is negligible compared to the data processed by typical machine learning applications. Although the number of macro variables for which data is collected is large, the amount of the data per variable can be quite limited. For example, three decades of quarterly GDP data provides only 120 observations. Going further back in history and not questioning the applicability of remote data to current macro-financial environments will not resolve the data issue. The data scarcity concern is amplified by the fact that machine learning algorithms are rich in their number of parameters, which scale up with the input dimension and number of hidden layers considered. In the absence of sufficient data, the performance of machine learning algorithms to generalise is bound to suffer.

Second, the complexity of time series modelling under non-stationary conditions such as those implied by utility maximising agents in a market economy poses a challenge to apply these techniques. Third, in general, it is difficult to tell from the parameters of a trained neural network which ones are responsible for which statistical features of the output time series. In practice, tractability of statistical features such as expectation, volatility or mean reversion properties are useful to impose forward-looking views on the projected time series.

To illustrate the application of machine learning to macro-financial modelling, we consider neural networks as an example of supervised learning. We assume k input variables $x_{i,t}$ with $i = 1, \dots, k$ and the corresponding labels y_t. The input of neural network may consist of $x_{i,t}$, their past values $x_{i,t-d}$ and the past values of the label y_{t-d}. In contrast to image recognition applications, where the input is well defined, the input structure in case of macroeconomic modelling is a question of model design. The network is then trained with a large subset of the data while the remaining part is used to validate and test the generalisation performance of the network.

More specifically, we consider a shallow feedforward neural network with two hidden layers where the first hidden layer has ten neurons and the output layer one neuron (James et al., 2017). The number of neurons in the hidden layers is often determined heuristically. Each neuron has an activation function. The activation function prescribes whether a neuron should fire (+1) or not (−1). There is a range of activation functions used in different learning applications. We use a sigmoid activation function for the first layer and a linear activation function for the output layer, leading to the following network:

$$y_t = vf(Wz_t + b) \tag{5.11}$$

where f is the sigmoid activation function, the matrix W and the vectors v and b comprise the weights of the neural network. The network is trained using the N dimensional input vectors z_t, the labels y_t and the back-propagation training algorithm (Hastie, Tibshirani, and Friedman, 2008). The back-propagation algorithm is an iterative algorithm obtained by minimising the following cost function:

$$E(W,v,b) = \sum_t (y_t - vf(Wz_t + b))^2 \tag{5.12}$$

The iteration process is repeated until the training goal of a small error rate is reached.

To compare the results of the neural network to the macroeconomic model in Equation (5.7), we trained the neural network with the Brexit data of Section 5.5.2. The input of the neural network is assumed to be:

$$Z_t = (\text{US CPI}_t, \text{UK CPI}_t, \text{US PR}_t, \text{UK PR}_t) \tag{5.13}$$

with the corresponding label $y_t = \text{GBPUSD}_t$. Higher input dimensions, including additionally lagged values of the variables, were tried but did not lead to an improved performance of the neural network. From Equation (5.11) follows that the number of parameters to be trained is 60. Figure 5.5 depicts the generalisation results of the network for several parameter initialisations. Although the training is performed each time successfully, the generalisations are quite poor and exhibit high sensitivity to initialisation.

To exclude the possibility of overfitting, the number of neurons in the hidden layer is varied. The network is trained with 8, 6 and 4 neurons in the hidden layer, however, with insignificant gain in generalisation performance of the network. This suggests two possible reasons for the poor generalisation. First, the optimal region of solutions is a plateau and different parts of the plateau lead to different generalisation patterns. Second, due to the insufficient amount of the data, particularly for stress events, the network is not able to learn such patterns from the data.

Broader application of machine learning to macroeconomics will require a paradigm change to macro data collection. A higher frequency macro data collection will not only require a technology solution to obtain data at source but it will also require data cleansing, standardisation and, in some cases, data anonymisation. In contrast to financial data, where exchanges act as a platform to collect and distribute high-frequency financial data by creating a marketplace for trading financial instruments, there is no comparable approach to macro data.

5.7 A Hybrid Approach to Scenario Generation

In previous sections, we considered some shortcomings of macroeconomic and machine learning methods to model macro-financial variables, particularly in times of economic stress. In this section, we consider a hybrid modelling approach that combines techniques from econometrics, financial engineering and risk management to model macro-financial variables and generate scenarios. Key features of the hybrid approach include an integrated approach to macro-financial variables, parsimonious model selection, flexibility to account for regime differences between countries and, in particular, its suitability for stress testing applications.

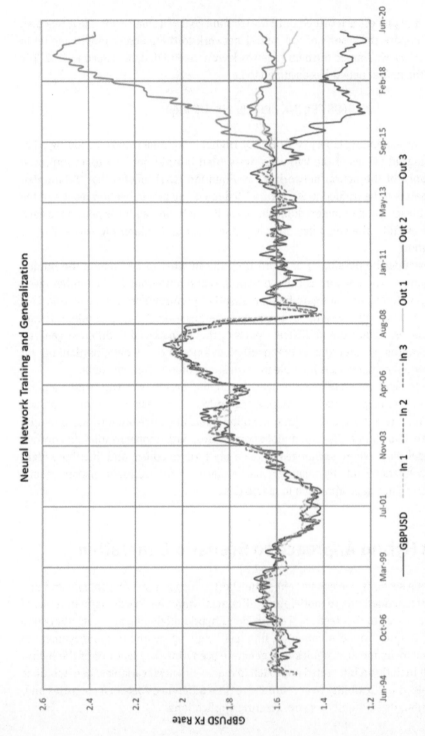

Figure 5.5: Training and generalisation performance of a feedforward shallow neural network with 3 parameter initialisations.

The hybrid approach considers stochastic dynamic models that replicate the characteristics of the macro-financial variables. These characteristics, in financial literature also referred to as stylised facts (Cont, 2000), are manifold and depend on the type of the macro-financial variable. Typical stylised facts include heavy and asymmetric return distributions, volatility clustering, mean-reversion, conditional dependence, return autocorrelation in case of macroeconomic variables and absence of it in case of financial variables. In addition, the hybrid approach captures the multivariate aspects by differentiating between relationships that are broadly and manifestly observed in the data and those that hold for specific macroeconomic regimes. This approach provides the needed flexibility to accommodate a wide range of macro-financial variables within a unified stress testing framework.

We confine ourselves here to a brief outline of the hybrid approach and refer to (Hovhannisyan, Mirzai, and Müller, 2008) for details. The common modelling equation is a stochastic dynamic equation defined for the returns of the variables:

$$r_t = \mu_t + \sigma_t \, \varepsilon_t$$

$$\mu_t = \mu_t(x_t, r_{t-1}, r_{t-2}, \dots, y_{1,t}, y_{2,t}, \dots) \tag{5.14}$$

where r_t is the return of a transformed variable x_t and μ_t, σ_t, and ε_t correspond to the expected return, return volatility and residual distribution, respectively. The manifestly observed relations with variables $y_{1,t}, y_{2,t}, \dots$ are modelled through the return expectation while the specific relations are considered through the correlations of the residual distributions. Equation (5.14), despite its apparent simplicity, allows for a unified multivariate modelling of macro-financial variables with completely differing dynamics including all variables in Table 5.3. Moreover, it encompasses risk management techniques needed to appropriately model stress events (Embrechts, Klüppelberg, and Mikosch, 2011).

The hybrid model is compared to the models described in Equations (5.7) and (5.12) by the example of FX rate GBPUSD using the GFC and Brexit data sets described in Section Introduction 5.5.1. The results are depicted in Figure 5.6. As seen in the figure, for both data sets, the calibrated hybrid model shows better out-of-sample performance compared to the macroeconomic and neural network models. Moreover, the responses of the model for both calibrations based are stable and consistent.

5.8 Reverse Stress Testing

In previous sections, we discussed the necessary tools for implementing a practical RST process. To summarise, there are three key steps. First, the specification of an appropriate loss measure to set the severity of RST by assuming a critical loss level. The critical loss, in turn, will imply the severity of the scenarios. Second, a segmentation of

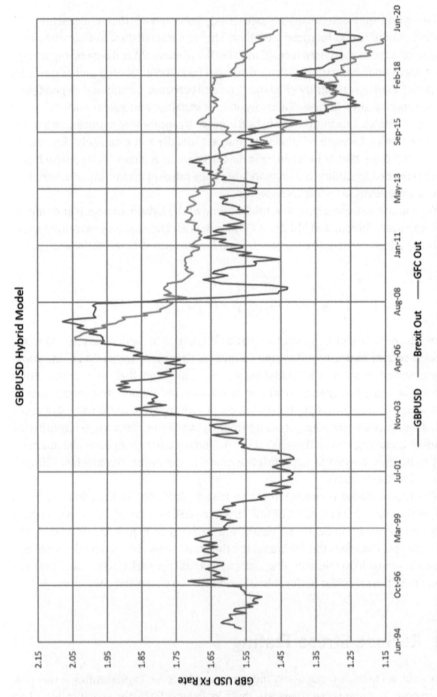

Figure 5.6: Out-of-sample results of the hybrid model for FX rate GBPUSD using the GFC data and Brexit data.

assets and liabilities in homogenous portfolios and specification of proxy models that replicate their risk profiles. Third, the ability to generate consistent macro-financial scenarios as inputs to proxy models to perform a valuation and identify RST scenarios that meet the critical loss conditions.

In this section, we formalise RST process and apply it to an example. We consider only assets and assume an asset portfolio segmentation consisting of N segments that are fully described by k time dependent and correlated macro-financial variables $X_t = (X_{1,t}, \dots, X_{k,t})$. The value of segment i at time t is denoted by $V_{i,t}$ and is assessed by a proxy model assigned to the segment i. We assume $V_{i,t}$ to be a function of the macro-financial variables at time t, i.e. $V_{i,t} = V_{i,t}(X_t)$. The value of the asset portfolio at time t is then given by $V_{pf,t} = \sum_i V_{i,t}$.

We denote the space of RST scenarios by Ω and apply the measure in Equation (5.3) to obtain RST scenarios $S \in \Omega$. Each scenario S is a random realisation of X_t that meets the condition:

$$\Omega = \arg_X \left(V_{pf,o}(X_0) - V_{pf,t}(X_t) \geq C_{V_0} \right) \tag{5.15}$$

The structure of Ω can be complex and depends on the portfolio assets. Therefore, a clustering of Ω into groups of similar scenarios that share a common narrative can be helpful to visualise and analyse RST scenarios. The more homogenous a portfolio is, the less fragmented the structure of Ω will be. Identification of RST scenarios requires knowledge of the entire scenario space, as we do not know in advance which combinations of the macro-financial variables will exceed the critical loss.

In the example provided in Table 5.4, we consider stylised portfolios consisting of loan business, treasury and proprietary trading activities. The loan portfolios consist of mortgage, consumer, and corporate loans. The loans are subject to interest rate risk

Table 5.4: Stylised asset portfolio.

Asset	Risk Factors	Proxy Model	Weight
Mortgage loans	Mortgage credit cycle, interest rates	USD A 15Y Mortgage Loan Portfolio	40%
Consumer loans	Consumer credit cycle affected by unemployment rate, interest rates	USD BB 3Y Consumer Loan Portfolio	12%
Corporate loans	Corporate credit cycle affected by corporate bond spreads, interest rates	USD BBB 5Y Corporate Bond Portfolio	30%
Treasury operations	Swap rates, swaption implied volatilities, Treasury rates	USD Swap 3M10Y USD Swaption 3M10Y USD Govt 10Y Bond	0% 0% 8%
Traded securities	Dow Jones equity index	Equity index model	5%

and counterparty default risk. In practice, the interest rate risk is hedged by treasury. The credit risk, however, may not be hedged. In the case of mortgages, for example, the collateral is an implicit hedge which is taken into account by an appropriate loss given default (LGD). During a stress period, however, the loan to value is subject to increase due to the likely decline of real estate prices. Such effects can be modelled by introducing a stochastic LGD that is linked to the real estate prices. In our example, we will assume both risks to be unhedged.

Using the hybrid approach introduced in Section 5.7, 100,000 paths with a quarterly frequency are simulated for the relevant macro-financial variables. The simulated variables are either required to perform proxy model valuations or they are used as economic indicators. The simulated variables include US real GDP, US unemployment rate, US HPI index, Dow Jones, US treasury yields for maturities 3M, 1Y, 5Y, 10Y, 30Y, swap yields for 3M floating and 1Y, 5Y and 10Y fixed, swaption implied volatilities, and credit cycles for the three loan portfolios. The starting point of simulation is assumed to be 31st of December 2016 with a one-year horizon for RST, and a rollover strategy for the portfolio assets is adopted.

The proxy models in Table 5.4 are assumed to consist of diversified assets. The level of diversification is assumed to be moderate, representing a level between fully dependent and fully independent assets in the portfolio. The rating and maturity of the proxy loan models are set equal to the average rating and average time-to-maturity of the assets in the respective portfolios. The assets in a proxy loan portfolio are subject to rating migrations. As the simulation step size is quarterly, migrations are modelled stochastically from one quarter to the next. In a contracting economy, the downgrade and default probabilities are higher than in an expanding economy. The magnitude of the change in migration and default probabilities is rating-dependent and is calibrated using Standard and Poor's historical migration and default data (Hovhannisyan, Mirzai, Müller, 2018). Moreover, the correlations between defaults and macro-financial variables are modelled through the correlations between the credit cycles and macro-financial variables. The default correlations within and between different loan portfolios are similarly modelled using the respective credit cycles.

For the purpose of RST, we assume both credit and interest rate risks not to be hedged. Although this assumption is not realistic for interest rate risk, in absence of a hedge, the structure of the risk mitigation strategies required to manage the interest rate risk within the limits set by the committees becomes visible. This assumption can be easily relaxed by considering appropriate interest rate derivative contracts in the RST process.

RST scenarios are computed for a critical loss of 10%. To visualise and to analyse the resulting RST scenarios, it is convenient to use a clustering of the scenarios. Clustering is an example of unsupervised learning which is applied to categorise data by groups of similar items. Clustering also allows to assign each group of RST scenarios a narrative or macro description. RST macro descriptions may correspond to economic, financial market, or geopolitical events. For the purpose of RST analysis, the particular event is often difficult to predict and, in fact, is of little interest. However, the macro description together with the quantitative measures derived from RST provide valuable and actionable information.

We apply the k-means clustering algorithm with a Euclidian distance measure (Witten, Frank, and Hall, 2001) to group the RST scenarios into similar categories assuming three clusters. Figures 5.7–5.9 show the results of the clustering algorithm by projecting RST scenarios into two-dimensional hyperplanes where the axes correspond to macro-financial variables. The square points in black indicate the values of the variables at the start of RST. The coloured plus markers show the values of the variables for different clusters. The cluster centres are shown as coloured cross markers.

In Figure 5.7, RST scenarios are projected to the plane spanned by Dow Jones and US Real GDP. Relative to the state of the economy at the start of RST (black square), the blue cluster represents higher growth levels, the green cluster comparable growth levels, and the red cluster lower growth levels. In this projection, the three clusters are clearly separated. The impact of growth levels on equity index is apparent from the cluster centres – particularly the red cluster, which has an average drop of about –45% for Dow Jones and –3% for Real GDP. As the proprietary trading has only a weight of 5%, the critical loss of 10% in case of red and blue clusters is only in part driven by the equity index drop. The large portion of the loss is due to credit risk.

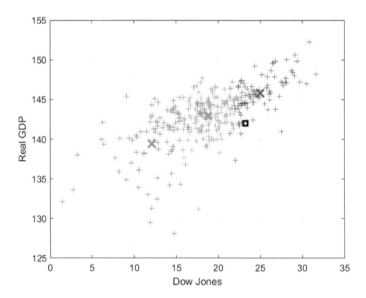

Figure 5.7: Cluster representation of RST scenarios after projection to the plane spanned by Dow Jones and US real GDP. The three clusters have different levels of growth relative to the start point of RST, which is depicted as a black square.

The hybrid approach assumes credit cycle as a factor in modelling counterparty default and credit spread risks. By doing so, for loan products the correlation between market and migration and default risks is consistently modelled. The credit cycle is normalised to mean 0 and variance 1. A credit cycle value of zero describes an average credit environment. Positive values of the credit cycle correspond to credit contraction, an environment with higher default rates, the higher the value the more contraction. Similarly, its negative values correspond to credit expansion, an environment with lower default rates, the more negative the more expansion. As depicted in Figure 5.8, for blue and red clusters, the credit cycle values for consumer and mortgages loans increase relative to their values at the start of RST. The increase in the credit cycle value implies, in turn, an increase in downgrade and default probabilities. For example, in the case of the red cluster, the change in the credit cycle implies an increase in default probability of an A-rated counterparty on average by a factor of 3 relative to its starting value.

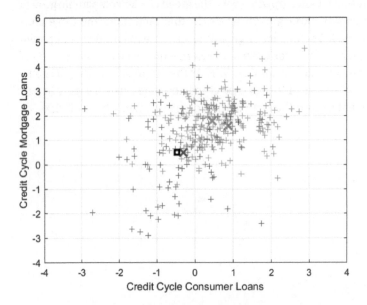

Figure 5.8: The green and red clusters represents RST scenario with increase in credit cycle value which indicate a contraction of the credit markets.

Figure 5.9 shows the impact of the credit contraction on spreads of BBB 10Y corporate bonds. The spread is on average at least twice higher for green and red clusters compared to the blue cluster. In the case of the blue cluster, RST loss is driven by a hike in the interest rates, as shown in the example of Govt 10Y yield. Therefore, to manage interest rate risk exposure to scenarios that can result in loss levels exceeding the critical loss, the strike value of the hedge for the relevant maturities should be aligned with the cluster centre value, which is 4% for the 10Y maturity, as shown in Figure 5.9.

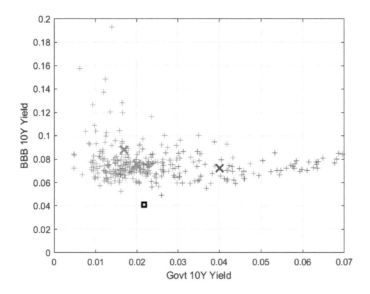

Figure 5.9: The blue cluster represents RST scenarios with high interest rates. The green and red clusters represent RST scenarios with higher bond spreads.

The results of RST and clustering suggest that for the assets in Table 5.4, the critical loss of 10% is either obtained by an increase in interest rates or by an increase in asset defaults in loan portfolios. Although the macro descriptions obtained from the clustering analysis seem intuitive and expected, the actual value of RST arises from the additional information that RST scenarios provide.

First, the values of the macro-financial variables in RST can be used for setting objective limits for risk management and mitigation strategies. Alternatively, the effectiveness of risk mitigation strategies, such as an interest rate risk hedge, can be analysed by considering RST with varying levels of critical loss. Similarly, for a given level of critical loss, different risk mitigation strategies can be compared to identify those strategies that remain within risk appetite limits. Second, the values of the macro indicators implied by RST provide quantitative benchmarks that can be used in an early warning process. As forecasts for macro indicators are readily and widely available, they can be monitored and compared to internal benchmarks obtained from RST. Third, the hybrid approach also allows one to compute scenario probabilities, enabling one to prioritise RST scenarios by their likelihood of occurrence.

5.9 Summary

A successful reverse stress testing methodology requires a number of ingredients. First, a definition of an appropriate risk measure together with a critical loss that allows to select RST scenarios in accordance with risk management and mitigation strategies. Second, a comprehensive portfolio segmentation for assets and liabilities in form of a stylised portfolio that can be modelled using proxy models. Third, realistic scenarios representing possible outcomes of the macro-financial variables as inputs to proxy models to perform valuation of assets and liabilities. For the scenario generation macroeconomic modelling techniques, neural networks and a hybrid approach are compared. The hybrid approach turns out to be more suitable for RST applications due to its robust modelling of stress events in the presence of limited historical data, its modularity, and the ability to model a large number of macro-financial variables within a unified and consistent framework.

To analyse the RST scenarios, k-means clustering is performed. The clustering groups RST scenarios into categories of similar events. Clustering enables the development of intuitive macro descriptions for RST scenarios within each group. Moreover, the cluster centres and the distribution of scenarios around these centres provide quantitative measures to support risk management and mitigation strategies.

Bibliography

Alexander, B. S., Smola, J. (2002). *Learning with Kernels, Support Vector Machines, Regularization, Optimization, and Beyond*, The MIT Press.

Brookings Institution (2014). Central Banking after the Great Recession – A Conversation with Ben Bernanke.

Cont, R. (2000), Empirical properties of asset returns: Stylized facts and statistical issues, Research Paper, Centre de Mathmatiques Appliquées, Ecole Polytechnique, France.

ECB (2017) Introducing ECB's global macroeconomic model for spillover analysis, Working Paper Series, No. 2045.

Embrechts, P., Klüppelberg, C., and Mikosch, T. (2011). *Modelling Extremal Events for Insurance and Finance*, Springer.

Hamilton, J. D. (1994) *Time Series Analysis*, Princeton University Press.

Hastie, T., Tibshirani, T., and Friedman, J. (2008). *The Elements of Statistical Learning*, Springer Series in Statistics.

Hovhannisyan, E., Mirzai, B., Müller, U. (2018). *Stress Testing Methodology*, EVMTech.

James, G., Witten, D., Hastie, T., and Tibshirani, R. (2017). *An Introduction to Statistical Learning*, Springer Series in Statistics.

Maugis, Pierre-André G. (2016). *Event conditional correlation*, University College London.

Moody's Analytics (2014). Global Scenario Development Using Moody's Analytics Country Models.

Sak, H., Senior, A., and Beaufays, F. (2014). Long Short-Term Memory Recurrent Neural Network Architectures for Large Scale Acoustic Modelling, Conference of the International Speech Communication Association.

S&P Global Ratings (2018). Default, Transition, and Recovery: 2018 Annual Global Corporate Default and Rating Transition Study.

Taylor, J. B. (1993). Discretion versus policy rules in practice, Carnegie-Rochester Conference Series on Public Policy, Volume 39.

Witten, I. H., Frank, E., and Hall, M. A. (2001). *Data Mining: Practical Machine Learning Tools and Techniques*, Third Edition, The Morgan Kaufmann Series in Data Management Systems.

Daniel Almehed, Torsten Pfoh, Thomas Steiner

6 Reverse Liquidity Stress Testing

A Practical Framework Based on the Danger Zone Approach

6.1 Introduction

Reverse stress testing (RST) is a method for decision-makers in a bank to understand what chain of events might lead to a situation where an institution is unable to continue operating. In general, RST starts from the definition of a pre-defined outcome, such as the default of an institution, within a given time frame (or maybe a less severe situation) and tries to identify possible chain of events that could lead to such an outcome. In essence, decision-makers face a simple question: What does it take to realise a certain, unfavourable situation, even after risk mitigation actions have been executed?

This simple question is not simple to answer. There could be plenty of reasons that lead to the same outcome. Therefore, one must sharpen the question and put it into the context of certain types of events. For example, one of the biggest threats to banks' continuity of business is the drying out of funding sources in a stress event. This can turn into a liquidity crisis where a bank is struggling to meet its contractual cash-flow obligations.

Reverse liquidity stress tests can support the decision-making process, both by providing insight into how future stress events could evolve and what could be done to identify and manage them, as well as providing input to the design of stress scenarios for the regular use of stress testing. This may include questions regarding indicators suitable for monitoring changes in the availability of funding, critical values that signal a severe deterioration of the availability of funding, appropriate selection of events for stress test scenarios and choice of early warning indicators in order to be able to react in a timely manner, such that mitigating actions have time to become effective.

Even in the context of a single risk category like liquidity risk, it is not straight-forward to give sophisticated answers to these questions. This is essentially related to the fact that RST is an inverse problem with many possibly interrelated risk drivers as well as non-linear effects and potential feedback loops associated with the economic environment. For practical reasons, even though the question itself is backward-looking, the analysis has to be done in a forward-looking manner. It is not meaningful to investigate all possible constellations of risk factors – instead, a smart choice has to be made about which factors are considered and how they are assumed to interact with each other. The outcome of the RST analysis should be a list of likely or unlikely (but not completely implausible) scenarios, including sets of critical values.

Note: Edited by Michael Eichhorn

https://doi.org/10.1515/9783110647907-006

System-wide dynamics and contagion effects of funding crises have been discussed in a series of working papers by the Bank of England (Aikman et al., 2009; Kapadia et al., 2012). We have previously adopted the "Danger Zone" (DZ) approach proposed by the respective authors to be used by banks as method for parametrisation of funding liquidity stress, based on the idea that different funding markets close sequentially as the stress level increases. The DZ approach is suitable for performing the RST analysis too. Its huge benefit is that a bank's access to different funding sources is summarised by a single parameter, the so-called DZ score. Rather than running complex cash flow and new business simulations across a number of risk parameters, banks could perform impact analyses for different DZ scores. As a first step, decision-makers could consider possible remediation actions and conclude on possible meaningful constellations of risk factors that contribute to the respective DZ score in a second step. The challenge of simulating cash flows under funding stress therefore decouples from the underlying risk factor analysis.

The rest of the chapter is organised as follows. In Section 6.2, we briefly summarise the general idea of the DZ approach and how it can be used to parametrise funding liquidity stress. We present how the DZ approach is used in normal liquidity stress testing and how the model and assumptions of the DZ approach work. The approach will be illustrated by a simple example of a small bank with corporate clients. In Section 6.3, we elaborate how to perform reverse liquidity stress testing using the DZ approach in general and for the example described in Section 6.2. Our conclusion is set out in Section 6.4.

6.2 Parametrisation of Funding Liquidity Stress

Imagine an economic stress situation or idiosyncratic stress in which a bank's solvency is questioned by its competitors, maybe expressed through a significant downgrade by external rating agencies. In such a situation, the bank is susceptible to an increase in the funding costs of its long-term assets. At a certain point, long-term unsecured funding may no longer be available (or affordable) to the institute, which therefore triggers refinancing of larger volumes of its liabilities in short-term markets. As the trust of market participants and clients to the institute's solvability further deteriorates, additional sources of funding become unaffordable and deposits start to flow out. At a certain point, the funding cost problem turns into a liquidity problem.

When the bank is hit by its liquidity constraints, it will take actions to improve its situation. Depending on the size of the institution and the concentration of its business, some of these actions can have a direct adverse impact on its economic environment, and even aggravate its own financial situation. This could be related to a reduction in value of its own assets and pledged collateral (for example, due to fire sales of correlated assets) but also to further loss of confidence of other market participants in the bank itself or in the market as a whole. This in turn might quickly lead to a further increase of funding costs, accelerated outflow of deposits and, subsequently, to the closure of further funding markets for the institute, as indicated in Figure 6.1. Ultimately, the institute might not be able to satisfy its liquidity needs, e.g. it is unable to meet its contractual obligations, and thus defaults.

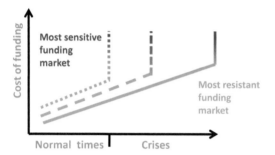

Figure 6.1: Closure of different funding markets, indicated by dotted and solid lines, over deterioration of funding.

To model the impact of the liquidity risk factors on different types of funding, one needs to cluster all potential types of funding into a set of funding markets. A funding market in this sense represents funding transactions that can be expected to react in a similar fashion during a liquidity stress event. The funding markets are bank-specific and should be defined granular enough so that the assumption that the constituents of the market will behave in the same way during a crisis is applicable. One could, for example, distinguish between long-term unsecured bond issuances, central counterparty repo funding, or issued foreign currency CPs/CDs. The final number of funding markets relevant to a bank will vary depending on the size and complexity of the bank. While a bank with a simple funding structure might only need to include a handful of funding markets, a large complex bank might need several times that.

The DZ approach provides a method for the parametrisation and modelling of such a situation where funding stress turns into liquidity stress. It is based on the idea that funding markets close sequentially as the funding situation deteriorates. To that end, one identifies relevant risk factors which can be used to quantify the simulated danger level regarding solvency, liquidity and confidence (for example, own credit rating, ratio of non-performing loans, PMI Manufacturing Index, government debt as percentage of gross domestic product, credit default index, funding spread, etc.). These risk factors can be internal, e.g. based on the bank's portfolio, or based on external market data. For each of these DZ factors, a metric needs to be defined which, for example, consolidates balance sheet information into a single number or combines certain external measures and data. Based on historic observations and expert judgement, one estimates the critical levels at which the individual factors can close a funding market or at least contribute to its closure.

A DZ score is introduced to sum up the contributions from several DZ factors. For each funding market, a critical score value is defined for which the market closes for the bank. The lower the value, the earlier the closure of the market. In addition, the expected gradual outflow of retail and wholesale deposits is mapped to several score levels. Finally, a mapping needs to be done to translate the DZ factor metric value ranges to DZ scores. The total Danger Zone score is calculated by summing up the DZ score values from all DZ factor metrics. The calibration of the individual score values is refined in an iterative manner.

The DZ parametrisation and calibration can be summarised by four steps:
1. Identification and ordering of funding markets
2. Definition of DZ factors and metrics
3. Estimation of critical and safe DZ levels
4. DZ normalisation

The last two steps are done in an iterative manner, where the model is calibrated to fit against historic liquidity stress events. Details of the process are given in Figure 6.2.

As an example, we look at a small bank with small- to mid-size corporate clients whose funding structure can be summarised as 40% from covered bond issuance, 30% from senior unsecured bond issuance, 20% corporate deposits and 10% repurchase agreements (repos). This bank identifies that the main liquidity risk drivers (risk factors) consist of its own rating, the non-performing loans ratio, change in own market capitalisation over that last three months, the Purchasing Managers Index, and market spread in short term repos vs. deposits. For each of these factors, a mapping prescription is defined that translates the risk factor metric value (e.g. percentage number of non-performing loans) into a score value. The prescription needs to identify three values for each metric: the maximal score that the risk factor can contribute to the overall DZ score, the upper critical value where the risk factor is mapped to the maximal score, and a lower critical value, below which the risk factor contributes 0 (see Figure 6.3 and illustrative examples in Table 6.1). This is done independently for each risk factor.

Of the four relevant funding markets in this example, the covered bond issuance, senior unsecured bond issuance and repo market can be expected to be either fully available or fully closed in a crisis. This is because the counterparties are professional investors who monitor the (liquidity) situation of their counterparties very closely and can therefore be expected to be well informed and react quickly in a crisis. It is not expected that the corporate deposits funding depletes as quickly because many of the bank's clients are small corporates with an operative relationship which they use for their transactions and their own liquidity needs. Once the crises reaches a level where the first funding market closes, it is assumed that the withdrawal starts with a constant outflow rate proportional to the DZ score. The calibration of the outflow rate

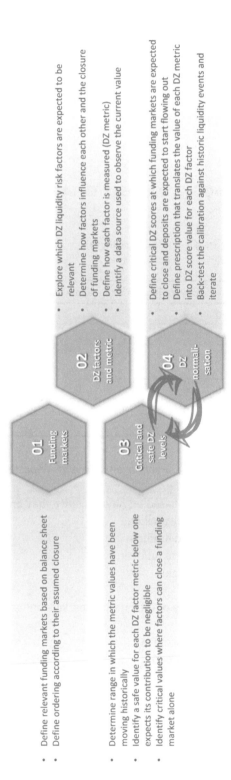

- Define relevant funding markets based on balance sheet
- Define ordering according to their assumed closure

- Determine range in which the metric values have been moving historically
- Identify a safe value for each DZ factor metric below one expects its contribution to be negligible
- Identify critical values where factors can close a funding market alone

01 Funding markets

02 DZ factors and metric
- Explore which DZ liquidity risk factors are expected to be relevant
- Determine how factors influence each other and the closure of funding markets
- Define how each factor is measured (DZ metric)
- Identify a data source used to observe the current value

03 Critical and safe DZ levels

04 DZ normali- sation
- Define critical DZ scores at which funding markets are expected to close and deposits are expected to start flowing out
- Define prescription that translates the value of each DZ metric into DZ score value for each DZ factor
- Back-test the calibration against historic liquidity events and iterate

Figure 6.2: Order of steps to the funding liquidity stress parametrisation and calibration using the DZ approach, where the third and fourth step are done iteratively.

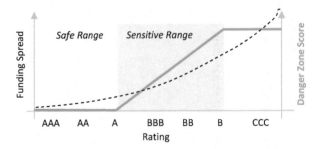

Figure 6.3: Example for identification of critical and safe ranges of DZ factors for the risk factor "own rating".

Table 6.1: Examples of liquidity risk factors and their assigned critical DZ metric values for a small bank with corporate clients.

Risk factor	Maximal score	Lower critical value	Upper critical value
Own Rating	20	A	B
NPL ratio	15	5%	30%
Change in own market capitalisation over 3 months	10	−10%	−50%
Purchasing Managers Index	10	50	30
Secured/unsecured money market spreads (repo/depo)	20	0bp	200bp

could be based on information on how corporate clients have withdrawn deposits during historical crises.

The four relevant funding markets are ordered based on how sensitive they are expected to react in a crisis. Here, three principles are applied:

– Secured funding is less sensitive than unsecured funding
– Short-term funding is less sensitive than long-term funding
– Sophisticated counterparties will react more quickly

These three principles lead to the following ordering of the funding markets and an assignment of a critical score value:

1. Senior unsecured bond issuance – closes at DZ score 25
2. Corporate deposits – starts flowing out at DZ score 25
3. Covered bond issuance – closes at DZ score 35
4. Repo – closes at DZ score 45

In a mild scenario, one could, as an example, assume a 2-notch downgrade (from A to BBB+), an increase of non-performing loans (from 6% to 10%), a drop in the PMI from 51 to 44, a drop in market capitalisation of 30% and an increase in secured/unsecured money market spreads (repo/depo) spread (from 20bp to 100bp). If this would result in an overall DZ score of 28, we would assume that the senior unsecured market is closed and there is an initial moderate outflow of corporate deposits.

In a severe scenario, one could, for example, assume a 4-notch downgrade (from A to BBB-), an increase of non-performing loans (from 6% to 15%), a drop in the PMI from 51 to 44, a drop in market capitalisation of 50% and an increase in secured/unsecured money market spreads (repo/depo) spread (from 20bp to 100bp), leading to an overall DZ score of 42. This means that the senior unsecured market and the covered bond market is assumed to be closed and there is a severe (for example, 6 times faster than in the mild scenario) outflow of corporate deposits. Only rolling of existing repo funding would still be available in this scenario.

Of course, this is a simplified example, e.g. we do not discuss the treatment of the liquidity buffer and credit and liquidity facilities. However, the DZ approach can be expanded to include such and other types of liquidity flows as well.

Once the DZ calibration has been set up, future cashflows are simulated under the constraint imposed by the overall DZ score value. The following new business assumptions should be applied:

- Funding positions related to open funding markets are rolled over.
- Funding positions related to closed funding markets mature and are not rolled over.
- Deposit outflows are included according to the prescribed outflow rates.
- Funding gaps are closed by selling liquidity buffer assets with haircuts related to the relevant DZ score.
- Possibly include further scenario elements such as increased funding costs for new business given the current DZ score value.

6.3 Reverse Liquidity Stress Testing Based on the DZ Approach

The first decision in the context of any RST is the choice of the target state one wishes to analyse. This could be the default of the institution within a specified time frame, but also a less severe situation like the realisation of a certain critical risk metric value, which is of special interest to risk control or the management body. The second decision is the choice of risk parameters one wishes to use for analysis. The great benefit of the DZ approach is that it allows for the aggregation of the impact of several risk factors into a single number, the DZ score.

The approach divides the calculation into two major steps. In the first step, all the funding risk drivers and their interdependencies are modelled into the DZ score using the approach described in Section 6.2. In the second step, that DZ score is used to determine the digital status (open or closed) of each material funding market. Based on that, the liquidity metric applied for the RST exercise can be calculated. An illustration is given in Figure 6.4.

The reverse liquidity stress testing analysis can now be done as follows:

1. Choose a liquidity metric and define the outcome that corresponds to the selected RST target state.
2. Calculate the liquidity metric for a range of DZ scores until the expected RST outcome is reached. This requires assessing the status of each funding market and recalculating the liquidity metric multiple times. This will be the computationally most demanding step. However, since we are only varying a single parameter (DZ score), the effort will likely correspond to recalculating the liquidity metric a handful of times.
3. Estimate the combination of funding risk factors that could lead to the critical DZ score. This will typically involve varying all relevant funding risk drivers and determining which combination of factors can lead to the critical score. In general, several combinations of different parameters can lead to the required outcome.
4. Depending on the outcome in Step 3 and the type of decision-making that the RST exercise is trying support, one could now revisit some of the assumptions that were used to determine the behaviour of funding risk drivers, the calculation of DZ metric values or the modelling of funding markets. After adaptations have been made, one would iterate back to Step 2.

For the example of a small bank given in the previous section, we will now investigate how the reverse liquidity stress test can be used to analyse the potential impact of different risk factors.

Assume that the target state of the RST is the loss of 100% of available liquidity within 90 days (i.e. survival period of 90 days). One would now need to calculate the survival periods for different DZ scores to identify which score corresponds to the target outcome (see Table 6.2). In this case, a DZ score of 45 corresponds to the target state.

Already for this simple example with only five risk factors, there are naturally many combinations of risk factors values that can lead to the target state. In practice, it can be helpful to focus on the impact of just a few key risk factors. In this case, we choose to focus on the secured/unsecured money market spreads and the non-performing loans ratio. For the other risk factors, we are not varying the values we described in Section 6.2 as a default value for the mild stress scenario.

Based on this simple calculation and the results in Table 6.3, we can conclude that using the mild stress scenario as starting point, it takes a combined deterioration of the internal non-performing loan ratio and the market depo/repo spread to come to survival horizon of 90 days or less. Neither of the two risk factors can achieve this on their own. This type of analysis can be used to identify which combinations of risk factors need to be analysed particularly carefully when doing future adjustments of the stress scenarios or early warning indicators.

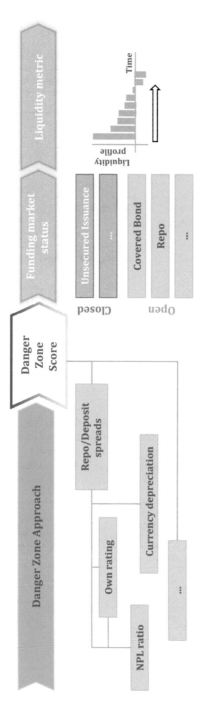

Figure 6.4: The DZ approach separates the liquidity stress testing into 2 distinct major steps. The first major step represents a multi-dimensional model of all material liquidity risk factors including interdependencies. The outcome of this step is the DZ score. The next major step generates a unique outcome the liquidity metric for each of value of the DZ score.

Table 6.2: Illustrative examples of survival periods and related DZ scores for a small bank with corporate clients.

Danger Zone Score	Affected of funding	Calculated survival period
25	Senior unsecured bond issuance – closed	>360 days
30	Senior unsecured bond issuance – closed Corporate deposits – 10% outflow per month	260 days
35	Senior unsecured bond issuance – closed Corporate deposits – 20% outflow per month Covered bond issuance – closed	180 days
40	Senior unsecured bond issuance – closed Corporate deposits – 30% outflow per month Covered bond issuance – closed	120 days
45	Senior unsecured bond issuance – closed Corporate deposits – 40% outflow per month Covered bond issuance – closed Repo market – closed	90 days = RST target state
50	Senior unsecured bond issuance – closed Corporate deposits – 50% outflow per month Covered bond issuance – closed Repo market – closed	70 days

Table 6.3: Examples of the DZ score for varying non-performing loan ratio and secured/unsecured money market spreads (repo/depo) spread. The combination of risk factors that lead to the selected RST target state (DZ Score ≥ 45) is highlighted in the lower right corner. The other risk factors are assumed to be as in the mild scenario mentioned in Section 6.2 – i.e. the rating is BBB+; PMI is 44; and the drop-in market capitalisation of 30%.

DZ Score		NPL Ratio						
		0%	5%	10%	15%	20%	25%	30%
Repo/Depo Spread (bp)	0	15	15	18	21	24	27	30
	25	18	18	21	24	27	30	33
	50	20	20	23	26	29	32	35
	75	23	23	26	29	32	35	38
	100	25	25	28	31	34	37	40
	125	28	28	31	34	37	40	43
	150	30	30	33	36	39	42	45
	175	33	33	36	39	42	45	48
	200	35	35	38	41	44	47	50

6.4 Summary

Liquidity stress that originates from funding markets becoming unavailable is one of the biggest threats for the continuity of business and should therefore be subject to reverse stress testing analysis. We have argued that the Danger Zone approach, which was introduced for the investigation of system-wide funding liquidity risk, is also an elegant method for institution-specific parametrisation of funding liquidity stress. The basic assumption is that available funding markets close suddenly but at different times as the funding stress increases. As the observed or assumed impact of several risk factors is harmonised and aggregated into a single Danger Zone score, the analysis of relevant root causes simplifies considerably.

The Danger Zone framework simplifies both the normal and reverse stress test analysis since it separates the complex dependencies of the risk factors from the cash flow simulations. While running complex simulations with several risk parameters, the calculation-intensive liquidity profile calculations are done under the constraints imposed by the Danger Zone score level. As a first step of the reverse liquidity stress test exercise, the critical Danger Zone score, which leads to the specified failure of business, is determined. In the second step, a risk factor analysis is done based on the metrics and mapping rules defined within the Danger Zone approach. This two-step approach facilitates flexible analysis where a great deal of understanding can be achieved with limited effort.

The Danger Zone-based reverse liquidity stress test results are relatively easy to interpret as the liquidity impact is driven by the closing of funding markets. This helps the management to gain an intuitive insight into how changes of the stress test scenarios or the steering of liquidity impacts the liquidity risk metrics. The result should provide the risk management and risk control functions with sufficient information to, for example, update limits or early warning thresholds such that threats are recognised at an early stage and counter measures have time to become effective. It also provides insight into how the stress testing framework can be further developed.

Bibliography

Aikman, D., Alessandri, P., Eklund, B., Gai, P., Kapadia, S., Martin, E., Mora, N., Sterne, G., Wilison, M. (2009). Funding liquidity risk in a quantitative model of systemic stability, Bank of England Working Paper No. 372.

Kapadia, S., Drehmann, M., Elliott, J., Sterne, G. (2012). Liquidity risk, cash-flow constraints and systemic feedbacks, Bank of England Working Paper No. 456.

Fabio Caccioli

7 Reverse Stress Testing Banking Networks

A Quantitative Approach

7.1 Introduction

Systemic risk is the risk associated with the collapse of the financial system, and it emerges from the interactions and interconnections between different market participants.

A clear example is the subprime crisis of 2008, where an exogenous shock affecting 5% of the US real estate market caused a systemic crisis because of endogenous amplification due to interactions between different constituents of the financial system.

Interconnectivity and endogenous amplification are not incorporated into traditional tools to assess financial stability, which typically consider financial institutions as isolated and adopt a microprudential perspective according to which it is enough to make each individual institution safe to guarantee systemic stability.

Since the subprime crisis, a lot of effort has been devoted to the development of macroprudential stress testing frameworks that explicitly account for interactions and interconnections (see Aymanns et al., 2018 for a recent review).

A large part of the literature in the field has focused on the modelling of the interbank system as a financial network (see Glasserman and Young, 2016 and Caccioli et al., 2018 for recent reviews). Financial networks are networks where nodes represent financial institutions – in the following section, we will focus on banks – and links represent relationships between them. In this context, one is interested in understanding under what condition an exogenous shock that hits a part of the system will be amplified and will spread to the rest of the system.

Network models have first been built to provide an intuition about the mechanics of shock propagation and to understand how the topological properties of the network (its "shape") affects its robustness (see for instance Gai and Kapadia, 2010), and they have subsequently been refined and incorporated into network-based stress testing frameworks.

Given a scenario of an exogenous shock that hits the system, these frameworks allow us to compute systemic losses due to network effects.

One concern associated with stress testing is the arbitrariness of the scenario that is used to shock the system in the first place (Wiersema et al., 2019).

Reverse stress testing, akin to solving the problem of finding patient zero in epidemiology, can remove this arbitrariness through the identification of the smallest

Note: Edited by Tiziano Bellini

https://doi.org/10.1515/9783110647907-007

exogenous shocks that would lead to given final loss. In the following, we will refer to these shocks as worst-case shocks.

In Section 7.2, we will review a stylised network-based stress testing framework and discuss how the stability of a network can be characterised in terms of a quantity that measures the tendency of the system to endogenously amplify shocks.

In Section 7.3, we will discuss a simplified version of the reverse stress testing framework introduced in Grigat and Caccioli (2017). In both cases, we will apply the methodology to stress testing an interbank exposure network of the largest European banks.

7.2 Network-based Stress Testing

We present in this section a stylised stress testing methodology for interbank networks.

The idea of a network-based stress test can be formulated in the following way: Given a network that represents interactions between banks, and a dynamic that models how shocks propagate between banks, we are interested in computing the final losses associated with an initial exogenous shock (see Figure 7.1).

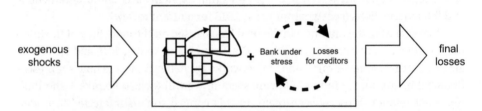

Figure 7.1: Pictorial representation of a network-based stress test. An exogenous shock is given as input to a dynamical model. The model consists of a network of exposures between banks, and a rule that dictates how losses are propagated between connected banks (e.g. a bank is under stress, which causes losses to its creditors, some of which may go under stress, and so on). The network model outputs the final loss of each bank.

In this chapter, we consider the network of direct interbank exposures between banks, and we present a specific dynamic of shock propagation known as DebtRank (Battiston et al., 2012). In Section 7.2.2, we will apply this methodology to the network of the 44 European banks included in the STOXX Europe 600 Banks index.

7.2.1 DebtRank

The method has been originally developed in Battiston et al. (2012), but here we present the extension proposed in Bardoscia et al. (2015).

We consider a network of N banks. Each bank is characterised by a balance sheet (see Figure 7.2, left panel). On the asset side of a bank's balance sheet, there are interbank assets A_i^{int} and external (non-interbank) assets, denoted as A_i^{ext}. On the liability side, we have liabilities L_i and equity E_i.

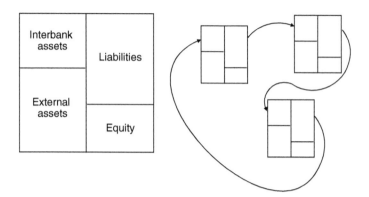

Figure 7.2: Left panel: representation of the stylised balance sheet of a bank. Assets are divided into external and interbank. Right panel: Pictorial representation of the network of interbank exposures. The interbank assets of a bank are associated with interbank liabilities of other banks.

We will consider in the following a discrete time dynamical evolution, so these quantities depend on time, and at each time the following balance sheet identity must be satisfied for each bank.

$$E_i(t) = A_i^{ext}(t) + A_i^{int}(t) - L_i(t) \tag{7.1}$$

It is important to notice that, here, t labels the iterations of the contagion algorithm, not necessarily the physical time.

Banks interact because the interbank assets of a bank correspond to interbank liabilities of other banks. In the following, we will refer to interbank loans for the simplicity of exposition, but everything applies to interbank exposures in general. These interactions can be represented in terms of a network of interlinked balanced sheet (see Figure 7.2, right panel).

We will denote by $W_{ij}(0)$ the exposure of bank i towards bank j, so that the balance sheet at time $t = 0$, before any shock is applied to the system, reads:

$$E_i(0) = A_i^{ext}(0) + \sum_{j=1}^{N} W_{ij}(0) - L_i \tag{7.2}$$

where we have dropped the time dependency for liabilities, as we assume them to be constant over time.

We now assume that a shock hits the system at time $t = 1$, and we want to model the dynamic of shock propagation. The idea is that when a bank's equity is reduced, its creditors suffer losses associated with the credit quality deterioration of the exposures towards the bank. Models of default cascades typically assume that losses are propagated from a borrower to the lender only after the borrower becomes insolvent (Furfine, 2003), so no loss is propagated if the loss of a bank is smaller than its equity. DebtRank considers instead the situation in which losses are propagated to lenders as soon as borrowers experience losses. More specifically, DebtRank assumes that losses are propagate linearly: An x % devaluation of the equity of bank i translates into an βx% devaluation of the interbank assets of i's creditors associated with their exposure towards i (see Figure 7.3).

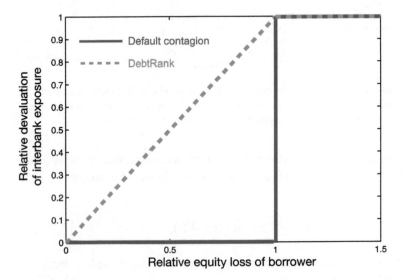

Figure 7.3: Contagion dynamic: According to default contagion dynamics, a bank propagates shocks to its creditors only after its default. DebtRank considers instead the effect of credit quality deterioration, and assumes a linear propagation of shocks. The recovery rate is set to zero in this example.

In formulas, this is expressed as

$$\frac{W_{ij}(0) - W_{ij}(t)}{W_{ij}(0)} = \beta \frac{E_j(0) - E_j(t-1)}{E_j(0)} \tag{7.3}$$

Here β is a non-negative parameter related to the recovery rate of the interbank assets: If a bank defaults its creditors recover a fraction $1 - \beta$ of the original exposure.

Inserting expression (3) into the balance sheet identity, we obtain that

$$E_i(t) = A_i^{ext}(t) + \sum_{j=1}^{N} W_{ij}(0)\left[1 - \beta\frac{E_j(0) - E_j(t-1)}{E_j(0)}\right] - L_i(t) \tag{7.4}$$

If we now define the relative equity loss between times 0 and t as $h_i(t) = \dfrac{E_i(0) - E_i(t)}{E_i(0)}$, the matrix of interbank leverage as $\Lambda_{ij} = W_{ij}(0)/E_i(0)$, and the relative exogenous shock as $u_i = \dfrac{A_i^{ext}(0) - A_i^{ext}(1)}{E_i(0)}$, equation (7.4) can be written as

$$h_i(t) = \sum_{j=1}^{N} \beta\Lambda_{ij}\, h_j(t-1) + u_i \tag{7.5}$$

This expresses the fact that the relative loss of bank i at time t is the sum of an exogenous shock occurring at $t = 1$ affecting its external assets, and an endogenous component that depends on the losses experienced by i's creditors at time $t - 1$.

The matrix Λ is called matrix of interbank leverage (D'Errico et al., 2016), because its element (i,j) is equal to i's exposure towards j divided by i's equity, that is the contribution to i's leverage of its exposure towards j (here, we define leverage as assets over equity).

The response of the system to an exogenous shock depends on the product between the largest eigenvalue of Λ, which we denote by λ_{max}, and the parameter β. $\beta\lambda_{max}$ is a real number that has a role similar to the basic reproduction number of epidemiological models. The larger $\beta\lambda_{max}$, the more shocks propagate between subsequent iterations of equation (7.5). Moreover, if $\beta\lambda_{max} > 1$ the network is unstable, meaning that losses will keep being amplified at every step of the dynamic. Otherwise, losses between two subsequent time steps will be progressively reduced over time.

Equation (7.5) is actually valid as long as no bank becomes insolvent. When a bank becomes insolvent, according to equation (7.3), the value of the interbank exposures towards that bank becomes smaller than the recovery rate. However, a creditor cannot lose more than the recovery rate, so equation (7.5) is modified as

$$h_i(t) = \min\left\{1, \sum_{j=1}^{N} \beta\Lambda_{ij}\, h_j(t-1) + u_i\right\} \tag{7.6}$$

We now look at one example where we apply this methodology.

7.2.2 Use Case

We consider balance sheet data of 44 European banks included in the STOXX Europe 600 Banks index. These are publicly traded companies, and they are among the biggest European banks.

For each bank, we know its total assets, equity (tier 1 capital), total interbank assets and liabilities. We do not know the matrix of interbank exposures. This can, however, be inferred using the RAS algorithm (Bacharach, 1965). The algorithm reconstructs the matrix of interbank exposures by spreading exposures as evenly as possible while ensuring that the total amount lent and borrowed by each bank is consistent with the data.

We now consider a simple exercise in which a bank is defaulted at time $t = 1$, we run the algorithm by iterating with equation (7.6), and we measure the final losses of the system. We repeat this exercise 44 times, each time defaulting a different bank at $t = 1$.

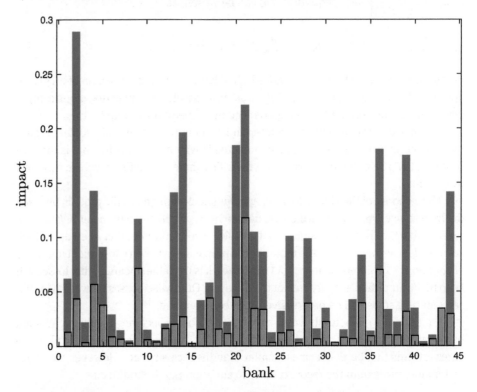

Figure 7.4: Blue bars represent the systemic impact of banks, i.e. the fraction of equity that would be lost should they default. Red bars represent the relative size of banks. Banks with similar sizes can have very different impact. This is because the position that a bank occupies in the network contributes to its impact.

Figure 7.4 shows a measure of the impact associated with each bank (blue bars), where the impact is measured in terms of the fraction of equity lost by the other banks as a consequence to the shock, i.e.:

$$I_i = \frac{\sum_{j \neq i}(E_j(0) - E_j^*)}{\sum_{j=1}^{N} E_j(0)} \qquad (7.7)$$

where E_i^* is the equity of i computed at the fixed point of iteration (6). Note that in equation (7.7), we do not include the loss due to the exogenous shock into the definition of impact, which only accounts for losses due to endogenous amplification.

For this analysis, we assumed a recovery rate of 50%, so we set $\beta = 0.5$. From the figure, we see that banks have quite heterogeneous impacts.

Figure 7.4 also shows the relative size of banks (red bars). By comparing the size of a bank with its impact we see that, while there is certainly a correlation between the two, there is more to a bank's impact than just its size. For instance, we see that the most impactful bank is not the largest one, and we see that banks with a similar size can have quite different impacts (which is the case for instance of banks 43 and 44), signalling the fact that the position that a bank occupies in the network is important to determine its systemic impact.

7.3 Network-based Reverse Stress Testing

In this section, we consider a reverse stress testing framework based on the DebtRank methodology explained in Section 7.2. In particular we will identify the smallest exogenous shocks that should hit the system to generate final losses larger than a given threshold, and how this shock is distributed across banks.

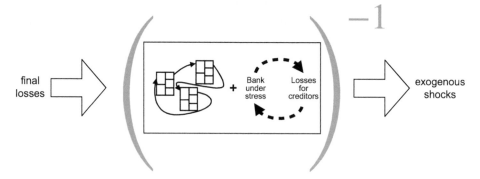

Figure 7.5: Pictorial representation of a network-based reverse stress test. Final losses are now the input to an optimisation problem where the dynamical model is reverse engineered. The output is the exogenous shock that would lead to the final losses.

7.3.1 Methodology

The methodology we present is related to the one introduced in Grigat and Caccioli (2017). The simplification comes from the fact that here we consider an exogenous shock occurring only at $t = 1$, while in Grigat and Caccioli (2017), a trajectory of shocks occurring at all steps of the dynamic was considered.

In order to define the stress testing framework, we write a constrained optimisation problem where the objective function minimises the size of the worst-case shock, while the constraints are provided by the target final losses and the dynamic of shock propagation.

We will look in the following at identifying the smallest shock that would lead over a time horizon T to final relative losses larger than a given threshold, i.e.

$$h_i(T) \geq \ell_i \text{ for } i=1, \dots, N \tag{7.8}$$

where ℓ_i is the threshold for bank i.

If we use equation (7.5) to compute the final loss of bank i, equation (7.8) can be written as

$$\sum_{t=1}^{T} \sum_{j=1}^{N} \beta^{T-t} (\Lambda^{T-t})_{ij} u_j \geq \ell_i \text{ for } i=1, \dots, N \tag{7.9}$$

As a measure of the size of the shock hitting the system, we introduce the following quantity:

$$K(\vec{u}) = \sum_{i=1}^{N} u_i^2 \tag{7.10}$$

where $\vec{u}$ denotes the vector of entries u_i for i = 1, ... N.

Since our objective is to find the smallest shocks, the optimisation problem that defines our stress testing framework is therefore:

$$\min_{\vec{u}} \sum_{k=1}^{K} K(u)$$

$$s.t. \tag{7.11}$$

$$\sum_{t=1}^{T} \sum_{j=1}^{N} \beta^{T-t} (\Lambda^{T-t})_{ij} u_j \geq \ell_i \text{ for } i=1,\dots, N$$

We denote by $\vec{u}^*$ the worst-case shock corresponding to the solution of this optimisation problem.

It has to be noted that to properly invert the contagion dynamic of equation (7.6) one would need to consider the fact that h_i should not exceed 1. This, however, would make the optimisation problem more complicated, while (11) has the advantage of being a quadratic programme, for which fast algorithms are available. The approximation is exact as long as:

$$\sum_{t=1}^{T} \sum_{j=1}^{N} \beta^{T-t} \left(\Lambda^{T-t}\right)_{ij} u_j^* \leq 1 \text{ for } i=1,\dots, N \tag{7.12}$$

and it becomes worse the more these inequalities are violated. These conditions can be checked after solving the optimisation problem (11). Should the conditions (12) be violated for some banks, one would assume their default, update the balance sheet of the remaining banks to account for the losses induced by such defaults, and then re-run the reverse stress test (11) on the remaining banks. Should the conditions still be violated for some other banks, the procedure would be repeated.

7.3.2 Use Case

In this section, we perform a reverse stress test of the same system considered in Section 7.2. As before, we reconstructed the network of interbank exposures from partial information on total interbank assets and liabilities using the RAS algorithm.

As an example, to illustrate the output of the methodology, we consider the simple case in which $\ell_i = 0.1$ for all banks, and we consider $T = 10$. Although the outcome of the reverse stress test depends on the target losses, the properties that we are going to discuss in the following do not dependent on this specific choice.

Here, we mainly want to discuss how the properties of the worst-case shock identified through the reverse stress test are affected by the endogenous amplification of the system, which, as explained in Section 7.2, is measured in terms of $\beta\lambda_{max}$.

Since we have one specific network, λ_{max} is given, so to generate the following plots we actually tune the parameter of β. In general, however, different systems will be characterised by different values of λ_{max}, and the endogenous amplification depends on the product $\beta\lambda_{max}$.

In Figure 7.6, we report the value of the objective function K computed in the solution of the optimisation problem (11). The larger K, the larger the size of the aggregate worst-case shock. The figure shows that K decreases monotonically as $\beta\lambda_{max}$ increases. This is due to the fact that, as the endogenous amplification of shocks becomes larger, a smaller exogenous shock is required to reach the same final losses.

Figure 7.6 refers to the aggregate shock, but how is this shock distributed across banks? To quantify this, we define the following quantity:

$$C_i = \frac{\sum_{i=1}^{N} u_i^{*2}}{K(\vec{u}^*)} \tag{7.13}$$

which measures the concentration of the aggregate worst-case shock on bank i.

Figure 7.7 shows the distribution of C_i for two different values of $\beta\lambda_{max}$, chosen to represent the regime of small ($\beta\lambda_{max} = 0.2$) vs. large ($\beta\lambda_{max} = 1.5$) endogenous amplification.

We observe that in the regime of small amplification, while there is a bank that contributes to the aggregate shock twice as much as the others, the shock is more or less homogeneously distributed across banks. In the regime of large amplification, in contrast, the shock is mostly concentrated on smaller number of banks, with most banks not contributing to it.

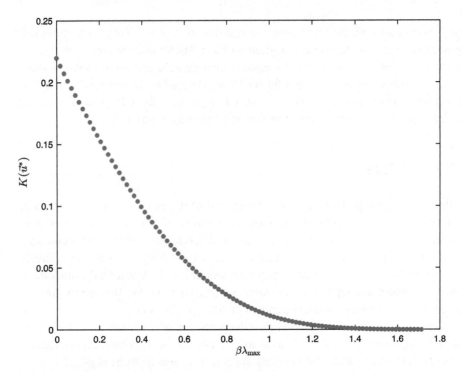

Figure 7.6: Cost function as a function of λ_{max}. The size of the shock decreases as endogenous amplification becomes stronger.

For Figure 7.7, the target losses were the same for all banks. We can, however, use the methodology to identify what are the shocks that could lead to the default of a bank. We now consider a situation in which $\ell_j = 0$ for all $j \neq i$, while $\ell_i = 1$, asking therefore what is the shock that would lead to the default of a given bank.

Figures 7.8–7.11 shows the distribution of worst-case shocks that would lead to the default of bank 1 (Figures 7.8 and 7.10) and bank 6 (Figures 7.9 and 7.11) in our sample for $\beta\lambda_{max} = 0.1$ (Figures 7.8 and 7.9) and $\beta\lambda_{max} = 0.8$ (Figures 7.10 and 7.11). Similar plots can be obtained for the other banks. We selected banks 1 and 6 because they are representative of two different common patterns observed also for the others, while the two values of $\beta\lambda_{max}$ represent small vs. large endogenous amplification.

For small endogenous amplification, we see that the worst-case shock that would make a given bank fail is mostly an idiosyncratic one affecting that bank.

For large endogenous amplification, different patterns emerge. For bank 1, we see that the worst-case shock is again mainly an idiosyncratic one, where about 75% of its equity is eroded by the exogenous shock, while the rest is lost because of contagion effects due to other banks being hit by a relatively small common shock. For bank 6, instead, the shock is distributed across more banks, and most of bank 6's equity is lost because of network effects. In fact, in this example, bank 2 is more affected than bank 6 by the exogenous shock, but bank 6 eventually defaults because of network effects.

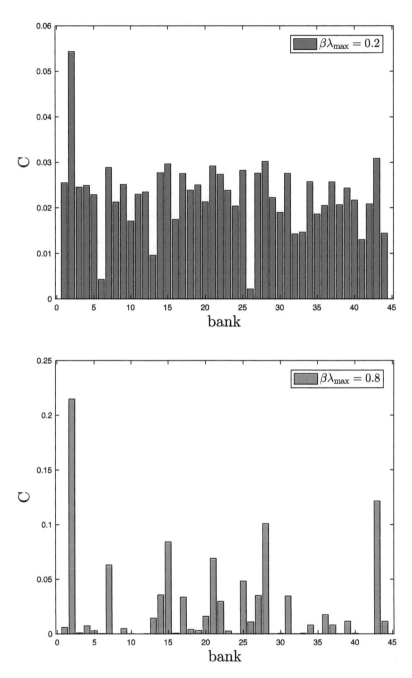

Figure 7.7: Concentration of the aggregate worst-case shock on individual banks. For small endogenous amplification, the worst-case shock is homogenously distributed across many banks. For large endogenous amplification, the worst-case shock is concentrated on fewer banks.

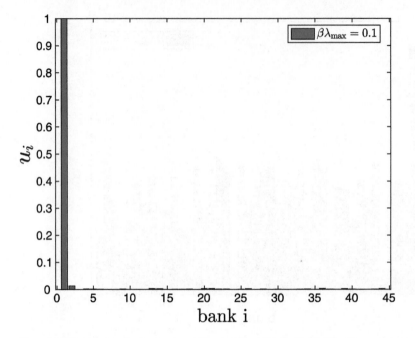

Figure 7.8: Worst-case shocks that would lead to the default of bank 1 for $\beta\lambda_{max} = 0.1$.

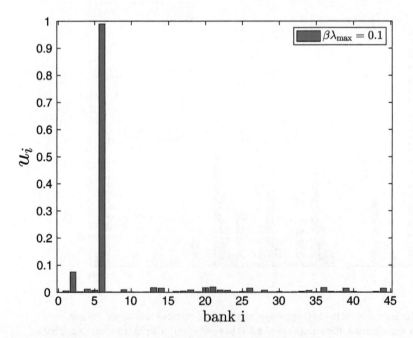

Figure 7.9: Worst case shocks that would lead to the default of bank 6 for $\beta\lambda_{max} = 0.1$.

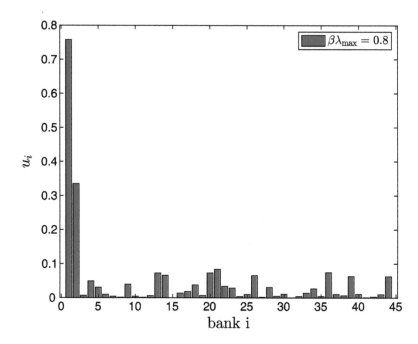

Figure 7.10: Worst-case shocks that would lead to the default of bank 1 for $\beta\lambda_{\max} = 0.8$.

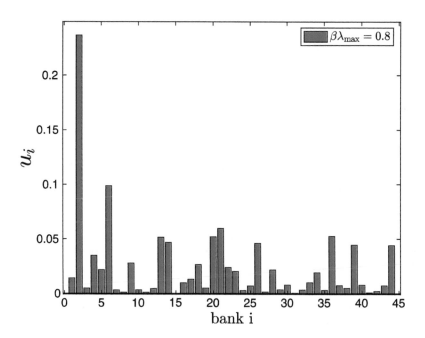

Figure 7.11: Worst case shocks that would lead to the default of bank 6 for $\beta\lambda_{\max} = 0.8$.

7.4 Summary

Financial institutions are not isolated but interact with each other. Some of these interactions can be represented as networks, and network models can be developed to quantify systemic risk.

Several network-based stress testing methodologies have been proposed in the literature. Here, we have discussed one of them, the so-called DebtRank, and we have shown how it can be used to measure the impact of a bank's default.

We then turned to the opposite question, which is the one of identifying the smallest exogenous shocks that would lead to final losses larger than a given threshold. We called such shocks worst-case shocks.

We have shown how the size of the worst-case shocks and their distribution across banks depend on the endogenous amplification of the network.

In both cases – reverse and direct stress testing – we have considered as a use case the network of 44 European banks that belong to the STOXX Europe 600 Banks index, for which we used balance sheet data dating to 2014. The same analysis can be carried out for different years, leading to similar results.

In this chapter, we focused on direct exposures between banks, such as those due to interbank lending. It is important to note that banks also interact indirectly through their common asset holdings: If a bank is in trouble and liquidates part of its assets, these will be devalued, which causes a mark-to-market loss to other banks holding those assets (Caccioli et al., 2014; Cont and Schaanning, 2018). Our methodology can be extended to account also for this contagion channel.

Bibliography

Aymanns, C., Farmer, J. D., Kleinnijenhuis, A. M., and Wetzer, T. (2018). Models of financial stability and their application in stress tests. In *Handbook of Computational Economics* (Vol. 4, pp. 329–391), Elsevier.

Bacharach, M. (1965). Estimating nonnegative matrices from marginal data. *International Economic Review*, 6(3), 294–310.

Battiston, S., Puliga, M., Kaushic, R., Tasca, P., and Caldarelli, G. (2012). DebtRank: too central to fail? Financial networks, the Fed and systemic risk. *Scientific Reports*, 2, 541.

Bardoscia, M., Battiston, S., Caccioli F., and Caldarelli, G. (2015). DebtRank: A microscopic foundation for shock propagation. *PLoS One*, 10, 0130406.

Caccioli, F., Barucca, P., and Kobayashi, T. (2018). Network models of financial systemic risk: a review. *Journal of Computational Social Science*, 1, 81–114.

Caccioli, F., Shrestha, M., Moore, C., and Farmer, J. D. (2014). Stability analysis of financial contagion due to overlapping portfolios. *Journal of Banking & Finance*, 46, 233–245.

Cont, R., and Schaanning, E. (2017). Fire sales, indirect contagion and systemic stress testing. Indirect Contagion and Systemic Stress Testing. Available on SSRN.

D'Errico, M., Battiston, S., and Gurciullo, S. (2016). DebtRank and the Network of Leverage. *The Journal of Alternative Investments*, 18(4).

Furfine, C. H. (2003). Interbank exposures: Quantifying the risk of contagion. *Journal of money, credit and banking*, 111–128.

Gai, P., and Kapadia, S. (2010). Contagion in financial networks. *Proceedings of the Royal Society A: Mathematical, Physical and Engineering Sciences*, 466, 2401–2423.

Glasserman, P., and Young, H. P. (2016). Contagion in financial networks. *Journal of Economic Literature*, 54, 779–831.

Grigat, D., and Caccioli, F. (2017). Reverse stress testing interbank networks. *Scientific reports*, 7, 15616.

Wiersema, G., Kleinnijenhuis, A. M., Wetzer, T., and Farmer, J. D. (2019). Inherent Instability: Scenario-Free Analysis of Financial Systems with Interacting Contagion Channels. Available on SSRN.

Jérôme Henry
8 Reflections on Macroprudential Reverse Stress Testing

8.1 Introduction

Over the recent period, marked by the coronavirus pandemic, system-wide stress testing, a legacy of the Great Financial Crisis (GFC), attracted renewed attention (e.g. Bank of England 2020 "desktop" stress test, US Federal Reserve 2020 DFAST update or the ECB 2020 Vulnerability Analysis – see Henry (2020) for a comparative assessment of these) due to the prevailing crisis situation. Dealing with extreme events, low-probability and high-impact episodes such as the highly unexpected coronavirus outbreak, and their potential impact on the banking sector is consubstantial to stress testing. This was a very special and rather unique context – for one thing, the coronavirus-triggered crisis had led to widespread and far-reaching revisions of all forecasts (EU, ECB, IMF, OECD, just to mention the international institutions) both on real economy and financial markets. The effects on the latter can be evaluated using dedicated models, pretty much those used in standard macroprudential stress tests, as in fact conducted by some of these authorities (in particular, the IMF or the ECB).

The coronavirus crisis was characterised by quite specific features, such as a very high uncertainty on current health developments and subsequent impacts on the economy, but also the huge size of the shocks involved and their impressive scope. The world experienced a truly global shock – at about the same point in time (as flagged by the IMF, see WEO, 2020). In any case, the observed and implied shocks go well beyond those usually accounted for in standard stress test exercises, even when considering the most severe scenarios in the US Fed or BoE exercises. The shock (e.g. to GDP) is indeed far from any historical previous crisis; even the GFC fares poorly in this respect, with the 2018–2019 trade halt weighing less than what has been observed as a result of the coronavirus-triggered worldwide lockdown. It was also a very sudden shock, originating outside the banking sector.

Being in a position to assess how such real activity sudden interruptions and the accompanying surge in unemployment would affect the banks' situation is essential with a view to preventing or at least mitigating a further spread of the crisis, via banks' failures or procyclical deleveraging. The impacts on the real economy are subject to highly unusual uncertainty, not to mention on banks themselves. There was first an immediate financial market unrest, reflecting expectations of forthcoming banks' (and other firms) losses. Asset prices have not always fully recovered, so that banks' balance sheets are

---

Note: Edited by Tiziano Bellini

https://doi.org/10.1515/9783110647907-008

also more permanently affected – after having faced temporary liquidity issues that were addressed thanks to central banks' interventions. In the subsequent stages of the crisis, solvency would come to the forefront, with defaults in the real economy affecting banks via degraded credit risk positions. The extent to which banking systems will prove resilient to this remains surrounded by a wide margin of uncertainty.

Facing such a joint real and financial crisis, Schuermann's (2015) dichotomy between stress testing in war versus peace times comes to mind. Now is certainly not a peace time, given the magnitude of the shocks hitting the economy, as well as the systemic aspect of their impacts. This is where microprudential and macroprudential authorities get together to join forces and combine policies. In the particular case of stress testing, both can use the latter for their now common objectives of preserving individual banks and the whole system stability. A number of policy steps were taken in a variety of constituencies, such as releasing or relaxing macro or micro buffers, postponing or alleviating regulation implementation (e.g. IFRS9, moratoria of various kinds) – all in conjunction with fiscal support such as for loan guarantees or with monetary policy moves, helping banks to get adequate funding.

Stress testing is a tool readily available to complement, or at least inform, the implementation and calibration of policy measures, even if it may not be as necessary as back in 2009 to use such exercises as a tool to enhance confidence in banks and support a system-wide recapitalisation.

In such an uncertain and severe context, a banking system-wide exercise could help identify trigger points in terms of real side developments, beyond which banks will not be sufficiently preserved, check whether capital shortfalls and the potentially resulting deleveraging be excessive for the real economy to grow, assess the extent to which procyclical effects of regulation or requirements deepen the downturn, and so on. There is value in quantifying both the impact of the ongoing crisis on banks as well as how they could react – for example, by shrinking their assets and possibly generating a credit crunch. In this connection, the US Fed 2020, BoE 2020 or ECB 2020 results provided valuable information to policy-makers but also to the general public – particularly on banks' resilience, and thereby on the economy going forward, given the essential role of credit in such phases.

As informative as they might be, these exercises still remain in the domain of standard stress testing, whereas the magnitude of the shock as well as the uncertainty surrounding developments going forward could call for differing exercises, giving more room to unusual and large events, not necessarily specified in advance. This connects to the Worst-Case Scenario (WCS) terminology and academic literature. Osborn (2020) envisaged for the real side a range of possible outcomes, grouped under such a header. Having a stress test framework capable of handling such huge and uncertain systemic events would be clearly valuable. It could also be attuned to cater for the "unknown unknowns" (Danielsson, 2019), in the form of scenarios that never occurred in the past, not only in terms of size but also of the combination of underlying risk factors. Scenarios that would endanger the system stability could be thereby identified and precautionary measures best prepared. This would then be a new kind of exercise, a Reverse Stress Test (RST) for the system – i.e. a macroprudential one – that could be carried out using macroprudential stress test models, such as those documented in Hesse et al. (2014) or Dees et al. (2017).

This paper presents further reflections on why and how such a macroprudential RST could be conducted. First, we focus on supervisory microprudential RST – there are EBA guidelines 2018, where such exercises are defined and framed for individual banks to conduct. In the second section, by contrast, we try to define a macroprudential RST, and how a corresponding framework can be set up, taking inspiration from the way in which standard system-wide stress tests are designed (see Baudino et al., 2018), focusing on implementation aspects. Naturally, scenarios would appear as the cornerstone of the exercise – as is the case for any regular stress test in fact, but even more for RST as finding "a" or "the" scenario(s) is the end objective. We dedicate the third section to a discussion on how a scenario search exercise can be analytically embedded in a macro set-up. Finally, we present illustrative hypothetical simulation results, using bank-level data and a specific large scale model, STAMP€ (Dees et al., 2017).

8.2 RST Micro to Macro Concepts and Toolkit

There is a very limited literature on RST, even less so with macroprudential applications, and there is no clear consensus on how to define such an exercise. A very generic definition could be to consider equation (8.1), whereby the stress-test process or model ST delivers an *Output* as a function of an *Input*:

$$Output = ST\,[Input] \tag{8.1}$$

For a regular stress test, the input will be bank-data and a scenario, with the output being the end-of horizon capital ratio. The RST in turn would correspond to the inversion of this relation:

$$Input = ST^{-1}\,[Output] \tag{8.2}$$

A first remark is that this generic formulation would apply to also non-extreme cases, which may not necessarily be looking for a single WCS. The inversion may but likely would not yield a unique solution, given the multi-dimensional feature of the usual stress testing inputs. This is one of the standard problems to be addressed when considering RST, as evidenced by the literature. RST are used in the micro space to find out what can go really wrong in the firm and where, up to causing the failure of the entity but also looking at close-to-default resulting situations, all of which can prove useful to define resolution and recovery plans. Distress situations could result from a variety of causes that trigger and propagate their impact through diverse channels.

Solution(s) to (8.2) moreover depend on a number of features of the problem summarised in equation (8.2). The targeted output could be a variety of outcomes, such as a given capital level or a loss amount, which could lead to differing inverted inputs. Solution(s) may also heavily depend on the properties of the ST transducer (in other words, on the reactions of the given bank or banking sector or of whatever agent to input shocks, as captured or proxied by the ST operator).

While the RST approach is closely connected to the WCS body of work – to the extent that it involves searching across events and scenarios – it also distinguishes itself by not necessarily having an extreme outcome as a target nor seeking a single solution either.

8.2.1 From Microprudential to Macroprudential RST

Turning to what supervisors specifically mention with reference to RST, in terms of requirements or advice, relevant references are the FSA 2020 Handbook dedicated to such exercises, as well as the EBA 2018a stress test guidelines or the BCBS 2018 principles that both include a part dedicated to RST. In all cases, the aim is to identify weaknesses in the bank and its deeper vulnerabilities with a view to developing mitigation strategies and/or resolution and recovery plans as a sequel.

The EBA document in particular provides a set of recommendations and requirements which are worth recalling. They relate to the objective and the implementation of the RST – borrowing from the typology used in both the BCBS 2018 principles and the BIS FSI survey (Baudino et al., 2018) on the design of banking system-wide stress tests. We focus in what follows on implementation features; the governance elements that are also needed to complete the framework are left aside, as they are not in scope now.

The EBA publication states that all banks should include RST and RST scenarios in their stress-testing programmes. Some additional guidance is provided on how this can be achieved. Banks should look at near-default scenarios, so as to identify critical risk factors and to develop recovery plans. Banks are also advised to use RST as a tool to gauge the severity of scenarios used in their ICAAP/ILAAP. Another use of RSTs can be to test the models that need to be employed to carry out the exercise. On the qualitative side, banks are moreover required to employ a well-defined narrative as well as an understanding of feedback and non-linear effects, also considering combinations or risk factors (all elements that are not that straightforward technically). A final important practical recommendation is to conduct sensitivity analyses – based on "push" to a single factor or a set thereof, resorting to a joint statistical analysis covering all factors, including judgmental assumptions. Even though RST remains a largely quantitative exercise, the prescribed approach therefore should include qualitative considerations, since it will eventually not be a pure modelling exercise.

All in all, with such a recommendation to include RST in the firms' strategies on stress testing, it should closely relate to other regular exercises such as ICAAP/ILAPP. Given the somewhat still loose supervisory guidance on technical aspects, firms' approaches are admittedly less harmonised for RST than is the case for other stress tests. The consensus that has been built over time on best practices for standard stress testing – see Moody's 2020 for an updated overview of what this implies, including in comparison with macroprudential stress test and RST – is not yet available for RST.

Turning to macroprudential RST, there is even less of a consensus – the definition of the term itself is not crystal clear. In the process of transferring or adapting a concept from the micro to the macro sphere, a key (and obvious) dimension is to consider the whole system. While it is relatively easy, albeit incomplete or unduly simple, to just aggregate individual institutions' results to get to a first system-wide view in regular stress tests, this is not feasible for RST. For one thing, the formal solution of the aggregate inversion will generally not be a simple aggregation of the bank-by-bank inversion. In practice, the micro bank-by-bank specific events that would to the failure of a given bank would not necessarily coincide with those affecting others. Any aggregation would be a complex exercise, requiring for instance the compilation of a superset of the bank's own factors and, then, rerunning an impact analysis to also identify what subset of those factors could combine and be common enough to put the whole system at risk. This would be tantamount to actually having an authority in charge of directly conducting a (top-down) RST, with the authority taking a more efficient route. In addition, a macroprudential RST should involve feedback and spillovers, which is more than challenging for a single bank to capture in its own modelling (in spite of it being requested by EBA).

A macroprudential RST would also require running a stress test under many different scenarios for the whole system, which then renders it close to unfeasible for a "bottom-up" (BU) approach to be taken – in line with the BIS BCBS or FSI terminology, BU is when banks produce stress test results on the basis of their own models. Supervisors have to then closely review the outcome. EBA BU stress tests employ only a limited number of scenarios, largely due to the large sample of banks they have to scrutinise. As a result, a "top-down" (TD) approach seems better suited for an RST, whereby a "centre" authority, supervisor or central banker would be best placed to run the exercise, using models that should also be appropriate for macroprudential stress testing.

Typically, a macroprudential TD stress test framework involves a complex process and a suite of models that would need also to be inverted to produce an RST – see Figure 8.1 for a standard process (similar across the ECB, IMF or BoE). The workflow depicted in the chart goes from the scenario assumptions to the final macro results, going via first the translation of scenarios into banks' risks parameters, then via quasi-accounting equations the impact on individual banks' balance sheets, which are then aggregated before finally supplemented with a range of spillovers to complete the macro picture. In case feedbacks and spillovers are sizeable enough to warrant a change in the scenario

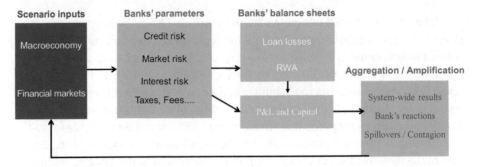

Figure 8.1: A standard macropru stress-test process.

initially considered, iterations are required in such a set-up. Even if a closed-form solution is available for this system, its inversion would not be trivial.

8.2.2 Lessons from the Academic and Institutional Literature on RST

Reviewing the limited but now burgeoning literature can help in this respect, with WCS morphing over time into RST – academics but also central bankers (to a sizeable extent) have contributed to this field, where a few key pieces stand out. To begin with, Cihak (2004) and Breuer et al. (2009) can be seen as seminal pieces. Cihak (2004) in particular introduces, in a paper otherwise generally dedicated to macroprudential stress testing, a number of concepts that will prove critical to the WCS analysis but also to RST work at a later stage. He takes a macro perspective upfront and considers WCS versus threshold metrics, and suggests selecting a scenario generating a maximum loss or the most likely scenario resulting in a given loss amount. Technically, he also introduces equiprobability ellipsoids (to represent the joint probability of possibly correlated risk factors) and their intersection with loss curves – a toolkit still at the core of the work in this area at present.

Breuer et al. (2009) explore further the trade off loss-probability in seeking a WCS, namely the fact that a more damaging scenario would be less probable, which warrants the existence of an optimum. He also promotes specific tools, such as the Mahalanobis (probability) distance within ellipsoids, the latter representing sets of equiprobable shocks in a multivariate setting. He also simplifies the multi-factor problem by allocating a conditional expected value to shocks not calibrated in the set of scenarios under review that provide the initial conditioning factor set. He also decomposes WCS outcomes into respective risk factor contributions.

An important subsequent step was to introduce distributions on scenarios themselves and not factors, which is done by Abdymomounov et al. (2011) – considering for each scenario a range of impacts (i.e. higher and lower bands) and a frequency of occurrence. He then picks the WCS as the higher lower band event at a given frequency. Breuer and Csiszar (2013) also revisit the scenario selection issue using distributions – with a distance this time to a reference distribution that has to be minimised by the selected scenario (an entropy criterion). The applications reported also include macroprudential stress tests.

Another further development in the WCS area related to work on metrics to be employed in the underlying optimisation exercise, reflecting its objective. Pritzker (2012) defines systemic (i.e. macro) objectives, introducing a Maximum Loss as opposed to a Constrained Maximum Loss. The former is the result of an unconstrained optimisation, whereas the latter involves the use of a threshold such as the number of banks remaining above a given capital level even in the WCS.

A final key paper is Glassermann et al. (2014), which properly introduces the very notion of RST and applies it to equity portfolios, presenting a methodology to select shocks to risk factors on the basis of a Maximum Expected Shortfall (similar in spirit to Breuer et al., 2009). In addition, the paper also accounts for non-linearities in the shock distributions, and adjusts outcomes for tail events.

With all these fundamental building blocks available, a number of research pieces or applications could be produced either by the industry or the academia. On the micro front in particular, there is already a close to standardised process (see for example Gea-Carrasco and Nyberg, 2013) resorting to a BU risk analysis. Contrary to the similar terminology for stress testing which qualifies who produces the results, in the case at hand, i.e. in risk management terms, BU means to process individual sources of risks (credit, market, interest), but modelling them and their interaction directly at the instrument or asset level (terminology then close to that employed for forecasting techniques). Grundke (2011) presents the details of such a methodology for WCS. McNeil and Smith (2012) use equi-proba ellipsoids, and focus on the Maximum Likelihood Ruin Event for a given bank, thereby bridging the gap between WCS and RST. Other notable contributions are Grundke and Pliszka (2017), who use a Principal Component Analysis (PCA) to simplify the analysis of the impact of macro factors such as interest rates on a bank portfolio – thereby reducing the dimension of the problem by diminishing the number of factors (again akin to Breuer et al., 2009). Finally, further technical refinements are ongoing, with Tracucci et al. (2019) introducing non-linear P&L functions in the McNeil and Smith (2012) approach and Finck (2019) efficient optimisation algorithms to most efficiently search for the WCS.

On the macroprudential side, there are fewer pieces and progress has been witnessed only recently. Dridi (2015) presents an original application of the RST approach to a banking system (Tunisia) looking at losses from GDP and interest rates, in a credit risk VaR modelling set-up. Kapinos and Mitnik (2015) is an important step forward for top-down RST of banking systems, as they conduct an ex ante PCA on macro variables – similar to Grundke and Pliszka (2017), in both cases to reduce input dimensionality. Breuer and Summer (2018) use a large stress test model to conduct scenario selection, again in a risk impact versus plausibility approach. Baes and Schaanning (2020) conduct a similar system-wide simulation exercise, focusing on market price dynamics and fire sales with many assets and banks, but without considering the full set of risks faced by a banking system under stress. Flood et al. (2020) extends Pritzker (2012) with system-wide simulations, using PCA this time ex post – i.e. not to reduce the dimension of the risk factors ex ante, but to summarise instead the main drivers of the WCS (in an RST).

8.3 A Tentative Set-Up for Macroprudential RST

Next to the previously mentioned literature, further ideas can be put forward with a view to developing an adequate macroprudential RST framework. A critical point is the system-wide dimension which calls for the introduction of dynamic features in simulations – this holds generically for macroprudential stress testing (see in particular Constancio, 2015). The critical step in this respect is to consider banks' reactions to stress – in particular, how they would adjust asset and liability. Once accounted for, such reactions would modify their own capital position but, most important, would form a macro perspective and also trigger a number of externalities within the banking system, as well as affecting agents outside the system. Channels at work that lead to such spillover-contagion-feedback effects would comprise market prices, credit supply or liquidity and funding actions. This has implications for the models to be employed – reactions would affect others via price and quantity mechanisms. For instance, banks' asset deleveraging with a view to restoring capital levels at their pre-stress level could trigger a price shock via fire sales (mark-to-market mechanism with lower valuation for commonly held assets) or affect real demand via credit supply shrinkage (with then downward pressure on activity).

Such requirements explain why a TD approach is largely favoured in macroprudential stress testing (Baudino et al., 2018), which would be even more the case once envisaging a corresponding RST. Leaving aside the (theoretical) idea of having all banks running a multiplicity of alternative prescribed scenarios, BU RST results for individual banks would never be aggregated in a straightforward manner. They can nonetheless provide information on how to set a system-wide critical scenario by identifying across banks a set of critical risk factors or narratives.

A macroprudential RST would be conducted with also a different objective, by nature – that is, instead of focusing on a single bank failure, its objective would be expressed in terms of what occurs to the whole system, or even the economy at large, with failure or distress not having in that case a readily available definition or even set of criteria identifying them. Somewhat contrary to micro RST, the objective could be to invert the ST process to get outcomes other than a "failure". This can be summarised, adapting (8.1) and (8.2), by introducing the scenario as an input along with the set of banks subject to stress – which is a singleton in a micro case versus the whole system in the macro one:

$$Micro\ ST\ (bank,\ scenario) = Bank\ failure/distress \tag{8.3}$$

$$Macro\ ST\ (\{banks\},\ scenario) = Outcome \qquad (8.4)$$

Taking the specific example of a given stress test operator *ST* and assuming that the macro authority has settled the desired outcome for its RST in terms of a "target", the problem can be restated:

$$Scenario = ST^{-1}\,(Outcome) \qquad (8.5)$$

The specific target picked should be aligned with the objective of the exercise, a non-exhaustive list of which could be: checking up to where the system stays robust, identifying pockets of vulnerabilities (in terms of critical risk factors and/or critical banks), get a desired effect of policy measures (e.g. a hurdle rate or macro buffer), preserving a given level of credit or activity, including by identifying a given level of loan guarantees take-up (a relevant current example) and so on.

All of these objectives would then require appropriate metrics, some of which could be employed for more than one of these objectives. These could be the share of banks above a given capital level, individual risk factor system-wide impacts, implied stress for specific risk types or geographies, the overall capital ratio or total shortfall to a given threshold or a specific level of credit or economic growth. Flood et al. (2020) present some RST applications that, like Pritzker (2012), distinguish between Maximum Losses and so-called Constrained Maximum Losses, echoing Cihak (2004) and the difference between the Maximum Loss and Threshold determinations of the WCS.

As for a micro RST, there will not be a single solution to (8.5), which therefore creates the need for a selection or at least sorting process among the (multiplicity of) found solutions. An option is to develop a probabilistic framework – inspired by the WCS literature, especially Breuer et al. (2009) and Glassermann et al. (2014) – whereby each scenario can be attributed a probability and then ranked against others yielding the same outcome. From a purely statistical perspective, however, this is not problem-free, as Data Generating Processes are not usually known, there are non-linearities especially for tail events, and crises are characterised by breaking correlations, not to mention that some scenarios would or even should – as mentioned in EBA (2018a) – include judgmental elements, the probability of which remains unknown. The relevance of these considerations moreover increases with stress, i.e. when the outcome sought for reflects an extreme "failure"-type target.

8.3.1 Scenario Design for a Macroprudential RST

While the essence of RST, scenarios are also the cornerstone of any standard stress test, since the latter is always a conditional exercise – some useful lessons from employed practices in standard stress-testing can therefore be drawn for RST. In system-wide stress test exercises, next to historical developments, reviews of banks portfolios or macroeconomic analyses, RST can also be employed to design scenarios (as flagged in Baudino et al., 2018). This could be done by gathering RST information from individual banks or having previously run macro TD simulations that exemplified how some crisis events would lead the system or a good chunk of it in a distress state. Another observation is that among strategies followed to design scenarios, while some focus on the probability of the scenario (e.g. IMF, setting a GDP target at 2 standard errors, which is then tantamount to inverting the macroeconomic model but not the stress test one), others also fix the exogenous risks drivers at a given probability level (e.g. ESRB 2018, this can then be a first step towards implementing a probabilistic approach to selecting risk factors, but only ex ante then). For regular EBA stress-tests, however, there are also judgmental calibrations for some risks that are then not directly connected to a probability distribution.

RST can be seen as one specific approach to scenario design, involving, however, a differing process. Figure 8.2 – inspired by Gross et al. (2020) – recalls the standard process generally followed to design macroprudential scenarios. Starting from the left-hand side of the workflow, adapting it for the purpose of RST would imply skipping the first (Risk identification) step or have it only setting a list of candidate risk factors, with possibly also range of values each of these could take (to make the exercise bounded and tractable). Severity would have to be ignored in Step 2 (Shock definition) given the essence of an RST. Step 3 and 4 (System response and Impact assessment) would need to be run for all admitted scenarios. Once all results are collected, focusing on the outcome to be inverted in the light of an agreed metric, the set of possible solutions would have to be reviewed and possibly sorted (e.g. to reach some WCS).

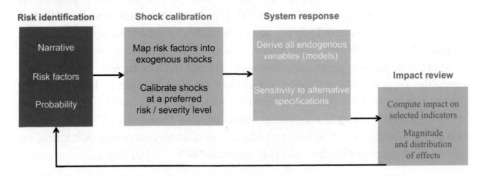

Figure 8.2: A schematic standard ST scenario process.

Scenario design for stress testing has a number of implementation issues (see Henry, 2015 and Gross et al., 2020), which would also affect RST endeavours, but the latter would also have to face specific challenges. Standard challenges arise for instance in Step 1, such as balancing micro versus macro risks, assessing the relevance of risks, accounting for correlations, and also in Steps 2–4 with respect to severity levels. For one thing, this latter issue is not affecting RST, as being of an utmost severity is usually not a problem – the likelihood of the solution scenario remains a concern, however. Risk identification issues also arise to a much lesser extent with RST, even though a model-based exercise would have to operate with a pre-defined set of risk factors. A Monte Carlo exercise could reduce the dependence of results on pre-assigned probabilities to given events, but this may lead to solutions reflecting only statistical artefacts (as can happen in factor-based forecasting, where the best predictor may be, in theory or practice, cumbersome to relate to the predicted variables). Finally, non-standard correlations or behaviour can also be tackled in an RST, but this may render the model required to obtain results overly complex. Such generic or specific problems are, as for the EBA exercise, magnified within a multi-country set-up.

Coming up with a strategy for generating scenarios in an RST may also help to bridge the gap between various approaches taken across institutions. In spite of the broad consensus when it comes to design scenarios across a number of institutions, there are still significant differences. EBA stands out in this respect, and this is again largely related to the necessary multicountry nature of their stress test exercises as well as the bottom-up nature of their exercises – that is, numbers are produced by banks using their models. Figure 8.3 – using the infomation in Gross et al. (2020) – shows, for instance, that many institutions use more than one adverse scenario (none use many, though) and have a dynamic balance sheet assumption. On the other hand, EBA is the only one in this table which does not come up with an ex ante target for the scenario, i.e. the narrative guides the shock calibration – itself however influenced by a probabilistic approach to set some of the inputs (see ESRB, 2018). In the case at hand, on top of obviously multiplying the number of scenarios, an RST may then employ (especially for macroprudential purposes) a Dynamic balance sheet approach, but possibly being more parsimonious with respect to external factors or focus on overall aggregate indicators for the whole population of banks – all features that could reduce complexity.

Stress Test Scenarios	EBA	US Fed	BoE
countries covered	28	1	1
risk narrative	detailed	high level	high level
adverse scenarios	1	2	2
severity calibration	assumptions	outcome	outcome
ST bank behaviour	static BS	dynamic BS	dynamic BS
ST models	BU	TD	TD

Figure 8.3: Features of standard stress test scenario design for some institutions.

8.3.2 Options for a Practical Implementation of a Macroprudential RST

Once the scenario generator is set, subsequent steps in the process can be envisaged in different ways. A first line of divide would again be whether the risk identification step would be completely or only partially ignored, with a corollary issue – namely, whether simulations hinge on single-risk factors (i.e. what is the major risk?) or a combination (what is the most damaging combination of events?). The latter would be more complex – also due to the need for specific correlations to be assumed. A range of assumptions could be tested, but this would further increase the dimensionality of the problem. This connects to the so-called BU approach in risk management that, as we recalled, is being employed for bank-level RSTs.

A particular aspect of an RST carried out for macroprudentia purposes is that the tool to be employed in Step 4 of the process, a block translating shocks/inputs into impacts/outputs, would have ideally to be comprehensive enough to cover the so-called first- and second-round effects that shape results in a standard macroprudential stress test. In this vein, risk parameters for banks and the system should be modelled as well as the impact of the various externalities at play, including for non-banks.

After all results have been collected, the selection step would have to take place, optimally and practically reflecting a mix of ex ante and ex post decisions. The set of factors itself has possibly been derived from prior risk analyses. Whether the probability of occurrence is seen as a more relevant criterion than the damage done also matters. The metrics and target choice similarly influence the modelling and also the channels to be specifically reviewed and assessed. The focus could be on markets, banks or the real side. Correspondingly, the outcome of interest could be, for example, equity prices or CDSs, weaker banks and overall capital needs, or credit and GDP.

Overall, the RST process could follow three main avenues that can be seen as options for the modeller, depending on a variety of criteria, such as the connection to a given narrative, time available, the complexity of the models and the weight granted to probability, just to name a few aspects that could play a role in the decision to engage in whatever process.

Option 1 would be to take a given scenario, consistent with a pre-defined narrative, and push it to extreme values by multiplying all risk factor shocks by a given scaling factor. This homothetic or scalar approach has pros and cons. The pro is that the link to the narrative, and likely to the standard stress test, is also easier to implement and document. On the cons side, it cannot by construction capture any unknowns (be it for rare set of events, broken correlations, shifting probabilities, etc.).

Option 2 would be to experiment with no ex ante identified risks, running many (e.g. Monte Carlo) stochastic simulations. It has the advantage of limiting priors to the choice of risk factors to be shocked. It would, on the other hand, produce a mass of results that may be hard to summarise and interpret – even if employing a probability-based selection process. The latter would itself heavily depend on the distributions assumed or the samples used to generate the cloud of results. The computational requirements may also be such that the model to be employed to translate the input into a relevant output would have to be simplified, possibly overly so in economic terms, to become tractable.

Option 3 would represent a mixed strategy whereby factors could be grouped, submitting each group to shocks of various probability size – moments needed can be empirically estimated. On the pros side, it would keep a link with risk identification and macroeconomic mechanisms, with more room for unknown (magnitude of and correlations among) shocks than in Option 1. It would also allow the modellers to still run a very large and complex model. At the same time, it would still have the disadvantage of not being as generic as Option 2 while still needing some probabilistic selection.

An example of the type of models that could be used is the financial simulator used in generating market price shocks in the EBA scenario (see ESRB, 2018). It is inspired by Breuer et al. (2009) ("setting the values of non-stressed factors to their conditional expected value, given the value of the stressed risk factor maximises plausibility") and Glassermann et al. (2014) using the Multivariate Expected Shortfall – capturing tail dependencies via conditioning. A specific aspect of this tool is that it generates observations by bootstrapping real data to generate a cloud of observations. For each risk factor – there can be thousands – a value at any probability level can then be empirically determined. As illustrated in Figure 8.4, for any given shock on a specific factor at a given probability level (x axis), the corresponding shock can be calibrated for any other factor (y axis) at the Expected Shortfall value, computed as the average of values for the sub-cloud located in the south-east quadrant of the chart.

The EBA market risk scenario can then be interpreted as a WCS for market prices, given specific shocks sets beforehand, such as to the US bond rate. The latter also appears as such in the macro scenario, in line with the ESRB official financial stability risk assessment and identification, and therefore a first candidate for a conditioning variable. Alternative results can also be derived from an initial dataset corresponding to crisis periods, which then would modify correlations and bring them close to those observed during market turmoils (with specific tail cross-dependencies). It would, however, remain a reflection of historical albeit selected data – no unknowns would then be accounted for in this approach. The modelling also does not include scenario assumptions other than financial market prices (e.g. GDP, inflation, real estate prices), let alone bank variables that are all needed for a full-fledged macro RST to be operational.

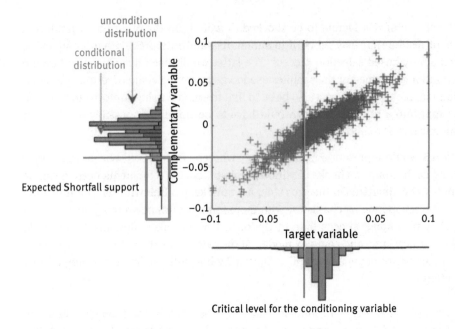

Figure 8.4: Conditional Expected Shortfall in scenarios.

8.4 Illustrative Model-Based Implementation of a Macroprudential RST

This section presents an application of the Option 3 introduced previously, reported for purely illustrative methodological purposes, from which therefore no inference can be made with respect to actual system-wide stress test results. Our simulations first of all cover only a random anonymised sub-sample of EU banks, use outdated data for banks' balance sheet (2017) and stress test methodologies (2018), as well as a dated (pre-coronavirus) baseline (2018 forecasts). Most important, at this juncture, these simulations in addition do not account for policy measures that are taken by regulatory, macroprudential, monetary and fiscal authorities – an extremely strong limitation during a crisis. A comprehensive re-run of such an approach based on updated comprehensive data, policy assumptions, scenarios and methodologies would potentially yield very different results and conclusions. In any event, as is generally the case for RST, using different models or alternative probabilistic assumptions could drastically change the results. The ensuing methodological exposition and related discussion, however, remains fully valid.

8.4.1 The Methodology for Scenario Generation and Sensitivity Analyses

The practical, model-based illustration now presented makes use of the STAMP€ Dees et al. (2017) framework, comprising a suite of stress-test models, using both macro and micro data. The simulations are run on a random non-representative subset of EU banks, that are moreover anonymised for this purpose. The set of models used concentrates on the first-round impact of stress – i.e. the effect of shocks to macro-financial variables on each bank's risk parameters. In contrast with the EBA set-up, computations are done conditionally on an aggregate credit supply set to be consistent with macro-financial assumptions – i.e. a dynamic balance sheet assumption replaces the static one that characterises the EBA microprudential exercise. Credit supply is then re-allocated on a pro-rata basis to all banks in the overall sample. Such a dynamic approach is also used is the ECB FSR (e.g. FSR, 2017), in order to bring the stress test results closer to a realistic macro picture, in which, at times of stress, credit supply mechanically declines. While available in the framework, second-round effects also typically included in macroprudential stress-tests are switched off for the sake of the simplicity of conducting the exercise but also to render its interpretation easier to convey.

From a scenario perspective, the shocks typically underlying the EBA scenario are a starting point for the simulations conducted (see ESRB 2018). For macrofinancial variables, we have used a scenario generator similar to that employed for EBA exercises (see Henry, 2015 and Gross et al., 2020), with inputs' size and profile calibrated to deliver a path roughly similar to that of EBA 2018, without any judgmental adjustments. While this first instance scenario can be interpreted as a "reference" point corresponding to shocks individually calibrated at a 5% level (in line with the input approach mentioned in the previous section), the resulting path differs from that of EBA and is eventually slightly more severe – in fact, it is closer to the unused EBA (ESRB) 2020 scenario in terms of deviation from baseline GDP after three years. The set-up differs for market risk and market prices shocks – there, we have simply taken the financial simulator outcome as used in the EBA 2018 exercise, itself also assumed to be broadly consistent with a two standard error approach (see the previous section).

The RST proceeds as follows: We first group the risk factors in three sub-sets (domestic denoted d, external e and financial f). This is tantamount to having implemented an ex ante PCA a la Kapinos and Mitnik (2015) – sparing us the cost of computations, with a likely good match between components that would be accurately computed (see Angelini et al., 2001, for an application to inflation). The factors comprise for instance investment and housing prices in the domestic set, world demand and competitors' prices in the external one, or interest rates and equity prices in the financial one.

We then run a sequence of scenarios where for all three groups, reference shocks in a given group are all rescaled in a homothetic fashion, for various levels of risk, expressed in terms of multiple of the underlying shocks' standard errors, denoted σ. We then can generate a grid of scenarios along two dimensions, number of factor groups and rescaling factors (the "scalar", set at 2 for all reference shocks).

The set of risk factors $e \times f \times d$ is then associated to $(Scalar_e, Scalar_f, Scalar_d)$. The shock sizes and the corresponding scalars considered are the following:

$$\forall\ i \in \{e, f, d\},\ Scalar_i \in \{\ 0, 0.5, 1, 1.5, 2\ \} \Rightarrow Size \in \{\ 0, \sigma, 2\sigma, 3\sigma, 4\sigma\ \}$$

This approach also allows the modeller to experiment with alternative profiles for the shocks over the three-year horizon. A typical EBA scenario can be said to exhibit a U or L shape – i.e. shocks kick in gradually and are protracted, slowly diminishing at horizon-end. In view of the coronavirus crisis, and to reflect ongoing reflections on what a WCS could be on the macroeconomic side going forward, we have also investigated the impact on GDP of redistributing the shocks again using a scalar approach – whereby all shocks are re-scaled with respect to the reference U-shape profile consistent with the reference set:

Reference input U-shape over the 3 years, scalar annual profile (1 – 1 – 1)
V-shape over 3 years, scalar annual profile (2 – 1 – 0)
W shape over 3 years, scalar annual profile (2 – 0 – 1)

Running the models, we can then generate for each combination of macrofinancial and market prices shocks, specific outcomes from which we can derive by interpolation the whole surface of outcomes over a range of shocks sizes (assuming local continuity in partial derivatives). The metrics we focus on for illustrative purposes are the average capital ratio post stress and the share of the sample of banks that end with a capital ratio below 8% under stress (was 25% in the EBA 2018).

Two scalar configurations are of specific relevance and interest in the factor group space, namely:

$$V0 = (0, 0, 0)\ \text{and}\ V1 = (1, 1, 1)$$

The first three-dimensional scalar vector by construction reproduces for the adverse a set of values for macrofinancial and market variables that are exactly identical to that in the baseline. At the same time, given that this is an input to a model proxying the EBA methodology (see EBA 2017) – which is more punitive in the adverse than under the baseline – the outcome will be more severe than processing this scenario configuration as a baseline. This affects a number of risk factors, such as NII with caps and floors but also Credit risk with minimum PDs and LGDs, or also NFCI or NTI with constraints on income if under an adverse configuration. The impact of such constraints varies with the scenario and the bank, but can reach a couple of ppts of capital. The other vector of scalars, with values all set at 1, then reproduces the reference scenario whereby all risk factors are assumed to be subject to a 5% level shock.

8.4.2 Scenarios and their Impacts on Banks for Various Metrics

The resulting map of scenarios can be illustrated by looking at the GDP path over alternative scalar vector configurations. Figure 8.5 shows only a sub-set of the generated scenarios – all for "symmetric" cases, i.e. resulting from the same scalar used for all three groups of factors (tantamount to an Option 1 approach). Series 1 is for all shocks set at 0, ie the baseline. Series 3 in the middle of the range corresponds to the reference 2σ case, while Series 6 and 7 represent the V and W shape respectively. Other lines show rescaled U-shaped scenarios for alternative scalar values. The reference case ends up with a deviation from the baseline GDP at about 9% at the end of horizon ie at Year3Q4, slightly more severe than EBA 2018 for the EU. Series 5 shows the path for the risk level set at 4σ, a practically zero-probability case, i.e. a lower band one. Series 3 and 5 represent configurations in which respectively GFC and coronavirus profile of shocks would be sustained over a three-year period – i.e. without any subsequent recovery after the year of the shock – a rather extreme assumption, characterised in effect by an extremely low, quasi-0 probability.

The outcome of our experimental set-up is for each metric is a three-dimensional manifold in the 4-dimensional space ($Scalar_d$, $Scalar_e$, $Scalar_f$, Outcome). The representation we chose is a 3D one, which implies plotting the outcome expressed in a given metric against two sets of scaling factors. The latter then need to be grouped further – so that the outcome can be (scatter) plotted against two groups of factors.

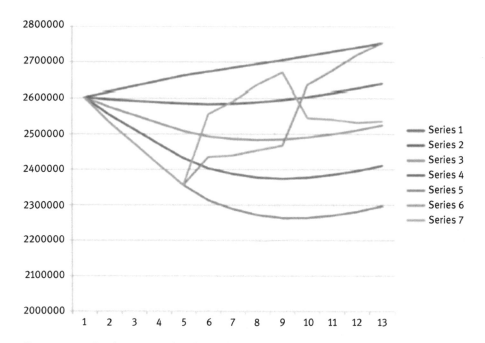

Figure 8.5: GDP level – 3-year path under a sub-set of the input scenarios.

For an outcome equal to the capital ratio, we have provided two of the three possible groupings, namely ({*Scalar$_d$*, *Scalar$_e$*}, *Scalar$_f$*, Outcome) where Scalar$_d$ equals Scalar$_e$, to illustrate the role of financial factors in shaping the surface of results, along with ({*Scalar$_e$*, *Scalar$_f$*}, *Scalar$_d$*, Outcome) where Scalar$_e$ equals Scalar$_f$, to highlight in turn that of domestic shocks. For an outcome equal to the share of banks in the sample whose capital post-stress is below 8%, only the former grouping is reported.

Figures 8.6, 8.7 and 8.8 have the 2 horizontal axes with a grid starting from 0 at the origin (the baseline ie 0-shock scenario as in Series 3 beforehand) and lines that materialise scalar values in the set {0.5, 1, 1.5, 2}. The point opposite to the origin on the floor of the diagram corresponds to scalar values set at 2 for all risks and 0 capital. The mid-point on each horizontal axis therefore represents the reference scenario. The outcome is on the vertical axis, the capital ratio in Figure 8.6 and the share of banks in the sample whose capital ratio is under 8% in Figure 8.8.

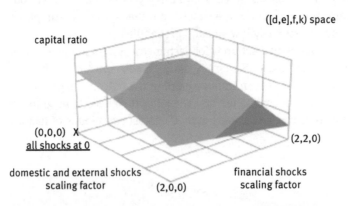

Figure 8.6: Capital ratio surface for various scalars and factor combinations.
NB: Based on hypothetical data for a random anonymised sample of banks

For both Figures 8.6 and 8.7, the surfaces appear smooth, with clearly a downward slope as we go along any of the 2 horizontal axes, which means increasing stress along a given dimension, i.e. for a given set of risk factors. The capital ratio remains positive over the whole surface, maximal for $(x,y) = (0,0)$, ie the baseline, and reaching its minimum when all risk factors are set at a level consistent with four standard errors (the configuration $(x,y) = (2,2)$ with practically zero probability). Additional observations are that a stress increase in the combinations comprising external shocks (at the same time decreasing the corresponding probability) has a quicker and stronger impact than doing the same for the other factor – the slopes of the surfaces on the visible sides are steeper on the left-hand side of the surface.

Albeit not fully obvious graphically, the partial derivatives of the capital ratio with respect to stress factors are not constant, i.e. there is some non-linearity and not only around the origin, where a visible kink appears. Partial derivatives with respect

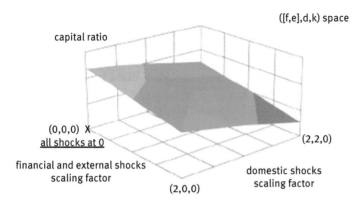

Figure 8.7: Capital ratio surface for various scalars and factor combinations.
NB: Based on hypothetical data for a random anonymised sample of banks

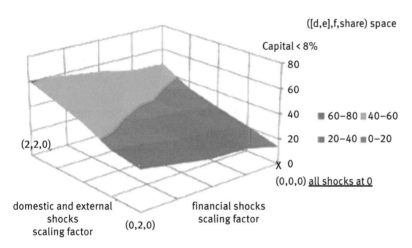

Figure 8.8: Share of banks in the sample with capital below 8% for various factor combinations.
NB: Based on hypothetical data for a random anonymised sample of banks

to factors have a local maximum around scalar at 1 or 1.5, i.e. for stress between 2σ and 3σ. Such derivatives are a good indicator of the trade-off risk-probability, as a maximum value means that at this point the increase in stress (i.e. a given probability loss) results in the most sizeable capital loss. This "efficient" region in terms of getting to a constrained WCS appears in that case in the vicinity of the reference scenario location. Another related observation is that increasing stress has so to say decreasing returns in terms of capital decline – this reflects the methodology but also the fact that many variables of interest are bounded (e.g. PDs or LGDs will not be below a 0 value even ever-increasing stress).

The other metric we focused on – namely, the share of weaker banks in the sample, whose capital ratio is beyond 8% under stress – can be represented in a similar 3D fashion (see Figure 8.8). The resulting surface is then not smooth, since the variable of interest is a discrete binary one for each bank (contrary to capital), and there are therefore threshold cliff effects (non-linearity) that result in kinks at various locations on the surface. An interesting observation is that having 50% of the banks with lower capital than 8% requires scalars on both axes to go beyond the mid-point, that is, having the shock size for all three groups of factors beyond those under the reference case – in other words, a highly improbable conjunction of shocks. More specifically, this would necessitate shocks size beyond 2σ for domestic and external shocks and even higher than 3σ for financial ones. The mid-point result is at about 30% whereas it was about 25% for EBA 2018, bearing in mind that the latter had a smaller GDP shock and that samples are also not comparable anyhow.

8.4.3 From Sensitivity to RST, a Probabilistic Illustration

A last element to include to complete the journey from the sensitivity analysis to an RST is a discussion on probability – which we will conduct very much along the lines of Cihak (2004). We will moreover use a simplified set-up, with a view to better illustrating how the approach can generate results, and also make additional assumptions on results to facilitate closed-form resolution. More specifically, we will produce equicapital loci in the scaling factor space, from the simulated data and consistent with the surface graphs just reported. These we will confront with equi-probability ones, using in both cases a simple proxy instead of directly relying on simulated data.

The construction of equiprobability loci in particular requires specific assumptions on the respective probability distribution function of each factor. In the above Figures, each point on the surfaces can be projected on the (x, y) floor space, which then provides the two scaling factors it is associated with. To simplify the representation and computations, we will assume that each factor axis corresponds to a Gaussian distribution $N(0, \sigma)$, moreover with no correlation with the other, i.e. the DGP is a bivariate normal with a correlation factor $\rho = 0$.

For a generic bivariate normal with correlation, equiprobability curves should satisfy for (x, y) in the floor space:

$$Constant = x^2 - 2\rho . x.y + y^2 \tag{8.6}$$

This equation defines an ellipse which reduces to a circle in the no-correlation case.

Once these two sets of loci are available, the WCS analysis and similarly RST can be fully conducted. It is best illustrated by considering a graphical representation in the (x, y) scaling factor – see Figure 8.9. The diagonal is the support for all symmetric shock configurations – i.e. when the risk level is identical across all risks as all shocks are set with the same factor multiplying 2σ. We will be searching for each capital ratio level, the factor configuration generating this capital ratio (the RST part) with the highest probability, i.e. that corresponds to jointly lowest shocks on both factors (the WCS, conditional part).

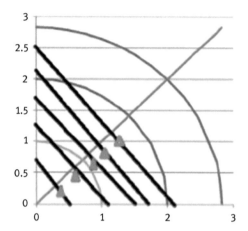

Figure 8.9: Equi-proba circles and equi-capital lines, WCS for given capital ratios (y=fin versus x=dom-ext).
NB: Based on hypothetical data for a random anonymised sample of banks

The WCS problem is then to maximise probability under the equicapital constraint, i.e. along the corresponding locus. In the (x, y) space, the Euclidian distance to the origin – namely $x^2 + y^2$ – also provides the equiprobability circle on which a given point (x, y) in the scaling factor space is located, representing (8.6) when $\rho = 0$. This distance is a degenerated lower dimension version of the Mahalanobis one in the generic multivariate and elliptic case (as in Breuer et al., 2009). The WCS point for a given capital level is therefore the one on the corresponding equicapital locus that is closer to the origin. It will then be geometrically equivalent to locating the orthogonal projection of the origin on the equicapital line.

Even though equicapital loci are not straight lines in practice, they can be represented as such to simplify exposition and also allow for a full and simple graphical and analytical resolution. We also can assume accordingly that for a given capital level, the equicapital line in the (x, y) factor space is defined by $(y = -\alpha.x + \beta)$. Linking this to the already mentioned partial derivatives of the outcome to factors, the slope of the line materialising the relation between y and x can be derived for a given k^* from the implicit function defining the corresponding equicapital line, namely on the $(k = k^*)$ line, where the total derivative will be 0:

$$k(x, y) = k^* \Rightarrow \partial k/\partial x.dx + \partial k/\partial y.dy = dk_{k=k^*} = 0 \tag{8.7}$$

$$\Rightarrow -\alpha = dy/dx = -(\partial k/\partial x)/(\partial k/\partial y) \tag{8.8}$$

Since the capital ratio declines with the stress on any of the two factors the two partial derivatives of k in (8.8) are negative and therefore the slope of the (y, x) line is always negative (and α positive). In addition, a slope of absolute value higher (resp lower) than 1 for a given capital outcome indicates that an increase in factor y has a weaker (resp stronger) impact on capital for a given shift in probability than for the same move along the x axis, as the slope is the ratio of the two partial derivatives.

The bivariate optimisation problem to solve to get the minimum distance reads:

$$\text{Min } (x^2 + y^2) \text{ s.t. } (y = -\alpha . x + \beta) \tag{8.9}$$

$$\textit{Lagrangian } L = x^2 + y^2 - \lambda . (y + \alpha . x - \beta) \tag{8.10}$$

$$\partial L / \partial x = 2x - \lambda . \alpha \text{ and } \partial L / \partial y = 2y - \lambda \tag{8.11}$$

For 0 values of the Lagrange derivatives, i.e. at the optimum, then the following relation holds:

$$x = \alpha . y \tag{8.12}$$

The minimum distance will then be reached on a straight line starting from the origin of equation $(y = \gamma . x)$, with $\gamma = 1/\alpha$. Geometrically, this line is indeed orthogonal to the equicapital line, itself of slope -α, since their dot product $(1, 1/\alpha) . (1, -\alpha)$ is 0.

The slope of a given equicapital locus plays a critical role in defining the WCS location, i.e. for $\alpha = 1$, this point is on the diagonal and is therefore a "symmetric" scenario with the same scaling factor on both axes and risk factors. For slopes higher (resp lower) than 1, as in Figure 8.9, the WCS is located below (resp above) the diagonal – i.e. where locally the domestic and external factors shocks on the x axis have a stronger (resp weaker) impact on capital than financial ones, on the y axis. As expected in the light of the shape of the capital surfaces on Figures 8.6 and 8.7, and the corresponding properties of partial derivatives of the capital ratio, slopes of equicapital lines are generally higher than one, and the WCS for a given target ratio therefore gives less weight to financial factors.

For a given capital target, here with equicapital loci all straight lines, there exists a unique optimal factor combination which delivers the target, materialised by the triangles on Figure 8.9. In most cases moreover, the solution to the WCS substantially differs from a symmetric shock – i.e. there is almost always an asymmetric factor combination which delivers the same level of severity as the symmetric one but with higher probability (whenever the slope on the given equicapital line differs from 1).

The picture would rather dramatically change, however, in the event where a non-zero correlation would be assumed or deemed appropriate – orthogonality between domestic, external and financial (unconditional) shocks seems at best a heroic assumption, which was used to facilitate understanding and exposition. If this were

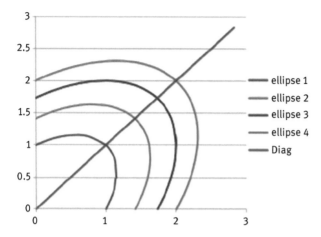

Figure 8.10: The case of ellipsoid equiprobability- loci, for ρ = 0.5.

not the case, equi-probability loci would constitute a family of ellipses, symmetric around the diagonal, as in Figure 8.10 (for a correlation between the two distributions set at 0.5). Most important, at a given probability level for a single risk factor, there will be equiprobable configurations with stronger shocks on both risk factors with clearly a stronger impact regardless of the model multipliers.

Needless to say, the dimensionality of the problem is also a major element, rendering such exercises challenging to not only solve but also interpret. Hence the value that can be seen in reducing the rank of the space to be covered, by focusing as suggested on a couple of main families of driving risk factors. Of course, specifying these introduces restrictions to the set of possible solutions investigated, which is also very dependent on the probability distributions postulated.

8.5 Summary

We have attempted to demonstrate that the microprudential RST approach and related technologies can be adapted to define an analogue RST for macroprudential purposes.

We have proposed a methodology to implement such a macroprudential RST, with a (light) mid-ground option proven feasible and fruitful, particularly in delivering WCS information including under constraints.

The approach builds on Cihak (2004) adapted with a structural (heavier) model, rendered tractable by grouping risk factors and running a relatively small number of simulations.

RST and WCS helps identify more likely and equally damaging combinations, hence stress the need to focus on multiple risks – but also guide on setting priorities, i.e. which risk should be mitigated first as well as the areas where outcomes may become seriously worrying.

The simple model-based exercise carried out was meant to be essentially illustrative and has therefore a number of limitations that would need to be further addressed in a real-life RST. Only three sets of factors were used in the illustration – against a multiplicity of factors in reality (even viewed by modellers); shocks would likely be correlated; and would need some more refined probabilistic approach, as any probability discussion also hinges on distributions, moreover with non-Gaussianity likely.

At the same time, a full probabilistic multivariate approach, albeit computationally heavy, could still be conducted; Monte Carlo simulations could be feasible if the model is parsimonious enough – optionally with no prior distributions, e.g. of a non-parametric copula type.

To achieve this, it would be possible to consider adapting Glassermann et al. (2014), augmented with macrofinancial variables; even though such a set-up would be of a reduced form kind. In addition, it would be heavy computationally and would likely face mixed-frequency issues (daily versus quarterly or even annual) across financial, real, and banking variables.

More fundamentally, running a macroprudential RST would moreover need to fulfil requirements not addressed in the application presented, that are crucially needed for full relevance at the macroprudential level: policy measures, second-round effects, other real financial sectors, and so on.

In the case of the ongoing improvements on the modelling and computational side, such additional features are not to be seen as obstacles. As long as the resulting model is tractable and can be solved in a reasonable fashion, all should be open.

Bibliography

Abdymomounov et al. (2011) Worst-case scenarios as a stress testing tool for risk models, Federal Reserve of Richmond, mimeo.

Angelini et al. (2001) Diffusion index-based inflation forecasts for the euro area, ECB WPS # 61.

Baes and Schaanning (2020) Reverse stress testing, ECB Macroprudential stress testing conference, February.

Bank of England (2020) UK banking sector resilience and Covid-19, Interim Financial Stability Report, May.

Baudino et al. (2018) Stress testing banks: a comparative analysis, FSI Insight #12, BIS.

BCBS (2018) Stress-testing principles, BIS.

Breuer et al. (2009) How to Find Plausible, Severe, and Useful Stress Scenarios, *International Journal of Central Banking*, vol. 5(3).

Breuer and Csiszar (2013) Systematic stress tests with entropic plausibility constraints, *Journal of Banking & Finance* 37.

Breuer and Summer (2018) Systematic systemic stress tests, WP # 225, OeNB.

Cihak (2004) Stress-testing: a review of key concepts, Research and Policy Notes, 2004/02, Czech National Bank.

Constancio (2015) The role of stress testing in supervision and macroprudential policy, Keynote speech at the LSE conference on "Stress-testing and macroprudential regulation: a transatlantic perspective".

Danielsson (2019) *Global financial systems: Stability and risk*, Pearson.

Dees et al. (2017) *Stamp€ – Stress Test Analytics for Macroprudential Puroposes in the € area*, ECB.

Dridi et al. (2015) On reverse stress testing for worst case scenarios: An application to credit risk modelling of Tunisian economic sectors.

EBA (2017) 2018 EU-wide stress test: methodological note, November.

EBA (2018) 2018 EU-wide stress-test: results, November.

EBA (2018a) Guidelines on stress-testing.

ECB (2017) Financial Stability Review, May.

ECB (2020) COVID 19 Vulnerability Analysis – Results overview (ppt), July.

ESRB (2018) Adverse macro-financial scenario for the 2018 EU-wide banking sector stress test, January.

ESRB (2020) Adverse macro-financial scenario for the 2020 EU-wide banking sector stress test, January.

Finck (2019) Worst Case Search over a Set of Forecasting Scenarios Applied to Financial Stress-Testing. *GECCO'19 Proceedings*.

Flood et al. (2020), The Role of Heterogeneity in Macroprudential Stress Testing, forthcoming in Farmer, Kleinnijenhuis, Schuermann and Wetzer (eds.), *Handbook of Financial Stress Testing*, CUP.

FSA (2020) Reverse Stress Testing, Chapter 20, FSA Handbook.

Gea-Carrasco and Nyberg (2013) Is Reverse Stress Testing a Game Changer? Moody's Analytics Risk Perspectives.

Glassermann et al. (2014) Stress scenario selection by empirical likelihood, Columbia, published in *Journal of Quantitative Finance*, 15(1).

Gross et al. (2020) Macrofinancial scenario for system-wide stress tests, for banks and beyond, forthcoming in Farmer, Kleinnijenhuis, Schuermann and Wetzer (eds.), *Handbook of Financial Stress Testing*, CUP.

Grundke (2011) Reverse stress tests with bottom-up approaches, *Journal of Risk Model Validation* 5(1).

Grundke and Pliszka (2017) A macroeconomic reverse stress test, published in *Review of Financial Quantitative Accounting* N. 50.

Henry (2015) Macrofinancial scenario for system-wide stress tests: Process and challenges, Risk. Quargliariello Ed. *Europe's new supervisory toolkit*, Risk.

Henry (2020) Banking system-wide stress testing and Corona: a first summary appraisal, forthcoming in *Journal of Risk Management in Financial Institutions*.

Hesse et al. (2014) How to capture macro-financial spillover effects in stress tests, IMF WP 14/103.

IMF (2020) WEO update: A crisis like no other, an uncertain recovery, June.

Kapinos and Mitnik (2015), A top-down approach to stress-testing banks, WPS 2015-02, FDIC.

McNeil and Smith (2012), "Multivariate stress scenarios and solvency," *Insurance: Mathematics and Economics*, 50(3).

Moody's Analytics (2020) ICAAP/ILAAP – Unlocking business value from capital and liquidity assessment, Risk.net.

Osborn (2020) Covid scenarios: finding the worst worst-case, Risk.net.

Pritszker (2012) Enhanced Stress Testing and Financial Stability. mimeo, Federal Reserve Bank of Boston.

Schuermann (2015) Stress testing in wartimes and peacetimes, LSE conference on "Stress-testing and macroprudential regulation: a transatlantic perspective", October.

Tracucci et al. (2019) A triptych approach for reverse stress testing of complex portfolios. e-version. arXiv: Risk Management.

US Federal Reserve (2020) Assessment of Bank Capital during the Recent Coronavirus Event, June.

Konrad Wälder, Olga Wälder

9 Reverse Stress Testing: Reliability Analysis

9.1 Introduction

Reliability analysis is well known in engineering sciences. Reliability analysis is the quantitative analysis of survival and hazard rates. Typical finance applications are the prediction of loan default rates or fair pricing of credit default swaps. From a theoretical point of view, the reliability analysis is closely related to survival analysis in the life sciences. Both approaches deal with lifetimes of objects and even with failures or deaths of these objects. Reverse stress testing in financial sciences is defined as the method of identifying the point at which a financial institution's business model becomes unviable and the identifying scenarios, events and circumstances that might cause this to happen. In other words, reverse stress testing is based on observed or modelled failures in a broader sense and tries to analyse the behaviour of usefully defined time depending parameters leading to the failures. This corresponds to the approach of reliability. With this chapter, we would like to contribute to the connection of reliability analysis and reverse stress testing and to show the applicability of methods from reliability analysis in reverse stress testing.

The chapter starts with necessary definitions, especially with respect to corresponding approaches from statistics. Subsequently, we discuss useful lifetime distributions like Weibull and IDB distributions. Modelling the so-called hazard rate is of great importance, especially with respect to the aims of reverse stress testing. Therefore, we discuss the behaviour of hazard rates, even to describe different types of failures. Section 9.7 deals with fitting techniques. In conclusion, the general idea of combining reliability analysis and reverse stress testing is discussed in more detail.

9.2 Terms and Definitions

An exact definition of reliability is needed. Reliability is defined in the ISO standard 9000 (ISO 9000, 2015); however, the definition of reliability in this norm is only non-quantitative as a summary expression for the availability, functionality and maintainability of products, processes and technical systems.

This is usually quantified in quality assurance, which leads to the following definition.

Note: Edited by Daniel Mayenberger

https://doi.org/10.1515/9783110647907-009

From a statistical point of view, reliability is defined by the reliability function $R(t)$ which describes the probability that the lifetime T exceeds a given period t

$$R(t) = P(T > t) \tag{9.1}$$

If $F(t)$ is the distribution function of T, the reliability function is given by

$$R(t) = P(T > t) = 1 - P(T \leq t) = 1 - F(t) \tag{9.2}$$

Lifetime is not to be understood literally here. The lifetime of a system can be the downtime in operating hours, the mileage in km, the number of load changes and so on.

Although the normal distribution is the most frequently used distribution, it is not necessarily suitable for modelling lifetimes, since the normal distribution is also defined for negative values of t. Therefore, only distribution models for non-negative lifetimes are useful. Some appropriate models are discussed in the following sections. If a distribution model is used, the parameters of the distribution have to be fitted. For this, a sufficient number of observed lifetimes is necessary. Specific fitting methods are discussed in connection with the distribution models.

In Figure 9.1, the reliability function of a normally distributed lifetime T is given. From the chart, it can be seen that $R(t)$ is a monotonously decreasing function.

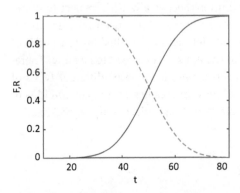

Figure 9.1: Distribution (solid curve) and reliability function (dashed curve) of a normally distributed T with $\mu = 50$, $\sigma = 10$.

If $f(t)$ is the density function of T, distribution and reliability function are given by

$$F(t) = \int_{-\infty}^{t} f(x)dx \text{ and } R(t) = 1 - F(t) = \int_{t}^{\infty} f(x)dx \tag{9.3}$$

Figure 9.2 shows the density functions of a normally distributed T. For $t=60$, we get $F(t)=0.84$ and $R(t)=0.16$ which corresponds to the shaded area.

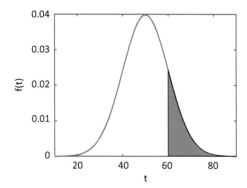

Figure 9.2: Density function (solid curve) and reliability function for x=60 (coloured area) of a normally distributed T with $\mu = 50$, $\sigma = 10$.

The empirical distribution function as non-parametric estimate of F can be considered. It is given by

$$F_{emp}(t) = \frac{Number\ of\ times\ smaller\ as\ or\ equal\ to\ t}{n} \tag{9.4}$$

The empirical reliability function is then obtained by

$$R_{emp}(t) = 1 - F_{emp}(t) \tag{9.5}$$

Table 9.1: Cancellation dates of annuity loans (in months from beginning).

i	1	2	3	4	5	6	7	8	9	10
t_i	80	12	62	15	70	62	67	70	20	45

Example:
The data from Table 9.1 leads to the empirical distribution function:

$F_{emp}(t) = 0$ for $t < 12$ and $F_{emp}(t) = 1$ for $t > 80$, respectively

$R_{emp}(t) = 1$ for $t < 12$ and $R_{emp}(t) = 0$ for $t > 80$.

The empirical functions are shown in Figure 9.3.
So far, only the lifetime of one object has been considered. From a practical point of view, it also makes sense to consider technical or even financial systems including several components with corresponding lifetimes. In the easiest case, we consider a redundant system, whose N components have the same lifetime distribution $F(t)$, and thus also the same reliability function $R(t)$. Let $FS(t)$ and $RS(t)$ be the distribution function and the reliability function of the system. If the systems work, if at least

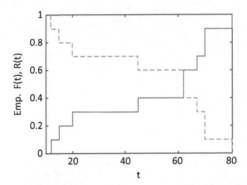

Figure 9.3: Empirical distribution (solid curve) and empirical reliability function (dashed curve) for the data from Table 9.1.

M<N components work, the system is redundant and *RS(t)* is defined by the binomial distribution:

$$R_S(t) = \sum_{k=0}^{N-M} \binom{N}{k}(1-R(t))^k R(t)^{N-k}$$

If there are N components with different reliability functions $R_1(t), \cdots, R_N(t)$ without redundancy, the reliability function of the system is given by $R_S(t) = \prod_{i=1}^{N} R_i(t)$.

In finance, redundant systems are given by web servers for online banking, file server for customer data storage and multiple ATMs.

9.3 Exponentially Distributed Lifetimes

The exponential distribution is defined for non-negative values. The distribution function is given by

$$F(t) = P(T \leq t) = 1 - e^{-\lambda t}, t \geq 0 \tag{9.6}$$

This leads to the reliability function

$$R(t) = e^{-\lambda t}, t \geq 0 \tag{9.7}$$

From its definition, the exponential distribution only depends on parameter λ. This parameter determines the mean and the variance:

$$E(T) = \frac{1}{\lambda}, \ Var(T) = \frac{1}{\lambda^2}$$

9.4 Weibull-Distributed Lifetimes

The Weibull distribution is a general distribution model in reliability analysis. Especially, there is a two-parameter and a three-parameter model. The two-parameter distribution function depends on the scale parameter a und the shape parameter b. For a Weibull-distributed T, i.e. $T \sim Weibull(a,b)$ with $a,b > 0$, the distribution function is defined by

$$F(t) = 1 - \exp\left(-\left(\frac{t}{a}\right)^b\right)$$

(9.8)

So, the reliability function equals

$$R(t) = \exp\left(-\left(\frac{t}{a}\right)^b\right)$$

(9.9)

The mean of T can be calculated with

$$E(T) = a\Gamma\left(1 + \frac{1}{b}\right)$$

where $\Gamma(x)$ is the Gamma function defined by

$$\Gamma(x) = \int_0^\infty t^{x-1} \cdot e^{-t} dt$$

The Gamma function is tabulated and can be calculated with mathematical and statistical software tools like Matlab and R. Differentiating (9.8) leads to the density function

$$f(t) = F'(t) = \frac{b}{a}\exp\left(-\left(\frac{t}{a}\right)^b\right) \cdot \left(\frac{t}{a}\right)^{b-1}$$

(9.10)

Figure 9.4 shows the density function of Weibull distributions with different shape parameters. For $b \leq 1$ the density function is monotonously decreasing. An increasing shape parameter leads to a density function similar to the density of the normal distribution (see the density in Figure 9.4 with $b=2$).

The three-parameter Weibull distribution depends on an additional t_0, sometimes referred to as the minimum lifespan.

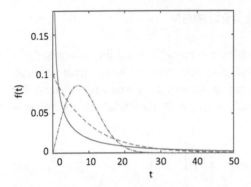

Figure 9.4: Density function of Weibull distributions with a=10 and b=0.5 (solid curve), b=1 (dashed curve) and b=2 (dot dashed curve).

The reliability function is given by

$$R(t) = \begin{cases} P(T>t) = \exp\left(-\left(\dfrac{t-t_0}{a-t_0}\right)^b\right), & t \geq t_0 \\ 1, & t < t_0 \end{cases} \tag{9.11}$$

By definition, the reliability functions equal 1 for $\leq t_0$. Therefore, t_0 can be understood as an amount of damage which is survived with certainty or probability 1.

The corresponding mean depends on the Gamma function:

$$E(T) = t_0 + (a - t_0)\Gamma\left(1 + \frac{1}{b}\right)$$

9.5 IDB Distributed Lifetimes

The IDB distribution is also known as Hjorth distribution as a tribute to J.S. Urban Hjorth (Hjorth, 1980). IDB stands for increasing, decreasing and bathtub. This is explained in Section 9.6.

The distribution function is given by

$$F(t) = 1 - \frac{\exp\left(-\dfrac{at^2}{2}\right)}{(1+bt)^{c/b}}, \quad t \geq 0 \tag{9.12}$$

Therefore, we obtain the corresponding reliability function

$$R(t) = \frac{\exp\left(-\dfrac{at^2}{2}\right)}{(1+bt)^{1+c/b}}$$

(9.13)

and the density function

$$f(t) = F'(t) = \frac{at(1+bt)+c}{(1+bt)^{1+c/b}} \exp\left(-\frac{at^2}{2}\right)$$

(9.14)

Figure 9.5 shows the density functions for different parameters. The mean and the variance have to be calculated numerically. Further useful distribution models can be found in (Wälder and Wälder, 2017).

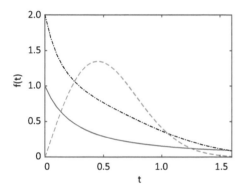

Figure 9.5: Density functions of IDB distributions with a=0, b=3, c=1 (solid curve), a=2, b=3, c=2 (dot dashed curve) and a=5, b=2, c=0 (dashed curve).

9.6 Considering the Conditional Risk

The reliability and unreliability functions introduced in Section 9.2 naturally model a risk aspect, but do not cover the complete type of failure. This should first be explained using an insurance example. The lifetime distribution of an insured person in this sense is important for calculating the premiums of a life or pension insurance. However, the lifetime distribution does not take into account the age of the policy-holder when the contract was concluded or the annual risk, which is, however, of crucial importance in the performance of annual premiums. The premium calculation is therefore based on a so-called mortality table. This contains probabilities q_x separately for men and women. q_x is the probability that a person who has reached the age of x will die in the following $(x+1)$ year. With $p_x = 1-q_x$ then the probability is given that this person will also survive the $(x+1)$ th year of life or accomplished. A mortality table valid for Germany can be found on the website of the Federal Statistical Office (Statistisches Bundesamt, 2018).

The generalisation of such an approach to other fields of engineering or finance is straightforward: The probability is considered that an object or unit that has survived a certain period will fail within the next period.

This conditional risk is described with the so-called hazard rate.

$$\lambda(t) = \frac{f(t)}{1 - F(t)} = \frac{f(t)}{R(t)} \tag{9.15}$$

Let T be the distribution of the considered lifetime. The hazard rate at t times multiplied by an infinitesimally small time period δt corresponds to the probability that the objects fails between t and δt. This leads to

$$\lambda(t) = \lim_{\delta t \to 0} \frac{P(T \le t + \delta t | T > t)}{\delta t} \tag{9.16}$$

In (9.15) $P(T \le t + \delta t | T > t)$ is a conditional probability. From (9.16)

$$P(T \le t + \delta t | T > t) = \frac{P(T \le t + \delta t \text{ and } T > t)}{P(T \le t)} = \frac{\int_t^{t+\delta t} f(x)dx}{P(T > t)} = \frac{F(t + \delta t) - F(t)}{R(t))} \tag{9.17}$$

is obtained easily. From calculus the definition of the first derivative is well known, i.e.:

$$F'(t) = \lim_{\delta t \to 0} \frac{F(t + \delta t) - F(t)}{\delta t} = f(t)$$

This leads to the definition (9.15).

The hazard rate determines the type of failure. A monotonously decreasing hazard rate models so called early failures. For example, this can be useful for technical devices whose operation requires experience and training, which are only acquired over time. Failures resulting from operating errors can then be reduced with increasing time.

Random failures are failures not depending on time t, i.e. $\lambda(t) = \lambda$ holds. Random failures often occur with electronic components. From a theoretical point of view, radioactive decay is subject to a constant failure rate. A monotonously increasing hazard rate leads to so called late failures. This is typically given if failures are caused by wear.

All three cases are shown in the so-called bathtub curve (see Figure 9.6). The bathtub curve can also describe the product life cycle: Operating errors cause failures of new products. After eliminating these errors, only random failures remain. With an increasing operating time, additional failures caused by wear occur.

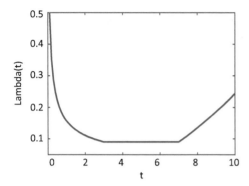

Figure 9.6: Bathtub curve for Weibull distributions with b=0.5, b=1 and b=3.

For the Weibull distribution, the hazard rate can be calculated easily. In the case of the two-parameter distribution:

$$\lambda(t) = \frac{b}{a}\left(\frac{t}{a}\right)^{b-1}$$

(9.18)

follows from (9.9) and (9.10). The hazard rate from (9.18) has an interesting property: For b=1, we obtain a hazard rate not depending on t. In the special case of b=1, the Weibull distribution reduces to an exponential distribution with constant hazard rate. For b<1, the hazard rate is monotonously decreasing and describes early failures. For b>1, the hazard rate increases. Therefore, late failures can be modelled. So, all types of failure can be modelled with corresponding Weibull distributions. But it is not possible to represent the curve, i.e. to model the life cycle, with one model with fixed parameters a and b.

For the sake of completeness, the hazard rate of a three-parameter Weibull distribution is given by

$$\lambda(t) = \begin{cases} \left(\dfrac{b}{a-t_0}\right)\left(\dfrac{t-t_0}{a-t_0}\right)^{b-1} & , t \geq t_0 \\ 0, t < t_0 \end{cases}$$

(9.19)

Consequently, no failures are available for $t<t_0$.

A more general approach is given by the IDB distribution, see Section 9.5. Equations (9.13) and (9.14) lead to the hazard rate

$$\lambda(t) = \frac{f(t)}{R(t)} = at + \frac{c}{1+bt}$$

(9.20)

For a=b=0, the hazard rate is constant. In this case the IDB distribution corresponds to an exponential distribution. For *a=0* and *c,b>0* a monotonously decreasing hazard rate is obtained. The most interesting case is given for

0<a<bc. Then the hazard rate corresponds to the bathtub curve, i.e. the hazard rate depends on *t*. Thus, the IDB distributions reflect the entire product life cycle (see Figure 9.7).

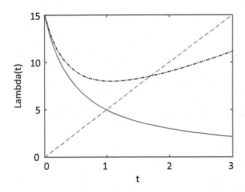

Figure 9.7: Hazard rates of IDB distributions with a=0, b=2, c=15 (solid curve), a=3, b=2, c=15 (dot dashed curve) and a=5, b=2, c=0 (dashed curve).

9.7 Model Fitting

If $t_1, \dots, t_n$ is a sample of observed lifetimes, the Maximum likelihood method can be applied to fit the corresponding model parameters. Let *F(t)* be a distribution function depending on parameters $\alpha_1, \dots, \alpha_m$ with density function *f(t)*. Estimates of the parameters are obtained by maximising the Likelihood function

$$L(\alpha_1, \dots, \alpha_m) = \prod_{i=1}^{n} f(t_i)$$

(9.21)

or by maximising the Loglikelihood function

$$logL(\alpha_1, \dots, \alpha_m) = \sum_{i=1}^{n} \log(f(t_i))$$

(9.22)

Usually, maximisation of (9.21) and (9.22) requires numerical methods. Well-suited is Nelder-Mead Simplex Method (Lagarias et al., 1998), realised in many software tools. From a practical point of view, using software tools like Matlab, R or JMP is recommendable. For numerical reasons, maximising the Loglikelihood function is more stable.

The Maximum likelihood method can be applied to fit parameters of different distribution models. Therefore, the problem arises of choosing the best model. Now, there are different methods to solve this problem.

As mentioned, it is useful to maximise the Loglikelihood function. Therefore, it is possible to choose the model with maximum Loglikelihood. Often software tools provide $-2*Loglikelihood$. In this case, the model with minimum value has to be chosen.

The choice based on maximising the Loglikelihood ignores that the Likelihood as well as the Loglikelihood increases with an increasing number of model parameters. The so-called Akaike information criterion (AIC) takes the number of model parameters into account by adding a penalty term depending on this number to $-2*Loglikelihood$ (see Akaike, 1974). The resulting value is even denoted by AIC. Further, it is possible to calculate the correlation between empirical quantiles and the quantiles determined by the fitted distribution. In this case, the correlation coefficient has to be maximised. Millar (2011) discusses the Maximum likelihood method in more detail.

Example: We use the data from Table 9.1. Fitting a two-parameter Weibull distribution leads to $a = 57, b = 2.2$.

In the case of fitting an exponential distribution we obtain $\lambda = 1/50$.

For this example, the Weibull distribution is more useful considering both criteria (see Table 9.2). Figure 9.8 shows the fitted Weibull distribution.

Table 9.2: Goodness of fit.

	Weibull distribution	Exponential distribution
AIC	97,97	100,86
−2*Loglikelihood	92,25	95,37

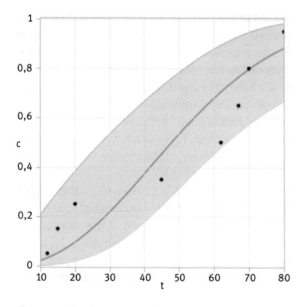

Figure 9.8: Fitted Weibull distribution.

So-called censored lifetimes are of great importance in reliability and survival analysis. A censored lifetime t refers to a lifetime, the corresponding object exceeds or survives. In this case, not a failure is observed but an exceeded lifetime. Therefore, we have two types of data: survival times and failure times. To avoid an underestimating of the mean lifetime, censored time has to be considered in fitting the parameters of the corresponding distribution. This can be done by generalising the Likelihood function: To consider a censored lifetime t_i in (9.21) and (9.22), $f(t_i)$ has to be replaced with $R(t_i)$.

9.8 Reliability Analysis with Respect to Reverse Stress Testing

Reliability analyses models' failures and describes the type of failure by analysing the corresponding lifetime distribution and the corresponding hazard rate. The behaviour of the hazard rate, especially the type of failure, can lead to the causes of failure. This retrograde view is typical for reverse stress testing. With respect to financial sciences, reverse stress tests require a firm to assess scenarios and circumstances that would make its business model unworkable, identifying potential business vulnerabilities. To apply models and methods of reliability analysis, corresponding lifetimes, however, have to be defined. Reverse stress testing is based on a failure – for example, the collapse of a bank caused by withdrawal of client deposits. In the context of reliability, the amounts of withdrawals can be interpreted as lifetimes in some broader sense. In reliability and survival analysis censored lifetimes are of great importance. A censored lifetime is a lifetime that will be survived. In contrast to a normal lifetime, a censored lifetime provides direct information regarding reliability. Especially, censored lifetimes have to be considered to avoid an underestimation of the mean lifetime.

In our case, censored withdrawals have to be considered, which do not destroy the business model but are needed to fit the distribution model correctly.

Example: Table 9.3 presents fictional data of client withdrawals in a meaningful unit which can cause a failure or collapse of a bank. In the context of this scenario, a withdrawal can be interpreted as an observed lifetime or as a censored lifetime in the case of surviving.

Fitting a Weibull distribution for the data from Table 9.3 leads to the parameters $a = 263$, $b = 7.1$. Figure 9.9 shows the corresponding distribution function. For $t=180$, we have $F(t)=0.065$ and $R(t)=0.935$ (see Figure 9.9). The mean of this distribution equals 246. So, on average, a withdrawal of 246 units causes the failure.

Figure 9.10 presents the corresponding, monotonously increasing hazard rate. Unsurprisingly, we are faced with late failures: Increasing withdrawals increases the risk for a failure caused by the next withdrawal of a monetary unit. Therefore, monitoring the withdrawals in combination with an analysis of the hazard rate can help to

Table 9.3: Withdrawals leading to a failure of the bank (censor=0) or not (censor=1).

Withdrawal	Censor
100	0
120	1
80	1
140	1
200	1
240	0
250	0
80	1
90	1
280	0
270	0
220	1
275	0
267	0

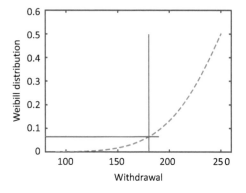

Figure 9.9: Weibull distribution for the withdrawals from Table 9.3.

develop a strategy to reduce the risk. Further, factors influencing the distribution and thus the hazard rate should be analysed.

In a financial sciences context, many lifetimes in the discussed sense are thinkable: the duration of low interest periods, amounts of damages caused by natural disasters, and so on. Considering several risks is possible by analysing the reliability of systems, see Section 9.2.

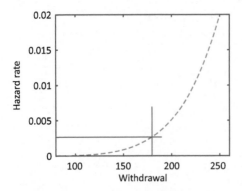

Figure 9.10: Hazard rate for a Weibull distribution with a=263 and b=7.1.

Many lifetimes expressing effects like loadings, amounts of damages or stress in the literal sense lead to increasing hazard rates and late failures like overload. So, the Weibull distribution with shape parameter *b>1* seems to be an obvious approach. But also, in classical reverse stress testing scenarios decreasing hazard rates are possible. Maybe, falling deposits lead to the failure of a bank. In this case the Weibull distribution with *b<1 can be applied.*

Therefore, the choice of the Weibull distribution is useful in many cases. Like the IDB distribution the Weibull distribution is sufficiently general, see Figure 9.4. But fitting the Weibull distribution is more stable than fitting the IDB distribution.

9.9 Summary

Reliability analysis as well as survival analysis were introduced to model lifetimes of technical components systems and organisms or creatures. Lifetime must be understood in a more general sense: loadings of materials until they break, mileage of engines, amount of damages leading to some kind of failure, stress, burden, and so on. The corresponding distribution of such generalised lifetimes and even the reliability function in connection with the hazard rate help to understand the behaviour of failure processes. Reverse stress testing starts in a very similar way, possibly with the failure of a bank. So, for both methods, the failure in whatever sense has to be modelled. Both reverse stress testing and reliability analysis start at the end point and work back to the input that leads to a specified outcome.

Therefore, we want to contribute to a further development of reverse stress testing considering methods from reliability analysis with this chapter. Analysing the hazard rate and thus the type of failures can especially help to understand causes of failure. For this, the Weibull distribution and the IDB distribution are useful to model all types of failure.

Bibliography

Akaike, H. (1974). Stochastic theory of minimal realization. *IEEE Transactions on Automatic Control* 19: 667–674.

Hjorth, U. (1980). A reliability distribution with increasing, decreasing, constant and bathtub-shaped failure rates. *Technometrics* 22: 99–107.

ISO 9000: 2015-09. (2015). Quality management systems – Fundamentals and vocabulary. https://www.iso.org/obp/ui/#iso:std:iso:9000:ed-4:v1:en

Lagarias, J. C., Reeds, J. A., Wright, M. H. and Wright, P. E. (1998). Convergence properties of the Nelder-Mead Simplex method in low dimensions. *SIAM Journal of Optimization* 9: 112–147.

Millar, R. B. (2011). *Maximum Likelihood Estimation and Inference: With Examples in R, SAS and ADMB*. John Wiley & Sons. New York.

Statistisches Bundesamt (2018). Sterbetafel 2016/18. https://www-genesis.destatis.de/genesis//online?operation=table&code=12621-0001&levelindex=0&levelid=1588349511902

Wälder, K., Wälder, O. (2017). *Methoden zur Risikomodellierung und des Risikomanagements*. Springer Vieweg. Wiesbaden.

Part III: **Qualitative Use Cases**

Michael Eichhorn, Philippe Mangold

10 Qualitative Reverse Stress Testing

A Process-Orientated Generic Approach

10.1 Introduction

Reverse stress testing (RST) is, in a narrow sense, defined as the analysis of scenarios that render the business model unviable (see Part I and chapter Lodha/Eichhorn in Part III of this book for wider definitions).[1]

A decade ago, few, if any, banks worked on RST. After the financial crisis, regulators and de-facto regulatory bodies introduced different requirements and recommendations for banks to perform RST. In 2013, in a survey of major international financial institutions, Ernst & Young noted that the importance of RST as a tool for risk measurement and risk management strongly increased. However, as discussed by Eichhorn/Romano in Part I of this book, there is still neither detailed regulatory guidance nor an industry standard or "best practice" on how to meet the expectations.

While both traditional stress testing and RST involve scenarios and scenario-related impacts, they differ in two key aspects. The first difference relates to the *direction*: in traditional stress tests, banks start with defining a (macro-financial) scenario and then assess its impact on their business, typically, in terms of earnings, capital and liquidity. RST starts with defining the outcome followed by reverse-engineering scenarios that, should they unfold, lead to the specified result. The second difference relates to the *severity* of the stress: RST can go further into the tail end of the probability distribution compared to other risk measures since RST scenarios can be designed to be so severe that they "break the bank".

The primary challenge in RST is usually not a lack of imagination of individual stakeholders within any bank. Often, it is rather the *process* to collect and aggregate the knowledge and potential contributions that are spread across the bank in a consistent and coherent manner.

Against this background, this chapter proposes a framework for RST that shall provide a generic approach to support deep and deliberate thinking around scenarios – most notably, low-probability high-severity scenarios. Since there is usually a plethora of scenarios that could lead to a specific outcome, we advocate beginning at a generic level, followed by deeper examination of specific scenarios.

---

[1] This chapter is an updated and extended version of an earlier contribution published in the *Journal of International Banking Law & Regulation* 31(4), pp. 237–40 (2016). We thank Sweet & Maxwell for the permission to reproduce.

https://doi.org/10.1515/9783110647907-010

Finally, if the likelihood of a given scenario is deemed unacceptably high, management actions to mitigate impacts should be developed in order to make the analysis meaningful in practice.

10.2 A Generic Framework for Reverse Stress Testing

The proposed process for collecting and aggregating the knowledge and potential contributions across the bank entails the following steps: 1. definition of points of failure, 2. vulnerability analysis and creation of a risk inventory, 3. generic storyboards, 4. scenario design and parametrisation, 5. plausibility checks and management actions, 6. monitoring and reporting. This should form the fundamental basis for RST discussions across the bank and involve the respective functional representatives. These steps are shown in Figure 10.1.

Figure 10.1: Six-step approach in sequential order as a generic approach to reverse stress testing.

The following sub-sections walk through the process. The chapter closes with a summary. It is complemented by appendices. The appendices offer various literature references and recommendations for the practical implementation. The references and recommendations are organised under the following questions:
- What can be learned from regulatory requirements?
- What can be learned from practitioners?
- What can be learned from past failures?
- What can be learned from recent research?
- What can be learned from preparatory work for (near) failures?

10.2.1 Step 1: Definition of Failure Points

The first step is the definition of so called "failure points", defined here as the points at which a bank's business model becomes unviable. In the following, we distinguish three perspectives: Firstly, a failure from an earnings perspective, secondly, from a capital perspective, and thirdly, from a liquidity perspective. While there may be interlinkages, it is important to consider those as separate perspectives.

Earnings failures involve sustained low or deteriorating pre-tax income (PTI) over a number of quarters or years for a cluster, business area or the bank. It could call into question whether a business should continue to operate from a commercial point of view. The earnings failure point could be reached well before a bank's capital is exhausted. For example, regulators have stressed that reputational risk may break a bank even if it has sufficient capital and liquidity (see appendices).

From a capital perspective, the bank may become insolvent. Prior to reaching insolvency, however, the capital figures may breach internal thresholds, which may therefore also be used as failure points in the context of RST. For example, capital losses that exceed the risk appetite may trigger actions to restore the capital base while a further decline in capital levels could trigger mandatory conversions of convertible instruments into equity or breach regulatory thresholds. Accordingly, the failure points could be linked to the recovery and resolution Plans (RRP); the linkage between RST and RRP is discussed further by Eichhorn/Romano in Part I and Dengler in Part V of this book. However, the business model can also become unviable without a reduced capital base. This may be the case if the capital requirements increase, e.g. due to a loss of an internal model waiver or new regulation that results in higher capital requirements. In this case, RST may be cross-linked to other plans – for example, trigger points of the Solvent Wind-Down Plan.

Thirdly, the bank may become illiquid. This may occur, for example, at the point when the High-Quality Liquid Asset (HQLA) buffer drops below or net outflows exceed a pre-defined level, again potentially linked to either Risk Appetite or Recovery triggers. Alternatively, liquidity failure points may be linked to a minimum day-count survival horizon.

10.2.2 Step 2: Vulnerability Analysis and Risk Inventory

The purpose of the vulnerability analysis is to identify the primary material risks to which the bank is exposed to through the business it conducts and the clients it serves. As demonstrated by the use cases in Part II and III of this book, there are multiple ways to perform a vulnerability analysis. It can be performed top-down or bottom-up and combine various qualitative or quantitative techniques.[2]

Whatever techniques are used, the output should be a comprehensive list of vulnerabilities that are material to the bank under consideration. This list should feed into a bank-wide vulnerabilities inventory. Ideally, specific risk inventories exist for different business units or risk types, which are then aggregated into a bank-wide risk inventory maintained by an enterprise-wide risk function.

---

[2] Techniques may range from qualitative expert interviews to quantitative risk factor modelling using VaR type (Monte Carlo) simulations, maximum loss analytics, error trees and impact chains with a critical path. Likewise, a bank may think about an executive offsite workshop that uses strategic management tools such as SWOT analysis, Porter's 5 Forces, PESTEL analysis, scenario planning, possibly supported by creativity techniques such as the Delphi-Method.

In the example of a Private Banking & Wealth Management business unit, we used qualitative expert interviews. With the support of two members of senior management, 15 business and risk executives were asked in a series of bilateral semi-structured interviews what could cause the business model to become unviable from their perspective.

In the next step, we clustered the responses by risk type and established a two-dimensional heat map. Depending on the frequency with which the different risk types were mentioned during the interviews and the perceived severity of the events, they were assigned to the red, amber or green zone of the heat map.

Prior to clustering the vulnerabilities by risk type and assigning each risk type to a position on the heat map, we analysed the interview responses in detail.[3] For example, it became clear that the framework needed to differentiate between pure reputational risk incidents and reputational risk incidents as a domino effect of operational or conduct risk incidents. Particularly, most of the executives emphasised this domino effect. Another result of the analysis was that it is important to consider certain types of operational risk giving rise to conduct risk. We also noted other sequential patterns – i.e. some risks were repeatedly seen as a consequence of the materialisation of other risks.

Depending on the position of each risk type on the heat map, we distinguished between "key vulnerabilities" and "other vulnerabilities" of the business model. Key vulnerabilities were mentioned most frequently and were estimated to be very severe during the interviews. Other vulnerabilities were risks that were mentioned not as frequently and could be relevant in combination with key vulnerabilities. Therefore, they were kept in the inventory.

We also examined patterns. For example, the vulnerability analysis may suggest that most key risks in the red zone of the heat map are idiosyncratic in nature whereas risks in the other zones of the heat map are more systemic in nature or vice versa.

Another interesting finding resulted from the question over which time horizon the business model becomes unviable. We distinguished between incidents where the point of non-viability is reached over a period of days or months ("a sudden fatal punch") and incidents where non-viability is reached over a period of years ("a slow bleeding out").

The output of Step 2 was not simply a list of relevant incidents but a risk inventory and a corresponding classification. This is displayed in Figure 10.2, where the rows differentiate the various time horizons over which the failure point is being reached and the columns display the different dimensions of failure. As shown, we added a

---

3 In parallel, we reviewed historical cases of banks that failed (e.g. Northern Rock and different US banks) and incidents that recently brought financial companies close to failure (e.g. "balance sheet holes" identified by UK financial firms). We also conducted an extensive literature review. For example, triggered by the interviews, they reviewed empirical studies on the reputational damage caused by certain types of operational incidents.

	Liquidity failure	Capital failure	Capital induced liquidity failure	Earnings failure
Instantaneous	Case 1a Severe reputational risk event results in liquidity failure (impact on capital is minor)	Case 2a Sudden exhaustion of capital basis	Case 3a Sudden deterioration of capital base raises substantial doubt about future viability of business, leading to liquidity failure	Case 4a Sudden changes resulting in negative PTI impact for the foreseeable future making business model unviable
Bleeding out	Case 1b Series of reputational risk events result in liquidity failure (impact on capital is minor)	Case 2b Gradual exhaustion of capital basis, emergency liquidity facility still available	Case 3b Continued deterioration of capital base raises substantial doubt about future viability of business, leading to liquidity failure	Case 4b Continued changes resulting in negative PTI impact making business model unviable

Time horizon of scenario

Figure 10.2: Classification of scenarios by reason of failure and time horizon.

fourth dimension called "capital-induced liquidity failure" which will be explained later. This classification allows achieving some degree of completeness, given the wide range of possible scenarios. It will also be useful for subsequent steps where storyboards need to be identified, as discussed in Step 3.

10.2.3 Step 3: Generic Storyboards

The storyboard encompasses the development of scenario narratives (from status quo to the point where the business model becomes unviable). One obvious and to some extent trivial way is to derive scenarios by scaling single or multiple risk factors to extreme (and probably absurd) levels, which generally seems overly simplistic in that it is restricted to a sensitivity analysis.[4]

Regulatory requirements and recommendations provide high-level guidance on storyboards. Among others, regulators usually expect banks to review a range of scenarios, including the failure of major counterparties and coinciding idiosyncratic and macro-financial events (see appendices).

We also spoke to different consultancies. They recommended developing 6 to 12 well-defined storyboards. Even this number may prove challenging in practice, while potentially still being insufficient. As discussed at the outset, there may be hundreds or thousands of relevant scenarios for each business model. Considering all of them is likely to prove impractical and difficult to handle computationally.

Therefore, the framework proposes to obtain a big-picture perspective first (and not to get lost in detail by many possible storyboards). By drawing from the classification displayed in Figure 10.2, we differentiate eight groups of storyboards. Having specified, say, one storyboard for each group results in a manageable number of scenarios, while providing some comfort around the degree of completeness. The objective of the next step is to develop scenarios for each of the eight case groups. However, instead of jumping straight to one specific scenario and calibrating the full set of variables, we propose to start with the development of so-called "generic scenario storyboards".

Figure 10.3 illustrates an example for a generic storyboard. The timeline in the middle divides the graph into upper and lower parts. The length of the arrow illustrates the time horizon as per the vulnerability analysis. The upper part shows generic event types, e.g. a macro-economic crisis and an idiosyncratic operational risk event. The lower part of the graph shows how the capital and liquidity resources develop over time and it uses red, amber and green traffic light zones. The solid black lines

---

4 Even if a single risk factor is identified to have a sufficiently high impact to break the bank by itself, it then should become a scenario in its own right. However, it would still need to be complemented by multifactor cross risk scenarios.

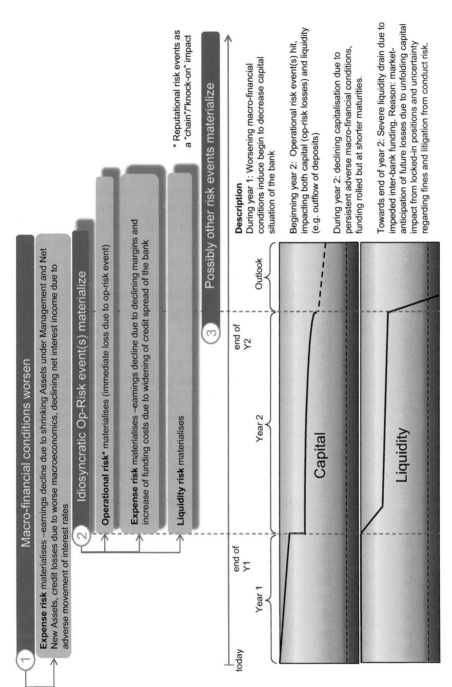

Figure 10.3: Illustrative example of a generic storyboard.

illustrate how the capital and liquidity resources are projected to behave over time while the storyboard specified in the upper part of the graph unfolds. In Figure 10.3, we illustrate the generic storyboard for case group 3b from Figure 10.2, which is a capital-induced liquidity failure unfolding over time – i.e. a "bleeding out" type of scenario.

In this example, the storyboard is as follows: In year 1, the worsening macro-economic conditions negatively affect the capital situation of the bank. However, the capital resource is still in "green territory". As can be inferred from the box at the bottom, there is no significant impact on the HQLA buffer during year 1. At the beginning of year 2, an idiosyncratic operational risk event materialises in a loss that induces a drop in the capital buffer. With a time-lag, this also results in a reduction of the liquidity buffer, which can be seen in the bottom box showing the liquidity perspective. During year 2, the persistent adverse macro-economic conditions cause a further gradual decline in capital, leading to both capital and liquidity ending up in the amber zone at the end of year 2. At this point, however, the market starts to anticipate the materialisation of future losses, which would lead to insolvency. This may be associated with other risk events materialising (e.g. anticipation of further operational risk incidents, which may also give rise to conduct and reputational risks) or with losses from locked-in positions that cannot be unwound. This anticipation of a future deterioration of capital is illustrated by the dotted line in the capital box. However, before this impact can materialise, the bank suffers a severe liquidity drain and hits a liquidity failure point. The reason is that certain counterparties are, within this scenario, not willing to roll existing or provide new funding because of the depressed capitalisation associated with the anticipated future losses. Therefore, this is what we label a "capital-induced liquidity failure".

10.2.4 Step 4: Scenario Design and Parametrisation

To give more meaning and content to the storyboards[5] and their building blocks, the next step in the framework is to specify the building blocks of the scenario – i.e. to provide specific calibration of the scenario. This step will provide further insight into the range of risk factors contributing to the scenario, their financial impacts, and how they would change under stress. The calibration may, but is not required to, rely on guidance derived from standard scenario analysis, such as historically observed or regulatory-imposed. This is followed by the next step: plausibility checks and management actions.[6]

---

5 Generic storyboards should support and not restrict discussions. Scenarios developed outside the scope of the generic storyboards are equally valid, and should trigger the same monitoring and escalation action discussed later.

6 Steps 5 and 6 of the proposed framework are based on the scenario planning work by Schoemaker.

10.2.5 Step 5: Plausibility Checks and Management Actions

With regard to plausibility checks, the calibration should be carefully sense-checked and, where possible, back-tested against existing stress events. If the likelihood of an RST scenario, and hence the risk of business failure, is deemed to be unacceptably high, the bank must take mitigating actions. In fact, without deriving tangible action, RST may be perceived as a "purely academic exercise" and lack credibility with stakeholders, including regulators.

The open-ended nature of RST means that appropriate mitigating management actions should depend very much on the type of the scenario identified and its constituent material risk-drivers. The proposed framework differentiates between actions that address the cause of risks, and actions that primarily address the effect of a risk materialisation.

In our view, banks should think broadly and deeply at this stage. For example, instead of just asking whether the bank should restructure the business, it may also consider the following questions:

- Can decisions be postponed until a point in time where a major uncertainty will be resolved (e.g. the outcome of a pending regulation or litigation)?
- Can tests be created to probe and reduce uncertainties surrounding decisions?
- Can the bank create real options that give the right but not the obligation to take certain actions?

With regard to the effects of risks that are assumed to materialise, the bank may consider changes to their capital planning, liquidity planning, contingency planning and living will. Furthermore, management should use the knowledge gained by RST to improve the existing risk management. For example, a bank may decide to review netting agreements with counterparties or initiate systems and process enhancements to reduce identified operational risks.

Management actions should consider the likelihood. Immediate mitigating actions should be taken for scenarios close to materialisation. Given that RST in a narrow sense focuses on "very severe but plausible" scenarios, it would be very rare for a scenario to appear in this high likelihood category. Lower likelihood scenarios may not be escalated but should be monitored so that any change in scenario impact or likelihood is captured.

On the identification of a new scenario, the first action should be to check whether the current risk management framework provides sufficient coverage. Then a decision should be made on whether the scenario should be part of the ongoing monitoring and reporting, which represents the final step in the framework.

10.2.6 Step 6: Monitoring and Reporting

RST scenarios and vulnerabilities should be monitored regularly to trigger management discussions and actions. Over time, users will observe changes of likelihood levels. If, for a given RST scenario, overall scenario likelihood levels increase above a pre-defined threshold, managers should propose formal mitigating actions and escalate to the relevant governance body.

Scenario monitoring may be conducted primarily through indicators linked to their constituent risk factors. If a risk is particularly unquantifiable or hard to monitor empirically, a specific risk management function may be required to assess its status (e.g. reputational risk). Ideally, the bank should establish dashboards and combine them with top-down judgement and qualitative reports (e.g. from functional area heads) to monitor whether the real world is moving away from or towards a generated scenario.

Besides scenarios, the bank should also directly monitor the vulnerabilities identified in Step 2. For example, the Operational Risk function should constantly monitor their top ten operational risks.

Finally, the overall RST owner, usually a working group or a committee, should be responsible for consolidating the RST results for presentation to the governing bodies. Reports should be produced at least annually to achieve awareness of the gained insight from both the findings as well as from running the process itself.

10.3 Summary

Reverse stress testing can be a powerful tool to improve our understanding of exposures of the bank. As the starting point is the result rather than the scenario, it averts the danger of scenario creep.[7] In particular, it can help to identify so-called hidden risks that are not considered when running traditional stress tests. Furthermore, it can facilitate a better understanding of the dynamic interplay of risks over time.

From our experience, we believe that when it comes to RST, the *process* is actually more important than the exact figures or detailed scenarios that are being derived. The process should have led senior executives and senior risk managers through the relevant thought process and thereby have spread risk awareness across the organisation.

---

7 Analysing scenarios that are not bound by historic precedence is a good complement to stress testing that is often relying implicitly or explicitly on historically observed scenarios.

The proposed framework provides a structured process and facilitates discussions on a deeper level. The generic set up means that the framework introduced here can be stable over time while its content is continually evolving. For example, banks may accommodate new vulnerabilities and different scenarios with the potential to break the bank. As Lodha/Eichhorn demonstrate in Part III of this book, the framework can also be used for less severe configuration sets (Mild RST).

Nevertheless, we appreciate that there is no "one size fits all" framework. Like other risk management tools, banks should modify and extend the framework to suit their specific needs. For example, the proportionality argument seems also relevant in the context of RST. "For smaller, simpler firms, reverse stress-testing may primarily be an exercise in senior management judgement focused on scenario selection. For very small firms, the submission may be a short written explanation of these factors, which would simply need to be periodically refreshed. It does not necessarily involve detailed modelling. For larger, more complex firms, a more structured and comprehensive approach to reverse stress-testing is expected" (Katalysys Ltd, n.d.).

We believe that banks need to be much more creative in the way they use RST to evaluate the strengths and deficiencies of business models. The proposed generic framework may serve as a starting point.

Appendix 10.1: What can be learned from regulatory requirements?

In Chapter 3 of this book, Eichhorn/Romano summarise the development of the regulatory guidance, identify development lines and reference publications which answer frequently asked questions. The following Appendix 10.1 complements Chapter 3.

Table 10.1 maps regulatory guidance to each step of the proposed six-step approach – in particular, those requirements issued by the Basel Committee on Banking Supervision (BCBS), European Banking Authority (EBA), Financial Conduct Authority (FCA), Federal Reserve (FED) and Islamic Financial Services Board (IFSB).

Table 10.1: Regulatory guidance.

Overall framework		
EBA	Para 84 p. 30	Institutions should perform adequate reverse stress tests as part of the stress testing programme, sharing the same governance, an effective infrastructure and quality standards, and to complement other types of stress testing, taking into account the nature, size, scale and complexity of their business activities and risks. Small and less complex institutions may focus more on the qualitative aspects of reverse stress testing while more sophisticated reverse stress testing techniques are required of larger or more complex institutions. The reverse stress testing should be clearly defined in terms of responsibilities and resources allocated and should be supported by an infrastructure that is suitable and flexible and by written policies and procedures. Reverse stress testing should be carried out regularly by all types of institutions and at the same level of application as ICAAP and ILAAP (e.g. institution-wide and covering all relevant risk types).
FCA	SYSC 20.2.2	The reverse stress test must be conducted on a solo basis as well as on a consolidated basis in relation to the UK consolidation group or the non-EEA sub-group.
FCA	SYSC 20.2.5G	Reverse stress testing should be appropriate to the nature, size and complexity of the firm's business and of the risks it bears.
FCA	SYSC 20.2.7 (1)	The appropriate regulator may request a firm to submit the design and results of its reverse stress tests and any subsequent updates as part of its risk assessment.
Failure points		
BCBS	p.14	Reverse stress tests start from a known stress test outcome (such as breaching regulatory capital ratios, illiquidity or insolvency) and then asking what events could lead to such an outcome for the bank.

Table 10.1 (continued)

FCA	SYSC 20.2.1	A firm must reverse stress test its business plan; that is, it must carry out stress tests and scenario analyses that test its business plan to failure.
FCA	SYSC 20.2.4 (1)	Business plan failure in the context of reverse stress testing should be understood as the point at which the market loses confidence in a firm and this results in the firm no longer being able to carry out its business activities. Examples of this would be the point at which all or a substantial portion of the firm's counterparties are unwilling to continue transacting with it or seek to terminate their contracts, or the point at which the firm's existing shareholders are unwilling to provide new capital. Such a point may be reached well before the firm's financial resources are exhausted.
FCA	SYSC 20.2.4 (2)	The appropriate regulator may request a firm to quantify the level of financial resources which, in the firm's view, would place it in a situation of business failure should the identified adverse circumstances crystallise.
FCA	SYSC 20.2.4 (3)	In carrying out the stress tests and scenario analyses required by SYSC 20.2.1 R, a firm should at least take into account each of the sources of risk identified in accordance with GENPRU 1.2.30R (2).
FCA	SYSC 20.2.5 (3)	The appropriate regulator recognises that not every business failure is driven by lack of financial resources and will take this into account when reviewing a firm's reverse stress test design and results.
IFSB-13	Section 3.4.2 Para 126	Institutions offering Islamic financial services (IIFS) should determine what scenarios could challenge their viability and thereby uncover hidden risks and interactions among risks (i.e. developing reverse stress testing). Reverse stress testing starts from a known stress test outcome (such as breaching regulatory capital ratios, or a liquidity crisis) and then asking what events could lead to such an outcome for the IIFS.
IFSB TN-2	Para 49 p. 24	This is a method under which the IIFS assumes a specific adverse outcome, such as suffering losses to cause a breach in regulatory capital ratios, and then deduces the types of events that could lead to such an outcome.
Vulnerabilities		
BCBS	p. 15	A good reverse stress test also includes enough diagnostic support to investigate the reasons for potential failure.
CRR	p. 219, article 368, para 1(g)	This process shall particularly address illiquidity of markets in stressed market conditions, concentration risk, one-way markets, event and jump-to-default risks, non-linearity of products, deep out-of-the-money positions, positions subject to the gapping of prices and other risks that may not be captured appropriately in the internal models.

Table 10.1 (continued)

EBA	Para 87 p. 31	Institutions should use reverse stress testing as a regular risk management tool in order to improve their awareness of current and potential vulnerabilities, providing added value to institutions' risk management.
EBA	Para 91 p. 31	Institutions with particular business models, e.g. investment firms, should use reverse stress testing to explore their vulnerabilities to extreme events, in particular where their risks are not sufficiently captured by more traditional (e.g. solvency and liquidity) stress scenarios based on macroeconomic shocks.
EBA	Para 92 p. 32	Institutions using internal models for credit risk, counterparty credit risk and market risk … should endeavour to identify severe, but plausible, scenarios that could result in significant adverse outcomes and potentially challenge an institution's overall viability. Institutions should see these reverse stress tests as an essential complement to their internal models for calculating capital requirements and as a regular risk management tool for revealing the possible inadequacies of these internal models. In severe stress scenarios, even though this should not necessarily be taken as an indication that the modelling of the inputs into the IRB formula are inadequate, model risk will increase and may lead to a breakdown in the model's predictability.
FCA	SYSC 20.2.4	In carrying out the stress tests and scenario analyses, a firm should at least take into account each of the sources of risk.
FCA	SYSC 20.2.6	In carrying out its reverse stress testing, a firm should consider scenarios in which the failure of one or more of its major counterparties or a significant market disruption arising from the failure of a major market participant, whether or not combined, would cause the firm's business to fail.
IFSB 13	Section 3.4.2 Para 128	Areas that may benefit from the use of reverse stress testing are business lines where traditional risk management models indicate an exceptionally good risk/return trade-off; new products and new markets which have not experienced severe strains; and exposures where there are no liquid two-way markets.
Storyboards		
BCBS	p. 14	Considered events could include not only events that inflict large losses but which subsequently cause damage to the bank's reputation

Table 10.1 (continued)

BCBS	p. 15	Reverse stress testing [focus should be] business lines where traditional risk management models indicate an exceptionally good risk/return trade-off; new products and new markets which have not experienced severe strains; and exposures where there are no liquid two-way markets
EBA	Para 86 p. 30	In carrying out their reverse stress tests, institutions should also consider whether failure of one or more of their major counterparties or a significant market disruption arising from the failure of a major market participant (in a separate or combined manner) would cause the pre-defined outcome.
EBA	Para 89 p. 31	Institutions should use reverse stress testing in planning and decision-making and to challenge their business models and strategies in order to identify and analyse what could possibly cause their business models to become unviable, such as the assessment of both the ability to generate returns over the following months and the sustainability of the strategy to generate returns over a longer period based on strategic plans and financial forecasts.
EBA	Para 96 p.33	Institutions should use reverse stress testing as a tool to gather insights into scenarios that involve combinations of solvency and liquidity stresses, where traditional modelling may fail to capture complex aspects from real situations. Institutions should use reverse stress testing to challenge their capital plans and liquidity plans. Where appropriate, institutions should identify and analyse situations that could aggravate a liquidity stress event and transform it into a solvency stress event, and vice versa, and eventually to a business failure. Institutions should endeavour to apply reverse stress testing in an integrated manner for risks to capital or liquidity with a view to improving the understanding and the management of related risks in extreme situations.
FCA	SYSC 20.2.1 (1)	The firm must identify a range of adverse circumstances which would cause its business plan to become unviable and assess the likelihood that such events could crystallise.
FED SR 12-7	Appendix p. 12	Reverse stress testing is a tool that allows a banking organisation to assume a known adverse outcome, such as suffering a credit loss that breaches regulatory capital ratios or suffering severe liquidity constraints that render it unable to meet its obligations, and then deduce the types of events that could lead to such an outcome. This type of stress testing may help a banking organisation to consider scenarios beyond its normal business expectations and see the impact of severe systemic effects on the banking organisation.

Table 10.1 (continued)

FED SR 12-7	Appendix p. 12	Given the numerous potential threats to a banking organisation's viability, the organisation should ensure that it focuses first on those scenarios that have the largest firm-wide impact, such as insolvency or illiquidity, but also on those that seem most imminent given the current environment. Focusing on the most prominent vulnerabilities helps a banking organisation prioritise its choice of scenarios for reverse stress testing. However, a banking organisation should also consider a wider range of possible scenarios that could jeopardise the viability of the banking organisation, exploring what could represent potential blind spots.
FED SR 12-7	Appendix p. 12	This type of stress testing also helps a banking organisation evaluate the combined effect of several types of extreme events and circumstances that might threaten the survival of the banking organisation, even if in isolation each of the effects might be manageable. For instance, reverse stress testing may help a banking organisation recognise that a certain level of unemployment would have a severe impact on credit losses, that a market disturbance could create additional losses and result in rising funding costs, and that a firm-specific case of fraud would cause even further losses and reputational impact that could threaten a banking organisation's viability. In some cases, reverse stress tests could reveal to a banking organisation that "breaking the bank" is not as remote an outcome as originally thought.
IFSB-13	Section 3.4.2 Para 128	A reverse stress test induces an IIFS to consider scenarios beyond its normal business settings and highlights potential events with contagion and systemic implications.
IFSB TN-2	Para 75 p. 21	At times, reverse stress tests may also be conducted [by Regulatory and supervisory authorities (RSA)] that aim to identify the extreme shock scenarios that have the potential to cause a financial system failure in the concerned jurisdiction.
Calibration		
CRR	p. 219, article 368, para 1(g)	The shocks applied shall reflect the nature of the portfolios and the time it could take to hedge out or manage risks under severe market conditions
EBA	Para 85 p. 30	Reverse stress testing should be useful for assessing the severity of scenarios for ICAAP and ILAAP stress tests. The severity of reverse stress testing scenarios can also be assessed by comparing it to, inter alia, historical or other supervisory and publicly available scenarios.
EBA	Para 87 p. 31	The principle of proportionality applies to all aspects of the use of reverse stress testing. Institutions should also consider that the pre-defined outcome of reverse stress testing can be produced by circumstances other than the circumstance analysed in the stress test.

Table 10.1 (continued)

EBA	Para 94 p. 32	Institutions should perform quantitative and more sophisticated analyses, taking into account the institution's size as well as the nature, scale, complexity and riskiness of its business activities, in setting out specific loss levels or other negative impacts on its capital, liquidity (e.g. the access to funding, in particular to increases in funding costs) or overall financial position. Institutions should work backwards in a quantitative manner to identify the risk factors, and the required amplitude of changes, that could cause such a loss or negative impact (e.g. defining the appropriate loss level or some other measure of interest on the balance sheet of the financial institution such as capital ratios or funding resources). Institutions should understand and document in detail the drivers of risk (e.g. outputting the exact factor draws that had the most impact on the portfolio tail region), the key business lines and a clear and consistent narrative around weaknesses and the corresponding scenarios (e.g. about the underlying assumptions and sensitivity of the results to those assumptions over time) that cause the pre-defined outcomes and the events chain and the likely flow through (e.g. the most important factors may be mapped to macroeconomic variables according to the combinations for a given target loss/capital in a portfolio), identifying hidden vulnerabilities (e.g. hidden correlations and concentrations) and overlapping effects.
EBA	Para 95 p. 32/33	Institutions should, where appropriate, use sensitivity analyses as a starting point for reverse stress testing, e.g. shifting one or more relevant parameters to some extreme to reach pre-defined outcomes. An institution should consider various reverse sensitivity analyses for credit risk (e.g. how many large customers would have to go into default before the loss absorbing capital is lost), market risk, liquidity risk (e.g. stress on deposits in the retail sector and circumstances that would empty the institution's liquidity reserves) and operational risk, among other risks, and a combination analysis where all risks are covered simultaneously. However, an institution should not primarily use a sensitivity analysis and simple metrics to identify the scenario relevant for the reverse stress test. The qualitative analysis should lead to the identification of the relevant scenario, combining expert judgement from different business areas, as thinking might be the most effective way to prevent a business model failure. A joint stressing of all relevant risk parameters using statistical aspects (e.g. volatility of risk factors consistent with historical observations supplemented with hypothetical but plausible assumptions) should be developed. The plausibility of the parameter shifts required to reach the pre-defined outcome gives a first idea about possible vulnerabilities in the institution. To assess the plausibility, historical (multivariate) probability distributions – adjusted, where deemed necessary, according to expert judgements – should, inter alia, be applied. Qualitative analyses and assessments, combining expert judgements from different business areas, should guide the identification of relevant scenarios.

Table 10.1 (continued)

Management actions		
EBA	Para 90 p. 31	Where reverse stress testing reveals that an institution's risk of business model failure is unacceptably high and inconsistent with its risk appetite, the institution should plan measures to prevent or mitigate such risk, taking into account the time that the institution should have to react to these events and implement those measures. As part of these measures, the institution should consider if changes to its business model are required. These measures derived from reverse stress testing, including any changes to the institution's business plan, should be documented in detail in the institution's ICAAP documentation.
FED SR 12-7	Appendix p. 12	It also allows a banking organisation to challenge common assumptions about its performance and expected mitigation strategies.
FED SR 12-7	Appendix p. 12	Reverse stress testing can highlight previously unacknowledged sources of risk that could be mitigated through enhanced risk management.
FCA	SYSC 20.2.1 (2)	Where those tests reveal a risk of business failure that is unacceptably high when considered against the firm's risk appetite or tolerance, adopt effective arrangements, processes, systems or other measures to prevent or mitigate that risk.
FCA	SYSC 20.2.5	Where reverse stress testing reveals that a firm's risk of business failure is unacceptably high, the firm should devise realistic measures to prevent or mitigate the risk of business failure, taking into account the time that the firm would have to react to these events and implement those measures. As part of these measures, a firm should consider if changes to its business plan are appropriate. These measures, including any changes to the firm's business plan, should be documented.
FCA	SYSC 20.2.7 (2)	In the light of the results of a firm's reverse stress tests, the appropriate regulator may require the firm to implement specific measures to prevent or mitigate the risk of business failure where that risk is not sufficiently mitigated by the measures adopted by the firm in accordance with SYSC 20.2.1 R, and the firm's potential failure poses an unacceptable risk to the appropriate regulator's statutory objectives.
IFSB-13	Section 3.4.2 Para 127	Financial institutions (including IIFS) need to examine high-impact "tail" events and to assess the actions required to deal with them … . Though reverse stress testing is a useful tool in risk management, IIFS should note that reverse stress testing is not expected to result in capital planning and capital add-ons. Instead, its use as a risk management tool is in identifying scenarios, and the underlying dynamism of risk drivers in those scenarios, that could cause an IIFS's business model to fail. This analysis will be useful in assessing assumptions made about the business model, business strategy and the capital plan.

Table 10.1 (continued)

IFSB TN-2	Para 213 p. 62	The results of liquidity tests based on the top-down approach provide information for RSAs in these areas: ... They show the counterbalancing ability of IIFS (and their specific limits in the case of reverse stress tests) to remain liquid.
Governance		
BCBS	p. 14	Exercise requiring involvement of senior management and all material risk areas across the firm.
BCBS IFSB	p. 14 Section 3.4.2 Para 128	Reverse stress testing has important quantitative and qualitative uses, such as informing senior management's assessment of vulnerabilities.
CRR	p. 219, article 368, para 1(g)	The institution shall frequently conduct a rigorous programme of stress testing, including reverse stress tests, which encompasses any internal model used for purposes of this Chapter and the results of these stress tests shall be reviewed by senior management and reflected in the policies and limits it sets
EBA	Para 88 p. 31	As part of their business planning and risk management, institutions should use reverse stress testing to understand the viability and sustainability of their business models and strategies, as well as to identify circumstances where they might be failing or likely to fail ... It is important that institutions identify indicators that provide alerts when a scenario turns into reality.
EBA	Para 89 p. 31	The engagement of the management body and senior management throughout the [reverse stress testing] process is expected.
FCA	SYSC 20.2.3	The design and results of a firm's reverse stress test must be documented and reviewed and approved at least annually by the firm's senior management or governing body.
FCA	SYSC 20.2.3	A firm must update its reverse stress test more frequently if it is appropriate to do so in the light of substantial changes in the market or in macroeconomic conditions.
FCA	SYSC 20.2.5	These measures should be documented as part of the results document.

Appendix 10.2: What can be learned from practitioners?

Practitioners frequently offer valuable help on the visualisation and aggregation of information. In this chapter, we used different techniques (heatmaps, generic storyboards, etc.). Table 10.2 maps further observed practices to the steps of the proposed RST approach.

Table 10.2: Observed industry practices.

Step	Observed practice
Failure points	– Use of different levels of severity, e g distinction between significant adverse outcome and business model failure
Vulnerability Analysis	– Top down analysis of specific vulnerabilities (e.g. risk of sudden earnings drops by analysing how much of 100 units of profit is generated on day 1 and how much is accrued over multiple years) – Analysis of vulnerabilities gross and net/before and after hedges to understand where hedges (over/under) compensate or may not be rolled in stress – Top down development of macro-economic scenario and bottom up gathering of vulnerabilities by risk function – Bottom up gathering of vulnerabilities and risk inventory generation through gathering of vulnerabilities based on standardised and granular risk taxonomy – Bottom up gathering of vulnerabilities includes request for top vulnerabilities ranking – Bottom up gathering of vulnerabilities with two-dimensional impact-likelihood matrix. Based on thresholds vulnerabilities are mapped to one of twelve combination fields (e.g. minor/moderate/significant /major financial or non-financial impact and probable, possible, remote likelihood) with visualisation of loss potential through size of dots – Aggregation and visualisation of vulnerabilities with the help of a dartboard like risk radar with distinction of Group/Division) in the top half and external/internal in the bottom half of the radar diagram
Storyboards and scenario design	– Compilation of risk inventory/vulnerability list followed by inter-risk assessment to derive storyboards (e.g. elimination of mutually exclusive events, identification of correlated events) – Vulnerabilities mapped to main macro-economic scenarios – Vulnerabilities ranked and reported as percentage of CET1 for capital failures and percentage of HQLA buffer for liquidity failure (allowing report reader to identify which combinations would breach the failure points) – Storyboard presented as batch of events with impact layers – Test of vulnerability groupings against failure points (e.g. design starts with systemic scenario and then adds idiosyncratic events to push through the failure threshold)
Plausibility check and Management Actions	– "Backtesting" of scenarios and risk factor calibrations against traditional stress tests – Comparison of identified scenarios and proposed management actions with RRP
Monitoring and reporting	– Scenario narrative and aggregation of potential impacts compared to RST failure points, Risk Appetite, limit calibrations, ICAAP/ILAAP and Pillar 2 scenarios (in the same report) – RACI matrix defines in detail RST roles and responsibilities of all stakeholders

Practitioners also offer hands-on experiences on the do's and don'ts – a selection of these "lessons learned" are shown in Table 10.3.

Table 10.3: Lessons learned – A practitioner's view.

Step	Theme	Practical take-away and example
Definition of points of failure	It may be challenging to identify scenarios that reach failure thresholds	Explain ex ante that capital and liquidity failures often require large exogenous shocks and challenging assumptions (or use less severe failure points). Example: Every position in the bank is within the defined risk limits. These limits are derived from the overall capital and liquidity buffers, which are already calibrated to cover extreme losses.
Vulnerability analysis	Positions which provide large gains	Challenge positions that provide large gains to stress scenarios. Investigate the assumptions that give rise to those gains. Example: An RST working group asked if these positions should be considered to design shocks and pathways that push through the failure points.
Vulnerability analysis	Structural hedges of tail risks	Challenge the reliability of structural hedges for the overall portfolio. Example: An RST working group examined the behaviour of structural hedges in a suite of stress scenarios. The group explored the consequences of the failure of those structural hedges, discussed any amplification mechanisms for systemic risks and possible management actions.
Vulnerability analysis	Second order losses	Consider losses even if the bank may not be legally liable. Example: A bank's special purpose vehicles (SPVs) are off-balance sheet and bankruptcy remote. Failure of these SPVs should normally not impact the capital position but non-support may drive regulatory and reputational risk.
Vulnerability analysis	Second order losses	Consider (credit) contingency risks and network impacts. Example: Collateral concentration from margin financing business. Failure of a counterparty can lead to material exposure to the underlying securities.

Table 10.3 (continued)

Step	Theme	Practical take-away and example
Storyboard and scenario design	Simplistic storyboards	Avoid simplistic storyboards.
		Example: An RST users informed his CRO that the loss of an internal model waiver may equate to a capital failure. The CRO answered that he was well aware of this without RST and that this one-off 'capital hit' would not represent a storyboard that lends itself to deeper RST discussions. By contrast, another RST users considered the loss of the internal model waiver alongside changes in the Risk Weighted Asset quantification under the standard approach, capital reductions through defaults, further losses resulting from the reduced monetisation value of collateral and adverse FX moves.
Storyboard and scenario design	Number of scenarios	Develop multiple scenarios, potentially 6 to 12, including a shortlisting of a few key scenarios, to consider a sufficient multitude of vulnerabilities.
		Example: An RST user received very positive feedback from his board. He presented multiple scenarios to discuss with his Board which of the scenarios require the most management attention and why.
Plausibility check	Underestimation of risks	Check, if parallels can be drawn (e.g. from existing businesses) and if chain effects need to be considered.
		Example: For some banks, regulatory fines have been significantly higher than expected and operational incidents also triggered conduct and reputational risks.
Plausibility check	Overestimation of risks	State points of comparison to explain the plausibility of the applied shocks.
		Example: In one bank, the RST scenario assumed that spreads for government bonds widen to levels multiple times higher than observed during the financial crisis in 2007/2008. The board challenged this assumption and later dismissed the entire RST work.
Management actions	Narrow focus and poor definition of management actions	Consider management literature (e.g. on scenario planning) and other tools to facilitate broader discussions on management actions.
		Example: RST discussions only focussed on the reactive measures following the risk materialisation in the assumed crisis. It was not discussed how these risks can be avoided or hedged, such as building optionality and flexibility into strategic plans.

Table 10.3 (continued)

Step	Theme	Practical take-away and example
Management actions	Execution risks	Use range estimates for management actions instead of the spurious accuracy of (subjective) point estimates.
		Example: An RST user had intense debates with regulators and auditors around the credibility of his management actions. As management actions are subject to different sources of uncertainty (e.g. feasibility, implementation time required, governance approvals needed), a range allows better to reflect execution risks.
Monitoring and reporting	Dashboards and ownership	Regularly report if the 'real world' is moving towards or away from the 'scenario world'.
		Example: A working group assigned ownership at different levels (e.g. scenarios, vulnerabilities, risk factors) and continuously asked each owner for regular updates to get a granular and differentiated picture where the 'real world' is moving.

Note: We would like to thank Shan S. Wong for her input on the table. She also shared her experience at a Liquidity Management conference in London in June 2017.

Appendix 10.3: What can be learned from past failures?

Historical market-wide crises (e.g. 1866, 1907, 1914, 2007/2008, 2020) and (near) failures of individual firms (see Figure 10.4 for examples) offer regularly well-documented evidence on causes and event chains – that is, why and how risks unfolded.

Literature on past failures exists in various forms, from macro- or micro-prudential analyses of crisis events to hearings by parliaments and select committees. From the plethora of publications, a few recommendations are detailed in the bibliography. (See Basu, 2003; Government Accountability Office, 2013; House of Commons Treasury Committee, 2012; Kohn, 2018; Office of the Comptroller of the Currency, 1998; Rose et al., 2009; Shin, 2008; UK Parliament, 2012; Vaz, 1999.)

When studying past failures, RST user may find the following questions helpful:
- Which (business model) assumptions were made and turned out to be wrong?
- What was the exact chronology of events? How did risks unfold and interact? Which actions did the management take and what were the impacts of the latter?
- Which mitigating actions gained traction in helping institutions regain liquidity, raise capital or re-emerge from recovery back to a going concern status?

A History on Losses of Financial Institutions

1974 Herstatt Bank: $620 mn (foreign exchange trading)	2001 Dexia Bank: $270 mn (corporate bonds)
1994 Metallgesellschaft: $1.3 bn (oil futures)	2006 Amaranth Advisors: $6.5 bn (gas forward contracts)
1994 Orange Country: $1.8bn (reverse repo)	2007 Morgan Stanley: $9.0 bn (credit derivatives)
1994 Procter & Gamble: $160 mn (ratchet swap)	2008 Société Générale: $7.2 bn (rogue trading)
1995 Barings Bank: $1.3 bn (stock index futures)	2008 Madoff: $65bn (fraud)
1997 Natwest: $ 127 mn (swaptions)	2011 UBS: $2.0 bn (rogue trading)
1998 LTCM: $4.6 bn (liquidity crisis)	2012 JPMorgan Chase: $5.8 bn (credit derivatives)

Financial institutions in distress or bankruptcy

Barings Bank (1995): bankruptcy	Wachovia (2008): major distress
HIH Insurance (2001): bankruptcy	Depfa Bank (2008): major distress
Conseco (2002): bankruptcy	Bear Stearns (2008): bankruptcy
Northern Rock (2007): major distress	Lehman Brothers (2008): bankruptcy
Countrywide Financial (2008): major distress	Washington Mutual (2008): bankruptcy
Indy Mac Bank (2008): major distress	DSB Bank (2008): bankruptcy
Fannie Mae/Freddie Mac (2008): major distress	Fortis (2009): major distress
Merrill Lynch (2008): major distress	Icelandic banks (2008-2010): major distress
AIG (2008): major distress	Dexia (2011): major distress

Figure 10.4: List of historical case studies.

This may lead to:
- Which (business model) assumptions are we making right now (that, if wrong, can contribute to a failure)?
- How should risks be addressed – through additional controls, reduced business activity or through risk acceptance?

Answers to these questions can inter alia help to derive deep, coherent and relevant RST narratives in step 3 of the proposed approach; anecdotally, regulators frequently criticise that narratives would lack depth, suffer from biases and would not be sufficiently relevant for the firm's business model.

Appendix 10.4: What can be learned from planning work for (near) failures?

The term *recovery and resolution planning* (RRP) summarises preparatory planning work for a near failure (Recovery) or actual failure (Resolution) of an institution. The cross-linkage and co-integration with RST is discussed in Chapter 3 and, in particular, in Part V of this book. The authors inter alia recommend an RST user to familiarise themselves with the respective in-house plans. Besides the latter, the Board of Governance of the Federal Reserve System (2020) offers free access to the public part of regulated banks' resolution plans. The database allows users to search resolution plans by name, asset size and submission date. The information can be helpful across all six steps of the proposed RST approach, including governance protocols and playbooks.

Appendix 10.5: What can be learned from recent research?

Recent research can help RST users to, amongst others, identify 'white spaces' and hidden vulnerabilities (step 2) as well as to inform and develop new narratives (step 3). This is exemplified by research work in chapter 25 of this book. In 2019, as a guest speaker of the RST Masterclass event in London, the academic inter alia argued a risk manager would frequently search in the wrong places:

- Risk has two faces – a perceived face (as reported by risk models), and an actual face that is hidden but ever present. Thereby the actual risk would arise before a risk manager can perceive it. The suite of current risk indicators (Vol, VIX, CDS, etc.) would provide a signal too late for meaningful reaction.
- High volatility is not a good predictor of risk. It would typically result in preparation for known unknowns (while unknown unknowns would be the most damaging). Risk would build up during a period of low volatility and perceived stability and then materialise in recessions. Fast growth and perceived low risk would be the best risk predictor.
- Banks tend to accurately measure and manage short-term risk (i.e. what they can see), while the typical OECD country would suffer a systemic crisis every one out of 43 years.
- Risk is endogenous. While common stress tests may focus on exogenous shocks to the financial system (which arrive from outside the system like an asteroid), risk would be largely created by the interaction of market participants. Thereby, the typography of financial system could decide on the propagation of risks.

RST users may search for areas which are growing fast while perceived to be of lower risk, and factor in time delays with which risk may emerge and consider counterparties' counterparties as well as the industry position in the systemic risk cycle as part of their RST work.

Recent research on new risk stripes and "hot topics" can equally inform RST work. For example:

- Catastrophic risks (see, for example, Kunreuther/Useem, 2018)
- Novel risks (see Kaplan et al., 2020)

- Sustainability risks,[8] including Climate risks/"green swans" (see Basel Committee on Banking Supervision, 2020)
- Systemic risks (see, for example, chapter 7 in Part II and chapter 24 in Part V of this book).

Besides, selected working papers and bulletins from central banks can support RST users:
- For example, Working Paper No. 456 "Liquidity risk, cash-flow constraints and systemic feedbacks" introduces the danger zone concept. The latter consists of failure points (danger zone thresholds), vulnerabilities (indicators), storyboards (propagation channels), management actions (defensive actions) and monitoring activities (at indicator level). The paper applies the concept to the actual failure of Continental Illinois. In Part II of this book, Almehed et al. develop the concept further towards a Reverse Liquidity Stress Test approach.
- As part of a quarterly Bank of England bulletin, Beau et al. (2014): visualises the dynamic nature of funding and lending with an analogy (buckets filled with water on a scale). Assuming a funding cost shock, their contribution derives storyboards and discusses the merits of different management actions. RST practitioners may use the analogy to facilitate workshops, e.g. to illustrate RST objectives and derive different scenario narratives.

Overall, RST can incorporate these and other ideas, potentially better than most traditional stress tests. Most important, it can link them directly to the business model whereby the flexibility allows for bespoke test designs and configuration sets. At the same time, the future of RST may depend on how well users master this integration and evolve existing practices.

Bibliography

Basel Committee on Banking Supervision (2009). Principles for sound stress testing practices and supervision, May 2009, https://www.bis.org/publ/bcbs155.pdf
Basel Committee on Banking Supervision (2020). The green swan: Central banking and financial stability in the age of climate change, January 2020, https://www.bis.org/publ/othp31.pdf
Basu S. (2003). Why do Banks Fail?, International Review of Applied Economics, 17(3), pp. 231–248.
Beau, E., Hill, J., Hussain, T., Nixon, D. (2014). Bank funding costs: What are they, what determines them and why do they matter? Quarterly Bulletin 2014 Q4, Published on 08 December 2014.

---

8 Sustainability risks can result from different conflicts (e.g. conflicts between land usage change and conservation, energy and climate change, business and human rights). Transactions are often closely related to reputational risks and may be assessed within the reputational risk review process.

Board of Governance of the Federal Reserve System (2020). Resolution Plans, https://www.
federalreserve.gov/supervisionreg/resolution-plans-search.htm, Last Update: July 23, 2019.

Danielsson, J. (2019). Short- and Long-Term Risk, Measurement, and Technology, Presentation given
at 2nd Annual Reverse Stress Testing Masterclass, 18 June 2019, London.

Ernst & Young (2013). Remaking financial services: risk management five years after the
crisis, http://www.ey.com/Publication/vwLUAssets/Remaking_financial_services_-_
risk_management_five_years_after_the_crisis_-_Complete/$FILE/EY-Remaking_financial_
services_risk_management_five_years_after_the_crisis.pdf

European Banking Authority (2018). Final report: Guidelines on institutions' stress testing,
July 2018, EBA-GL-2018-04, https://eba.europa.eu/sites/default/documents/files/
documents/10180/2282644/2b604bc8-fd08-4b17-ac4a-cdd5e662b802/Guidelines%20
on%20institutions%20stress%20testing%20%28EBA-GL-2018-04%29.pdf?retry=1

Federal Reserve (2012). Supervisory Guidance on Stress Testing for Banking Organizations with More
Than $10 Billion in Total Consolidated Assets, May 14, 2012, https://www.federalreserve.gov/
supervisionreg/srletters/sr1207.htm

Financial Conduct Authority (2020). SYSC 20.2 Reverse stress testing requirements, June 2020,
https://www.handbook.fca.org.uk/handbook/SYSC/20/2.html

Government Accountability Office (2013). Causes and Consequences of Recent Bank Failures,
GAO-13-71: Published: Jan 3, 2013, https://www.gao.gov/products/GAO-13-71

House of Commons Treasury Committee (2012). The FSA's report into the failure of RBS, Report,
together with formal minutes, oral and written evidence, 16 October 2012.

Islamic Financial Services Board (2012). Guiding Principles on Stress Testing for Institutions offering
Islamic Financial Services, IFSB-13 (March 2012), [https://ifsb.org/standard/IFSB-16%20
Revised%20Supervisory%20Review%20Process_March%202014%20(final-clean).pdf

Islamic Financial Services Board (2016). TN-2, Technical Note on Stress Testing for Institutions
Offering Islamic Financial Services, https://www.ifsb.org/; December 2016.

Kapadia, S., Drehmann, M., Elliott, J. Sterne, G. (2012). Liquidity risk, cash-flow constraints and
systemic feedbacks, Bank of England Working Paper No. 456.

Kaplan, R., Leonard, H., Mikes, A. Novel Risks, Harvard Business School, Working Paper 20-094,
Revised May 2020.

Katalysys Ltd. Reverse Stress Testing (n.d.): Tool to improve business planning and risk
management, http://www.katalysys.com/reverse-stress-testing.html

Kohn, D. (2018). From the great moderation to the great recession and beyond: How did we get
there and what lessons have we learned? Speech given at the 200th Anniversary of Danmarks
Nationalbank, Copenhagen, Published on 07 September 2018, https://www.bankofengland.
co.uk/speech/2018/donald-kohn-200-anniversary-conference-of-danmarks-nationalbank

Kunreuther, H., Useem, M. (2018). *Mastering catastrophic risk: how companies are coping with
disruption*, Oxford, New York.

Office of the Comptroller of the Currency (1998). Bank Failure: An Evaluation of the Factors
Contributing to the Failure of National Banks, June 1998, https://www.occ.treas.gov/
publications-and-resources/publications/banker-education/files/bank-failure.html

Rose, C., Bergstresser, D., Lane, D. (2009). The Tip of the Iceberg: JP Morgan Chase and Bear Stearns
(A), Harvard Business School Case 309–001, January 2009. Revised November 2011.

Shin, H. (2008). Reflections on Modern Bank Runs: A Case Study of Northern Rock, Working Paper,
Princeton University, August 2008.

UK Parliament (2012). The FSA's report into the failure of RBS – Treasury Contentshttps://publications.
parliament.uk/pa/cm201213/cmselect/cmtreasy/640/64004.htm, 19 October 2012.

Vaz, D. (1999). Four Banking Crises – Their causes and consequences; *Revista de Economía –
Segunda Epoca*, Vol. VI, No. 1, Banco Central del Uruguay.

Jean-Pierre Charmaille

11 Reverse Stress Testing with Cognitive Maps

A Use Case at the UK Pension Protection Fund

11.1 Introduction

In this chapter, we look at reverse stress testing in a non-banking context. The case under consideration here is that of the Pension Protection Fund, referred to as 'PPF' in the rest of the chapter.

The PPF is a statutory body that was created by the Pensions Act 2004 to protect members of private Defined Benefit (DB) pension schemes. It is led by a board and accountable to the Parliament through the Secretary of State for the Department for Work and Pensions (DWP). In Section 11.2 of this chapter, we describe the mission, operations and risk profile of the PPF and provide some background data about the organisation. As the PPF is a creature of the Parliament, it can only be dissolved by an act of Parliament. This feature makes the PPF an interesting case for reverse stress testing. For a commercial organisation (financial or otherwise), its survival depends in essence on its commercial viability. When one is reverse stress testing a commercial organisation, one is looking for scenarios leading for non-economic viability of the organisation and ultimately its bankruptcy. In the case of a bank or an insurance company, we would typically look for scenarios leading to a breach of minimum solvency capital where the bank or insurance is not solvent enough to be allowed by the Regulator to carry on its operations. In order to reverse stress test the PPF, one has to look for scenarios of catastrophic failure that would persuade the Parliament to vote the dissolution of the PPF. How we can look for such scenarios of failure is explored in Section 11.4. In Section 11.5, we look at how we can use the outputs of a stochastic models when events of failure can be defined quantitatively. In Section 11.6, we look at techniques that can be applied to reverse stress testing the organisation when no quantitative threshold of failure is available.

11.2 The Context: The Pension Protection Fund (PPF)

11.2.1 The Mission of the PPF

The PPF is an organisation that was created by the Pensions Act 2004 to protect members of private Defined Benefit (DB) pension schemes.

Note: Edited by Tiziano Bellini

https://doi.org/10.1515/9783110647907-011

Following the creation of the PPF, when the employer of a DB pension scheme becomes insolvent, that pension scheme is wound up and its trustees make a claim on the PPF. Once a claim is made, the scheme enters a so-called assessment period, during which the PPF checks whether there are enough resources in the fund to secure, with an insurance company, the level of compensation that would be provided by the PPF. If the total of the assets of the fund and the proceeds from the insolvency procedure of the employer is not enough to secure this minimum level, the assets and liabilities of the schemes are transferred to the PPF and members of the scheme are paid the PPF level of compensation.[1]

All eligible pension schemes, i.e. all UK private DB pension schemes, can and must make a claim on the PPF if their employer or employers get insolvent, but they must also pay a premium, the 'PPF Levy'.

The resources of the PPF are the assets of schemes that transfer to the PPF, recoveries from the insolvencies of sponsoring employers of schemes that transfer and the levy collected from all eligible pension schemes. With these resources, the PPF pays compensations to its present and future pensioners.

The mission of the PPF, as stated on its website, is "to pay the right people, the right amount at the right time".[2] Then follows the statement: "Our mission means making sure we can protect people with defined benefit pension when an employer becomes insolvent, today, tomorrow and for as long as they need us."[3]

The mission of the PPF is focused on the effective payment of compensations over the long term, for as long as the PPF is needed.

11.2.2 The PPF Business and Risk Profile

One can view DB pensions as debt that is owed by the employer to the members of the schemes (current and/or past employees) that is collateralised with the assets of the scheme. These assets that serve as collateral, have been accumulated over time through employer's and employees' contributions and compounded return on invested assets.

When the employer of a DB scheme becomes insolvent, the pension scheme must be wound up and members of the scheme make a claim on the employer as senior unsecured creditors for the amount of assets that would be necessary to secure the pension liability with an insurer.[4]

If the assets of the schemes are sufficient to secure pensions in full with an insurer, the scheme is bought out by that insurer.

---

1 For details on PPF compensations, see https://ppf.co.uk/what-it-means-ppf.
2 See https://www.ppf.co.uk/our-mission-and-values.
3 See https://www.ppf.co.uk/our-mission-and-values.
4 See section 75 of Pensions Act: http://www.legislation.gov.uk/ukpga/1995/26/section/75/enacted.

However, in the vast majority of cases, schemes are not sufficiently well-funded to be bought out in full by an insurer. If there are not enough assets to secure with an insurer, the level of pension provided by the PPF, the assets and liabilities of the schemes are transferred to the PPF and members of the scheme are compensated with PPF benefits. As such, the PPF provides an insolvency insurance to DB pension schemes.

Once schemes have transferred, the PPF's operations are that of an annuity provider. Therefore, the business profile of the PPF can be viewed as the combination of:
- An insolvency insurance that underwrites policies insuring the credit risk of sponsoring employers of DB schemes
- An annuity provider that manages the assets and liabilities of claimant schemes.

Concepts traditionally applied to credit risk of a bank loan book can easily be transposed to the case of the PPF when we analyse the risk profile of the insolvency insurance business. The aggregate credit risk the insolvency insurance is exposed to can be quantified by:

$$\sum_{i=1}^{\# \, of \, DB \, schemes} PD_i \times EAD_i \times LGD_i$$

Where:
- Probability of Default (PD_i) corresponds to the probability of scheme i making a claim, in effect, the probability of its employers getting insolvent
- Exposure at Default (EAD_i), the present value of the pension liabilities of scheme i at PPF level of compensation
- Loss Given Default (LGD_i) scheme i deficit (asset shortfall relative to the liabilities) as a proportion of the liabilities

The product $EAD_i \times LGD_i$ corresponds to scheme i deficit when a claim is made expressed in monetary amounts. This quantity is highly volatile as the pension schemes funding position fluctuates according to changing values of assets and liabilities. Pension liabilities are very long streams of payment (typically of over a 20-year duration), hence they are highly sensitive to interest rates and partly indexed to inflation. But as many schemes do not or only partially hedge interest rates and inflation risks, for many schemes, the assets are only loosely correlated to the liabilities. This mismatch of pension assets to liabilities leads to a volatile funding level. The PPF7800 tracks changes to the aggregate funding level of DB schemes universe. Figure 11.1[5] shows how volatile this index has been.

---

5 PPF 7800 31 December 2019, https://www.ppf.co.uk/sites/default/files/file-2020-01/ppf_7800_at_31_december_2019_for_january_update.pdf.

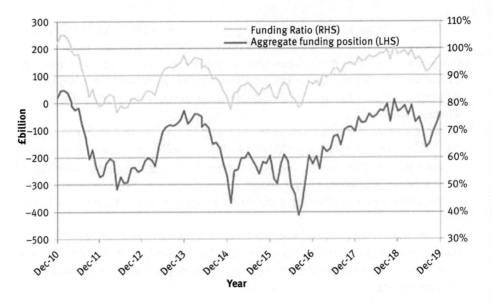

Figure 11.1: Historical aggregate funding pension and funding ratio schemes in the PPF universe.

The probabilities of default of the employers are related to the state of the economy. As the global economy (and the UK economy in particular) weakens, probabilities of insolvency tend to increase. Moreover, because the universe of DB pension schemes is highly concentrated. There are only 196 schemes (out of a total 5,422) with more than 10,000 members. But they concentrate over 60% of the total liabilities of the universe.[6] Therefore, the PPF is also subject to the idiosyncratic risk of one or more large schemes falling into the PPF regardless of the state of the economy.

For the annuity insurance side of the PPF, the two main risks are:

- The Asset-Liability Mismatch (ALM) risk – i.e. the risk the assets of the PPF do not grow as fast as its liabilities. This could happen if the liabilities were under-hedged with respect to inflation and/or interest rate risk or if growth assets (equity and alternative assets) performed poorly.
- Longevity risk, which is the risk that members of the PPF live longer than anticipated and therefore are paid pensions for longer than expected.

These two risks are not necessarily correlated but they compound themselves. This is because if longevity materialises, the liabilities would be longer than expected, creating an unintended under-hedged position and exposing the fund to declining interest rates and/or increasing inflation.

Longevity risk also affects the funding position of all DB schemes. If it materialised, the exposure of the insolvency insurance side of the PPF to insolvency risk would also grow.

The risks affecting both aspects of the PPF – the insolvency insurance and the annuity business – are corelated to an extent. We have seen that longevity risk affects both sides, but also investment risks affecting the assets of the PPF and therefore the annuity business is to an extent correlated with the investment risk faced by UK DB pension schemes. Indeed, when equity markets perform poorly, deficits of DB pension schemes tend to grow and with it grows the potential loss as a result of a claim made on the PPF. At the same time, when equity markets perform poorly, the growth assets of the PPF are more likely to underperform.

Finally, equity risk and the risk of employers getting insolvent are also correlated. This is because a weak global or UK economy is likely to simultaneously increase the risk of employers getting insolvent and weaken the performance of global and/or UK equity markets which in turn will impact negatively on pension funds funding and the performance of PPF growth assets.

11.3 Key Statistics

11.3.1 The Universe of Pension Schemes Protected by the PPF

As of 31 March 2019, there were 5,436 schemes protected by the PPF.[7] These schemes have 10.1 million members, of which 4.2 million are pensioners, 4.7 million are deferred members and only fewer than 1.2 million are active members with benefits still accruing. The universe of DB pension schemes covered by the PPF has been shrinking ever since the creation of the PPF. In 2006, just one year after the creation of the PPF, there were 7,751 schemes with 14 million members. This attrition of the number of DB schemes is the result of mergers, schemes being bought out and claims on the PPF while no new DB schemes have been opened. The sharp reduction in the number of members is the result of closures of schemes to new entrants and new accruals. As of 31 March 2019, 44% of the 5,436 schemes were closed to new entrants, 44% closed to new accruals and only 11% were still open to new members.

As of 31 March 2019, the total of the assets of UK DB schemes was £1,615 billion whilst the cost of securing liabilities of UK DB schemes at PPF level of compensation was estimated at £1,628 billion. Of the 5,436 schemes, 3,066 were thought to be in deficit, with a combined deficit of £160 billion.

---

7 See https://www.ppf.co.uk/sites/default/files/2020-01/Purple-Book-2019_1.pdf.

11.3.2 Key Statistics Relative to the PPF[8]

As of 31 March 2019, the total assets of the PPF were valued at £38.7 billion, of which £32.2 billion were directly under the management of the PPF and £6.5 billion belonged to schemes in assessment, schemes that have not yet transferred to the PPF but are expected to do so at the end of their assessment period.

On the liabilities side, the total of the pension liabilities of schemes that have transferred to the PPF was £23.1 billion and the liabilities of schemes in assessment and expected to transfer were estimated at £9.5 billion making a total of £32.6 billion and an estimated reserve (assets minus liabilities) of £6.1 billion.

As of 31 March 2019, the PPF had nearly 250,000 members and there were a further 150,000 members of schemes in assessment, expected to be transferred to the PPF.

11.4 The Definition of Failure

As stated in the introduction of this chapter, because the PPF was created by an Act of Parliament, it could only be dissolved by another act of Parliament. Moreover, unlike banks and insurance companies, the PPF is not regulated. It is therefore not subject to minimum solvency requirements and we cannot use any prescribed ratio as the minimum threshold below which the organisation would be forced to wind-up. The closure of the PPF could only be the result of a decision by policymakers or lawmakers. Because of that, there is no prescribed definition of failure and the first step to the reverse stress-test exercise is to come up with a definition of failure, collectively agreed upon by the senior management and the board of the organisation.

To come up with an agreed definition of failure, we consulted with internal stakeholders (internal Subject Matter Experts, senior management of the PPF and the Board) and external stakeholders (the Department for Work and Pensions, the Pensions Regulator and pension industry bodies).

The outcome of this consultation was two broad definitions of failure:

– First failure to accomplish PPF's mission of "Paying the Right People, the Right Amount, at the Right Time". Here in particular we look at the long-term financial strength of the PPF which in some scenarios could become insufficient to pay the level of compensation that the PPF is currently committed to pay.
– Second losing the support of our stakeholders, first UK DB schemes and/or members of the PPF and ultimately, DWP, the Government and Parliament.

The process of consultation and discussion that leads to the definition of failure is in itself a very useful risk management exercise that helps risk practitioners, members

---

8 See https://www.ppf.co.uk/sites/default/files/file-2019-07/annual_report_2018-2019_2.pdf.

of senior management and the Board think about the risks that really matter for the organisation. And as we will see in the next section, it also leads to risk measures that are well understood by stakeholders and that are not externally imposed but chosen freely by Senior Management and the Board.

11.5 Reverse Stress Test When a Failure Event can be Defined Quantitatively

The PPF describes the level of benefits provided to its members on its website.[9] However, in some severe economic scenarios where the performance of PPF assets would be poor, scheme funding, low and many insolvencies leading to claims on the PPF would occur, the PPF might no longer be able to pay compensations at the level currently described on its website.

In such extreme circumstances, the board of the PPF would have to take drastic actions, either reducing compensations or future compensation indexation or increasing the levy beyond its current boundaries.[10] In such scenarios, the PPF would fail to accomplish its mission because it would no longer have the financial resources to do so.

We estimated a threshold of funding level below which the PPF is unable to pay compensations at the current level and using the PPF stochastic model, the long-term risk model[11] (LTRM), we were able to quantify the risk of such scenarios (estimate a probability) and characterise them.

Out of the 1,000,000 scenarios generated by the LTRM, we selected a (small) subset of scenarios, the RST subset, where at some point over the projection horizon, the funding level of the PPF falls below the threshold of funding level defined in the previous paragraph. We were then able to calculate a probability (number of scenarios in the RST subset divided by 1,000,000) and describe the scenarios of the reverse stress test using descriptive statistics on the RST subset. For example, we could easily calculate the average performance of equity markets and the claim experience in the RST subset and compare these to the average across the entire set of 1,000,000 scenarios, the expected scenario.

---

9 https://ppf.co.uk/what-it-means-ppf
10 For example, the PPF levy cannot exceed a levy ceiling set in 2020 at £1.099 billion (see http://www.legislation.gov.uk/uksi/2020/101/made) and indexed to the Average National Earning.
11 For more information about the Long-Term Risk Model, see section 5 of https://ppf.co.uk/sites/default/files/file-2018-11/ppf_funding_strategy_document.pdf.

11.6 Approaches to the Non-Quantitative Definitions of Failure

11.6.1 Cognitive Mapping

In the previous section, we looked at the RST when there is a quantifiable definition of failure – in this instance, scenarios in which the PPF does not have enough assets to accomplish its mission of paying the promised level of compensation. However, there is a multitude of scenarios of failure that cannot be identified quantitatively by simply measuring one or more financial variables such as the level of funding or the size of the deficit. This is particularly the case for failures of the second type – i.e. scenarios when the organisation loses the trust of its stakeholders.

There is no quantitative method of measuring the trusts of stakeholders. Therefore, risk practitioners have to resort to qualitative approaches. And yet these approaches still need to be objective and systematic.

The PPF, like any organisation interacting with multiple stakeholders, is a complex system. Complexity arises from the dynamic nature of the interactions between all actors. Each of them reacts differently and often in an unpredictable way to external events and the actions of other stakeholders. It is extremely difficult or even impossible to model such a system.

One alternative to mathematical modelling is to employ a technique called cognitive mapping. This is the technique that was chosen by the PPF to develop its first RST scenarios in 2012. The PPF was supported by Milliman in this project. The paper "An Application of Modern Social Sciences Techniques to reverse stress testing at the UK Pension Protection Fund",[12] by N. Cantle, J. P. Charmaille, M. G. Clarke and L. M. K. Currie is devoted to this approach and this project in particular.

As described in Allan, Cantle, Godfrey, and Yin (2012), "A concept map is a model which allows complex interconnected factors to be shown in a simplified diagrammatic form, so that the overall picture can be understood and communicated to a wide audience. Such maps are particularly useful for identifying and analysing strategic issues, as these are often complex in nature and contain a wide range of factors interacting in a nonlinear manner. Also, they can help visualise the complex and nonlinear relationships between different concepts." The approach used was derived from Cognitive Mapping (Eden, 1988).

---

12 See https://www.soa.org/globalassets/assets/files/resources/essays-monographs/2013-erm-symposium/mono-2013-as13-1-clarke.pdf.

The technique essentially permits the structured compilation of the views of knowledgeable stakeholders on the PPF, in such a way that their individual contributions can be recombined to form a holistic view. In this objective way, individual biases are largely removed and any gaps in narrative identified.

11.6.2 Drawing the Cognitive Map

A series of workshops were held with key PPF stakeholders, including internal Subject Matter Experts (SMEs) and external parties such as government departments, consultants and representative bodies. Stakeholders were asked to discuss the PPF and the features of, and influences upon, its strategic delivery. They were also asked to identify the outcomes that would be achieved through successful strategic delivery.

Each discussion was converted by Milliman consultants into a graph called cognitive map where each key concept is represented by a vertex and is linked to other vertices to reflect the manner in which the experts made verbal links between them in the discussion. The map is organised into a hierarchy so that concepts tend to flow upwards towards the outcomes of the scenario. To illustrate the structure of such a map, an example is shown in Figure 11.2. (Note that vertex descriptions have been blurred for reasons of business confidentiality.) Figure 11.3 shows a small section of a map to illustrate the types of vertices created.

The cognitive maps of individual discussions were then combined to form an aggregate map representing the collective input of all stakeholders. This is shown illustratively in Figure 11.4.

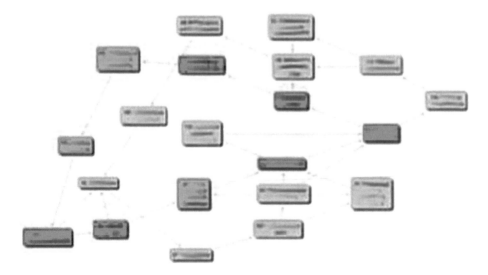

Figure 11.2: A sample cognitive map (the picture is blurry because it is only illustrative).

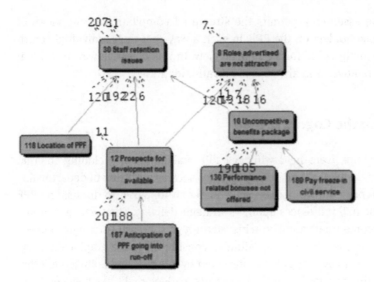

Figure 11.3: Extract from a map (the picture is blurry because it is only illustrative).

Figure 11.4: The aggregate cognitive map combining all stakeholder input (the picture is blurry because it is only illustrative).

The cognitive map now represents a form of system description of the PPF's strategy which shows the non-linear interactions between relevant factors and the ways in which they combine to produce outcomes.

The original narrative necessarily contains a lot of "context" which is useful but not essential to the understanding of the underlying system mechanism producing outcomes. It is, therefore, helpful to reduce the summary to a "minimally complex" form which removes as much context as possible without losing the critical dynamic features that the experts have explained. This is achieved by identifying the most highly connected vertices in the map, the critical nodes and their most common precursors, the potent nodes. See Figure 11.5.

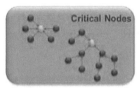 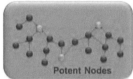

Figure 11.5: Critical nodes are highly globally and/or locally connected vertices. Potent nodes are vertices that lead to such critical nodes.

Vertices can be important (highly connected) if they are referenced immediately by many other vertices, and also if many vertices from the overall map ultimately link to them. This high level of connectivity implies that they are "critical" to the narrative of PPF's organisational dynamics because many parts of the map link to them. Identifying the "potent" vertices, which leads to a number of these "critical" vertices, captures the beginnings of dynamics which could lead to critical behaviours unfolding. By focussing on the smaller set of critical, potent and outcome vertices, it is possible to make the most important behaviours of PPF's strategic dynamics more visible.

11.6.3 Making Sense of the Cognitive Map

The cognitive map of the PPF was then further analysed to elicit an understanding of the key features that reverse stress scenarios might have. Concepts were clustered into broad strategic risk themes, which helped to identify the nature of developments that could lead to reverse stress situations. For example, some vertices related particularly to political considerations, others to internal operations and others to economic considerations. Studying the dynamics in this way reveals not only the obvious "large event" causes of reverse stress (e.g. large market falls) but also the more subtle combinations of factors which, in themselves, are not obviously leading to a disastrous outcome, but which create a sensitivity to otherwise benign conditions (e.g. a series of operational processes may take paths which combine to generate sensitivity to a political event).

The cognitive mapping exercise revealed the complexity of the risk profile of the PPF. From the transcripts of the workshops, 176 concepts or vertices were identified and these were connected by 349 edges.

Table 11.1 shows how the concepts discussed by the Subject Matter Experts in the workshops relate to the PPF's strategic Risk Areas. It shows the number of vertices/ nodes per risk category as well as the number of edges between each pair of risk categories. For example, the cell intersecting the row "Reputational" and column "Investment Operations" shows that there are four edges between these two risk categories.

Table 11.1: Frequency and interconnectivity of strategic risk themes.

	Number of nodes	Funding and Investment Strategy	Investment Operations	Strategy/ Environmental	Legal	Operational	Reputational	Organisational Design/Culture
Funding and Investment Strategy	21	1	3	18	3	35	15	24
Investment Operations	11	3	6	13	1	14	4	2
Strategy/Environmental	50	18	13	40	3	41	45	15
Legal	6	3	1	3	0	2	2	1
Operational	44	35	14	41	2	17	15	16
Reputational	27	15	4	45	2	15	4	6
Organisational Design/Culture	17	24	2	15	1	16	6	2

Detailed analysis of the cognitive map was carried out by identifying the critical nodes. These were defined in more detail in previous sections but can be best described as the key risk drivers of the PPF, as they are the most connected vertices.

In all, there were 16 critical nodes identified on the cognitive maps. Each of them is directly connected to at least 8 neighbouring vertices and connected indirectly (within 3 edges) to at least 20% of the whole map.

For risk management purposes it is also useful to understand which are the "potent" nodes that have the most influence on the set of critical nodes. In the case of Reputational Damage, an example of critical node, the risk is an outcome that cannot itself be controlled directly. It arises as a result of other events that might be controllable. With the knowledge of all the main precursors to Reputational Damage, i.e. the potent nodes connected to Reputational Damage, the organisation can be better equipped to mitigate the risk of Reputational Damage by applying risk mitigation strategies to the drivers of the risk.

Seventeen potent nodes were identified in total. Table 11.2 provides an overall summary of the PPF cognitive map and includes examples and definitions of the various features described in this section.

Table 11.2: Summary of PPF cognitive map.

Cognitive map feature	Definition	Number	Example
Vertices/ nodes	Represent each of the ideas or concepts mentioned in the workshops	176	−Inappropriate people recruited −Payment mechanism failure
Edges	The link between vertices, elicited from ways in which ideas/concepts were discussed in the context of each other	349	Weak candidate selection process => Inappropriate people recruited
Critical Nodes	Drivers and mitigants which are key to describing the risk scenario, and which are identified by looking for the most connected vertices in the map	16	−Knowledge gap −PPF deficit increases
Potent Nodes	Vertices influencing the most critical nodes	17	−PPF staffing cuts −Increase in interest rates
Loops/Cycles	Connected subsets of the map that are cyclical and which represent processes or chains of events that may spiral out of control	>1000	See chart 5

11.6.4 Loops and Scenario Design

Loops or cycles in graph terminology, are subsets of the cognitive map which are cyclical. They can start and end on the same vertex. Of particular interest in risk management are the loops containing several critical nodes and potent nodes. Taken individually, the risk represented by any one vertex of the loop may not necessarily be very detrimental. But when these events are combined together, they could easily spiral out of control or reach an extreme state.

The cognitive map developed for the PPF's risk exposure contains over a thousand cycles, indicating there to be a high degree of complexity within the system, as defined by the workshop participants. Figure 11.6 represents an example of a cycle where the red boxes correspond to critical nodes and the dark red boxes correspond to potent nodes.

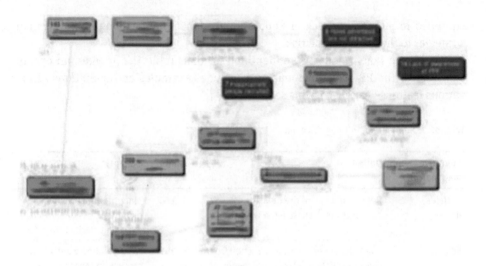

Figure 11.6: Example of a cycle within the cognitive map (the picture is blurry because it is only illustrative).

The loops were used to develop reverse stress test scenarios that might be seen to be closer to "real-life" examples of failures. Because of their greater complexity and realism, the reverse stress scenarios that were derived from this analysis of the cognitive map proved to be more engaging for members of the board.

11.6.5 The Stakeholders Map

In the previous section, we looked at the use of cognitive mapping to compile the knowledge of internal and external SMEs and develop plausible but very damaging scenarios that can count as reverse stress test scenarios.

In this section, we look at how cognitive mapping can be used to graph all the stakeholders of the organisation and how they interact together. Here again, the organisation and its stakeholders are viewed as a complex system. The diagram in Figure 11.7 represents a simplified view of the PPF and its stakeholders.

At the centre of the system is the PPF with its three actors:
- The board with both executive and non-executive members, that is the external face of the PPF
- Senior Management acting as an interface between the Board and staff of the PPF
- PPF staff

Outside of the PPF are various stakeholders who interact with the PPF and often between them. The whole system is open as it is affected by its environment – be it the economy, social and political developments in the UK, demographics, and so on. An obvious example of dependency on the environment is poor economic conditions

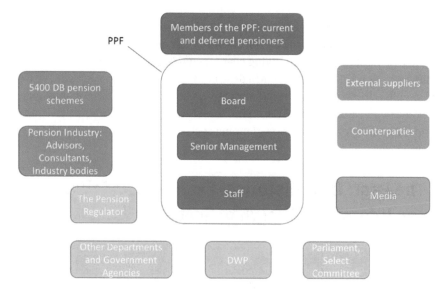

Figure 11.7: Stakeholder map.

leading to insolvencies of employers of DB pension schemes (green box on the upper left) and poor asset performance of pension funds. This could then lead to large claims made on the PPF, which in turn could weaken the funding level of the PPF and its ability to pay compensation to its members (blue box at the top).

By systematically listing all the stakeholders and the interactions between them, we can analyse this system like a network or graph similar to the cognitive map discussed in the previous section. In this graph, stakeholders are vertices and the interactions between them are edges. This mapping of the stakeholders of the organisation can be achieved through workshops gathering internal and external SMEs who will systematically list stakeholders and examine all the interactions between them.

The resulting graph will have much fewer vertices than the cognitive map, as vertices will only represent stakeholders but will be likely to be much denser as most if not all vertices will be connected to more than one edges. With fewer vertices and more edges per vertex, there is no need to identify critical and potent nodes. Most vertices (stakeholders) will be connected directly or indirectly to a large part of the map, if not all of it.

But the identification of cycles or feedback loops that incorporate DWP and/or the Parliament and the PPF is very useful for the development of RST scenarios. Such cycles suggest the existence of scenarios of events looping over a number of stakeholders including DWP and/or the Parliament and spiralling out of control until public confidence that the PPF can perform its operations is significantly eroded.

As with the cognitive map, feedback loops are necessary for a scenario to be disastrous enough to count as a scenario of failure. For example, an operational failure of the payment system of the PPF is insufficient in itself to cause the PPF to collapse. But in combination with other events, the effect of such an operational failure could be amplified. Example of such amplifying events could be poor crisis management or poor communication with stakeholders, a deterioration in the relationship with some external suppliers, deterioration in staff morale, and so on. A plausible but damaging enough scenario to count as an RST scenario is a story or chain of events that loops more than once over a cycle or over overlapping cycles.

11.7 The Past: How Historical Examples of Failure can Inform the Design of Scenarios

Past failures are also a source of inspiration for the design of RST scenarios. In their 2012 report "Roads to Ruin: A Study of Major Risk Events: Their Origins, Impact and Implications", Cass Business School analyse 18 historical failures. The authors identified seven broad categories of event that led to failure in these cases:
A. Events causing major loss of life, including transport accidents
B. Fire and explosion, including terrorism
C. Regulatory action, including criminal prosecution
D. Management behaviour, including fraud and mismanagement
E. Employee behaviour, including fraud or other misbehaviour
F. Product liability, product recall and supply chain failures
G. IT failure, including breach of data confidentiality

Table 11.3 shows how the 18 case studies are mapped against these seven categories of events

This categorisation of events is useful for the development of scenarios. All organisations are susceptible to management or employee misbehaviour but not all would be exposed to events such as major loss of life or fire or explosion. The categories of events that may apply to an organisation like the PPF are management misbehaviour, employee misbehaviour and IT-related failure. For a bank or an insurance company, regulatory action would also be relevant.

To make the most of historical examples of failures, practitioners should first select the examples which are the most relevant to their organisations. For example, for a retail bank, cases 14. Northern Rock (2007) and 10. HSBC/Nationwide/Zurich Insurance (2006–2008) are likely to be more relevant than case 17. Société Générale (2007), which would be better suited for an investment bank. In the case of the PPF, case 18. UK Passport Agency (1999) of a government agency undertaking a major IT change was found to be relevant to design a scenario of major operational failure.

Often, risk practitioners and/or senior management would find it difficult to believe that a scenario similar to some past failure could develop in their organisa-

Table 11.3: 18 historical failures analysed in the "Roads to Ruin".

Event/ Case study (date)	A Major loss of life	B Fire or explosion	C Regulatory action	D Managmt. behaviour	E Employee behaviour	F Product related	G IT related
1 AIG and AIG Financial Products (2005 & 2007)			✓	✓	✓		
2 Arthur Andersen (2001)				✓	✓		
3 BP Texas City Refinery(2005)	✓	✓					
4 Buncefield (HOSL) explosion (2005)		✓					
5 Cadoury Schweppes (2007)						✓	
6 Coca-Cola Dasani (2003)						✓	
7 EADS Airbus A380(2006)			✓	✓		✓	✓
8 Enron (2001)		✓	✓	✓			
9 Firestone (2000)						✓	
10 HSBC/Nationwide/ Zurich Insurance (2006–8)							✓
11 Independent Insurance(2001)			✓	✓			
12 Land of Leather (2008)						✓	
13 Madaren Pushchairs (2009)						✓	
14 Northern rock (2007)			✓	✓			
15 Rail disasters: Great Heck, Haltfield, Potters Bar (2000–2)	✓		✓				
16 Shell (Oil & gas reserves) (2004)				✓			
17 Soété Générale(2007)				✓	✓		
18 UK Passport Agency (1999)				✓			✓

tion. The most common assumption is that the controls in place in the organisation would not let such scenario develop. However, to learn from past failures, risk professionals need to challenge this assumption by asking themselves and other SMEs in the organisation:

–   What are the controls that would effectively prevent such scenario from developing?
–   Do they work effectively?
–   Can we conceive a scenario where those controls do not work as they should because of some other events that unexpectedly occur?

Answering this last question is often the beginning of an interesting RST scenario. This draft of a scenario can then be used and redevelop to follow some cycles found on a cognitive map.

A scenario inspired by historical failure(s), but derived primarily from the analysis of the cognitive map of the organisation exhibits the attributes of an interesting RST scenario.

–   It is relevant: It is based upon the characteristics of the organisation, its stakeholders and environment, which were systematically analysed through cognitive mapping.
–   It is plausible: It has happened in the past and there are reasons to believe that under particular circumstances, it could happen to the organisation under consideration.
–   It should be damaging enough to lead to failure: A similar chain of events has led to failure in the past.
–   It gives valuable insights to risk managers: The root causes of this failure were clearly identified – therefore, if we act now, we will be able to prevent it from happening or at least mitigate its impact.

11.8 Summary

In this chapter, we looked at reverse stress testing for a non-banking and unregulated government related organisation. This organisation is the Pension Protection Fund for which two types of failures were identified: first, the failure to accomplish its mission of "Paying the Right People, the Right Amount at the Right Time" mainly by not having enough assets to pay compensations at the agreed level over the long-term, and second, failure by losing the trust of stakeholders that the PPF can deliver its mission.

For the first type of failure, we can identify thresholds of funding below which the PPF is at great risk of not paying compensations at their agreed upon level, and we explained in Section 11.4 how a stochastic model can be used to identify and characterise scenarios of failure.

The main focus of this chapter was the other type of failure – i.e. losing the confidence of stakeholders and ultimately the licence to operate. For this type of failure, there is no quantifiable failure threshold that can be used to identified scenarios of failure with a stochastic model. But there are techniques used in social sciences that can be applied to perform an RST exercise. In Section 11.6, we introduced such a technique, cognitive mapping, to design RST scenarios. The principle of cognitive mapping is to systematically map a system or network on a graph.

In the context of RST, two types of cognitive maps are of interest. One is about systematically mapping the knowledge of a wide range of SMEs of an organisation by using the transcript of workshops with these SMEs. The second type of mapping consists of drawing an exhaustive graph of all the stakeholders of the organisation and their existing and potential interactions.

In the analysis of the cognitive map, we then look for cycles or feedback loops which can be used as a basis for the design of a scenario or chain of events that amplifies over time and eventually spirals out of control.

The scenarios that are obtained through the analysis of the cognitive map can be further enhanced by examples of past failures to make the stories more plausible and engaging when they are played back to the Senior Management that would include mainly non-risk professionals.

Bibliography

Allan, Cantle, Godfrey, & Yin (2012), A review of the Use of Complex Systems Applied to Risk Appetite and Emerging Risks in ERM, 2013.

Cantle, N., Charmaille, J. P., Clarke, M. G., and Currie, L. M. K. (2013). An Application of Modern Social Sciences Techniques to Reverse Stress testing at the UK Pension Protection Fund.

Cass Business School, Roads to Ruin. A Study of Major Risk Events: their Origins, Impact and Implications.

Charmaille, J. P. and Clarke, M. G. (2012). Enterprise Risk Management at the U.K. Pension Protection Fund.

Eden, C. (1988). Cognitive Mapping, European Journal of Operational Research.

Pension Protection Fund (2010). PPF Long-Term Funding Strategy, 2010.

Pension Protection Fund (2019). PPF 7800 Index, 31 December.

Pension Protection Fund (2019). The Purple Book 2019 – DB pensions universe risk profile, 2019.

Magdalena Kolev

12 Reverse Stress Testing with Strategic Management Tools

A Case Study of FinTech Banks in the Vulnerability Analysis Phase

12.1 Introduction

"The current body of literature on Reverse Stress Test [RST] is still sparse" (Grundke/ Pliszka, 2015, p. 1). It deals primarily with financial risks such as credit and market risks, usually with a quantitative, model-based approach. However, the turbulences observed over the past few years show that the risks of a bank's business model are not necessarily limited to quantitative financial risks. A considerable part of the causes for failure were related to non-financial risks and business strategy. These risks are often insufficiently considered. For example, in June 2020, confronted with the Covid-19 crisis, the Chief Risk Officer of a G-SIB bank assessed in an interview with Osborn/Mourselas (2020): "We do a good job of understanding financial risk. You saw that in 2008 and afterwards. I think our biggest failing was on the non-financial side." Regulators also ask for the integration of non-financial risks in RST but provide little guidance on the practical implementation (see also Chapter 3 by Eichhorn/Romano).

Against this background, the aim of the following chapter is to assess whether strategic management tools are helpful in the process of identifying vulnerabilities of a bank's business model for RST purposes. Using expert interviews, financial statements and other publicly available information, two strategic management tools – a PESTLE and a SWOT-analysis – are tested to identify the vulnerabilities of FinTech banks. The chapter is organised in four parts: Section 12.2 introduces the PESTLE and SWOT-analysis as well as FinTechs and their business models. Next, a PESTLE-analysis in combination with a SWOT-analysis is conducted. This is followed by a synthesis of the results in Section 12.3. The chapter closes with a summary in Section 12.4.

12.2 Context

12.2.1 RST Design and Configuration

The following chapter applies RST at an enterprise-wide level. It uses a top-down perspective with a focus on the business model and strategy. In terms of severity, it

---

Note: Edited by Michael Eichhorn

https://doi.org/10.1515/9783110647907-012

asks what can potentially "break the bank". In the six-step RST approach proposed by Eichhorn/Mangold in Part III of this book, this chapter focuses on phase 2, the vulnerability analysis, and indicates the links to the other steps:

1. Definition of points of failure
2. Vulnerability analysis
3. Generic storyboards
4. Scenario design and parametrisation
5. Plausibility check and management actions
6. Monitoring and reporting

The vulnerability analysis is performed with the help of the PESTLE and SWOT analyses. Given the RST test design and configuration, both analyses focus exclusively on potential "Achilles heels". The author chose the FinTech industry and specifically one European FinTech bank due to the strong public perception of their business models. However, the results of the PESTLE and SWOT analyses are limited, as the latter were performed using only publicly available data.

12.2.2 PESTLE and SWOT

PESTLE considers an organisation's environment by looking at the Political, Economic, Social, Technological, Legal and Environmental factors surrounding it. SWOT analyses an organisation's Strengths, Weaknesses, Opportunities and Threats. PESTLE frequently has more of an outside-in view, whereas SWOT often takes more of an inside-out view. As such, PESTLE analysis was chosen to identify potential external influences that affect the business model and over which the bank may have limited or no control. The SWOT analysis was chosen to assess to which extent external influences, derived from the PESTLE analysis, may impact the bank. As the aim is to identify vulnerabilities, the chapter focuses on adverse influences (PESTLE) and Weaknesses and Threats (SWOT).

12.2.3 FinTech Banks

Atom Bank, Tandem Bank, Starling Bank, N26, Monzo and Revolut are only a few examples of (fast) growing European FinTech banks. Most of them were founded in the middle or later part of the current decade and are digital-only banks. Often UK-based, they did not always start as a licensed bank. For example, one FinTech only issued prepaid cards where customers could upload a certain amount of money and budget it within the firm's app, which became the company's unique selling proposition. After obtaining a banking license, the FinTech is now able to offer other products, e.g. current accounts. The main selling point is usually technology – for example, an app which offers customers various smart features, such as being able to set budgets for their spending and set limits for categories such as groceries, eating out and transportation. The app will recognise a payment and subtract the sum from the budget. Furthermore, the app shows spending in real-time. As soon as a payment is made, it appears on the app and sends a push notification to the owner. Thanks to a partnership with the transfer service, customers are also able to make overseas payments for a low fee (see Mazurek, 2019, The Economist, 2019a, 2019b and Woodford/ Darrah, 2019, for details on the business model of British, European and overseas FinTechs).

FinTech banks often acquire their capital from crowdfunding. For example, in February 2016, one bank caused a sensation with its first crowdfunding campaign. It set a record as quickest crowdfunding campaign in history when it raised £1 million in just 96 seconds. This was followed by several other crowdfunding rounds. In June 2019, the bank raised £113 million and subsequently increased its firm valuation to £2 billion.

Using PESTLE and SWOT, the following section will provide a vulnerability analysis. The analysis was largely conducted prior to the Brexit agreement and the outbreak of the Covid-19 crisis. As noted, it used expert interviews (see Appendix), financial statements and other publicly available information.

12.3 Vulnerability Analysis for FinTech Banks

12.3.1 PESTLE Analysis

As London is the European FinTech hub, the following uses the UK as an example for illustration purposes.

Political: The UK's overall political stability index decreased within the past few years. In 2015, the UK was still ranked number 70 in the world's political stability ranking. Two years later, in 2017, it descended to rank number 80 (The Global Economy, 2018). Most political challenges UK FinTech banks are, or might be, facing in the near future are Brexit-related.

Economic: Great Britain's economy was relatively stable. The country's GDP reached $2,808.899 billion in 2018 (International Monetary Fund, 2018). Prior to the Brexit agreement, the Bank of England predicted that the entire UK economy might shrink by about 0.75%–1.75% by 2023. In case of a no-deal Brexit, the economy could possibly shrink by 7.7% in 15 years. Furthermore, "the value of the pound would slump by as much as 25%" (Kottasová, 2018). Whatever the actual impact will be, customers of UK FinTech banks, and thus the banks themselves, would be influenced by an economic downturn. On the other hand, many FinTech banks do not seem to hold any material market risk positions yet.

Social: An important social aspect influencing FinTech banks is demography. FinTech banks are often considered banks for millennials (i.e. people born between 1981 and 1997). Currently, about 30% of the world population falls in the range of millennials (Hechler-Fayd'herbe, 2017). In the UK, 13.9% of the population are so called millennials (Brown/Apostolova, 2017). The willingness of people to manage their finances over their smartphone via an app evidently affects UK FinTech banks. The attitude towards new technology is strong amongst millennials. They are undeniably attached to their smartphones and even trust them with their finances. However, other generations (born before 1981) who make up a large part of populations, are often more sceptical, e.g. because of data protection concerns.

Technological: Constant changes in technology have a strong impact on FinTech banks. Businesses that are entirely based on technology need to constantly evaluate their business model to keep up with the latest technological trends. There are various examples in the past where technology-based companies failed because they were not able to keep up with the fast pace of technological change. For example, some leading social media platforms were not agile enough to cope with technological trends and were outperformed by Facebook and other social media platforms. Technological change also influences FinTech banks from a direct competitive perspective. For example, London is a FinTech hub and banks face quite a few competitors which also keep abreast of technological developments. Furthermore, FinTech banks are facing the threat of cyber-attacks on a daily basis. According to *Cybercrime Magazine* (Herjavec Group, 2020), "cybercriminal activity is one of the biggest challenges that humanity will face in the next two decades", with cybercrime damages equating $6 Trillion by 2021. Another technological influence is social media. A bank's reputation gets particularly influenced by what users comment about the bank online, both positively and negatively.

Legal: The business model is usually heavily dependent on the banking licence. Thus, FinTech need to fulfil and maintain all legal and regulatory requirements, including labour and employment rights. Since the banks usually handle large amounts of customer data, it is expected to adhere to customer data regulation, which is currently the General Data Protection Regulation (GDPR). The regulation aims to give individuals more control over their data, making it possible to withdraw consent and delete or edit personal data.

Environmental: Environmental factors seem to affect many FinTech banks to a lesser extent at the moment. However, this may change in the future, as banks start to build out their product mix on the asset side of the balance sheet (e.g. loans).

12.3.2 SWOT Analysis for FinTech Banks

Table 12.1 summarises the results of the SWOT analysis. For the reasons previously mentioned, this chapter focuses on the weaknesses and threats listed on the right-hand side.

Table 12.1: Nucleus SWOT analysis.

Strengths:	Weaknesses:
Strong IT expertise	No secure cyber security system
Rapid growth	Dependence on internet connectivity
	Limited customer segment
	Limited product offer
	Dependence on crowdfunding/weak finances
	Location: Based in UK
Opportunities:	**Threats:**
High level of automation and cost-saving potential	Cyber attacks
High demand for mobile payment → operating in a growing market	Reputational damage
	Customers switching over to competitors
	Loss of passporting rights
	Stop in growth
	Shrinking capital due to unsuccessful (crowd)funding

12.3.2.1 Weaknesses

Cyber security system under attack/high exposure to cyber fraud: Since many FinTech banks operate entirely through online platforms, they are a target for hackers and cyber criminals. For example, in its 2017 annual report, the CEO of one European FinTech bank stated: "There are clearly potential risks and pitfalls here. Who gets to access customer data? What purposes can they use it for? Is it stored securely after it's shared? These are questions we will need to address before these third-party services can be offered to all customers" (Monzo Bank Ltd, 2017, p. 3). As such, FinTech banks may be exposed to weaknesses in their cyber security systems. A bank may also cooperate with companies that do not have safe cyber security systems and thus allow customers to become the victims of attackers.

Dependence on internet connectivity: For many FinTech banks, the core of the business model is an application or platform where customers can control their finances. The app must be connected to the internet in order for it to work. In these instances, it is not possible to use the bank's services without an internet connection.

Limited customer segment: Another weakness is that FinTech banks often still work with a relatively narrow customer segment. The banks, in some cases, call themselves a bank for millennials. By only attracting young customers, some banks limit their potential client base to a small group.

Limited product and service range: Individual banks still have a limited product and service range on offer. For example, one bank still primarily offers current accounts that only work in connection with the app. It does not yet provide traditional banking offers such as mortgages or credit cards, at least not in material size. The offerings tend to appeal to young people and may be seen as inaccessible for some members of older generations.

Dependence on crowdfunding/weak earnings: Individual FinTech banks are still entirely dependent on crowdfunding. They also do not yet generate enough revenue or have a large enough equity base to operate without capital raised by crowdfunding. While some FinTechs have already broken even, others remain loss-making companies.

Location: From a European perspective, being based in the UK currently creates additional political, economic and legal uncertainties (e.g. passporting rights).

12.3.2.2 Threats

Figure 12.1 summarises the results of the prior analyses in a joint graphic. The bottom right section lists the key threats, which are explained in detail.

Cyber attacks: Financial crime, cyber security and operational process risk are frequently seen as the main risk exposures of FinTech banks. Individual banks had to deal with major cyber-attacks during the last few years. Thereby they became a victim through direct attacks on the bank and through co-operations with third-party firms that suffered from weaknesses in their cyber security systems. Furthermore, FinTech banks' business models are usually dependent on internet connectivity. If an attacker gets access to the application, manipulates it or even makes it potentially unusable, customers could be unable to manage their accounts. The app is needed to block debit card transactions, which would no longer be possible if the app was compromised. As such, the risk that customer data is misappropriated and/or fraudulently used is often still one of the main risks to consider.

Reputational damage: A resulting threat is reputational damage. Start-ups need a strong reputation in order to grow. FinTech banks' reputations are particularly influenced by social media. Since some banks communicate to customers primarily via a blog, cyber security incidents have a risk of creating panic among current and potential customers. While transparent communication of incidents is generally seen as a positive, precipitated information may leave the impression amongst clients that

External Influences: PESTLE-Analysis	
PESTLE-factor	**Criteria**
Political	• Brexit/No-deal Brexit
Economical	• Economic slowdown by up to 7.7% due to Brexit
Social	• Demography: 13,9% millennials in UK • People's attitude towards mobile banking
Technological	• Technological change • Technological competition • Existence of hackers/cyber fraud • Social Media
Legal	• GDPR
Environmental	Not applicable

Internal Weaknesses	
Criteria	
• *Increased exposure to cyber attacks* • *Dependence on internet-connectivity* • *Limited customer segment* • *Limited offer* • *Dependence on crowdfunding* • *Location: Based in UK*	

Threats	
Criteria	**Threat**
Existance of hackers/cyber fraud +*No safe cyber security system* + *Dependence on internet-connectivity*	Cyber attacks
Social Media + *No safe cyber security system* GDPR + *No safe cyber security system*	Reputational damage
Technological change + Technological competition + *Limited offer*	Customers switching over to competition
No-deal Brexit + *Location: Based in UK*	Loss of passporting rights
Demography: 13,9% , illennialsin UK + *Limited customer segment* + *Limited offer* Economic slowdown by up to 7.7% due to Brexit + *Location: Based in UK*	Stop in growth
Economic slowdown by up to 7.7% due to Brexit + *Dependence on crowdfunding*	Shrinking capital due to unsuccessful crowdfunding

Figure 12.1: Nucleus PESTLE analysis and partial SWOT (Weaknesses and Threats) analysis.

their money is not safe with the respective FinTech bank. With social media, news spreads rapidly, which – in terms of bad news – may quickly damage a FinTech bank's reputation and may make current customers cancel their existing accounts as well as prevent potential customers from joining. Furthermore, data protection law breaches call into question an individual bank's cyber security system, threatening a bank's reputation with customers.

Customers switching to competitors: London is the FinTech hub of the world. More people than anywhere else in the world work in FinTech roles. Many FinTech banks still have a relatively limited offering. For example, one bank's main offer is a current account where customers can deposit money, which comes with a debit card and an app. This individual bank does not yet offer other common, traditional, banking products, such as mortgages. However, mortgages and credit cards are valuable products for creating additional income. Several competitors offer nearly the same products and services, while some main competitors offer exactly the same range of products. If competitors offer more and better products and services, the threat of customers switching over to competitors could materialise. At the same time, many business models are influenced by fast technological change on a daily basis.

Loss of passporting rights: Losing the passporting rights after the Brexit transition is another specific threat to many UK FinTech banks. The loss of passporting rights will make it more difficult to grow and operate in any other European country. UK FinTech banks may have to obtain a banking license for every European Union country in which they want to expand.

Slow growth: As previously mentioned, individual FinTech banks have a limited customer segment. Since only a fraction of customers (e.g. 13.9% of all UK citizens) are considered millennials, the idea of attracting new customers could be exhausted quickly. Furthermore, the product offering is often still limited. Banks headquartered in the UK might also be facing slowed economic growth environment as a result of Brexit.

Shrinking capital due to losses and unsuccessful crowdfunding: As noted, individual FinTech banks are dependent on crowdfunding. While leading FinTech banks have so far been able to achieve their targeted funding levels, this is a process subject to a multitude of external factors. Many investors are based in the same country and would be affected if a recession occurred (e.g. because of Brexit). Most importantly, banks could be subject to idiosyncratic issues impacting their ability to raise funding (in particular if they remain loss-making). Without crowdfunding capital, the risk of running out of money could materialise. The banks are also exposed to the sharing of intellectual properties. On the crowdfunding platform, they need to reveal business model information, which can make it an easier target for competition. Equity crowdfunding brings along additional administrative costs. In addition, the capital base is spread wider with every additional investor.

As part of the vulnerability analysis, these results can be further classified – for example, into financial and non-financial vulnerabilities, or mapped to heatmaps using severity and other criteria – and serve as input for the next steps in the RST process (see also Mazurek, 2019, The Economist, 2019a, 2019b and Woodford/Darrah, 2019 for further considerations on opportunities and threats of the FinTech industry and individual banks).

12.3.3 Linkage to Other RST Steps

In this section, the earnings, liquidity and capital position – typical RST failure points – are further assessed.

Earnings capability: As noted, leading FinTech banks continue to be in a growth phase and are not yet profitable. In some cases, the loss before tax increased multi-fold over the last years. The net operating income can still be a fraction of the total operating expenses, mainly caused by investments in the banking operations. At the same time, staff costs tend to grow as the number of employees increases rapidly in individual banks. While individual banks are able to decrease the costs of holding an account year-on-year, they often either suffer a net loss per account or make a low single-digit gain. At the moment, different FinTech banks do not have any products that create significant revenue. Individual banks plan to break even soon by cutting costs and adding revenue-generating services, such as fees on overdrafts. However, overdrafts bring along a risk of credit default. The scope to improve the current earnings situation is also limited due to the highly competitive environment. FinTech banks need to attract customers by offering products with low margins in order to remain in line with competitors, which is not beneficial for profitability.

Liquidity adequacy: In some FinTech banks, the 'cash and balances at bank' are higher than their customer deposits – i.e. these banks are holding more liquidity than needed to cover the immediate outflow of all customer deposits. However, the individual customer account size often remains small in overall notional terms.

Capital adequacy: Leading FinTech banks currently have strong equity ratios, often due to the successful crowdfunding campaigns. In some cases, the equity ratio decreased due to high growth strategies, which generated a high negative return on capital employed, meaning the bank generates losses with the acquired capital from crowdfunding. This leaves banks vulnerable to investors unwillingness for further investments, since the latter cannot expect dividends if a bank does not reach profitability. Some banks started giving out loans to customers for the first time. While there is limited information on whether any of the loans might be considered problem-loans, the risk that customers borrowing money will not repay or do not pay on time, causing financial loss, may be one of the main risks that FinTech banks are exposed to in the near future.

In practice, the next steps may depend on the chosen failure points, their calibration and the categorisation of the aforementioned vulnerabilities. However, applying the four failure types (earnings, liquidity, capital- and liquidity-induced failure) distinguished by Eichhorn/Mangold in Part III of this book leads to the following:

- The prospect of future earnings failures seems very real. Many FinTech banks have not yet reached profitability. In some cases, losses increase year on year. Even though losses during the first few years of operation are to be expected, the vulnerabilities identified here may give rise to scenario narratives such as the failure of the planned growth strategy.
- A capital failure cannot only result from continued losses. As highlighted, some banks are entirely capitalised by crowdfunding. While the crowdfunding campaigns were often very successful in the past and individual banks hold very healthy equity ratios at the moment, crowdfunding can be considered a volatile means of financing. Investments generally depend on the current phase of the economic cycle and may be impacted by the vulnerabilities previously identified.
- With regard to a liquidity failure, several FinTech banks have been rather successful in growing their deposit portfolio. However, as some banks are only developing loan products, at times, most of these funds are held at a central bank which also contributes to earnings weaknesses. While vulnerabilities such as cyber attacks and data incidents may cause the withdrawal of funds (especially if they reoccur), a pure liquidity failure may be more remote than, for example, an earnings failure, given current overall liquidity positions.
- A capital-induced liquidity failure seems more relevant than a 'pure' liquidity failure, especially if the capital risks outlined here materialise and possibly even coincide with other (non-financial) vulnerabilities such as cyber attacks or data confidentiality breaches.

These considerations suggest focusing the subsequent steps in the RST approach proposed at the outset (high-level storyboards, scenario calibration, mitigating actions and so on) on capital and earnings considerations. While these steps require further management insight, the results identified so far seem rich enough to support initial management discussions with content and structure.

12.4 Summary

Reverse stress tests are intended to provide insights into a bank's susceptibility to developments that could endanger its existence and thus facilitate the identification of potential threats for the bank's business model. The purpose of strategic management tools, overlaps, in part, with this objective. This leads to the question of whether they can be leveraged for RST.

The results of this high-level experiment suggest that strategic management tools like SWOT and PESTLE can indeed help to detect and categorise vulnerabilities. Despite the strong public perception and arguably solid capital and liquidity positions of leading FinTech banks, the work identified multiple vulnerabilities (of which various may also be relevant for more mature banks). In the analysis process, the tools helped to ask the "right" questions and to map back and classify the resulting answers. The results can in turn help to derive relevant RST storyboards and prioritise mitigating actions.

On the contrary, only publicly available data was considered. The results are therefore by no means representative and should instead be considered a test run. The latter also highlights the following limitations:

- Like other tools, PESTLE and SWOT are dependent on the quality of their inputs. This chapter used expert interviews, financial statements and other publicly available information. This helped to identify initial themes and to classify them. However, there is no substitute for inside knowledge.
- The tools can only satisfy certain aspects, which should be considered in a vulnerability analysis. A PESTLE analysis only deals with political, economic, social, technological, legal and environmental influences. In order to gain broader insight, a bank should consider observing further external influences such as ethical or geographical aspects, as well as internal factors (e.g. corporate culture and stakeholder motives).
- In this analysis, the SWOT analysis was further restricted to weaknesses and threats. In practice, banks may take a sense of false security from supposed strengths and opportunities without scrutinising them further. A well-known example is assumptions made on the risks inherent in certain credit derivative products prior to the financial crisis. The "euphoria" over these products often meant that managers did not challenge them sufficiently. Therefore, a possible extension would be to critically examine a bank's strengths and to check whether or not the perceived opportunities bear any potentially overlooked risks.
- The test only used two strategic management tools to identify business model vulnerabilities. In practice, it seems advisable to include further strategic management tools (e.g. scenario planning) to gain insight from different perspectives. Interestingly, both tools crystallised similar vulnerabilities without one tool being clearly superior to the other. Banks may therefore consider using only one of these two tools.
- The usage of strategic management tools seems more relevant for qualitative RST. Since most UK FinTech banks are still relatively small banks, a qualitative analysis may be considered adequate. In larger institutions, a combination of qualitative risks and quantitative elements may be required (Grundke/Pliszka, 2015). The implementation of a quantitative and qualitative stress test, however, is very complex and requires the help of many departments and experts. It would therefore be accompanied by a lot of effort (Gann, 2012).

On balance, especially smaller banks and users who look for a qualitative RST approach may consider strategic management tools as an easily accessible starting point from which the organisation can collaboratively think about business model vulnerabilities in a structured way. Like RST, strategic management tools have a dedicated business model focus – they are designed to examine the fundamental assumptions of the business model, how vulnerable these assumptions are to stress and to capture business model uncertainties and strategic risks.

Going back to the beginning of this chapter, the tools may be particularly helpful to capture non-financial risks – an area where, as highlighted, RST approaches are less advanced. The relevance of this chapter for the future advancement of RST is finally underlined by the following considerations:

- According to Kastner (2012), the root cause for many earnings, liquidity, capital and other failures are strategic misallocations and misguided actions. These strategic errors often precede and ultimately lead to capital and/or liquidity failures.
- Quagliariello (2019) argues that capturing strategic risks and uncertainties in stress tests "requires long-term horizons and it is more about the sustainability of a business model rather than immediate capital needs". He makes the argument in context of climate change. However, it seems equally true for other political, economic, social, technological and legal risks and uncertainties previously discussed.
- For Slywotzky/Drzik (2005, p. 78), "most managers have not addressed in a systematic way", what they call "the greatest threat of all" – "the array of external events and trends". Strategic management tools like scenario planning help to analyse external trends and uncertainties in a structured manner using a defined sequence of steps and a forward-looking enterprise-wide perspective.
- Beyond vulnerabilities, strategic management tools can offer insights into scenarios where the bank can profit from uncertainty, addressing the "downside only" limitation of RST stated in Chapter 1. For example, Schoemaker (2002), in his book *Profiting from Uncertainty: No Matter What the Future Brings*, proposes a scenario planning approach which starts with the identification of the two most relevant uncertainties. This leads to a 2x2 matrix consisting of four distinct scenarios. Each scenario combines different binary realisations of the two main uncertainties – from a best-case scenario (positive/positive) to a worst-pain scenario (negative/negative). The scenarios represent the cornerstones of a scenario canvas which projects possible future states of the world. After a further enrichment of each scenario, the approach pressure-tests the viability of the firm's current business model, key financial plans and strategic initiatives under each of the four hypothetical scenarios. For each scenario, preparatory management actions (e.g. purchase of real options) are assessed. Without the latter, at least, the worst-pain scenario tends to bring (parts of) the bank to its knees.
- The examined integration of SWOT and PESTLE into RST is only exemplary. An RST user can choose from a large group of strategic management tools. For example, Evans (2013) references over 80 key strategy tools.

Appendix 12.1: Interview with Vladimir Ivanov (SEC Washington DC) 04/03/2019

Vladimir Ivanov works as a Senior Financial Economist for the Securities and Exchange Commission (SEC) in Washington D.C. He works with start-ups and FinTechs and authored different publications based on his experiences (see, for example, Na Dai, Vladimir Ivanov and Rebel Cole (2017): Entrepreneurial optimism, credit availability, and cost of financing: Evidence from U.S. small businesses, in *Journal of Corporate Finance*, vol. 44, issue C, 289–307; Anzhela Knyazeva and Vladimir Ivanov, Soft and hard information and signal extraction in securities crowdfunding. 2nd Emerging Trends in Entrepreneurial Finance Conference, 2018).

Interview

Block 1: Vulnerabilities

Author: As the first step, I would like to hear a few opinions based on your own experience working with FinTechs. What are the main vulnerabilities/external risks in general for a FinTech bank's business models? You can for example think of capital related issues, fundraising, legal or political issues, etc.

Ivanov: One major risk is regulation. Currently most FinTechs are lightly regulated compared to traditional financial institutions because of the types of services they provide and the risks they pose to the financial system. If a FinTech bank is to branch out into more traditional banking services such as deposit taking, lending, securities underwriting, etc., that may lead to a higher regulatory regime that may decrease the profit margins. Competition is another major risk because of low barriers to entry. What leading FinTech banks do does not seem to be difficult for potential competitors to replicate. Plus, their technology cannot not be easily protected by a patent or some other type of intellectual property that could hold competition at bay for a while. Why can't a large bank like Citi or JP Morgan, with their enormous resources, replicate FinTech banks' business model? Yet another risk is the macroeconomic cycle. FinTech has been thriving over the last few years, but that has coincided with an economic boom. It remains to be seen how FinTech perform in a recession. If capital dries out during a recession, a FinTech bank may find it difficult to finance its activities.

Author: The main vulnerabilities for FinTech banks can be found in the field of technological threats. Which technological threats do you see for FinTech banks?

Ivanov: The development of substitute products that could take away customers from the bank. Also, technological shocks that may render a FinTech bank's technology obsolete and allow other FinTechs or even traditional financial institutions to offer the same types or even a broader spectrum of services, maybe at a lower price.

Author: FinTech banks tend to have a very young customer base. The average user is between 25 and 35 years old. Since this age group is usually not very wealthy and often dependent on loans, do you believe the young customer base is a threat to a FinTech bank?

Ivanov: I do think that the younger customer base is a potential threat because millennials are not very wealthy. This is especially true when combined with the limited scope of services that many FinTech banks are offering. At some point, a bank will have to reach out to wealthier/institutional investors or customers because those could provide much more capital.

Author: Is it more likely that a FinTech bank fails due to a fatal sudden punch (e.g. a sudden technological threat) or a slow bleeding out (e.g. long-term capital failure)?

Ivanov: It could be both. I don't think one is more likely than the other.

Author: If a FinTech failed, what would be the reasons for the failure? What factors usually let a FinTech's business model become unviable?

Ivanov: Competition, technological changes, inability to raise enough capital to stay afloat, inability to reach profitability quickly, a regulatory shock that negatively affects its profitability.

Author: In the second step, I would like to ask you one specific question about one specific UK FinTech bank.

The bank is not profitable yet. Due to the high competition, the bank follows a growth strategy rather than a profit strategy. Looking at its financial statements, do you believe the big losses might already be an indicator for them to fail soon? From your personal experience, is it normal for start-ups to have such big losses during their first years, and do you believe that the bank will become profitable soon?

Ivanov: It is normal for start ups to be unprofitable and stay unprofitable for a while, and a large current loss is not necessarily an indicator of an imminent failure, provided that at some point they expect to become profitable, and that they are able to raise capital to stay afloat until they reach profitability. So continued access to financing will be crucial. And it has to be institutional capital (e.g. venture capital, bank loans, etc.) which could bring in large amounts of money. From its financials, it appears that the main source of revenues is fees from services provided to customers. With a lean cost structure, fee income may be enough to lead to positive profitability. However, the bank may need to consider whether shifting to high profit margin services and products may be a way to survive in the long run.

Block 2: Mitigating Management Actions

Author: Based on the vulnerabilities you mentioned, which mitigating actions should the bank's management check in order to prevent its business model from becoming unviable?

Ivanov: The bank in question may want to think about offering high profit margin services and products that could allow it to break even sooner. Also, it has to develop some type of competitive advantage that would allow it to ward off competitors – brand name, product quality, innovative products and services, scalability or similar. Maybe it can expand its customer base. Lastly, making sure that the company has access to capital while pursuing its growth strategy will be crucial to survival.

Appendix 12.2: Interview with Kalin Tintchev (IMF Washington DC) 17/02/2019

Kalin Tintchev is currently a Senior Economist at the European Central Bank in Frankfurt, Germany, on secondment from the International Monetary Fund (IMF) in Washington, DC.[1] During his career at the International Monetary Fund, he has conducted stress tests and financial stability analysis for the IMF's Financial Sector Assessment Program and has co-authored publications on these topics. (See Rodolfo Maino/ Kalin Tintchev, 2012: From Stress to Costress, Stress Testing Interconnected Banking Systems, February 2012, IMF Working Paper No. 12/53; Kalin Tintchev, 2014: Interconnectedness, Vulnerabilities, and Crisis Spillovers: Implications for the New Financial Stability Framework, The George Washington University); Canetti et al., 2017: Financial Interconnectedness in the Caribbean: Challenges for Financial Stability (in Srinivasan et al: *Unleashing Growth and Strengthening Resilience in the Caribbean.*)

Interview

Block 1: Reverse Stress Testing

Author: Do you believe reverse stress tests can help a young start-up like a FinTech bank in detecting its vulnerabilities and preventing the business model from becoming unviable?

---

[1] This interview should not be reported as representing the views of the IMF or the ECB. The views expressed in the interview are those of the interviewee and do not necessarily represent those of the IMF or IMF policy as well as the ECB or ECB policy.

Tintchev: I believe that reverse stress testing is important for start-ups as they operate in a very volatile environment. Thus, it is important to know your vulnerabilities.

Author: Where do you see potential limits of reverse stress testing?

Tintchev: The scenarios used in reverse stress testing are typically severe and it is important that they are also plausible in order to be able to provide reliable information about the stress tested companies' financial viability. Data limitations could constrain our ability to quantitatively implement the reverse stress testing scenarios and assess their impact.

Author: Do you believe that FinTech banks are usually concerned about stress testing (or even reverse stress testing) or do they not deal with it at all?

Tintchev: FinTech banks are still more lightly regulated than traditional banks and may not be subject to mandatory stress testing requirements. Furthermore, many FinTech start-ups have yet to become profitable and face more volatile business conditions, which could pose new, unique challenges to stress testers. FinTech companies have to cope with multiple challenges during their initial years and may not have the resources and skilled personnel to conduct stress tests.

Block 2: Vulnerabilities

Author: Which external risks in general do you see for a leading UK FinTech bank's business model?

Tintchev: External risks could arise from various channels – for example, structural changes in the regulatory regime or macroeconomic shocks.

First, FinTech companies could face a potentially more challenging regulatory and operational environment, especially after Brexit, which could lead to uncertainty about the future relations with the EU. UK-based FinTech companies would have to adapt to the new trade and financial arrangements between the UK and the EU. Their EU operations are also likely to face new regulatory barriers.

Second, macroeconomic shocks – for example, an upcoming recession – could pose significant risks to more fragile FinTech companies. FinTech start-ups have to mainly rely on equity funding given their weak balance sheets and profitability, which constrain their ability to tap the debt markets. They may need additional rounds of equity financing to expand their market share and invest in technology in order to remain competitive. Raising equity financing is more difficult and more costly than debt financing – especially during recessions, when equity investors become more risk averse.

A recession could also undermine the creditworthiness of the FinTech bank's customers. Its customer base represents primarily millennials, who could face difficulties finding and retaining employment during recession given their lack of experience. Thus, its more volatile and financially fragile customer base could render the bank more at risk than other banks with a more mature customer base. Finally, the FinTech bank needs to grow fast in order to reach profitability. A recession would reduce its business volumes and fee income, with negative repercussions for its financial condition.

Author: Where do you believe are weaknesses?

Tintchev: The bank's low profitability is a major weakness, especially in a more volatile macroeconomic environment. Its dependence on external financing (crowdfunding capital) is another source of risk. Furthermore, its business model is heavily dependent on technology. This renders the bank vulnerable to technological failure. A cyber-attack that compromises the FinTech bank's firewalls could lead to reputational damage as customers might lose savings and become subject to identity theft. Another weakness stems from the bank's limited product diversification. The bank relies on a narrow range of products – mainly checking deposit accounts – and earns small margins. Diversifying into higher-margin products (e.g. consumer loans, mortgages) could help support growth and profitability. Finally, the FinTech bank operates in an area where regulations are still under development. A potential tightening of FinTech regulations would increase the bank's compliance costs, with negative repercussions for profitability.

Author: The main vulnerabilities can be found in the field of technological threats. Which technological threats do you see for the bank?

Tintchev: The main technological threat comes from the possibility of a cyber-attack. There are many examples of breaches that have occurred in bank security systems. Breaches could cause customers to lose trust in the FinTech bank's ability to meet data protection regulations. Since the bank is heavily dependent on retail deposits, a run on the bank could be very dangerous.

Another major threat stems from competitive pressures. Competitors could develop better technological solutions and take away customers from the bank. For example, they could develop better, faster, more reliable applications. Another risk is related to the possibility of a technological failure of the bank's applications. If there are glitches in the bank's applications, customers would temporarily lose access to their money, leading to reputational damage for the bank.

Author: The bank has a very young customer base. The average user is between 25 and 35 years old. Since this age group is usually not very wealthy and is often dependent on loans, do you believe the bank's customer base is a threat to the business model?

Tintchev: The volatility of the bank's customer base is a big threat. Young customers are volatile because of lower earnings, which negatively affects their ability to save and service loans. The bank should develop products that appeal to members of higher age brackets who have more savings and, from a banking perspective, are safer customers. The bank could attract customers from higher age groups by offering traditional banking products such as credit cards and mortgages.

Author: The bank is not profitable yet. Due to the high competition, the bank follows a growth strategy rather than a profit strategy. Looking at the bank's financial statements, do you believe the big losses might already be an indicator of an upcoming failure?

Tintchev: It is typical for start-ups to operate at a loss in the initial stages of their development because they have to make large investments in infrastructure and technology platforms that would lay the foundation for future growth. The question is whether they will become profitable over time. The bank does not have brick-and-mortar branch operations – which would be very expensive – since it only operates via its application. Still, it has other operational expenses and costs related to licensing requirements. So far, the bank has managed to keep a very lean balance sheet structure. It goes without saying that crowdfunding is a very volatile way of funding. Retail investors are particularly risk averse and could withdraw from the market if economic growth falters.

Author: Can you please rank your top 5 vulnerabilities?

Tintchev: Low profitability, a weak capital position (crowdfunding-based), technological risk (a potential for reputational damage), volatile customer base and insufficient diversification.

Block 3: Storyboards

Author: Which storyboards do you believe are relevant to the bank's business model? Examples could be a long-term capital failure storyboard or a short-term reputational damage storyboard.

Tintchev: I consider the long-term capital failure option relevant, because the bank is not making profits and relies on external financing to support operations and investments. If the bank is unable to reach its crowdfunding target at some point in the future, capital failure is very likely. The bank should seek to become profitable to reduce its dependence on crowdfunding. Crowdfunding is relatively expensive and can dilute the bank's ownership over time. Crowdfunding is just not a long-term way of financing. Furthermore, a short-term liquidity failure due to reputational damage is very likely because of the technological risks the bank is exposed to, like cyber threats or technological failure. A technological breach could erode the bank's customer base.

Author: When you think about the vulnerabilities and the storyboards you mentioned, do you believe it is rather likely that the bank's business model becomes unviable by a fatal sudden punch (e.g. a sudden technological threat) or a slow bleeding out (e.g. a long-term capital failure)?

Tintchev: Both scenarios are plausible. A slow bleeding out could occur if the bank fails to broaden its customers' base and reach profitability while it is faced with reduced fresh capital as investors gradually lose confidence in its growth prospects or become more risk averse if the economy enters a recession. Internal errors that damage its reputation and lead to a sudden fatal punch are also possible. The management might engage in excessive risk-taking, while staff could commit costly operational errors. A fatal sudden punch is particularly likely to occur if there is an application failure or a cyber-attack that breaches the bank's firewalls and impedes the customers' ability to use the bank's services. This could permanently tarnish its reputation, causing customers to switch over to competitors.

Block 4: Mitigating Management Actions

Author: Based on the vulnerabilities you mentioned, which mitigating actions should the management consider?

Tintchev: The bank in question should strengthen its IT security and keep up with the latest technology to ensure reliability of its application. Meeting cyber-safety compliance requirements would help reduce technology failure risks. It should also keep cash buffers to be able to meet unexpected expenses due to such risks. To improve profitability, the bank should broaden its client base – for example, by gradually diversifying in more traditional banking products. The bank could expand its advertising to increase brand recognition and market share. This is important for achieving profitability and earning customer loyalty. Expanding the customer base to other age groups and business customers would strengthen its deposit funding and lead to more stable revenue generation. To mitigate risks, management should strive to reach the stage of stable revenue growth and profitability. This would allow the bank to raise longer-term debt financing, reducing its overall cost of borrowing and improving cash flow. Debt financing offers also tax advantages. However, the bank should be cautious against assuming excessive leverage as it could magnify its vulnerability and losses during economic downturns. To support profitability, the bank should invest in higher-margin products and expand interest income to reduce its reliance on third-party fees. Gradually, it could exploit its online platform to expand to other countries. This would broaden its growth opportunities and help diversify external risks.

Bibliography

Brown, J., Apostolova, V. a.o. (2017). Millennials, in: House of Commons Library, Vol. CBP7946.

Browne, R. (2018), Digital banking start-up Revolut breaks even as it prepares global expansion. Available at: https:// www.cnbc.com/2018/02/26/fintech-lender-revolut-breaks-even-as-it-prepares-global-expansion.html [Accessed 2 February 2019].

Canetti et al. (2017). Financial Interconnectedness in the Caribbean: Challenges for Financial Stability, in: Srinivasan et al: *Unleashing Growth and Strengthening Resilience in the Caribbean.*

Eichhorn, M. and Mangold, P. (2017). Reverse Stress Testing: Linking Risks, Earnings, Capital and Liquidity –A Process-Orientated Framework and Its Application to Asset–Liability Management: Edited by Andreas Bohn and Marije Elkenbracht-Huizing. *Handbook of Asset Liability Management in Banking* (2), pp. 511–531.

Evans V. (2013). *Key Strategy Tools: The 80+ Tools for Every Manager to Build a Winning Strategy*, Harlow.

Gann, P. (2012). Inverse Stresstests in Kreditinstituten: Ein quantitativ orientierter Ansatz, in: CFB0483574 6/2912, pp. 285–299.

Grundke, P., Pliszka, K. (2015). *A macroeconomic reverse stress test*. Deutsche Bundesbank: Frankfurt am Main.

Hechler-Fayd'herbe, N. (2017). Millennials: Besser als ihr Ruf. Available at: https://www. credit-suisse.com/about-us-news/de/articles/news-and-expertise/millennials-better-than-their-reputation-201710.html [Accessed 30 January 2019].

Herjavec Group (2020). Available at: https://www.herjavecgroup.com/the-2019-official-annual-cybercrime-report/ [Accessed 13 December 2020].

International Monetary Fund (2018). Report for Selected Countries and Subjects. Available at: https://www.imf.org/external/pubs/ft/weo/2018/02/weodata/weorept.aspx?pr.x=84&pr.y=9&sy=2017&ey=2018&scsm=1&ssd=1&sort=country&ds=.&br=1&c=112&s=NGDPD%2CPPPGDP%2CNGDPDPC%2CPPPPC&grp=0&a= [Accessed 11 February 2019].

Kastner A. (2012). Der Einsatz von Krisenindikatoren im Rahmen des Firmenkundenkreditgeschaeftes, in: Becker A., Gruber W., Wohlert D. (2012). *Handbuch MaRisk und Basel III*, 2nd edition, S.467–500 Frankfurt am Main.

Kottasová, I. (2018). The impact of Brexit on the UK economy, CNN. Available at: https://edition.cnn.com/2018/11/28/economy/brexit-economic-impact/index.html [Accessed 30 January 2019].

London & Partners (2018). London's fintech scene at a glance, https://www.thepower50.com/wp-content/uploads/2018/04/london-fintech-scene-2017-2.pdf [Accessed 7 July 2020].

Maino, R./ Tintchev, K. (2012). From Stress to Costress, Stress Testing Interconnected Banking Systems, IMF Working Paper No. 12/53

Mazurek, M. (2019). Revolut, N26 and the others: The arms race among European banking challengers accelerates (LinkedIn), [Online] Available from https://www.linkedin.com/pulse/revolut-n26-others-arms-race-among-european-banking-marcin-mazurek/ [Accessed 2 February 2019].

Monzo Bank Ltd. (2017). Annual Report 2017.

Morgan S. (2020). Cybercrime Damages $6 Trillion By 2021, https://cybersecurityventures.com/hackerpocalypse-cybercrime-report-2016/ [Accessed 24 July 2020].

Quagliariello M. (2019). The impact of climate change on financial system stability, referenced in: Plochan P.: *Climate Change, Strategy and Stress Testing*, PRMIA, November 2019.

Osborn T., Mourselas C. (2020). Stuart Lewis, Deutsche's survivor, confronts Covid-19, https://www.risk.net/risk-management/7654716/stuart-lewis-deutsches-survivor-confronts-covid-19 [Accessed 25 July 2020].

Schoemaker, P. (2002). *Profiting from Uncertainty: Strategies for Succeeding No Matter What the Future Brings*, New York.

Slywotzky, A., Drzik, J. (2005). Countering the Biggest Risk of All, in *Harvard Business Review*, April 2005, pp. 78–89.

The Global Economy (2018). Political stability by country, around the world, TheGlobalEconomy. com. Available at: https://www.theglobaleconomy.com/rankings/wb_political_stability/ [Accessed 11 February 2019].

The Economist (2019a). Tech's raid on the banks, May 4–10, 2019 p. 13.

The Economist (2019b). A bank in your pocket, Special Report: Banking, May 4–10, 2019, pp. 1–12.

Woodford, I. and Darrah, K. (2019). Digital banks Monzo, Revolut, Starling and N26 compared. Available at: https://sifted.eu/articles/challenger-banks-monzo-starling-revolut-n26-compared/ [Accessed 7 July 2020].

Meha Lodha, Michael Eichhorn

13 Mild Reverse Stress Testing

An Innovative Configuration Set

13.1 Introduction

Imagine you are invited to a meeting with your bank's board to present the annual reverse stress testing (RST) results. You have spent many weeks preparing for this by going through regulatory and industry recommendations and articles on RST. Accordingly, you determined the points of failure that could render your bank's business model unviable – for example, in terms of earnings failure, capital failure and liquidity failure. You have also analysed the vulnerability of your bank's business lines, checked if the chosen scenario narratives are plausible and determined management actions. Now, what is the board's reaction? To say the least, the board is unimpressed. They say the probability of such adverse scenarios is too remote and that they would be more interested in scenarios that are more likely to occur. A member of the board also comments that if we were to manage life focusing solely on extreme tail events, then we would never be able to move forward.

Traditionally, RST is performed at group-level to identify scenarios that, should they unfold, can lead to a bank's business failure and render the business model unviable. In practical terms, the probability of such severe business failure or tail events may not rank high. On the other hand, an innovative configuration set called "mild RST" aims to identify those vulnerabilities and risk factors that are likely to cause a pre-determined moderate but significant loss which has a higher chance of occurring. Like RST, "Mild RST" can use various calibrations and test designs across the dimensions laid out in Part I of this book.

13.2 Definition

RST is generally defined as the analysis of scenarios that render the business model unviable. RST scenarios are often designed to be so severe that they "break the bank". Hence, the question arises: Is RST able to capture only those scenarios that can cause a bank's failure, or can RST also be used to discuss scenarios that cause moderate yet more probable losses?

This chapter goes to show how RST, in a less severe form referred to as Mild RST (MRST), can prove to be a useful and versatile risk management tool. Section 13.3 of the chapter narrates the six steps to perform RST and how these can be applied to

https://doi.org/10.1515/9783110647907-013

MRST. Section 13.4 focusses on defining a framework for an individual MRST exercise, wherein the different dimensions of RST, as discussed in Part I, are deliberated. Section 13.5 describes three different approaches to performing MRST– a simple quantitative goal seek approach, a historical risk factor analysis and a qualitative approach by conducting iterative expert interviews. Section 13.6 introduces different ways to present the resulting findings. The chapter closes with a summary in Section 13.7.

13.3 Six Steps to Reverse Stress Testing

As exemplified by Eichhorn/Mangold in Part III of this book, RST can follow a stepwise approach, starting with defining the points of failure, then performing vulnerability analysis, leveraging the risk inventory and deriving generic storyboards. This is followed by scenario design and parametrisation, plausibility checks and management actions and finally, monitoring and reporting. Functional representatives from across the bank's management should be involved in RST discussions.

Figure 13.1 shows the six steps to perform RST. MRST can principally follow these steps. Where relevant, the nuances to consider in the case of MRST are also described, in the step descriptions in the following sections.

Figure 13.1: Six steps to reverse stress testing.

13.3.1 Definition of Points of Failure

The first step is the definition of the so called "failure points", defined, for example, as points at which a bank's business model becomes unviable. In MRST, these failure points are chosen to be significantly less severe than in RST. However, like RST, MRST may distinguish different types of failure, including a failure from a liquidity perspective, a failure from a capital perspective, and a failure from an earnings perspective. While there can be interlinkages between these perspectives, MRST may consider them separately (similar to a sensitivity analysis). These aspects are further illustrated in Section 13.5.

13.3.2 Vulnerability Analysis and Risk Inventory

The purpose of the vulnerability analysis is to identify the primary material risks to which the bank is exposed through the business it conducts and the clients it serves.

Like for RST, the vulnerability analysis can combine various qualitative techniques, like expert interviews, or quantitative techniques. In MRST, the vulnerability analysis tends to be performed with a narrower scope and at a more granular level (for example, at desk or portfolio level).

13.3.3 Generic Storyboards

The storyboard encompasses the development of scenario narratives from status quo to the point where the business model becomes unviable. For MRST, the scenarios would narrate events from status quo to the point where a pre-determined range of mild losses (as opposed to complete business model failure) are generated, for example, in terms of the liquidity, capital and earnings losses noted here. While there may be a plethora of scenarios leading to such outcomes, the focus can be on novel risks or on risks that are currently tolerated but where reassurance is needed that governance bodies feel comfortable with current risk management practices (e.g. to accept and not hedge risk even if this results in a loss specified in the failure point determination).

13.3.4 Scenario Design and Parametrisation

The next step in the aforementioned RST approach from Eichhorn/Mangold is to specify and calibrate each element of the big picture storyboard. In MRST, a further calibration may not be performed as the narrative may allow for the intended discussion on the current risk management practices. In other examples, the analysis of historically observed risk factors moves may be performed to inform a scenario narrative and its relevance. This is followed by the next step, plausibility checks and management actions.

13.3.5 Plausibility Checks and Management Actions

With regard to plausibility checks, the narrative and calibration should be carefully sense-checked. In RST, the bank must take mitigating actions if the likelihood of an RST scenario, and hence risk of business model failure or monetary loss, is deemed to be unacceptably high. In MRST, the likelihood is by design high(er). Therefore, the focus should typically be on a decision to either maintain or modify current risk-taking practices. Examples of management actions include a decision to keep a particular position (un)hedged, to (no longer) accept a certain operational risk or to (not) build new risk management capabilities (e.g. controls).

13.3.6 Monitoring and Reporting

Scenarios and vulnerabilities should be monitored regularly to trigger timely management discussions and actions. Over time, users will observe changes of likelihood levels. If, for a given RST scenario, overall scenario likelihood levels increase, managers should propose formal mitigating actions and escalate to the relevant governance body. MRST scenarios can also be stable over time. However, a user may instead focus on a few scenarios at a time, especially where they would like to receive guidance or influence a management decision.

13.4 Defining the MRST Framework

Defining the framework for an RST exercise involves thoughtful deliberation by managers into various dimensions laid out at beginning of this book. As noted there, the very essence of RST is that it is a versatile risk management tool and hence there is no "one size fits all" approach. If a user accepts this and experiments with the different dimensions, a great variety of RST applications can be constructed.[1]

Out of the dimensions shown in Figure 13.2, MRST primarily adjusts the severity – i.e. it uses lower failure vulnerability thresholds. It also often chooses a narrower scope – for example, a single parameter or a combination of parameters may be selected. However, even within MRST, different calibration sets and test designs can be used, as the following approaches illustrate.

Scope		Events		Cause of Failure		Vulnerability Threshold		Time Horizon		Approach	
☐	Group	☐	Macro-economic	☐	Earnings	☐	1–5 mn USD	☐	Short/fast burn	☐	Qualitative
☐	Entities			☐	Capital	☐	5–10 mn USD			☐	Quantitative
☐	Portfolio	☐	Idiosyncratic	☐	Liquidity	☐	>10 mn USD	☐	Long/bleed-out	☐	Combination
☐	Books					☐	Other _____				

Figure 13.2: Building blocks to define the framework for a Mild Reverse Stress Test.

13.5 Approach for MRST

Given that RST is a versatile thinking tool, there can also be different approaches to performing MRST. Described in this section are a simple quantitative goal seek method

---

1 This may be compared to preparing different meals by varying the combination of ingredients or building different structures by selecting different combinations of the same set of interlocking bricks.

and a more complex quantitative approach as well as a qualitative approach by conducting and analysing (iterative) interviews of experts.

13.5.1 Quantitative Approach – Goal Seek Concept

In its simplest form, MRST can be a "goal-seek" of individual sensitivities. This is in many ways comparable to an inverse what-if analysis. Even though this doesn't call for much time and effort, it requires expert judgement to pick the most relevant risk factors and vulnerabilities which can be based on historical movements of sensitivities. In the goal seek concept, key vulnerabilities or risk factors that could affect an entity, portfolio or book are identified and then linked to a generically designed storyboard.

Figure 13.3 illustrates the goal seek concept for liquidity, capital and earnings failure. In each case, there is a vulnerability and a generic storyboard. The vulnerability can be derived from a material risk inventory and denotes the movement of a risk factor or a combination of risk factors. The generic storyboard is framed as a question querying which risk factors would need to change, and by how much to arrive at the goal i.e. a given point of failure. If the likelihood of occurrence of such moves is high, it is recommended that the bank reviews mitigating actions and monitors the risk factor's movement on a frequent basis.

13.5.1.1 Liquidity Failure

In the first case, we look at liquidity failure. The identified vulnerabilities are the reduction of assets held in liquidity buffer and liquidity outflow caused by liquidity risk factors. The storyboard poses the question: Changes or stress to which risk factors and by how much could trigger a wipe-out of USD 10bn of the bank's liquidity buffer? For this, the risk managers would need to assess the risk inventory and identify combinations of risk factors and/or scale each factor, such that the resulting loss lands at USD 10bn. An assessment should then be made to understand how often these losses are likely to occur. Accordingly, mitigating actions would need to be reviewed.

13.5.1.2 Capital Failure

For capital failure, in Figure 13.3, we identify the vulnerability as a mismatch in the currency composition for Risk Weighted Assets (RWAs) and Common Equity Tier 1 (CET1). For example, if 50% of RWAs are in USD but the bank holds only 30% of CET1 in USD, the CET1/RWA ratio is vulnerable to moves in the major currencies' exchange rates. The storyboard poses the question: What size of shocks to the foreign exchange

Liquidity failure: Net outflows beyond regulatory and internal metrics	
Vulnerability	Haircuts to assets held in liquidity buffer and/or sizeable net out-flows by liquidity risk factors.
Generic Storyboard	Which liquidity risk factors need to change, and by how much, to reduce the liquidity buffer below a given amount, e.g. USD 10bn (failure point)?

Capital failure: Immunization of CET1 Ratio against FX moves	
Vulnerability	Mismatch between risk-weighted assets (RWA) by currency and CET1 composition by currency
Generic Storyboard	Which size of shocks of one or multiple currencies cause a reduction of CET1 ratio leading to dropin the ratio of 0.1% (10 bps)?

Earnings failure: Non-Maturing Deposits	
Vulnerability	Larger than expected shifts from modelled non-maturing deposits into maturing deposits.
Generic Storyboard	What size of unexpected outflows of non-maturing deposits could result in a loss of USD 1mn (failure point), e.g., due to the need to unwind hedges at a loss that are no longer matched but become open positions?

Figure 13.3: Examples of goal seek approach to MRST.

rates could lead to a reduction of CET1 by 10 bps? Based on this, the bank would need to take appropriate mitigating or hedging actions to minimise the exposure to the currency risk.

13.5.1.3 Earnings Failure

In the third case for earnings failure, the vulnerability is a larger than expected shift from modelled non-maturing deposits (NMD) into maturing deposits. The storyboard queries what size of unexpected outflows of NMD could result in a loss of USD 1mn. This should be followed by an analysis of how often such losses could occur and what actions may be taken to prevent such losses in the future.

The reader can observe that in each perspective analysed here, the magnitude of losses can be tailored to the user's need, thereby reiterating the point that MRST is a versatile tool and can be used for various scenarios and not only for extreme out-comes. Also, the simple quantitative goal-seek approach underlines the importance of detecting vulnerabilities and posing the "right" questions so that remedial actions may be taken.

13.5.2 Quantitative Approach – Historical Risk Factor Analysis

At the other end of the complexity spectrum is the historical risk factor analysis approach for MRST. As an example, a user of the approach first identified business units with the largest losses in traditional stress tests. From this, risk factors with the biggest impact were isolated and scaled up or down to reach specified loss levels (e.g. USD 100mn) with the following test design:

- Stress scenario results from the Group Capital and Earnings Scenarios were used
- Only Market Risk, Credit Risk and Operational Risk were considered in the scope of the analysis as they are more likely to materialise compared to Business Risk which materialises over a longer horizon
- Capital scenario losses were observed, for example, over the previous 24 months
- The observed scenario losses for each of the business lines were bucketed into USD 100mn–200mn, 200mn–300mn and 300mn–500mn
- For Market Risk, key risk factors affecting the business with a breach loss of USD 100m under stress scenario were identified. Furthermore, based on linear approximation, shocks were scaled to tune the business to lose USD 100mn
- Based on the above, the frequency of such movements in the past were highlighted

Figure 13.4 illustrates the historical risk factor analysis approach for Market Risk. The resulting grid containing the magnitude of risk factors moves was checked against actual historical moves to establish how often the risk factor moves reached the pre-defined loss level in the past. As illustrated, a drop in the S&P 500 index by 17% would cause a loss of USD 100mn in an Asset Management business line. Such a drop had been observed twice in the past ten years.

From this MRST test, different usages can be established. If the results are stored in a database, further analyses are possible – e.g. key risk factors by business line. This could feed a "cheat-sheet", allowing executives to instantly pinpoint which business lines are exceeding the loss threshold given the recent risk factors moves. An example of a visual representations, a risk radar, is provided in the next section.

13.5.3 Qualitative Approach – (Iterative) Expert Interviews

The qualitative MRST approach of conducting interviews of experts and analysing their responses may require significant effort depending on various aspects including the size of the stakeholder group, the time taken to conduct each interview and the time taken to analyse the results. There are many ways to conduct MRST interviews, including online surveys, questionnaire emails, group interviews and individual interviews. If the size of the stakeholder group is manageable, conducting one-to-one interviews with stakeholders is an effective way of performing expert interviews. This

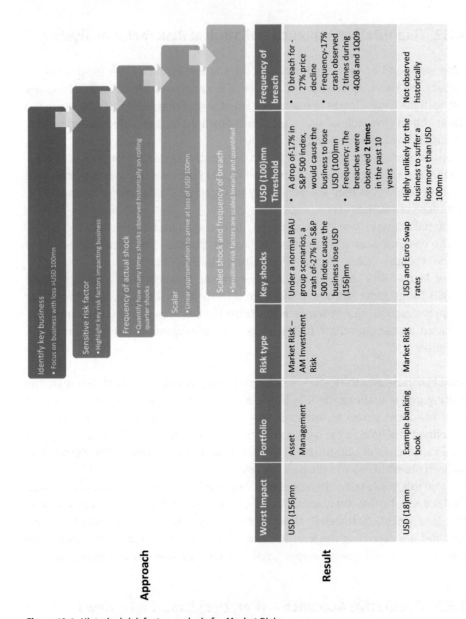

Figure 13.4: Historical risk factor analysis for Market Risk.

is because such an approach encourages candid input on business vulnerabilities which may not come to fore with the use of other offline or group interview methods. Here again, either a one-time interview or an iterative interview may be used, depending on the stakeholder group and time constraints.

For the approach detailed here, as an example we assume the following building blocks for the MRST framework, as referred to in Figure 13.2:

- **Scope:** The MRST exercise is performed for a specific business line spanning a cluster of trading desks
- **Events:** Both macro-economic and idiosyncratic events shall be considered depending on the input of the interviewed stakeholders
- **Cause of failure:** The cause of failure, whether liquidity, capital or earnings related may be determined by the interviewees
- **Vulnerability threshold:** This is assumed as a range of USD 100mn–200mn
- **Time horizon:** Both time horizons (i.e. short burn out and long bleeding out) may be applicable
- **Approach:** The qualitative expert analysis interview method is used

This approach to MRST begins with a scoping exercise followed by expert interviews, analysis of results and presentation of key findings and mitigating actions to a governance body for decision.

13.5.3.1 Scoping Exercise

The aim of the scoping exercise is to get buy-in from the management before conducting the MRST exercise. This involves laying out the purpose and expected output of the exercise, getting inputs on the stakeholder list and interview questions and identifying the appropriate vulnerability threshold.

The purpose of such an exercise would be to recognise the material vulnerabilities of the specific business line which could, for instance, result in losses to earnings to the range of USD 100mn–200mn. The output of such an exercise would include a comprehensive list of material risk factors which the business line is particularly sensitive to, and a proposal of mitigating actions for the management to consider.

For our example, the proposed stakeholder list of interviewees may include global and regional heads of the business line, product managers, the relevant risk managers (spanning all risk types who form the second line of defence), IT platform owners, as well as selected senior and junior traders from the trading desks specific to the business line. The vulnerability threshold (quantified loss value that could result from the RST scenarios, should they unfold) should be sense checked. For MRST, it is recommended that the vulnerability threshold should be high enough to be material but not too high to make the possibility of such a loss occurring remote.

13.5.3.2 Expert Interviews

The interviewees should be informed of the purpose of the exercise, the approval from the management to conduct such an exercise and should be encouraged to provide candid input. All responses should be collected to aid further analysis. Samples of interview questions are listed in Table 13.1. Additional questions may be posed depending on the flow of the interview, feedback received from the interviewee and the specific nature of the role of the interviewee.

Table 13.1: Sample set of expert interview questions.

Stakeholder Type	Interview question
Role	What is your role? What are your responsibilities pertaining to this specific business line?
Risk area	In your opinion, by order of materiality, please rank the key risk areas (Market Risk, Credit Risk, Non-Financial Risk, Treasury Risk, Liquidity Risk etc.) this specific business line is exposed to.
Risk area	From a historical perspective, which risks or vulnerabilities has this business line been afflicted with and what losses to liquidity, capital or earnings has this resulted in?
Scenario	What scenario of events could lead to a potential loss of USD 100mn–200mn for this business line in the future?
Scenario	In what sequence could these events unfold?
Scenario	As a result of such events occurring, would losses be more likely to be incurred over a short or long period of time?
Mitigants/ Controls	Are there any mitigating actions or controls already in place to minimise or prevent losses from the occurrence of identified vulnerabilities? Have these actions been effective?
Stakeholders	Are there other stakeholders who would be worth interviewing for this exercise?

Time and stakeholder group permitting, an iterative approach could be used as described in Section 13.5.3.3.

13.5.3.3 Iterative Expert Interviews

The difference of the iterative approach to conventional one-time expert interviews is the repeated execution of the same process which is illustrated in Figure 13.5. The quality of the result improves step by step as a result of repetitive validation. According to Lucht (2019), the integration of new knowledge that arises in the course of these cycles, such as deviations in results or changes in the environment, favours the accumulation of learning effects. There is a clear discussion and thus more reflection on the topic than would be possible with a normal one-time expert interview.

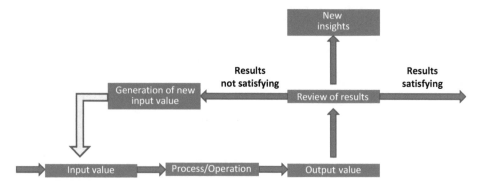

Figure 13.5: Control loop of iterative expert interviews.

As noted in Section 1.4. of this book, RST should help to mitigate cognitive biases in traditional stress tests but may itself be challenged by cognitive biases. Iterative expert interviews are one way to (partially) mitigate this challenge.

13.6 Analysis of Results and Presentation of Findings

The results from quantitative and/or qualitative MRST can be presented in multiple ways, from graphical depictions (e.g. heatmaps, logic trees) to the presentation in narrative form (e.g. storyboards for discussion with the board).

Figure 13.6 provides an example of a risk radar in which material risk factors, including macro-economic and idiosyncratic risk factors, are arranged. The top half of the radar displays risk factors specific to the business line, while the bottom half shows risk factors which are bank-wide and also affect the business line in question. The severity of risk factors is arranged outward from the bull's eye of the radar – high-severity factors in the bull's eye, followed by medium- and low-severity risk factors in the subsequent rings of the radar. Probability of occurrence of the risk factors are colour coded for convenient spotting. The risk radar provides a summary of the (historical) analysis and can be presented to management or the appropriate governance body for deliberation – e.g. if a risk is considered more probable and/ or severe compared to the last report. For this, individual risks could be mapped to trends and scenarios.

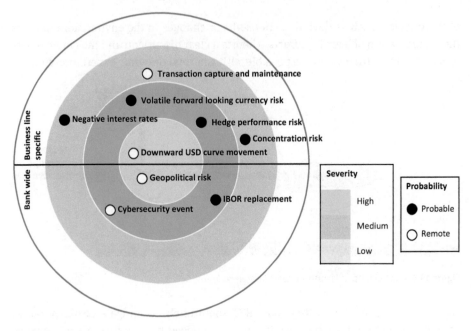

Figure 13.6: An illustrative risk radar depicting key risk factors which could cause a loss of USD 100mn–200mn.

Based on the analysis of the risk radar in Figure 13.6 and other analytics, the management or governance body can decide to take further action. When it comes to the high-severity risk factors, both factors depicted – downward USD curve movement and geopolitical risk – are assessed to have a low probability of occurrence. Such factors would need to be monitored and actions pre-defined for when such risks materialise. Of the medium- and low-severity risk factors, five have a reasonable probability of occurrence, while two have a remote probability of occurrence. The nature and magnitude of losses which could occur from the high probability of occurrence risk factors should be quantified and understood. The management or governance body should enquire into the robustness of existing mitigating actions and put new actions in place if required. Risks with a high probability of occurrence should be continuously monitored and reported.

Figure 13.7 provides an exemplary storyboard for the term out of non-maturing deposits.[2] These storyboards can be derived from (iterative) expert interviews.

---

2 Non maturing deposits can be withdrawn overnight. However, banks know from experience that parts of these deposits tend to stay for a longer term, often years. Banks hedge these parts with the term reflective of the actual client behaviour. Assuming a normal interest rate curve, these hedges improve the net interest income (NII) and protect margins against falling rates. However, in case of a sudden, sharp drop, the NII can still reduce if the deposit pricing cannot be reduced in a timely manner – for example, due to low-rate environment, this may require passing on negative rates.

Mild Reverse Stress Testing
Illustrative example: USD 100mn NII Loss

Portfolio composition –Vulnerability

Assume a significant portion of the retail /private banking NII is given by **USD non-maturing deposits** . Assume such positions are currently showing a materially positive contribution to margins, mainly due to the **term replication benefit**. Losses may be incurred in case reference rates move down faster than the client rate, compressing the firm's margins. Due to the floor embedded in the client rates and the close proximity of the strike level, **any significant USD down movement can generate NII losses** on these positions.

Scenario Narrative

A loss of USD 100mn NII over a one-year horizon is achieved due to an **abrupt USD yield curve down movement** – for example, due to an unanticipated economic slowdown . For example, it could be triggered by the ongoing tariff dispute and the internal US political situation.

The US Federal Reserve therefore harshly reduced the interest rates by 2.5% as an economic stimulus. At the same time, the ECB reacts with a small drop in rates. The reaction is limited – the EUR rates regime is already low and the ECB's range of action is bounded.

The currency rates are unaffected, as well as the respective business units.

Impacts on other risk factors have yet to be considered (particularly on foreign exchange rates).

Mitigation Actions

- USD margins are protected by term replication of deposits. A longer term replication is more favorable to decreasing rates but can be punishing under increasing ones. The term replication maturities are set once a year through a divisional management process, supported by Global governance in Risk and Finance.

  IN PLACE

- In case downward USD curve movements are considered particularly likely, intensified discussions between the Business, Finance and Risk should occur, including the development of dedicated monitoring to enable a timely reaction.

  Longer-term NII compression may not be always avoided.

  DEVELOPMENT

Status:	Live
Owner:	Div. Finance
Timeline:	Yearly
Status:	Development
Owner:	EORM CRO
Timeline:	Monthly, 3Q19

Governance /Management

Develop a radar scenario likelihood measure – for example, making the introduction of specific preemptive mitigation actions mandatory at the executive committee level.

Governance process: In case the leading indicator of scenario likelihood increases, executive committee discussions are triggered. The divisional executive committees will be allowed and will be required to provide feedback to group committees, considering the potential threats to the firm's NII.

The process should work out as follows: In case the leading indicator of scenario likelihood increases, executive committee discussions are triggered. **The divisional executive committees will be involved and will be required to provide feedback to group committees, considering the potential threats to the firm's NII.**

Figure 13.7: Illustrative example of MRST storyboard.

The example demonstrates how MRST can help to identify hidden vulnerabilities.[3] Based on the storyboard, management can discuss if additional processes and controls should be established.

13.7 Summary

MRST demonstrates that RST can be adapted by using different configuration sets and test designs with adjustments to severity and scope. As shown, MRST can use quantitative as well as qualitative approaches. The spectrum of quantitative approaches ranges from simple goal seek to expansive risk factor analysis. Likewise, qualitative approaches can vary in complexity. The chapter discussed expert interviews in a standard and iterative form.

This versatile nature makes MRST a useful complement. Coming back to the situation highlighted in the abstract of this chapter, imagine again that you go back to the board meeting and this time, you present the results of the MRST exercise you performed. You present a moderate loss outcome for an entity or a portfolio, the vulnerable risk factors the bank is exposed to and the mitigating actions the management can take. This time, the board feel the exercise is more relevant and are ready to discuss if the analysed risks should be accepted or mitigated.

Bibliography

Eichhorn, M., Mangold, P. (2016). Reverse Stress Testing for Banks: A Process-orientated Generic Framework, in *Journal of International Banking Law & Regulation*, 2016, Vol. 31 Issue 4, pp. 211–217.

Eichhorn, M., Mangold, P. (2017). Reverse Stress Testing: Linking Risks, Earnings, Capital and Liquidity – A Process-Orientated Framework and Its Application to Asset Liability Management, in *Handbook of Asset Liability Management in Banking*, Edited By Andreas Bohn and Marije Elkenbracht-Huizing, 2017, 2nd Edition, pp. 511–533, London.

Lucht, D. (2019). Theorie und Management komplexer Projekte. Wiesbaden.

---

3 Usually, the risk focus is on an increase in interest rates resulting in larger than expected deposit outflows and the need to unwind positions, often interest rate swaps, at a loss.

Part IV: **Application of Artificial Intelligence, Quantum Computing and Technology**

Daniel Mayenberger

14 Application of Artificial Intelligence and Big Data to Identify Business Vulnerabilities

Identification of a Firm's Specific Vulnerabilities with Natural Language Processing

14.1 Introduction

The goal of reverse stress testing (RST) is to find an event that leads to the non-viability of a given business. Depending on the scope, this business may be the whole firm, certain legal entities, a particular business or a specific book.

The focus is on the aspects of the failure and the cause, as the interest lies in identifying events that are relevant to the firm:

- Failure: The type of failure is given by the event. Determining this type from the raw text or data given is in itself an AI/ML application, a classification task. The focus will be on the identification of themes rather than their precise classification.
- Cause: Both bottom-up and top-down construction are relevant since it is a theme that is identified. Likely, AI/ML techniques are most successful at identifying a discrete event, though with the construction of additional context, it is possible to detect sequences of related events, too.

An algorithm will be useful to overcome known cognitive biases. Particularly relevant for RST are:

- Availability Bias: Tendency to overestimate the likelihood of more recent events.
- Clustering Illusion: Overestimate the importance of small streaks in large samples of data, even if the data are random. The observer sees non-existent pattern in data.
- Salience Bias: Focus on events that are more emotionally charged or vivid rather than unremarkable events, although both sets of events are of the same severity by objective standards.

Reverse stress testing (RST) is difficult, as it is a search for an extremely rare event with a massive financial impact. This search is made more difficult by cognitive biases. This chapter shows how to use techniques from artificial intelligence/machine

https://doi.org/10.1515/9783110647907-014

learning (AI/ML) and big data sources to identify themes for RST and their relations to such events.

The AI/ML techniques shown here will help produce narratives for reverse stress testing and facilitate the comprehensive identification of themes for these narratives by generating or inspiring themes and topics that may lead to non-viability. Quantification of impacts on liquidity and capital for an individual institution will require application of specific models that are beyond the scope of this chapter.

Section 14.2 gives an introduction to potential data sources and techniques to use these data: The elementary sentiment analysis is described in Section 14.3, word embeddings in Section 14.4, followed by techniques to mine operational risk events in Section 14.5 and concluded by identification of themes and relevant events from newsfeeds in Section 14.6. Section 14.7 summarises the content and provides outlook into further development and research.

14.2 Data Sources

First, the terms referring to the two main data types are defined for future reference.
- On one side, there are data whose purpose is to provide themes, events or a storyline that are related to the non-viability of a bank or a specific entity within the bank. These will be referred to as *event data*.
- On the other side, there are data that directly indicate the non-viability of a specific financial institution or extreme systemic stress in which at least one bank becomes non-viable. These are called *indicators*.

The event data describe what is happening and an indicator measures the impact of these events and quantifies how detrimental they are for the entity in scope.

Event data are:
- *Newspaper articles* with a date, or live news with a timestamp. Their primary purpose is the mining of events and themes that lead to specific or system-wide financial distress.
- *Social media streams*: Content posted on social media may be used paired with a sentiment analysis to identify themes that are of particular concern to the users of the platform.
- Anonymised *credit/debit billing and payment data*: The transactions, particularly when purchases are categorised, may reveal spending patterns in good or bad economic times.
- *Mobile phone location data*: In addition to the types of places at which the population spend their time and the frequency and distance of travel, these may indicate economic activity when located in shops.

Indicators are:

- *Bankruptcy events*: Records of banks taken into administration or receivership, with additional data for the size of the failure, usually the asset of the bank. For instance, the FDIC maintains a register of such banks in the US.
- *Economic cycles*: These are officially determined by a cycle dating committee (see, for instance, National Bureau of Economic Research, 2010 and Economic Cycle Research Institute, 2020) – and indicate times of a recession or economic growth. To further differentiate the different severities of recessions, additional data such as changes in real GDP should be used. In case GDP is not directly available or the level of economic activity is required at higher frequency, it can also be approximated – for example, by household electricity consumption (Lacko, 2000).
- *Volatility indices*: These are also known as "fear indices" as they signal market distress through their levels or sharp increases.
- *Social media streams*: Sentiments of short submissions, such as tweets or posts on social media, indicate general unease in the population. Normalisation is required to reflect the general level of debate as certain platforms are more geared towards business discussions and others set up to encourage more direct debate.
- *Online search phrases*: A sentiment analysis detects the level of distress among users.
- *Anonymised credit/debit payment data*: Transactions that are stopped for lack of funding or different stages of delinquencies (from 30 days past due to default) indicate consumers' financial distress at an aggregate level.

It must be assumed that different types of data – for example, the mobile phone location and spending through application on the same phone – cannot be connected for individuals because of data protection laws and regulations. Connections may be made in the aggregate, such as footfall in shops and payments at the same time. In any case, given the materiality required of an RST event, the data of a single person will not be relevant.

14.3 Technique 1: Sentiment Analysis

This technique is one of the mature natural language processing (NLP) tasks in sentiment analysis for texts (see Figure 14.1). Such an analysis determines whether a piece of text has overall positive or negative sentiment and provides a quantification of the extent of positivity or negativity, too. The machine classification algorithms detect sentiments at the same level of precision as humans.

In case the text data covers topics that are not relevant for the financial system, the data must be categorised into topics first. Particularly for more recent data, such tags are already available, for instance for news feeds. Otherwise, the categorisation

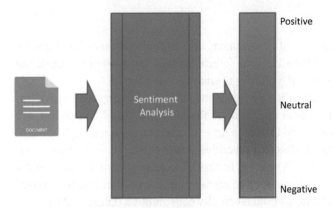

Figure 14.1: Sentiment analysis illustration.

of the data is another classification task to which the same techniques can be applied, such as Naïve Bayes or Support Vector Machines (SVM).

For example, the Natural Language Toolkit (NLTK) (Steven Bird, 2009) makes available tools with which a sentiment analyser can be constructed with less than 20 lines of code, see (Goodger, 2013). NLTK provides a set of text examples to which the sentiment analyser can be calibrated ("trained"). For a specific set of texts, e.g. financial news articles, it is advisable to use texts of the same type for calibration. This requires that the sentiments of the calibration texts are already determined which can be done manually or with a separate indicator, as described in Section 14.6.

A good illustration that sentiment analysis requires specific calibration to the type of texts that are subject of the analysis is an application of the VADER sentiment analyser (Gilbert, 2014) to summary description of recessions in the US from the 18th century to the present, including the Covid-19 crisis, sourced from Wikipedia (Wikipedia, 2020). According to the VADER documentation, the sentiment analyser is "specifically attuned to sentiments expressed in social media, and works well on texts from other domains". An application of VADER to the description of the 50 crises yields the results shown in Figure 14.2.

To summarise the results:
- For 80% of the descriptions, the sentiment is correctly shown as negative.
- For the 11 recessions that are not correctly detected as negative, most occurred in the 18th or 19th century.
- A closer examination of the description for the other three recessions shows that one of them was mild (1926–27), and for the second and third ones (1953–57 and 1957–58) the description does not mention an economic slowdown.

In conclusion, economic news which in general is more neutral in its tone requires a more fine-tuned algorithm.

Such a fine-tuning would specifically detect that the following phrases that are clearly associated with economic contraction are assigned a more negative sentiment.

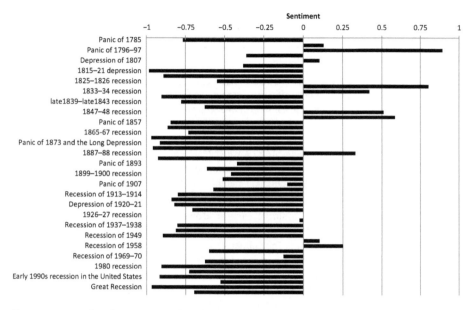

Figure 14.2: Results of sentiment analysis for wikipedia descriptions of US recessions.

With the default calibration, all of these expressions score neutrally, and the last one even slightly positively, because of the word "asset":
- Restrictive monetary policy
- Austerity programme
- Deflationary cycle
- Asset price bubble burst

More generally, sentiment analysis can be applied to identify pieces of text connected to negative sentiments in social media posts, news or online search phrases. These text pieces are then further analysed by finding common themes. Already, the default configuration produces useful themes by zeroing in on the most negative scores. The words that trigger the negative scores are emphasised.

Specifically, the following topics are highly relevant.
- Real estate price collapses with subsequent foreclosures.
- Sharp reduction in agriculture and manufacturing. Before Covid-19, this may have appeared anachronistic, though precisely the primary and secondary economic sectors are at risk, as they require a physical presence of workers that is severely restricted (BBC News, 2020).

An examination of the next five most negative scores (see Table 14.1) identifies a further theme preceding economic slowdowns: Restrictive monetary policy through high interest rates.

In summary, sentiment analysis is a simple and fast technique that already enables identification of potential themes for an RST narrative. In its scoring of single words,

Table 14.1: Description of crises with words emphasised that trigger sentiment scores.

Recession Name	Time Period	Description
1815–21 depression	1815–1821	Shortly after the *war* ended on March 23, 1815, the United States entered a period of financial *panic* as bank notes rapidly depreciated because of inflation following the *war*. The 1815 *panic* was followed by several years of mild *depression*, and then a major financial crisis – the *Panic* of 1819, which featured widespread *foreclosures*, bank *failures*, *unemployment*, a *collapse* in real estate prices, and a slump in agriculture and manufacturing.
1869–70 recession	June 1869– Dec 1870	A few years after the Civil *War*, a short *recession* occurred. It was unusual since it came amid a period when railroad investment was greatly accelerating, even producing the First Transcontinental Railroad. The railroads built in this period opened up the interior of the country, giving birth to the Farmers' movement. The *recession* may be explained partly by ongoing financial *difficulties* following the *war*, which *discouraged* businesses from building up inventories. Several months into the *recession*, there was a major financial *panic*.
1882–85 recession	Mar 1882– May 1885	Like the Long *Depression* that preceded it, the *recession* of 1882–85 was more of a price *depression* than a production *depression*. From 1879 to 1882, there had been a boom in railroad construction which came to an end, resulting in a decline in both railroad construction and in related industries, particularly iron and steel. A major economic event during the *recession* was the *Panic* of 1884.
1890–91 recession	July 1890– May 1891	Although shorter than the *recession* in 1887–88 and still modest, a slowdown in 1890–91 was somewhat more pronounced than the preceding *recession*. International monetary *disturbances* are *blamed* for this *recession*, such as the *Panic* of 1890 in the United Kingdom.
Great Recession	Dec 2007– June 2009	The subprime mortgage crisis led to the *collapse* of the United States housing bubble. *Falling* housing-related assets contributed to a global financial *crisis*, even as oil and food prices soared. The *crisis* led to the *failure* or *collapse* of many of the United States' largest financial institutions: Bear Stearns, Fannie Mae, Freddie Mac, Lehman Brothers, and AIG, as well as a *crisis* in the automobile industry. The government responded with an unprecedented $700 billion bank bailout and $787 billion fiscal stimulus package. The National Bureau of Economic Research declared the end of this *recession* over a year after the end date. The Dow Jones Industrial Average (Dow) finally reached its *lowest* point on March 9, 2009.

this technique is also completely transparent. The method may be improved further by not scoring single words but by word groups or complete sentences to add context. For example, "like" and "well" produce positive sentiment scores, but have neutral meaning in phrases such as, "Like the long depression ... " and " ... as well as ... ". A method to add context is introduced in the next section.

14.4 Technique 2: Word Embedding

A word embedding converts a word into a semantic vector which is a vector of real numbers with a dimension of several hundred. While a dimension of hundreds may appear high, it is already substantially reduced from the hundreds of thousands of different words, much more from the different number of combinations of words in sentences that easily go into the order of billions. The task is to perform this conversion of word to vector of in such a way that semantically similar word groups are close to one another in their vector representation. To achieve this, the method uses the context of each word – i.e. the words before and after that word – to determine its semantic vector representation as illustrated in Figure 14.3.

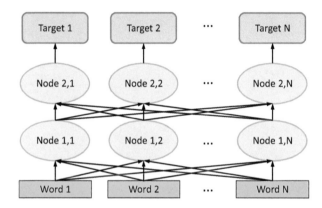

Figure 14.3: Stylised schema of continuous word representation.

A broad variety of methods is available, and at the time of writing, the Bidirectional Encoder Representations from Transformers (BERT) method (Jacob Devlin, 2019) is the most recent, most performant algorithm and used to improve the accuracy of Google searches. The same technique also performs at the same level as humans for reading comprehension tasks.

To visualise word embedding in order to detect themes, a dimensionality reduction technique, such as Principal Component Analysis (PCA), UMAP or t-SNE is then applied to the semantic vector to find words that are semantically close. For example, the word (group) "climate change" produces the following (Ikuya Yamada A. A., github.io, 2020):

The particular illustration shown in Figure 14.4 is based on work published in (Ikuya Yamada A. A., arXiv:1812.06280v3, 2020) and (Ikuya Yamada H. S., 2016). Word embedding is also an important constituent of the algorithms for NLP tasks, as will become clearer in the next sections on data mining and identification of events.

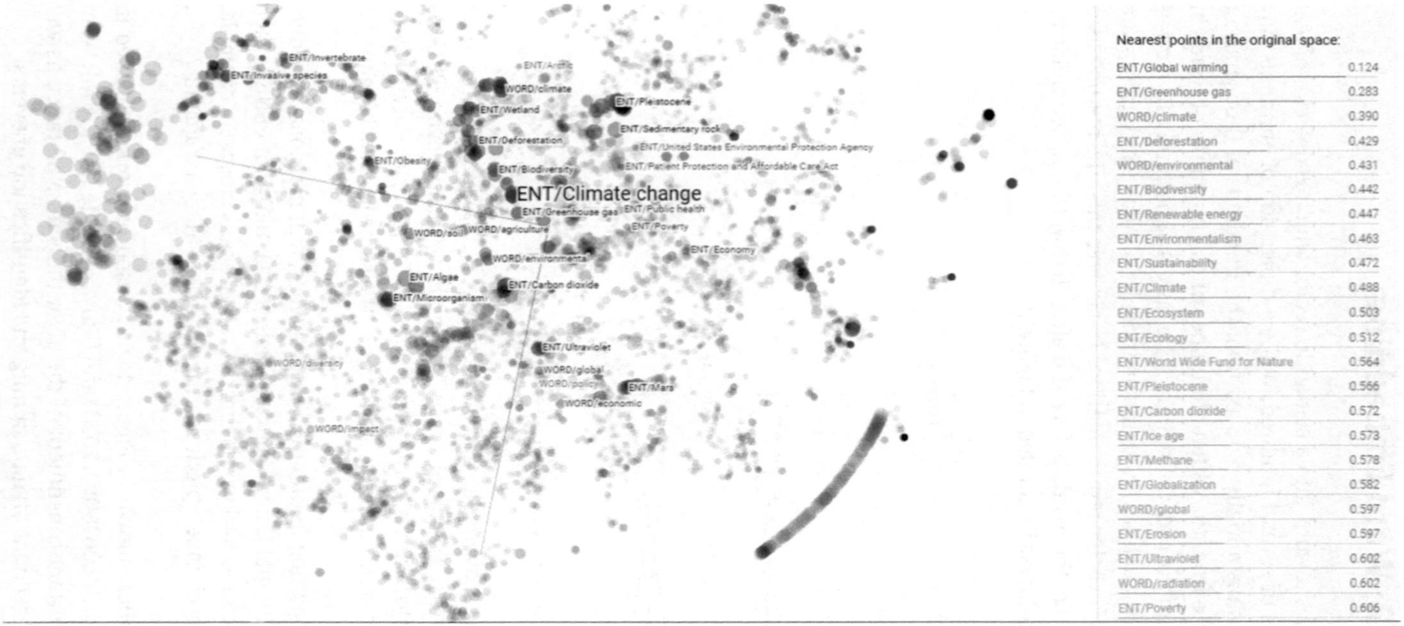
ENT/Invertebrate
ENT/Invasive species
ENT/Arctic
WORD/climate
ENT/Wetland
ENT/Deforestation
ENT/Obesity
ENT/Biodiversity
ENT/Pleistocene
ENT/Sedimentary rock
ENT/United States Environmental Protection Agency
ENT/Patient Protection and Affordable Care Act
ENT/Climate change
ENT/Greenhouse gas
ENT/Public health
ENT/Poverty
WORD/soil
WORD/agriculture
WORD/environmental
ENT/Economy
ENT/Algae
ENT/Microorganism
ENT/Carbon dioxide
ENT/Ultraviolet
WORD/diversity
WORD/global
WORD/policy
ENT/Mars
WORD/economic
WORD/impact
Nearest points in the original space:
ENT/Global warming 0.124
ENT/Greenhouse gas 0.283
WORD/climate 0.390
ENT/Deforestation 0.429
WORD/environmental 0.431
ENT/Biodiversity 0.442
ENT/Renewable energy 0.447
ENT/Environmentalism 0.463
ENT/Sustainability 0.472
ENT/Climate 0.488
ENT/Ecosystem 0.503
ENT/Ecology 0.512
ENT/World Wide Fund for Nature 0.564
ENT/Pleistocene 0.566
ENT/Carbon dioxide 0.572
ENT/Ice age 0.573
ENT/Methane 0.578
ENT/Globalization 0.582
WORD/global 0.597
ENT/Erosion 0.597
ENT/Ultraviolet 0.602
WORD/radiation 0.602
ENT/Poverty 0.606

Figure 14.4: Word embedding example for “climate change”.

14.5 Technique 3: Data Mining of Operational Risk Events

The obvious advantage of operational risk or loss data is that, by definition, they already constitute material loss events and the size of each loss is given. In addition, because of the additional categorisation information that includes business lines, financial products and processes, it is easier to dissect or filter the data to identify themes relevant for a certain business. Operational risk data are already available to banks because of existing requirements to estimate and manage operational losses.

However, one limitation of operational risk data is that some events are deliberately excluded as they do not constitute operational loss events. For example, ORX data do not contain strategic risks, project risks related to strategic decisions or business risks (Operational Riskdata exchanged Association [ORX], 2016).

An example of applications to reverse stress testing follows these steps:
1. Pre-filter the loss events by
    - The targeted aspects, which can be one or several of entity, business unit or product.
    - Setting a threshold loss, which may need to be normalised for the entity, usually by the annual revenue.
2. Identify common themes: For each event, use the event description to identify themes with a frequency analysis. Term frequency–inverse document frequency (TF-IDF) (P. Jackson, 2007) is a widely used method to determine the most important words or phrases for the event relative to the other pre-filtered events, or relative to the whole set of operational risk events.
3. Identify related topics: Using the visualisation of word embedding from the previous section, review phrases in the vicinity of these common themes which are related topics.

14.6 Technique 4: Use of Indicators for Detecting Relevance

Often the massive losses that are of interest in RST are not as conveniently in direct relation to given events as is the case for operational risk events. For the general task of identifying themes related to such losses, there are two sets of data:
1. Event data that contain a mixture of positive occurrences, neutral affairs and negative incidents.
2. Indicators that record extreme losses or general economic distress.

These two datasets must be connected for the model. Typically, this connection will be through occurrence around the same time or in the same location. For example, the VIX is a volatility index for the US market and has a time dimension. It is worth trying a different granularity of time, as daily granularity may produce a lower signal/noise ratio and annual data may lose too much temporal context.

There may also be a time lag for an event to affect the observed indicators. This time lag can be incorporated into the model calibration – for example, for subsequent events.

The identification of relevant themes then follows this procedure:

1. Choose the subset of event data, the training set, for the model calibration.
2. Take a word embedding that is pre-trained on a large text corpus, ideally the same type of text as in the event data.
3. Fine-tune the pre-trained model using the stress indicator. Consider calibration in a more specific context, such as a particular type of banks, business lines or geographies.
4. Use the fine-tuned model to produce a short list of relevant themes.
5. Optional: Inspect related themes using a 2D projection, see Technique 2 in Section 14.4.

14.6.1 Choice of Training Set

As usual in the training of a model, only part of the whole text corpus, the training data, should be used for the calibration. Since this search aims to detect rare events, it is also worth trying out different samples of training data or use an ensemble technique such as bootstrap aggregation (also known as 'bagging') to achieve greater stability.

14.6.2 Choice of Pre-Trained Word Embedding

Language-based tasks are performed better if the word embedding is pre-trained on a large body of text before fine-tuning it to the necessary task. Pre-trained word embedding not only encodes sentences into a numerical vector, but also detects relationships between sentences – for instance, whether one event immediately follows another one (Devlin, 2019).

14.6.3 Fine-Tuning to Indicator or Specific Scope

The most important step is the fine-tuning of the word embedding. The objective is to award the semantic sentence vector a high score if it occurs during a period of economic distress, as measured by the chosen indicator. This calibration need not be done from scratch. In fact, there are pre-calibrated word embeddings available that provide a good starting point (Devlin, 2019).

The fine-tuning of the calibration, illustrated in Figure 14.5, depends on the particular scope of the RST task, so fine-tuning can be made specific to:

- Banks that operate a similar business model (e.g. broker-dealer, retail, commercial) or firms that offer a close substitute (exchanges, credit unions, investment funds).
- A business line or a type of business such as consumer lending, mortgage lending or brokerage.
- Products offered – for example, trading products by asset class; for trading products, there is a more granular specification for their use, such as risk transfer/hedging, short-term speculation, investment or retail brokerage.

Such a specification is more likely to be trained on events that are particularly relevant for RST, as the scope is more limited. The specification also drives the indicator, for example:

- Unemployment rate for retail credit products such as credit cards and consumer loans.
- General economic activity (GDP, purchasing managers' index – PMI) and funding conditions (interest rate level, BBB credit spreads) for corporate banking activities.
- General economic activity (GDP), retail funding conditions (policy rate, prime rate) and financial wealth indicators (household disposable income) for mortgages.

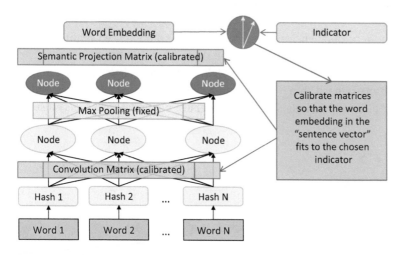

Figure 14.5: Stylised schema for fine-tuning of word embedding to indicator.

Often, these drivers may be derived from existing revenue or risk models that are required for capital and financial planning or regulatory capital calculations. As always with the calibration of models, the event data should be split into a training set and test set for the assessment of its performance. In making this split, there should be sufficiently representative data which can be more easily achieved by determining whether the indicator data in the training set covers the complete range of values from the total indicator data set. Note that it is not required, and may even be counter-productive, that the training set contain only extremely negative data. The power in the model comes for the differentiation and this requires the complete range of outcomes.

14.6.4 Shortlist of Relevant Events

The fine-tuned model is then used to filter through (ideally) a completely different set of data of the same type to identify sentences that correspond to the most extremely negative indicators. These then provide a shortlist of themes for the RST narrative. One can think of this filtering of events as a bias-free comprehensive search for RST themes for the specific scope.

After the filtering, pieces of text are rank-ordered by the aggregate score of the sentences they contain. In the aggregation, different weights may be assigned to parts of the text piece. For instance, the headline is of particular importance in a news article, as is the URL or title of a website for the whole webpage.

14.6.5 Inspection of Related Events

To produce a more comprehensive list of topics in the computerised brainstorming, the topics that lie close to the already identified themes are included into the list. An illustration of such topics that are close to a specific theme was shown in Section 14.4, Figure 14.4. Such an extended search can be automated by specifying the distance within which is searched. For a relatively short list of themes, a manual search may also be effective.

14.7 Summary

The publicly available toolkit of AI/ML techniques provides natural language processing (NLP) methods that are directly applicable to the complex task of identifying extreme events for RST. The methods can be used to mitigate cognitive biases that constrain the choice of themes for RST.

While sentiment analysis in its simplest form is transparent and useful to obtain a first collection of themes, it often lacks context. This context is added through word embedding that increases the accuracy in the selection of relevant themes. Word embedding also helps identify topics that are similar to already identified themes to achieve a more comprehensive brainstorming of events.

NLP methods can also be used to mine known extreme events such as operational risk incidents with a focus on a specific type of banking operations, legal entity or business line. The analysis that uses the well-established method of term frequency–inverse document frequency (TF-IDF) determines the themes of highest importance for a specific set of events.

Lastly, to use the most extensive variety of text corpuses available to achieve the broadest possible list of extreme events, the word embedding technique can be refined further by enriching the data with indicators from economics or alternative data. In this way, themes can be extracted from the wealth of information provided by news or social media to facilitate identification of potential RST events.

Further development may be possible in generating a set of storylines from the list of themes. At present, there are already AI/ML algorithms that write poems (Marjan Ghazvininejad, 2016) or compose music (Kaleagasi, 2017) so convincingly that humans cannot tell whether a human or a machine produced the work. Another line of development is the quantification of losses, since cognitive biases often get in the way of achieving realistically extreme results. The resulting bias-free narrative of salient vulnerabilities is a very useful tool for senior management decision-making.

Bibliography

BBC News. (2020, April 16). Retrieved April 16, 2020, from Eastern Europeans to be flown in to pick fruit and veg: https://www.bbc.co.uk/news/business–52293061

BBC News. (2020, March 24). Retrieved April 18, 2020, from Fruit and veg growers call for workers to 'feed the nation': https://www.bbc.co.uk/news/uk-england-cambridgeshire–52019810

Economic Cycle Research Institute. (2020). *Economic Cycle Research Institute*. Retrieved April 02, 2020, from The ECRI Approach: https://www.businesscycle.com/ecri-about/forecasting-approach

Gilbert, C. H. (June 2014). VADER: A Parsimonious Rule-based Model for Sentiment Analysis of Social Media Text. *Eighth International Conference on Weblogs and Social Media (ICWSM-14)*. Ann Arbor, MI.

Goodger, D. (2013, Feb 21). *nltk.org*. Retrieved April 4, 2020, from Sentiment Analysis: https://www.nltk.org/howto/sentiment.html

Ikuya Yamada, A. A. (2020, Jan 30). *arXiv:1812.06280v3*. Retrieved March 18, 2020, from Wikipedia2Vec: An Efficient Toolkit for Learning and Visualizing the Embeddings of Words and Entities from Wikipedia.

Ikuya Yamada, A. A. (2020). *github.io*. Retrieved March 12, 2020, from Wikipedia2Vec Demonstration: https://wikipedia2vec.github.io/demo/

Ikuya Yamada, H. S. (2016). Joint Learning of the Embedding of Words and Entities for Named Entity Disambiguation. *Proceedings of The 20th SIGNLL Conference on Computational Natural Language Learning* pp. (250–259). Association for Computational Linguistics.

Jacob Devlin, M.-W. C. (2019, May 24). *arXiv:1810.04805v2*. Retrieved March 18, 2020, from BERT: Pre-training of Deep Bidirectional Transformers for Language Understanding: https://arxiv.org/abs/1810.04805

Kaleagasi, B. (2017, March 9). *futurism.com*. Retrieved April 17, 2020, from A New AI Can Write Music as Well as a Human Composer: https://futurism.com/a-new-ai-can-write-music-as-well-as-a-human-composer

Lacko, M. (2000). Do Power Consumption Data Tell the Story? Electricity Intensity and Hidden Economy in Post-Socialist Countries. In E. M. Simonovits, *Planning, Shortage, and Transformation: Essays in Honor of János Kornai* p. (457). Cambridge, MA: MIT Press.

Marjan Ghazvininejad, X. S. (2016). Generating Topical Poetry. EMNLP.

National Bureau of Economic Research. (2010, September 20). *National Bureau of Economic Research*. Retrieved April 02, 2020, from Business Cycle Dating Committee: https://www.nber.org/cycles/sept2010.html

Operational Riskdata exchanged Association (ORX). (2016, December 1). *www.orx.org*. Retrieved January 6, 2020, from Operational Risk Reporting Standards: https://managingrisktogether.orx.org/standards

P. Jackson, I. M. (2007). *Natural Language Processing for Online Applications: Text retrieval, extraction and categorization*. Amsterdam/Philadephia: John Benjamins Publishing Company.

Steven Bird, E. K. (2009). *Natural Language Processing with Python* (1st ed.). Sebastopol, CA: O'Reilly Media.

Wikipedia . (2020, April 3). Retrieved April 4, 2019, from List of recessions in the United States: https://en.wikipedia.org/wiki/List_of_recessions_in_the_United_States

Iulian Cotoi, Robert Stamicar

15 Reverse Stress Testing Using Artificial Intelligence Techniques

Use of Gaussian Process Regression

15.1 Introduction

Under a reverse stress test (RST) platform, we search for scenarios that generate a given portfolio loss.[1] A key challenge is not only the generation of these scenarios, but also the pricing of securities for these scenarios. Furthermore, the computational cost for a full revaluation of a portfolio comprised of nonlinear positions is expensive. In this chapter, we present an RST framework based on Gaussian Processes to tackle both of these challenges. A Gaussian Process Regression (GPR), which is a machine learning regression technique that defines probability distributions over sets of functions, can be used to learn pricing functions. GPRs will not only ease the computational burden for pricing, but (unlike neural networks) will also provide uncertainty estimates that help guide the search for reverse stress test scenarios.

RST platforms are typically independent of Monte Carlo VaR (or CVaR) platforms. However, a GPR-based RST framework can be integrated as a module within a VaR platform. Under VaR platforms, risk factor scenarios are generated via Monte Carlo simulations, and full pricing models re-price securities. Instead, once pricing functions are trained via GPRs, costly calls to the pricing functions are replaced with GPR approximations, reducing the computational cost. In addition, VaR scenarios that are near a given portfolio loss threshold can be used as initial starting points for the GPR-based RST search algorithm.

Reverse stress testing is a separate and complementary approach to regular or traditional stress and scenario testing. Instead of specifying the risk factor shifts and computing the loss of a portfolio (as in a traditional stress test), reverse stress testing approaches from the opposite perspective. Under a reverse stress test, we specify the portfolio loss as an *input*, and then find scenarios that can generate this loss. For instance, for a 10% portfolio loss, what economic scenarios can contribute to this loss? Once these scenarios are identified, the plausible scenarios are selected.

Regulators have strongly endorsed reverse stress testing programmes within financial institutions since reverse stress tests can explicitly examine the solvency of

---

[1] The first author would like to thank Microsoft and notably Lindsey Allen, Xiaoyong Zhu, Jim Williams and Andrew Comas for their help on training, setting up computations in Azure ML and the joint presentation at the Ai4 Finance conference.

Note: Edited by Daniel Mayenberger

https://doi.org/10.1515/9783110647907-015

a firm. (See, for example, BCBS, 2009.) In this context, reverse stress tests are designed to identify economic scenarios that will threaten a firm's survival and potentially help managers hedge against hidden scenarios. Along with regulatory stress tests such as CCAR, reverse stress tests can overcome the limitations of risk models, which break down in periods of crisis. Another key benefit to a reverse stress is that it overcomes a manager's biases in stress test specifications. In particular, under a regular stress test, it is difficult to verify that the magnitudes of stress factor shocks have been unbiasedly selected.

A key challenge for reverse stress testing, as the authors acknowledge in Cotoi and Stamicar (2018), is the generation of scenarios and the pricing of these scenarios. More precisely, identifying the scenario (or region of scenarios) that can induce a specific loss to a portfolio with high plausibility is challenging. In addition, the computational cost for a full revaluation of nonlinear positions within a portfolio is expensive. In this chapter, we outline how to search for scenarios using Machine Learning techniques. We advocate the use of Gaussian Process Regressions (GPRs) not only to ease the computational burden of pricing, but also since they provide uncertainty estimates, which guide the search for RST scenarios. Some preliminary results have been presented in Cotoi and Li (2019).

Our goal is twofold. First, once pricing functions are trained via GPRs, we replace costly calls of the pricing function with the GPR approximations. Second, the mean and pricing error of the GPR will be incorporated into the search algorithm that we present.

We now make some remarks regarding VaR models based on Monte Carlo simulations. In this setting, risk factor scenarios are generated, and securities are repriced with full pricing models to capture asymmetric profiles. Since VaR models output P&L scenarios, it seems that reverse stress testing can be embedded within a VaR framework. So, for a given loss L, we can find the scenario that produces the loss closest to L (or interpolate between adjacent scenarios).

However, VaR models typically do not generate enough hidden scenarios around a given loss level L. Hence, the requirements for different techniques are required for reverse stress testing. Note that we can interpret a scenario-based reverse stress test framework as an add-on or a complement to a VaR platform. With the use of GPRs, we could replace costly calls to the pricing functions and increase the number of risk factor simulations for VaR. The subset of scenarios near a given loss threshold can then be used as inputs for a reverse stress test search algorithm.

It should be noted that GPs are gaining in traction for financial applications. Typically, they are used for fast pricing of derivatives – for example, pricing of securities in the context of CVA computations (see Crepey and Dixon, 2019). In addition, some applications have been performed for credit modelling (see Strydom, 2017).

In Section 15.2, we outline the steps to identify the reverse stress test scenarios and provide some background for stress testing requirements. In Section 15.3, we recall a few important results about GPRs and describe the exploration-exploitation algorithm which allows us to search for RST scenarios. Section 15.4 provides some preliminary results for a portfolio of options. Finally, Section 15.5 provides concluding comments.

15.2 Reverse Stress Tests Based on GPs

The implementation of an RST framework is challenging. As noted in an earlier paper by the authors Cotoi and Stamicar (2018), the generation of scenarios and pricing within an RST framework can be computationally expensive. This chapter focusses on the efficient pricing of assets for plausible and adverse scenarios. The two main steps of the algorithm which will allow us to extract these plausible and adverse scenarios are:

1. Construct GPR price approximations for instruments in the portfolio.
2. With the aid of GPR (under *exploitation-exploration*), identify scenarios x that are both adverse and plausible:
   - *High Plausibility Region:* $\{x \in \mathbb{R}^n \mid M(x) \tilde{p}\}$
   - *Adverse Neighbourhood of Loss:* $\{x \in \mathbb{R}^n \mid P \& L(x) \in (L-\epsilon, L+\epsilon)\}$

The plausibility region is specified by constraining the Mahalanobis radius $M(x) = \sqrt{x^T \Sigma^{-1} x}$ within a threshold $\tilde{p}$. Here, the covariance matrix of risk factor returns is denoted by Σ.

A novel feature of the RST algorithm is that both of these steps are interconnected. GPs provide not only an expectation for the forecast but a distribution of prices. Thus, we can specify a confidence interval for forecasting prices, and moreover, we can use GPs to help search for the region of interest defined in Step 2. The search algorithm is based on reinforcement learning where learning is based on its environment. Here, we deploy an exploitation–exploration algorithm which will allow us to explore the space of scenarios that are near the loss level set. This will minimise the computational burden as we search for candidate scenarios that are plausible and adverse.

15.2.1 Background

Before we describe our algorithm in more detail, it is useful to first highlight the desired properties of any stress test (see BCBS, 2009 or Cotoi and Stamicar, 2017). Under any stress testing requirement, we desire that stress tests are:

- *Adverse:* Under traditional stress tests, we select risk factor scenarios that will have an adverse impact on a given portfolio. Here, we reprice securities using pricing models for the risk factor shocks. With reverse stress testing, we simply state the loss as an input.

- *Plausible:* Whether explicitly specified under a traditional stress test or inferred from a reverse stress test, is the scenario plausible?

In addition, reverse stress tests should be:
- *Exhaustive:* A sufficient number of risk factor scenarios needs to be generated in order to find hidden scenarios that have a negative impact on the portfolio P&L. Scenarios should uniformly span the loss region of the risk factor space.

This condition adds to the computational expense of identifying RST scenarios. Our algorithm utilises GPRs to efficiently price instruments with complex payoffs, making RST more efficient, leading to the benefits listed in Table 15.1.

Table 15.1: Benefits of reverse stress testing.

Systematic Framework	Provides a systematic approach to stress testing that complements traditional stress tests.
Risk Decomposition	Enhance risk decomposition by examining plausible scenarios (around the gradient of VaR).
Biases	Eliminates manager's biases into stress test specifications. However, modelling choices need to be selected – thus, we are not completely bias-free.
Risk Mitigation	Aids hedging and overlay analysis by identifying hidden scenarios that adversely impact the P&L of the portfolio.

15.2.2 Standard Formulation and Motivation of Our Approach

We can formulate an RST procedure as finding the most plausible scenario that produces a given loss L as

$$\min_{P=P_0(1-L)} M(r) = \min_{P=P_0(1-L)} \sqrt{r^T \Sigma^{-1} r} \tag{15.1}$$

where P_0 is the initial portfolio value and Σ is the covariance matrix of risk factors. Note that the portfolio value p is determined from the pricing function of its securities, which in turn are functions of the risk factors r. Under this setting, we find the most plausible scenario by minimising the Mahalanobis radius. We assume that risk factors are multivariate normal but that pricing functions are nonlinear – i.e. asymmetric payoffs are embedded in the pricing functions. This is the standard methodology for large-scale Monte Carlo VaR platforms where risk factors are assumed multivariate and pricing functions are nonlinear. Note that the algorithm we propose is also suitable when the risk factors follow a Student t distribution.

15.2.2.1 Linear Setting

Before outlining our general setting for reverse stress testing, which utilises GPRs for identifying plausible and adverse scenarios, we discuss reverse stress testing under a linear setting. In this section, we follow the treatment outlined by Kopeliovich, Novosyolov, Satchkov and Schachter (2014).

Here the asset returns $r = (r_1, \ldots, r_n)^T$ are assumed to be multivariate normal with covariance matrix $C = E[rr^T]$. Consequently, plausibility of scenarios will then be modelled using the probability density from the multivariate normal distribution. The portfolio return is $r_p = w^T r$, where $w = (w_1, \ldots, w_n)^T$ are the portfolio weights.[2]

Under reverse stress testing, we specify a loss L, and determine which scenarios r^* would lead to this loss

$$L = -w^T r^*. \tag{15.2}$$

The portfolio loss also corresponds to VaR at some confidence level α, i.e.

$$L = \mathrm{VaR}_\alpha \triangleq q_\alpha \sqrt{w^T C w} = q_\alpha \sigma_p, \tag{15.3}$$

where q_α is the quantile of the standard normal distribution at level α, and σ_p is the portfolio volatility. The scenarios from Equation (15.2) are represented as a hyperplane in R^n as $H = \{r : w^T r = -L\}$. Figure 15.1 illustrates the case for two asset returns.

Which scenarios r^* should we select from H?

The hyperplane H contains all scenarios that give a portfolio loss of L. We know examine which subset of scenarios on the hyperplane is plausible. Given $r \in H$, the conditional distribution of r is normal with mean $\bar{r}_H$. It can be shown that the mean of this conditional distribution is in fact the gradient of VaR:

$$\bar{r}_H = q_\alpha \frac{C w}{\sqrt{w^T C w}}. \tag{15.4}$$

The gradient of VaR is used to compute risk contributions of positions. For example, the risk contribution for the first position is given by $(q_\alpha / \sigma_p) \times (w_1) \times \sum_i^n C_{1i} w_i$.

Note that (15.4) is the solution to (15.1). Geometrically, the vector $\bar{r}_H$ is tangent to the ellipsoid $r^T C^{-1} r = k$, for some constant k (see Figure 15.1). In fact, $\bar{r}_H$ is also the maximum of the conditional distribution density over the hyperplane H, and consequently is the most plausible scenario.[3]

---

2 Note that asset returns can be generated from a linear factor model of the form , where is the exposure matrix, is a vector of factor returns, and is a vector of idiosyncratic returns.
3 The term appears in the Gaussian density function; hence, the level sets of these ellipsoids are iso-probability contours.

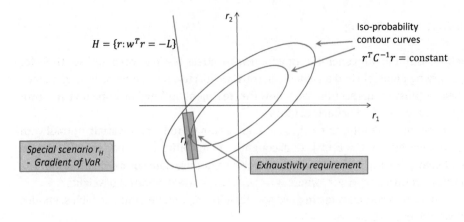

Figure 15.1: Elliptical distribution and hyperplane of losses for a linear portfolio.

Instead of just focusing on this single scenario, it is useful to examine slightly less plausible scenarios that produce the same loss (exhaustivity condition). We can include more scenarios in the vicinity around $\bar{r}_H$ that lie on H. Moreover, we can explicitly compute the likelihood of these scenarios since the conditional distribution can be estimated.

From Figure 15.1, we see that H is a line for two assets and that equally plausible scenarios are pairs of points on this line that intersect with iso-probability ellipses. In general, H is a $(n-1)$-dimensional hyperplane for n assets, and equal probability scenarios will lie on a $(n-1)$-dimensional ellipsoid.[4] Figure 15.2 provides the cases for $n=3$ and $n=4$.

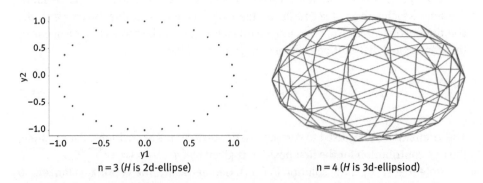

$n = 3$ (H is 2d-ellipse) $n = 4$ (H is 3d-ellipsiod)

Figure 15.2: Iso-probability ellipsoids lying in hyperplane H.

An obvious application, as suggested by Kopeliovich et al. (2014), is to enhance standard risk contribution analysis. The vector $\bar{r}_H$ corresponds to the most plausible scenario and is used to compute risk contributions. In addition, we can supplement this vector

---

4 This is a direct result of modelling plausibility via a multivariate normal distribution.

with nearby plausible scenarios that lie on H to provide more insight. (See Figure 15.1.) By examining more scenarios, we can ascertain the stability and relevance of standard risk contributions. For instance, if the risk contribution of a position or risk factor is relatively small under the standard risk contribution, but significant for nearby scenarios, then we should not neglect its risk contribution to the portfolio.

In Table 15.2, we consider a portfolio of equities, government bonds, FX forwards and commodity futures. In this report, we examine the stability of the standard risk contribution (labelled as "Base") with six nearby scenarios that are each 10% as likely as the base scenario.[5] All scenarios are chosen to have a portfolio loss of 12%. Here, we observe that the standard risk contributions across asset classes are fairly stable.

Table 15.2: Enhanced risk contributions.

Reporting Levels	Scenario Loss (%)						
	Base	1	2	3	4	5	6
Global Portfolio	12.00	12.00	12.00	12.00	12.00	12.00	12.00
▸ US Bonds	0.94	0.96	0.90	0.94	0.91	0.96	0.94
▸ UK Bonds	1.99	1.99	1.95	1.99	1.90	2.09	2.03
▸ FX	1.73	1.87	1.76	1.78	1.73	1.68	1.57
▸ US Equity	1.23	1.15	1.34	1.15	1.30	1.25	1.20
▸ UK Equity	2.06	1.88	2.14	2.13	2.06	2.00	2.17
▸ Commodity	4.05	4.15	3.90	4.02	4.10	4.02	4.09
Relative Likelihood	100%	10%	10%	10%	10%	10%	10%

Under a stress test framework, we typically think of generating adverse scenarios. In this section, we have made no explicit assumptions about *adverse* scenarios, other than the choice of L (which is a simple scaling of the portfolio volatility under the linear setting). We can embed adverse scenarios by utilising a *stressed* covariance matrix, perhaps computed from periods of market turmoil, or conditioned from a latent marker factor.

The notions of adverse and plausible are interconnected. Note that the covariance matrix is an input for the Gaussian multivariate density function. Hence, it determines the plausibility of scenarios. Even though a particular covariance matrix can reflect adverse conditions, we will consider it to be an input that defines the dependence structure – in this case, a Gaussian copula with normal marginals.

---

5 The relative likelihoods in Table 2 were computed by taking ratios of the conditional density function.

15.2.2.2 Incorporating Nonlinear Positions

Not only is it useful to examine nearby scenarios with the same loss (on the hyperplane), but scenarios in a neighbourhood of the portfolio loss L. Figure 15.3 depicts the nonlinear case where the loss level sets are curved surfaces. With this in mind, our approach is not to strictly solve (1), but instead search for scenarios with a given plausibility threshold and within a neighbourhood of losses within $(L-\varepsilon, L+\varepsilon)$.

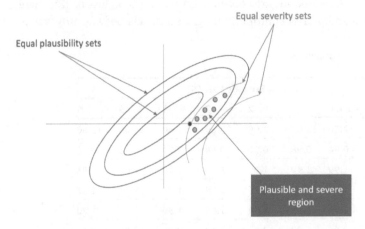

Figure 15.3: Adverse and Plausible Region of losses.

For linear portfolios, we modelled the dependence structure with a multivariate normal distribution. In addition, grid pricing can be systematically formulated by constructing a uniform mesh on iso-probability ellipsoids.

For portfolios that contain nonlinear positions, it is common to generate risk factor scenarios and reprice securities with full pricing models to capture asymmetric profiles. In fact, most VaR and CVaR applications operate in this fashion. Risk factor scenarios are generated from Monte Carlo simulations and pricing functions are applied to each risk factor scenario to produce a distribution of portfolio P&Ls. For example, consider an equity call option. We first simulate its risk factors, which include the underlying stock price, interest rates and its implied volatility surface. Then a pricing function, such as Black-Scholes, is used to capture the call's asymmetric profile.

Since VaR models output P&L scenarios, it seems that reverse stress testing can be embedded within a VaR framework. So, for a given loss L, we can find the scenario that produces the loss closest to L (or interpolate between adjacent scenarios). For instance, a loss L might correspond to VaR at the 98.3% confidence level.

But VaR models typically do not generate enough *hidden* scenarios (exhaustive condition) around a given loss level L. Although quasi-Monte Carlo techniques can be used for reverse stress testing, we advocate identifying scenarios in a systematic procedure using a GPR-based approach.

In the previous section, we identified plausible scenarios that gave the same loss. From Figure 15.1, these are scenarios on a hyperplane H, where $L = -w^T r$. Under the nonlinear setting, the level sets (of equal losses) are no longer hyperplanes, but rather curved surfaces. Identifying the associated iso-probability contours is nontrivial, and would require many scenarios. In addition, given simulation error, we will identify scenarios not only on the level sets but *off* the level set. As a depiction, this amounts to examining scenarios lying on and off the hyperplane.

15.3 A GPR-Based RST Algorithm

15.3.1 Linking RST with Artificial Intelligence (AI) Techniques

Recall from Section 15.2, under our GP-based RST approach, we search for scenarios that are both adverse and plausible:
- *Plausible Region:* $\{x \in \mathbb{R}^n \mid M(x) \leq \tilde{p}\}$
- *Adverse Loss Region:* $\{x \in \mathbb{R}^n \mid P \& L(x) \in (L - \dot{o}, L + \dot{o})\}$

To make the search for RST scenarios computationally efficient, we replace costly calls to the pricing functions with ML approximations. Thus, the first step is to train the pricing functions prior to the search algorithm.

In the next subsection, we will describe the GPR pricer and compare it with a deep neural network (DNN). As we will later discuss in more detail, the GPR-based approach, unlike DNN, provides uncertainty estimates as we search for scenarios.

A useful concept in Machine Learning is meta-learning. Meta-learning is the general idea of *learning how to learn* or *learning to learn fast*, which is useful under reinforcement learning (learning based on feedback from its environment). In this spirit, our search algorithm utilises the exploitation–exploration trade-off where the learning system (search algorithm) has to make choices at each step with uncertain pay-offs (incomplete knowledge). The exploitation component repeats decisions (searches) that have worked well (in this case sampling near the level loss set) while the exploration component makes novel or exploratory decisions, with the goal of greater rewards.

15.3.2 GPR Pricer Approximation

A Gaussian process is a collection of random variables indexed by time or space, in which any finite subset of these random variables is a multivariate Gaussian distribution. Gaussian Process Regression (see Rasmussen and Williams, 2006) is a nonparametric[6] Bayesian technique which works well on small data sets and has the added benefit of providing uncertainty measurements on predictions. This last property makes it ideal to be used on the exploration of the risk factor space for RST scenarios. Furthermore, GPR approximation/interpolation can be order of magnitude faster than full revaluation when it comes to complex instruments.

A GP is an infinite-dimensional extension of the multivariate Gaussian distribution. A GP is specified by its mean m, and covariance or kernel function k:

$$f(x) \sim GP(m(x), k(x, x')) \tag{15.5}$$

In our setting, a GP takes risk factors as inputs and outputs a price – i.e. it is a map $x \in \mathbb{R}^d \to f(x)$. Any finite collection $(f(x_1), \dots, f(x_n))$, by definition, is multivariate Gaussian with covariance k.

Given a set of evaluations $(x_i, f(x_i)), i = 1, \dots, n$ we can estimate a prediction of f^* at a new point $x^* \notin \{x_1, \dots, x_n\}$ by assuming a Gaussian process prior:

$$f^* \mid X, f, x^* \sim \mathcal{N}(k(x, x^*)k(x, x)^{-1}f, k(x^*, x^*) - k(x^*, x)k(x, x)^{-1}k(x, x^*)) \tag{15.6}$$

where $(X = [x_1, \dots, x_n]^T, f = [f(x_1), \dots, f(x_n)]^T)$ is the training data, and k is a kernel function. The kernel function $k(x, x^*)$ gives the covariance between $f(x)$ and $f(x^*)$, and this in turn specifies the smoothness of f. For instance, a kernel function that outputs a correlation near one for input values x and x^* that are close, will produce output values that are close. For all examples in this chapter, we use the radial basis function (RBF) with a length parameter of one as our kernel:

$$k(x, y) = \sigma^2 e^{-\frac{1}{2}|x - y|^2}$$

From equation (15.6), the prediction given x^* will take the form $\mathbb{E}[f^* \mid X, f, x^*]$ and the corresponding confidence interval comes from the covariance function.

In order to learn the pricing functions correctly, the design scenarios $S = \{x_1, \dots, x_n\}$ need to accurately represent the scenario space. For accurate approximations of the pricing function, it is more desirable to perform an interpolation between the training scenarios instead of an extrapolation. Thus, searches inside the convex hull of S will produce accurate portfolio revaluations. In Section 15.4, we will discuss how to extend scenario searches under extrapolation.

---

6 Parametric models have a finite number of model parameters whereas nonparametric models have an infinite number of model parameters.

15.3.2.1 Example: Learning Call Pricing Functions for the Heston Model

The pricer for a financial instrument can be seen as a function from the set of inputs (terms and conditions, model parameters) to the price of the contract. We assume that any market data necessary is included in the T&Cs and for the calibration of the model parameters. Note that model calibration can be learned separately using supervised learning and we assume this is already performed.

Throughout this chapter, we will use the Heston model to illustrate how GPRs can increase the speed of pricing. The Heston model is a stochastic volatility model that is used to price equity derivatives. It is given by:

$$dS_t = (r-q)S_t dt + \sqrt{v_t} S_t dW_t^S, S_0 \text{ given} \tag{15.7}$$

$$dv_t = \kappa(\theta - v_t)dt + \xi\sqrt{v_t} dW_t^v, v_0 \text{ given} \tag{15.8}$$

$$<dW_t^S, dW_t^v \geq \rho dt \tag{15.9}$$

Here S is the underlying stock price, r is the risk free rate, q is the dividend yield, v is the variance, θ is the mean reversion value, ξ is the volatility of volatility, κ is the reversion speed, and ρ is the correlation between the Brownian motions W^S and W^v.

The parameters of the model are labelled as $\mathcal{M} = (\kappa, \theta, \xi, \rho, v_0)$ while the T & Cs are described by $T \& C = (r, q, T, K)$, this includes both T&C and relevant market data. We generate a sequence of input values $\mathcal{I}_i = (\mathcal{M}_i, T \& C_i) \rightarrow p_i$ for $i = 1, \dots, N$.

First, consider learning the input prices from deep learning. One-layer neural networks provide an approximation to any function, given enough regularity assumptions (see Universal Approximation theory, Kratios, 2020). However, the single layer might require the number of nodes to approach infinity for the desired results to approximate prices within the bid-ask spread. Deep learning allows for the approximation of non-integrable functions with a finite number of jumps (see Kratios, 2020). Figure 15.4 depicts a neural network model with four hidden layers.

Once the DNN is trained (from the training data $(\mathcal{I}_i, p_i)_{i=1,\dots,N}$) it can be saved and used as needed. One advantage of the DNN is the ability to create as much data upfront "as needed", especially when historical data may be limited. Figure 15.5 plots the predicted values of implied volatility of call options against the actual values for a test set of data. Here, we see that the DNN accurately prices the call option using the Heston Model.

The top right plot of Figure 15.7 compares the GPR approximation with the actual call prices. Like the DNN, it provides an accurate fit of the call pricing function. We also provide the implied volatility calibration relative errors in Figure 15.6.

In addition, the top left and bottom right plots of Figure 15.7 provide predictions for the American put and down-and-out barrier put prices. Here, we observe that the GPR can price exotic derivatives with highly asymmetric pay-off profiles. Moreover,

Parameters	Options
Hidden Layers	4
Neurons (each layer)	200
Activation	Elu
Dropout Rate	0.0
Batch Normalisation	No
Optimiser	Adam
Batch Size	1024
Epoch	1000

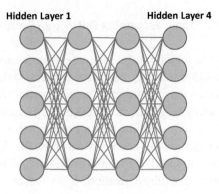

Figure 15.4: Structure of the neural network model.

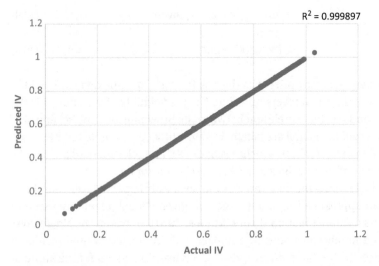

Figure 15.5: Neural network accuracy for Heston model.

computing Greeks using GPRs comes for *free*, but one should keep in mind that computing the derivative of an approximation is generally not the same as computing an approximation of a derivative, as the two do not commute for nonlinearity.

15.3.2.1.1 DL vs GPR: Which One?

One of the main differences between neural networks and GPRs is that neural networks are parametric models while GPRs are nonparametric models. For a DNN, the number of parameters is fixed once the topology and the activation functions are chosen. For GPRs, the number of parameters increases with the data. More precisely, additional information is added by priors, and GPRs typically work better with smaller samples. To obtain a nonparametric version of a neural network would require an

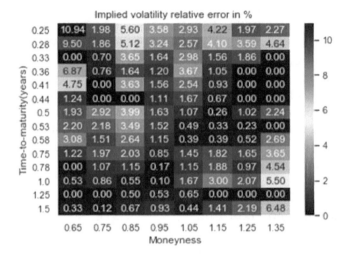

Figure 15.6: Implied volatility calibration relative error if Heston model for GPR.

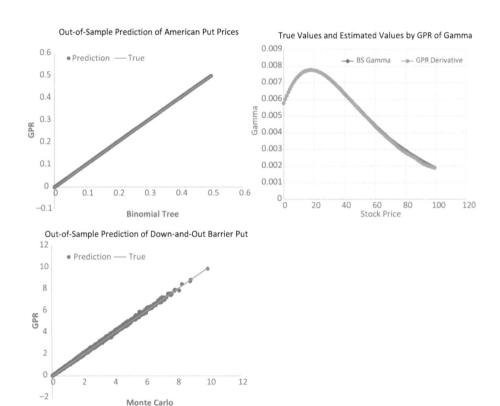

Figure 15.7: GPR approximations for American put, European call, and down-and-out barrier put prices.

infinite length (single) layer. Although DNN and GPR are apparently different from a methodological point of view, there is a link between them (see Lee et al., 2018).

The choice of the kernels for GPRs is important since they provide a trade-off between data fitting and smoothness. One disadvantage of GPRs can be the high computational burden in the calculation of the inverse of the covariance matrix but there are solutions to alleviate this problem.

From our perspective, one of the search requirements is to have enough information to direct the search towards the region of interest, and GPRs satisfy this requirement since they automatically output a confidence interval.

15.3.3 Level-Set Computation Algorithm

Meta-modelling has become an increasing trend in prediction and optimisation of expensive black-box functions in many fields such as finance, environmental science and engineering. A surrogate (meta-model) is an approximation of a complex system response from a small number of selected inputs. In this context, the surrogate model is the GPR approximation of the pricing function. Selecting the inputs is known in engineering as design of experiments (DoE). Selecting the experiments (i.e. risk factors scenarios in our case) coupled with the computationally inexpensive surrogate model is the desired recipe for sampling around the level set of interest while keeping plausibility as a constraint. Starting from different points in the sample space, we can sequentially look for the interesting scenarios, keeping a trade-off between exploration and exploitation within a computational budget.

Consider the scenario that is most plausible for a given portfolio loss. This was formulated in equation (15.1) and can be re-written as the solution to the following quadratic optimisation problem with equality constraint:

$$\min M_{\Sigma}(x), \text{s.t.} \ f(x) = L \tag{15.10}$$

Here f represents the valuation function of the portfolio and L is the level of interest (e.g. VaR, % of loss from current value). We will present a result in the next section where we replace f by a meta-model (or a surrogate).

15.3.3.1 The Acquisition Function

For meta-modelling, GPR has become the most popular nonparametric approach for both deterministic and stochastic black-box functions. GPs are used with a sequential algorithm using their rich uncertainty quantification which can be used analytically.

The algorithm can be described as sequentially sampling:

$$x_{n+1} = \arg\max_{x \in D} \mathcal{H}_n(x) \qquad (15.11)$$

where we maximise the acquisition function $\mathcal{H}(z)$ conditional on the current information that takes into account the closeness to the target and the uncertainty (variance).
Another approach uses ranking and selections (see Chen, 2008). The acquisition
function specifies how the parameter space should be explored during Bayesian optimisation. The predicted mean and predicted standard deviation generated by the GP
model is used for the exploration–exploitation algorithm.

One of the first acquisition methods, called the Maximum Contour Uncertainty
(MCU) (Upper Confidence Bound strategy) that expresses the exploration and
exploitation trade-off through the posterior mean (exploitation) and standard deviation (exploration) is given by

$$\mathcal{H}_n(x) = -|m_n((x)| + \lambda_n s_n(x) \qquad (15.12)$$

where the mean $m(x)$ and standard deviation $s(x)$ of the GP are given by equations
(15.5) and (15.6). A large step λ_n leads to a space filling sampling that minimises the
MSE while a small step aggressively samples along the boundary of interest. A constant choice, $\lambda_n = 1.96$ leads to the straddle method, whereby we look for a 95% band
around the level set of interest.

In order to align our search with equation (15.10) (conduct our search near the
level set that is plausible), we modify the acquisition function by adding a term for
the Mahalanobis radius:

$$\tilde{\mathcal{H}}_n(x) = -\left|m_n(x)\right| + \lambda_n s_n(x) - \lambda_2 \left\|x\Sigma^{-1}x\right\|_2^2 \qquad (15.13)$$

15.4 Numerical Results for Search Algorithm

In this section, we examine how the term in (15.13) behaves for a portfolio of options.
We consider a portfolio with three options (two calls and one put) where the risk
factors are the underlying stock returns. We look for a loss of 10% from the initial
value of the portfolio.

Three Heston models with the following parameters are used for pricing the
options:

$$\theta = [0.2957, 0.04, 0.04], \ \kappa = [0.9626, 2.0, 2.0], \ \sigma = [0.0208435, 0.1, 0.3]$$
$$v_0 = [0.0983, 0.04, 0.04], \ \rho = [-0.2919, 0.0, -0.5]$$

The maturity of all the options is one year, the starting values for the underlying stock price is 100, and the strikes are [99.5, 101.5, 100.0]. The risk-free rate is 0.02 and the continuous dividend yield is assumed constant at 0.01. We generate correlated scenarios for the underlyings $(S_i)_{i=1,\ldots,3}$ and split the data into a training and a test set. We price the options using QuantLib with a Fast Fourier Transformation (FFT) pricer for the training data.

Using 500 training points we learn the portfolio pricer. Figure 15.8 shows the out-of-sample performance and that the GPR prices the portfolio accurately. It is worth noting that we observe a speed-up of an order of 30 to 40 times using the GPR.

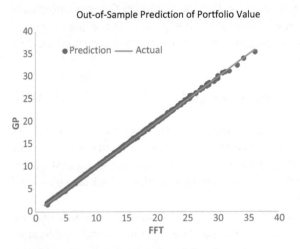

Figure 15.8: GPR approximation of portfolio value.

We set the portfolio loss at 10% and identify the scenario in the training set that is closest to this loss and use it as a starting point for the search. This initial scenario can be interpreted as VaR at some confidence level. A VaR framework gives us a single scenario, whereas an RST framework will extract more scenarios.

We optimise (15.13) using a global differential evolution (DE) optimisation algorithm and the output of each optimisation is used as the next starting point. We run the algorithm and present the first twenty iterations in Figure 15.9.

We can define the region of interest by specifying plausibility and a neighbourhood of losses:
- *Plausible Scenarios:* Set the Mahalanobis radius to 0.5
- *Adverse Neighbourhood:* Losses are contained in the P&L interval (−11%, −8%)

With this region of interest, we examine scenarios 7–20, which came from the iterations of the search algorithm. But this is just one sample path. We can sample with many more paths that start at the Mahalanobis threshold or VaR scenarios near 10%.

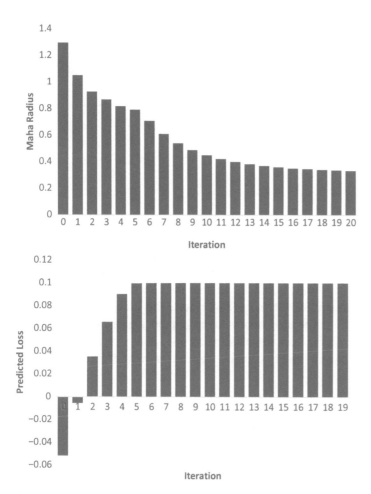

Figure 15.9: Mahalanobis radius and predicted losses from a single path.

As an illustration, Figure 15.10 depicts five sample paths. In a similar fashion, we examine the scenarios that are within the region of interest defined here. Note that running the algorithm with adaptive λ parameters and in parallel from different starting points will increase efficiently.

15.4.1 Extrapolation of Scenarios and Asymptotic Approximations

For the illustrative example in this section, the RST scenarios were contained in the convex hull of the training scenarios $S = \{x_1, \dots, x_n\}$. As a result, interpolation rather than extrapolation was performed. Pricing scenarios accurately under extrapolation is more difficult and we briefly discuss techniques that extend the GPR-based search algorithm outside its initial training set.

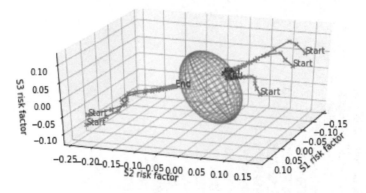

Figure 15.10: RST sample paths.

Deep Learning is making a big impact in the pricing of derivatives and risk, including extrapolation outside the training set. More precisely, how do we replace a (model) pricer with its surrogate model outside the convex hull of the training samples? Antonov, Konikov and Piterbarg (2020) tackle this problem by introducing a neural network that incorporates large-value asymptotics over the extrapolation region. They introduce a spline interpolator with prescribed asymptotics and the addition of a neural network layer that guarantees zero asymptotic behaviour in any prescribed directions.

For GPRs, the mean (which is set to zero in our case) can be used to control the asymptotic behaviour outside the region that we learn. In addition, we can directly apply an *asymptotic* function outside the training scenario space. Even though this requires domain knowledge about the particular pricing function, there are asymptotic results available for many pricing models (see Antonov et al., 2020, Kienitz et al., 2020).

Finally, we can combine the asymptotic behaviour to the *initial* training set by Local Gaussian Regression (LGR) to tackle both the extrapolation and computational cost/complexity (cubic inference costs), a topic that we will explore in future work. Using a localising function basis and inference techniques, the computational complexity can be reduced to that of a locally weighted regression which would be a step forward toward real-time algorithm.

15.5 Summary

Reverse stress tests are simple in concept. Under an RST, we first specify the portfolio loss, and then find scenarios that generate this loss. However, the implementation of RSTs is nontrivial, especially when the portfolio is comprised of nonlinear positions. A search algorithm for scenarios will encompass the pricing of positions that can be computationally expensive.

We presented a GPR-based search algorithm to find scenario that are both adverse and plausible. In this setting, the adverse losses are specified as a neighbourhood around the given loss and plausibility was specified by containing scenarios within a Mahalanobis radius. Prior to the search, complex pricing functions are first trained by GPRs. Consequently, this will dramatically speed up the portfolio valuation during the search. Moreover, the GPR provides both an expectation and distribution for the portfolio loss for a given scenario. The search algorithm is based on reinforcement learning, in which an exploitation and exploration algorithm explores the space of scenarios that are near the loss level set.

It should be noted that the Mahalanobis radius can be used for other elliptical distributions such as the Student distribution. We considered a more general dependence structure of risk factors modelled using vine copulas in an earlier paper (Cotoi and Stamicar, 2018). In this setting, we could still use the GPR-based algorithm but replace the Mahalanobis radius with a half-depth measure for plausibility.

Bibliography

Antonov A., Konikov, M., and Piterbarg, V. (2020). Neural networks with asymptotic control, preprint, 2020.

Basel Committee on Banking Supervision (2009). Principles for sound stress testing practices and supervision, Consultative Document, Bank for International Settlements.

Chevallier, C., Picheny, C., Ginsbourger, D. Kriging: An efficient and user-friendly implementation of batch-sequential inversion strategies based on kriging, *Computational Statistics & Data Analysis*, 71 (2014), pp. 1021–1034.

Chen, C.H., et al. (2008). Efficient simulation budget allocation for selecting an optimal subset, *INFORMS Journal on Computing*, 20, pp. 579–595.

Cotoi, I. and Microsoft (2019). Reverse Stress Testing and AI, Ai4 Finance conference, New York.

Cotoi, I. and Stamicar, R. (2017). Stress testing best practices, *Axioma In-Practice Series*.

Cotoi, I., Stamicar, R. (2018). Towards a RST framework, *Axioma-In-Practice Series*.

Crepey, S. and Dixon, M. (2019). Gaussian process regression for derivative portfolio modelling and application to CVA computations, SSRN.

Kopeliovich, Y., Novosyolov, A., Satchkov, D., and Schachter, B. (2014). Robust risk estimation and hedging: a reverse stress testing approach.

Micchelli, C.A., et al. (2006). Universal kernels, Journal of Machine learning Research 7, pp. 2651–2667.

Rasmussen, C., E., Williams, K., I. (2006). *Gaussian processes for Machine Learning*, The MIT Press.

Kienitz, J. (2020). New stochastic volatility models: PDE, approximation, deep pricing and calibration, Thalesian presentation.

Kratios, A., (2020). The Universal Approximation Property: Characterizations, Existence, and a Canonical Topology for Deep-Learning, arXiv:1910.03344.

Lee, J., Bahri, Y., Novak, R., Schoenholz, S., Pennington, J., Sohl-Dickstein, J. (2018). Deep neural networks as Gaussian processes. Conference paper at ICLR 2018.

Li, T., Cotoi, I. (2019). GPRs applied to quantitative pricing and risk analytics, QPRA ML day, Axioma Inc.

Ludkovski, M. (2018). Kriging metamodels and experimental design for Bermudan option pricing, *Risk*, vol. 22.

Horvath, B. et al. Deep learning volatility, SSRN paper.

Liu, M., Nelson, B., L., Staum, J., Simulation on Demand for Pricing Many Securities, Proceedings of the 2010 Winter Simulation Conference.

Lyu, Y. et al., Evaluating Gaussian Process Metamodels and Sequential Designs for Noisy Level Set Estimation, arXiv:1807.06712v2.

Picheny V., et al., Adaptive Designs of Experiments for Accurate Approximation of a Target Region, https://hal.archives-ouvertes.fr/hal-00319385v2 QuantLib, https://www.quantlib.org

Strydom, P. (2017). Macroeconomic cycle effects on mortgage and personal loan default rates, *Journal of Applied Finance and Banking*, vol. 7, no. 6, pp. 1–27.

Tong, W, Cotoi, I. (2019). GPRs applied to quantitative pricing and risk analytics, QPRA ML day, Axioma Inc.

Williams, J. (2019). Microsoft AI overview, QPRA ML day, Axioma Inc.

Zhu, X. (2019). Azure Machine Learning Service, QPRA ML day, Axioma Inc.

Claudio Albanese, Stefano Iabichino, Paolo Mammola,
Ashutosh Nawani

16 Reverse Stress Testing and Funding Sets

The Evolving Challenges of OTC Portfolios

16.1 Counterparty Credit Risk

Financial crises have historically had a far-reaching impact on risk management practices, and the Covid-19 turmoil is not likely to be an exception to the rule.[1]

Losses in mortgage lending triggered the 2008 crisis and exposed the inadequacy
of counterparty credit risk management in swap markets. The ex-post fix resulted
in a general overhaul of Counterparty Valuation Adjustment CVA capital reserves,
portfolio-wide risk capital cushions, and a host of collateral requirements to "bubble
wrap" the financial system. The Covid-19 crisis, which originated even farther afield
in the realm of microbiology, is causing the methods for liquidity risk management to
evolve and include reverse stress testing RTS.

Liquidity risk was largely anticipated at the policy level – the justification for
imposing collateral requirements which converted credit risk to liquidity risk was that
governments had the tools to act quickly and with determination to pump liquidity
into the system at the crisis point, as indeed happened. Nevertheless, the toolkit of
risk managers may have to be enhanced once again.

The issue of wrong-way risk as a critical focus area for risk management was
first brought out in the Basel requirements. Counterparty Specific Wrong-Way-Risk
(SWWR) emerged in the late 1990s along with CVA,[2] and has been routinely assessed
at the netting-set level.

Collateral posting obligations heighten the liquidity pressure on bank counterparties as they face margin calls against volatile exposures. Liquidity concerns,
credit deterioration and unprecedented volatility establish a self-reinforcing loop. An
acronym for this turn of events already exists: General Wrong Way Risk (GWWR), the
sort of wrong-way risk which is tied to macroeconomic factors and has a pervasive
impact across the entire bank portfolio. GWWR manifests itself as a wrong-way correlation between the cost of funding, market risk and default risk.

---

1 Author Stefano Iabichino is Vice President at JP Morgan Chase, London. This paper represents the opinions of the authors and it is not meant to represent the position or opinions of JP Morgan or their members.
2 Winters, W. Wrong Way Exposure, *Risk Magazine*, July 1999.

Note: Edited by Daniel Mayenberger

https://doi.org/10.1515/9783110647907-016

Portfolio-level GWWR is considered a strategic risk and did not gain much momentum until recently due, in part, to regulatory initiatives and, in part, to the Covid-19 crisis, which brought liquidity management in the spotlight as a central focus area for risk managers. As macro-economic uncertainty seeps through counterparty balance sheets in a heightened volatility environment, the squeeze on the ability to meet funding requirements causes exposures to reach unprecedented levels.

Stress testing is the instrument in the toolset of risk managers designed for the specific purpose of assessing, anticipating, quantifying and possibly mitigating events of extreme systemic risk. Unfortunately, models for counterparty and liquidity risk are often out of alignment and do not capture economic risk. Silos-specific analytics generate numbers that do not capture portfolio-wide inter-relations. Stress scenarios for counterparty specific default risk are client-centric. However, stress scenarios for liquidity shocks should model conditions of systemic market strain, disruption severity and the impact of the duration of the crisis period. These events must be considered on a portfolio-wide mix of assets, collateral and capital positions, where detailed interlinkages between tightening liquidity and exposures to both specific and general wrong-way risk are explicitly captured.

Historical precedent is a useful guide, as well as a scarce resource. Instead of accurately capturing correlation risk, historical scenarios outline an episodic narrative, which is a far cry from being systematic. Risk managers like generals tend to model (or fight) the last war. As we have learned from experience, the full effect of correlation and systemic risk should not be underestimated, as the sheer variety of its potential manifestations will never cease to surprise us.

A more proactive strategy to manage liquidity risk will be more beneficial than reactive decision-making, but to be useful it must be based on a methodology that accurately captures economic risk drivers.

The FVA (Funding Valuation Adjustment) is a fundamental metric, potentially possessing all the right features for liquidity risk management since it combines the bank funding spread and balance sheet exposure over future time horizons. However, FVA must be appropriately defined based on true economic drivers. Definitions currently used for either accounting or transfer pricing are not necessarily suitable for liquidity modelling.

Specific counterparty credit is eminently bilateral in nature and can be analysed at the aggregation level of netting-set exposure specific to each counterparty. However, netting-set analytics are intrinsically inadequate when assessing the cost of funding employing either debt or equity for the most lapalissian reason: collateral can be rehypothecated across the entire portfolio, and capital models are meaningful only at the portfolio-wide level. This motivated some of us to introduce the notion of "funding-set" (in contrast to netting-set) as a portfolio sharing the same funding strategies in debt and equity.[3] Not only do netting-set specific metrics and accounting numbers do not capture economic risk (e.g. ignoring client-wide default times correlations), but the impact of macro-economic drivers underlying GWWR requires a holistic portfolio view. A coherent portfolio view of the true risk cannot be adequately represented as a linear sum over independent netting-sets. Notwithstanding the different causes, all crises exhibit strong correlations between both credit spreads and default arrival times, which the netting-sets view does not capture.

It will take time for the FVA acronym to shake-off the black-art label granted by Risk Magazine. The "FVA debate" that took place from the years 2013 to 2016 around the definition of FVA and KVA (Regulatory Capital Valuation Adjustment) metrics might have been perceived by the general public as an alien argument among practitioners, tweaking CVA models to capture liquidity, and disgruntled academics complaining about theoretical inconsistencies. Although subtleties surrounding the Modigliani-Miller theorem excited only adepts, the core of the debate revolved around the appropriateness of using netting-set aggregation typical to CVA analytics in a context that clearly required funding-set metrics.

A proper GWWR framework for liquidity management contains all the key features of the CCR framework but supersedes it with a more comprehensive and consistent modelling approach. It combines exposure, collateral, and defaults into a single paradigm to assess the funding implications for the bank's obligors experiencing funding distress in an environment with widening credit spreads.

Funding strategies for financial institutions are articulated across the entire breadth of the capital structure, ranging from equity liabilities to debt tranches of various degrees of subordination and seniority. The automation in TLAC conversion establishes a further degree of interconnectedness, so that losses offset by risk capital have immediate implications on funding spreads with senior unsecured debt. This mechanism makes it impossible to pinpoint the cause of bank failure to a specific event such as a drop in their CET1 or sudden widening of CDS spread rates. The path to default resembles a cascade of interconnected events leading to that pivotal moment where the bank is incapable to promptly raise funding across any segment of its capital structure. Once a dealer is shut out of the secured financing market, and institutional investors, private equity funds, and governments signal their unwillingness to fund the bank, the stock price falls, and the overall funding rate is pushed beyond the point of no return, triggering bank default.

The bank's overall funding rate is primarily driven by underlying capital requirements and possible default loss or market risk the bank is expected to suffer. Funding requirements are a function of overall balance-sheet exposure, accounting for offsets between assets and liabilities. The FVA number supposedly captures the present value of funding costs by projecting out into the future requirements and credit spreads.

---

3 Albanese, C., Andersen, L., and Iabichino, S. FVA: Accounting and Risk Management, *Risk Magazine*, February 2015.

The KVA number instead is a cost of capital metric designed as an overall proxy for shareholder return and for general guidance on a broad spectrum of strategic actions from hedging to executive compensation, credit limits and dividend policy. A GWWR methodology can be added to a simulation framework, which generates synthetic scenarios and then pinpoints the ones with the most significant single impact on the relevant economic numbers such as KVA and FVA. A coherent GWWR framework generates room for endogenous modelling of the bank spread by simulating the waterfall of revenues, trading and capital losses.

By simulating various market states via a nested Monte-Carlo, holistic reverse stress testing is finally available, and a bank could gather which future market scenarios would lead to an unacceptable (or "catastrophic") level of funding risk, and dynamically hedge the tail risk. Dynamic hedging could involve either forward CVA market risk hedges or long-term unsecured financing strategies. A quantitative assessment of the latter using FVA projections is also part of the regulatory requirements for the calculation of metrics such as RLAP or S2.

Regulatory metrics such as RLAP or S2 are backward-looking in nature, while the coronavirus crisis has significantly different dynamics than the 2008 crisis. We require a more systematic approach based on a comprehensive set of synthetic scenarios. As we embrace the funding-set level portfolio simulations, we then also must be particularly careful about model risk in all its elements, from pricing models to risk metrics, passing by the accounting methods' snare.

16.2 Model Risk

The 2008 crisis triggered a shift from trade-specific pricing to netting-set CVA analytics. In the process, it also created a hiatus between trading models and CVA models since high-quality pricing models could not be used at the netting-set level because of performance limitations. This fundamental inconsistency between high-quality and low-quality models used simultaneously was one of the drivers that brought a renewed attention on model risk, which inspired parts of the FRTB.

Model risk is a concept that does not apply only to derivative pricing models but extends to accounting methods and risk management analytics. The FVA debate that unfolded on the pages of Risk Magazine in the years 2013 to 2015 revealed an example of model risk for accounting models.

The initial approach to FVA by Pieterbarg[4] was trade-centric and inspired by the pricing practice with cross-currency swaps. The netting-set view by Burgard and

---

4 Pieterbarg, V. Funding Beyond Discounting: Collateral Agreements and Derivatives Pricing, *Risk Magazine*, February 2010.

Kier[5] appeared later and quickly became the industry standard in the XVA (Valuation Adjustment) space, as it could be easily shoehorned into a CVA calculator.

Although both arguments are heuristic approximations motivated by system limitations and although they are mutually exclusive, the two practices succeeded to coexist, leading to double-counting of funding costs and triggering uncontrolled wealth transfers dependent on the net directionality of trades and Credit Support Annex (CSA) terms. Ad-hoc patches and adjustments aimed at mitigating side effects ultimately have a corrosive system-wide impact and fall short of a robust resilient solution.

A certain degree of imprecision of FVA accounting rules based on netting-set metrics was tolerated for seven years because the numbers were not particularly material. However, the eightfold widening of credit spreads we have observed during the Covid crisis combined with tighter capital positions and the impending IBOR transition serve as a stimulus to advance the state of the art. Interestingly enough, a revision of FVA methodologies is set to have an impact in the more general context of liquidity risk management.

In a nutshell, within the limits of netting-set aggregation, the funding cost specific to a netting-set is approximated by the so-called symmetric FVA, expressed as

$$FVA = FCA - FBA$$

The FCA accounts only for states of the world where the netting-set in question is an asset. In contrast, the FBA accounts for the funding benefit deriving from holding liabilities and receiving variation margin, which can then be rehypothecated against other margin requirements. This is theoretically inconsistent, as based on the assumption that the variation margin received through netting-sets which are a liability is entirely offset by the netting-sets which are assets. Although typically valid during tranquil times, whereby bank balance sheets have a systematic tilt in favour of assets, when the bank is in distress the combined effect of mark-downs and defaults can potentially reverse the balance sheet and generate excess cash which is not of much use and would not count as a source of stable funding.

In the more consistent funding-set approach, the FVA is computed asymmetrically – the entire funding-set is simulated going forward, and the cost of funding is accrued only over states of the world where the funding-set in its entirety necessitates funding.

Because of the known inconsistencies of the netting-set symmetric FVA, accounting and hedging practices are warped in a peculiar way. While the FBA does not contribute to CET1 capital, the P&L ex DVA number is used for hedging. At first sight, this is rather counterintuitive – executives are mandated to maximise shareholder value,

---

5 Burgard, C. and Kjaer, M. In the Balance, *Risk Magazine,* 2011.

which is best approximated by CET1, not by the P&L ex DVA. Furthermore, why would one subtract the DVA from the GAAP P&L number and not the FBA if both numbers have the exact same accounting treatment?

The justification of this practice is that, in tranquil time and with normal portfolio positioning, the asymmetric funding-set FVA is approximately equal to the symmetric FVA. If asymmetric funding-set FVA is the only capital deduction, then the CET1 number one obtains is remarkably close to the P&L ex DVA.

At times of crisis, however, if the bank is distressed and with an anomalous balance sheet position dominated by liabilities, the P&L ex-DVA number diverges from asymmetric funding-set FVA. More seriously, any attempt to model General Wrong Way Risk (GWWR) for liquidity risk and navigate turbulent times is doomed to failure if only siloed netting-set analytics are available.

As capital buffers tighten at times of crisis, and banks start considering the prospect of emergency recapitalisation, the FVA capital deduction suddenly becomes more visible. It was noticed that the FVA capital deduction for a representative portfolio, in calm markets, was overstated by a factor 3. Risk[6] recently reported FVA losses triggered by the Covid-19 crisis and that have been realised using the traditional FCA/FBA method.

Funding-set analytics that are appropriate for rigorous FVA accounting are a fundamental necessity, but yet are not sufficient for GWWR modelling and reverse stress testing unless further conditions are also met.

The CVA is often computed with only market risk factors and deterministic credit defaults to obtain a more stable result based on just a few thousand scenarios. However, realistic liquidity risk modelling requires a simulation including both market and credit risk factors for each counterparty and the bank itself. This complexity level makes the computation harder because one must simulate ten times more risk factors and generate 100 times more scenarios.

To model GWWR for liquidity risk accurately, size matters. Market scenarios whereby many small counterparties default and a situation where a large bank defaults are quite different in the way contagion spreads and liquidity dries up. For liquidity management, it is crucial to analyse in detail events of default of the largest and most significant counterparties. The inclusion of binary default events is straightforward at the condition that one makes use of 10 to 100 times more scenarios than one would use otherwise.

An accurately calibrated simulation is essential if liquidity risk ought to be risk-managed by hedging strategies – optimal hedge ratios can only be calculated by an engine that correctly fits their present and future conditional valuation. A possible approach is to calibrate stochastic processes to derivatives for each risk factor and then join the processes with a dynamic copula construct, which is guaranteed

6 Becker, L. FVA Losses in Spotlight after Coronavirus Stress, *Risk Magazine*, April 2020.

to preserve the marginals. Wrong-way risk can be built into the correlation model to reflect macro-economic correlations, e.g. between interest rates and credit spreads or between FX risk and country-specific risk.

Correlations themselves, however, are stochastic in nature and are subject to wrong-way risk driven by portfolio composition. The funding spread of the bank used in the FVA calculation is intertwined with the size of funding requirements at times of stress. In these periods, if funding requirements increase at times of stress, because of the peculiar portfolio exposures, then the funding spread of a bank approaching the market in search of liquidity can blow up substantially. Ideally, the bank funding spread should be modelled endogenously along with the entire capital structure of the bank from equity to senior debt, and accounting for the TLAC conversion mechanics.

A standard dynamic copula cannot model stochastic correlations driven by portfolio composition. They can, of course, be shaped by hard-coding scenario changes, however, at the cost of affecting calibrated marginals for the funding curve of the bank itself. As a compromise solution, one can hard code wrong-way correlation risk only in low-probability extreme scenarios, which have a minor overall impact on present values. This way, one is well-positioned to hedge future liquidity risk events, consistently with the currently observed funding curve of the bank.

The Covid-19 turbulence and the IBOR transition, similarly to all past crises, will be an incentive to ultimately strengthen the resilience of the financial system. Reverse stress testing methodologies play a central role in the required holistic funding set analytics. A case study and more details on reverse stress testing for funding sets including Specific and General Wrong Way Risk are in Chapter 17.

Claudio Albanese, Stéphane Crépey, Stefano Iabichino

17 Capital and Collateral Simulation for Reverse Stress Testing

Chapter 16 introduced a holistic framework for reverse stress testing (RST), based on accurate data mining of large-scale synthetic scenarios.[1] The current section takes a step closer to the operational reality of a market maker, shedding light on the theoretical and computational framework for the analysis of extreme events in the form of forward-looking RST. The framework builds on a large-scale Monte Carlo simulation, thus, targeting the bespoke characteristics of the portfolio held. The Monte Carlo, relying on models calibrated to option prices, is used to propagate all the risk factors the portfolio is exposed to, while the RST aims to gather those future economic states under which bank solvency could be impaired. Specific and General Wrong Way Risks effects are injected through dynamic market-credit and credit-credit correlations.

Throughout this chapter, which provides a roadmap on the implementation of C. Albanese,[2] C., S. Crépey,[3] and S. Iabichino (2020),[4] we introduce the main ingredients and mechanics required to achieve such a holistic framework, which coherency extends to the entire banking book. While driving the reader throughout the framework's alchemy, we will present numerical results collected on a representative portfolio. We refer the interested reader to Albanese, C., S. Crépey, and S. Iabichino (2020) for details on the possible scope of applicability, of the presented framework, to the reality of a market-maker.

17.1 Setting the Stage

For the sake of simplicity, we use the risk-free (OIS rate) asset growing as a numeraire, and we assume equality between physical and pricing measures, denoted by P and Q respectively. The latter assumption is justifiable by the absence of reliable knowledge about the discrepancy between P and Q at the large horizons, which are typical of

1 The authors of this chapter are thankful to Alex Miscampbell for discussions.
2 Global Valuation, London.
3 University of Evry in Paris-Saclay. The research of Stéphane Crépey benefited from the support of the Chair Stress Test, RISK Management and Financial Steering, led by the French Ecole polytechnique and its Foundation and sponsored by BNP Paribas.
4 JP Morgan, London. This paper represents the opinions of the authors and it is not meant to represent the position or opinions of JP Morgan or their members.

Note: Edited by Daniel Mayenberger

https://doi.org/10.1515/9783110647907-017

an OTC derivative portfolio. Furthermore, we indicate with $E^Q[\cdot \,|F_t] = E_t^Q[\cdot]$ the conditional (to the σ-algebra F_t) risk-neutral expectation.

Consider a portfolio composed by a set N_c of counterparties. A counterparty can be characterised either by an individual netting-set, or by a collection of netting sets,[5] for which a Credit Support Annex (CSA) characterises collateral posting obligations.

For each counterparty, the characteristics of an individual netting-set are analysed in terms of risk-factors drivers and future cash-flows. This information is then sourced to the Monte Carlo based environment to generate counterparty-specific CCR, and portfolio-wide funding exposure profiles. Therefore, for each counterparty, the distribution of future CCR losses as well as its present expected value, i.e. the CVA (Counterparty Valuation Adjustment), are computed.

The (unilateral) CVA for a counterparty c is defined as

$$UCVA_{t_0}(c) = E_{t_0}^Q\left[e^{-\int_{t_0}^{\tau_c} r_{OIS}(s)ds}\,1_{\{t_0 < \tau_c < T\}}LGD(c)(V_{\tau_c}(c) - CSA_{\tau_c}(c))^+\right]$$

$$= E_{t_0}^Q\int_{t_0}^T e^{-\int_{t_0}^t r_{OIS}(s)ds}\,1_{\{t_0 < t < T\}}LGD(c)(V_t(c) - CSA_t(c))^+ \delta_{\tau_c}(dt)$$

where:
- t_0 and T are the computation date and the final maturity of the portfolio
- τ_c is the default time of the counterparty c
- r_{OIS} is the risk-free rate
- 1_A is an indicator function, subject to the A condition
- $LGD(c)$ is the counterparty-specific Loss Given Default, i.e. one minus the counterparty-specific recovery rate
- $V_t(c)$ is the counterparty specific aggregated Mark-to-Market
- $CSA_t(c)$ is the collateral posted by the client c according to the counterparty specific Credit Support Annex
- $v^+ = \max(v, 0)$

Additionally, the present value of the Funding Valuation Adjustment (FVA), computed at the funding-set level, is determined. Following Albanese, Andersen, and Iabichino (2015), the FVA is defined as:

$$FVA_{t_0} = E_{t_0}^Q\int_{t_0}^T e^{-\int_{t_0}^t r_{OIS}(s)ds} S_t(B)\left(\sum_{c=1}^{N_c}(V_t(c) - CSA_t(c))1_{t<\tau_c}\right)^+ 1_{t<\tau_B}\,dt$$

---

5 However, for the sake of narration simplicity, in the following, we will adopt the simplifying view that a counterparty has only one netting set with a CSA.

where:

- τ_B is the default time of the bank
- $S_t(B)$ is the funding spread of the bank

17.1.1 Tensor Algebra, CVA and FVA Computations

Define a set of epoch dates t_h, with $h \in \{1, 2, \dots, N_h\}$, and a set of primary scenarios $s \in [1, N_s]$. For each risk factor characterising the portfolio, define a set of discrete state variables r_x, with $x \in \{1, 2, \dots, N_x\}$. The dynamics of each risk factor are described in terms of a transition probability tensor, representing a collection of kernels $(T_{\delta t}(x, x'; t_h))$ whose elements specify the transition probabilities to evolve from the state x to the state x' at any given epoch-date t_h. The validity conditions for a transition probability tensor are:

1. Positivity: $T_{\delta t}(x, x'; t_h) \geq 0, \forall x$
2. Probability Conservation: $\sum_x T_{\delta t}(x, x'; t_h) = 1, \forall t_h$

The first condition implies the non-negativity of the elements of the tensor, while, for each epoch-date t_h, the second imposes the additivity to one of the kernels.

For each epoch-date, counterparty, and scenario, we store in-memory all the relevant counterparty-specific information – e.g. conditional default probabilities $(PD(h, c, s))$, OIS discounted exposures $(\hat{V}(h, c, s))$ and collateral amounts $(\widehat{CSA}(h, c, s))$.

In order to compute the CVA, following Albanese and Pietronero (2010), define a loss lattice $l \in \{1, 2, \dots, N_l\}$. At each epoch, the scenario conditional portfolio default loss distribution $(\Lambda(h, s, l))$ is calculated, taking the convolution product over individual counterparty losses conditioned to a scenario (assuming that the individual counterparty losses are independent given the realisation of a scenario):

$$\Lambda(h, s, l) = \Lambda(h, s, c_1, l) * \Lambda(h, s, c_2, l) * \dots * \Lambda(h, s, c_{N_c}, l)$$

where

$$\Lambda(h, s, c_i, l) = (1 - PD(h, c_i, s))\, \delta(l) + PD(h, c_i, s)\delta(l - (\hat{V}(h, c_i, s) - \widehat{CSA}(h, c_i, s))$$

is the probability that the loss triggered by the possible default of counterparty c_i at time h equals l, conditional on the realisation s of the economic drivers at time h (with δ for the Dirac measure at 0).

The (unconditional) point-in-time Default-Loss-Distribution, is deduced as:

$$\Lambda(h, l) = \frac{1}{N_s} \sum_{s=1}^{N_c} \Lambda(h, s, l)$$

from which cumulative portfolio losses between time 0 and H are computed by summation between epochs $h=0$ and H (see Figure 17.1). Figure 17.1 represents the expected loss level, for each epoch, using white pins, which converges to the time 0 CVA in the large horizon limit.

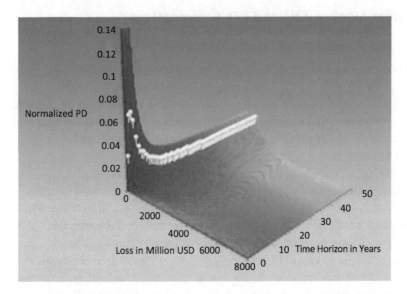

Figure 17.1: Cumulative portfolio default loss distribution. The white pins indicate the corresponding expected portfolio Default Loss at each epoch date.

At this point, the definition of a suitable scenario ranking criterion (i.e. a merit function) takes a pillar role.

17.2 The KVA

A holistic RST framework, which scope of applicability extends to the entire derivative book, requires a merit function sensitive to all the risk sources characterising the book, including CVA and FVA volatility. As we will discuss, the KVA owns all the desired properties.

The Regulatory Capital Valuation Adjustment (KVA) is a risk margin metric representing the expected remuneration of bank shareholders for their posted loss-absorbing capital, at some hurdle rate (h). However, instead of considering Pillar I regulatory capital models, following Albanese, Caenazzo, and Crépey (2016, 2017), Crépey, Sabbagh, and Song (2020), Albanese, Crépey, Hoskinson, and Saadeddine (2019), and consistently with IFRS17 (see IASB (2017)), we use a more comprehensive definition of KVA in terms of Pillar II economic capital.

The reason to favour a KVA defined in compliance with the Pillar II economic capital rests on the fact that, while Pillar I Regulatory Capital is consistent in intent with the Pillar II economic capital, Pillar I Regulatory Capital is characterised by several modelling assumptions. These assumptions, proposed to reduce computation times, strongly shrink the risk factors which the Pillar I Regulatory Capital is able to capture. For example, the Expected Effective Positive Exposure (EEPE),[6] based on an individual counterparty viewpoint, neglects General Wrong-Way Risk (GWWR), default clustering, as well as complex tail dependencies, while the usage of Gaussian copulas (in the default RWA) highly stylises default occurrences. Remarkably, the possibility of creating doom loops (e.g. between Capital Requirements and CCR hedges) and the losses triggered by the volatility of CVA and FVA are completely neglected.

Instead, Pillar II economic capital strongly tights to the shareholder's Core Equity Tier 1 capital (CET1), which is allocated to absorb any form of unexpected losses. CET1 depletions are given by

$$-dCET1_t = dD(t) + dF(t) + dUCVA_t + dFVA_t \tag{17.1}$$

where $dD(t)$ and $dF(t)$ are the shorthand notation for the integrands in the $E^Q_{t_0} \int_{t_0}^T \cdots$ formulations of the CVA and FVA, i.e. the future losses realised by the bank due to defaults and funding expenses. The Pillar II economic capital (EC) profile at time t is specified as the one year 97.5% expected shortfall depletion of CET1, i.e.

$$EC(t) = E^Q[CET1_t - CET1_{t+1} \,|\, CET1_t - CET1_{t+1} \geq VaR(t)] \tag{17.2}$$

where $VaR(t)$ is the 97.5% Value-at-Risk of the $CET1_t - CET1_{t+1}$ distribution. The present value of the KVA is then given by

$$KVA_0 = h \int_0^\infty EC(t)dt \tag{17.3}$$

where h is the inter-temporal hurdle rate, representing shareholder's expected reward for unit of capital invested.

Therefore, the KVA_0, which equals zero if and only if the CET1 is a constant function through time, represents the present value of the weighted average of future economic capital needs. It is, therefore, an organic metric to express the inter-temporal risk of the bank.

The computation of equations (17.1) and (17.2) requires the knowledge of the conditional future $UCVA_t$ and FVA_t terms. These future conditional metrics are computed

---

6 The EEPE, for an unsecured portfolio, is defined as:

$$\int_{t_0}^{1year} \max_{s \in [t_0, t]} E[(V_s)^+]dt$$

through nested Monte Carlo, where, for each epoch date and primary scenario, a set of secondary scenarios are branched-off (see Figure 17.2).

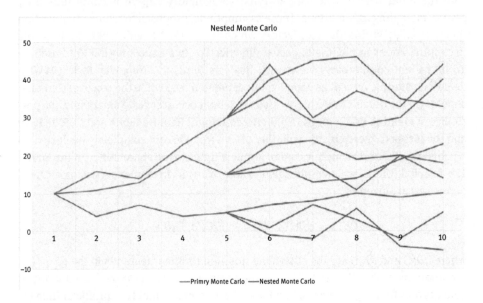

Figure 17.2: Nested Monte Carlo.

See Figure 17.3 for the resulting CET1 distribution at one epoch date.

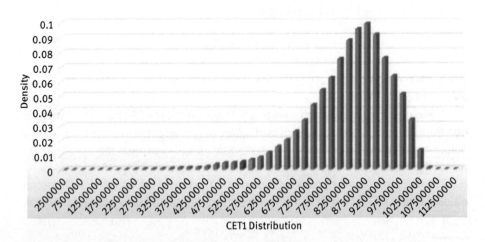

Figure 17.3: The CET1 distribution for one epoch date. The red bin marks the EC profile at the 97.5% confidence level.

17.3 The KVA as Merit Function and the Reversing Problem

The definition of KVA, anchoring to those CET1 losses exceeding their 97.5% VaR, naturally focuses on those stress scenarios where the whole portfolio suffers from severe default and/or market losses. However, before risk-factor data-mining, all the scenarios that composed the CET1 distribution need to be ranked in terms of their riskiness.

We define the scenario $(s \in [1, N_s])$ incremental KVA as the marginal contribution of a given scenario to the overall KVA_0, i.e. as:

$$\delta_s KVA_0 = KVA_0 - KVA_0(-s) \forall s \qquad (17.4)$$

In other words, the scenario incremental KVA is defined as the difference between the KVA and the KVA recomputed excluding scenario s. $\delta_s KVA_0$ thus, captures the dividend stream accrual requested by the capital market to lend capital to the bank to cover unexpected losses. Therefore, $\delta_s KVA_0$ represents a suitable merit function, as each incremental scenario will collect the additional capital requirement needed to cover any type of future losses.

17.3.1 Risk-Factors Inversion and Data Mining

Among the pool of scenarios, we select stress scenarios in the confidence interval [99%, 99.9%]. We thus select the 200 most adverse scenarios out of the original pool of primary scenarios (see Figure 17.4).

An interval-by-interval drill-down analysis, among the pool of gathered CET1 absorbing scenarios, identifies the points in time where the most significant CET1 depletions occur (see Figure 17.5).

The knowledge of the scenario-epoch date tuple, representing the most substantial CET1 depletion, allows to perform a scenario drill-down analysis. We therefore gather the set collecting the risk-factor state underneath the CET1 depletion spike.

Figure 17.6 depicts a bivariate projection of such an analysis. Each rhomboid pinpoints the risk factor state where the most material CET1 depletions manifest.

17.3.2 Counterparty Inversion and Data Mining

After identifying the most adverse economic states, we can proceed with a further data-mining analysis. We therefore expand the analysis to identify the counterparties which exacerbate the CET1 depletion in the identified states (see Figure 17.7).

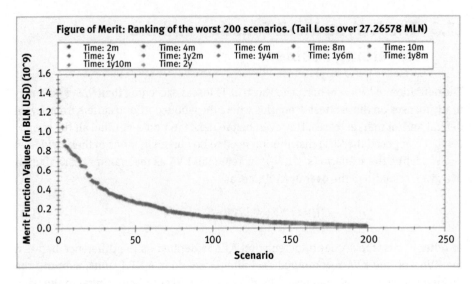

Figure 17.4: Figure of merit ranking criterion.

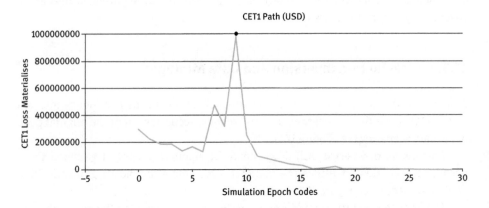

Figure 17.5: Time point where the most significant CET1 loss materialises.

The possibility to identify the counterparties that impair the capital demand (see Figure 17.7) sets the base to formulate a new credit limit metric based on counterparty incremental KVA. Taking the difference between the KVA_0 of the entire portfolio and the KVA of the portfolio obtained by removing the counterparty c, we compute the incremental counterparty KVA ($\Delta_c KVA_0$).

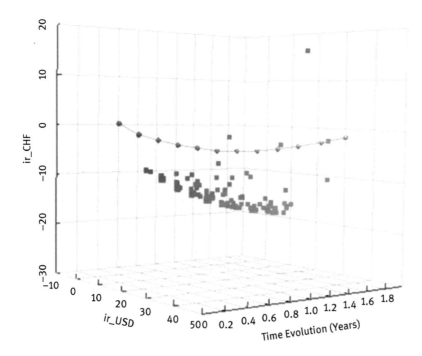

Figure 17.6: USD OIS vs. CFH overnight rates (in BPS) for stress scenarios on a representative fixed-income portfolio.

Top 5 Countrparties for CET1 Deplition (in MLN $) -- Scenario 18, Epoch-Date 2 years

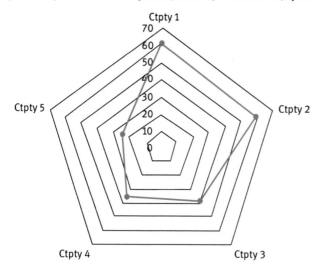

Figure 17.7: Extreme stress scenario – Top name.

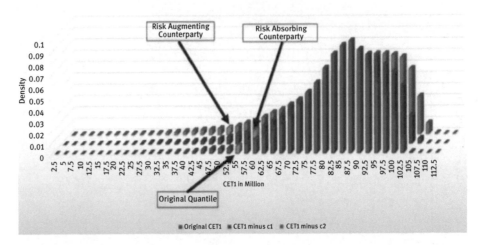

Figure 17.8: Incremental counterparty KVA.

Similar to the potential future exposure (PFE),[7] the $(\Delta_c KVA_0)$ assumes going-concern' and a run-off basis portfolio holding. However, differently from the PFE,[8] which concerns only MtM losses, the $(\Delta_c KVA_0)$ reflects all the potential sources of future losses, and it carries the intuitive meaning of the incremental demand for CET1 capital generated by a counterparty (see Figure 17.8). $(\Delta_c KVA_0)$ could thus naturally take a fundamental spot for setting limits on idiosyncratic risk appetites. Accounting for the full-term structure of economic capital, as opposed to just the current value, is in line with regulatory directives, such as CRR 292.7(b) (see European Banking Association, 2013). The CRR 292.7(b) explicitly prescribes to monitor and potentially capitalise on the concentration of exposure beyond the first year of credit exposure.

Current Credit Limit practices relay on metrics which are limited, as often based on a counterparty-centric view. As for Regulatory Capital metrics, correlated losses triggered by GWWR, or convexity concentrations for exotic derivative, are neglected. The lack of a comprehensive risk view, typical of MtM centric metrics, can thus obfuscate

---

7 An extreme quantile (typically ranging between 95% and 99%) of the counterparty specific time-t MtM distribution defines the PFE. The risk metric used for credit limit monitoring is typically the maximum PFE ($\max_{te}[0,T](PFE(t))$, where T is either the residual life of the netting set or its first year of credit exposure.

8 The PFE, currently used to impose Credit Limits, is based on primordial RST exercises, as it concerns potential future extreme MtM losses. To prevent risk concentrations, which might threaten bank solvency, credit risk officers set limits based on extreme exposure levels. These limits are used to bound the accepted total exposure over the lifetime of a netting set.

solvency risk.[9] The higher risk sensitivity of $\Delta_c KVA$ makes KVA based credit limits a substantial addition to a PFE-based system.

Bibilography

Albanese, C., L. Andersen, and S. Iabichino (2015). FVA: Accounting and Risk Management. *Risk*.

Albanese, C., S. Caenazzo, and S. Crépey (2016). Capital and funding. *Risk Magazine*, 71–76.

Albanese, C., S. Caenazzo, and S. Crépey (2017). Credit, funding, margin, and capital valuation adjustments for bilateral portfolios. *Probability, Uncertainty and Quantitative Risk 2*(7), 26 pages.

Albanese, C., S. Crépey, R. Hoskinson, and B. Saadeddine (2019). XVA analysis from the balance sheet. Working paper available on https://math.maths.univevry.fr/crepey.

Albanese, C., S. Crépey, and S. Iabichino (2020). Reverse Stress Testing. ssrn.3544866.

Albanese, C., G. Pietronero (2011). Coherent Global Market Simulations and Securitization Measures for Counterparty Credit Risk. *Quantitative Finance* 11(1), 1–20.

Crépey, S., W. Sabbagh, and S. Song (2020). When capital is a funding source: The XVA Anticipated BSDEs. *SIAM Journal on Financial Mathematics* 11(1), 99–130.

European Banking Association (2013). Capital requirements regulations, Article 292. http://eur-lex.europa.eu/legalcontent/EN/TXT/PDF/?uri=CELEX:32013R0575&from=EN.

IASB (2017). IFRS 17 for Insurance Contracts. https://www.ifrs.org/-/media/project/insurance-contracts/ifrs-standard/ifrs-17-effects-analysis.pdf.

---

9 For example, fully collateralised derivative portfolios result in a zero PFE, although there is collateral funding risk, so that the risk embedded could be far different from zero.

Assad Bouayoun

18 Multi-Period Reverse Stress Testing Using Quantum and Simulated Annealing

Application to XVA

18.1 Introduction

Financial stress testing is becoming a dominant part of the arsenal built by regulators to protect the economic stability against the fall of one or a series of financial institutions.[1] To avoid a combinatorial explosion, a number of arbitrary choices are usually made in relation to the level of each shock, their combination and the time horizon. These assumptions, although necessary, are limiting the effectiveness of this technique. Simulated and quantum annealing techniques provide significant speed gains as computational time grows linearly with the number of risk factors and not exponentially as with conventional optimisation techniques allowing for exhaustive search. This chapter investigates the possibility of reverse stress testing by inferring the combination of shocks maximising the XVA loss at a particular time horizon using simulated and quantum annealing. XVA is simply the generic name referring to the different costs and benefits linked to the risk management of derivative products (see Green, 2015). A reformulation of the reverse stress testing as a quadratic unconstrained binary optimisation and its resolution using first and second derivatives is proposed.

Whether managing a portfolio, a business unit or a bank, one must make sure that a sudden shock in the markets provoking a large loss, a jump in your capital utilisation or in your funding consumption will not drive you out of business. That is where reverse stress testing can help.

Financial stress testing is a necessary extension to the regulatory framework as it reveals vulnerabilities that were not identified with traditional sensitivity analysis. It is also a useful decision tool for senior managers and heads of desk who must assess the size of their provisions and manage their tail risk.

To avoid a combinatorial explosion, a number of arbitrary choices are usually made in relation to the level of each shock, their combination and the time horizon. These assumptions although necessary, are limiting the effectiveness of this technique. It is, for example, difficult to determine the correct combination of realistic stress scenarios causing the maximum loss. A historical analysis can help but will

---

[1] The author would like to thank Andrew Green and Ryan Ferguson, Andy Mason and Alexei Kondratyev for their help and guidance.

Note: Edited by Daniel Mayenberger

https://doi.org/10.1515/9783110647907-018

not be sufficient as these relations are rarely stationary. This article investigates the possibility of inferring the worst-case combination of scenarios maximising the XVA loss at a particular time horizon using simulated annealing and quantum annealing. Indeed, quantum annealing (QA) developed by the company D-Wave[TM2] is an algorithm close to simulated annealing but running on quantum processing unit (QPU). It uses the properties of its quantum bits to speed up the resolution of a range of binary optimisation problems.

It is indeed possible to benefit from the speed and power of QA by expressing the XVA reverse stressing as a Quadratic Unconstrained Binary Optimisation (QUBO) problem. As of today, few attempts to exploit quantum annealing in finance have been successful. A good example for a more classic case is presented in (Venturelli & Kondratyev, 2019). One of the reasons is the difficulty to find and formulate a problem in a shape that could be solved particularly well with this technique but not or less with other techniques. The model is implemented using D-Wave[TM] API site and the results are compared to those of simulated annealing benchmark written in Matlab[TM].[3]

A reformulation as a QUBO problem is proposed where each scenario is represented as a set of binary variables multiplied by a shock. A concrete illustration using simulated annealing is finally proposed as a benchmark to test the benefits of QA. In particular, we show that if simulated annealing is appropriate for low-dimension problems, it becomes unpractical for realistic use cases where the dimension can increase to the several hundred.

18.2 Reverse Stress Testing

Quantitative reverse stressing a derivative portfolio valuation is finding systematically and for a set of time horizons, the realistic scenario inflicting the highest loss. A realistic scenario can be represented as a series of shocks on all risks factors that have been previously occurred either independently or together. When closely linked, risk factors must be shocked together. For a typical portfolio of several hundreds of trades, we must shock around hundred risk factors. The set of realistic scenarios is in nature infinite and difficult to comprehend. The most popular method is to rely on the historical distribution of each factor and their correlation in order to group and compute the size of each shock at several time horizons (e.g. one week, one month, one year). Principal component analysis is often used to reduce the dimension of the problem. The structure of complex risk factors like interest rates can then be preserved (see Grundke & Pliszka, Semantic Scholar, 2012).

---

2 dwavesys.com.
3 www.matlab.com.

Another aspect of the problem is the nonlinear aspect of the derivative portfolio valuation functions. A combination of big shock will not necessarily provoke the biggest lose. Indeed, as the portfolio becomes more complex, embedding products with payoff singularities, the hyper plan representing the aggregated value taken into account all risk mitigants (e.g. netting, collateral) in function of all pseudo-independent risk factors resembles a rugged landscape.

For a particular set of singular payoffs on different currencies, we can see characteristic crevasses as we change the correlation between the foreign currency interest rate and the foreign exchange rate (IR EUR vs FX EURUSD). As described in Denchev et al. 2016, quantum annealing is performing particularity well for this kind of optimisation problem.

18.2.1 Application to Total Valuation and XVA

Define XVA as the valuation adjustment necessary to account for all credit, funding and capital costs:

$$XVA = CVA + FVA + MVA + KVA \tag{18.1}$$

The losses due to XVA are the right metric for several reasons. Indeed, the computation of XVA includes all the mitigants put in place by the bank:
- Agreements on netting, collateral and close out
- Aggregation respecting netting, funding and capital sets
- Inclusion of regulatory constraints like different financial ratios

The market and credit risks of a portfolio values are hedged. VAR models tend to capture the eventual mismatch between value and hedges in case of extreme scenarios. This measure is managed effectively on a daily basis in most institutions and can be negligible for our initial study. On the contrary, XVA are not or are partially hedged. It can be explained by several factors:
- The output of the XVA model are often used only to size a reserve
- Some sensitivities cannot be hedged because the market is not liquid (credit derivatives) or does not exist (long maturities)
- Parameters like correlations are obtained historically and cannot be hedged at all
- Some calibration parameters are simply interpolated, extrapolated and there are no liquid financial instrument systematically offsetting their change

Reverse stress testing can be applied also to other financial aggregates:
- The loss on a trading book not, partially, or fully hedged
- Loss on a banking book not, partially, or fully risk managed
- The retained earnings

- The respect of the regulatory ratios, aggregate loss on all books including XVA
- Purely regulatory capital

18.3 Modelling

This section shows how the XVA reverse stress testing problem can be defined and how it can be reformulated into a QUBO problem.

18.3.1 XVA Reverse Stress Testing Formula

As part of the XVA risk management (see Green, 2015), we want to identify the worst-case market scenarios at several given time horizons for a group of portfolios of financial derivatives.

A worst-case market scenario can be defined as the scenario maximising the losses due to XVA variation. This loss can be computed as a function of its aggregated partial derivatives (known in finance as the sensitivities or Greeks) by Taylor expansion:

$$XVA(t+dt, \vec{x}+d\vec{x}) = XVA + \frac{\partial XVA}{\partial t}dt + \sum_{i=1}^{N}\frac{\partial XVA}{\partial x_i}dx_i + \frac{1}{2}\sum_{i=1}^{N}\sum_{j=1}^{N}\frac{\partial^2 XVA}{\partial x_i\partial x_j}dx_idx_j \quad (18.2)$$

$XVA = XVA(t,x)$ is the sum of all value adjustment following the standard convention of negativity for costs and positivity for benefits.

x is the vector corresponding to all the credit market and correlation factors influencing the XVA. This vector can have different representation. It is possible to switch from one representation into another by Jacobian transformation.

- $\frac{\partial XVA}{\partial t}$ is theta, the sensitivity of XVA with respect to time. It can be computed analytically.

- $\frac{\partial XVA}{\partial x_i}$ are the delta or Vega sensitivities with respect to the factors. They usually are computed analytically using finite difference or AAD.

- $\frac{\partial^2 XVA}{\partial x_i\partial x_j}$ are the gamma or cross gamma sensitivities with respect to the factors. They are computed in the same way as delta.

Choosing x is not a trivial exercise as factors are linked by no-arbitrage rules. Other relations that are more difficult to ascertain can hold as well. For example, a strip of interest rate future prices may appear independent, but their movement are in general highly correlated. A scenario where each future price is bumped independently will therefore not be realistic. A reasonable remediation would be a historical principal component analysis to select the most important independent factors and their share of the variability of the original data. It is then easy to change variable in Equation (18.2) from the original set of factors to the principal factors. A welcomed consequence is the reduction of the dimensionality of the problem.

This solution would then use historical data to determine the set of independent factors and the size of the shocks.

If we assume that *XVA* is regular enough over one day, we can inject daily shocks in the Taylor approximation to compute the stressed *XVA* for $t + \Delta t$ and $\vec{x} + \vec{\Delta} x$.

If we define the absolute relative daily shock on x_i as Δx_i, the corresponding scenario would be:

$$XVA(t+\Delta t, \vec{x} + \vec{\Delta} x) \approx XVA + \frac{\partial XVA}{\partial t} \Delta t + \sum_{i=1}^{N} \frac{\partial XVA}{\partial x_i} \Delta x_i + \frac{1}{2} \sum_{i=1}^{N} \sum_{j=1}^{N} \frac{\partial^2 XVA}{\partial x_i \partial x_j} \Delta x_i \Delta x_j$$

These factors are then employed in the calibration of the stochastic risk factors: interest rate and foreign exchange rate principally. This could extend to inflation credit and equity as well. The model can produce the XVA and sensitivities of each value adjustment with respect to each factor. This computation is expensive; it is therefore preferable to find a short optimisation path for the maximisation of the loss due to XVA.

The regularity assumption relies on the fact that the XVA function is a sum of composition of smooth functions. It is not totally true, as we must distinguish here between the risk factor functions and the payoff functions. The former functions are indeed mostly smooth functions of the market data but the latter ones can exhibit all sorts of discontinuities (barrier options). These discontinuities are less likely to be crossed for a small period of time.

Traditionally, financial institutions rely on a small set of market scenarios chosen by practitioners in cooperation with regulators. This can be problematic, as future stresses will not necessarily be assembled in the same manner as those driven by past experience. For XVA in particular, computing impacts for all combinations of scenarios would be too expensive.

To circumvent these limitations, we investigate the use of several search algorithms. In this regard, quantum annealing seems to be particularly powerful for the resolution of quadratic unconstrained binary optimisation. For this, the reverse stress testing problem defined precedingly must be reformulated into a QUBO problem.

18.3.2 QUBO Formulation

Quantum annealing is a technique used to solve quadratic unconstrained binary problems. It is minimising an energy function $E(X)$ over a set of binary variable X (see McGeoch, 2015), with:

$$E(X_1, X_2, \ldots, X_N) = \sum_{i=1}^{N} c_i X_i + \sum_{i=1}^{N} \sum_{j=1}^{i} Q_{ij} \times X_i \times X_j \qquad (18.3)$$

$$X_i \in \{0,1\}; c_i Q_{ij} \in \mathbb{R} \qquad (18.4)$$

18.3.3 XVA Reverse Stress Testing as a QUBO Problem

Each shock Δx_i, once determined can be applied positively or negatively. If we define the absolute relative shock on x_i as Δx_i, then the binary variable X_i can take the value 0 if the shock is Δx_i or 1 if the shock is $-\Delta x_i$. We can then write that the total shock for the factor i is $(2X_i - 1)\Delta x_i$. As XVA is defined as a cost when negative, the loss is maximised when the XVA is minimised:

$$\arg\min[XVA(t + \Delta t, x + \Delta x \cdot X)] \approx$$

$$XVA + \frac{\partial XVA}{\partial t} \Delta t + \sum_{i=1}^{N} \frac{\partial XVA}{\partial x}(2X_i - 1)\Delta x_i + \frac{1}{2}\sum_{i=1}^{N\setminus}\sum_{j=1}^{N} \frac{\partial^2 XVA}{\partial x_i \partial x_j}(2X_i - 1)(2X_j - 1)\Delta x_i \Delta x_j$$

$$(18.5)$$

This formula does not change as long as we include in the argmin function only factors that are independent from the argument X_i of the minimisation.

The equation is then equivalent to:

$$\arg\min\left| XVA(t + \Delta t, x + \Delta x \cdot X) + XVA(t + \Delta t, x + \Delta x) - 2XVA - 2\frac{\partial XVA}{\partial t}\Delta t \right| \approx$$

$$(18.6)$$

$$\sum_{i=1}^{N} \frac{\partial XVA}{\partial x_i} X_i \Delta x_i + \frac{1}{2}\sum_{i=1}^{N\setminus}\sum_{j=1}^{N} \frac{\partial^2 XVA}{\partial x_i \partial x_j} X_i X_j \Delta x_i \Delta x_j$$

If we use the following notation:

- $c_i \in \mathbb{R}$ the linear coefficients, $c_i = \dfrac{\partial XVA}{\partial x_i}\Delta x_i$,

- $Q_{ij} \in \mathbb{R}$ the quadratic coefficients, $Q_{ij} = \dfrac{\partial^2 XVA}{\partial x_i \partial x_j}\Delta x_i \Delta x_j$,

- $E(X) \in \mathbb{R}$ the energy to minimise,

$$E(X) = -\left| XVA(t + \Delta t, x + \Delta x \cdot X) + XVA(t + \Delta t, x + \Delta x) - 2XVA - 2\frac{\partial XVA}{\partial t}\Delta t \right|$$

We finally obtain the QUBO formulation:

$$\underset{X}{\mathrm{argmin}}[E(X)] = \sum_{i=1}^{N} c_i X_i + \sum_{i=1}^{N} \sum_{j=1}^{N} Q_{ij} X_i X_j \qquad (18.7)$$

18.3.4 Generation of Risk Factor Shocks

Generating the shocks can be carried out using historical distributions of the risk factors. Shocks are ultimately related to the input used by the model.

Relations between these input and macro or micro scenarios are often difficult to comprehend. A simple approach would be to determine the historical distribution of each input and how it relates to all the others. If some inputs have similar distribution and have high correlation with some others, they should be grouped together. If not, they can be considered independent and can be shocked separately. If not, they can be included in principal component decomposition where the eigenvalues become the variable to shock.

In most banks, the generation of the shocks is done first by mapping a set of liquid financial instrument to each risk factor affecting the portfolio valuation. These risk factors must be defined consistently across businesses as proposed in FRTB (Fundamental Review of the Trading Book, see Basel Committee on Banking Supervision (2019). For example, a set of interest rate swaps will be mapped to a particular interest rate risk factor. Then we compute historical percentiles of movement in returns of the risk factors. The objective is to capture extreme moves at a high confidence level for several time horizons. Shocks can then be deduced easily.

For commercial banks, several hundred risk factors can be needed. To reduce this number, several methods can be used. They often involve a spectral decomposition for all risk factors as explained in Grundke & Pliszka (2015).

Another method consists of using Bayesian nets to build a graph of risk factors. One of the major advantages of this methodology is the association of conditional probability to the realisation of a particular shock (see Rebonato, 2017).

18.4 Optimisation using Annealing

18.4.1 Simulated Annealing

Simulated annealing is an algorithm used for solving unconstrained optimisation problems. The method models the physical process of heating a material and then slowly lowering the temperature to decrease defects, thus minimising the system energy.

A binary version of this algorithm is used to solve the QUBO system. This algorithm can be described as follows (see illustration in Figure 18.1): the neighbouring function returns a list of vectors where at most one binary variable has changed. For each neighbouring vector, the energy is computed. One of them is selected randomly. If its energy is lower than the previous state, it is replaced. Otherwise, it is replaced with a probability, depending on the difference of energy between the two states and the number of iterations of the algorithm. It means that the algorithm's acceptance of non-optimal states is decreasing as it converges in time and energy.

As the number of iterations grows, the probability of selecting an optimal state converges to one. The optimal solution is found when there is no better neighbour and the probability of choosing the best is one.

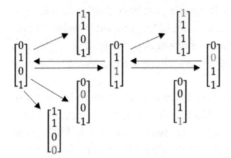

Figure 18.1: Simulated annealing selection of solution process.

The selection of the different solutions is presented in Green (2015).

18.4.2 Quantum Annealing

Recent advances in commercial quantum technologies have given rise to widespread industry investigation into their practical usefulness. Quantum computing holds particular promise, as the field aims to tackle the most difficult computational problems known in mathematics, computer science and physics. Specifically, the quantum processing units (QPUs) produced by D-Wave Systems have been subject to research in a variety of areas, such as the automotive industry, quantum simulations of materials, operations research and more.

These QPUs implement a quantum annealing algorithm, where qubits (quantum bits) can be prepared in a simple initial energy configuration where all qubits are both 0 and 1 (quantum superposition) and are then evolved to a final configuration corresponding to a combinatorial optimisation problem. It has been shown that if this quantum system is evolved carefully enough, the qubits remain in the minimum energy configuration.

The qubits can therefore be used to represent variables, whose values (0 or 1) are determined by the QPU in an attempt to minimise the energy of the system. The quantum properties of the qubits, such as entanglement, superposition and tunnelling, are used during the annealing process to compute solutions, and can potentially provide a speed-up over classical algorithms.

The functional form of the objective function the QPU is designed to minimise is:

$$Obj(Q) = x^T Q x$$

where x is a bit-string vector of length N, and Q is an $N \times N$ matrix of real-valued numbers. The entries in the matrix Q represent the optimisation problem that is being solved: diagonal elements (Q_{ii}) are the variable weights, and off-diagonal elements (Q_{ij}) are interactions between variables. This is known as a quadratic unconstrained binary optimisation (QUBO) problem. Minimising this objective function is equivalent to minimising an Ising Hamiltonian (McGeoch, 2015), which is known to be NP-hard (and the decision version is NP-complete). Therefore, many interesting and difficult problems can be mapped to this form.

The newest commercial QPU, the D-Wave 2000Q, has 2048 functioning qubits, and implements a specific graph structure (or a graph topology) called Chimera. This graph is composed of a 16×16 square lattice of $K_{4,4}$ unit tile graphs.[4] Thus, each qubit in the Chimera graph is connected to 6 other qubits at most.

Since the QPU is a physical implementation of this graph, the connectivity of each qubit (and therefore variables in an optimisation problem) cannot be changed. However, it is possible to "chain" multiple qubits together, forcing them to act as a single "logical" qubit, by adding additional constraints enforcing these restrictions. Using these techniques, it is possible to minor-embed arbitrarily structured graphs into the Chimera topology.

Once a QUBO problem has been formulated, classical software tools must be used to communicate with the QPU to solve it. D-Wave Systems provides a client library, SAPI (Solver API), that allows low-level access to the QPU. In this library, there are tools that help create the QUBO, minor-embed the graph directly onto a QPU graph and submit/ obtain results from the QPU directly. There are also a number of pre- and post-processing tools that can be used to enhance performance of the QPU. While this is limiting in terms of the size of problems that can be solved (limited by the number of physical qubits on the QPU), this is the most powerful form of using the quantum computer.

When attempting to solve problems with more variables than the QPU, it is possible to use a decomposition algorithm and incorporate the QPU in a hybrid manner. In particular, there is an open-source decomposition algorithm qbsolv[5] that uses Tabu

---

4 $K_{n,n}$ is a bipartite graph of size $2n$, meaning two groups of nodes of size n where every node for the first group is connected to every node in the other group.

5 The public GitHub repository for qbsolv can be found at github.com/dwavesystems/qbsolv.

search in combination with the QPU in order to solve problems. This method has the advantage of using the QPU in the inner loop of the algorithm to solve the most difficult part of the optimisation problem, and uses classical algorithms to implement the sliding window approach to finding the sub-problems. Recently, another higher-level software package has been developed as an extension to the Python graphical package NetworkX.[6] This package has two important use cases: the first is the natural representation of QPU-related graphs in Python (for example, generating Chimera graphs for visualisation and experimentation), which makes it easier to understand the issues related to the topology of the QPU. There is also a Matlab version of the library available upon request.

From a computational perspective, there are extensions of the graph properties methods that are built in to NetworkX that use the QPU – due to the nature of NP-complete problems, many graph property calculations can be formulated as QUBOs and solved by the QPU. For example, given a random graph, D-Wave NetworkX can be used to calculate important graph properties like minimum vertex cover, maximum independent set and max-cut, all of which are NP-complete.

Table 18.1: Different parts of the QUBO equation.

QUBIT	q_i	Quantum bit which participates in the annealing cycle and settles into one of the two possible final states: 0,1
COUPLER	$q_i q_j$	Physical device that allows one quibit to influence another qubit
WEIGHT	a_i	Real-valued constant associated with each qubit which influences the qubit's tendency to collapse into its two possible final states; controlled by the programmer
STRENGTH	b_{ij}	Real-valued constant associated with each coupler which controls the influence exerted by one quibit on another; controlled by the programmer
OBJECTIVE	Obj	Real-valued function which is minimised during the annealing cycle

QA will be used to solve the QUBO previously defined in Table 18.1. Once the QUBO on a graph G is defined, we must run the algorithm finding a minor embedding G_{emb} in a sub graph consistent with the current topology of the quantum computer by contracting edges. Once returned, the solution has to be converted to the initial problem.

The run time is distributed between each part of the workflow. The minor embedding and the conversion of the result back to the original problem can take several seconds for high dimension. The resolution of the minor embedded problem by the quantum computer takes on average 20 microseconds. The communication is taking 100 milliseconds.

---

6 D-Wave's extension to NetworkX can be found at github.com/dwavesystems/dwave networkx.

For problems with large and tall barriers between minimums, this technique performs particularly well according to Denchev et al. (2016). Figure 18.2 shows a comparison that was conducted in 2016:

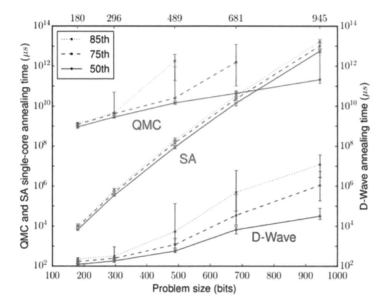

Figure 18.2: Comparison of the time to find the optimal solution of a weak strong cluster problem using simulated annealing (SA), quantum Monte Carlo (QMC), and quantum annealing (QA) see (Denchev et al., 2016).

A speed up of 10^6 for a dimension of 500 at most can be achieved from simulated annealing to quantum annealing under very restrictive conditions.

18.5 Illustration

The numerical experiment is based on a simple implementation of a three-factor model for interest rates and foreign exchange:
- USD and EUR interest rates follow each a Hull and White process
- EURUSD foreign exchange rate follows a pseudo lognormal process

There are 12 different risk factors:
- USD short interest rate
- USD volatility of the short interest rate
- EUR short interest rate
- EUR volatility of the short interest rate
- EURUSD foreign exchange spot

- EURUSD volatility of the foreign exchange spot
- Correlation EUR/USD
- Correlation EUR/EURUSD
- Correlation USD/EURUSD
- Funding spread
- Credit spread
- Recovery rate

18.5.1 Portfolio Definition

We build randomly a portfolio of interest rate swaps with random type, maturity, payment frequency and currency.

Simulated market values, CVA and FVA, are computed for a particular portfolio. The corresponding Jacobian (first-order derivatives) vector and the Hessian matrix (second derivatives) are also computed.

18.5.2 Numerical Results

The partial derivatives are computed with respect to each active variable.

The first and second derivatives of each risk factor are multiplied by the corresponding shock. A test is performed to remain within the range defined by Table 18.2. Running the model, we obtain the vector and the matrix of the QUBO.

Table 18.2: Active input variables.

name	initial value	minimum	maximum	sensitivity bump	stress bump
FUNDING	0.10 %	1.00 %	0.01 %	0.01 %	0.10 %
CREDIT	0.10 %	1.00 %	0.01 %	0.04 %	0.40 %
RECOVERY	40.00 %	100.00 %	0.00 %	0.10 %	1.00 %
IRDOM	3.00 %	10.00 %	0.10 %	0.10 %	1.00 %
IRFOR	3.00 %	10.00 %	0.10 %	0.10 %	1.00 %
FX	1.2	0.20	5	0.1	0.2
IRDOMVOL	4.00 %	10.00 %	0.01 %	0.01 %	0.10 %
IRFORVOL	2.00 %	10.00 %	0.01 %	0.01 %	0.10 %
IRFXVOL	1.00 %	10.00 %	0.01 %	0.01 %	0.10 %
IRIRCORR	20.00 %	100.00 %	−100.00 %	0.10 %	1.00 %
IRDOMFXCORR	40.00 %	100.00 %	−100.00 %	1.00 %	10.00 %
IRFORFXCORR	−20.00 %	100.00 %	−100.00 %	1.00 %	10.00 %

The yellow elements of the matrix in Figure 18.3 are close to zero. This will be used to reduce the coupling of the problem when the QUBO will be mapped to the topology of the quantum machine.

	Jacobian x Shock c_i	Hessian x Shock I x Shock j Q_{ij}										
FUNDING	0.47	0.00	68.97	0.08	228.41	109.67	0.52	3.89	1.10	0.19	0.27	0.20	0.21
CREDIT	57.19	68.97	0.00	69.29	282.01	35.79	68.62	70.67	68.34	69.34	69.37	69.34	69.35
RECOVERY	0.24	0.08	69.29	0.00	228.42	109.56	0.43	3.96	1.01	0.27	0.35	0.28	0.30
IRDOM	455.68	228.41	282.01	228.42	2.32	338.14	228.92	224.51	229.50	228.21	228.14	228.21	228.19
IRFOR	219.58	109.67	35.79	109.56	338.14	0.46	108.97	113.56	108.57	109.86	109.94	109.87	109.88
FX	1.43	0.52	68.62	0.43	228.92	108.97	0.00	4.41	0.58	0.71	0.78	0.71	0.73
IRDOMVOL	8.14	3.89	70.67	3.96	224.51	113.56	4.41	0.04	4.99	3.70	3.62	3.69	3.68
IRFORVOL	2.71	1.10	68.34	1.01	229.50	108.57	0.58	4.99	0.01	1.29	1.36	1.30	1.31
IRFXVOL	0.01	0.19	69.34	0.27	228.21	109.86	0.71	3.70	1.29	0.00	0.07	0.01	0.02
IRIRCORR	0.12	0.27	69.37	0.35	228.14	109.94	0.78	3.62	1.36	0.07	0.00	0.07	0.05
IRDOMFXCORR	0.02	0.20	69.34	0.28	228.21	109.87	0.71	3.69	1.30	0.01	0.07	0.00	0.02
IRFORFXCORR	0.01	0.21	69.35	0.30	228.19	109.88	0.73	3.68	1.31	0.02	0.05	0.02	0.00

Figure 18.3: Illustration of the QUBO vector and matrix.

It is indeed important to understand that the graph of qubits is not complete as all the possible couplers are not present in the hardware graph. The working graph is described in detail in D-Wave (2018). Using unoptimised code for 1,000 simulations and 120 dates on Matlab™, the computation takes 37 seconds. If we compute all the set of possible scenarios ($2^{12} = 4096$), we obtain easily the minimum energy. It took 0.291389 seconds on average to compute all of them with a powerful personal computer (Intel™Xeon E5 3.6 GHz 64 GB RAM on Windows™7 Enterprise).

A simple observation of the distribution of energy levels confirms the difficulty to approximate the negative tail having an isolated scenario at the far end of this tail. This is consistent with the presence of large and tall barriers between minimums.

The simulated annealing algorithm chooses the best of three different mutations of the scenario with a probability increasing with iteration (time) to avoid local minimums at the start.

We obtain the result using simulated annealing. It is consistent with the exhaustive computation but, as expected, takes less time: 0.024930 seconds on average.

Simulated annealing is converging in this case really fast as only 70 iterations are needed to reach the minimum energy. However, it is difficult to extrapolate. QA will be tested against this small-scale example.

It is possible to improve the performance of the algorithm by using GPU™ (from NVIDIA™) and parallelising the search. Depending on the actual performance, it could be a better benchmark.

18.5.3 Quantum Annealing Results

Interacting with the D-Wave™ system is extremely simple and can be done in python or Matlab by just creating a DWaveSampler, populating with the correct biases (vector) and couplers (matrix), sending a request and receiving the response. The response contains several results, shown in Table 18.3, Figure 18.4, Figure 18.5 and Table 18.4, and guarantees that the optimum solution is included with a high probability. It is therefore necessary to check which solution is the best.

Before interacting with the machine, the QUBO needs to be mapped to the topology of the machine. Indeed, the working graph representing all the qubits and their connections is not fully connected, as shown in Figure 18.7.

The qubits are organised in unit cells with 5 connections by qubit. A technique known as "Minor Embedding" is used to merge nodes in the graph to increase the graph connectivity. They need to be "non-embedded" when we obtain the result. Our problem, if we accept to concentrate on material element of the QUBO matrix, can be simplified by requiring only 3 qubits (credit, interest rate domestic and foreign) with 11 couplers, 2 (funding and recovery) with 5. The other variables have enough couplers. We can then find a mapping that uses a minimum number of qubits. As the maximum coupling is close to the dimension of the problem ($11 \approx 12$), it is equivalent to consider it as fully connected. We can therefore use the software provided by DWave™ to automatically find a correct embedding. The embedded problem is then solved by the QPU. The problem must be non-embedded from the output to get the answer to the original problem. For our simple test example, the quantum annealing results are as follows.

It is the correct solution of equation (18.5), as it is corresponding to the result from simulated annealing and the exhaustive computation of all combinations. It has been obtained after post processing of 100 solutions for less than hundred runs (97 runs). The post processing here consists in taking the lowest energy after evaluation of the all the solutions. For this particular example, we find that the total real time is really close to the compute time using simulated annealing ($0.023361 \approx 0.024930$). This shows that QA is at least as fast as SA. It is important to carry out further tests but with an increasing number of factors to confirm the superiority of QA over SA as shown in Denchev et al. (2016). A simple way to increase the number of risk factors is to increase the number of currencies and interest rate swaps dependent on them, outlined in Table 18.5.

For another problem, this time involving four currencies, we have 38 risk factors (4 interest rates, 3 foreign exchanges) we obtain the following performances using the exhaustive algorithm computing all the combinations of shocks and simulated annealing. The computer used limits the dimension to 20 because the maximum length of a vector is $2.^{20}$ It is compared to a simulated annealing algorithm which has been tuned to hit almost certainly the minimum. It is difficult to compare the performance of simulated annealing with anything else when the optimal solution is not known (dimen-

Table 18.3: Extract of all different risk factor scenarios and their energy.

Scenario	Energy	FUNDING	CREDIT	RECOVERY	IRDOM	IRFOR	FX	IRDOMVOL	IRFORVOL	IRFXVOL	IRIRCORR	IRDOMFXCORR	IRFORFXCORR
1	–	0	0	0	0	0	0	0	0	0	0	0	0
2	-0.02	0	0	0	0	0	0	0	0	0	0	0	1
3	-0.02	0	0	0	0	0	0	0	0	0	0	1	0
4	-0.05	0	0	0	0	0	0	0	0	0	0	1	1
5	0.13	0	0	0	0	0	0	0	0	0	1	0	0
6	0.26	0	0	0	0	0	0	0	0	0	1	0	1
7	0.26	0	0	0	0	0	0	0	0	0	1	1	0
8	0.38	0	0	0	0	0	0	0	0	0	1	1	1
9	-0.03	0	0	0	0	0	0	0	0	1	0	0	0
1277	-2,393.20	0	1	0	0	1	1	1	1	1	1	0	0
1278	-2,812.43	0	1	0	0	1	1	1	1	1	1	0	1
1279	-2,812.40	0	1	0	0	1	1	1	1	1	1	1	0
1280	-3,231.64	0	1	0	0	1	1	1	1	1	1	1	1
1281	-257.78	0	1	0	1	0	0	0	0	0	0	0	0
1282	-3.04	0	1	0	1	0	0	0	0	0	0	0	0
1283	-3.04	0	1	0	1	0	0	0	0	0	0	1	0
1284	251.69	0	1	0	1	1	0	0	0	0	0	1	1
4095	-61.99	1	1	1	1	1	1	1	1	1	1	1	0
4096	-25.64	1	1	1	1	1	1	1	1	1	1	1	1
Min = 1280	-3,231.64	0	1	0	0	1	1	1	1	1	1	1	1

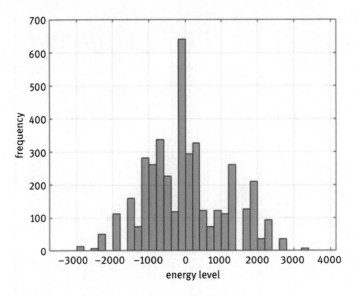

Figure 18.4: Energy distribution of the QUBO.

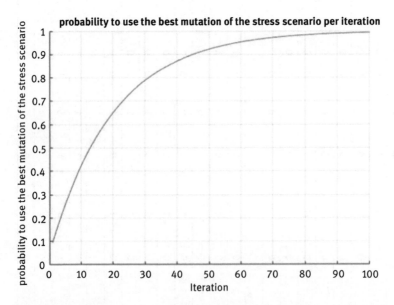

Figure 18.5: Evolution of the probability of selecting the best solution as the number of iterations increases.

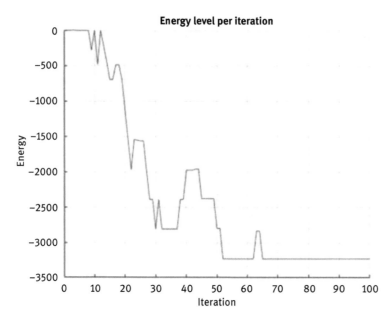

Figure 18.6: Energy per iteration.

Table 18.4: Results from QA.

FUNDING	CREDIT	RECOVERY	IRDOM	IRFOR	FX	IRDOMVOL	IRFORVOL	IRFXVOL	IRIRCORR	IRDOMFXCORR	IRFORFXCORR
0	1	0	0	1	1	1	1	1	1	1	1

sion more than 20 here). Indeed, tuning the acceptance criteria probability and the maximum error, allowing for the termination of the algorithm, give very different timing and results.

We therefore slice the vector and the matrix of our QUBO to build smaller equivalent problems from dimension 5 to dimension 20. We obtain the following results, charted in Figure 18.8.

The exhaustive algorithm time consumption is increasing exponentially. The simulated annealing seems to perform better as the time consumption is increasing linearly. The overhead of simulated annealing algorithm is compensated only when the dimension is greater than 15. It is also important to note once more that this algorithm is not always converging to the global optimum.

The same QUBO can be solved on the QPU.

Figure 18.9 shows that the QPU time seems to be the same for all dimensions when taking only one sample. Indeed, the different QUBOs, even for the maximum

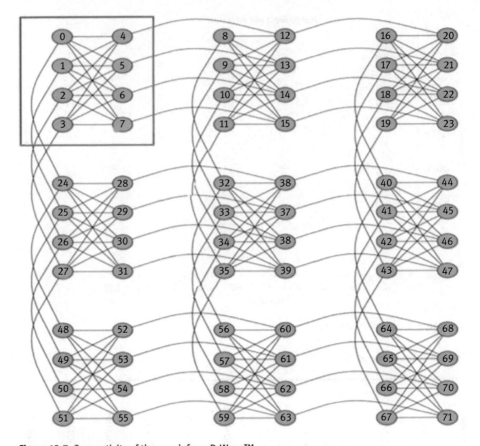

Figure 18.7: Connectivity of the graph from D-Wave™.

Table 18.5: Risk factors count.

Number of currencies	Total number of risk factors	Valuea djustments	interest rates	Foreign exchange	Correlations
1	5	3	2	0	0
2	12	3	4	2	3
3	19	3	6	4	6
4	38	3	8	6	21

dimension, are too small. Therefore, the problem does not need to be broken down into smaller pieces ran separately and then put back together. The time shown here is the usual compute time necessary for the resolution of a QUBO of dimension – i.e. a little bit less than 211 = 20148, due to errors on some qubits.

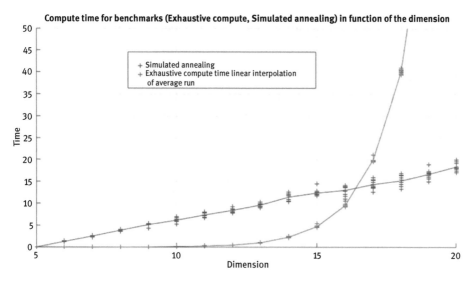

Figure 18.8: Time consumed on the CPU to solve the QUBO from dimension 5 to 20.

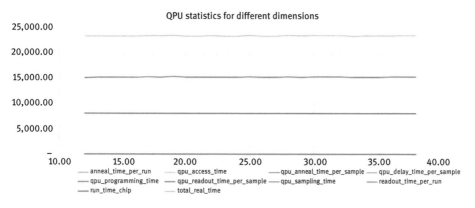

Figure 18.9: QPU performances for different numbers of risk factors.

It is also important to note that the QPU time depends only on the number of samples taken, and not on the input size n. As a rule of thumb, we expect for smaller problems to find the ground state in about 1 run out of 100 but for larger problems, the ground state might be present in 1 run out of 100,000, especially when we approach the limit of fully connected graphs.

The QPU results are consistent with the CPU results for small dimensions. It is not possible to validate the results for higher dimensions, but it is reassuring to see the energy decreasing smoothly as the number of dimensions decreases, almost linearly.

For dimension greater than 12, the QPU is faster than the CPU as the compute time on the QPU side does not seem to increase substantially. If we take into account the time spent to embed and reconstruct the solution, then the compute time increases linearly with the dimension.

A small number of risk factors do not need any kind of optimisation because the number of scenarios to compute is small. A realistic number of risk factors can increase to several hundred for real portfolios. Based on precedent computations with different numbers of risk factors, the exhaustive method can take one day for a dimension of 29, simulated annealing performs better but reaches one day as well for a dimension of 32. Current QA can be used up to 65 factors. Issues linked to error

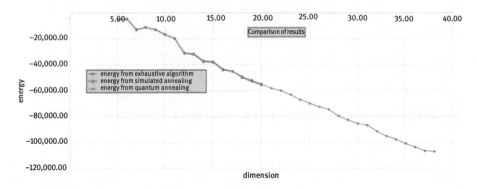

Figure 18.10: Minimum energy computed using exhaustive, simulated annealing and quantum annealing algorithms for different dimensions.

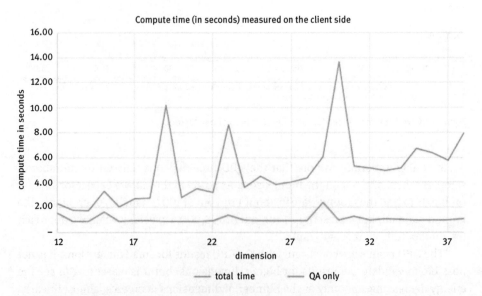

Figure 18.11: Compute time from the client's point of view, embedding and reconstruction of the solution for different dimensions.

correction are then becoming a limiting factor. It is an important area of research and development currently.

Benefits from QA are already visible for small dimensions, as demonstrated in the results in Figure 18.10 and 18.11. The experiment must be carried out on higher dimensions to establish whether it is a viable method. QA can also be used in conjunction with a greedy local search algorithm to perform reverse annealing. For instance, Choi (2008) shows an improvement by two orders of magnitude.

18.6 Potential Problems

Several potential problems need to be addressed. This methodology is maybe too pessimistic as it relies on the portfolio suffering a loss due to the realisation of the worst combination of factors at each date. The underlying assumption that the worst-case scenario over a long period of time is attainable by applying successive worst-case scenario can be accepted intuitively but is not proven. It is even possible to find counter examples where, for example, exercisability can change the direction of sensitivity. For example, the exercise condition can have a short-term effect which has an opposite direction to its long-term effect.

The dynamic aspect of portfolio management is not included. This could be reduced by auto hedging some risk factors with some counterparties. We may need to review the size of shocks as they realise at successive time steps of the simulation. For this, we should use the serial correlation of risk factors or a series of realised historical shocks of a particular stress period.

18.7 Summary

Quantitative reverse stress testing as a tool to identify the scenario provoking the largest loss has been described and a resolution using simulated and quantum annealing have been proposed. This article has also shown the expected benefit from the speed of QA by expressing the XVA reverse stressing as a QUBO (quadratic unconstrained binary optimisation) problem.

The next stage is to compare simulated annealing with quantum annealing results and performances by implementing this model using D-wave API on a real-world case.

The XVA reverse stress testing can also be generalised to multi-period case by running successively the XVA and sensitivity calculation on the worst-case combination of scenario computed by quantum annealing for the preceding day.

Direct reverse stress testing XVA over a longer period is not possible for several reasons. First, the XVA function is not regular enough to be approximated by a Taylor expansion for large changes in its variables. Second, the XVA computation can run in the future only if each trade is ageing correctly. It means that the correct population of the different fixings and the application all exercise conditions. This can be done only if the shocks have been identified for each day preceding the stress run.

This issue can be solved by iterating through the computation of the worst-case scenario and using it as the base case for the next day. This leads to the construction of the path to the worst loss for a long period that could extend to one month or even one year. The solution is then a sequence of binary numbers for each factor.

Finally, a financial interpretation of the binary variables can lead to their utilisation in the context of a particular firm or as a tool for regulatory systemic stress aggregation.

Bibliography

Basel Committee on Banking Supervision. (2019). *Basel III: International Framework for Banks*. Retrieved October 7, 2020, from Minimum capital requirements for market risk: https://www.bis.org/bcbs/publ/d457.pdf

Choi, V. (2008). Minor-embedding in adiabatic quantum computation: I. The parameter setting problem. *Quantum Information Processing, 7* (5), pp. 193–209.

Denchev, V. S., Boixo, S. I., Ding, N., Babbush, R., Smelyanskiy, V., Martinis, J., et al. (2016). *ArXiv*. Retrieved October 7, 2020, from What is the Computational Value of Finite Range Tunneling?: https://arxiv.org/abs/1512.02206

D-Wave. (2018). *Getting Started with the D-Wave System, User Manual*. D-Wave.

Green, A. (2015). *Credit Funding and Capital Valuation Adjustments*. Wiley.

Grundke, P., and Pliszka, K. (2015). A macroeconomic reverse stress test. *Deutsche Bundesbank Discussion Paper*.

Grundke, P., and Pliszka, K. (2012). *Semantic Scholar*. Retrieved October 7, 2020, from Empirical implementation of a quantitative reverse stress test for defaultable fixed-income instruments with macroeconomic factors and principal components: https://www.semanticscholar.org/paper/Empirical-implementation-of-a-quantitative-reverse-Grundke-Pliszka/4b895006f212ae2c73e39fe832b181e0457278ca

McGeoch, C. C. (2015). *Adiabatic Quantum Computation and Quantum Annealing: Theory and Practice*. Wiley.

Rebonato, R. (2017). ress Testing with Bayesian Nets and Related Techniques: Meeting the Engineering Challenges. In M. Pompella, and S. N. (eds), *The Palgrave Handbook of Unconventional Risk Transfer* pp. (537–575). Palgrave Macmillan.

Venturelli, D., and Kondratyev, A. (2019). Reverse quantum annealing approach to portfolio optimization problems. *Quantum Machine Intelligence, 1,* 17–30.

Sidhartha Dash

19 Reverse Stress Testing and Technology

Optimal Configuration of Hardware and Software to Achieve Best Acceleration Results

19.1 Introduction

A key challenge to implementing a quantitative approach to reverse stress testing (RST) is that the presence of multiplicity – i.e. the same outcome such as expected loss rate, portfolio loss or liquidity shortfall – could be obtained with multiple combinations of risk factors or macroeconomic scenarios. Finding the inverse function in RST creates the problem of multiplicity and can be several orders of magnitude more computationally intensive than usual stress testing. This chapter focuses on the various technology alternatives to accelerate reverse stress testing.

The solution to this challenge in the author's view is to leverage technology, however, the appropriate choice of hardware or software is highly dependent on the specifics of the portfolio to reach the required acceleration. This chapter shows how to make this optimal choice.

The PRA defines reverse stress tests as "tests that require a firm to assess scenarios and circumstances that would render its business model unviable, thereby identifying potential business vulnerabilities. Reverse stress-testing starts from an outcome of business failure and identifies circumstances where this might occur. This is different to general stress and scenario testing which tests for outcomes arising from changes in circumstances."

The financial and economic crisis of 2007–2008 has shown that, for various reasons, the models' risk predictions are not always reliable. Banks and taxpayers had to bear huge losses that should not have been possible according to the risk models. As a consequence, stress tests have gained importance for banks and bank supervisors as a supplement to quantitative risk management approaches. Meanwhile, supervisory authorities also stress that it is necessary to carry out the so-called reverse stress tests (for example, Basel Committee on Banking Supervision, 2009, Committee of European Banking Supervisors, 2009 or Financial Services Authority, 2008, 2009). While, for regular stress tests, scenarios are chosen based on historical experience or expert knowledge and their influence on the bank's survivability is assessed, reverse stress tests aim to find exactly those scenarios (i.e. combinations of realisations of relevant risk factors or risk parameters) that cause the bank to cross the

Note: Edited by Daniel Mayenberger

https://doi.org/10.1515/9783110647907-019

frontier between survival and default. Afterwards, the most likely of these scenarios must be found. Reverse stress tests are not intended to be a substitute for regular stress tests – rather, they are intended to be a supplement.

Reverse stress can be applied at a variety of levels of granularity. It is of course, possible to reverse stress capital calculations and overall solvency of an institution, but it is also possible to reverse stress specific portfolios, individual instruments and portfolios which have been approximated by specific instruments (i.e. payoff function). The critical element is that there must be an evaluation function for which we can generate the inverse.

At its core, reverse stress testing proposes to invert the standard process, starting now from an outcome (business failure) with the aim of finding potential states-of-nature (scenarios) consistent with such an outcome. When implementing RST in a quantitative way, multiplicity emerges as a challenge. The same outcome (say, high expected losses or liquidity shortfall) could materialise under multiple combinations of risk factors (say, PDs, EADs and LGDs) and alternative macroeconomic scenarios.

This is a concern since the reverse engineering exercise can end up identifying only a subset of scenarios that are consistent with the starting assumption. The challenge faced is that those scenarios that were not found could be of more relevance and severity compared to the ones that were identified by the process. The granularity by which the reverse stress tests are generated and which of the individual paths are evaluated will be crucial in determining the quality of the test. However, granularity brings forward other issues, such as the availability of computational resources.

Thus, for reverse stress tests to be practical and to become a fundamental part of the financial computational arsenal, it is crucial to leverage the full technological capabilities available.

This chapter seeks to explore various options, choices and strategies that can be adopted. It will also make the case that it is important for risk analysts and quantitative specialists to look at the underlying technology infrastructure – such as hardware options, messaging interconnects, data grids, computational grids, cloud infrastructure, databases and programming languages – not just as background information, but as fundamental building blocks that drive the level of performance of the analytics. The gap between the best case and the worst case can be significant and is additive.

The first contribution of this chapter is to look at technology tools to overcome the multiplicity issues inherent in RST. The tenet of this chapter is that inverse, and mapping functions can be solved using many approaches, several of which are inherently data parallel. However, there are many options and approaches. These may range from conventional loosely coupled computational grids to more data parallel approaches leveraging GPUs and Field-programmable Gate Arrays (FPGAs). Equally, the data architecture and choice of database has considerable impact on the efficiency of execution. The current chapter outlines the technology options and drills down into the tradeoff that different technologies impose. It concludes by outlining an overview of the relative applicability of different technologies in different RST contexts.

Section 19.2 outlines why there is a need to utilise the full potential of different varieties of computational hardware options and makes the case that these technologies are currently viable and ready for large-scale production and deployment.

Section 19.3 provides the various ways RST can be accelerated using some combination of high-performance hardware, new deployment architectures (cloud) and new code development framework (new programming languages and ecosystems).

Section 19.4 outlines the options enabled by the cloud and makes the case that the cloud is not just a cost reduction platform but that it provides new computing strategies.

Section 19.5 focuses on the evolution of the graphics processing unit (GPU) and choices provided by GPUs and other hardware alternatives.

Section 19.6 takes a quick look at the impact of data and data technologies on analytical efficiency and outlines tradeoffs.

19.2 Hardware (chips) and New Ways of Combining them (clouds) are Powerful but Underestimated Tools

Traditionally, most of the High-Performance Computing (HPC) systems in finance have been loosely coupled grids (nodes which run largely independent process) – however, in the last few years, more data parallel options have become available. The widespread availability of graphics processing units (GPUs) and parallelism on the CPU and more customisable forms of parallelism (FPGA), have ensured that it is increasingly imperative to examine the nature of the algorithms that are core to different kinds of reverse stress testing problems. Additionally, general technology trends are creating an environment with much broader and varied ways of accessing HPC capabilities:

- High-performance computing is increasingly more widely available, and most HPC platforms are built up from cots (commonly off the shelf) hardware components. The programming tools too are more generic.
- Cloud platform abstracts hardware choices and complexity. Allow heterogeneous options to co-exist.
- High-performance is built into many elements of the cloud fabric.
- Programmers need to know where to look and how to leverage it.
  - Hardware is increasingly programmable. Many such programmable components exist even on public cloud platforms.
  - New languages are available as full ecosystems (DSL, workflow, etc.). Well-designed domain-specific languages allow experts (not programmers) to access cloud resources in a flexible but constrained way.

- However, algorithms that worked well in the CPU do not necessarily work well in the GPU or any of the new hardware paradigms.
- Cloud brings a new way of thinking about data.
- Cutting the stack (the hardware and software stack) and building bespoke systems software requires new ways of mapping business problems back to technology and data constructs. Financial engineers are, however, for the most part, still betting on Moore's law. Figure19.1 shows the evolution of hardware and computational elements.
- Quant strategy needs to be integrated with data management and programming strategy.

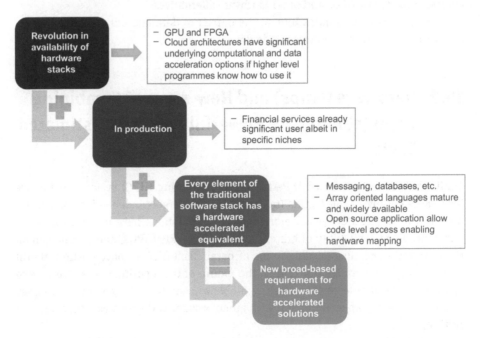

Figure 19.1: Evolution of hardware and software stacks.

19.2.1 Many Options to Accelerate Reverse Stress Testing Applications

GPUs are not the only option to accelerate reverse stress testing applications. Nor is focusing on the hardware the only way. Finally, it is important to understand the alternative ways we can explore performant systems.

Table 19.1 shows a selection of alternative options that are available for acceleration. Powerful new open source languages such as Python, Julia, OCAML R, Scilab have increasingly become tools of quantitative programming. What is striking about

Table 19.1: Components and their acceleration effects.

Component	Acceleration Effect
Cloud and special purpose data centre	Scalable and burstable compute solve the inversion problem in shorter time by running on much larger set of set nodes.
Languages and their ecosystems	New language ecosystem allows array-orientated programming, allowing easier access to high-performance matrix algebra.
Databases	Database choices impact performance of speed of Monte Carlo simulation and approximation functions in several ways – Access time i.e. the time to link up with and operate on the data set – Tight coupling of the data set i.e. building the functions within the database environment and running computational and data query processes in the same operating process
Hardware specialty chips and core compute systems	Accelerating the computational algorithm directly, particularly for data parallel type functions

the growth of these new languages is not just the availability of new or more powerful compilers, but the availability of a new computational ecosystem (many numerical and computational packages include array orientated special purpose programming environments and matrix management tools).

New languages now have a full ecosystem including multi-dimensional array stores, GPU accelerators, and array management components. There has been an explosion in types of data management tools and databases available either as open source or in the commercial vendor market (or as a combination of both). With the advent of many new tools, the boundaries of structured and unstructured data have become blurred. New types of data management tools allow the efficient and effective manipulation of complex graphs, networks, arrays or documents.

The cloud is the new operating system. It is fundamentally heterogeneous. The cost reduction element of the cloud is, in the long-term, a trivial element largely overshadowed by the flexibility and on-demand dynamics of the cloud economy.

The cloud is currently misunderstood as a cost cutting tool. However, the cloud allows a fundamentally new approach to development. A more flexible approach where applications link up on a more on-demand and just-in-time basis. Equally, many complex technologies (such as new hardware) can be abstracted and exposed as resources. This means that the most successful organisations (whether vendors or end users) are those who understand how business functions map into abstract resources and functions (arrays, data sets, graphs, dependency graphs, etc.). This is because those who do will have much higher productivity than those who do not.

So overall, there are many components of the application stack whose optimal choice can accelerate performance. Cloud computing enables the interoperability of these different choices and as such is more than a mere cost-saving technology.

19.2.2 The Technology Choices are Multi-Dimensional

There are many ways one can trade off the various technology choices based on the core target and the nature of the reverse stress.

Figure 19.2 Shows the different computational acceleration options available. The nature of the technology choices is also significantly impacted by the nature of the data required and the pre-processing required.

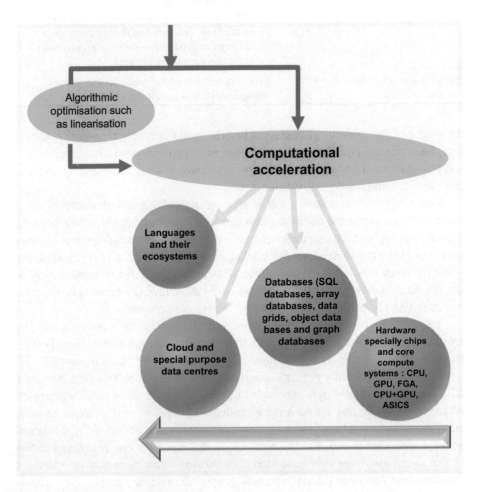

Figure 19.2: Computational acceleration.

Granularity of evaluation: Reverse stress tests can be run with very different levels of evaluation and different levels of restriction on the evaluation function. For example, when running RSTs to evaluate an interest rate environment that can provide a specific portfolio pay off and impact, the evaluation may use linear approximations instead of full revaluation of the positions. This would reduce the computational overhead – however, it radically reduces the overall accuracy, particularly if the portfolio contained a lot of non-linear products and path-dependent products. The various dimensions on which technology can be chosen is shown Figure 19.3.

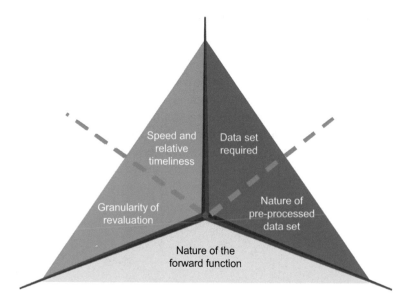

Figure 19.3: Technology choices.

Nature of the data: The processed data can take many different forms. It could be a graph, an array, time series, complex array objects, and so on. These determine what type of database is required. With over 200 open source options available, developers are spoilt for choice, but the performance gap between appropriate database support and poor support for the required data can be hundred-fold. A relatively simple example of this performance would be to implement a highly granular time series database in a SQL environment. Reverse stress tests that focus on reliability analysis of systems will benefit from the presence of graph database.

Nature of the forward function: The nature of the forward function is critical in determining the optimal technology support. Many functions can be highly non-linear (complex path dependent options, networks, calculations that may require an optimisation to be performed, etc.). These can be very hard to manage on the GPU which has a very small memory and is relatively rigid in its memory management.

Equally, if the problem can be efficiently partitioned into a linear component and a non-linear component then, a CPU+GPU combination could be the optimal option.

Nature of pre-processing: It is required for some kinds of problems that the number of transformations applied to raw market data be limited (e.g. RST for an interest derivative portfolio). In this example, the data used by the evaluation function is largely directly available without significant pre-processing from market, reference and derived data repositories.

19.3 Cloud Provides Many Options and Several Challenges

Cloud resources are one powerful way to scale the computational requirements. The cloud as such is hard to define. In the new software, as a service environment, there are a range of options that quantitative developers can take advantage of. Equally, developers must be aware of the limitations and the pitfalls of the cloud environment they have access to and to understand where the challenges and pitfalls to computational scalability are. Range and variety of cloud types is shown in Figure 19.4.

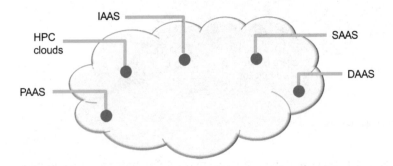

Figure 19.4: Cloud services.

Definition: Analytics functions are said to have been delivered *as a service*, when any one of the aforesaid functions is delivered largely remotely, and not as an in-premise application with most of the application logic, computational capacity and/or data residing in a remote data centre and being delivered through telecommunication networks. It could involve operational involvement of human beings and a central processing hub or could entirely be a single set of software applications.

Traditionally, the flexibility, depth and structure of this service was restricted by the nature of the telecommunication (mostly delivered around a wire protocol), however, with the evolution of sophisticated types of high-performance transmission networks and development of server technologies, this has opened the category, and modern service bureaus are immeasurably more sophisticated than its predecessors.

As mentioned previously, cloud technology offers not only cost reduction. It is also a fundamentally new developmental paradigm – with the cloud, everything is an API. The cloud environment allows resource abstraction and heterogeneity.

It is important to understand what commercial (private or public) clouds actually offer. Some clouds offer simply remote hosting, while others have built many of their core technical components on high-performance computing technologies. Most commercial clouds have an HPC hidden in its internals.

It allows for new flexible architectures and new hybrid architectural options such as GPU+CPU hybrids, multi-paradigm data storage and database support, multi-paradigm internal application messaging, and so on.

Cloud environments allow discrete and continuous application updates, abstract and create clear separation of concerns for all elements of an application: middleware, databases, analytics, GUI, and so on.

There are many cloud options. Cloud technologies span from general purpose public clouds serving a primarily Infrastructure as a Service (IAAS) version to highly customised custom clouds with many options in between. The appropriateness of the specific type of the cloud depends on the specific nature of the reverse stress test process. Generally, most organisations will prefer a standard basic infrastructure as a service (IAAS)cloud version for their grids, since this will allow almost all standardised grids to work with no major changes. Thus, reverse stress tests for portfolios with large sets of nonlinear products fit well in this environment. Additionally, they can now leverage the burst-ability of cloud to allow the RSTs to be run whenever and however appropriate. If, on the other hand, there is a very large amount of data to process (say, operational risk type scenarios or balance sheet construction) before the RST can be run, it will be worthwhile to consider the nature of the Platform as a service (PAAS) solution and the data support provided. If the data type is predominantly unstructured (lots of documents which need to be parsed with natural language processing (NLP), for instance), a Hadoop style grid within a PAAS environment is a good solution, however, if the preprocessed data is predominantly graphs, which requires the execution of some form of graph database (such as neo4j, tiger graph) on IAAS will be a better fit.

19.4 A Brief History of GPU in Time

GPUs have come of age and today provide programmability, performance and scalability. Additionally, they are no longer exotic devices. There is a vast library of GPU programmes, both open and commercial, which provide a strong foundation to start with. Even though data parallel programming is inherently hard, there is a large pool of programmers who have grown with the "GPU coding style" in a variety of industries.

No longer can quants and risk managers claim that GPU requires an all new coding style or that GPU frameworks are exotic. The increasing availability of general purpose, programming tools and libraries makes GPU far more easily accessible to the broader quantitative analyst community.

As can be seen from Figure 19.5, GPUs have defied Moore's law and have been the platform of choice for a variety of computationally intensive tasks.

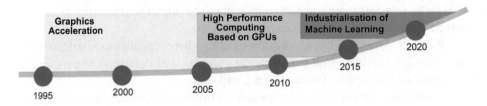

Figure 19.5: History of GPUs.

GPUs and GPU grids have however several structural restrictions given the relatively rigid memory framework. They provide a direct and straightforward platform for Monte Carlo simulations and are somewhat challenged with tree-based option pricing, particularly for complex path-dependent options.

19.4.1 CPU and GPU can be Leveraged to Handle a Variety of Complex Tasks

The key driver in deciding whether to use CPUs or GPUs is the nature of the evaluation function. If the evaluation function is linearisable, then GPUs are the obvious choice. If they are not linearisable without substantial loss of information or structure, then CPUs will win from a performance perspective (largely because most modern CPUs have data parallel add-ons, allowing accelerating some segments of the algorithm). However, there are vast ranges of uses where part of the problem may be expressible as a set of linear structures whilst the rest have to be treated as highly non-linear and as path-dependent functions.

Portfolios of convertibles, CDOs, CLOs or MBS are all good candidates. However, most portfolios of path-dependent options can be expressed as simplified portfolios of relatively simple options.

Equally, there are many optimisations that can be run which allow simulations and functional evaluation to be accelerated on standard CPUs and CPU+GPU combinations. The central issue is that the programmers have not always explored the full availability of data parallelism available on the CPU. Traditionally, CPU programmers have heavily relied on increasing the clock frequencies to improve performance and have not optimised their applications. However, CPUs are evolving to incorporate more cores with wider SIMD units, and it is critical for applications to be properly parallelised. In the absence of such optimisations, CPU implementations are sub-optimal in performance, and can be orders of magnitude off their attainable performance.

We believe many factors contributing to the underperformance are in the non-exploitation of the parallelisation possibilities on the CPU, and indeed lack of exploration of whether CPU can handle sequential threads while allowing the GPU (on board or external) to handle the large data parallel (such as dense matrix operations). The potential of combining GPU and CPU grids is shown in Figure19.6.

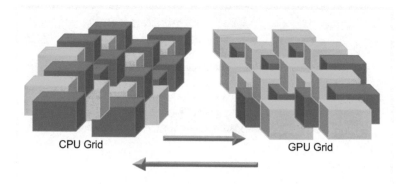

CPU Grid   GPU Grid

Figure 19.6: Combination of CPU and GPU grids.

19.4.2 FPGA and GPU Clouds

Field-programmable gate arrays (FPGAs) come in many flavours and can be customised to any specific problem type. However, they generally have much more flexible and complex (and larger) memory management contexts and, compared to GPUs, are more suitable for solving data-intensive problems. However, programmability is a very strong challenge, with different platforms having somewhat different programmability models (additional to the fact that the programming model is at a very low level). Without specific design, FPGAs are generally poorer than GPUs in handling large matrix operations.

19.4.2.1 FPGA and GPU Clouds

FPGA and GPU can be made available in a wide variety of ways. They can be a single co-processor to a single CPU or a co-processor to a CPU grid. But increasingly, they are available in custom grids. Indeed, the majority of the new supercomputers in the Top

500 are GPU-based. GPU (and FPGA) grids have their own specific software stack and many of these grids are "enhanced" by specific hardware such as high-speed interconnects like Mellanox. Possible components of such a grid is shown in Figure 19.7.

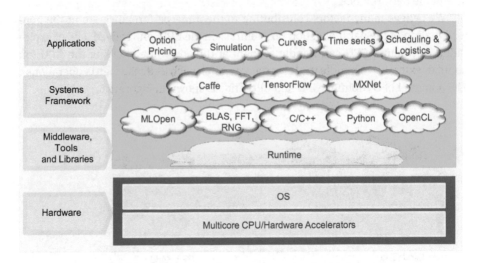

Figure 19.7: FPGA and GPU clouds.

19.4.3 Memory Hierarchy: A Very Fundamental FPGA Advantage

The complexity and size of the memory that FPGAs support allows for a more nuanced computational pipeline and more sophisticated parallelism architectures.

It also allows hybrid models and allows the FPGA designer/programmer to determine the granularity of the parallelism. It follows, that in complex multistep problems, it is thus possible to partition the problem into many components. For instance, in a portfolio of convertibles, it may be possible to partition the interest rate risk from the credit risk.

19.5 Collect and Prepare Pre-Processing Data Optimally

Data comes in many formats. The format in which the evaluation functions can absorb data may not be the format in which the data is available or is commonly visible throughout the IT infrastructure. Most pricing and market data are usually available as time series, however, many instruments such as OTC derivatives, fixed income and commodities are generally available as complex time series. In these instances, a different kind of database is required to work optimally, especially a database that handles array sequences.

In many operational risk contexts, a very significant amount of unstructured data often is required to be parsed and ingested. These types of reverse stress tests will typically leverage a standard SQL-oriented extract, transform, load (ETL) process and document object databases. However, in a context where a large set of regulatory data (such as CRD IV data) is leveraged to build balance sheet analysis and optimisation functions in order to identify scenarios where a bank's solvency or profitability is unacceptable, the focus will be on ETLs that handle complex array data. Additionally, they may leverage array-orientated object databases with an attached relational component. Different data processing workloads are shown in Figure 19.8.

19.6 Summary

Different technologies have differential relevance across a broad range of RST problems. RST problems where the inversion function is linearisable are good GPU candidates. Portfolios that have a large number of fixed-income securities, credit or path dependent OTC derivatives, require some CPU+GPU blend or FPGAs. Equally, highly dense graphs can leverage graph databases which themselves can be implemented on either GPUs, CPU+GPU combination hybrids or FPGAs. This depends on the nature of the graphs to be analysed.

In Table 19.2, we have outlined the level of fit of different technologies to specific types of reverse stress testing applications.

In quantitative arenas, it is common for risk managers, quants, and analysts to focus on the regulatory and business contexts as well as the details and "abstract" efficiency of the analytical models. But models do not exist in abstraction, but in a real world where hardware, infrastructure (data centre, cloud, interconnections, messaging) and databases make a difference. Additionally, different kinds of algorithms have different optimal implementations. In computationally intensive application areas such as reverse stress testing, to not keep this perspective in mind can be disastrous and a significant roadblock. In some contexts, the most optimal implementation can be a thousand times more performant than standard naïve implementations.

Equally, there are many algorithmic workarounds that can dramatically accelerate the analysis or even change the optimal technical implementation. The precise nature of the workaround can influence the choice of technology components. A powerful example of this occurs when reverse stress testing a portfolio of path-dependent contingent claims (knock in swaptions, certain classes of convertibles, most RMBS tranches). Directly applied, these are highly unsuitable for GPUs. However, as linearised, they become suitable for the GPUs (either as standalone or in conjunction with CPUs or FPGAs).

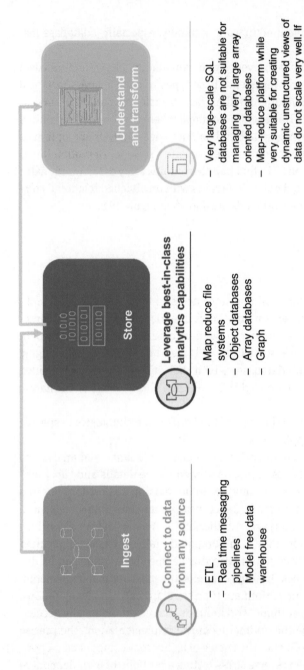

Ingest

Connect to data from any source

- ETL
- Real time messaging pipelines
- Model free data warehouse

Store

Leverage best-in-class analytics capabilities

- Map reduce file systems
- Object databases
- Array databases
- Graph

Understand and transform

- Very large-scale SQL databases are not suitable for managing very large array oriented databases
- Map-reduce platform while very suitable for creating dynamic unstructured views of data do not scale very well. If the problem in question is handling graph it is imperative that the system leverages graph databases

Figure 19.8: Data processing.

Table 19.2: Optimal selection of hardware by context.

Reverse stress testing context	Cloud [1]	Database	GPU	FPGA	CPU+GPU	Languages
Default scenario of bank from mix of credit conditions	●	●	●	●	● [2]	●
Operational failure evaluated to specific operational risk	●	● [3]	●	● [3]	●	●
Interest risk challenges from specific combination of interest rates	●	● [4]	●	●	● [4]	●
Reverse stress testing in ALM context	●	●	●	●	●	●
Reverse stress testing of traded portfolios	●	●	●	●	●	●
Reliability analysis	●	●	●	●	●	●
Investment portfolios	●	●	● [5]	●	●	●

Scores

5 Perfect fit

4 Very good fit

3 Good fit

2 Poor fit

Notes:

1. Cloud is a general-purpose good fit allowing burstability and scale. However, using anything but the base cloud capability (IAAS) can create structural complexity.
2. While CPUs are good for complex processes, general default calculations and complex default structures, GPUs can process relatively simple default structures at scale. A combination of a CPU+GPU grid is the best fit, as it can handle a broad range of complex credit risk functions at scale.
3. Operational failure analysis often requires a very significant amount of data pre-processing, including the conversion of unstructured data to structured data sets. FPGAs can target specific data structures such as graphs.
4. In-database computational models are a poor fit for interest rate simulation, whilst CPU+GPU combination is required to potentially address scalability and path dependence.
5. Investment portfolios depend on the asset mix – however, generally some degree of linearisation is acceptable for individual assets as long as they do not make up an unreasonable percentage of the portfolio.

Equally, when a very large data preprocessing is required for every compute step, it is far more appropriate to leverage specially designed FPGAs rather than GPUs. Many systemic risk reverse stress testing frameworks (or any frameworks that leverage graphs) are much better off using dedicated graph databases (of which there are many, and the optimal choice depends on many factors, including depth and complexity of graph leveraged in the framework).

This chapter provides an introduction to the options, choices and challenges which quants and risk managers need to look at. Technology is a critical resource and a powerful enabler.

The current trends outlined in this chapter are likely to accelerate. Hardware options providing different types of parallelism are already proliferating, specialist cloud services enabling a broader set of computational strategies continue to expand and the choices available to storage and manage data (and support a variety of data types) continue to increase. Another area in which we expect significant change will be growth in ways to linearise path-dependent non-linear pay offs.

Bibliography

https://www.nvidia.com/en-gb/data-center/data-center-gpus/
https://www.nvidia.com/en-gb/data-center/gpu-cloud-computing/
https://aws.amazon.com/hpc/#:~:text=HPC%20on%20AWS%20eliminates%20the%20wait%20
    times%20and,new%20technologies%20like%20Artificial%20Intelligence%20and%20
    Machine%20Learning
http://on-demand.gputechconf.com/gtc/2018/presentation/s81047-introduction-to-deep-
    stream-sdk.pdf

Daniel Mayenberger

20 Robust Model Development in Reverse Stress Testing

How to Build Resilient Models for Reverse Stress Tests –
and in Real Economic Stress Situations

20.1 Introduction

The goal of reverse stress testing (RST) is to find an event that leads to the non-viability of a given business. Depending on the scope, this business may consist of the whole firm, certain legal entities, a particular business or a specific portfolio.

This chapter illustrates how reverse stress testing (RST) has a distinct place in model development and model risk management. Specifically, stress-proof model design is fundamental to avoiding model failures by determining the boundaries of model validity as an integral part of model design and setting up alternative models as a fallback solution. The stress-proof design goes much further and makes the case for rigorous model standardisation and automation for superior outcomes in financial terms, in regulatory examination outcomes, and above all, to enable ad-hoc scenario analyses for real economic stress. Two examples serve as an illustration to showcase the conceptual changes and the firm-wide implementation.

As in all quantification tasks, models have an important role since they are used in RST to determine a scenario that leads to non-viability. As a model is typically set up to consume inputs from a scenario and produce an output that is a metric of the non-viability assessment (e.g. P&L or capital), the model use in RST is distinctly different: It is an exhaustive search for the input that leads to an output consistent with non-viability, requiring the model to be run more than once. This search in itself may be based on additional assumptions to ensure convergence, or another exit criterion to stop the search, and exhaustiveness.

Consequently, the RST model use may require additional modelling activities:
- Ensure that the higher frequency of model evaluations is supported by the given infrastructure.
- In case the infrastructure bandwidth only supports an approximate model implementation, determine the impact on the accuracy of the model and compare this against the accuracy requirement.
- Test the additional assumptions made for convergence/exit and exhaustiveness of the search.

https://doi.org/10.1515/9783110647907-020

In addition, the model may break or become unreliable under a stress scenario which requires additional preparation to prevent such model failures.

In each of the subsequent section, there will be separate considerations for

1. Maintaining model validity.
2. Additional modelling activities for more frequent model evaluation, model proxies and any additional assumptions.

Relevant regulatory guidance has been issued by supervisors in the US (Board of Governors of the Federal Reserve System, Office of the Comptroller of the Currency, 2011), the UK (Prudential Regulatory Authority, 2018) and the EU (European Banking Authority, 2018).

The chapter gives a general outline of the aspects of stress-proof model design in Section 20.2. The subsequent sections go into further details of these different aspects, conceptual soundness in Section 20.3, developmental evidence in Section 20.4, implementation in 20.5, ongoing monitoring in 20.6, model use in 20.7, governance in 20.8 and documentation in 20.9. Section 20.10 provides a summary and an outlook into further developments.

20.2 Preparation for Stress: Examples

In its core, each model consists of simplifying assumptions to mimic real-world events and calculations that are consistent with these assumptions. The model will only work if the assumptions continue to hold. It will become clear that stress tests, including reverse stress tests, are key preparation tools to ensure models continue functioning.

For a specific demonstration, consider the two examples in the following sections.

20.2.1 Example 1: European Option Pricing

A European option, named a *call* (*put*), is a contract to buy (or sell) a standardised asset (the *underlying*) at a predetermined price (the *strike price*) on an agreed future date (*maturity* date). The buyer (or holder) of the option has the right, but not the obligation, to transact (buy/sell) under this contract specifications, whilst the seller of the option has the obligation to enter into this transaction if so instructed by the option buyer. Typically, a European option assumes the underlying asset S to follow a Geometric Brownian motion with drift:

$$\frac{dS}{S} = \mu dt + \sigma dW$$

The drift parameter μ is computed as the net cost of carry (funding costs of the asset less yields from the asset) and can be considered given. The volatility parameter σ is taken depending on the strike price and time to maturity. Usually, the option price is translated into this volatility parameter to construct a surface $\sigma(K, T)$ with strike price K and time to maturity T which follows an assumed parameterisation and/or interpolation method. Upon moves of the underlying, this surface may move with the underlying ("sticky delta" rule) or remain in place ("sticky strike" rule) or anything in-between. This assumption about the *volatility dynamic* must be defined and tested. (See Derman, 1999).

Even without additional considerations for portfolio valuation adjustments such as CVA, DVA, and FVA or single-instrument adjustments for prudential valuation (in the UK), there are several assumptions which may no longer hold under stress:
- Asset prices are log-normally distributed. This implies that they are positive.
- The volatility parameterisation/interpolation remains stable (at least for a certain time period).
- The volatility dynamic is as previously tested.

Specifically, the Western Texas Intermediate (WTI) oil price became negative on 20 Apr 2020, unprecedented in history. With that, usual volatility parameterisations or dynamics are not only different from the assumed ones, but may not even be defined. This is particularly the case if a logarithmic transformation is applied for the volatility parameterisation which is very common (Natenberg, 2014).

20.2.2 Example 2: Credit Card Probability of Default (PD) Estimation

Banks routinely estimate a single customer's probability to default (PD) on a payment under a credit card contract to decide whether to issue a credit card, determine the interest rates and fees on this card, or to calculate the (regulatory) capital to hold under Basel regulations for an existing card contract.

A widespread model to estimate the PD assumes that the log-odds of the PD are linearly related to risk drivers x_1 through x_n, in a so-called logistic regression:

$$\ln\left(\frac{PD}{1-PD}\right) = \beta_0 + \beta_1 x_1 + \ldots + \beta_n x_n$$

There are several obvious assumptions in this model:
- This relationship between log-odds and drivers is and remains linear.
- The coefficients $\beta_0, \ldots, \beta_n$ remain stable over a certain time period (for example, one year).
- The only factors determining default are $x_1, \ldots, x_n$ and no others.

To ensure validity of these assumptions, a common technique is to segment customers into groups that behave similarly and/or have contracts with similar terms and conditions. Such segmentation itself constitutes an assumption which may be tested using a *population stability index* (PSI).

In the recent Covid-19 crisis, several observations were made resulting from government assistance:

- Drivers such as real disposable personal income spiked because of government assistance programmes.
- The same government assistance has a larger effect on low-income borrowers than it has on high-income card holders.
- Drivers such as delinquencies may no longer be observable because of help through government assistance or through credit modifications that do not flag payment delays as delinquencies.

These observations call into question at least the coefficient stability assumption, if not all the other assumptions, too:

- The relationship may no longer be linear but follow a step pattern or take on another functional form.
- Government assistance itself may be an additional factor.
- Customer segmentation may be affected if creditworthiness rank-ordering of customers is affected through asymmetric effects of the government assistance.

Also, the unemployment rate, which is an important driver for these types of models, was incorrectly measured during the crisis (U.S. Bureau of Labor Statistics, 2020), which would for instance result in an unemployment rate of 16.1% for May 2020 in the US instead of the official reported rate of 13%. This raises the question of whether the unemployment rate should be adjusted for this period, and if so, by how much.

These examples of option pricing and credit card PD estimation illustrate that model assumptions may and do break down under a real stress test, so in an RST setting, these assumptions must be dealt with accordingly.

20.2.3 Stress Preparation Steps

Key to any crisis even is comprehensive preparation. For model testing, this includes identification of assumptions, formulation of tests, definition of performance criteria and tests, setup of ongoing monitoring and outcomes analysis. The ongoing monitoring is the crucial component which, if correctly designed, may indicate issues with the model at an early stage. It will also become clear that for optimal crisis preparation, RST must be built into the testing at the point of model design – otherwise, ongoing monitoring is only detective, but not preventative.

Identification of Assumptions: As seen in the two illustrative, but real examples, assumptions may be too obvious (positive asset prices or a linear dependency) or not explicit (stability of parameters over time). Nonetheless, they are important for the model to work, so comprehensive identification of assumption is of key importance.

Assumption Tests: Once assumptions are identified, tests must be devised to verify the assumptions. If possible, tests should be statistical or otherwise quantitative. Also, a variety of tests should be employed to test more complex assumptions as different tests may perform better or worse under different conditions. For example, there is a large variety of statistical methods to test the normality of a random variable (Razali & Wah, 2011).

Performance Tests: For each model, performance is measured depending on its purpose. Also, different aspects require a variety of tests even though there is only a single output of the model – for instance, the PD in the second example. For this model, the aspects that are covered in performance tests include accuracy of the PD estimate, discriminatory power (the ability to correctly rank-order borrowers) and population stability over time.

Ongoing Monitoring: All assumption and performance tests may be included into ongoing monitoring. In doing so, the following must be decided for each test:
Purpose: What does the test intend to verify?
–   Method: Which methods are employed? As mentioned, there may be a variety.
–   Results: What types of results are produced? (e.g. p-values for a hypothesis test)
–   Evaluation: What is the criterion for success of the test? (e.g. upper threshold for a p-value)
–   Action: Which action(s) must be taken if the test fails?

The scale for such testing operations becomes large very quickly – for example, on a daily basis, modern broker/dealer businesses process millions of trades on hundreds of thousands of underlying assets. Automation enables the execution of these tests on a large scale as well for all parts but the action – this can only be automated to the degree that the action entails increased monitoring activities or other tests that do not yet require human intervention. Therefore, the critical test design components are the evaluation criteria and actions which must be set up to allow effective intervention by the available staff.

Now, even if all assumptions are identified, tests are set up for assumptions and performance and are expansively captured in the ongoing monitoring, models may still break – the only difference is that the ongoing monitoring reports the break when it happens.

As models tend to break down in times of economic stress, testing the model under a set of economic stress scenarios is good practice and is required by most regulations anyway, particularly for regulatory capital models. So, all assumption and performance tests must be conducted under such stress scenarios before the model goes live to ensure it will continue functioning under these conditions.

However, since any crisis is different from both real and hypothetical scenarios, any such set of stress testing that provides preparation for the actual stress event is still limited at best. In the event, the current Covid-19 crisis is remarkably distinct from any regulatory stress scenario defined over the past two years. In a much more insidious case, the model may continue working, but produce unreliable results. The case in point is, for example, real disposable personal income that spiked to previously unobserved levels because of governance assistance programmes. This is where model RST comes in, also known as the boundary of model validity.

The following Sections 20.3 to 20.9 will describe in more detail how to incorporate model validity boundaries into the preparation of the single aspects, form conceptual soundness to testing, implementation, ongoing monitoring, model use, governance and documentation.

20.3 Conceptual Soundness

20.3.1 Maintaining Model Validity

The boundaries of model validity determine the range of inputs for which the model is valid, or at least performs effectively. For the two examples, these model validity boundaries are straightforward to determine:

European Option Pricing:
- Price of underlying asset is positive: $S > 0$.
- Volatility is positive: $\sigma > 0$. A negative volatility may occur as a result of parameterisation, so then the task becomes deriving conditions for the parameterisation to ensure strict positive volatility.

Credit Card PD Estimation:
- All inputs are within the (x% confidence) range of previously observed values.

The confidence range for the PD estimation model may be necessary since outliers by any definition are worth flagging for specific investigation.

So, once the model validity boundaries are determined, the harder part is devising a strategy for their breach. In general, one may determine the breach to be a "one-off" case. Then, the last available inputs may be used as fallback or the offending input may be adjusted within a small margin to the right side of the validity threshold. Alternatively, if the model is deemed inoperable, it will require an alternative model that can handle the data points that caused the breach.

European Option Pricing:
- Shifted log-normal model – This was used when interest rates became negative. The model equation changes to

$$\frac{dS}{S+S_0} = \mu dt + \sigma_{DD} dW$$

with an appropriate shift S_0 so that the shifted price is a positive number at each point in time.
- Normal model: $dS = mdt + sdW$. This model can consume negative asset prices and will continue functioning.

Both models allow a straightforward calculation of Black-Scholes type formulae for the prices of European options. See for example Rubinstein (1983) and Kuklinski, Negru, & Pliszka (2014).

Credit Card PD Estimation:
- The model itself remains, but
    - Either the input is recognised as a requiring adjustment and the adjustment brings the input back into the accepted range, or
    - The input is a genuine data point and the model requires recalibration with inclusion of the new data point.
- An indicator variable for regime shift (e.g. for government assistance) is introduced into the model.

In the case of the model change for option pricing, all related parameters require changing, as indicated by the use of σ_{DD} or s instead of σ. This has wide-reaching consequences that must also be included in the preparation and includes the following effects:
1. Volatility parameters for the calibration of the risk models change, including value-at-risk, counterparty credit risk and valuation adjustments such as CVA and FVA. The related risk parameters and capital charges may change substantially, too.
2. Volatility dynamics change. In fact, both alternative models introduce a skew in terms of the implied (Black-Scholes) volatility, which is also equivalent to a change in the static distribution assumption of the asset price. Therefore, also the dynamics of the new volatility σ_{DD} or s may differ and require separate testing to confirm that the assumed dynamics are consistent with the observed ones.

The regime shift model variant in the credit card PD model essentially knits two models together, one without governance assistance and one with it. This regime shift also constitutes a new input variable that must be covered in scenario design, deciding whether government assistance will occur. For an automated search in pursuit of RST scenarios, such a decision may be designed as rule-based – for instance, triggered by a drop in GDP below a certain threshold or a spike in unemployment above a threshold.

20.3.2 Additional Modelling Activities

Since the evaluation of either example model is not computationally intensive, there is no need for additional modelling activities resulting from multiple model evaluations.

However, there may be additional assumptions to ensure that the search has been exhaustive. In case the possible model inputs from this exhaustive search are outside the model validity boundaries, the evaluation results in the use of a different (or recalibrated) model. This case is already covered in the preceding section.

In contrast to the European option in the example, any derivatives that require a numerical solution, such as a PDE solver or a Monte Carlo simulation, incur higher computational costs. In particular, if valuation adjustments such as CVA or capital calculations for counterparty credit charges (CCR) require another Monte Carlo simulation of the inputs, the choice of the calculation method may already be approximate for the CVA or CCR calculations under normal conditions, and all the more so for multiple evaluations under an RST use case. Examples for approximate models are regression-based approaches. More recent machine learning (ML) techniques such as Gaussian Process Regression or neural nets offer a better approximation than linear or logistic regressions as they are more flexible. Furthermore, quantum computing techniques may be applied to a Taylor expansion to achieve acceleration by several orders of magnitude. Applications are shown in Chapters 15, 18 and 19.

20.4 Developmental Evidence and Independent Testing

20.4.1 Maintaining Model Validity

Assume that a choice has been made on the pre-empted breaches of model boundary validity. Whichever choice is made, including the acceptance as a "one-off" event, it must be well justified and supported by tests and impact analyses.

In terms of additional developmental evidence and testing, this means:

Assumption testing: In reaction to breaches of model validity boundaries, an alternative model may be introduced. This model may have different and/or additional assumptions. These assumptions must be tested in the same way as the assumption of the primary model. In the examples, these assumptions change in the following way:

–   European Option Pricing: The alternative models imply a different distribution assumption of the underlying asset. As a consequence, the implied volatility changes and, with that, the dynamics of that implied volatility. It is a possibility that the alternative model fits the observed market data less well than the primary model, which introduces a trade-off. This trade-off becomes even starker in the performance.

–   Credit Card PD Estimation:

–   The recalibrated model itself is of the same form, but may produce different outputs for the same inputs. Also, the recalibration implies that all related tests such as significance tests must be re-run, and there may be a worse fit to previous data introduced by the structural break.

–   The regime-switch model introduces a new variable of government assistance on/off, creating an assumption for its values in hypothetical future scenarios.

Performance testing: All performance tests must be conducted for the model alternatives, at least for the possible inputs which may trigger their use as the primary model becomes invalid or unreliable. This may introduce another trade-off between a primary model that is deemed invalid but has better performance and an alternative model that may handle extreme inputs but performs worse overall in the domain in which both models are valid.

Outcomes/Output Analysis: Similar to performance testing, the outcomes analysis compares model outputs to actual outcomes. Sometimes, outcomes analysis takes hypothetical inputs and compares the outputs to realised outcomes for comparable inputs (e.g. for stress scenarios of a similar severity). As with performance testing, this may give rise to a trade-off in which the model alternative for a model validity breach can handle the data that caused the breach, but produces outputs that are less consistent with real outcomes than the outputs of the primary model.

In summary, whenever alternative models must be introduced to deal with inputs under which the primary model becomes invalid, there may be a trade-off between:

1.   The primary model that does not handle all inputs, but overall passes assumption tests better, performs better and/or produces outputs more consistent with real outcomes, and

2.   The alternative model that is more robust with respect to inputs, but has additional assumptions that are inconsistent with observed data and/or is worse in performance and outcome analysis.

If such a trade-off does not exist, the alternative model becomes the clearly superior choice and should replace the primary model.

20.4.2 Additional Modelling Activities

These additional activities are required if the RST-driven search for a sufficiently detrimental scenario requires an approximate model to handle the computational effort. Note that an *approximate* model is usually different from the *alternative* models such as those described in Section 20.3.1. As explained in Section 20.3.2, an approximate model is not required for the two examples, but is typically required for valuation and risk calculation of more complex derivatives. Those approximate models require additional modelling development:

Assumption Testing: Identify the assumptions changed by the approximate model and test them under a representative range of inputs.

Performance Testing: It is of particular interest how well the approximate model performs compared to the primary model. For stress tests in particular, accuracy is of lower importance, as it is only relevant whether P&L or other financial metrics move sufficiently much. For example, large investment banks require a P&L move of hundreds of millions of dollars for a measurable impact of 0.1% to the CET1 ratio. It is advisable, though, to keep track of all accuracy effects as they may become material in the aggregate.

Outcomes Analysis: This involves qualitative evaluations comparing the approximate model to both the primary model and realised outcomes. Such comparisons investigate the direction of change in output to a change in inputs as well as the overall magnitude of the output. For stress tests, conservatism is usually a safe option, and approximate methods may typically be configured for conservatism. As with accuracy, it is also sensible to quantify the conservatism since the cumulative effect may become material to important metrics such as the CET1 ratio or liquidity ratios.

Particularly if any capital or liquidity thresholds are breached, one course of action is to revise or change the approximate models to determine whether replacing conservatism with higher accuracy will change the result sufficiently.

20.5 Implementation

20.5.1 Maintaining Model Validity

From the previous considerations, it is apparent that that even for elementary models, many situations can arise in which alternative models are required. Therefore, any implementation must offer a high degree of flexibility. This can be achieved through a model application programming interface (API) or modular design.

Such a model API must offer the following functionalities:

1. Replacement of the model throughout the implementation as a matter of configuration, not of coding.
2. Production of audit trails for such configuration changes.
3. Execution of testing, distinguishing applicable tests for the specific model. This is part of static setup and covers assumption testing, performance testing and their implementation in ongoing monitoring.

In general, implementation must be set up in a standardised way as standardisation enables automation and makes the overall model operations more efficient. Often, standardised infrastructure is not in place, particularly in large organisations as these have grown through acquisitions, accumulating a variety of different technology stacks. Cost-cutting measures then constrain investment, even though standardised setup saves cost and, over the course of at least two years, is actually cheaper than the maintenance of a large number of legacy technology components. With the growing utilisation of cloud technology, model interfaces and APIs in general become more flexible, as discussed in more detail in Chapter 19. The migration to cloud technology may ultimately enable migration away from legacy infrastructure onto more recent and standardised technology.

For maximum efficiency, the following aspects of model operations should be standardised and subsequently automated:

1. Sourcing of inputs: Different inputs must be sourced from their respective single source.
2. Storage of outputs that capture the data lineage, are searchable and are indexed to facilitate results analysis.
3. Mapping of assumption tests and performance tests to each model type.
4. Setup of a schedule of such tests for ongoing monitoring, as justified by model developers as the first line of defence and confirmed by the model risk function as the second line of defence.
5. Generation of text blocks that describe the results of tests, based on set thresholds. For hypothesis tests, this will require two variants for a pre-set confidence level. For other tests, the text variations may be more nuanced. However, since it is important to maintain consistency, there is an incentive to keep the number

of variations to a reasonable level and typically ranges from 3 in a traffic-light approach to 5 for more granular distinction of test results.

6. Generation of audit trails that incorporate production model runs, inputs and outputs of models, production of tests with their exact configurations, inputs and outputs as well as test results.

Not only will this standardised setup enable efficient operations, but it will also ensure consistency, which is a standing aspect of regulatory exams. Such so-called horizontal checks are easy to conduct and often turn up inconsistencies. As remediation work is significantly more expensive than a consistent setup from the outset would have been, this may also constitute an argument for funding of the up-front infrastructure investment.

In the context of RST for models, the criteria listed here ensure that any change of a model that was triggered by inputs lying outside the validity boundaries of the primary model can be comprehensively verified and analysed. It also ensures that if a model fails despite all the preparations, identification of the root cause will be much easier. Finally, the flexible and standardised setup also supports any ad-hoc runs of the model infrastructure for scenario analysis much more efficiently. The Covid-19 crisis is again a case in point as banks' senior management and regulators across the globe requested scenario-based stress tests to gain additional comfort in the stability of individual institutions and the financial system.

20.5.2 Additional Modelling Activities

Infrastructure Bandwidth: Apart from the model validity, it must be determined whether the number of model evaluations that are required under a stress test, and even more under a reverse stress test, can be handled by the infrastructure. For a typical regulatory stress test, instead of one set of inputs, there are multiple sets of inputs from at least four different scenarios – internal and regulatory baseline and internal and regulatory stress. For a reverse stress test that involves an exhaustive search, the number of different scenarios is many times larger. Therefore, the existing bandwidth is often not enough to process stress testing requirements or requires additional time for production.

Approximate Model Implementation: In case the infrastructure bandwidth is not sufficient for the primary model, approximate models are used. This includes models that mimic the input-output relationship without the economics that often underlie the full models. Instead, ML methods such as neural nets are a flexible family of functions that have a universal approximation property, see for instance (Cybenko, 1989). If properly calibrated, they provide sufficiently accurate implementations of the primary model at a fraction of the runtime, a factor of 30–40 (see Chapter 15).

Flexibility of Model Implementation: To fully embed such models will require the flexible setup described in Section 20.5.1. As in banks, the full incorporation of a model into the system requires an overhead that is a multiple of the actual programming and configuration effect. The implementation of additional models often takes place in end-user developed applications, mostly spreadsheets. This is at first glance more flexible than the fully-fledged system implementation, but often comes at the cost of key person dependencies and with substantial control deficiencies.

Robustness of Model Implementation: In the absence of a fully integrated model infrastructure that is sufficiently flexible to accommodate alternative or approximate models, banks often resort to spreadsheets or scripts outside the business-as-usual systems to run. Such an implementation choice is often done under the time constraints and effectively transfers development activities from IT specialists to other functions. Compared to a native IT implementation, the effort including the overhead is comparable while controls are inferior and an audit trail is not fully implementable.

In summary, if additional models are implemented, the most frequent implementation choice is outside the bank's system of records because of time constraints. This comes at the cost of additional development burden in non-IT functions, which is usually not captured in transfer pricing. From an efficiency, implementation flexibility and robustness perspective, the system-bound implementation would be superior.

20.6 Ongoing Monitoring

Setup of a model infrastructure as described in Sections 20.4.1 and 20.5.1 also ensures that any human activities can focus on the value-added aspects. These include:

1. Identification of root causes for remaining failures and subsequent fixes and patches of the code base.
2. Analysis of validity-boundary-induced model changes with respect to their performance metrics.
3. Analysis of test results that indicate deterioration in model performance or failure of crucial model assumptions.

Since the infrastructure setup also substantially facilitates the testing of entirely new model methods, it is also a productive testing ground for such methods. For example, ML methodologies are more flexible and may produce a superior model performance. Such parallel runs will also go a long way towards obtaining buy-in from the business and regulators. In any case, business models that do not require regulatory signoff and have immediate impact on profits are the better place to start for any fundamentally new model methods.

20.7 Model Use

20.7.1 Maintaining Model Validity

With trigger-based changes of models, it is vital that all stakeholders be informed of any such model changes induced by inputs that would render the primary model dysfunctional or unreliable and the financial impact they generate.

In addition, any comprehensive reporting of changes that prevent model failures caused by breach of model validity boundaries serves multiple purposes. First, it creates transparency for the business and other stakeholders about the financial impact. Second, it demonstrates the stability of the setup, as without the change there would not be any financial results or they would not be reliable. Therefore, such events also create the opportunity to showcase opportunity profits due to the superior setup of an automated switchover to an alternative model. Such a setup prevents model failures, and patching these ad-hoc as they arise is costly, both financially and reputationally.

20.7.2 Additional Modelling Activities

Similar to the use of alternative models, relevant stakeholders must be included in the decision-making process for the use of approximate models. In addition to creating a clear governance structure that establishes clear accountability for decisions, the ultimate owner of the modelled result has an innate interest in a result that is reliable and reproducible. As such, it is rational for the result owner to support a model implementation that can both maintain model validity and is robustly implemented.

20.8 Governance

Robust governance is fundamental for the successful implementation of the stress-proof model design described in the previous sections. Governance starts from the top with senior management and permeates all aspect of model operations.

Senior management buy-in is vital to realise the model design. To obtain this buy-in requires a concise case that demonstrates the cost benefits, profit opportunities, operational stability and the resulting reputation gains with investors and regulators. Presentation of this case also ensures that senior management is aware of the related model assumptions and limitations that necessitate fallback solutions.

Governance meetings represent the formal forum to argue the case for stress-proof model setup. These meetings also ensure that all affected stakeholders are included and provide their input into the decision-making process. Typically, a hierarchy of such meetings from committees down to working groups is the most effective way to involve different levels of seniority into the process. Finally, governance meetings produce the documentation for a continuous information flow to senior management and for external scrutiny by providing an audit trail of discussions and decisions.

Roles and responsibilities must be clearly defined. For each aspect, from decisions on model design to model operations to sign-off of modelled result, there must be a single person who is accountable. This person must have the authority to directly influence the relevant aspect. This sounds simple and effective, but is often not the case for large organisations as matrix structures and decisions made by committees diffuse accountability. Another issue that arises often is the responsibility for testing of models that depend on other models, so-called feeder models. The cleanest solution is to have the dependent-model developer accountable for requesting tests from the model developers of feeder models. The feeder-model developer is then accountable for producing these tests and including them into the model documentation. The documentation is made available to all relevant stakeholders, including the developer of the dependent model.

Data completeness, accuracy and timeliness must be governed in two facets: people and infrastructure. Working groups and governance meetings cover the people aspect. The infrastructure side is put in place through the implementation of the infrastructure requirements from Section 20.4.2.

Ongoing monitoring requires a broad variety of decisions, from the choice of tests to the selection of pass/fail thresholds or the definition of more granular outcome ranges to the frequency of monitoring to the actions to take upon negative test results. Robust governance clearly defines who is accountable for these decisions, ensure the relevant stakeholders are involved through the appropriate governance meetings and produces documentation to ensure the entire process is reproducible and comprehensible to third parties.

In summary, governance is important to initiate stress-resistant model design through senior management backing, efficiently involve the important decision-makers and relevant stakeholders throughout the organisation and create efficient transparency for internal and external scrutiny.

20.9 Documentation

The recurring documentation mantra is "If something is not written up, it does not exist". This goes beyond the pure necessity for external audit or regulators and starts

by compelling model developers to clarify their thought process through laying it out in writing. Other obvious benefits of documentation are:
- demonstration of financial profits for senior decision-makers
- establishment of clarity and avoidance of ambiguity
- efficient communication with affected stakeholders
- creation of transparency for internal and external control functions
- training material for junior staff or new joiners

For each of the aspects from Section 20.3 to 20.8, it is vital to have comprehensive but concise documentation in place. In addition to the already existing documentation, stress test and RST uses of the model give rise to additional model development and testing activities that must be documented.

Conceptual Soundness: Any alternative or approximate model approaches are compared side-by-side with the primary model, laying out the pros and cons of each model choices. Such a comparison strongly supports the choice of the primary model as well as the other model approaches and efficiently informs all stakeholders about this choice. This also includes a concise mathematical description of each model choice that allows independent reconstruction.

Developmental Evidence: Any conceptual choices of alternative or approximate models are supported by tests of the additional or different assumptions inherent in these models. In addition, all different models must be evaluated with respect to their calibration and performance, providing as customary for each test its purpose, the methods used, the result, its evaluation and any action to be taken as a consequence.

Implementation: Of particular importance for operations functions is a comprehensive description of the running of the model, with the dependencies, the processing procedures and the interpretation of the final output. Other ancillary information supporting the model output includes the model versions, overlays and the data flow.

Ongoing Monitoring: Any ongoing monitoring results must include a full description of the test. This is the same information as produced for the developmental evidence, supporting again the benefits of standardisation. The important difference is that the developmental evidence documentation is static, while the documentation produced for ongoing monitoring changes depending on new inputs and position information. The most important part of the documentation is the last part of the test, the actions taken upon the evaluation of results.

Model Use: All model uses must be shown. This includes the use in stress testing and RST in particular. As sometimes model choices differ not only by their use in stress testing versus business-as-usual contexts, a map or table is useful for an overview.

In summary, documentation is a must, with clear benefits for all additional aspects that arise from the use of models in stress testing. A well-structured documentation template significantly facilitates producing the documentation whilst enforcing minimum standards and enhancing readability.

20.10 Summary

The current Covid-19 crisis has made apparent the need for ad-hoc and exhaustive stress testing. At the same time, it has shown that in a real crisis, models fail in ways which are avoidable. This chapter shows how to create a robust setup that prevents model failures, to ensure that models work under hypothetical stress tests and identify scenarios for RST-severity outcomes. The necessary setup requires as much conceptual work in designing and testing alternative models as fallback and approximate models for shorter runtimes, as it needs a flexible infrastructure architecture that can accommodate these additional models.

In particular, the current infrastructure setup in banks, often due to inherited and fragmented systems, requires further work to fully realise this type of model setup. Such an infrastructure is more robust and simultaneously more cost-efficient over a typical software lifecycle of three to five years. Ultimately, the setup facilitates use of the best models, so new modelling methodologies as well as cloud technologies may enable the migration to this future-proof architecture.

Bibliography

Board of Governors of the Federal Reserve System, Office of the Comptroller of the Currency. (2011, April 4). *Federal Reserve*. Retrieved May 29, 2020, from Supervisory Guidance on Model Risk Management: https://www.federalreserve.gov/boarddocs/srletters/2011/sr1107a1.pdf

Cybenko, G. (1989). Approximation by superpositions of a sigmoidal function. *Mathematics of Control, Signals and Systems, 2*, 303–314.

Derman, E. (1999). Regimes of Volatility – Some Observations on the Variation of S&P 500 Implied Volatilities. *Goldman Quantitative Strategies Research Notes*.

European Banking Authority. (2018). *European Banking Authority*. Retrieved May 29, 2020, from Model validation: https://eba.europa.eu/regulation-and-policy/model-validation

Kuklinski, J., Negru, D., and Pliszka, P. (2014). *arXiv.org*. Retrieved June 19, 2020, from Modelling the skew and smile of SPX and DAX index options using the Shifted Log-Normal and SABR stochastic models: https://arxiv.org/ftp/arxiv/papers/1404/1404.4659.pdf

Natenberg, S. (2014). *Option Volatility and Pricing: Advanced Trading Strategies and Techniques* (2nd ed.). New York: McGraw-Hill.

Prudential Regulatory Authority. (2018). *Bank of England*. Retrieved May 29, 2020, from Model risk management principles for stress testing: https://www.bankofengland.co.uk/-/media/boe/files/prudential-regulation/supervisory-statement/2018/ss318.pdf

Razali, N. M., and Wah, Y. B. (2011). Power comparisons of Shapiro–Wilk, Kolmogorov–Smirnov, Lilliefors and Anderson–Darling tests. *Journal of Statistical Modeling and Analytics, 2*(1), 21–33.

Rubinstein, M. (1983). Displaced Diffusion Option Pricing. *The Journal of Finance, XXXVII*(1), 213–217.

U.S. Bureau of Labor Statistics. (2020). *BLS*. Retrieved June 24, 2020, from Frequently asked questions: The impact of the coronavirus (COVID-19) pandemic on The Employment Situation for May 2020: https://www.bls.gov/cps/employment-situation-covid19-faq-may-2020.pdf

Jon Danielsson, Robert Macrae, Andreas Uthemann

21 The Role of Artificial Intelligence as Central Banker and in the Stability of Markets

21.1 Artificial Intelligence and the Stability of Markets

Artificial intelligence is increasingly used to tackle all sorts of problems facing people and societies.[1] This section considers the potential benefits and risks of employing AI in financial markets. While it may well revolutionise risk management and financial supervision, it also threatens to destabilise markets and increase systemic risk.

Artificial intelligence (AI) is useful for optimally controlling an existing system with clearly understood risks. It excels at pattern matching and control mechanisms. Given enough observations and a strong signal, it can identify deep dynamic structures much more robustly than any human can and is far superior in areas that require the statistical evaluation of large quantities of data. It can do so without human intervention.

We can leave an AI machine in the day-to-day charge of such a system, automatically self-correcting and learning from mistakes and meeting the objectives of its human masters.

This means that risk management and micro-prudential supervision are well suited for AI. The underlying technical issues are clearly defined, as are both the high- and low-level objectives.

However, the very same qualities that make AI so useful for the micro-prudential authorities are also why it could destabilise the financial system and increase systemic risk (discussed in Danielsson et al., 2017).

21.1.1 Risk Management and Micro-Prudential Supervision

In successful large-scale applications, an AI engine exercises control over small parts of an overall problem, where the global solution is simply aggregated sub-solutions.

1 The two sections in this chapter have been published on VoxEU under Jon Danielsson's column at https://voxeu.org/users/jondanielsson0 and are reproduced here with the kind permission of Mr. Danielsson and VoxEU. Jon Danielsson is the sole author of Section 21.1; Section 21.2 is the joint work of Jon Danielsson, Robert Macrae and Andreas Uthemann.

Note: Edited by Daniel Mayenberger

https://doi.org/10.1515/9783110647907-021

Controlling all of the small parts of a system separately is equivalent to controlling the system in its entirety. Risk management and micro-prudential regulations are examples of such a problem.

The first step in risk management is the modelling of risk and that is straightforward for AI. This involves the processing of market prices with relatively simple statistical techniques, work that is already well under way. The next step is to combine detailed knowledge of all the positions held by a bank with information on the individuals who decide on those positions, creating a risk management AI engine with knowledge of risk, positions, and human capital.

While we still have some way to go toward that end, most of the necessary information is already inside banks' IT infrastructure and there are no insurmountable technological hurdles along the way.

All that is left is to inform the engine of a bank's high-level objectives. The machine can then automatically run standard risk management and asset allocation functions, set position limits, recommend who gets fired and who gets bonuses and advise on which asset classes to invest in.

The same applies to most micro-prudential supervision. Indeed, AI has already spawned a new field called regulation technology, or 'regtech'.

It is not all that hard to translate the rulebook of a supervisory agency, now for most parts in plain English, into a formal computerised logic engine. This allows the authority to validate its rules for consistency and gives banks an application programming interface to validate practices against regulations.

Meanwhile, the supervisory AI and the banks' risk management AI can automatically query each other to ensure compliance. This also means that all the data generated by banks becomes optimally structured and labelled and automatically processable by the authority for compliance and risk identification.

There is still some way to go before the supervisory/risk management AI becomes a practical reality, but what is outlined here is eminently conceivable, given the trajectory of technological advancement. The main hindrance is likely to be legal, political and social rather than technological.

Risk management and micro-prudential supervision are the ideal use cases for AI – they enforce compliance with clearly defined rules, and with processes generating vast amounts of structured data. They have closely monitored human behaviour, precise high-level objectives, and directly observed outcomes.

Financial stability is different. There the focus is on systemic risk (Danielsson and Zigrand, 2015), and unlike risk management and micro-prudential supervision, it is necessary to consider the risk of the entire financial system together. This is much harder because the financial system is, for all practical purposes, infinitely complex and any entity – human or AI – can only hope to capture a small part of that complexity.

The widespread use of AI in risk management and financial supervision may increase systemic risk. There are four reasons for this.

21.1.2 Looking for Risk in all the Wrong Places

Risk management and regulatory AI can focus on the wrong risk – the risk that can be measured rather than the risk that matters.

The economist Frank Knight established the distinction between risk and uncertainty in 1921.[2] Risk is measurable and quantifiable and results in statistical distributions that we can then use to exercise control. Uncertainty is none of these things. We know it is relevant but we can't quantify it, so it is harder to make decisions.

AI cannot cope well with uncertainty because it is not possible to train an AI engine against unknown data. The machine is really good at processing information about things it has seen. It can handle counterfactuals when these arise in systems with clearly stated rules, like with Google's AlphaGo Zero (Silver et al., 2017). It cannot reason about the future when it involves outcomes it has not seen.

The focus of risk management and supervision is mostly risk, not uncertainty. An example is the stock market, and we are well-placed to manage the risk arising from it. If the market goes down by USD $200 bn today, it is going to have a minimal impact because it is a known risk.

Uncertainty captures the danger we don't know is out there until it is too late. Potential unrealised losses of less than USD $200 bn on subprime mortgages in 2008 brought the financial system to its knees. If there are no observations on the consequences of subprime mortgages put into CDOs with liquidity guarantees, there is nothing to train on. The resulting uncertainty will be ignored by AI.

While human risk managers and supervisors can also miss uncertainty, they are less likely to. They can evaluate current and historical knowledge with experience and theoretical frameworks, which is something AI can't do.

21.1.3 Optimisation against the System

A large number of well-resourced economic agents have strong incentives to take very large risks that have the potential to deliver large profits at the expense of significant danger to their financial institutions and the system at large. That is exactly the type of activity that risk management and supervision aim to contain.

These agents are *optimising against the system*, aiming to undermine control mechanisms in order to profit, identifying areas where the controllers are not sufficiently vigilant.

These hostile agents have an inherent advantage over those who are tasked with keeping them in check, because each only has to solve a small local problem and their computational burden is much lower than that of the authority. There could be many

---

2 In his work *Risk, Uncertainty, and Profit*, Houghton Mifflin.

agents simultaneously doing this and we may need few, even only one, to succeed for a crisis to ensue. Meanwhile, in an AI arms race, the authorities probably lose out to private sector computing power.

While this problem has always been inherent in risk management and supervision, it is likely to become worse the more AI takes over core functions. If we believe AI is doing its job, where we cannot verify how it reasons (which is impossible with AI), and we only monitor outputs, we have to trust it. If it then appears to manage without big losses, it will earn our trust.

If we don't understand how an AI supervisory/risk management engine reasons, we better make sure to specify its objective function correctly and exhaustively.

Paradoxically, the more we trust AI to do its job properly, the easier it can be to manipulate and optimise against the system. A hostile agent can learn how the AI engine operates, take risk where it is not looking, game the algorithms and hence undermine the machine by behaving in a way that avoids triggering its alarms or, even worse, nudges it to look away.

21.1.4 Endogenous Complexity

Even then, the AI engine working on the behest of the macroprudential authority might have a fighting chance if the structure of the financial system remained constant, so that the problem is simply of sufficient computational resources.

But it isn't. The financial system constantly changes its dynamic structure simply because of the interaction of the agents that make up the system, many of whom are optimising against the system and deliberately creating hidden complexities. This is the root of what we call endogenous risk (Danielsson et al., 2009).

The complexity of the financial system is endogenous, and that is why AI, even conceptually, can't efficiently replace the macro-prudential authority in the way that it can supersede the micro-prudential authority.

21.1.5 Artificial Intelligence is Procyclical

Systemic risk is increased by homogeneity. The more similar our perceptions and objectives are, the more systemic risk we create. Diverse views and objectives dampen out the impact of shocks and act as a countercyclical stabilising, systemic risk minimising force.

Financial regulations and standard risk management practices inevitably push towards homogeneity – AI even more so. It favours best practices and standardised best-of-breed models that closely resemble each other, all of which, no matter how well-intentioned and otherwise positive, also increase pro-cyclicality and hence systemic risk.

21.1.6 Summary

Artificial intelligence is useful in preventing historical failures from repeating and will increasingly take over financial supervision and risk management functions. We get more coherent rules and automatic compliance, all with much lower costs than current arrangements. The main obstacle is political and social, not technological.

From the point of view of financial stability, the opposite conclusion holds.

We may miss out on the most dangerous type of risk-taking. Even worse, AI can make it easier to game the system. There may be no solutions to this, whatever the future trajectory of technology. The computational problem facing an AI engine will always be much higher than that of those who seek to undermine it, not the least because of endogenous complexity.

Meanwhile, the very formality and efficiency of the risk management/supervisory machine also increases homogeneity in belief and response, further amplifying pro-cyclicality and systemic risk.

The end result of the use of AI for managing financial risk and supervision is likely to be lower volatility but fatter tails – that is, lower day-to-day risk, but more systemic risk.

21.2 Artificial Intelligence as a Central Banker

Artificial intelligence, such as the Bank of England Bot, is set to take over an increasing number of central bank functions. This section argues that the increased use of AI in central banking will bring significant cost and efficiency benefits, but also raise important concerns that are so far unresolved.

Artificial intelligence (AI) is increasingly useful for central banks. While it may be used only in low-level roles today, technological advances and cost savings will likely embed AI deeper and deeper into core central bank functions. Maybe each central bank will have their own AI engine – maybe a future "BoB" (the Bank of England Bot).

What will be the impact of BoB and its counterparts?

BoB could today, or soon, help with many central bank tasks, such as information gathering, data analysis, forecasting, risk management, financial supervision and monetary policy analysis.

The technology is mostly here; what prevents adoption are cultural, political and legal factors. Perhaps most important is institutional inertia. However, the considerable cost savings from the use of AI will likely overcome most objections.

In some areas of central banking, BoB will be particularly valuable, such as in crisis response. If the central bank is facing a liquidity crisis and has hours or days to respond, speed of information gathering and analysis is critical. Having a standby

AI engine that is expert in situational assessment is invaluable, freeing the human decision-makers from data crunching so they can make timely decisions, advised by BoB.

At the same time, the increased use of AI raises critical questions for economic policymakers (Agrawal, 2018). Within central banking, four questions are particularly important (Danielsson et al., 2020).

21.2.1 Procyclicality

BoB, when used for financial supervision, will favour homogeneous best-of-breed methodologies and standardised processes, imposing an increasingly homogeneous view of the world on market participants.

That amplifies the procyclical impact of the banks' own AI engines, which all have the same objective: profit maximisation subject to constraints. 'Better' solutions are closer to the optimum and, consequently, closer to each other.

The consequence is crowded trades because of crowded perception and action. When new information arrives, all AI engines, in both the private and public sectors, will update their models similarly. All will see risk in the same way, and the banks' AI will want to buy/sell the same assets.

The result is procyclicality – short-term stability and high profits but at the cost of increased systemic risk.

21.2.2 Unknown-unknowns

One of the most challenging parts of the central bankers' job is dealing with 'unknown-unknowns'. Vulnerabilities, especially of the dangerous systemic type, tend to emerge on the boundaries of areas of responsibilities – the silos. Subprime mortgages put products with hidden liquidity guarantees into structured credit, crossing multiple jurisdictions, agencies, institutional categories and countries. These are areas where humans and AI alike are least likely to look.

Current AI can easily be trained on events that have happened ('known-knowns'). BoB can perhaps be trained on simulated scenarios ('known-unknowns').

However, our financial system is, for all practical purposes, infinitely complex. Not only that, but every action taken by the authorities and the private sector changes the system – the complexity of the financial system is endogenous, a consequence of Goodhart's (1975) law: "[a]ny observed statistical regularity will tend to collapse once pressure is placed upon it for control purposes".

BoB will, by definition, miss the unknown-unknowns, just like its human counterparts. After all, the machine can only be trained on events that either have already happened or are generated from simulations of fully specified model economies.

For exactly the same reason, it will be really good at dealing with known-unknowns much better than its human counterparts. Yet, it is the unknown-unknowns that cause crises.

21.2.3 Trust

BoB will likely keep the financial system safe most of the time, most likely much better than a purely human-staffed supervisory system, and we will consequently increasingly rely on and trust BoB. That can both undermine contingency planning and preventative regulatory measures, while also creating a false sense of security that may well culminate in a Minsky moment: perceived low risk that causes crises (Danielsson et al., 2018).

In the 1980s, an AI engine called EURISKO used a cute trick to defeat all its human competitors in a naval war game. It simply sank its own slowest ships so that its naval convoy became faster and more manoeuvrable than the competitors', ensuring victory (for a list of similar examples, see Krakovna, 2018).

This example crystallises the trust problems facing BoB. How do we know it will do the right thing? A human admiral doesn't have to be told they can't sink their own ships. They just know; it's an ingrained part of their humanity. BoB has no humanity. If it is to act autonomously, humans will have to first fix its objectives. But a machine with fixed objectives, let loose on an infinitely complex environment, will have unexpected behaviour (Russel, 2019). BoB will run into cases where it takes critical decisions in a way that no human would. Humans can adjust their objectives. BoB cannot.

How then can we trust BoB? Not in the same way we trust a human. Trust in human decision-making comes from a shared understanding of values and a shared understanding of the environment. BoB has no values, only objectives. And its understanding of the environment will not necessarily be intelligible to humans. Sure, we can run hypotheticals past BoB and observe its decisions, but we cannot easily ask for an explanation (Joseph, 2019).

Does this mean we will only use AI in central banks for simple functions? Unlikely. Trust creeps up on us. We suspect most people would have baulked at managing their personal finances online 20 years ago. Five years ago, most would not have trusted self-driving cars. Today, we have no problem entrusting our lives to AI-flown aircraft and AI-controlled surgical robots.

As AI proves its value to central banks, they will start trusting it, facilitating BoB's career progression. After all, it will be seen as doing a great job much more cheaply than human central bankers.

Then, if a crisis happens, and we see that the AI is doing something unacceptable – perhaps the central bank version of sinking its own slowest ships – we might want to hit the kill switch. Except it will no longer be that simple. Its growing reputation will have reduced incentives for other contingency measures, and, thereby, our ability to interfere with Bob's behaviour. Switching it off might endanger critical systems.

21.2.4 Optimise against the System

The final area of concern is how BoB would deal with 'malicious actors': those taking unacceptably high risk, those creating instability to profit, or even those whose main objective is to damage the financial system.

Here, BoB is at a disadvantage to its opponents' AI engines. It faces what is, in effect, an infinitely complex computational problem, as it has to monitor and control the entire system.

The opponent only has to identify local loopholes that can be exploited, and so will always have the advantage.

This advantage is amplified by AI's intrinsic rationality. Its objectives drive its actions. It makes BoB predictable, giving its adversaries an edge. Fixed objectives paired with a complex environment create unpredictable behaviour, regardless of whether we use AI or not. Now, however, rational behaviour within a well-defined environment allows for reverse-engineering of BoB's objectives via repeated interactions.

Certainly, countermeasures already exist. The standard defence is for AI to react randomly in interactions with human beings or other AI, limiting their ability to game it. This mimics the natural defence provided by humans – they create randomness, nuance and interpretation, which vary across individuals and time.

There are at least two reasons why such countermeasures would not work in practice for BoB.

First, randomised responses would have to be programmed into the central bank AI, which would be unacceptable except in special cases. Regulations and supervision need to be transparent and fair.

Second, randomisation requires the AI designers to specify a distribution for BoB's actions, and this distribution can be reverse-engineered as regulated entities observe repeated decisions.

BoB's innate rationality coupled with demands for transparency and fair play put it at a disadvantage when it is used for supervision. Interestingly, constructive ambiguity is accepted in monetary policy, so may be less of a problem there.

21.2.5 Summary

AI will become very helpful to central banks. Microprudential AI ("micro BoB") will reduce costs and increase efficiency, help with crisis response, and be highly successful on 999 days out of 1,000.

AI will be similarly beneficial to monetary policy, handling data collection and policy forecasting, and improving the information flow to the monetary policy committees at a much lower cost than with current infrastructure.

It is in macroprudential regulations and crisis management where AI raises the most critical questions. BoB will increase procyclicality and the likelihood of Minsky moments, and cannot be trusted. It will facilitate optimisation against the system.

Macro BoB needs a kill switch, but probably will not get one.

The use of AI for control purposes can increase systemic risk, reducing volatility and fattening the tails.

Bibliography

Agrawal, J. G., and A. Goldfarb (2018). Economic policy for artificial intelligence, VoxEU.org, 8 August.

Chakraborty, C., and A. Joseph (2017). New machines for the Old Lady, BankUnderground.co.uk, 10 November.

Danielsson, J. and J.P. Zigrand (2015). A proposed research and policy agenda for systemic risk, VoxEU.org, 7 August.

Danielsson, J., H. S. Shin and J.P. Zigrand (2009). Modelling financial turmoil through endogenous risk, VoxEU.org, 11 March.

Danielsson, J., R. Macrae and A. Uthemann (2017). Artificial intelligence, financial risk management and systemic risk, LSE Systemic Risk Centre special paper 13.

Danielsson, J., R. Macrae and A. Uthemann (2019). Artificial intelligence and systemic risk, SSRN.

Danielsson, J., M. Valenzuela and I. Zer (2018). Low risk as a predictor of financial crises, VoxEU.org, 26 March.

Goodhart, Charles (1975). Problems of Monetary Management: The U.K. Experience. Papers in Monetary Economics, Reserve Bank of Australia.

Jon Danielsson, Robert Macrae, Andreas Utheman: Artificial Intelligence and Systemic Risk, https://ssrn.com/abstract=3410948.

Joseph, A. (2019). Opening the machine learning black box, BankUnderground.co.uk, 24 May.

Knight, F. H. (1921). *Risk, Uncertainty and Profit*, Houghton Mifflin.

Krakovna, V. (2018). Specification gaming examples in AI, blog post, 2 April.

Russel, S. (2019). *Human compatible*, London: Allen Lane.

Silver, D. et al. (2017). Mastering the game of Go without human knowledge, *Nature* 550: 354–359.

Part V: **RST and Its Link to Recovery and Resolution Planning**

Nasir Ahmad

22 Reverse Stress Testing and Recovery and Resolution Planning: An Implementation Perspective

A Pledge for an Integrated Approach

22.1 Introduction

A resolution scenario describes how a firm will fail or will become likely to fail. This means it describes events leading to a point where the firm's business model has become unviable despite some management actions being taken. This is the goal of a reverse stress test – to find events that lead to non-viability. This chapter highlights the similarities between the recovery and resolution planning process and the reverse stress testing process, both from a framework and an implementation perspective. It also shows how these two processes can mutually leverage and enrich each other; especially once reverse stress testing has been properly extended/generalised. The synergies cover identification of vulnerabilities, selection of scenarios, choice of metrics and corresponding thresholds, reinforcement of the control framework, scope and impact of management actions, and the creation of a firm-wide database of scenario case studies (in a standardised format).

The goal of this chapter is to show that RST and RRP are related processes and can reinforce each other both from a framework as well as an implementation perspective. We also show how these two processes can mutually leverage and enrich each other, especially once reverse stress testing has been properly extended/generalised. We call this generalisation Extended Scenario Analysis (ESA).

Conceptually and practically, ESA is useful for all scenario-based processes such as business planning, regulatory or ICAAP stress tests, IFRS 9 forecasting – and not only for recovery and resolution planning (see Figure 22.1). The synergies cover identification of vulnerabilities, selection of scenarios, choice of metrics and corresponding thresholds, reinforcement of the control framework, and scope and impact of management actions. It leads to the following benefits:
- Consistency across processes (e.g. annual regulatory stress tests and business planning).
- Significantly lower costs (same infrastructure is used across several processes and calculations that need to be done once rather than multiple times as is often the case).

Note: Edited by Daniel Mayenberger

https://doi.org/10.1515/9783110647907-022

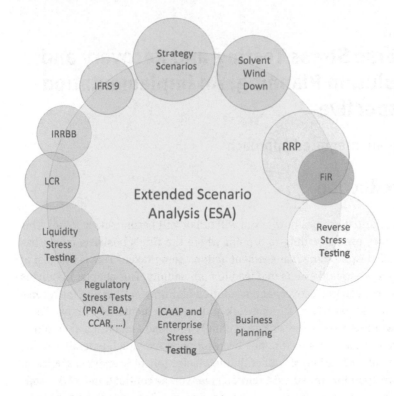

Figure 22.1: Processes requiring scenario analysis.

–   Quick turnaround times and ease of use, as a database of standardised scenarios and their impacts (case studies), is maintained and regularly referred to.

Despite its importance, RST is not yet widely used as a risk management tool. This can seem surprising as the main goal of RST is to find the causes (scenarios) that lead to bad outcomes (failing of a firm) – which is surely an important piece of the puzzle in managing risk. However, there are understandable reasons for this lack of success:

1.   Limited regulatory guidelines and push (e.g. as compared to the annual stress tests), with unclear specifications regarding the extent to which quantitative analysis is necessary.
2.   Often, the focus is to find only very improbable scenarios.
3.   A consequence of 1) and 2), RST is often not fully embedded in a firm – i.e. it is not linked as closely as it should be to other/all scenario-based processes or decision-making in general. As such, it fails the "use test".
4.   Another consequence of 2) is that standard/regular bank models are sometimes not valid in extreme scenarios and hence it is very difficult to quantify the consequences.

In Section 22.2, we briefly recall the most relevant sections of regulation (from the original sources) covering RST, recovery and resolution planning (RRP) and funding in resolution (FiR, the "liquidity part of RRP"). Section 22.3 lists those processes in a bank that requires scenario analysis. Section 22.4 describes Extended Scenario Analysis (ESA), a framework inspired from RST and generalising it. In Section 22.5, we show what a database of scenario case studies looks like and how it will help the firm in its risk management in general and RRP in particular. Section 22.6 describes how ESA can be implemented as a versatile tool. Section 22.7 covers the specifics of FiR, and we show how ESA can be leveraged to find scenarios that will be used in FiR (the latter is taken as a representative sub-case of RRP, illustrating both the quantitative and qualitative sides of implementation). The chapter ends with Section 22.8, which summarises the benefits of the approach. To make the chapter self-contained, further relevant extracts from original regulatory texts are included in the Appendix.

22.2 Relevant Regulatory Background

Whilst RST has not had the regulatory push and has not become as integral as other forms of stress testing, there are regulatory requirements and guidance. This is especially the case in the context of RRP, where RST is often used as an analytical tool to find scenarios. For ease of reference, we briefly recall the salient features of requirements for RST, RRP, and FiR that are directly relevant for our discussion. To make this chapter self-contained, some additional useful regulatory aspects are included in the Appendix.

22.2.1 Reverse Stress Testing

Note the following points from (Financial Conduct Authority, 2020) which encourages a quantitative approach to RST in certain contexts.
- *We would expect larger, more complex firms to undertake more detailed analysis, incorporating quantitative analysis from the outset.*
- *We expect larger, more complex firms to undertake more extensive quantitative analysis in their reverse stress testing as appropriate, relative to smaller, less complex firms.*
- *Firms must, therefore, consider both slow- and fast-crystallising events that might cause the business model to become unviable.*

Note the following points from (European Banking Authority, 2018a) which positions RST as an important risk management tool, link it to other scenario-based processes, and recommend a quantitative approach for certain aspects.

- *Reverse stress tests applied in a wider context can be used to inform a recovery plan stress test by identifying the conditions under which the recovery might need to be planned.*
- *Reverse stress testing should be useful for assessing the severity of scenarios for ICAAP and ILAAP stress tests.*
- *Institutions should use reverse stress testing as a regular risk management tool in order to improve their awareness of current and potential vulnerabilities, providing added value to institutions' risk management.*
- *As part of their business planning and risk management, institutions should use reverse stress testing to understand the viability and sustainability of their business models and strategies.*
- *Institutions should work backwards in a quantitative manner to identify the risk factors and the required amplitude of changes that could cause such a loss or negative impact (e.g. defining the appropriate loss level or some other measure of interest on the balance sheet of the financial institution such as capital ratios or funding resources).*
- *A joint stressing of all relevant risk parameters using statistical aspects (e.g. volatility of risk factors consistent with historical observations supplemented with hypothetical but plausible assumptions) should be developed.*

22.2.2 Recovery and Resolution Planning

The following points are taken from The European Parliament and The Council (2014) and refer to an appropriate choice of metrics and quantification of resolution strategies.

- *Competent authorities shall require that each recovery plan includes a framework of indicators established by the institution which identifies the points at which appropriate actions referred to in the plan may be taken.*
- *The resolution plan shall include, quantified whenever appropriate and possible a detailed description of the different resolution strategies that could be applied according to the different possible scenarios and the applicable timescales and a description of critical interdependencies.*

22.2.3 Funding in Resolution

FiR is the "liquidity part of RRP". It is the requirement to determine the funding need, both internal and public support that will be required by a bank in resolution. In an ideal scenario, the public amount is zero, hence protecting the taxpayer. A bank needs to demonstrate which scenarios will lead it into resolution, what actions it will take during that path (i.e. during recovery and resolution), how it will manage the process during recovery (metrics driven) and how the regulator can manage during resolution by implementing the playbook.

New resolution planning concepts were introduced in the Fed/FDIC Guidance for 2017. The following points are taken from Federal Deposit Insurance Corporation, (2017).

- *The firm should have the liquidity capabilities necessary to execute its preferred resolution strategy, including those described in SR Letter 14–1.7 For resolution purposes, these capabilities should include having an appropriate model and process for estimating and maintaining sufficient liquidity at or readily available to material entities and a methodology for estimating the liquidity needed to successfully execute the resolution strategy.*
- *Resolution Liquidity Adequacy and Positioning (RLAP)*
  - *With respect to RLAP, the firm should be able to measure the stand-alone liquidity position of each material entity (including material entities that are non-US branches) – i.e. the high-quality liquid assets (HQLA) at the material entity less net outflows to third parties and affiliates – and ensure that liquidity is readily available to meet any deficits.*
  - *Additionally, the RLAP methodology should take into account (A) the daily contractual mismatches between inflows and outflows; (B) the daily flows from movement of cash and collateral for all inter-affiliate transactions; and (C) the daily stressed liquidity flows and trapped liquidity as a result of actions taken by clients, counterparties, key financial market utilities (FMUs), and foreign supervisors, among others.*
- *Resolution Liquidity Execution Need (RLEN)*
  - *The firm should have a methodology for estimating the liquidity needed after the parent's bankruptcy filing to stabilise the surviving material entities and to allow those entities to operate post-filing. The RLEN estimate should be incorporated into the firm's governance framework to ensure that the firm files for bankruptcy in a timely way, i.e. prior to the firm's HQLA falling below the RLEN estimate.*
  - *The firm's RLEN methodology should*
    a. *Estimate the minimum operating liquidity (MOL) needed at each material entity to ensure those entities could continue to operate post-parent's bankruptcy filing and/or to support a wind-down strategy.*
    b. *Provide daily cash flow forecasts by material entity to support estimation of peak funding needs to stabilise each entity under resolution.*
  - *The peak funding needs estimates should be projected for each material entity and cover the length of time the firm expects it would take to stabilise that material entity. Inter-affiliate funding frictions should be taken into account in the estimation process.*
  - *The RLEN estimate should be tied to the firm's governance mechanisms and be incorporated into the playbooks as discussed below to assist the board of directors in taking timely resolution-related actions.*

22.3 Commonalities across Frameworks and Processes

The regulatory requirements and internal processes in Figure 22.1 require some sort of scenario analysis at their core.

The common elements of these processes are: scenarios, aggregation of exposures, incorporation of dependencies, use of models, and impact analysis via chosen metrics. Even though it may look different in this regard, RST blends in well except that the order of things is reversed – the outcome is given and one finds the events that caused it. This implies a need for two-way leveraging: RST can benefit from the existing scenario analysis infrastructure and its results can be used to generate scenarios for other exercises (e.g. ICAAP, ILAAP, FiR, IRRBB, and so on).

In addition, banks have increasingly felt the need to have consistency across the various processes and, with cost cutting pressures, to be able to do the calculation as few times as possible and use it multiple times. This has led some banks to develop a technology infrastructure that allows them to leverage calculations across several of these processes, with the intention of increasing the coverage over time.

22.4 Extended Scenario Analysis

RST provides an objective scenario selection process given the exposure and risk profile of the firm. It can be used far more extensively than currently typical. It can become a very powerful and central risk management tool if its methodology and process are extended as described in this section. We call the resulting process Extended Scenario Analysis (ESA).

Methodology extensions:
- RST includes BAU and mild stress events rather than only extreme events (the so called "Mild Reverse Stress Testing"). Extending RST to cover milder scenarios will link it more closely to regulatory/ICAAP/liquidity stress testing and covering (even milder) BAU scenarios will link it closely to financial planning.
- Instead of asking which scenarios correspond to a high-percentile loss one should ask which scenarios correspond to a selected set of values for P&L, CET1 ratio, leverage ratio, LCR, etc. The starting point of a "given loss level" is generalised to "given a set of values for chosen metrics", of which loss can be one.

The scenario is described over multiple time steps – it moves from a one-period narrative to an explicit multi-period description.

Process extensions:
- RST is subjected to similar rigorous analysis (including quantitative) and the same technological infrastructure as for regulatory or ICAAP stress tests.

- All scenarios are articulated in a standardised manner.
- A superset of metrics is chosen at the firm level and depending upon the scenario and use case, a subset of these metrics is used to describe the impacts in a standardised format.

In other words, ESA is about finding scenarios (which can be mild or extreme) that lead to a given sequence of metrics (dashboards) and about creating a database as part of the process. This is shown in Figures 22.2 and 22.5.

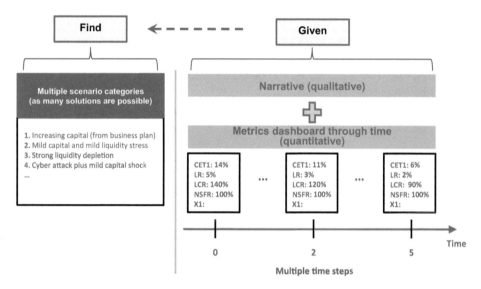

Figure 22.2: Extended Scenario Analysis (ESA).

The actual calculations are done in "direct mode" (as opposed to reverse) – i.e. many scenarios will be chosen (with judicious starting points) and then their impact (metric dashboard) will be calculated through time. In other words, the reverse problem is solved in practice by trial and error of the direct method. Broad themes are initially identified along with reasonable starting points. Then a "generalised solver" is used to find multiple solutions through an iterative process.

22.4.1 Choice and Standardisation of Metrics

The state of a firm (capital adequacy, liquidity adequacy, profitability, and so on) can be reasonably gauged by a comprehensive set of metrics. These metrics neatly fall into a handful of categories, such as capital, liquidity, profitability and asset quality. Each category generally has between three to seven metrics. Different processes – such as financial planning, stress testing and Recovery Planning – make use of several of these metrics. This is shown in Figure 22.3.

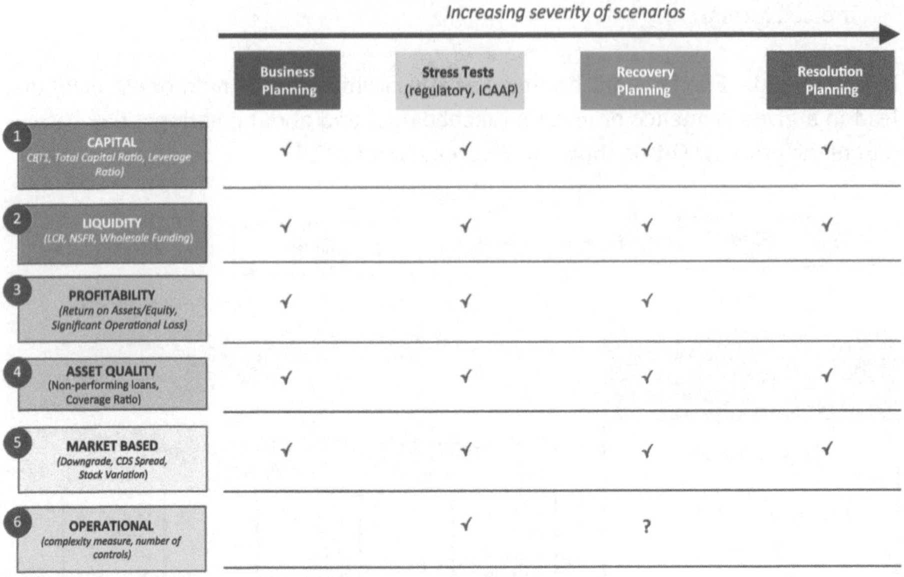

	Business Planning	Stress Tests (regulatory, ICAAP)	Recovery Planning	Resolution Planning
1 CAPITAL (CET1, Total Capital Ratio, Leverage Ratio)	✓	✓	✓	✓
2 LIQUIDITY (LCR, NSFR, Wholesale Funding)	✓	✓	✓	✓
3 PROFITABILITY (Return on Assets/Equity, Significant Operational Loss)	✓	✓	✓	
4 ASSET QUALITY (Non-performing loans, Coverage Ratio)	✓	✓	✓	✓
5 MARKET BASED (Downgrade, CDS Spread, Stock Variation)	✓	✓	✓	✓
6 OPERATIONAL (complexity measure, number of controls)		✓	?	

Increasing severity of scenarios

Figure 22.3: Firm-wide metric categories and relevance by process.

The evolution of the state of a firm whether under benign BAU conditions or under the effect of an imposed adverse scenario, is then described by the evolution of the relevant metrics. This evolution can be backward-looking or forward-looking. Two common examples where metrics are described through time are: the work of equity analysts (e.g. free cash flows from pro-forma P&L projections are used for firm valuation) or the regulatory stress testing templates (the evolution over five years of CET1 ratio under a regulatory prescribed scenario). A stylised example is shown in Figure 22.4.

22.4.2 Standardisation of Scenarios

For our purposes, a scenario describes the evolution over time of three categories of variables: macroeconomic, market and firm-specific. It is generally assumed that a firm cannot control this evolution – rather, this evolution is imposed on the firm. Under the effect of this scenario the firm evolves – in stages – as a function of its positions, risks, control infrastructure and sets of actions (taken by management over and above what would happen in BAU, i.e. management actions).

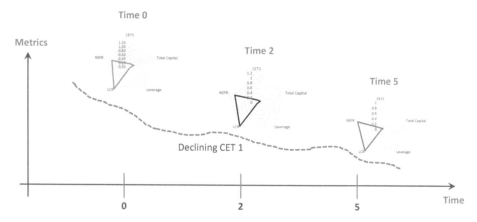

Figure 22.4: Evolution of a firm described using appropriate metrics.

The goal of classical stress testing, business planning and RRP is to describe the evolution of a firm via a comprehensive set of metrics under well-chosen or imposed scenarios.

22.4.3 Benefits of ESA

The benefits of ESA are many:
1. A scenario description is standardised (three categories and multiple time steps).
2. A comprehensive list of firm-wide metrics has been selected covering a wide range of use cases.
3. It establishes a mapping between scenarios description and its impact (measured via evolution of metrics).
4. It encourages the creation of multiple scenarios (BAU, mild, adverse, severely adverse, etc), i.e. a database of scenarios and corresponding impacts.
5. Many regulatory and internal processes (e.g. the ones described in Section 22.3) can be seen as particular cases of ESA. This leads to firm-wide consistency and better decision-making. It also leads to large cost savings as unnecessary duplication is eliminated.
6. Scenarios used for business planning and ICAAP have objective underpinnings and form part of a robust vulnerability identification process.

22.5 Database of Scenario Case Studies

Using ESA, a database of scenario case studies can be created over time. In this context, a case study includes four components:

a. A scenario narrative
b. A standardised description of the scenario using a predetermined set of variables (see Table 22.1)
c. A sequence of metrics dashboards (one for each time step) capturing evolution of the firm
d. Management actions that were taken or will be taken to move from one timestep to the next

The database is a collection of several such case studies. The actual number of scenarios will depend on the size and complexity of the firm. Typically, one would expect 10 to 30 categories of firm-wide scenarios with variations in each category. Examples of categories are: house price decline, large trading loss, large exposure default combined with a cyber attack, China recession, and so on. Certain categories may include many scenarios, e.g. market risk calculations for the trading book.

The following is a recipe for creating such a database:

We assume that the superset of metrics has been chosen and the standardisation of the scenario template has taken place.

1. Select a scenario and write a narrative – this can be a regulatory prescribed scenario. The narrative should describe the evolution over multiple time periods (e.g. what happens in the first year, between years 1 and 2, etc.).
2. Complete a standardised scenario description (see Figure 22.5). This is similar to how some regulators describe their scenarios for the annual stress tests.
3. Run the scenario. This can be done using a sophisticated tool if available (see Section 22.6) or, if unavailable, it can be done in a spreadsheet and with heavy use of expert judgement.
4. Create a metrics dashboard (for each time period, after selecting the appropriate ones from the superset).
5. Write the management actions that need to be (or were) taken. This includes playbook actions.

The scenario repository should include previous scenarios and metrics/results from:

1. Regulatory stress tests (PRA, EBA, CCAR, ...)
2. ICAAPs and ILAAPs
3. High-level or detailed scenarios used for financial planning
4. IFRS 9 macroeconomic forecasts
5. RRP, especially Recovery Planning
6. RST
7. High-level scenarios from strategy work

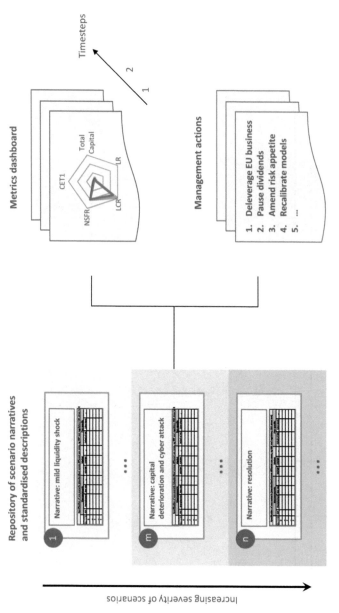

Figure 22.5: A database of scenario case studies.

Table 22.1: Standardised scenario description.

| Time | Macroeconomic | | | Market | | | Firm-specific | |
	GDP	Unemployment	Base rate	...	USD/GBP	EUR/GBP	...	Default of ABC	Cyber attack	...
0										
...										
2										
...										
5										

Specification of one scenario (standardised across different use cases, eg RRP and regulatory EBA stress test)

The main benefits of creating such a database are:
1. Easy access to a repository of case studies (some firms are unable to retrieve regulatory stress test scenarios from a few years ago)
2. Comparison across scenarios and critical review of metrics and management actions
3. Design of future scenarios for a wide variety of use cases
4. Consistency of scenarios and assumptions across use cases

Even when the database is partially complete it will help with decision-making and will allow to respond quickly to related questions from senior management and board.

As mentioned in article 85 in (European Banking Authority, 2018a): "Reverse stress testing should be useful for assessing the severity of scenarios for ICAAP and ILAAP stress tests. The severity of reverse stress testing scenarios can also be assessed by comparing it to, inter alia, historical or other supervisory and publicly available scenarios."

22.6 Example of an Extended Scenario Analysis Tool

The diagram in Figure 22.6 shows the typical set up of an ESA tool.

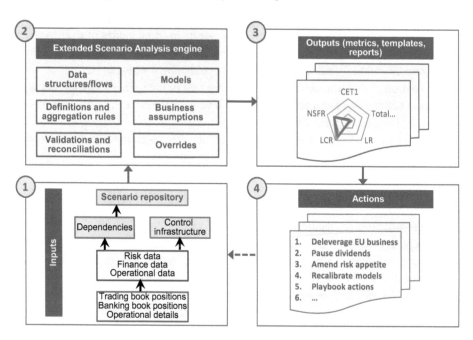

Figure 22.6: Typical extended scenario analysis tool.

The stages are:

1. The banking and trading book positions determine the credit, counterparty credit, market and liquidity risks. The operational infrastructure determines the operational risk. The dependency structure – across risk types and with certain other (e.g. finance) variables – is articulated. This information is sufficient to describe and generate scenarios (within a simulation). The control infrastructure is also taken into account, although it does not directly affect the scenario, in the sense that the impact of the scenario is calculated, where relevant, with different levels of controls. More controls lead to lower losses and such an exercise also allows to calibrate the control infrastructure, i.e. avoid excessive degree of controls. As per earlier discussion, it is of paramount importance, for the entire process to be efficient, that all scenarios are described in a standardised manner (see Figure 22.6). All components of stage 1 feed into stage 2.

2. The scenario analysis engine is essentially comprised of three parts:
   a. Models (including overrides) and business assumptions
   b. Metadata, data structures and flow, and definitions and aggregation rules, and
   c. Validations and reconciliations

3. The output of this stage is forecasted data at sufficient granularity to satisfy various regulatory and internal reporting requirements.

4. Stage 3 is where the output of the calculations is used to complete chosen regulatory and internal templates, e.g. the Bank of England STDF templates, the EBA's stress testing templates, a bespoke ICAAP template (or PRA's 111), a recovery plan template, etc. It is beneficial to produce results in three modes of risk: inherent (without the controls or management actions), with controls (but without management actions), and with controls and management actions.

5. Based on the results obtained, actions are determined. These include management actions (over and above BAU) and how to implement the certain processes via a playbook (e.g. resolution).

6. There can be a feedback loop if certain actions require changes to the assets and liabilities of the firm.

The implementation infrastructure at most European banks is often fragmented and generally has the following standalone components:
- A granular tool for regulatory stress testing
- A separate tool for ICAAP and internal stress tests, which used to be less granular than the regulatory stress tests one, but is becoming more granular as the regulatory guidance for ICAAP increases
- A third tool for RRP, much less granular than the above two, incorporating some liquidity capability and ECB mandated metrics for RRP
- A simplistic tool for RST
- A bespoke tool for liquidity stress testing

These five tools are often built on not fully aligned methodologies and take data from different sources, leading to inconsistent results which can be difficult to interpret for senior management. In addition, other typical shortcuts include qualitative estimates of financial metrics, manually run processes including "calculators/EUCs" for quantitative estimates.

To be able to properly address RRP, a tool that has been designed for regulatory capital and ICAAP stress tests will need to be extended to include liquidity metrics and liquidity stress testing. Such an integrated tool would then cover the majority of the use cases described in Section 22.3. Some further extensions are required to be able to do business planning under various scenarios. These include the inclusion of finance metrics and data, finance models (such as PPNR, PBIL), and ability to run the simulation at a less granular (i.e. more consolidated) level.

With these extensions the tool will be capable of handling regulatory stress tests, ICAAPs, liquidity stress tests, ILAAPs, Recovery Planning, resolution planning, funding in resolution and business planning. It would then be ready to be deployed in running quantitative reverse stress tests, as these require multivariate scenarios.

If a firm already had such a tool and was using it for quantitative RST, then it would be extremely useful for running FiR scenarios and see their evolution in terms of chosen metrics. In addition, such a tool will lead to significant firm-wide cost savings and consistency in results across the various scenario-based exercises.

22.7 Case Study: Funding in Resolution

The goal of this section is to describe in more detail the FiR requirements and how the ESA framework can help with the computations, MI and how the results obtained can then in turn enrich the ESA framework.

FiR is the requirement to determine the funding need, both internal and public support, that will be required by a bank in resolution (i.e. RLAP and RLEN, see Section 22.2.3). Banks must demonstrate that they have the ability to manage funding and liquidity in a resolution scenario, showing that their FiR plans are credible and have, where possible, been operationally proven ex-ante.

This links directly to the ESA framework (see Figures 22.5 and 22.10) as follows:
1. RST type analysis is required to determine scenarios that lead the firm into resolution (this is true for FiR requirements but also more widely for RRP computations, see Figures 22.7, 22.8 and 22.11). If the firm already has a database of scenarios, as described in Section 22.5, then the relevant scenarios will be available in it. In practice, these scenarios would be the same as or similar to RST scenarios reported in the ICAAP.
2. Suitable liquidity metrics need to be chosen for recovery and resolution phases (along with other metrics) and their evolution needs to be described during these

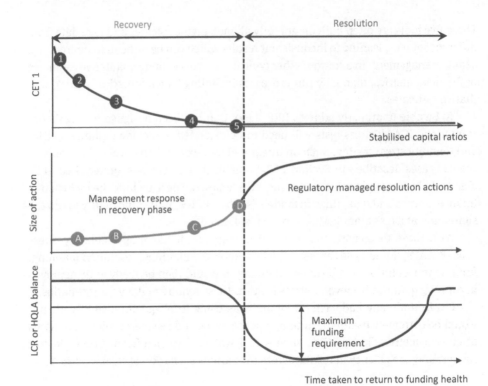

Figure 22.7: Background to FiR.

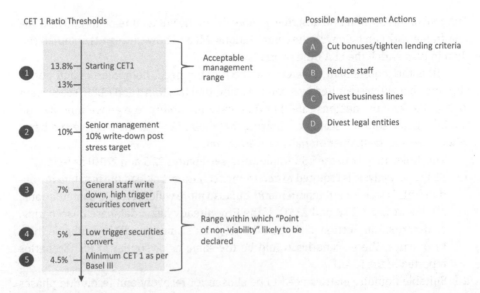

Figure 22.8: FiR scenario details.

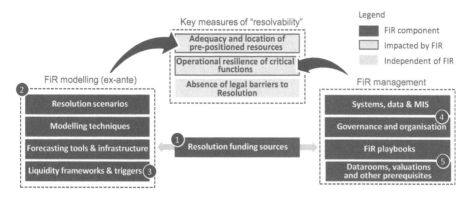

Figure 22.9: FiR framework.

two phases. For example, a daily liquidity profile, the liquidity position at the point of resolution, and so on. (See Figures 22.8, 22.12 and 22.13.)
3. Management actions through time need to be articulated that will be taken to deal with funding and liquidity shortfalls (see Figure 22.10).

The essential features of a typical dynamic leading a bank into resolution are shown in Figure 22.7.

The deterioration of CET1 ratio is shown in the top graph, and the corresponding management actions are summarised in Figure 22.8.

A robust FiR framework (See Figure 22.9) should demonstrate two elements of the resolution plan:
– The ability of the bank or relevant regulator to manage funding in resolution at each material entity
– The adequacy of pre-positioned liquidity (and capital) so that each entity remains solvent and liquid during the resolution process

The ideal FiR implementation has the following characteristics:
1. Funding sources to be used in resolution are clearly defined, with sufficient evidence of reliability having been provided.
2. Resolution forecasting capability is deployed into BAU with the regular recalculation of funding requirements based on the consideration of multiple scenarios, tailored to the bank's business model.
3. Framework and triggers are in place to adjust the pre-positioning of HQLA in response to the latest projection of resolution funding requirements.
4. Systems and processes required to measure and manage funding at "Resolution Entity" level are operational today.
5. Playbooks are in place, defining how key aspects of the resolution funding strategy will be executed with data rooms, valuations and other prerequisites for liquidating the balance sheet and moving intra-group funds as necessary.

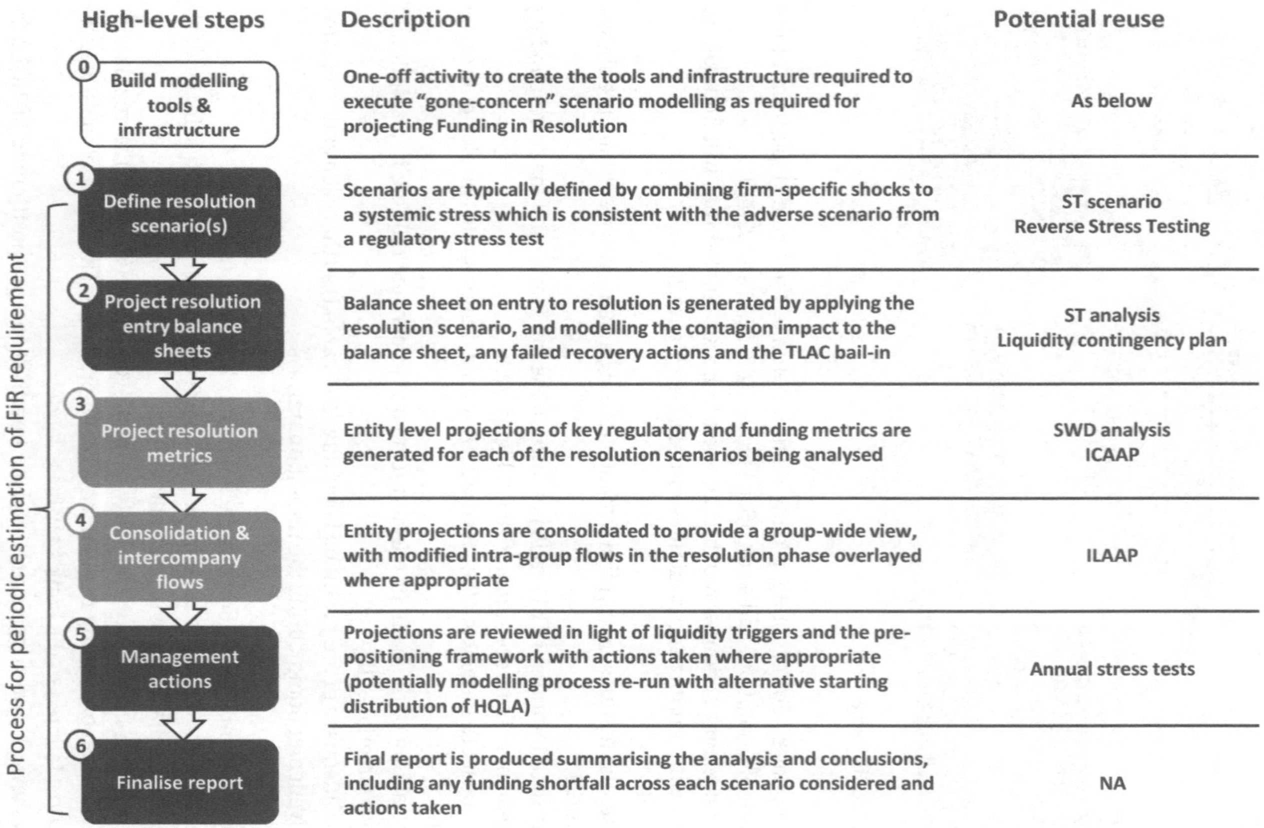

High-level steps	Description	Potential reuse
0 Build modelling tools & infrastructure	One-off activity to create the tools and infrastructure required to execute "gone-concern" scenario modelling as required for projecting Funding in Resolution	As below
1 Define resolution scenario(s)	Scenarios are typically defined by combining firm-specific shocks to a systemic stress which is consistent with the adverse scenario from a regulatory stress test	ST scenario / Reverse Stress Testing
2 Project resolution entry balance sheets	Balance sheet on entry to resolution is generated by applying the resolution scenario, and modelling the contagion impact to the balance sheet, any failed recovery actions and the TLAC bail-in	ST analysis / Liquidity contingency plan
3 Project resolution metrics	Entity level projections of key regulatory and funding metrics are generated for each of the resolution scenarios being analysed	SWD analysis / ICAAP
4 Consolidation & intercompany flows	Entity projections are consolidated to provide a group-wide view, with modified intra-group flows in the resolution phase overlayed where appropriate	ILAAP
5 Management actions	Projections are reviewed in light of liquidity triggers and the pre-positioning framework with actions taken where appropriate (potentially modelling process re-run with alternative starting distribution of HQLA)	Annual stress tests
6 Finalise report	Final report is produced summarising the analysis and conclusions, including any funding shortfall across each scenario considered and actions taken	NA

Process for periodic estimation of FiR requirement

Figure 22.10: FiR calculation steps.

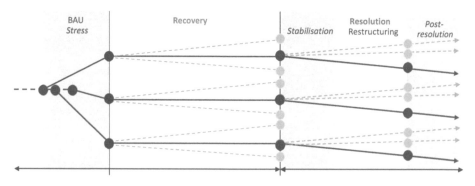

Figure 22.11: Selection of a small number of representative scenarios from a large set of possibilities.

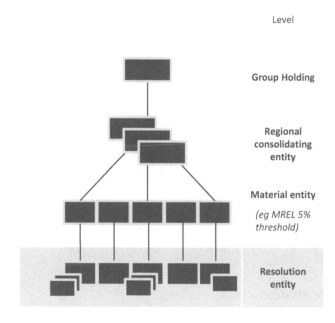

Figure 22.12: Entities to be modelled.

Once the tools and infrastructure have been created, banks need to periodically re-run the FiR modelling process so that an up-to-date view of funding require-ments in resolution can be maintained by senior management. This is described in Figure 22.10.

The process of modelling different resolution scenarios should be repeated on a regular basis in order to re-validate the robustness of the resolution plan. Although the

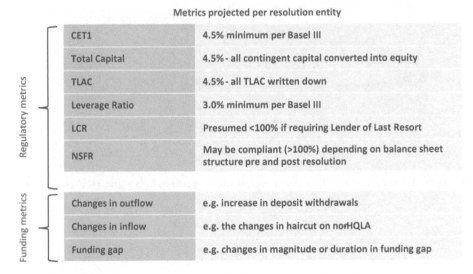

Figure 22.13: Typical metrics used in FiR.

material reuse of existing analytical processes is possible, Steps 2 and 3 in Figure 22.10 require bespoke resolution modelling tools and techniques (as the techniques used in a regulatory stress test may not be valid under more extreme conditions; furthermore, bespoke valuations/haircut estimation models are required to value portfolios that may be used as collateral for central bank funding, e.g. low LTV mortgages). Regulators now expect to see detailed evidence of this activity, therefore the final report (Step 6 in Figure 22.10) is likely to be tailored to local regulatory expectations. As with stress testing, it is likely that regulators will expect that resolution modelling forms part of strategic decision-making.

22.7.1 Choosing FiR Scenarios

Textbook FiR scenarios would be those that illustrate changes to RLAP and RLEN as the scenario evolves, finally leading the firm into resolution, and then how the liquidity resources and planning lead to a smooth restructuring. Typically, such a scenario would consider a systemic shock which is consistent with a severe adverse scenario from a regulatory stress test, plus a firm-specific shock. Multiple resolution scenarios should be considered, reflecting different firm-specific shocks originating in different areas of the firm. Existing scenarios from the database of case studies should be leveraged to inform the selection of firm-specific shocks.

Although there are multiple layers of optionality as a firm passes from BAU into resolution (see Figure 22.11), modelling should focus on a finite manageable list of scenarios which reflect the most plausible triggers of bank failure.

Examples of a severe adverse scenario are as follows:

1. For a broker dealer, trading losses (e.g. due to long positions in oil) and counterparty default combined with Covid-19
2. If exchanges are closed due to a pandemic, then positions cannot be hedged leading to further losses
3. Increasing margin calls as losses increase, depleting the firm's liquidity
4. The firm will go through the usual recovery actions, e.g. liquidation of HQLA, then collateral, restricted access to unsecured interbank funding, accessing central bank discount window, etc.

Multiple potential stress events will lead to different recovery entry points (see Figure 22.11). Theoretically, multiple paths through recovery could be modelled but a jump to resolution assumptions is likely to be more conservative. For each entry point into resolution, the optionality over what actions are taken and how will these be limited, a single central projection should be adopted leading to a single modelled resolution outcome for each stress scenario.

22.7.2 Choosing FiR Metrics and Thresholds

Section 22.2 and the Appendix provide relevant extracts of regulatory guidance on the choice and monitoring of metrics. Resolution financial modelling infrastructure and tools should be capable of producing granular daily projections at the resolution entity level for each of the scenarios being considered. Where a different resolution path is assumed for a business line within an entity, the entity should be divided into two, both for the purposes of ex-ante modelling and for ex-post reporting. These resolution paths affect all functions across risk and finance.

Appropriate metrics from the superset selected for the firm (see Figure 22.3) need to be chosen for FiR and will determine series of actions based on their values with respect to predetermined thresholds. For each resolution entity in each resolution scenario, the metrics in Figure 22.13 should be projected as a daily time-series. Regulatory metrics must be projected to identify when financial health is restored, and a restructured business could be returned to "BAU". Funding metrics must be projected to establish the peak funding requirement during the resolution phase – optimally, these would be produced by currency.

22.8 Summary

This chapter presented an extended scenario analysis framework, which generalises the thinking behind reverse stress testing. The essential features of this framework are:

1. The standardisation of scenario representation.
2. The choice of a superset of metrics that are used extensively to describe the evolution of various regulatory and internal processes such as RRP, FiR, ICAAP, regulatory stress tests.
3. The creation of a database of scenario case studies.

RRP and RST are closely linked processes and can leverage each other. Both can be seen as particular cases of ESA. RST can inform RRP/FiR in the choice and description of scenarios. With some adaptation, RRP infrastructure can be used to run quantitative implementations of RST.

This chapter used funding in resolution – the "liquidity part of RRP" – to demonstrate how RRP calculations could benefit from ESA's framework and implementation.

Bibliography

European Banking Authority (2015). EBA. Retrieved from Recovery planning. Comparative report on the approach taken on recovery plan scenarios.

European Banking Authority (2017). EBA. Retrieved from EBA recovery planning. Comparative report on recovery options.

European Banking Authority (2018a). EBA. Retrieved from Guidelines on institutions' stress testing. Final report. EBA/GL/2018/04.

European Banking Authority (2018b). EBA. Retrieved from Guidelines on the minimum list of qualitative and quantitative recovery plan indicators. Final report. EBA/GL/2015/02.

European Central Bank (2018). ECB. Retrieved from Report on recovery plans.

Federal Deposit Insurance Corporation (2017). FDIC. Retrieved from Guidance for 2017 §165(d) Annual Resolution Plan Submissions by Domestic Covered Companies that Submitted Resolution Plans in July 2015.

Financial Conduct Authority (2020). FCA. Retrieved from Reverse stress testing. SYSC 20/6, Chapter 20: https://www.handbook.fca.org.uk/handbook/SYSC/20.pdf

Financial Services Authority (2011). FSA. Retrieved from Reverse stress-testing surgeries – FAQs.

Financial Stability Board (2016). FSB. Retrieved from Guiding principles on the temporary funding needed to support the orderly resolution of a global systemically important bank ("G-SIB").

Financial Stability Board (2018). FSB. Retrieved from Funding Strategy Elements of an Implementable Resolution Plan.

The European Parliament and The Council (2014). The European Parliament and The Council. Retrieved from Directive 2014/59/EU (BRRD).

Appendix 22.1 Reverse Stress Testing

The following points are directly taken from (Financial Conduct Authority, 2020).

As part of its business planning and risk management obligations under SYSC, a firm must reverse stress test its business plan –; that is, it must carry out stress tests and scenario analyses that test its business plan to failure. To that end, the firm must:

1. *identify a range of adverse circumstances which would cause its business plan to become unviable and assess the likelihood that such events could crystallise; and*

2. *where those tests reveal a risk of business failure that is unacceptably high when considered against the firm's risk appetite or tolerance, adopt effective arrangements, processes, systems or other measures to prevent or mitigate that risk.*

Business plan failure in the context of reverse stress testing should be understood as the point at which the market loses confidence in a firm and this results in the firm no longer being able to carry out its business activities.

The following points are directly taken from (Financial Services Authority, 2011).

– *We would generally expect all firms to include a number of relevant scenarios in the submission, and larger, more complex firms to consider and submit more scenarios. Firms should undertake a filtering process, starting with a wide set of potential scenarios and narrowing these down until those that present the greatest threat to the failure of the business model are left for detailed analysis and for inclusion in the submission*

– *As a starting point, every scenario should be described in qualitative terms, with quantitative analysis where appropriate and possible*

– *Although firms should consider events that might occur at any time within a time horizon of three to five years, it may be that there is an event (or a set of events) that leads to the firm's business model failing more rapidly – e.g. discovery of a significant internal fraud event with resultant loss of market confidence*

The following points are directly taken from (European Banking Authority, 2018a).

– *Specific reverse stress testing can be also applied in the context of Recovery Planning*

– *Assess (depending on the institution's size, as well as the nature, scale, complexity and riskiness of its business activities) the likelihood of events included in the scenarios leading to the pre-defined outcome*

– *Institutions should see these reverse stress tests as an essential complement to their internal models for calculating capital requirements and as a regular risk management tool for revealing the possible inadequacies of these internal models*

– *Institutions should perform qualitative analyses in developing a well-defined narrative of the reverse stress testing and a clear understanding of its feedback and* non-linear effects, taking into account the dynamics of risk, and combinations of and interactions between and across risk types

- Institutions should perform quantitative and more sophisticated analyses, taking into account the institution's size as well as the nature, scale, complexity and risk-iness of its business activities, in setting out specific loss levels or other negative impacts on its capital, liquidity (e.g. the access to funding, in particular to increases in funding costs) or overall financial position
- Institutions should, where appropriate, use sensitivity analyses as a starting point for reverse stress testing, e.g. shifting one or more relevant parameters to some extreme to reach pre-defined outcomes. An institution should consider various reverse sensitivity analyses for credit risk (e.g. how many large customers would have to go into default before the loss absorbing capital is lost), market risk, liquidity risk
- To assess the plausibility, historical (multivariate) probability distributions – adjusted, where deemed necessary, according to expert judgements – should, inter alia, be applied.

Recovery and Resolution Planning

The following points are directly taken from (The European Parliament and The Council, 2014).

- A regime is needed to provide authorities with a credible set of tools to intervene sufficiently early and quickly in an unsound or failing institution so as to ensure the continuity of the institution's critical financial and economic functions, while min-imising the impact of an institution's failure on the economy and financial system. The regime should ensure that shareholders bear losses first and that creditors bear losses after shareholders, provided that no creditor incurs greater losses than it would have incurred if the institution had been wound up under normal insolvency proceedings in accordance with the no creditor worse off principle as specified in this Directive. New powers should enable authorities, for example, to maintain uninterrupted access to deposits and payment transactions, sell viable portions of the institution where appropriate, and apportion losses in a manner that is fair and predictable. Those objectives should help avoid destabilising financial markets and minimise the costs for taxpayers
- The ongoing review of the regulatory framework, in particular the strengthening of capital and liquidity buffers and better tools for macro-prudential policies, should reduce the likelihood of future crises and enhance the resilience of institutions to economic stress, whether caused by systemic disturbances or by events specific to the individual institution
- Authorities should take into account the nature of an institution's business, share-holding structure, legal form, risk profile, size, legal status and interconnectedness

to other institutions or to the financial system in general, the scope and complexity of its activities
- It is essential that institutions prepare and regularly update recovery plans that set out measures to be taken by those institutions for the restoration of their financial position following a significant deterioration. Such plans should be detailed and based on realistic assumptions applicable in a range of robust and severe scenarios
- Recovery and resolution plans should not assume access to extraordinary public financial support or expose taxpayers to the risk of loss
- The resolution framework should provide for timely entry into resolution before a financial institution is balance- sheet insolvent and before all equity has been fully wiped out. Resolution should be initiated when a competent authority, after consulting a resolution authority, determines that an institution is failing or likely to fail and alternative measures as specified in this Directive would prevent such a failure within a reasonable timeframe
- An effective resolution regime should minimise the costs of the resolution of a failing institution borne by the taxpayers. It should ensure that systemic institutions can be resolved without jeopardising financial stability
- Member States shall require that recovery plans include appropriate conditions and procedures to ensure the timely implementation of recovery actions as well as a wide range of recovery options. Member States shall require that recovery plans contemplate a range of scenarios of severe macroeconomic and financial stress relevant to the institution's specific conditions including system-wide events and stress specific to individual legal persons and to groups
- When assessing the appropriateness of the recovery plans, the competent authority shall take into consideration the appropriateness of the institution's capital and funding structure to the level of complexity of the organisational structure and the risk profile of the institution
- The resolution plan shall take into consideration relevant scenarios including that the event of failure may be idiosyncratic or may occur at a time of broader financial instability or system wide events.

Funding in Resolution

The following points are directly taken from (Financial Stability Board, 2016).
- Recapitalisation of a G-SIB in resolution is not, by itself, sufficient to ensure the continuity of a firm's critical functions if the firm cannot maintain access to liquidity to refinance its liabilities as they fall due. In the period following commencement of a resolution process, even a recapitalised G-SIB is likely to experience heightened liquidity needs generated by market volatility and by an asymmetry of information

regarding the firm's viability. Despite successful recapitalisation of the firm, private market participants may stand back from providing liquidity – and existing creditors may be motivated to run – if there is a lack of confidence stemming from uncertainty concerning the G-SIB's ability to meet its increased liquidity needs while in resolution

– *To satisfy the Key Attributes' objectives of conducting an orderly resolution that minimises any adverse impact on financial stability, ensures the continuity of critical functions, and avoids exposing taxpayers to loss, it follows, with respect to the matter of liquidity needs in resolution, that in resolution, a recapitalised firm's internal liquidity sources (e.g., cash and other liquid assets available for sale or use as collateral that are held by the firm) should be used to meet funding needs to the extent possible.*

New resolution planning concepts were introduced in (Federal Deposit Insurance Corporation, 2017).

– Resolution Liquidity Adequacy and Positioning (RLAP). Firms must "position" an appropriate balance of contributable and prepositioned (internal) liquidity resources during business as usual (BAU) to anticipate a stress scenario.

– Resolution Liquidity Execution Need (RLEN). When under financial stress, firms are required to make real-time projections of liquidity needs of OpCos during a resolution period. Projected liquidity resources needed at each OpCo after the BHC's bankruptcy filing to cover net liquidity outflows until liquidity levels stabilise (the "Stabilisation Date") must be sufficient to cover both: a) cumulative net outflows during period after commencement of bankruptcy or resolution proceedings (after offsetting inflows) until Stabilisation Date, and b) peak intraday liquidity needs. These projections need to be updated daily during the stress period.

The following points are directly taken from (Federal Deposit Insurance Corporation, 2017).

– *Recapitalisation of a G-SIB in resolution is not, by itself, sufficient to ensure the continuity of a firm's Resolution Liquidity Adequacy and Positioning (RLAP)*

  – *The RLAP model should cover a period of at least 30 days and reflect the idiosyncratic liquidity profile and risk of the firm. The model should balance the reduction in frictions associated with holding liquidity directly at material entities with the flexibility provided by holding HQLA at the parent available to meet unanticipated outflows at material entities. Thus, the firm should not rely exclusively on either full pre-positioning or the parent. The model should ensure that the parent holding company holds sufficient HQLA (inclusive of its deposits at the U.S. branch of the lead bank subsidiary) to cover the sum of all stand-alone material entity net liquidity deficits*

- *The stand-alone net liquidity position of each material entity (HQLA less net outflows) should be measured using the firm's internal liquidity stress test assumptions and should treat inter-affiliate exposures in the same manner as third-party exposures. For example, an overnight unsecured exposure to an affiliate should be assumed to mature*
- *Finally, the firm should not assume that a net liquidity surplus at one material entity could be moved to meet net liquidity deficits at other material entities or to augment parent resources*

- *Resolution Liquidity Execution Need (RLEN)*
  - *The firm's RLEN methodology should*
    a. *Provide a comprehensive breakout of all inter-affiliate transactions and arrangements that could impact the MOL or peak funding needs estimates, and*
    b. *Estimate the minimum amount of liquidity required at each material entity to meet the MOL and peak needs noted above, which would inform the firm's board(s) of directors of when they need to take resolution-related actions*
  - *The MOL estimates should capture material entities' intraday liquidity requirements, operating expenses, working capital needs, and inter-affiliate funding frictions to ensure that material entities could operate without disruption during the resolution.*
- *The firm's forecasts of MOL and peak funding needs should ensure that material entities could operate post-filing consistent with regulatory requirements, market expectations, and the firm's post-failure strategy. These forecasts should inform the RLEN estimate, i.e., the minimum amount of HQLA required to facilitate the execution of the firm's strategy.*

Heike Dengler

23 Reverse Stress Testing and Recovery Planning: A Conceptual Perspective

Scenario Design, Mitigating Actions and Challenges

23.1 Introduction

Regulatory requirements aim to stabilise the financial system by strengthening the balance sheet of banks and fostering a resilient environment.[1] As there are various angles pertaining to that aim, so are there various different regulatory guidelines. This chapter analyses the interplay between stress testing requirements and Recovery Planning. The former should pave the way towards a better understanding of the latter. As history – also recent history, given the effect of Covid-19 in the economy and the financial system – has proven though, imagination does not always capture the whole story. To that end, reverse stress testing has the aim to deal with the known-unknowns leading towards necessary recovery actions. This chapter assesses possible recovery actions in various stress scenarios, which would otherwise lead to a status 'fail' or 'likely to fail' as capital- and liquidity ratios are being jeopardised. It also discusses possible challenges met implementing those actions and points towards mitigation as part of the recovery plan as well as possible enhancements of the scenario landscape.

This chapter analyses the role of reverse tress testing within the banking recovery and resolution regulatory requirements. The regulatory stage is set by the following regulations:

- Directive 2013/36/EU of The European Parliament and of The Council of 26 June 2013 on access to activity of credit institutions and the prudential supervision of credit institutions and investment firms
- EBA/GL/2018/04 Guidelines on institutions' stress testing
- Directive 2014/59/EU of the European Parliament and of the council of 15 May 2014 establishing a framework for the recovery and resolution of credit institutions and investment firms
- EBA/RTS/2015/05 Regulatory technical standards on criteria for determining the Minimum Requirement for Own Funds and Eligible Liabilities under directive 2014/59/EU
- EBA/GL/2015/02 Guidelines on the Minimum List of Qualitative and Quantitative Recovery Plan Indicators

---

[1] The author would like to thank EY and in particular Dirk Brechfeld, Niklas Werner and Leonard Külpp for their support and guidance.

Note: Edited by Daniel Mayenberger

https://doi.org/10.1515/9783110647907-023

Reverse stress testing is explicitly mentioned in EBA/GL/2018/04 in order to analyse circumstances leading to a status 'fail or likely to fail' as per Art 32 of Bank Recovery and Resolution Directive (BRRD). Hence, reverse stress testing forms a risk management tool to explicitly identify and assess the scenarios including trigger events, which require the institution to take up measures to avert failing. Analysing potential recovery actions as well as feasibility, potential challenges and mitigations implementing them is a key component of the thought process.

The chapter continues with an assessment in Section 23.2, summarising remarks in 23.3 and outlook in 23.4.

As part of the assessment in 23.2, Section 23.2.1 presents the analysis and connection of the various regulatory requirements for reverse stress testing and Recovery Planning, which have been introduced in 23.1. It also touches on the role of capital- and liquidity ratios as key performance indicators (KPIs) and is the foundation for Section 23.2.2, in which possible approaches to fulfil the regulatory requirements are analysed. Section 23.2.2.1 carries forward the analysis on KPIs and presents details on their relation to minimum regulatory requirements. Section 23.2.2.2 analyses four exemplary KPIs. Section 23.2.2.4 presents and analyses various mitigation actions towards recovery, including their effect and limitations. In Section 23.2.2.5, the possible recovery paths for two exemplary crisis scenarios are analysed using the long list of recovery actions introduced in Section 23.2.2.4. The description and roll out of the crisis scenario are each followed by their impact on capital- and liquidity indicators and other impacts. Potential courses and limitations describe the impacts and well as challenges met when implementing the recovery actions during the roll out of the crisis scenario.

Finally, Section 23.3 gives a summary and Section 23.4 gives an outlook for further research.

23.2 Assessment

23.2.1 Analysis and Connection of Regulatory Requirements

The purpose of this section is to briefly explain the relation of current regulatory requirements on reverse stress tests and Recovery Planning. The analysis presented in this chapter is centred around the European Banking Authority (EBA) Guidelines on institutions' stress testing (EBA/GL/2018/04). Paragraph 88 of the EBA/GL/2018/04[2]

---

2 See (European Banking Authority, Final Report – Guidelines on institutions' stress testing, 2018), paragraph 88: "As part of their business planning and risk management, institutions should use reverse stress testing to understand the viability and sustainability of their business models and strategies, as well as to identify circumstances where they might be failing or likely to fail within the

states that the main objective of reverse stress tests is for institutions to grasp an understanding of the "viability and sustainability of their business models and strategies". This meets the stated objective in Article 32 paragraph 5 of Directive 2014/59/EU (BRRD) for institutions to "identify circumstances where they might be failing or likely to fail".

Hence, the status failing-or-likely-to-fail, or the lack of viability of the business model, should be the starting point for reverse stress testing, capital rations, liquidity ratios and positions to define key performance indicators (KPIs) in this process.[3] For a detailed assessment of "failing or likely to fail" and viability of business models, see Chapter 2.

In order to assess the capital and liquidity positions of an institution, quantitative triggers need to be defined. The obligatory ratios[4] defined by the supervisory authorities serve as one reference point. For complementary purposes, the triggers mentioned in the EBA Guidelines on minimum recovery indicators (EBA/GL/2015/02) are used in internal scenarios to gain further insight into potential weaknesses in the financial positions and/or the viability of the business model (see EBA/GL/2018/04 paragraph 96[5] regarding a better understanding and management of associated risks in

---

meaning of Article 32 of Directive 2014/59/EU. It is important that institutions identify indicators that provide alerts when a scenario turns into reality. To that end, institutions should:
1. identify the pre-defined outcome to be tested (e.g. of a business model becoming unviable);
2. identify possible adverse circumstances that would expose them to severe vulnerabilities and cause the pre-defined outcome;
3. assess (depending on the institution's size, as well as the nature, scale, complexity and riskiness of its business activities) the likelihood of events included in the scenarios leading to the pre-defined outcome; and
4. adopt effective arrangements, processes, systems or other measures to prevent or mitigate identified risks and vulnerabilities."

3 See European Banking Authority (2015b), Title II 1.14.: "For the purposes of making a determination that an institution is failing or likely to fail, in accordance with the circumstances laid down in Article 32(4)(a)-(c) of Directive 2014/59/EU, the competent authority and the resolution authority as the case may be should assess the objective elements relating to the following areas as further specified in these Guidelines:
–   the capital position of an institution;
–   the liquidity position of an institution; and
–   any other requirements for continuing authorisation (including governance arrangements and operational capacity)."

4 See (European Commission, Regulation (EU) No 575/2013 of the European Parliament and of the Council of 26 June 2013 on prudential requirements for credit institutions and in-vestment firms and amending Regulation (EU) No 648/2012 Text with EEA relevance, 2013b), (European Parliament, Directive 2013/36/EU of The European Parliament and of The Council of 26 June 2013 on access to activity of credit institutions and the prudential supervi-sion of credit institutions and investment firms, 2013) Article 128 et seq. and chapter 17.2.2.1 as well as chapter 17.2.2.2 of this article.

5 Institutions should use reverse stress testing as a tool to gather insights into scenarios that involve combinations of solvency and liquidity stresses, where traditional modelling may fail to capture

adverse conditions). Thresholds indicating a specific stress scenario should be determined[6] and institutions should utilise knowledge gained during reverse stress tests to develop, assess and calibrate "near-default" scenarios[7] and appropriate recovery actions that can be implemented upfront or during the course of a scenario leading to a status of "near default" (EBA/GL/2018/04 paragraph 100[8] and 101). This information should contribute to the Recovery Planning and include recovery triggers, recovery actions and their expected effectiveness, appropriate timing and required process as well as possible additional recovery actions, if further stress requires addressing of residual risks.[9]

Moreover, EBA/GL/2018/04 paragraph 88 (4) and paragraph 90[10] require institutions to take actions to "prevent or mitigate ... risks and vulnerabilities" identified in the reverse stress tests, especially in the case of an inconsistency with their risk appetite. Potential measures should be added to the institutions Internal Capital Adequacy Assessment Process (ICAAP) documentation. However, the supervisory authorities emphasise the importance of separate stress tests for ICAAP, Internal Liquidity

---

complex aspects from real situations. Institutions should use reverse stress testing to challenge their capital plans and liquidity plans. Where appropriate, institutions should identify and analyse situations that could aggravate a liquidity stress event and transform it into a solvency stress event, and vice versa, and eventually to a business failure. Institutions should endeavour to apply reverse stress testing in an integrated manner for risksto capital or liquidity with a view to improving the understanding and the management of related risks in extreme situations.

6 See (European Banking Authority, Final Report – Guidelines on institutions' stress testing, 2018), paragraph 88: "It is important that institutions identify indicators that provide alerts when a scenario turns into reality".

7 See (European Banking Authority, Final Report – Guidelines on institutions' stress testing, 2018), paragraph 99: "Institutions should use reverse stress testing to assist with the development, assessment and calibration of the 'near-default' scenarios used for Recovery Planning."

8 See (European Banking Authority, Final Report – Guidelines on institutions' stress testing, 2018), paragraph 100: "Institutions should use reverse stress testing to identify the risk factors and further understand and describe the scenarios that would result in 'near default', assessing effective recovery actions that can be credibly implemented, either in advance or as the risk factors or scenarios develop."

9 See (European Banking Authority, Final Report – Guidelines on institutions' stress testing, 2018), paragraph 101: "reverse stress testing should contribute to the recovery plan scenarios by using a dynamic and quantitative scenario narrative, which should cover: a) the recovery triggers (i.e. at which point the institution would enact recovery actions in the hypothetical scenario); b) the recovery actions required and their expected effectiveness, including the method of assessing that effectiveness (i.e. indicators that should be monitored to conclude that no further action is required); c) the appropriate timing and process required for those recovery actions; and d) in the case of further stress, points (b) and (c) for the potential additional recovery actions required to address residual risks."

10 See (European Banking Authority, Final Report – Guidelines on institutions' stress testing, 2018), paragraph 90: "Where reverse stress testing reveals that an institution's risk of business model failure is unacceptably high and inconsistent with its risk appetite, the institution should plan measures to prevent or mitigate such risk. ... These measures derived from reverse stress testing, including any changes to the institution's business plan, should be documented in detail in the institution's ICAAP documentation."

Adequacy Assessment Process (ILAAP) and Recovery Planning, which should then be compared against each other.[11] Furthermore, it is crucial to create a concisely formulated narrative for reverse stress testing, taking into account external exogenous events, risk factors and combinations thereof.[12]

The next section provides possible approaches of determining trigger points, scenarios and suitable recovery actions as well as an analysis of potential challenges.

23.2.2 Possible Approaches

As outlined in the introduction, the first step in reverse stress testing analysis is the definition of KPIs in mind, which indicate a status of failing or likely to fail. In order for these KPIs to fall below warning, recovery or resolution thresholds, crisis scenarios and adverse effects have to be simulated, taking into account the individual institute's risk profile and overall business model. In this chapter, we included a thorough analysis on an institute's ability to recover from two exemplary crisis scenarios (described in Section 23.2.2.5) with the help of a set of recovery options (described in Section 23.2.2.4) aimed at recovering the most important KPI dimensions capital and liquidity. These KPIs and corresponding thresholds indicating adverse stress scenarios are derived from regulatory minimum requirements (see Section 23.2.2.1) as well as from the institute-specific business model and risk profile (see Section 23.2.2.2).

23.2.2.1 Introduction into KPIs and Relation to Minimum Regulatory Requirements

The Core Equity Tier 1, Additional Tier 1 and Tier 2 Capital Requirements (Figure 23.1)[13] constitute the minimum requirements on total capital. The Capital Conservation Buffer

---

11 See (European Banking Authority, Final Report – Guidelines on institutions' stress testing, 2018), paragraph 98: "Because of the different objectives of the two sets of reverse stress tests, the stress tests for ICAAP and ILAAP purposes and Recovery Planning should not be interlinked but compared with one another."

12 See (European Banking Authority, Final Report – Guidelines on institutions' stress testing, 2018), paragraph 93: "When developing a well-defined narrative, an institution should consider external exogenous events such as economic events, an industry crash, political events, litigation cases and natural events, as well as risk factors such as operational risks, concentration and correlations, reputational risks and loss of confidence, and combinations of these events and factors."

13 See (European Commission, Regulation (EU) No 575/2013 of the European Parliament and of the Council of 26 June 2013 on prudential requirements for credit institutions and in-vestment firms and amending Regulation (EU) No 648/2012 Text with EEA relevance, 2013b) Article 92 (European Parliament, Directive 2013/36/EU of The European Parliament and of The Council of 26 June 2013 on access to activity of credit institutions and the prudential supervi-sion of credit institutions and investment firms, 2013) Article 128 et seq.

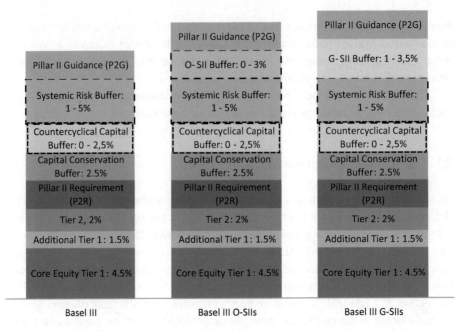

Figure 23.1: Regulatory minimum Capital Requirements.

was introduced to enhance the overall capacity of banks to absorb losses and must be met with an additional amount of Common Equity Tier 1 (CET1) capital. Besides, the countercyclical capital buffer is intended to counter pro-cyclicality in the financial system. Therefore, the buffer should account for a higher percentage during financial upturns to accumulate capital for downswings, where the buffer will be lowered.

Along with an update of the terminology, changed buffers for globally and other systemically important institutions (G-SII/ O-SII) were introduced. Both, G-SIIs and O-SIIs are institutions that, due to their systemic importance, are more likely to create risks to financial stability. "Whilst maximizing private benefits through rational decisions, these institutions may bring negative externalities into the system and contribute to market distortions".[14] However, the identification process differs in that G-SIIs are determined uniformly throughout the EU, while O-SIIs are subject to national discretion. Depending on the classification of institutions as G-SII or O-SII at consolidated or individual/sub-consolidated level, the higher of the systemic risk buffer and the G-SII/O-SII buffer applies or is cumulative.[15]

Additional capital requirements can apply as deemed necessary by EBA in terms of Article 104 (a) of Directive 2014/59/EU or resulting from the Supervisory Review and

---

14 See (European Banking Authority, Guidelines on the criteria to determine the conditions of application of Article 131(3) of Directive 2013/36/EU (CRD) in relation to the assessment of other systemically important institutions (O-SIIs), 2014a) and European Banking Authority (2020).
15 See European Parliament (2013), Article 133 (4 & 5).

Evaluation Process (SREP). The SREP was introduced on a national basis in 2004 within the framework of Basel II and uniformly implemented in the EU by 2015. Since then, the European Central Bank assesses and measures the risks for each individual bank on an annual basis and sends notices regarding respective additional requirements.[16]

The Basel III framework additionally introduces requirements on liquidity and loss absorption capacity.[17] Both play a vital role in terms of triggers and resolution actions in the context of BRRD II.[18] One of the minimum requirements regarding liquidity is the Liquidity Coverage Ratio (LCR). It is defined as the quotient of high-quality liquid assets and total net cash outflow in the next 30 days in stressed market conditions.[19] Further details about the regulatory requirements and the trigger points with regards to LCR used in the exemplary approach of this paper will be provided in Section 23.2.2.3 of this chapter.

Figure 23.2 gives an overview of the interconnectedness of the various regulatory requirements within the context of the SREP.[20]

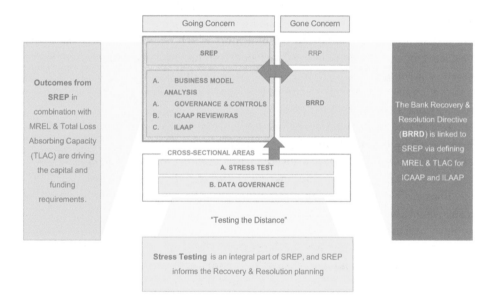

Figure 23.2: Overview of regulatory requirements within the context of SREP.

The regulatory requirements for capital and liquidity not only serve as a minimum value to be complied with, but also serve as a starting point for the alignment of indi-

---

16 See European Central Bank (2017).
17 See Basel Committee on Banking Supervision (2013).
18 See European Parliament (2014).
19 See European Commission (2013a).
20 See European Banking Authority (2014b).

cators based on them to assess performance and/or resistance to adverse business situations. The indicators are purposefully integrated into bank management so that they can have a certain signal effect on senior management depending on their design and connection to the corresponding governance processes. In order to do justice to this signal effect before a crisis scenario actually strikes and to trigger a timely escalation, the indicators are to be monitored within the scope of risk management at an appropriate frequency (liquidity indicators usually daily, others usually monthly/quarterly). In doing so, defined indicator clusters have to be used in certain phases of the business cycle (see Figure 23.3).

In the business as usual phase, a wide variety of indicators are used to assess performance and for general risk management purposes. In crisis phases, however, indicators for the assessment of the business cycle are primarily considered, which indicate the point in time of the transition from business as usual to the early warning phase and from the early warning phase to the recovery phase. A further deterioration would lead to the final stage of resolution. For an overall assessment of the prevailing risk situation of an institution, so-called early warning and recovery trigger levels are defined for a broad bandwidth of indicators which reflect the main risks of the respective business model (in the dimensions capital, liquidity, earnings, quality of assets, market and macro-economy).[21] The EBA Guidelines EBA/GL/2015/02 contain a minimum list of indicators institutes are expected to implement in their respective recovery plans (see Section 23.2.2.2).

A breach of the early warning or recovery threshold of an indicator, which usually have a sufficient control buffer above the regulatory minimum requirements (if available for this category), leads to a governance escalation process specified in the institute's recovery plan which is interlinked with the usual business processes.

In case of falling short of an early warning threshold, an immediate escalation to a specified circle of addressees will take place and, if deemed necessary, purposeful counter measures will be prepared.

If there is a further undercut of the recovery threshold, an immediate escalation to a specific internal and external circle of addressees (including the supervisory authorities) occurs, decision templates for suitable options of action will be prepared and, if deemed necessary, the implementation of these will be resolved by the management board.

It is possible that after a corresponding escalation in the recovery phase and the subsequent implementation of options for action, the viability is not sustainably restored. Furthermore, the indicators (capital and liquidity) relevant to the recovery plan may fall below the regulatory minimum requirements. In this event, an order by the supervisory authorities to resolve the institution is to be expected.

---

21 See European Banking Authority (2015c).

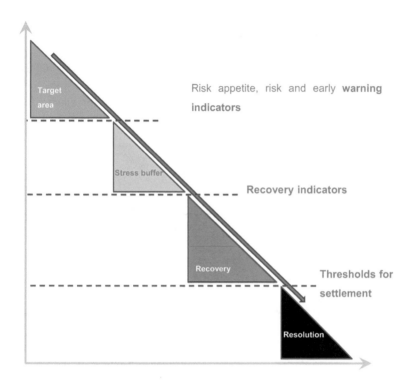

Risk appetite, risk and early **warning** **indicators**

Recovery indicators

Thresholds for settlement

Existing indicators, which are defined for risk management.

Quantitative definition of the point in time, across various categories (capital, liquidity, credit and market risk), at which options for action should be initiated. About a dozen recovery indicators suffice.

Quantitative definition of the point in time at which the supervisory authorities would take over the bank, i.e. wind up. One threshold value each for capital and liquidity.

Figure 23.3: Indicators in different phases of the business development.

23.2.2.2 European Banking Authority KPIs

The European Banking Authority (EBA) published a guideline (EBA/GL/2015/02) containing a minimum list of indicators to be implemented in recovery plans. Each indicator is subject to the possibility for an institution to justify that it is not relevant for it, however in such a case it should be substituted with another indicator which is more relevant for this institution. Please see Table 23.1 for a minimum list of KPIs.

Table 23.1: Minimum list of recovery plan indicators as defined by EBA.

1. Capital indicators	2. Liquidity indicators
a) Common Equity Tier 1 ratio	a) Liquidity Coverage Ratio
b) Total Capital ratio	b) Net Stable Funding Ratio
c) Leverage ratio	c) Cost of wholesale funding
3. Profitability indicators	**4. Asset quality indicators**
a) (Return on Assets) or (Return on Equity)	a) Growth rate of gross non-performing loans
b) Significant operational losses	b) Coverage ratio [Provisions/(Total non-performing loans)]
5. Market-based indicators	**6. Macroeconomic indicators**
a) Rating under negative review or rating downgrade	a) GDP variations
b) CDS spread	b) CDS of sovereigns
c) Stock price variation	

Source: See European Banking Authority (2015c) Annex II.

In the following, three of those KPIs, namely CET1, LCR and the Cost of wholesale funding, will be analysed in more detail. Additionally, the capital KPI Minimum Requirement for Own Funds and Eligible Liabilities (MREL) will be discussed.

23.2.2.2.1 Common Equity Tier 1 Ratio

For a general composition of the thresholds of the indicators, see Section 23.2.2.1. As an assumption for recovery and early warning thresholds for the normative capital requirements, in the subsequent examples, an average SREP score as defined by the supervisory authority as well as average values for further institute specific capital buffers not included in the SREP score are presumed. These specific buffers are the capital buffer for other systemically important institutes (O-SII-Buffer) in accordance with § 10g paragraph 1 KWG and the institute-specific countercyclical buffers laid down in § 10d KWG.

When deriving the respective thresholds, the following requirements concerning the common equity will be assumed:
- "Pillar 1 minimum requirements" of 4.5%
- "Pillar 2 requirement" of 2.1%[22]
- Capital buffer for other systemically important institutes of 1.1% (including the systemic risk buffer)[23]
- Countercyclical buffer of 0%[24]
- "Pillar 2 Guidance" of 1.5%[25]

Institutes would in practice include a "management buffer" on top of these minimum requirements and set the recovery point for the CET1 ratio to ~10.5%. The early warning threshold would likely be set above the total requirements to an amount of ~13%.

23.2.2.3 Liquidity Coverage Ratio

Since 2018, institutions have to comply with the supervisory minimum requirements of an LCR of 100%. In case of a short fall, organisations are obliged to send daily reports regarding the LCR to the supervisory authority. Additionally, a plan of action for returning to compliance with the LCR has to be coordinated with the supervisory authority.

For the exemplary approach, the recovery triggers as well as the early warning threshold for the LCR will be chosen as follows:

Institutes would in practice include a "management buffer" on top of these minimum requirements and set the recovery point for the LCR to ~102.5%. The early warning threshold would likely be set above the total requirements to an amount of ~110%. The calibration of the LCR thresholds is usually based on an institution's internal risk management.

23.2.2.3.1 Cost of Wholesale Funding

Wholesale funding constitutes a fundamental way for banks to ensure liquidity and conduct business. This can either take the form of unsecured or secured borrowing. During individual or systemic crisis though, banks might have trouble to attain funding via secured borrowing in the repo market and even more so in the inter-banking unsecured money market.

---

22 See (European Central Bank, Supervisory review (SREP) – Aggregate SREP outcome for 2019, 2020).
23 See (BaFin, Other systemically important institutions (O-SII), 2020b).
24 See (BaFin, Countercyclical capital buffer, 2020a).
25 See European Central Bank (2020).

Academic research indicates this risk as a crucial constituent for the severity of the financial crisis in 2008/2009.[26]

Therefore, the regulatory authorities included the cost of wholesale funding as a vital part of recovery plans to indicate, whenever actions concerning liquidity might be required.[27] However, these costs will depend on the institute-specific situation with regards to risk, capital and liquidity, among other things. Hence, there are no concrete regulatory requirements, that the early warning and recovery point could be based on and every institution will define their own thresholds.

23.2.2.3.2 Minimum Requirement for Own Funds and Eligible Liabilities

After the introduction in Article 45 of Directive 2014/59/EU to provide a risk measure independent from the Risk-Weighted Assets (RWA) calculation, the EBA has published guidelines regarding the calculation of MREL. These Minimum Requirements on Eligible Liabilities (MREL) serve to safeguard the institution's resolvability and make sure the institution holds enough bail-in able capital for this case. They are calculated as the amount of own funds and eligible liabilities expressed as a percentage of the total liabilities and own funds of the institution. Whilst the ratio is determined for each institute individually, the initial assumption in the BRRD is 10%.[28] The respective thresholds for risk control have to be appropriately defined by the institutes. According to the institution's notification by the supervisory authority, the minimum requirement of the MREL-ratio ranges between 6% and 10%.

In order to conduct reverse stress testing, firstly, the guiding KPIs have to be set. Secondly, a scenario possibly leading towards manifestation in those KPIs has to be determined. Thirdly, viable recovery actions have to be analysed. Sections 23.2.2.5.1 and 23.2.2.5.2 will deal with each step subsequently.

23.2.2.4 Mitigation Actions towards Recovery

In order to get a general idea of potential recovery actions, that is mitigation actions towards recovery, this chapter provides a summary of possible courses of action. In the course of the drafting of recovery plans institutions prepare recovery options aiming at averting the stage of "likely to fail and/or failing" in times of stress. These options are strongly dependent on the business model, risk profile and size of an institution. In the context of the analysis which recovery options are most likely to improve the capital or liquidity situation, institutions, in a first step, create a long list with potential recovery options. This list contains potential recovery options which

---

26 See Huang and Ratnovski (2011).
27 See European Banking Authority (2015c).
28 See European Banking Authority (2015a) Chapter 2.2.

would in general be suitable to recover an institution from capital and/or liquidity stress. From this base of potential recovery options, in a second step, the institution defines its most suitable options for implementation in times of stress which culminate in a recovery option short list. As no crisis scenario is foreseeable in its dimensions and characteristics but institutions need an indication whether they can successfully implement these measures, the recovery options are analysed in detail regarding their feasibility and impact in the general crisis categories system-wide and idiosyncratic as well as in a combination of both. In order to estimate the successful impact on the financial situation, all potential execution burdens and limitations are evaluated and – if possible – anticipated with additional preparation measures to ensure a successful execution when needed.

Though the catalogue in Table 23.2 is not exhaustive, it will suffice as basis for the analysis of scenarios in the following section. In this assessment, suitable measures for each individual scenario will be discussed. For individual institutions the likelihood of successful mitigation using each measure will differ.

Table 23.2: Catalogue of possible recovery actions.

Name of the measure	Description and effect
Capital recovery options	
Suspension of dividend payments	The reorganisation measure "Suspension of dividend payments" controls the payment of dividends. It thus increases the leeway for allocating reserves. It is also intended to contribute to an improvement in the CET1 ratio and risk-bearing capacity. Effect: – Improving the CET1 ratio – Improvement in risk-bearing capacity Limitations: – Positive annual surplus required – Shareholder meeting needs to approve of this option – Time from implementation to impact can be long depending on business year-end
Utilisation of credit enhancement and guarantees	The reorganisation measure "Utilisation of securities and guarantees" is aimed at the utilisation of provided securities and guarantees which have been issued in view of possible crises. Effect: – Improvement of the capital situation – Improvement of the liquidity situation Limitations: – Guarantee provider needs to be recognised as independent from the affected institute

Table 23.2 (continued)

Name of the measure	Description and effect
Increase in share capital	The reorganisation measure "increase in share capital" provides for an increase in the credit institution's share capital. This can be done by means of cash contributions as well as contributions in kind. The increase in capital can be carried out from among the existing owners or by taking on new owners. Effect: – Improvement of the risk-bearing capacity – Improvement in the CET1 ratio – Improvement of the liquidity situation Limitations: – Willingness and ability of potential investors
Restructuring of equity instruments	This recovery option provides for the conversion of equity instruments in order to be able to include them in CET1 in accordance with the requirements of the Capital Requirements Directive IV (CRD IV). Effect: – Improvement of the CET1 ratio Limitations: – Legal aspects of underlying instrument
Sale or securitisation of corporate loans	The recovery option provides for the sale of corporate loans in the bank's portfolio or their securitisation to reduce RWA and thus increase the CET1 ratio. Effect: – Improvement of the CET1 ratio – Acceptance of the RWA Limitations: – Legal burdens – Market conditions for successful sale/securitisation
Sale of subsidiaries	The reorganisation measure "Sale of subsidiaries" is intended to sell subsidiaries in order to support liquidity and capital positions. Realised hidden reserves can improve the liquidity position while the reduction in RWA by selling the subsidiary improves the capital situation. Effect: – Improvement of the capital situation – Acceptance of the RWA – Improvement of the liquidity situation Limitations: – Negative reputational effects – Strategic disadvantages – Timeframe

Table 23.2 (continued)

Name of the measure	Description and effect
Liquidity recovery options	
Discount window/ marginal lending facility	This measure provides the opportunity of short-term/overnight borrowing from a central bank against the presentation of eligible assets, in order to meet temporary liquidity shortages. The central bank can also function as a lender of last resort, borrowing money without eligible assets. Effect: − Improvement of the liquidity situation Limitations: − Availability of eligible assets − Negative reputational effects (for unsecured lending) − Confidentiality often impaired
Borrowing in inter-banking repo-market	This measure provides the opportunity of weekly borrowing (Main Refinancing Operation) from the European Central Bank against the presentation of eligible assets or balances on national bank accounts, in order to meet liquidity demands. Furthermore, money can be borrowed from the interbank market. Effect: − Improvement of the liquidity situation Limitations: − Availability of eligible assets − High borrowing costs for institutes under stress
Acquisition of customer deposits	This recovery option is aimed at attracting additional time deposits, which are preferably provided by institutional customers in sufficient amounts for a minimum period of 30 days. Effect: − Improvement of the liquidity situation Limitations: − Willingness and ability of customers depends on market conditions and offered rate
Sale of trading portfolios	The reorganisation measure "sale of trading portfolios" is aimed at the sale of the highly liquid securities held by a credit institution. This measure is intended to reduce risk positions and have a positive effect on core capital and risk coverage potential. Effect: − Improvement of the liquidity situation − Acceptance of the RWA − Increase in risk-bearing capacity Limitations: − Forfeit of future revenue − Limits ability to encumber assets for drawing liquidity − Ability to place in market

Table 23.2 (continued)

Name of the measure	Description and effect
Emission of structured covered bonds	The purpose of the measure is to issue covered bonds in times of crisis. The aim is to generate liquidity. Effect: – Improvement of the liquidity situation – Increase in risk-bearing capacity Limitations: – Experience and market knowledge required

The following subsections describe exemplary crisis scenarios which impact capital and/or liquidity KPIs as well as the successful and goal-orientated implementation of recovery actions to cope with near-default situations.

23.2.2.5 Crisis Scenarios

The focus of this section are possible recovery paths for two exemplary stress scenarios using the long list of recovery actions introduced in Section 23.2.2.4.

Any crisis scenario will evoke a broad bandwidth of possible effects that will negatively affect capital and/or liquidity KPIs. When creating a reverse near-default scenario, institutes focus on KPIs and related stress events most important regarding their business model and create the reverse scenario accordingly. Table 23.3 lists example events derived from the EBA guidelines on the range of scenarios to be used in recovery plans (EBA/GL/2014/06) that banks incorporate in their stress scenarios for the purpose of reverse stress testing.

Table 23.3: Examples of events and their impact on capital/liquidity KPIs.

Events with primary impact on capital KPI	Events with primary impact on liquidity KPI
– Default of significant counterparties – Macroeconomic downturn – Severe credit losses – Adverse development in the prices of assets	– Significant liquidity outflows (e.g. Bank run) – Severe operational risk losses – Decrease in liquidity available in the interbank lending market – Damage to the reputation of the institute or group

The most recent experience of a real-life stress scenario, namely the Covid-19 pandemic, illustrates that a stress scenario might incorporate various events – in this example, economic downturn, adverse development of prices of assets and significant liquidity outflows, just to name a few.

In order to portray the effects on the capital and liquidity position of an institute and the mitigating effects of countermeasures, we cover two specific crisis scenarios: one system-wide and one idiosyncratic.

23.2.2.5.1 System-Wide Crisis Scenario

In this section, the example of a market-wide scenario 'financial crisis' will be further analysed. This scenario would result in jeopardising the capital KPIs.

The 'financial crisis' constitutes a fast-acting and market-wide stress scenario. In analogy to the financial crisis of 2008/2009, the cause of the scenario is a default of a systemically important bank as well as a massive price correction of the Asset-Backed Security (ABS) markets. The crisis concerns the full global financial industry: Firstly, it strikes banks with a business model grounded on the structuring of securitisation as well as banks, that refinance very short-term on the interbank market. Secondly, it also hits banks, that invested in ABS.

In the short term, the crisis goes along with strong overreactions at the money- and capital markets. This leads to a gradual deterioration of the performance of banks and organisations and as a consequence to a dramatic global recession.

The significant risk drivers identified are the market risk and credit risk.

Phase 1

The initial situation can be described as such: Immediately after the default of a systematically important counterparty is announced, there is major market turbulence. Exaggerations on the bond markets lead to a massive widening of credit spreads and correspondingly to substantial valuation losses. The bank has comprehensive direct write-downs on positions with the failed bank as counterparty which puts pressure on its capital indicators.

Phase 2

During phase two, the scenario develops further. The continuing strong uncertainty leads to a worsening of the crisis, which now reaches its peak. Fixed income and ABS markets are at their lowest point. Refinancing bottlenecks occur due to the loss of confidence in the interbank lending market accompanied by substantial losses, particularly in receivables from banks and in the securitisation portfolios. Central banks decide on systematic countermeasures in the form of falling policy rates and the provision of short-term central bank money in unlimited amounts from quarter two onwards. The greatest effect comes from a suffering of massive valuation losses as well as considerable value adjustment requirements in the securities portfolios.

Phase 3

In the course of phase 3, the scenario develops as follows. Severe recession hits all industrialised countries accompanied by rising corporate insolvencies and increasing credit defaults, rising national debt and high uncertainty among companies. In order to combat the crisis, government economic stimulus programmes to stabilise the economic situation are introduced. Additionally, central banks decide on further interest rate cuts. However, economic stimulus programmes remain ineffective and the global recession deepens. This represents the climax of the crisis in the real economy. Write-downs on the carrying amounts of investments due to market value losses are still required. Furthermore, the bank records a significant decline in new business. The impact of the scenario before recovery actions on the capital indicators is shown in Figure 23.4.

		Phase 1		Phase 2		Phase 3	
Indicators	Core Tier 1 Ratio						
	Core Capital Ratio						
	Total Capital Ratio						
Overall status		Yellow	Yellow	Red	Red	Red	Red

Figure 23.4: Indicator levels according to the gross progress of the system-wide stress scenario.

Impact on Capital Indicators

As a consequence of the crisis, all capital reference numbers deteriorate rapidly, with the result that the rating indicators "CET1 ratio", "core capital ratio" and "total capital ratio" reach "yellow" status at the end of the first month and "red" status at the end of the first quarter. The deteriorating risk factors of credit risk and market price risk during the crisis have led to a drastic increase in the capital requirement for both risk types. Early warning indicators pre-empt the deteriorating prior.

Impact on Liquidity Indicators

The liquidity situation worsens noticeably in the course of the scenario, but the "LCR" indicator never breaches the early warning or recovery threshold in the overall course of the scenario. The "Cost of wholesale funding" increases, but it never reaches a critical point, where wholesale funding might not be feasible anymore.

Other Effects

Due to substantial credit defaults and significant valuation losses, particularly in the ABS portfolios, profitability has deteriorated massively. Combined with substantial stress effects on commission income and net income from investments, this results in huge losses in the after-tax result at the end of the scenario year.

Potential Courses of Action and Limitations

Since the effects of the scenario are mainly on the capital indicators and the recovery threshold for the "CET1 ratio", "core capital ratio" and "total capital ratio" is torn down in the short term, options for action are required which specifically improve these ratios. Before examining these in detail in the following paragraph, Figure 23.5 gives an overview over potential progresses of the scenario. It portrays possible developments of the capital position and indicates the points in time when suitable actions should be implemented.

Scenario-Specific Shortlist of Recovery Actions

Due to the impact on the ABS market, individual options for action are not applicable. Because of the market situation, a sale of the ABS portfolio would require high discounts on the selling price or would make them completely impossible. Hence, the application of it will be foregone in the scenario. Furthermore, the reduction of trading portfolios/business activities will be waived. Other own contribution measures are possible without restriction.

Scenario-Specific Effect of Recovery Actions

Particularly in the case of sales of subsidiaries and real estate, it can be assumed that in the event of a market-wide crisis situation, valuations and thus sales prices will fall. However, the extent to which the crisis affects individual institutions varies, so that asset managers and insurance companies in the group are less affected by potential losses of confidence than banks. Specific discounts are therefore taken into account in the scenario-specific stress values of the options for action, in particular the possible complete sale of subsidiaries and the sale of real estate. Other options (in particular other capital and liquidity measures) are not affected in their effect by the market-wide crisis.

Phase 1

In this phase, measures are mainly concerned with governance and communication. Immediately after the default of the globally systemically important bank has become known and the market distortions that are about to occur have become apparent, the situation is evaluated and a task force to manage the crisis is appointed. At this point, no further measures deem necessary.

Phase 2

When the recovery threshold of an indicator is fallen short of for the first time, the indicators are examined and far-reaching measures with a rapid effect as well as those requiring more time and/or preparation are taken. New business is reduced to the full extent compared to operational planning. Furthermore, the bank begins to

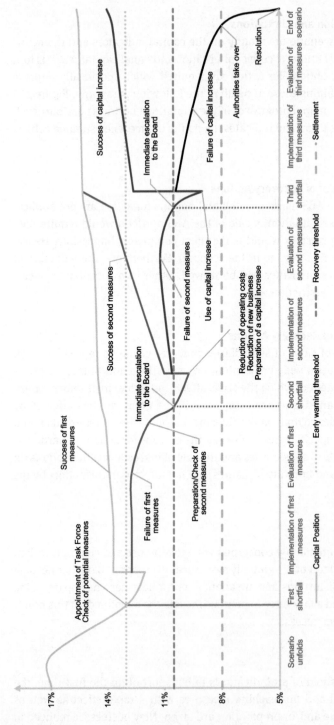

Figure 23.5: Timeline of the capital position and respective actions.

reduce operating costs with short-term effect. Because of necessary preparation the effect remains low throughout the first quarter and does not unfold considerably until the second quarter. Besides, a capital increase is prepared (effective from the end of quarter three at the earliest). Prior, the feasibility of that option has to be investigated thoroughly. The additional reputational risk of an unsuccessful capital increase must be added onto the possible lack of proceeds.

Phase 3
Due to the bank's improving situation, which is clearly reflected in the recovery indicators, no further recovery options are seen as necessary. All temporarily possible measures implemented to date will remain in effect until the end of the year. The cost measures and new business reductions will therefore have a full impact. However, as a result of the worsening crisis and fear of potential adverse effects on the capital position of the bank the prepared guarantees and capital increase will still be implemented.

After the options for action have been applied, a burden analysis is performed to prove that the affected indicators have returned to the target range and a stable financial position has been restored on a sustainable basis.

The impact of the possible courses of action on the capital indicators is shown in Figure 23.6.

Indicators		Phase 1		Phase 2		Phase 3	
	Core Tier 1 Ratio						
	Core Capital Ratio						
	Total Capital Ratio						
Overall status		Yellow	Yellow	Red	Red	Yellow	Green

Figure 23.6: Impact of possible courses of action on the indicators in the system-wide stress scenario.

23.2.2.5.2 Idiosyncratic Crisis Scenario
In this section the institute-specific scenario "Hacker Attack" will be further assessed. This scenario would result in jeopardising the liquidity as well as capital KPIs.

The "Hacker Attack" constitutes a fast-acting and institute specific scenario. A criminal organisation infiltrates the institute's payment system, manipulates the monetary transactions of the bank and publishes confidential customer data. This leads to huge cash outflows and a damaged reputation.

The impact of the scenario before recovery actions on the indicators is shown in Figure 23.7.

		Phase 1		Phase 2		Phase 3	
Indicators	Cost of wholesale funding						
	Liquidity Coverage Ratio						
Overall status		Red	Red	Red	Red	Red	Red

Figure 23.7: Indicator levels according to the gross progress of the idiosyncratic stress scenario.

Impact on Liquidity Indicators

The liquidity situation is under severe stress after the massive outflow of cash payments and the resulting reputational damage the institute suffers as a result. The "Cost of wholesale funding" indicator reaches "yellow" and the "LCR" reaches "red" status within the first week.

Impact on Capital Indicators

As a consequence of the huge liquidity losses due to the hacker attack, all capital reference numbers crash as well, with the result that the rating indicators "CET1 ratio", "core capital ratio" and "total capital ratio" reach "red" status within the first week. Recovery measures in this idiosyncratic scenario will focus on the improvement of the liquidity situation and consequently also improve capital ratios. In order to recover the capital indicators to the full extent in the target zone, distinctive capital recovery options can be implemented as well.

Other Effects

Due to the massive operational risk losses caused by the hacker attack, the scenario results in a significant annual loss. The fact that the institution became the target of such a massive hacker attack also leads to a massive loss of reputation among all customer groups, which has an additional negative impact on the earnings situation. Only after a targeted communication strategy has been put in place to provide transparent information, will the reputation of the institute slowly improve again.

Potential Courses of Action and Limitations

Since the effects of the scenario are massive on the liquidity indicators as well as on the capital indicators and thus the recovery threshold for "LCR", "CET1 ratio", "core capital ratio" and "total capital ratio" is torn down in the short term, options for action are required which specifically improve these ratios. With regards to liquidity various measures must be considered. Figure 23.8 portrays possible developments of the liquidity position and indicates the points in time, where suitable actions should be implemented.

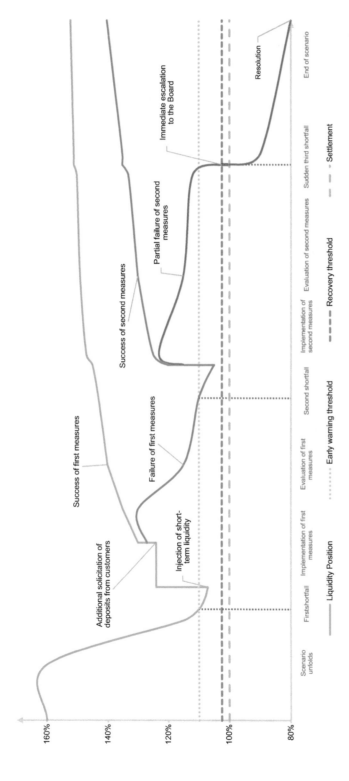

Figure 23.8: Timeline of the liquidity position and respective actions.

Scenario-Specific Shortlist of Recovery Actions

Due to the direct impact on some subsidiaries, certain options for action are not applicable. It can be assumed that the subsidiaries that are strongly affected by the hacker attack are not saleable in this scenario, or that the sale is economically extremely unattractive. However, it is presumed that, due to the unchanged market situation, the reduction of business activities and the external sales of the remaining subsidiaries are possible.

Scenario-Specific Effect of Recovery Actions

It is estimated that the effectiveness of most of the options on the shortlist will not be reduced due to the unchanged market situation. Only in the case of the sale of subsidiaries is it assumed that a discount on the calculated effect must normally be expected due to the damage to the Group's reputation and a lower interest of potential buyers.

Phase 1

Immediately after the hacker attack is, the situation is evaluated and a task force to manage the crisis is appointed. The overall damage of the attack is assessable within the first week, it becomes apparent, that far-reaching recovery options have to be taken. Firstly, there is a reduction of new business to the full extent compared to operational planning. Secondly, the bank starts to reduce operating costs with short-term effect from quarter one, even though this action is limited due to measures to increase IT-security. Thirdly, a sale of the ABS portfolio is prepared, which will impact the capital indicators from the first month on. Additionally, short-term liquidity is provided through the mobilisation of counterbalancing capacity. With a view to the capital indicators, a capital increase (effective from quarter 3 at the earliest) is prepared.

Phase 2

The hacker attack is under control, but still further measures have to be taken to increase the capital and liquidity situation. Therefore, the bank injects short-term liquidity through further mobilisation of counterbalancing capacity and acquisition of deposits.

In addition, the bank starts a sale of the ABS portfolio with an impact on the capital and liquidity indicators at the end of the first quarter.

Phase 3

Due to the bank's improving situation, which is clearly reflected in the indicators, no further recovery options are seen as necessary. All temporarily possible measures implemented to date will remain in effect until the end of the year. The cost measures and new business reductions will therefore have a full impact. However, the prepared capital increase will still be implemented at the end of the third quarter to further ease the situation.

After the options for action have been applied, a burden analysis is performed to prove that the affected indicators have returned to the target range and a stable financial position has been restored on a sustainable basis.

The impact of the possible courses of action on the indicators is shown in Figure 23.9.

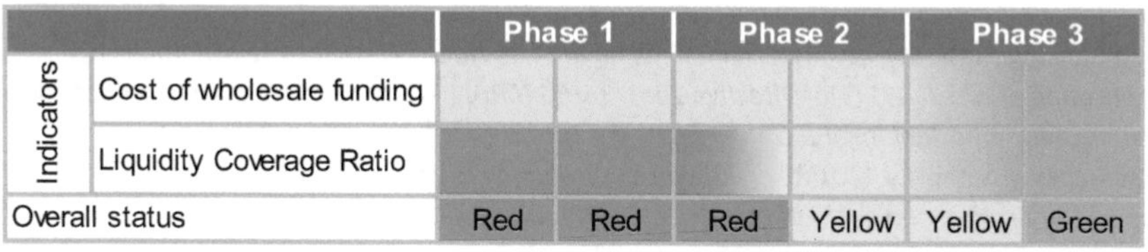

		Phase 1		Phase 2		Phase 3	
Indicators	Cost of wholesale funding						
	Liquidity Coverage Ratio						
Overall status		Red	Red	Red	Yellow	Yellow	Green

Figure 23.9: Impact of possible courses of action on the indicators in the idiosyncratic stress scenario.

23.3 Summary

In the understanding of and dealing with banking recovery in times of stress, it is important to have a sound process ready to be out of the gate when needed. A long list of possible and proven actions is important to that end. The long list has to be updated regularly, including additional experiences. One needs to be prepared for second-round effects and necessary additional recovery actions. Readiness crucially depends on the imagination regarding reverse stress scenarios. Banks can only prepare for specific scenarios.

23.4 Outlook

When compiling the narrative for a reverse stress test, the natural limit of imagination is shaped by one's experiences. Artificial intelligence in the form of both supervise and unsupervised learning might be able to point towards yet unknown drivers for risk factors. The limiting factor is the existence of biases as discussed in Chapter 14 when designing and coding the algorithm. These biases derive – yet again – from one's experience. It might be in the nature of things, that the unknown unknowns become known unknowns if and only if they have entered our knowledge via experience. This should not, however, stop us from extending the frontier of knowledge.

Bibliography

BaFin. (2020a). *Countercyclical capital buffer*. Retrieved April 17, 2020, from https://www.bafin. de/EN/Aufsicht/BankenFinanzdienstleister/Eigenmittelanforderungen/Kapitalpuffer/ antizyklischer_kapitalpuffer_node_en.html

BaFin. (2020b). *Other systemically important institutions (O-SII)*. Retrieved April 17, 2020, from https://www.bafin.de/EN/Aufsicht/BankenFinanzdienstleister/Eigenmittelanforderungen/ ASRI/asri_node_en.html

Basel Committee on Banking Supervision. (2013). *Basel III: The Liquidity Coverage Ratio and liquidity risk monitoring tools*. Bank for International Settlements.

European Banking Authority. (2014a). *Guidelines on the criteria to determine the conditions of application of Article 131 (3)of Directive 2013/36/EU (CRD) in relation to the assessment of other systemically important institutions (O-SIIs)*. EBA/GL/2014/10.

European Banking Authority. (2014b). *Guidelines on common procedures and methodologies for the supervisory review and evaluation process (SREP)*. EBA/GL/2014/13.

European Banking Authority. (2015a). *EBA final draft regulatory technical standards on criteria for determining the Minimum Requirement for Own Funds and Eligible Liabilities under directive 2014/59/EU*. EBA/RTS/2015/05.

European Banking Authority. (2015b). *Guidelines on the interpretation of the different circumstances when an institution shall be considered as failing or likely to fail under Article 32 (6)of Directive 2014/59/EU*. EBA/GL/2015/07.

European Banking Authority. (2015c). *Guidelines on the Minimum List of Qualitative and Quantitative Recovery Plan Indicators*. EBA/GL/2015/02.

European Banking Authority. (2016). *Final Guidelines – Revised guidelines on the further specification of the indicators of global systemic importance and their disclosure*. EBA/GL/2016/01.

European Banking Authority. (2018). *Final Report – Guidelines on institutions' stress testing*. EBA/ GL/2018/04.

European Banking Authority. (2020).*Other Systemically Important Institutions (O-SIIs)*. Retrieved April 27, 2020, from https://eba.europa.eu/risk-analysis-and-data/ other-systemically-important-institutions-o-siis-

European Central Bank. (2017). *What is the SREP?* Retrieved April 27, 2020, from https://www. bankingsupervision.europa.eu/about/ssmexplained/html/srep.en.html

European Central Bank. (2020). *Supervisory review (SREP) – Aggregate SREP outcome for 2019*. Retrieved April 24, 2020, from https://www.bankingsupervision.europa.eu/banking/srep/ srep_2019/html/aggregate_results_2019.en.html#toc1

European Commission. (2013a). *Commission Delegated Regulation (EU) No 2015/61 of 10 October 2014 to supplement Regulation (EU) No 575/2013 of the European Parliament and the Council with regard to liquidity coverage requirement for Credit Institutions Text with EEA relevance*.

European Commission. (2013b). *Regulation (EU) No 575/2013 of the European Parliament and of the Council of 26 June 2013 on prudential requirements for credit institutions and in-vestment firms and amending Regulation (EU) No 648/2012 Text with EEA relevance*.

European Parliament. (2013). *Directive 2013/36/EU of The European Parliament and of The Council of 26 June 2013 on access to activity of credit institutions and the prudential supervision of credit institutions and investment firms*. Official Journal of the European Union.

European Parliament. (2014). *Directive 2014/59/EU of the European Parliament and of the council of 15 May 2014 establishing a framework for the recovery and resolution of credit institutions and investment firms*. Official Journal of the European Union.

Huang, R., and Ratnovski, L. (2011). The dark side of bank wholesale funding. *Journal of Financial Intermediation, 20*(2), 248–263.

Part VI: **Governance**

Brandon Davies

24 On the Governance of Reverse Stress Testing

Finance is Different: Considerations of a Non-Executive Director (NED)

24.1 Introduction

One of the biggest issues I have often faced as a non-executive director (NED) but also as an economist and ex-banker is that board members have all the same failings in their technical knowledge of risk, as does the rest of society.

This should come as a surprise to no one. Who saw Covid-19 coming? How much was the effects on our economies already buried in our contingency planning? We do not have a crystal ball, though as treasurer of Barclays retail businesses, I kept one on my desk to point to when the inevitable questions about the future were asked of me. I had excellent academic credentials for my reticence in forecasting, including Keynes (1921) famous quote that "the future is not unknown it is unknowable". This was backed up by my knowledge of the first two features of risk I now teach students at Buckingham University: Risk is heterogeneous and idiosyncratic – i.e. it can come from any feature of your business model, and any one direction it can come from can be enough to destroy the business.

My belief in the importance of NEDs is not based on their superior theoretical understanding of the features of risk I will outline in this chapter but rather that I believe what they bring to the role is experience and especially, but certainly not exclusively, experience in the financial services. Experience, I contend, is a commodity that is far too undervalued in the risk management of a business. Few NEDs will be able to describe the economic theory behind the experiences they have had over a career in finance, and even less the mathematics, but many will have experienced them in their executive positions throughout their working lives. As such they should be able to challenge the executive as to how reliant the business is on the modelling of these risks and how good the models are, not least because many NEDs will have had experiences where risk models have failed to accurately predict either or both of business- and/or economy-wide risk. My favourite question to ask is: In what circumstances does a model not have accurate predictive power? Hesitation or, worse still, denial of such circumstances is, in my view, sufficient cause not to sign off on the model.

Because economics and finance use the same mathematics as are used in natural science disciplines there is no shortage of articles and indeed books that point out

Note: Edited by Michael Eichhorn

https://doi.org/10.1515/9783110647907-024

how practitioners in economics and finance can learn from the application of mathematics in natural science disciplines. Economics and finance are, however, very different from those disciplines that are based on the natural world. This chapter seeks to point out how important experience is and why the opportunities to learn from natural science may be very much less than is often supposed and where a better insight into economics and finance may require significant advances in the understanding of unique features of economics and finance.

24.2 How Finance Differs from Other Complex Systems

The difference between economics and finance and the natural world is an issue well understood by many bank board members who have plenty of experience in the industry. They have learned from their experiences and though they might not characterise the issues as an economist, their input is incredibly important in managing a finance business or indeed in managing the economy.

It is my contention that natural sciences such as geology or meteorology (I have chosen these disciplines as there have been recent articles making claims about how finance can learn from them) certainly have a long history of operating complex models efficiently, but economics and finance are different and are in many ways far more difficult to model than natural science disciplines.

Let us look at an example from geology. If one oil company drills into a certain rock structure, the rock does not change. If two, three, and so on join them, the rock is still the same rock. Contrast this with a financial market: If one financial institution makes a market in an asset and is then joined by others, the liquidity, price structure, size of individual purchases and sales will all change, and the market itself will change quite fundamentally. Finance is thus different from the natural world, and plenty of bank board members will have experienced the practical effects of these differences. Perhaps the major difference between the natural world and a financial market is the importance of liquidity to financial markets, which determines the ability of asset owners to convert their assets into cash when needed. Many NEDs will have had experience of what happens when liquidity drains away from a market and you hear that telling phrase, "offer, no bid" as asset holders attempt to sell their assets but cannot find a buyer, thus threatening their solvency.

Of even more concern and a growing field of research in economics is the example of how the modelling of an economy is very different from that of modelling weather. Weather has a big effect on people's moods – for example, a couple of months or so ago here in the UK, there was a prolonged period of pretty continuous rain and associated flooding, but however badly we feel about the weather, our collective mood will not have any effect upon it. But we know that the way we feel about an economy has a material effect on the level of investment and purchasing of goods and services across the economy. This is something that, especially in light of the Covid-19 pandemic, we need to bear very much in mind. No matter how fast the Central Bank prints money, it does not mean people will spend it or that commercial banks will turn base money into broad spending money (M0 to M4 in the UK, for those of a technical bent), something I will focus on later in this chapter. Indeed, the modelling of this effect is fundamental to understanding the feed-back and particularly the feed-forward effects of social developments on output and employment in the economy, the level of asset prices in markets and the level of defaults in banks' lending books.

The technical description for this is dynamic conditional correlation (DCC); that is that the relationship between assets change and the way they change is conditional upon certain events, but the conditionality is not stable. For example, when the US Federal Reserve Board initially dropped its interest rate by 0.5% in reaction to the Covid-19 crisis, the US stock market fell – the last time it took the same action, the US stock market rose. Whatever the sources of dynamic conditional correlation, its effects can be extreme.

Let us look at this in the case of a single trader holding a trading portfolio of both government and corporate bonds. The economy starts to falter; growth rates fall and with them, interest rates. The rise in expected default rates for companies outweighs the effect of falling interest rates, and consequently, the value of the corporate bond holdings falls. In contrast, government bonds are seen as credit-risk free (as the government is not expected to default on its debt), so the value of these bonds rises. These opposing effects determine the overall effect on the portfolio's value.

Let us now suppose that the bond holdings have been funded through the asset repurchase (repo) market and that the value of the corporate bonds falls such that it is both difficult to sell them, except at extreme loss, and they are subject to larger repo "haircuts" resulting in smaller loans against a given portfolio. Moreover, the fall in the corporate bonds' values are no longer cancelled out by the rise in government bond values. To fund the corporate book, it is necessary to start selling or pledging the government bonds to finance the now-illiquid corporate bond market. If enough market makers are in this position, the value of the government bonds will begin to fall, making funding more difficult and forcing the distressed sale of any bonds that can find a buyer. The previously offsetting effect of falling corporate bond values and rising government bond values has now become a re-enforcing effect as both corporate and government bonds begin to fall in value – that is, negative correlations between the asset classes have turned positive.

The result of this process of changes in correlations is that the shape of the distribution ceases to display the characteristics of a "fat-tailed" distribution (say a Student-t distribution) where observations of bad out-turns are more frequently observed than in the "normal" distribution which is the dominant distribution describing the observation of out-turns in the natural world (we often first encounter the normal distribution at school where the height of each member of the class is measured).

The fat-tailed distribution is the dominant class of distributions we observe in financial markets and they frequently appear in financial market models, but many NEDs will tell of their experience of what we may describe as a distribution with a "fat and fatter" tail. What they will describe is a set of circumstances where the dynamics of the situation, often driven by people's reaction to a bad outcome, make the situation worse and worse. A good example of this would be the "bank run" that precipitated the collapse of Northern Rock Bank in the UK in 2008. What is happening is that the likelihood of a very, very bad outcome, given that a very bad outcome has already happened, has risen substantially – i.e. the likelihood of a seven standard deviation (SD) event happening, given that a five SD event has happened, is very high. In diagrammatic terms, it looks like the "dotted" path in Figure 24.1.

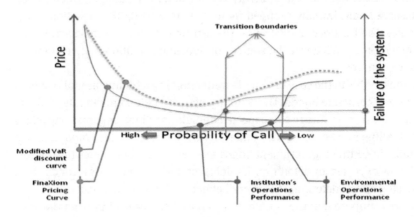

Figure 24.1: Probability of an option call ("fat and fatter tails").

Figure 24.1 shows the pricing curve (expected loss distribution) of a complex option. What is important to observe is the shape of the option pricing curve (the dotted yellow line). It shows that the value of the option is best described by a distribution that exhibits dynamic conditional correlation in that the likelihood of extreme loss rises over a significant part of the tail of the distribution.

Again, addressing the difference between the natural world and finance, the issue here is *not* analogous to the issue we have with understanding geometric rather than arithmetic progression. We have seen this problem all too clearly in relation to infection rates and the Covid-19 pandemic ravaging many parts of the world. Why is track and trace so important? Because once the virus gets ahead of your ability to track and trace those infected, its infection rate quickly becomes a geometric progression with tens of infections becoming hundreds the thousands then tens of thousands in very short order. However, this is not an example of DCC. DCC is far more dramatic – more as if some drug that suppressed the symptoms of Covid-19 suddenly changed sides and made the symptoms far worse!

We do not yet and indeed we may never fully understand the dynamic properties of the financial system, though work is progressing through a better understanding of network theory (the non-linear behaviour of the financial system in situations of stress) and the properties of financial networks are increasingly being put in the spotlight by researchers looking at systemic risks across markets (most notably by the Systemic Research Centre at the London School of Economics). Financial network systems are, however, complex and the interconnections between agents within them are in many instances not well understood, but the importance of network theory can be appreciated from the following simple diagrams.

Figure 24.2 shows two independent market systems with a number of institutions (agents) within them. Each system is independent as there are no connections between the two systems. An institution in the first system collapses but there is no contagion in this scenario.

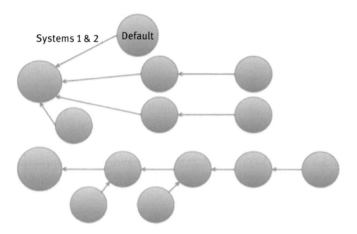

Figure 24.2: Illustration of an independent market system.

Figure 24.3 shows what happens in the same circumstances. However, in this diagram there are just two interconnections between institutions in each market system. The same institution defaults but this now results in all the institutions in both systems collapsing.

So, this is where we currently stand, and it is important to understand that far from looking to natural science, economics and finance are looking to a better understanding of the dynamic and conditional effects that drive economic and financial outcomes. In this quest, there is a great deal of analysis that a combination of big data and big data analytics of what we collectively read in public media and say through social media can allow us to look at the social circumstances in which market and economic outcomes occur. Indeed, these new studies of sentiment (e.g. Kabiri et al., 2020) and how they affect financial market and economic outcomes may add yet

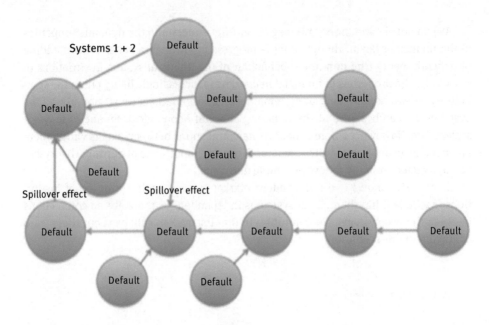

Figure 24.3: Illustration of a connected market system.

another layer of complexity to our understanding of the dynamic and conditional nature of financial systems. But all this is on the frontier of our research into financial markets and economy-wide out-turns. Interesting as it is, it may be some time before it creates any great breakthrough in our theoretical understanding of risk in financial markets, much less any new, practically useful analytical methods for looking at market- or economy-wide out-turns.

The best quote I can come up with on the current state of network theory is from Haldane (2009) at the Bank of England on the Sars and Lehman Brothers events is as follows:

> Both events were manifestations of the behaviour under stress of a complex, adaptive network. Complex because these networks were a cat's cradle of interconnections, financial and non-financial. Adaptive because behaviour in these networks was driven by interconnections between optimizing, but confused, agents. Seizures in the electricity grid, degradation of ecosystems, the spread of epidemics and the disintegration of the financial system – each is essentially a different branch of the same network family tree.

The danger, as I see it, is that of course the world and everything in it is connected and therefore is deterministic so long as we understand all the connections. However, the problem is we don't, and, in my view, it is unlikely that we will anytime soon, so we are better to deal with the problem by building probabilistic models based on abstractions from reality. They won't be perfectly accurate, but at least we stand some chance of getting a usable guide to our policy decisions.

In the meantime, we need to learn from experience, something NEDs are well-placed to provide, so we do need to choose them well. Indeed, it may be that we have little to learn from natural science disciplines, but a lot to learn through the way data-based companies such as Facebook or Amazon operate. An issue that again I would say is helped by having NED board members. At least some of the NED board members should come from different industries. They can bring this experience to bear on the strategic and business model questions that are fundamental to the direction a board gives to a business.

In the light of these factors, is there something else we might usefully try? I would suggest from my experience that focusing on either the theory or on the current practice has severe limitations. It is clear that the theory has a long way to go and is far from offering a solution, though I do think it can bring useful insights, so I am not at all dismissive of research.

These issues with the current state of the theory of risk have of course sent the regulators and the industry off on the course of stress testing and scenario analysis. This has led to requirements on commercial banks to increase their capital and improve their short-term cash positions and their long-term funding liquidity, but it doesn't seem to tell us much else and I think post–2008, we all knew this was necessary.

Scenarios, especially those looking at systemic risk in stressed markets are pretty much just a guessing game and passed the obvious messages on capital and liquidity. I am not always sure what they are telling us. However, I have a real concern where they are telling us something new and the latter is something we do not wish to hear. What do I mean by this? That in really extreme circumstances (such as we are experiencing now – none of any regulators stress tests got even close to this), no level of improved liquidity or capital is sufficient to preserve the current fractional reserve banking model without massive central bank and finance ministry support – and not simply commercial bank support, but support for a broad swathe of asset markets and institutions as well.

At the time of writing this, there is a broad range of support measures with banks capital ratios being reduced to encourage them to expand (or at least not reduce) their balance sheets at a time when risk in their existing portfolios is rising rapidly. Provisioning by US banks has risen by around 350% and European around 250%, despite the much larger balance sheet size in relation to GDP of European Banks (at around 350% of GDP versus 100% for US banks).

Banks are being used by finance ministries as ciphers for lending to companies on a variety of risk sharing basis, including a fully finance ministry guaranteed basis, thus dramatically lessening the capital and liquidity strains of new commercial bank lending. In the personal sector, the income support schemes financed by finance ministries have equally supported personal sector lending by commercial banks, vital in economies where personal consumption accounts for over 70% of GDP and where the personal sector is already highly geared. Asset markets have also benefited from central banks' and finance ministries' support with extensive central bank buying in credit markets, corporate bond, and securitisation markets. (Are equities next?)

This time around (as opposed to post–2008), the support for both banks and asset markets has been swift and plentiful, at least from the Federal Reserve and the Bank of England, though, as in 2008, it appears the European Central Bank will be playing catch up (somewhat inevitable given its legal structure). So, perhaps on this score, it is time to recognise that the markets and the banking system are vital components in maintaining our economies and it is time to drop the pretence they are simply commercial businesses that should stand or fall on their own merits. We should decide where competition is to be allowed and where it is not, but recognition of the "special" (in some instances, government underwritten) status of some institutions and the markets in which they operate, is simply a fact of life which we need to live with, at least until digital national currencies come along (which is another story for another time).

This should of course come with what many of these institutions would see as a level of invasive regulation of their activities, which they and possibly many governments will not welcome (e.g. taxation, domicile, remuneration, dividends and buy backs), though characterising it as a private/public partnership might help. This, I would argue, is, however, better than preserving the myth of independence in all circumstances which simply ignores the issue of government support until it is late in the day and support has to be provided but in an unplanned way, leading to supporting some institutions that really do not deserve support and the relaxation of capital regulation and even accounting standards in circumstances where this seems impossible to justify on any grounds but expediency.

Having addressed that problem, the next issue is how to tackle "operational resilience" for real. By this I mean that we should stop focussing on how each institution is to continue to operate in stressed circumstances within its own resources and start planning for how a combination of central bank and finance ministry support, along with actions by supported markets agents, should be implemented. I would liken this to a focus not on stopping a fire occurring but rather on ensuring the economy has a fully staffed and equipped fire service.

In a fractional reserve banking system where the commercial banks are also the primary source of credit and money to large swathes of the economy's preservation in economically challenging times, they are systemically vital. Above all, they play the major role in the functioning of a monetary economy. Central banks can create base money by buying assets (largely but no longer solely government bonds) from the commercial banks, but only commercial banks can turn this into the broad money we spend by making advances to the personal and corporate sectors of the economy, which will in turn appear as deposits on the other side of their balance sheets.

Two factors play a vital role in this process. First, the willingness of commercial banks to create broad money from base money is a factor largely driven by their perception of their need to preserve capital, which would otherwise be consumed by the capital backing for the increased size of their asset base and the likelihood of bad debts as well as the provisions they will need to accrue against them. This, in turn, will stem from the economic environment in which they are currently operating (see e.g. Morris/Storbeck, 2020). The views of bank directors play a crucial role here, and anything that reduces their appetites for risk at what is a crucial moment for an economy is likely to increase systemic risk. It is here that I feel a well-meaning regulation such as the Senior Manager and Certification Regime is playing a counter-productive role. Many NEDs in particular will have lived through enough of the bad times to know they do end, and, left to their own devices, they can play an important role in scrutinising overly pessimistic views of the future that may predominate in younger and often more risk-averse senior executives. This is far from a theoretical problem at the end of March 2020, when US banks held some $2.1tn of reserves against a requirement to hold £203bn (Hoisington Investment Management Company, 2020).

Second, the demand for loan finance from the corporate and personal sectors, which will propel the money created around the economy, is a factor. Basically, I assume that the velocity of circulation of broad money around the system is driven by how optimistic consumers and producers are about the future. Pessimism will lead to a low demand for loans and high savings rates to build precautionary balances; what money is created will not flow aggressively around the economy.

Whilst the operational resilience of any single bank matters, what matters much more is that the whole system is resilient. In this context the ability of a central bank to conduct monetary policy is critical, especially in a low interest rate environment.

24.3 Summary

Stress testing is currently the main way in which we look at the specific risk of an individual organisation. It is a way for regulators to establish a view of the risks to the system as a whole, so-called systemic risk. Reverse stress testing is a very important approach for both individual bank risk and systemic risk.

Our understanding of risk is, however, continuously subject to new insight. This chapter looked at the latest developments in our understanding of risk. It started from the position that, in the absence of a far more comprehensive understanding of risk, the importance of having experienced non-executive directors on the boards of financial institutions is vital to the better governance of financial institutions, including a better understanding of the risks they run both individually and collectively.

Risk in banking only really matters to society when it is systemic and when it is, we have no reliable modelling methodology to address it. In practice, this requires a partnership between the commercial banking system, the regulators, central banks and finance ministries. Within commercial banks, the lack of any robust analytical framework for understanding (let alone managing) extreme risk means that experienced board directors and especially NEDs can play a vital support role, as we must learn to manage what we cannot measure.

What we have today with stress testing, of which reverse stress testing is a key part, is an intuitive and easy to understand basis for setting a "state of the world" against which we can establish the regulatory capital requirements of banks. It is, however, a process that is increasingly far removed from our growing understanding of the extremely complex nature of risk in financial institutions and markets and of how financial risk can propagate through the economy to produce systemic risk. The challenge we face is to incorporate the results of research into system dynamics and how sentiment affects these dynamics into our construction of scenarios. This will result in a better understanding of how, the capital and liquidity requirements resulting from stress tests of individual banks will impact the banking system as a whole.

Bibliography

Haldane, Andrew G. (2009). Rethinking the Financial Network, Speech delivered at the Financial Student Association, Amsterdam, Published on 28 April 2009, https://www.bankofengland.co.uk/speech/2009/rethinking-the-financial-network.

Hoisington Investment Management Company (2020). In the two-week accounting period for reserve requirements in late March, the banks held $2.1 trillion of excess reserves and $203 billion of required reserves, Quarterly Review and Outlook First Quarter 2020.

Kabiri, A., Harold, J., Landon, J., Tuckett, D., Nyman, R. (2020). The Role of Sentiment in the Economy of the 1920s, CESifo Working Paper No. 8336, https://www.cesifo.org/en/publikationen/2020/working-paper/role-sentiment-economy–1920s

Keynes, J. (1921). *A Treatise on Probability*.

Morris, S., Storbeck, O. (2020). Big US and European banks book $50bn in charges to cover bad loans, *Financial Times*, 4 May 2020.

Jon Danielsson, Marcela Valenzuela, Ilknur Zer, Robert Macrae, Morgane Fouché, Hyun Song Shin, Jean-Pierre Zigrand

25 Reverse Stress Testing and Recent Research

Considerations on Vulnerabilities and Scenario Narratives

25.1 Introduction

In the context of RST, the following chapter exemplifies how research work can inter alia help to identify hidden vulnerabilities and inform new scenario narratives.[1] Topics covered include biases in risk measurement, cyber risk, political risk, model risk, systemic risk and the endogenous nature of the latter.

25.2 The Dissonance of the Short and Long Term

The type of risk we most care about is long-term, what happens over years or decades, but we tend to manage that risk over short periods. This section argues that the dissonance of risk is that we measure and manage what we don't care about and ignore what we do.

Most important financial concerns are long-term – perhaps whether banks fail, or pensions keep their value – or are about problems that may develop at any time, today or decades in the future. Short-term risk is not particularly important.

Even the perfect, and never achievable, knowledge of risks that will materialise in the next month is of very limited value in making a decision that will involve exposures over many years.

One might therefore expect that risk management techniques used by industry and regulators reflect the importance of the long term. Instead, standard practices focus almost exclusively on the recent past and only capture short-term risk.

---

[1] The six sections in this chapter have been published on VoxEU under Jon Danielsson's column at https://voxeu.org/users/jondanielsson0 and are reproduced here with the kind permission of Mr. Danielsson and VoxEU. Jon Danielsson is the sole author of Section 25.2 and Section 25.6. Section 25.3 is the joint work of Jon Danielsson, Marcela Valenzuela and Ilknur Zer. Section 25.4 is the joint work of Jon Danielsson and Robert Macrae, Section 25.5 of Jon Danielsson, Morgane Fouché, and Robert Macrae and Section 25.7 of Jon Danielsson, Hyun Song Shin and Jean-Pierre Zigrand.

Note: Edited by Michael Eichhorn

https://doi.org/10.1515/9783110647907-025

This dissonance in how we think about risk is a direct result of how risk is measured and managed in practice.

25.2.1 Measurement of Risk

The main reason is that it is really hard to measure long-term risk. After all, extreme infrequent events are by definition very scarce. Take systemic financial crises. An OECD country suffers a crisis in one year out of 43 on average; global crises are even less frequent. Consequently, systemic risk analytics – the statistical forecasting of systemic risk – is not easy (Giglio et al., 2015).

We are taught in first-year statistics that the sample size needs to be sufficiently large for accurate statistical analysis. But modern financial markets are less than two centuries old and give us only a handful of crises for each country – much too small of a sample to draw reliable statistical interference.

To bypass the problem of a lack of data, we usually resort to a statistical sleight of hand – a technique known as probability shifting (e.g. Boucher et al., 2014) – to estimate the distribution of higher frequency events, perhaps daily or monthly, and project those distributions onto longer time horizons (years, decades, or even centuries).

Technically, it's quite easy to do, as it is straightforward to model short-term risk. Once we have estimated a parametric stochastic process of daily or monthly outcomes, all we have to do is to plug in extreme probabilities. As some popular systemic risk models would have it, you model the distribution of daily stock prices and plug in a probability of 0.009% and voilà, you have a 43-year crisis.

Seductive ... but there is a problem. While the calculations are easy enough to do, for the numbers to have meaning, we need at least two strong assumptions. Obviously, we need *ergodicity* of the underlying stochastic process, but also the *correct parametric form* of the distribution (typically fat-tailed), because we will be using it to extrapolate far beyond the region in which evidence has been obtained.

In practice, these are heroic and non-verifiable assumptions at best. Financial markets are continually evolving, violating ergodicity, and the severity of the most extreme events is bounded by a complex and evolving social process, implying that tail distributions must also evolve because risk is endogenous.

In the real world, no purely statistical technique allows us to go from the short term to the long term in a reliable manner, and there is little economic or financial theory available to help.

Take the forecasting of systemic risk. We certainly observe extreme price movements when a crisis happens. However, those are only the consequences of a crisis, reflecting the specific portfolio holdings of financial institutions at the time. Any statistical measurements are therefore specific to that particular crisis. The same fundamental vulnerability, coupled with different holders of the affected assets, would lead to different price dynamics and different associations. Those differences can be very large.

After a crisis, with the benefit of hindsight, one can of course back out the cause of the given crisis from the observed price and quantity movements, but this should not be confused with any kind of predictive or forecasting ability. The distribution of events during the crisis is not only different from that of typical events, but observations of financial variables during crises are mostly idiosyncratic, with limited information value for analysing the likelihood of crises.

The consequence is that a projection of probabilities from day-to-day or month-to-month events onto the likelihood of crises, often done with market price data or accounting data, is not informative about the likelihood of the crisis.

25.2.2 The Problem of Risk Measurement is Entwined with that of Risk Management

Consider a sovereign wealth fund that cares about very long-term risk, decades into the future, where such a time perspective is written into its laws and mandates. However, the fund is monitored quarterly, and if it performs poorly over a few quarters, questions are raised. The effective time horizon moves to become quarters, not decades.

Similarly, many pension funds use value-at-risk or expected shortfall to monitor performance, motivated by these being state-of-the-art risk measures in banking. However, value-at-risk or expected shortfalls make no sense for most pension funds that have predictable inflows and outflows over many years. The main risk is not daily fluctuations as captured by value-at-risk, but investment performance over many years.

Daily price fluctuations should be irrelevant for funds with a long-term outlook, like pension funds and sovereign wealth funds, but because they *can* be measured, they *are* measured. The funds become shorter in outlook than they should be, and focussed on avoiding short-term losses rather than long-term performance.

25.2.3 Practical Implications of the Dissonance of the Short and Long Term

The dissonance of the short and long term has several negative consequences. To begin with, the performance of long-term investments like pension funds will likely suffer if short-term fluctuations in asset prices are a key driver of decisions.

Perhaps the asset managers will be biased towards short-term stable assets, avoiding those that can be expected to perform well in the long run even when fluctuating in the short term.

Alternatively, they may look for false diversification, perhaps buying private equity funds, which do not exhibit much short-term volatility even though they are long-term cointegrated with equity markets. They may accept the frictional costs of dynamic trading strategies or invest in assets with fat tails and little short-term volatility.

Excessive focus on the short-term risk can easily blind us to the risk in the long term. If the short-term risk dashboards are reassuring, as in 2006, we may easily take on undesirable levels of risk, oblivious to the dangers.

Buy low-volatility, very fat-tail assets, because volatility is what is specified in the mandate.

Such an eventuality becomes even more likely because risk is endogenous (Danielsson et al., 2009a and b.), created by the interaction of market participants. If we focus on the short term, we can become quite good at smoothing out fluctuations, and when such strategies are successful, we can expect more and more assets to be managed using them.

This can change the distribution of outcomes, lowering volatility – the probability of intermediate losses – but increasing the intensity of tail events, as most clearly demonstrated by the portfolio insurance crisis of 1987 and the quant crisis of 2007.

25.2.4 Conclusion

As the management of risk is increasingly formalised, and hence depends on statistical measurements of risk, decision-making becomes increasingly biased towards the short term, even if the ultimate objectives are long-term – the dissonance of the short and long term.

The consequence is the wasting of resources, procyclicality, poor performance, and insufficient attention towards important long-term risk. The short-term bias can even be a driver of systemic risk.

There are steps we can take to mitigate the dissonance of the short and long term: focus on resilience; avoid inferring long-run risk from the short-run; and use scenario planning.

25.3 Low Risk as a Predictor of Financial Crises

Reliable indicators of future financial crises are important for policymakers and practitioners. While most indicators consider an observation of high volatility as a warning signal, this section argues that such an alarm comes too late, arriving only once a crisis is already under way. A better warning is provided by low volatility, which is a reliable indication of an increased likelihood of a future crisis.

The Global Crisis in 2008 blindsided every observer. We had come to believe that crises were a thing of the past. The rules and institutional structure in place protected us. The crisis proved all of this wrong.

Since then, we have been searching for ways to predict that a crisis might be underway so that the policy authorities and private institutions can prepare.

One of the key tools is early warning indicators of crises, which gained some prominence after the Asia crisis of 1998. Those in place in 2008 did not work well (Rose and Spiegel, 2009), and to rectify that, a variety of indicators have been proposed.

At the risk of oversimplification, we can classify this work in two main categories. First is a group of early warning indicators that are purely data-driven and based on market data indicators, such as stock prices, volatility and CDS spreads. The second category uses economic theory to guide the indicator design, looking more fundamentally at how risk emerges in the first place.

25.3.1 Theoretical Background

Economic theory is quite clear on where we should look for indications of crisis. Both Keynes (1936) and Hayek (1960) suggest that perceptions of risk affect risk-taking behaviour, especially when they deviate from what economic agents have come to expect.

Perhaps the best expression of this view is Minsky's (1977) instability hypothesis, where economic agents observing low financial risk are induced to increase risk-taking, which in turn may lead to a crisis – the foundation of his famous dictum that 'stability is destabilising'.

The recent literature reaches the same conclusion, for example Brunnermeier and Sannikov's (2014) 'volatility paradox' and Bhattacharya's et al. (2015) examination of Minsky's hypothesis. Similarly, Danielsson et al. (2012) consider a general equilibrium framework with risk constraints, where upon observing low volatility, agents are endogenously incentivised to increase risk.

The basic mechanism for the relationship of risk to crisis can be seen in Figure 25.1.

At the start, economic agents observe that volatility is lower than what they have come to expect. This fuels optimism, making the agents more willing to take more risk. This is manifested within the banking sector, which will both lend more than it did before and also make riskier loans. Eventually, loan defaults mount and a banking crisis ensues – at which time, volatility increases sharply.

This chain of events implies that a considerable amount of time passes between an observation of low volatility and crises. By contrast, an observation of high volatility directly results from a crisis, implying that by the time volatility peaks, it is too late to react.

Figure 25.1: The relationship between volatility and financial crises.

25.3.2 The Empirical Data-Driven Literature

Most empirical literature on early warning indicators takes the opposite view that the likelihood of crises increases along with measured risk, typically measured by ex post outcomes in financial markets, price movements or volatility, VIX, CDS spreads, volumes, and other activity measures. Examples include SRISK (Acharya et al., 2012) and the ECB's systemic risk composite indicator.

The theoretical literature suggests that such indicators are likely to be of limited use. They signal high risk once a crisis is underway, but do not provide much in terms of prediction, limiting their usefulness.

A counter-argument might be that a particular indicator gave a good warning for the events of 2008 – however, that is one observation with multiple degrees of freedom for optimisation, calculated ex post. It is straightforward to use the benefit of hindsight to find a measure that predicts a single known crisis event in history. However, such indicators are unlikely to capture the build-up of systemic risk that leads to crises in the future.

25.3.3 Empirically Testing the Theoretical Literature

Several recent papers have been guided by the theoretical literature in the design of early warning indicators. The most promising ones are those that link credit expansions to crises, as for example Schularick and Taylor (2009), or Baron and Xiong (2017), where over-optimism increases the likelihood of a financial crisis.

In a recent paper, we take this one step further and formally investigate the mechanism in Figure 25.1 (Danielsson et al., 2018). We take a historical perspective to examine the likelihood of crises as a function of volatility, using data going back to 1800, where available, and from 60 countries.

To start with, we investigate the relationship between current volatility and the likelihood of future crisis – what could be called the *linear volatility crisis view*, as seen in Figure 25.2. This is rejected by the data. When coupled with macroeconomic variables to capture the state of the economy, volatility itself is not a significant predictor of crises.

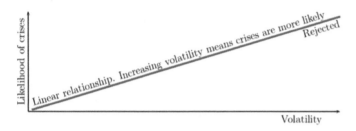

Figure 25.2: Volatility as predictor of crises.

However, by decomposing volatility into trend, and deviations from trend, a different picture emerges. The reason is that economic agents see the trend as 'usual/expected' volatility, and when it deviates from the trend, risk-taking behaviour is affected.

That leaves two forms of volatility: *low volatility* when it is below trend, and *high volatility* when above the trend. The relationship between low and high volatilities and the likelihood of crises can be seen in Figure 25.3.

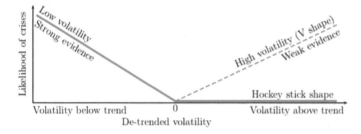

Figure 25.3: Low and high volatilities as predictors of crises.

The slope of the curve, which translates into regression coefficients in a statistical model, indicates the strength of the relationship. The higher the slope in absolute terms, the more likely a crisis becomes as volatility moves away from its trend. In Danielsson et al. (2018), we find strong evidence for low volatility but only weak evidence for high-volatility causing crises.

The economic impact is the highest if the economy stays in the low-volatility environment for five years: a 1% decrease in volatility below its trend translates to a 1.01% increase in the probability of a crisis.

We also show that the chain of causality in Figure 25.3, with low volatility leading to increased lending and excessive risk, holds empirically.

25.3.4 Volatility as an Early Warning Indicator

These results suggest that volatility would not be a good crisis indicator. It might tell policymakers that a crisis is underway, but we suspect that they will know that anyway.

A standard way to evaluate the quality of early warning indicators is the area under the receiving operating curve (AUROC). An AUROC of 0.5 means that an indicator is no better than random noise, while a value of 1.0 implies perfect predictability.

Low volatility has an AUROC value of 76%, with a 95% confidence interval of 72%, 80%. This means that it provides a reliable signal to policymakers for the incidence of future crisis.

25.3.5 Conclusion

Within the post–2008 crisis macroprudential agenda, policymakers are actively searching for signals of future financial and economic instability and developing policy tools to mitigate the most unfortunate outcomes.

Most early warning indicators of crises are founded on ex post market data, typically volatility in some form or another, where increasing volatility indicates that the financial system has become more risky and a crisis is therefore more likely.

However, an observation of high risk is the consequence of a stress event where financial instructions are in difficulties, not the causes.

It will be more fruitful to search for early warning indicators amongst the fundamental drivers of financial instability. A major cause of financial crises is excessive risk taking by economic agents. When they perceive a low-risk environment, they are endogenously incentivised to take more risk, which ultimately culminates in a crisis.

This view has been expressed by policymakers: "Volatility in markets is at low levels ... to the extent that low levels of volatility may induce risk-taking behaviour ... is a concern to me and to the Committee" (Former Federal Reserve Former Chair Janet Yellen, 2014).

The data confirms this view. An observation of low risk is a significant crises predictor and suitable for an early warning indicator. The policy authorities and private institutions would consequently benefit from using low volatility as a crisis indicator since an observation of current low volatility implies that a future crisis is more likely.[2]

---

2 Authors' note: The views in this column are solely those of the authors and should not be inter-

25.4 The Fatal Flaw in Macropru: It Ignores Political Risk

Political risk is a major cause of systemic financial risk. This section argues that both the integrity and the legitimacy of macroprudential policy, or "macropru", depends on political risk being included with other risk factors. Yet it is usually excluded from macropru, and that could be a fatal flaw.

The purpose of macroprudential policy is to identify financial risks and take corrective measures before it is too late. If the measures are effective, systemic risks will be diminished, the severity of any negative events already occurring in the financial system will be contained, and the wider economy will be protected.

The successful implementation of "macropru" demands three things of the financial authorities. First, they need estimates of systemic risk (and its impact on the real economy) from the early signs of a build-up of stress to the post-crisis economic and financial resolution. Second, they need the tools to implement effective policy remedies. Finally, given the power of the tools they wield, the authorities need legitimacy, a reputation for impartiality, and political support.

Most discussions about macropru focus on the first two conditions. Our concern is on the third. It is often assumed that macropru has a similar legitimacy as monetary policy, but we do not believe the comparison works.

For monetary policy, central banks have one measure (inflation) and two tools (interest rates and quantity of money) that have powerful but diffuse effects on the economy. The independent use of these tools by central banks is backed up by decades of research, including the work of Nobel Prize winners. Given the importance of the mission, the clear understanding of the problem, and the still-fresh memory of the 1980s, it is not remarkable that democratic societies choose to give this power to unelected bureaucrats.

In contrast, the macropru policymaker is faced with a complex, ill-defined policy domain in which there is not a clear consensus on either the problem or the objective. The indicators at this policymaker's disposal are often imprecise and conflicting. The surgical implementation tools are often ineffective, and the powerful implementation tools are too blunt. Macropru also tends to result in clearly identifiable winners and losers, perhaps even more so than monetary policy. As a result, it is subject to intensive lobbying and political pressure.

This adversely affects both the legitimacy of the macropru regulator, and the regulator's reputation for impartiality. It makes it harder to mobilise the sort of political support that monetary policy can get. As a consequence, as we argued (Danielsson et al., 2015), except in times of obvious, dire emergency, macropru is likely to lose out to policy objectives like micropru when they inevitably conflict.

This may well frustrate the preventive role of macropru, condemning it to be solely reactive. For example, Sebastian Mallaby writes in his recent autobiography of Alan Greenspan (Mallaby, 2015) that the Federal Reserve was aware of the risk from the volume of subprime mortgages. It was largely unable to act because Congress supported increased home ownership, and politicians feared a political backlash if this policy were curtailed.

It seems impossible to ignore the profound and intimate way that politics constrains macropru. Yet the macropru agenda typically takes little account of political risk, and when it does, the backlash may be immediate. Consequently, macropru regulators must tiptoe around politics, both as a major source of systemic risk and as the dominant constraint on their ability to act.

25.4.1 Why Political Risk Matters

When we look at major stress events in the financial system, only a few have arisen purely from excessive risk-taking by, and misbehaviour of, economic agents. Perhaps the best example is the 1987 stock market crash that originated in an automatic trading rule and portfolio insurance. This crash had a limited impact outside finance. Most other stress events, however, have been strongly influenced by politics. The biggest systemic financial crises in the world were caused by war or a transition between political systems, such as in Russia in 1919, Germany in 1923, Japan in 1945 and China in 1949. The severe financial and economic crisis currently occurring in Venezuela is largely political.

In events of this magnitude, the financial strains are merely one aspect of a near-total collapse of social institutions. It is unreasonable to expect any regulator to achieve much of value. There are, however, many less-seismic events that are also largely political in origin.

Take Brexit, for example. The only immediate financial or economic impact was a 20% drop in the value of the pound against major currencies. This is not in itself a systemic concern, but there were possible of systemic consequences via the fixed income markets (Csullag et al., 2016). During the referendum campaign, the Bank of England decided to warn of serious economic consequences if there were a vote for Brexit, putting itself on the losing side of an acrimonious political debate. As a consequence, it has come under repeated attacks from politicians. It is having to reaffirm its independence and request support from the post-Brexit UK government in a way that is unusual for a central bank. This clearly highlights the dangers facing central banks if they include politics in their macroprudential considerations.

Populist parties in Europe have the most realistic chance in a generation of achieving power. Given the strains and imbalances within the Eurozone, it is not clear how they could be accommodated, and if current assumptions – such as the fungibility of euros – were called into question, the consequences could easily be systemic. Populism must therefore be a source of systemic risk, but how far can (or should) a civil servant working on macropru venture into this domain?

Similarly, the election of US President Donald Trump appears to signal a dramatic change in US economic priorities, with the potential for the Fed to make much larger adjustments to US interest rates. Given the vulnerability of fixed income markets to rising interest rates, and with the dollar replacing the VIX stock market volatility index as the 'fear gauge' of the financial markets (as argued by Shin 2016), the consequences could well be systemic. This is exactly the type of scenario the macropru authorities should focus on. On the other hand, it is hard to see how the Fed could react.

25.4.2 The Limits to Macropru

Whatever independence is claimed, in practice, the financial authorities are authorised by, controlled by, and gain their legitimacy from the political leadership. Not surprisingly, the mandate from political leadership is to look at financial and economic risk, not to look at risk that has been created by politicians themselves. This makes it hard for the financial authorities to incorporate political risk as a determinant of systemic risk, despite its importance.

As a result, political risk is largely missing from the macroprudential debate, despite having always been a major cause of systemic risk. This makes it institutionally difficult for the financial authorities to publicly anticipate crises that have predominantly political causes, and also difficult to mitigate crises once they happen.

25.4.3 Conclusion

If financial regulators take steps to address political risk to achieve macropru stability, whether they succeed or fail, we are heading down a dangerous path. Being involved in a political debate with macroprudential consequences jeopardises their reputation for impartiality, threatens their independence, and affects their ability to execute both macropru and monetary policies.

If the authorities visibly react to political initiatives that affect financial stability, there is a danger this would be interpreted as frustrating or twisting democratic decisions. On the other hand, if the macropru authorities are not able to incorporate political risk in their analytic frameworks, how effective can they be?

The authorities face a dilemma. The inability to incorporate political risk in macropru but the ineffectiveness of macropru if political risk is ignored, may be a fatal flaw in macroprudential policymaking.

25.5 Cyber Risk as Systemic Risk

The threat to the financial system posed by cyber risk is often claimed to be systemic. This section argues against this, pointing out that almost all cyber risk is microprudential. For a cyber attack to lead to a systemic crisis, it would need to be timed impeccably to coincide with other non-cyber events that undermine confidence in the financial system and the authorities. The only actors with enough resources to affect such an event are large sovereign states, and they could likely create the required uncertainty through simpler financial means.

Various public and private authorities have come to see cyber risk – risk emanating from computer systems and computer networks – as a significant channel for systemic risk. Recent examples include the Bank of Canada (2014), the BIS (2014), the Bank of England (2015) and the SEC (Ackerman, 2016).

Cyber risk is certainly a real and growing threat to the well-being of financial institutions, with most months bringing news of a major systems failure, hack, or outright theft, like the recent $81 million theft from the Bangladeshi Central Bank. While obviously a microprudential issue, is it really a systemic concern?

As the argument goes, yes, because the increasing threat of failure of critically important computer systems threatens the internal operations of financial institutions and the plumbing of the system. Since everybody is interconnected, if systems fail, the consequence is a loss of confidence, disappearance of liquidity and hence, ultimately a systemic crisis.

We disagree. While one can certainly envision a cyber event so severe that it would cause a systemic crisis under the right circumstances, in normal times it is highly unlikely, almost no matter the severity of the cyber event.

25.5.1 Financial Systemic Risk

Systemic risk is generally seen as the potential for a major financial crisis adversely affecting the real economy, as defined by the IMF-BIS-FSB in 2009. Addressing such systemic risk – macroprudential policy – is one of the three planks of government financial policy, the others being monetary policy and microprudential policy – the protection of bank clients.

Systemic crises do not happen frequently. By studying the IMF-WB crisis database (Laeven and Valencia, 2012), we find they happen once every 42 years for OECD members. If anything, that is an overestimate, as the database includes relatively non-extreme events, like October 1987 and August/September 1998.

The fundamental cause of financial systemic risk is excessive risk-taking by financial institutions, where perhaps the best indicator of a future crisis is large credit growth, as shown by Taylor and Schularick (2009). This is especially dangerous when the resulting risk is undetected or ignored by the powers that be, creating the potential for an abrupt fall in confidence, as discussed here on Vox by Danielsson and Zigrand (2015).

25.5.2 The Root Cause of Systemic Crises is Risk-taking Behaviour of Economic Agents

In turn, the behaviour of these economic agents is directly motivated by confidence. It is a fundamental element of financial markets because we only participate willingly in the markets if we believe the financial system will continue to function in the same way as we have always seen it function. In particular, we need to have faith in what is often called the plumbing of the financial system, such as the payment system and the ability to trade and clear financial assets.

Conversely, the disappearance of confidence is a strong and often early indication of crisis. We have to believe that the financial edifice is at real risk of collapsing for a crisis to really turn systemic. The best example of this is 1914, where the assassination of the Archduke Ferdinand triggered a systemic crisis in global financial markets long before the actual war broke out. It was the anticipation of a war and failure of cross-border payments that was the main trigger of the crisis (Danielsson, 2013).

25.5.3 Timing Matters

When it comes to identifying the origins of cyber risk as systemic risk, it is important to distinguish between a trigger and a root cause, where in general triggers are irrelevant for policy purposes, since there is a very large number of potential triggers, unless both the timing is fortuitous and no other triggers exist.

We do not see how cyber risk could be the root cause of a systemic crisis because there is no direct connection between the failure of computer systems, no matter how severe, and the behaviour of those economic agents which ultimately culminates in a systemic crisis.

A cyber event could act as a trigger, provided the timing is just right. An exogenous crisis event, like a cyber attack, that results in a fall in confidence and liquidity would not be systemic, provided the levels of excessive risk-taking had not already reached a tipping point. If not, we can expect to recover on a timescale that makes real-world impact moderate, as in October 1987, LTCM in 1998 and the 2010 flash crash.

Consider a potential disaster scenario – the total failure of a country's ATM system, or even the payment system, for a few days. Would that be systemic?

Well, it depends. If it happened today, it is highly unlikely, because people would recognise that the disruption was temporary, and the end result would be a frustrating and costly but only temporary disruption. The failure would not trigger a crisis, provided that people believed that the authorities would react appropriately.

However, if the failure had happened on 1 October 2008, things could have been different. At that time, people everywhere were converting bank balances into cash in response to the Global Crisis, and both the Eurozone and the UK were not too far – perhaps only hours – away from running out of cash. Any disruption to the delivery of cash could have drained confidence, potentially turning existing problems into a systemic event.

The crucial role of timing means that any attacker must either be able to create a heightened state of financial market vulnerability, be very lucky, or else both be capable of maintaining their attack vectors in place for years or decades and be sufficiently patient to wait.

25.5.4 The Origins of Cyber Risk

There are four broad origins of cyber risk: technical computer system failures, theft, hacktivists and terrorists, and state actors.

Systems failures and theft can be expected at any time and have a very large microprudential impact. However, since the timing and victims are likely to be idiosyncratic, it is practically impossible for them to act as a trigger for a systemic crisis and they certainly cannot be a root cause.

Hacktivists and terrorists could subvert IT systems to promote a political agenda, possibly with multiple targets and as part of a broader strategy of disruption. They are very unlikely to have systemic consequences because they would have to combine the attack with other forms of aggression and can at best trigger a systemic crisis, provided the timing is absolutely right.

The only actors with sufficient resources to cause a systemic crisis are the largest sovereign states. They can spend years developing and deploying attacks, keeping them hidden until in a coordinated fashion they attack multiple IT systems. However, even in this case, a cyber attack would not be sufficient unless it was on a colossal scale, involving multiple computer systems and their backup mechanisms.

For a state actor with the necessary resources, however, it might be just as easy to manufacture the necessary uncertainty through financial means by, for example, making credible threats to world trade, the sequestration of foreign assets, or by the repudiation of international liabilities. If carried out on a sufficiently large scale, in our highly connected world, these could easily lead to a repeat of the experiences of 1914. All these attacks require is enough international connectedness to allow trust in domestic institutions to be destroyed by a foreign actor.

While financial warfare of this type would presumably be accompanied by a cyber attack, it is not clear that the cyber element would really be necessary, and even then, it would likely only play a secondary role.

25.5.5 Conclusion

While systemic risk is frequently invoked as a key reason to be on guard for cyber risk, such a connection is quite tenuous. A cyber event might in extreme cases result in a systemic crisis, but to do so needs highly fortuitous timing.

From the point of view of policymaking, rather than simply asserting systemic consequences for cyber risks, it would be better if the cyber discussion were better integrated into the existing macroprudential dialogue. To us, the overall discussion of cyber and systemic risk seems to be too focussed on IT considerations and not enough on economic consequences.

After all, if there are systemic consequences from cyber risk, the chain of causality will be found in the macroprudential domain.

25.6 Risk and Crises

Financial models are widely blamed for underestimating and thus mispricing risk prior to the crisis. This section analyses how the models failed and questions their prominent use in the post-crisis reform process. It argues that over-relying on market data and statistical forecasting models has the potential to further destabilise the financial system and increase systemic risk.

Statistical pricing and risk-forecasting models played a significant role in the build-up to the crisis. For example, they gave wrong signals, underestimated risk, and mispriced collateralised debt obligations. I am therefore surprised by the frequent proposals for increasing the use of such models in post-crisis reforms, and I am not alone (see for example, Leijonhufvud, 2011). If the models performed so badly, why aren't we questioning their increased prominence?

This may be because of the view that that we can somehow identify the dynamics of financial markets during crisis by studying pre-crisis data. That we can get from the failure process in normal times to the failure process in crisis times. That all the pre-crisis models were missing was the presence of a crisis in the data sample.

This is not true. The models are not up to the task. While statistical risk and pricing models may do a good job when markets are calm, they lay the seeds for their own destruction – it is inevitable that such models be proven wrong. The riskometer is a myth (Danielsson, 2009).

25.6.1 Models, Momentum and Bubbles

The vast majority of risk models are based on the following assumptions:
– Take a chunk of historical observations of the data under study.

- Create a statistical model providing the best forecasts.
- Validate the model out of the sample, but with historical data known to the data modeller.

This approach to modelling may be quite appropriate in the short run when there are no structural breaks in the data, so we can reasonably assume that data follows the same stochastic process during the entire sample period. Recent examples include the low-volatility periods of 1994 to 1997 and 2003 to 2007.

Even in such best-case scenarios, modelling is likely to deliver inferior forecasts. Data mining is rife; modellers tailor the model to the data in sample, resulting in the model performing well in the sample used for model validation but performing badly with new data.

The main problem, however, is that such modelling affects the behaviour of model participants. If market participants perceive risk as being low and returns high because that is what happened in the past, we get a positive feedback between continually increasing prices and decreasing risk.

This process is reinforced because of momentum effects induced by models. This was one of the main factors behind the asset price bubble before the recent crisis. Eventually this goes spectacularly wrong.

25.6.2 Models Lay the Seeds for Their Own Destruction

Over time, market prices lose connection with fundamentals, and the bubble bursts. Prices collapse and perceived risk increases sharply. Statistically, there is a structural break in stochastic processes governing prices, invalidating pre-crisis forecast models.

This process is reinforced by endogenous changes in the behaviour of market participants, e.g. because of external constraints. For example, margin requirements during times of financial turmoil can lead to a downward spiral in prices, induced by ever-increasing margins, as discussed by Brunnermeier and Pedersen (2008). Similarly, as noted by Danielsson et al. (2011), financial institutions are subject to capital requirements and thus may be caught out in a vicious feedback loop between falling asset prices, higher risk and increasing demands for capital, leading to sales of risky assets, further exasperating difficulties and leading to more demands for capital and reduced risk taking.

25.6.3 Overestimating Risk after a Crisis: Why the Banks aren't Lending

The risk forecast models provide an equally poor signal after a crisis has passed. Presumably, at that time, investment opportunities are ample. However, backward-looking statistical risk forecast models still perceive risk as being high because observations from the crisis remain in the estimation sample for a long time after a crisis passes.

Since risk forecasts are a major input in the determination of bank capital (calculation of risk weighted assets), so long as risk is perceived as high, risk-taking by banks is curtailed, such as lending to high-risk small and medium enterprises. This process is reinforced by current financial regulations, particularly Basel II, and remains in the Basel III proposals.

It is somewhat disingenuous for political leaders to complain about lack of bank lending, when an important factor is the financial regulations that they pass.

25.6.4 Data Fit for Purpose

These issues are exasperated by the quality of market data since risk and pricing models are estimated with a recent sample of market data.

Market prices reflect the value of assets at any given time, but that does not mean that they provide a good signal of the state of the economy or are a good input into forecast models. The reason is that market prices reflect the constraints facing market participants.

The presence of external constraints of the type discussed here, such as margin requirements and capital, can cause prices to be driven to much lower levels than they otherwise would because of the feedback loop between the constraint, prices and risk.

In such scenarios, market prices reflect the constraints faced by market participants, so that high risk and low prices at times when constraints are binding are unlikely to persist when constraints bind less. Therefore, data in times of crises provides a poor guide to the future – even future crises, because the nature of the constraints is likely to change. Similarly, pre-crisis data is not very informative about what happens in crises.

25.6.5 Models are Least Reliable When Needed the Most

The consequence of these issues is that the stochastic process governing market prices is a very different during times of stress compared to normal times. We need different models during crisis and non-crisis and need to be careful in drawing conclusions from non-crisis data about what happens in crises and vice versa.

This means that when we most desire reliable risk forecasts – i.e. during market turmoil or crises – the models are least reliable because we cannot get from the failure process during normal times to the failure process during crises. At that time, the data sample is very small and the stochastic process is different. Hence the models fail.

From a modelling point of view, this suggests that it may be questionable to use fat-tailed procedures, such as extreme value theory, to assess the risk during crises with pre-crisis data. Techniques such as Markov switching with state variables may provide a useful answer in the future. At the moment, such models are few and far between.

25.6.6 Implications for Policy

The problem of model reliability has been widely recognised following the crisis. Since then, there have been very few, if any, methodological improvements of note in practical risk-forecasting techniques.

Given the widespread recognition of the lack of reliability in risk-forecast models in the build-up to the crisis, their prominence in the post-crisis and regulatory reform process is surprising.

Many of the proposals for reform of bank bonuses call for more risk sensitivity. If the underlying risk models are unreliable and even subject to manipulation, as is usually the case, basing regulations on compensation in financial institutions on risk forecast models might seem rather counterproductive.

Similarly, the calculation of bank capital in Basel II and Basel III is based on risk models because the capital ratio is calculated by capital divided by risk-weighted assets. For this reason, the introduction of the leverage ratio (with total assets) in Basel III is welcome.

Furthermore, many approaches to macroprudential regulations are based on systemic risk measurements. To the extent such endeavours rely on market data and statistical models, policy based on those measurements is likely to be flawed.

25.6.7 Crisis will not Happen Where People are Looking

The challenge facing policymakers is even worse because they cannot look everywhere and will have to focus their attention on where they think systemic risk is most likely to arise. At the moment, a lot of attention is focused on the causes of the previous crisis, like the liquidity mismatches peculiar to the last decade.

However, the next crisis will not come from where we are looking. Just like last time where the danger of conduits and special investment vehicles caught everybody by surprise, the next crisis will also come from an area we are not looking at. After all, bankers seeking to assume risk will look for it where nobody else is looking.

25.6.8 Conclusion

Economic models have recognised the inherent challenges caused by intelligent agents reacting to model predictions ever since the pioneering work of Bob Lucas.

Most practical models for price and risk forecasting by the industry and supervisors do not incorporate such features, reflecting the state of the art of macro models' pre-rational expectations.

The presence of endogenous risk, and the resulting feedback effects between agent behaviour and model predictions, coupled with the low information content in market prices when agents are subject to external constraints undermine the reliability of most risk models. Because of the way they are constructed in practise, such models tend to be systematically wrong, over forecasting risk during crises and under forecasting risk at other times.

For these reasons, over-relying on market data and statistical forecasting models has the potential to further destabilise the financial system and increase systemic risk.

25.7 Modelling Financial Turmoil through Endogenous Risk

By incorporating endogenous risk into a standard asset-pricing model, this section shows how banks' capacity to bear risk seemingly evaporates in the face of market turmoil, pushing the financial system further into a tailspin. It suggests that risk-sensitive prudential regulation, in the spirit of Basel II, makes systemic financial crises sharper, larger, and more costly.

Financial crises are often accompanied by large price changes, but large price changes by themselves do not constitute a crisis. Public announcements of important macroeconomic statistics, such as the US employment report, are sometimes marked by large, discrete price changes at the time of announcement. However, such price changes are arguably the signs of a smoothly functioning market that is able to incorporate new information quickly. The market typically finds composure quite rapidly after such discrete price changes.

25.7.1 A Crisis Feeds on Itself

In contrast, the distinguishing feature of crisis episodes is that they seem to gather momentum from the endogenous responses of the market participants themselves. Rather like a tropical storm over a warm sea, they gather more energy as they develop. As financial conditions worsen, the willingness of market participants to bear risk seemingly evaporates. They curtail their exposures and generally attempt to take on a more prudent, conservative stance.

However, the shedding of exposures results in negative spillovers on other market participants from the sale of assets or withdrawal of credit. As prices fall, measured risks rise, or previous correlations break down, market participants respond by further cutting exposures. The global financial crisis of 2007–2009 has served as a live laboratory for many such distress episodes.

25.7.2 Modelling Endogenous Risk

In a joint paper (Danielsson, Shin and Zigrand, 2009b), we explicitly model the endogeneity of risk. The risks impacting financial markets are attributable (at least in part) to the actions of market participants. In turn, market participants' actions depend on perceived risk.

In equilibrium, risk should be understood as the fixed point of the mapping from perceived risk to actual risk. When banks believe trouble is ahead, they take actions that bring about realised volatility. So, market turmoil results because banks anticipate such turmoil. This is so even if the underlying fundamental risks are constant. Such a fixed point is the "endogenous risk" in our title.

25.7.3 Risk Appetite and Trading Constraints

A model of endogenous risk enables the study of the endogenous propagation of financial booms and distress. Among other things, we can make precise the notion that market participants appear to become "more risk-averse" in response to deteriorating market outcomes. For economists, preferences and beliefs would normally be considered independent of one another.

However, we can distinguish "risk appetite" which motivates traders' actions, from "risk aversion", which is a preference parameter hard-wired into agents' characteristics. A trader's risk appetite may change even if their preferences are unchanged. The reason is that risk taking may be curtailed by the constraints that traders operate under, such as those based on Value-at-Risk (VaR).

In our framework, all active traders are risk-neutral, but they operate under VaR constraints, which are widespread among financial firms and encouraged by the Basel regulations. The Lagrange multiplier associated with the VaR constraint is the key quantity in our model. It plays two important roles. First, it affects the portfolio choice of the traders. Second, we show that the Lagrange multiplier is related to a generalised Sharpe ratio for the set of risky assets traded in the market as a whole and hence depends on the forecast probability density over future outcomes.

Beliefs and risk appetite are thus linked through the Lagrange multiplier (see Figure 25.4). To an outside observer, it would appear that market participants' preferences change with minute-by-minute changes in market outcomes. Crucially, shocks may be amplified through the feedback effects that operate from volatile outcomes to

Beliefs and Preferences 1

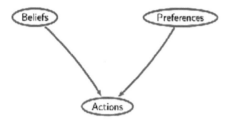

Beliefs and Preferences 2

Beliefs and Preferences 3

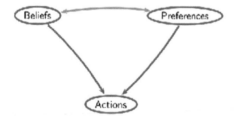

Figure 25.4: Market participants' beliefs and preferences.

reduced capacity to bear risk. In this sense, the distinction between "risk appetite" and "risk aversion" is more than a semantic quibble. This distinction helps us understand how booms and crises play out in the financial system.

25.7.4 Endogenous Volatility Clustering and Non-Linear Dependence

The model solution reveals several suggestive features that are consistent with empirical properties of asset returns found in practice.

The volatility of returns on financial assets generally changes over time, even though the fundamental shocks are constant. This is a well-known phenomenon known as volatility clustering. In the jargon, the model endogenously generates stochastic volatility.

Empirical evidence also suggests that option implied volatilities, and volatilities of volatilities, are shown to be high during market downturns, a result also predicted by our model.

Correlation also emerges where none exists at the fundamental level. During times of financial turmoil, correlations of returns are observed to increase with upward shifts in volatility. This phenomenon is known as non-linear dependence. We show that such features arise naturally in our model. Decrease in risk appetite and higher volatilities coincide with increased correlations, even though the underlying shocks are constant and independent across the risky assets.

25.7.5 Applying the Model to Financial Crises

A common feature of asset price bubbles followed by a financial crisis is that the markets go through long periods of high return amid low volatility, implying high Sharpe ratios. The bubble expands under tranquil conditions. Then suddenly, at the first hint of turbulence, the willingness of market participants to bear risk seemingly evaporates. The price path associated with a bubble exhibits the pattern traders describe as "going up by the escalator but down by the elevator".

However, the resulting shedding of exposures results in negative spillovers on other market participants from the sale of assets or withdrawal of credit. As prices fall, measured risks rise, previous correlations break down, or some combination of these occurs, market participants respond by further cutting their exposures. The global financial crisis of 2007–2009 is strewn with examples of such distress episodes.

Since our model explicitly captures such phenomena, it provides a useful framework for analysing outcomes in asset markets during financial crisis and could be a starting point for better analysis of financial stability.

25.7.6 Prudential Banking Regulations can be Destabilising

By pointing to the endogenous nature of risk, we highlight the role played by risk management rules used by active market participants, which serve to amplify aggregate fluctuations. Although it is a truism that ensuring the soundness of each individual institution ensures the soundness of the financial system, this proposition is vulnerable to the fallacy of composition.

25.8 Summary

Actions that an individual institution takes to enhance its soundness may undermine the soundness of others. If the purpose of financial regulation is to shield the financial system from collapse, it is a deeply flawed practice to base financial regulation on the "best practice" of individually optimal risk management policies, as is done under the current Basel II capital regulations. Risk is endogenous, and individually optimal risk management makes systemic financial crises sharper, larger, and more costly.

Bibliography

Acharya, V., R. Engle and M. Richardson (2012). Capital shortfall: A new approach to ranking and regulating systemic risks, VoxEU.org, 14 March.

Ackerman, A. (2016). Cyberattacks represent top risk, SEC chief says, *The Wall Street Journal*, 8 May.

Bank of England (2015). Financial Policy Report, July.

Bank of Canada (2014). Cyber security: Protecting the resilience of Canada's financial system, *Financial System Review*, December.

Baron, M. and W. Xiong (2017). Credit expansion and neglected crash risk, *Quarterly Journal of Economics* 132: 713–764.

Bhattacharya, S., C. Goodhart, D. Tsomocos, and A. Vardoulakis (2015). A reconsideration of Minsky's financial instability hypothesis, *Journal Money Credit and Banking* 47: 931–973.

BIS (2014). Cyber resilience in financial market infrastructures, BIS Committee on Payments and Market Infrastructure, November.

Boucher C., M., J. Danielsson, P. Kouontchou and B. Maillet (2014). Risk models–at–risk, *Journal of Banking and Finance* 44: 72–92.

Brunnermeier, M and LH Pedersen (2008). Market liquidity and funding liquidity, *Review of Financial Studies*, 22: 2201–2238.

Brunnermeier, M. and Y. Sannikov (2014). A macroeconomic model with a financial sector, *American Economic Review* 104: 379–421.

Csullag, B., J. Danielsson, and R. Macrae (2016). Why it doesn't make sense to hold bonds, VoxEU.org. 27 June.

Danielsson (2009). The myth of the riskometer, VoxEU.org, 5 January.

Danielsson, J. (2013). *Global financial systems*, Pearson.

Danielsson, J., M. Fouché, and R. Macrae (2015). The macro-micro conflict, VoxEU.org. 20 October.

Danielsson, J., H. S. Shin and J. P. Zigrand (2009a). Modelling financial turmoil through endogenous risk, VoxEU.org, 11 March.

Danielsson, J., H. S. Shin and J. P. Zigrand (2009b). Risk appetite and endogenous risk, https://riskresearch.org/papers/DanielssonShinZigrand2009b/

Danielsson, J., H. S. Shin and J. P. Zigrand (2011). Balance sheet capacity and endogenous risk, working paper, www.riskresearch.org.

Danielsson, J., H. S. Shin, and J. P. Zigrand (2012). Procyclical leverage and endogenous risk, Working Paper, Princeton University.

Danielsson, J., M. Valenzuela, and I. Zer (2018). Learning from history: Volatility and financial crises, *Review of Financial Studies*, forthcoming.

Danielsson, J. and J. P. Zigrand (2015). A proposed research and policy agenda for systemic risk, VoxEU.org, 7 August.

Former Federal Reserve Former Chair Janet Yellen (2014). https://www.federalreserve.gov/mediacenter/files/FOMCpresconf20140618.pdf

Giglio, S., B. Kelly and S. Pruitt (2015). Systemic risk and the macroeconomy: An empirical evaluation, VoxEU.org, 3 April.

Hayek, F. (1960). *The constitution of liberty*, Routledge.

International Monetary Fund, Bank for International Settlements and Financial Stability Board (2009). Report to G20 finance ministers and governors. Guidance to assess the systemic importance of financial institutions, markets and instruments: Initial considerations, Technical report.

Keynes, J. M. (1936). *The general theory of interest, employment and money*, Macmillan.

Laeven, L. and F. Valencia (2012). Systemic banking crises database: An update, IMF Working Paper.

Leijonhufvud, Axel (2011). Nature of an economy, CEPR Policy Insight 53 and VoxEU.org, 4 February.

Mallaby, S. (2015). *The man who knew: The life and times of Alan Greenspan*. London: Bloomsbury Publishing.

Minsky, H. (1977). The financial instability hypothesis: An interpretation of Keynes and an alternative to "standard" theory, *Nebraska Journal of Economics and Business* 16: 5–16.

Rose, A. and M. Spiegel (2009). Could an early warning system have predicted the crisis?, VoxEU.org, 3 August.

Shin, H. S. (2016). The bank/capital markets nexus goes global. Bank of International Settlements.

Taylor, A. and M. Schularick (2009). Credit booms go wrong, VoxEU.org, 8 December.

Evgueni Ivantsov

26 Reverse Stress Testing and Tail Risk

26.1 Introduction

The reverse stress test (RST) remains one of the key tools to address systemic or idiosyncratic tail risk. The banking sector has already acquired more than ten years of experience of using RST on a regular basis. Did this experience enrich tail risk management much? Unfortunately, less than it should. While in theory RST should be one of the most effective risk management tools decision-makers have in their disposal, in reality, decision-makers in many banks still consider RST an ancillary tool. They often treat RST as a purely regulatory exercise which should be run for the sake of ticking regulatory boxes. As a result, many banks fail to extract RST's real value that this tool can and should bring to the decision-makers.

In this chapter, we will analyse why RST's potential remains underused and offer some changes that should make RST much more useful for decision-makers.

Our analysis suggests that there are four areas of RST process that banks need to improve if they want to open up all potential of the RST as an effective risk management tool. The main weaknesses with a use of RST can be divided into the following groups:
- Weaknesses in the scenario development and scenario selection process
- Overreliance on stress impact quantification
- Oversimplification of RST methodology (e.g. ignoring the stress dynamics, interconnectedness and sequencing of events when modelling scenarios)
- Underestimation of the importance of a mitigating action plan, which leads to relegation of the contingency planning to an ancillary element of RST

In this chapter, we will focus on these four weaknesses and suggest improvements based on the industry's best practices. The most important improvements that we suggest include an enrichment of the RST scenarios, focusing on the RST process and senior management's dialogue, a transition to dynamic stress simulation and a development of credible and actionable contingency planning.

26.2 Who is Swimming Naked?

Warren Buffet famously said that "*It is only when the tide goes out that you learn who's been swimming naked!*" This is what we all can see when the systemic event struck

Note: Edited by Tiziano Bellini

https://doi.org/10.1515/9783110647907-026

the industry. The global financial crisis of 2007–2009 revealed it very clearly when a large number of banks that previously were regarded as "world's leading", "strong" and "innovative" miserably failed in a very short space of time and either disappeared or were bailed out by governments. The Covid-19 crisis also demonstrated how well different nations and their health systems were prepared to sustain extreme shock. Some countries which were previously regarded as having the outstanding health systems appeared to be ill-prepared to counter the global challenge.

The reverse stress test (RST) is an excellent tool to detect "who is swimming naked" before "the tide goes out". Large systemic or idiosyncratic risk events happen not so frequently. For example, the industry business cycle can last ten to fifteen years until the financial system accumulates a critical mass of disbalances that trigger a systemic shock. At this point, many firms already have fundamental business flaws like unsustainable business models, fatal investment errors and reckless risk cultures. It's already too late to stop these firms from crushing when the business environment starts becoming adverse.

RST, if done in a proper way, can help to uncover fundamental flaws and weaknesses that a firm already has until it's too late. In this case, the mitigating actions which should follow the RST can enormously reduce the risk for the firm becoming a victim of a systemic or idiosyncratic shock.

26.3 Enrichment of Stress Scenarios

As with any stress testing, the RST can be as valuable as its scenario. The wrong choice of a scenario diminishes the value of the whole stress testing exercise. A stress scenario that has been chosen is not a forecast. It is not the "base case". Moreover, the very definition of the RST dictates a choice of a high-severity scenario. The extreme stress scenario is always about the events that are highly unlikely to happen at all. Using the analogy, when an airline company trains their pilots on a flight simulator which simulates a failure of some critical systems during the flight (e.g. landing gear failure or engine failure), the company doesn't expects that this failure will necessarily happen during the next flight. But everyone understands that if this highly unlikely event occurs, it could result in a catastrophe, for which the airline company has zero tolerance. Hence, pilots need to be ready and able to prevent the worst. The same logic should apply for RST scenarios. These scenarios should provide an opportunity for decision-makers to be trained to deal with highly unlikely adverse events.

26.3.1 "Armageddon" Scenarios

The most popular scenarios for RST so far are major macroeconomic shocks (e.g. an extraordinary economic downturn), devastating geo-political events (social unrests, armed conflicts, trade embargos) and natural catastrophes or a combination of these events.

However, the prime purpose of RST is to uncover weaknesses in the existing business model using an exteme adverse scenario that would make this business model unviable. Ideally, this tail risk scenario should be rather company-specific than just a general "Armageddon" scenario.

The problem with an "Armageddon" scenario is that usually a such scenario means a devastation of the entire banking sector. Consider an economic disaster scenario with a drastic GDP drop, a skyrocket unemployment and a meltdown of residential and commercial real estate markets. Under this scenario, many players of the banking market would incur huge losses and fail without external support. The value of this scenario for an individual firm is quite limited as it hardly helps to uncover weaknesses of the specific business model that the firm relies on. The severity of the scenario is such that most of the business models would become unviable anyway in these harsh circumstances.

The task of RST scenario creation is to prepare and choose a set of scenarios which create stress situations targeting a specific business model, a specific business strategy or specific business portfolios.

Unfortunately, real-life Armageddon-type scenarios prevail in RST. It is not wrong to use Armageddon scenarios in RST. Armageddon-type scenarios can and should be considered but these scenarios should not be the only scenarios to be tested. We need to understand that Armageddon scenarios are only a subset of all severe but plausible scenarios that should be tested by running RST. The diversity of scenarios is an important factor of RST usefulness, and an overuse of one type of scenarios substantially diminishes the added value of the RST framework.

Why do banks like Armageddon scenarios so much? One of the reasons why it happens is a "corporate ego". Firms are often too reluctant to search weaknesses in their own strategies and business models. Scenario developers and scenario approvers prefer not to challenge a wisdom of their bosses who formulate the firm's business strategy and are responsible for the business model. Instead, they prefer to take a less risky stance by choosing a Armageddon-type scenario which, if unfolded, would be fatal for almost any other financial firm.

In addition, this "safe" scenario selection strategy helps banks to manage their relationships with regulators. Regulators are very interested in seeing results of internal stress tests done by regulated firms. If RST demonstrates a catastrophic failure of the firm's business model in a specific stress scenario when other firms are likely to sustain the shock, regulators would see this firm as an outlier. Therefore, regulators would immediately start asking the firm's top management difficult questions and request swift actions to remedy the situation. None of the firm's bosses want to inflict such a conversation with their regulators.

26.3.2 Past Experience is not a Good Guidance for Scenario Writers

When preparing tail risk scenarios for RST, it's important to keep in mind that past experience cannot be regarded as a reliable reference. A clear majority of historical stress events had rather mild severity. By definition, tail risk events are quite infrequent. Therefore, unlike the creation of "normal" stress scenarios, the extreme scenario writing requires more than just a utilisation of the historical experience and pure statistical modelling. The out-of-the-box thinking becomes an important condition for creating a robust extreme scenario.

Therefore, in order to develop a good extreme stress scenario, scenario writers should always think about the unthinkable and sometimes be "illogical", meaning they should include in the scenario events or risk drivers that may sound implausible at first glance.

The situation with the Covid-19 global pandemic is a good example. In the last several years, banks ran numerous stress tests. Some of them did an analysis of scenarios of different pandemics. But how many of them did a stress test for a global pandemic scenario with a complete lockdown of entire continents? Before the coronavirus outbreak starts, this scenario had a very low chance to be approved – people would discard such a scenario straight away as it would seem too harsh and entirely implausible. But this so-called implausible scenario has unfolded. And many banks didn't have contingency plans for this situation and found themselves in the uncharted territory when the global pandemic hit.

Quite often, the tail risk arises from several little-appreciated events (errors, failures) with very low individual probability, which could trigger a drastic event if they happen at the same time. In this sense, the extreme risk can be literally manufactured by sequences of several non-critical rare events.

This is another difficulty in preparing an extreme stress test scenario. Not only the scenario should be, to some extent "illogical" and "out of the box", but also the approval of such scenario is a very challenging process. "Illogical" scenarios have less of a chance to be accepted than a scenario which replicates a past event. Usually, these scenarios don't survive the approval process. It is so easy to apply the "general logic" and "demonstrate" that the extreme stress scenario which has had no precedents is illogical. It is so easy to label such scenarios implausible.

People do not always understand that proper risk management has already eliminated or substantially reduced the possibility for "logical" extreme events to materialise. In many highly regulated sectors like aviation, financial services, health care, a majority of "logical" and "plausible" tail risk events have been eliminated many years ago. If we want to develop an extreme stress testing scenario, we need to think out of the box and go beyond the conventional logic. Somebody needs to explain to key stakeholders the main principles of extreme scenarios. And key stakeholders need to fully recognise the difference between the normal and extreme stress test scenarios and accept the unusual logic as a necessary ingredient of any good tail risk scenario.

26.4 Four Types of Scenarios for RST

When preparing a scenario for RST, the focus should be on very severe and extreme events that can jeopardise the firm's existence. The widely used RST scenarios are external events (a very severe economic shock or a natural disaster) or acts of a third party (e.g. a terrorist or cyber attack) or a combination of these two events. In other words, the focus is on uncontrollable risks. While these are absolutely legitimate scenarios for RST, the focus on an external force doesn't allow to uncover some other potential weaknesses of the business model. A hidden assumption of such scenarios is that it implies that the firm could be a victim of external forces but can't create its own disaster.

However, the analysis of banking failures shows that failed banks are rare "innocent victims" of external forces, but more often, their failures are "hand-made" disasters. In reality, extreme risk events are often created as a result of the very basic and preventable actions like reckless behaviour of top management or an unsustainable business model.

The best way to illustrate what can cause an extreme risk event is to analyse the past history of the most severe nuclear reactor accidents. If we look at four the most severe accidents that happened with nuclear reactors to date (with severity ranked at a level of 5 to 7 points on the 7-grade scale known as the International Nuclear and Radiological Event Scale), we can notice that each case was triggered by a different cause. Yet, each one represents a distinctive category. These categories can apply to extreme events in another sector, such as the banking and financial services industry. When preparing a scenario of the RST, experts can use these four categories as a guidance for selecting the type of a scenario they would like to be tested.

26.4.1 Uncontrollable Risk Event

On 10 October 1957, the worst nuclear disaster in UK history happened at Unit 1 nuclear reactor at Windscale (Cumbria). The fire destroyed the reactor and led to the contamination of a large territory by radioactive materials. The investigation revealed that the fire and explosion of the graphite core was caused by the so-called Wigner effect – the spontaneous rush of heat from the graphite due to the accumulation of potential energy from the neutron flow in the nuclear reactor. As the Wigner effect was an unknown phenomenon in 1957, the explosion that happened in Windscale was an out-of-the-blue event and was entirely unpredictable, uncontrollable and almost unavoidable at the time.

If we think about uncontrollable risk events in the financial business, we might consider the Covid-19 global crisis which, for the banking sector, represents the uncontrollable and unavoidable financial shock. Let's look at the Covid-19 crisis from a perspective of a profitable European bank with a solid balance sheet, a diversified customer base, a well-performing credit portfolio and efficient customer services. When the global pandemic erupted, the bank had no chance to avoid the shock and had become a victim of the global health crisis. The bank suffered consequences from the lockdown of entire continents and a sudden stop of the global economy. Moreover, in this situation, the bank not only suffered from the direct financial impact of the crisis (e.g. interest rate cuts, a profit margin erosion, an increase of credit losses and RWA), but the bank also had to step in and take the burden of its social responsibility by helping its employees, community and customers (e.g. vulnerable individuals and SMEs).

26.4.2 The Chain of Non-Critical Errors

On 28 March 1979, a partial nuclear meltdown occurred at the Three Mile Island nuclear reactor – the worst accident in the US commercial nuclear power plant history. The accident was triggered by the jamming of the excess pressure released valve due to a mechanical fault. Also, despite the valve being stuck open, a light on the control panel indicated that the valve was closed. Operators failed to recognise the problem earlier. Therefore, two technical errors and the human error, albeit not critical in isolation, happened simultaneously and created a full-scale nuclear accident. In fact, many extreme events in different areas of human activity have been triggered by the coincidence of multiple non-critical errors.

Building a parallel between the events in the nuclear incidents and financial fiascos, we can mention the TSB Bank's outage, which put the bank on its knees and resulted in a huge reputational damage, £366m in direct costs and a resignation of the CEO. The meltdown of the banking IT system happened during the planned migration of the customer IT platform. According to the independent investigation report of the incident, the IT meltdown was a result of a range of technical issues rather than one big error. These technical issues all together made the new IT platform unstable and eventually led to a collapse of the IT system.

26.4.3 Deliberate Violation of Rules

Reckless behaviour was and remains the source of many extreme events. On 26 April 1986, the most devastating nuclear disaster in human history happened when the reactor at the Chernobyl nuclear power plant (Ukraine, former Soviet Union) exploded. While there is still no agreement on what fundamentally caused the accident, one thing remains clear – the accident was triggered by a human error. It was not just a mistake of the operators, but deliberate actions. In other words, the operators understood that they were breaking the operation rules.

In the financial industry, the most notorious examples of such extreme event causes are cases of rogue trading or large-scale frauds. We can mention here a case when a deliberate violation of the rules led to the collapse of an entire financial institution. The rogue trader destroyed Barings Bank in 1995 and the rogue boss bankrupted Bernard Madoff Investment Securities in 2008.

26.4.4 Strategic Mistake

Strategic mistakes are often the primary causes of failures, yet it is difficult to spot strategic errors ex ante. For many years, they remained uncovered until these mistakes became apparent by unfortunate coincidence. The Fukushima Daiichi nuclear disaster which happened on 11 March 2011 was this type of event. The fundamental cause of the accident was a string of strategic mistakes in both the plant location and its design. The most severe mistakes were:

- The plant was located in an area of high tsunami risk. The plant was not substantially affected by the earthquake but suffered from flooding caused by the tsunami.
- The switching stations for emergency generators of the cooling system were located in the poorly flood protected turbine buildings. This led to a cut of the emergency cooling system after the flooding, while cooling generators remained operational in the flood-protected area.

Interestingly, strategic mistakes are the most common cause of failures in the financial sector. Many remarkable banks' fiascos happened as a direct result of strategic mistakes made by the banks' bosses. The most nitrous examples of a strategic mistake of the financial institutions are a collapse of Northern Rock in 2007 and the failures of UBS, AIG, HBOS, RBS and Wachovia in 2008.

This classification of the four key underlying causes of extreme risk events not only helps to better understand the nature of tail risk, but also gives us a direction for RST scenario preparation. External and uncontrollable risks are not the only one category that should be addressed in RST.

The other three categories of tail risks are internal for the organisations. Errors and weaknesses of different elements of the management system, banking infrastructure or the governance framework (isolated or simultaneous) need to be uncovered during the RST. Human reckless behaviour, the violation of conduct and other existing rules and common sense should be also in the scope of RST scenarios.

Strategic mistakes and flaws of business models, albeit representing possibly the largest challenge to uncover, should be a prime focus of RST. While this category is also linked to human errors, these errors are not as obvious as those in the previous category when people knowingly violate regulatory requirements, internal instructions or safety rules. The problem with strategic failures is that it can take many years before these mistakes surface and become apparent. Moreover, quite often, an inherently dangerous strategy or a reckless business model once accepted by the organisation starts shaping the employees' behaviour. This risky strategy translates to the firm's instructions, business plans, employees' incentives and business culture. That is why for people inside the organisation, it is very difficult to spot the strategic error or business model's flaw before it triggers the extreme event.

26.5 Quantitative vs Qualitative

Unfortunately, RST is often treated as a predominantly quantitative exercise. Regulators focus on the quantitative side of the stress testing because they often see stress testing as a capital sufficiency measurement tool. The use of quantitative methods and historical data has become the central element of this approach.

The internal stress testing stakeholders, such as top management, and external bodies (regulators) make the stress testing results the top priority. These results signify the numbers of stressed balance sheet, profit & loss and cashflow statements, estimated stressed losses, impairments, figures of risk-weighted assets under stress, stressed capital ratios and so on. The desire to obtain a set of numbers dictates the prevailing stress testing process: the lion share of time and effort during RST is spent on number crunching and on discussions about how these numbers were derived and why. People who involved in stress testing can tell the stories of long battles around stress testing numbers – which number is wrong, which is right and why.

This great focus on numbers can be justified and accepted for scenarios emulating a mild stress when the aim is to test slight variations around the base case. In this case, we can rely on quantitative models and references to historical data because slight mild shocks happened many times in the past and we have a sound understanding of the sensitivities of the business with respect to mild shocks.

However, RST scenarios are fundamentally different as they focus on risk events with low likelihood but high severity. Quantitative models that can robustly assess an impact of mild stress scenarios appear ineffective and often useless for extreme ones. These models are built on large samples of data, which reflect the "normal" or close to normal relationships between risk drivers and dependent variables. The tail risk scenarios push the system to its new state where normal relationships do not hold anymore due to non-linearity and cliff effects. In addition, when we talk about the extreme scenarios, we can expect that the new state of the system can trigger new risk drivers, which are not visible in the normal situation (e.g. customer behaviour in the extreme stress situation can be unpredictable and very different from what we normally observe). In this situation, the number crunching technique is rendered unreliable due to high uncertainty regarding the potential outcomes.

A reliance on models for the extreme stress scenarios is questionable due to the non-linearity of relationships between risk drivers and dependent variables and paucity of data that doesn't allow to credibly amend the modelling results. Suppose for a UK bank you were tasked to model an impact of high unemployment on the retail credit portfolios. In this case, in your scenario you need to specify how key variables would move in case of an extreme increase of the UK unemployment rate. Based on the large number of observations, we have a pretty good understanding about the sensitivity of main economic parameters to the unemployment rate change. But most of these observations are concentrated in the area of minor deviations.

Therefore, we can easily model slight changes (e.g. the increase of the unemployment rate by 1 percentage point will lead to increase of impairment losses of the given credit portfolio by 2%). However, we have a very vague understanding about the impact of extreme shocks – for example, if the UK unemployment rate would increase from the level of 4% to 30% and remains at this peak for a prolonged period of time. The answer is difficult one. First, we have no historical precedents of such a shock. Second, due to the non-linearity of relationships, the extrapolation of the normal sensitivities becomes unreliable – it is likely that such an extreme spike in unemployment triggers the cliff effect when at a certain level of stress, all observed relationships suddenly brake and start moving unpredictably. But we don't know when this cliff effect would be triggered (or perhaps, several cliffs) and how the relationships would change by the cliff effect.

The rule of thumb that we use should be as follows: The more severe the stress scenario is, the less reliable models are. The exercise moves from the predominantly quantitative type for mild stress scenarios to the assumption-driven one for tail risk scenarios when numbers reflect opinions of experts. The power of analytics diminishes rapidly when we move to the territory of extreme events.

The whole idea of RST is to virtually simulate an event that does not occur often in real life but can be potentially very severe. How can we put together an exceptionally severe scenario of RST and our inability to reliably quantify its impact?

In our view, results (a set of numbers) should not be considered as the top priority for RST. The process itself should be the top priority. The stress testing process, if carried out correctly, creates the main added value for the organisation. The central part of this process should be a dialogue of the senior management of the organisation that should take place when RST is run. It's important to bring together the right decision-makers and initiate a serious discussion about what would happen to the organisation and its business should the stress scenario materialises. This dialogue should be supported by some calculations and estimations where possible. Yet the focus should be on mitigating actions that the organisation would take to defend its business, customers, employees and shareholders in the adverse situation.

Instead of a set of numbers, the main outcome of the RST it should be:

- an action plan for immediate implementation that addresses the business model flaws and weaknesses that have been identified during the discussions of the stress scenario
- a contingency plan which should be deployed if the stress scenario unfolds

Ironically, contingency plans, the most important result of RST, are often ignored or relegated to a box-ticking exercise. In fact, the development of a credible, effective and detailed contingency plan to mitigating tail risks is the most difficult and most important RST's task. In Section 26.6, we will provide more details on how a credible contingency plan should be produced.

Instead of crunching numbers, stress testing participants should allocate their time and intellectual capabilities to contingency planning. They should organise a thinking process focusing on what can be done to eliminate weaknesses of the business model and prevent the firm from a potential failure. Top management who review and approve the RST results should also worry much more about credibility and effectiveness of the proposed action plan and the contingency plan rather than about a set of numbers produced under particular assumptions.

A good contingency plan contains all of the necessary details which should guarantee its flawless implementation and ultimate efficiency. What an RST team needs is the WWWH plan: What, When, Who and How. The plan should contain not only what is required to implement, but also the clear assignment of responsibilities for carrying out each action point, estimation of timing, costs, resources and dependencies.

Therefore, when we run RST, we should spend less efforts and time on number crunching trying to figure out precisely the amount of potential loss or a capital shortfall due to stress. Instead, we should focus to the process of developing robust action plans and ensure that all stakeholders understand mitigating actions and how these actions should be rolled out.

This approach reinforces other important functions of RST. It can be and should be used as a "flight simulator" for people in the organisation. The RST simulates a stress environment and gives an opportunity to train staff to mitigate the impact of the adverse events. If RST's participants spend most of their time on number crunching, they miss the learning experience of RST. If we focus on the development of a credible action plan and robust WWWH contingency plan and engage all stakeholders to participate in this process, we, therefore, put these people in the "flight simulator". Because of this activity, people can obtain the "virtual" experience of dealing with extreme stress events.

26.6 Dynamic Simulation of Extreme Scenarios

As we know from the practice, when an extreme risk event unfolds, the most serious challenges that decision-makers need to deal with are a high level of uncertainty and the dynamic interconnectedness.

26.6.1 Dealing with High Uncertainty

High uncertainty is the most important characteristic of a tail risk event. Take the Covid-19 crisis. When the pandemic started spreading, the main problem for decision-makers was uncertainty with the speed of disease spreading, ways the virus infects people, the incubation period and symptoms, its impact on various communities, the mortality rate, the effectiveness of testing and treatment, and so on. Such information was absolutely vital for decision-makers who were responsible for developing a course of actions to stop the pandemic and to provide a robust medical response. However, even leading epidemiologists and health organisations straggled to get these vital pieces of information correct and their forecasts were so drastically different that decision-makers had no other choice but make heroic assumptions and a lot of guesswork. This high uncertainty explains why different countries have chosen such different strategies to fight the virus when the pandemic erupted. The different strategies varied from the very strict lockdown to a "herd immunity" approach.

We observed the similar situation during the global financial crisis in 2008, when decision-makers faced high uncertainty as well. The events unfolded so fast and unpredictably that decision-makers were straggling to rely on any forecast. The result was that many financial firms made very costly mistakes when they tried to mitigate the financial impact.

Based on the experience, we would expect that when running RST, banks should pay attention to this important characteristic of almost any tail risk event and simulate the high uncertainty environment. Yet, a majority of the banks don't proper incorporate a high uncertainty environment when running RST. The scenario writers prepare an RST scenario which includes all stages of the stress event and parameters from the start to the finish. This scenario then is given to stress testing team and key stakeholders. In other words, people who run the RST don't face uncertainty with regards to the sequence and magnitude of the stress event. The stress test scenario details are determined in advance and are fully disclosed to stress test participants. There is much uncertainty for decision-makers participating in such RST. They know what, when and how the crisis would unfold.

This artificial approach massively changes the focus of RST and makes the task of the stress testing team quite simple. The team should run quantitative models calculating the impact based on the known scenario and then to check whether the pre-defined outcome is reached. If not, then the scenario is corrected, and the process starts again.

Needless to say, this approach makes such RST unrealistic. When the extreme event strikes, decision-makers have no choice but to make their decisions based on limited information that they get. "Blindfolded" decision-makers often make errors and this can drastically affect the outcome and the ultimate impact of the adverse event. In reality, decision-makers after making a step can't rewind the situation and make a different step. Mistakes that are made in the situation of high uncertainty are often very costly or even fatal for the existence of the entire organisation. A typical example of the fatal error is a decision of Lloyds TSB's management to takeover HBOS after an unprecedented run on HBOS shares in September 2008. After this costly mistake, the bank found itself on the brink of a collapse and the UK government had no choice but to step in and bail out the bank.

26.6.2 Interconnectedness and Networking Effect

Another weakness of the traditional RST approach, which is logically linked to the first one previously described, is underestimation or even ignoring interconnectedness and the network effect in the banking business. The networking effect plays an especially important role during large market events (e.g. a macroeconomic shock, a global pandemic, a natural disaster). If banks underestimate the networking effect in their RSTs, it makes RSTs an "artificial" exercise detached from the reality of the business. The importance of the networking effect can be illustrated by the "Lehman Brothers" effect. After Lehman Brothers collapsed and filed for bankruptcy on 14 September 2008, it sent a shockwave which travelled across the financial world, and in the next two weeks, many financial institutions in the US and Europe collapsed. The casualties were AIG and Washington Mutual in the US, Lloyds TSB and Bradford & Bingley in the UK, Fortis, Hypo Real Estate, Dexia in the continental Europe and the entire Islandic banking sector.

The domino effect is an extreme manifestation of financial interconnectedness, but interconnectedness appears in many other forms during systemic shocks. There are many other forms of the networking effect that could play an important role and predetermine and escalate the crisis (fire sales of assets, market panics, bank runs).

If we consider a systemic event in RST, we must explicitly assume actions of competitors and systemically important market players which can substantially change the business environment in which the crisis is unfolding. Actions of regulators, policy makers and politicians are other key factors that can trigger substantial dynamic changes in the interconnected world and need to be considered. The behaviour of customers in stress situations plays a crucial role as well and their collective actions can become a game changer in the crisis situation (e.g. bank runs).

Even if RST focuses on the idiosyncratic risk event, we can't ignore the behaviour and reactions of internal and external stakeholders (employees, shareholders, regulators, customers, social media and press, competitors). Their actions (collective or individual) can substantially influence the direction, speed and severity of the shock.

26.6.3 Turning a War Gaming to Stress Simulating

If we think about a situation where high uncertainty is a natural factor, the perfect example is a war. Prussian general and military theorist Carl von Clausewitz wrote about war in the following terms: "War is the realm of uncertainty; three-quarters of the factors on which action is based are wrapped in a fog of greater or lesser uncertainty".

In addition, the interconnectedness of parties involved in a war and the networking effect are other dominant factors of a war. This is because a war is a complex social phenomenon and what happens in the war theatre is only a part of a complex war machine. An outcome of the war campaign depends not only on what the commander in chief has in their disposal when the war starts but also on their resources. The outcome of the war is often predetermined by the actions and behaviours of other actors during the war outside the war theatre. The Vietnam War is a good example of how the war outcome was decided not by the military power of two fighting armies but actions and behaviour of other actors outside the battle ground.

To deal with uncertainty and interconnectedness, the military invented a war gaming and has been successfully using it for more than 150 years. The concept of a war gaming should be applied for RST to substitute the prevailing traditional approach which often underestimates factors of uncertainty and interconnectedness. With necessary adjustments, the war gaming turns into the dynamic stress simulation, which works perfectly for RST for the banking business.

To simulate the interconnectedness in RST, a bank needs to have more than one stress testing team. Participants that are going to be involved in the RST should be divided in several teams, each of which will play a role of a designated entity or a group of market actors. For example, if an RST scenario is based around a big systemic event (e.g. a market crush, a global pandemic, a natural disaster, etc.), to simulate the networking effect, the participants should be divided in at least four teams which will play roles of the following market actors:
- Bank itself
- Competitors
- Regulators/policy makers
- Customers

Each group will work and act independently to make their own scenario analysis and propose actions responding to the crisis situation. It is also required to have a team which will be assigned to administrate the whole process of RST (the admin team).

To simulate the high uncertainty that decision-makers face during a severe risk event, the participants of RST should not be aware in advance about the scenario which will be tested. The admin team should keep the stress scenario confidential. The scenario should be broken down into several chronological phases (e.g. for a scenario covering one year, it could be four phases of three months each).

The dynamic simulation, therefore, should include several consecutive iterations. Each iteration includes one time period for which each participating team should make their own analysis of the stress situation and come up with the action plan (see Figure 26.1).

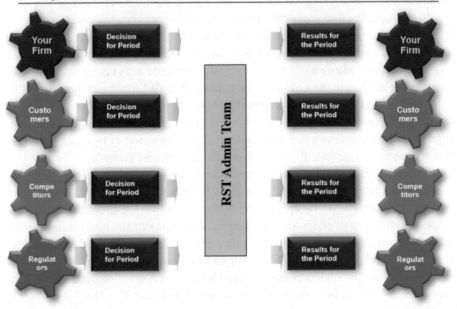

Figure 26.1: Algorithm of the dynamic simulation.

At the start of the RST, the admin team reveals only phase 1 of the scenario and asks participating teams who play roles of different market actors to make their own scenario analysis, assess the potential impact and come up with their mitigating actions. After all teams provide the admin team with the results and actions for phase 1, the admin team needs to analyse how collective actions of all market actors would impact the bank's position and how the initial scenario would change due to the cumulative effect in phase 1.

Based on the analysis of phase 1, the admin team amends phase 2 of the initial scenario to reflect actions of market actors in phase 1. They also amend the results for the bank after phase 1, taking into account actions of other teams which could affect the situation and financial position of the bank (e.g. changes in the pricing, product offerings and risk appetite of competitors). The updated scenario for phase 2 and the results of phase 1 are communicated to participants for their next phase analysis and mitigating actions. Therefore, the results of phase 1 and the amended scenario for phase 2 now become a starting point for the next iteration of the stress test. The process continues until the completion of the final iteration of the scenario or until a point of the banking failure (Figure 26.2).

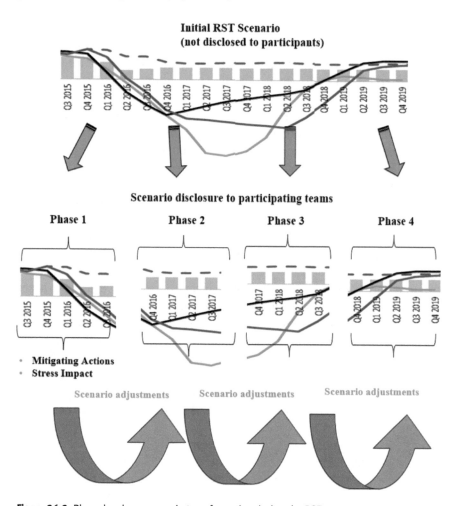

Figure 26.2: Phase by phase scenario transformation during the RST.

Therefore, the initial scenario is constantly amended during the RST, which creates the realism of the simulation. None of the participants (including the admin team which developed the initial version of the scenario) can know in advance the final scenario or even the scenario for the next phase. Like in real life, this "moving" scenario is shaped by the actions of market participants and other stakeholders involved in the crisis situation. The final scenario can only be seen retrospectively. The realism of the stress scenario is achieved due to its dynamic transformation based on the decisions made during the stress test.

26.6.4 Flight Simulator for Decision-Makers

The use of the dynamic simulation in RST fundamentally changes the quality of the test. It brings a much higher degree of realism in the simulation process. In fact, it turns the exercise into a "flight simulator" for bankers. The benefits of the dynamic simulation approach are not limited to simulating the uncertainty regarding the stress scenario. Like in real life, the firm's performance and ability to weather the storm depends, to a large extent, not on the overall firm's position before the stress, but on the effectiveness of decision-making and the robustness of mitigating actions during the stress period. Strategic mistakes or an inability to react fast or adequately enough on the changing environment can cost a fortune and be a decisive factor of a failure in the wilderness of the stress.

The dynamic simulation helps to reveal a level of preparedness of decision-makers in the organisation to mitigate extreme shocks. The management team participating in RST will not have a chance to "undo" mistakes that they can make during the simulation. It gives a valuable learning experience to participants. The dynamic simulation not only trains decision-makers to make the right decisions in situations of high uncertainty, but it also trains the management to uncover their mistakes faster once they are made, and to take appropriate measures to mitigate the damage.

The dynamic simulation tests not only the bank but robustness of decision-making in stress situations. Like in real life, in the RST under the dynamic simulation, the stress impact is driven to a large extent by management decisions made in a period of stress. Several errors or even one critical error made in the process of RST might lead to the immediate collapse of the firm. At the same time, a skillful management can allow the firm to stay aloft and sustain the stress much longer than the scenario developers could have expected.

Therefore, the dynamic simulation creates new utility of RST. The main value of the dynamic stress simulation is not in risk models' outputs nor in numbers produced by the RST team, but in the participants' intellectual output in a form of the scenario analysis, anticipations of behaviour and actions of key market players, proposed mitigating actions. The implementation of the dynamic simulation approach not only increases the realism of stress situations but also adds an important learning component which is otherwise missing. By training decision-makers to work in a stress situation, the dynamic simulation approach builds and enhances the management's capabilities to make decisions under stressed conditions. It shifts the priority from number crunching to strategic thinking and risk mitigation.

26.7 Contingency Planning

The dynamic stress simulation trains RST's participants to anticipate the unexpected and to make decisions in a situation of high uncertainty. At each iteration of the simulation process, RST participants need to propose their mitigating actions. These actions should be formalised and to be detailed enough for their integration into the dynamic simulation. In particular, it should include clear responsibilities and accountabilities, time required, expected outcomes, costs, implications for P&L and the balance sheet, and so on. In other words, these mitigating actions become a part of the WWWH contingency planning that we mentioned in Section 26.4.

The WWWH plan becomes one of the most valuable outcomes of RST. It provides a blueprint of actions that the firm should implement once the similar scenario unfolds in real life. When a crisis emerges next time, the WWWH plan developed during the RST should be deployed.

There is no doubt that in reality, the way of how the stress unfolds will be not exactly the same as it was simulated during the RST. Each stress has a potentially unlimited number of scenarios of how it can develop, depending on behaviour and the actions of all actors involved and the unpredictable nature of the networking effect. Therefore, we don't expect that all action points set out in the WWWH plan during the RST can be appropriate, feasible or achievable. Yet, the WWWH plan provides a good starting point for the crisis mitigation. When a tail risk event strikes, the bank should review its WWWH plans, select the appropriate one and update its action points considering the current circumstances. Without the readily available WWWH plan, the bank will likely be caught ill prepared, which could result in a slow crisis response and in costly errors.

The Covid-19 crisis confirmed the importance of having well-developed contingency planning not only for companies but also for countries. One of the reasons why South Korea has been so successful in fighting the coronavirus outbreak was that the country had a credible and well-resourced plan developed in previous years in response to failures in previous epidemics.

How can a firm ensure that the appropriate WWWH plan exists in the firm's depository? Indeed, the world of extreme and unpredictable events is massive. The life is the best and the most creative writer of stress scenarios. There is no guarantee that the next extreme shock has been already considered during one of the previous stress tests and the appropriate WWWH contingency plan is ready and waiting for the deployment. However, even if the crisis has new and previously unknown nature and risk drivers and never been analysed in the stress testing programme, WWWH contingency planning still can be very useful. The firm can take mitigating actions from different contingency plans and, like the Lego blocks, assemble them in the new contingency plan to address the previously unknown challenge.

26.8 Summary

After more than a ten-year period of using the RST, we should analyse the experience and identify areas for further improvements. Financial institutions still need to do quite a lot to improve their RST processes to ensure their effectiveness for decision-making. While there are many areas that firms should improve, we suggest that organisations should give propriety for the following four areas where their efforts will bring the crucial positive changes to RST effectiveness:

– *Scenario development and selection:* The process should be based on an understanding of the nature of tail risk events and should ensure the diversity of selected scenarios.
– *Qualitative scenario analysis:* An overreliance on a quantification of the RST impact and making the number crunching the central element of RST drains the firm's resources and distracts from the more important task. The senior management dialogue and qualitative scenario analysis should prevail in the RST process.
– *Dynamic stress simulation:* The transition to the dynamic stress simulation is a game changer for RST. It will allow a realistic simulation of uncertainty of the stress situation and the interconnectedness of the financial system. Subsequently, the dynamic simulation will turn RST into the "flight simulator" for decision-makers.
– *Contingency planning:* The implementation of WWWH contingency planning as a fundamental element of the RST process is necessary for firms to stay upfront to counter severe risk events once they unfold in real life.

Michael Eichhorn, Tiziano Bellini, Daniel Mayenberger

27 Summary and Outlook

What has been Learned and Where to go Next?!

27.1 Introduction

This book starts with three anecdotes which illustrate the relevance of RST and the timeliness of this book. The problem statement establishes that RST is still a "young child" with various challenges. Besides technical challenges, neither a detailed regulatory guidance nor an industry standard or best practice for is implementation exists.

Against a background of sparse literature, each chapter of this book has the objective to introduce ideas about how a user can address these challenges and build their own RST toolbox. This final section summarises the key learnings and offers insights into possible future development lines.

The chapter follows the book structure – which is organised in six parts – in a chronological order.

27.2 Fundamentals of Reverse Stress Testing (Part I)

Key takeaways:
- Users (regulators, practitioners, etc.) should experiment with different RST configurations and test designs across the dimensions laid out in the morphological box in **Chapter 1**.
- While regulatory guidance has been pivotal for the proliferation of RST across the globe, descriptions often remain high-level, in parts on purpose led by the principle of proportionality. However, examples of more detailed guidance can be found as can be reports on comparative practices. They should pave the way for the further evolution of the regulatory guidance on RST.
- Individual supervisory bodies have started to use specific RST configurations, specifically for Interest Rate Risk in the Banking Book and for Recovery Planning.
- Regulators and banks should work on the further cross-linkage and co-integration of RST and other crisis management frameworks, including resolution planning (see also Part V).

https://doi.org/10.1515/9783110647907-027

Part I introduces the Fundamentals of reverse stress testing.

In **Chapter 1** we outline the central idea of this book:

> *RST should be first and foremost considered a powerful thinking tool with versatile practical uses to support deep and deliberate thinking. Similar to the use of stress tests in material research, there are many different configurations and test designs available for RST.*

The chapter also provides an initial outline of key benefits and challenges. These are further deepened in **Chapter 2**, in which Gann lays out the fundamentals of RST. Following a summary of the central components of a comprehensive RST framework, the chapter discusses the term "failing or likely to fail" and potential approaches to identify and extract relevant scenarios which might threaten the survival of the bank. The chapter also focusses on the close relationship between RST, business model and risk strategy requirements. Gann presents a quantitative, cross-risk approach that enables the generation of economic control stimuli within the framework of value-based corporate management. He concludes that, correctly applied, RST can make a fundamental contribution to value-orientated corporate management that is geared towards the interests of investors, while ensuring creditors' claims can be met at all times. An elementary prerequisite for this would be to find an appropriate balance between the benefits and costs caused by reverse stress tests. Gann closes by expressing his hope that regulators acting with the objective of safeguarding financial market stability will use this balance as a guideline – both in the interpretation of the current requirements and in further specifications of the supervisory requirements in the future.

Building on this, Eichhorn and Romano summarise the evolution of the regulatory guidance with the help of a chronology in **Chapter 3**. They argue that RST is visibly growing in importance, as evidenced by the rapid, global proliferation since 2008. At the same time, the regulatory requirements would tend to remain high-level. Regulators seem to acknowledge challenges related with the implementation of RST. However, they would not tell users how to perform RST. Instead, a common message would be the principle of proportionality. In light of this, the chapter aims to contribute to future guidance in three ways. First, it identifies specific regulatory publications which provide answers to frequently asked questions and industry challenges. Together with rare publications on the range of practices, these publications may provide practitioners and supervisors with reference points for a deeper dialogue on mutual expectations and understandings. Second, it notes that whilst most regulators still choose a narrow definition, one national regulator started applying RST at risk type level too. Similarly, a supranational body distinguishes between a general usage of RST and the specific usage for Recovery Planning purposes. Both suggest a more versatile use of the RST (supporting the central idea of this book noted here). Finally, the chapter advocates the further cross-linkage and, where meaningful, co-integration of RST with other risk and crisis management frameworks, particularly recovery and resolution planning – a view further examined in Part V of this book.

27.3 Quantitative Use Cases (Part II)

Key takeaways:
- Suitable areas for quantitative RST are progressively crystallising from existing use cases (e.g. market, credit and systemic risks).
- Existing use cases demonstrate that different models can form part of RST test designs. However, model risk remains elevated and deserves further considerations.
- Frequently stated challenges (e.g. multiplicity, complexity) are increasingly addressed and may no longer be considered insurmountable "roadblocks". Besides methodological choices, technology may prove to be a catalyst in the future (see also Part IV).

Quantitative use cases on RST are still rare. The few existing cases can be classified across the dimensions scope (portfolio, bank, banking system) and approach (qualitative and/or quantitative). In particular, at portfolio and system-wide level quantitative approaches seem to be more common. At firm wide level primarily qualitative and combinations of qualitative and quantitative approaches seem more prevalent.

Chapter 4 introduces the key elements for quantitative RST. An important challenge in designing an effective stress test is to select scenarios sufficiently extreme and plausible to allow an understanding of the key weaknesses of a bank. RST pursues the goal to highlight circumstances causing the failure of a business. In this regard, both external conditions as well as bank internal sources of risk need to be considered. A first step in building a reverse stress test is to specify a suitable objective function to embrace external and internal potential sources of insolvency. Additionally, one needs to point out that both the long term as well as the short run bank's capability to face its obligations need to be scrutinised. Furthermore, given that a bank is exposed to many interdependent risk sources, risk integration is introduced as a key element for RST. The search for extreme circumstances leading to failure needs to be conducted by using both qualitative and quantitative statistical models. As a key element for the quantitative RST, a specific focus may be addressed on bank-specific features (e.g. concentration) investigated through what-if analysis and other expert-driven investigations. External macroeconomic conditions under which a bank fails to meet its obligations constitute the final step of this comprehensive introduction to quantitative RST.

In **Chapter 5**, the key requirements for a practical reverse stress testing of a banking portfolio are proposed. Different metrics are presented to measure the severity of the stress and to identify reverse stress test scenarios that meet specified levels of loss to the portfolio. It turns out that the ability to generate scenarios across a wide range of macro-financial variables is key to a successful reverse stress test. A comparison of different approaches is performed for showing scenario generation, including macroeconomic modelling techniques, supervised machine learning, and a hybrid approach. Moreover, we discuss how to visualise and analyse the results of a reverse stress test using clustering techniques in order to derive actionable risk management and mitigation information.

In **Chapter 6**, Almehed et al. argue that liquidity stress situations which originate from funding markets becoming unavailable is one of the biggest threats for the continuity of business for banks and should therefore be subject to reverse liquidity stress testing analysis. They propose the Danger Zone approach, which was introduced for the investigation of system-wide funding liquidity risk, and is also an elegant method for the institution-specific parametrisation of funding liquidity stress which facilitates reverse stress testing. The basic assumption is that each available funding market closes suddenly but at different times as the liquidity stress increases. As the observed or assumed impact of several risk factors is harmonised and aggregated into a single Danger Zone score, the analysis of relevant root causes simplifies considerably.

Chapter 7 proposes a framework for reverse stress testing networks of direct interbank exposures. It shows how the propagation of shocks between financial institutions can be modelled by means of dynamic processes on networks. The framework is based on the so-called DebtRank algorithm, which assumes that shocks are propagated linearly between interconnected banks. The framework computes the smallest exogenous shock that, given the dynamic of shock propagation, would lead to final losses larger than a given threshold. As a use case, an application is presented to a network of 44 European banks reconstructed from partial information.

Chapter 8 presents reflections on why and how a macro RST could be conducted. It argues that – in contrast to the microprudential side – no comparable commonly understood approach would exist on the macro side. It, therefore, defines a macro RST, and discusses how a corresponding framework can be set up, taking inspiration from the way in which standard system-wide stress tests are designed and focusing on implementation aspects. As finding "a" or "the" scenario(s) is the end-objective of RST, it discusses how a scenario search exercise can be analytically embedded in a macro set-up. Finally, the chapter presents illustrative hypothetical simulation results, using bank-level data and a specific model.

With **Chapter 9**, Wälder/Wälder aim to contribute to the further development of RST by considering methods from reliability analysis. Especially analysing the hazard rate and thus the type of failures can help to understand causes of failure. From a theoretical point of view, the Weibull distribution and the IDB distribution are useful to model all types of failure. Further work is needed to validate the applicability of these models. At the same time, future advancement may result from interdisciplinary work. For example, Wälder/Wälder introduce reliability analysis and survival analysis to model lifetimes of technical components systems and organisms or creatures.

Overall, the use cases demonstrate that RST can apply different test designs and configurations choices. At the same time, quantitative approaches seem to primarily apply RST to risk types such as market, credit and systemic risk (e.g. to model the amplification and propagation of shocks). For risk types that are more difficult to model, for example reputational risks, qualitative approaches are likely to prevail in the future.

27.4 Qualitative Use Cases (Part III)

Key takeaways:
- Suitable areas for qualitative RST test designs equally emerge (e.g. difficult to quantify risks like reputational risk, smaller institutions).
- As demonstrated by existing use cases, a variety of tools and techniques may be used (e.g. cognitive maps, error trees, iterative interviews).
- Given their focus on the business model in particular, the integration of Strategic Management tools into qualitative test designs seems to deserve further consideration.
- Qualitative test designs can use different configuration settings, as demonstrated by the Mild RST approach.

In **Chapter 10**, Eichhorn/Mangold introduce a generic process orientated approach to perform RST, consisting of six steps: 1. Definition of points of failure, 2. Vulnerability analysis, 3. Generic storyboards, 4. Scenario design and parametrisation, 5. Plausibility check and management actions, 6. Monitoring and reporting. Organised around these points, the Appendix provides practical tips about what can be learned from regulatory guidance, observed practices, past failures and recent research (e.g. identification of hidden vulnerabilities for the design of new storyboards and related scenarios). Smaller institutions are particularly likely to continue choosing qualitative test designs (in line with the aforementioned regulatory principle of proportionality). Other RST users can embed quantitative approaches in the proposed approach or use the qualitative test design to incorporate difficult to quantify risks.

In **Chapter 11**, Charmaille examines the case of the Pension Protection Fund, referred to as the 'PPF'. The PPF is a non-commercial organisation only accountable to the UK Parliament where situations of failure are in general non-quantifiable. A non-quantitative approach was therefore used to reverse stress test the PPF. This chapter covers the different steps of non-quantitative reverse stress testing, from the definition of failure to the design of scenarios, with particular attention given to the use of cognitive maps for scenario design and a more general understanding of the vulnerabilities of an organisation. We explain that we can use cognitive maps in two ways for reverse stress testing. First, we can use collective maps to plot the collective knowledge and ideas of a group of Subject Matter Experts who would be asked how the organisation could fail or more generally "what could go wrong". In effect, the cognitive map is a graph where the vertices are concepts or ideas of SMEs and the edges are links between these ideas, in general cause and effect. A second use of cognitive mapping is to map the key relationships of an organisation and the interactions between them. In this case, the cognitive map is a graph where vertices are internal and external stakeholders/relationships and edges are the interactions between them. The chapter explains how, by analysing the map and in particular by identifying loops (or cycles), one can build compelling scenarios of failure to support the identification of vulnerabilities and general risk management. The chapter contributes to the future advancements of RST well beyond the usage of cognitive maps. By way of extension, the chapter implies that a wider set of analytical tools can be integrated into RST in the future (e.g. Grundke uses hierarchical error trees to discuss failure causes and derive scenario narratives from combinations of the latter for an automotive financial firm).[1]

In **Chapter 12**, Kolev argues that strategic management tools like SWOT and PESTLE analysis can support the vulnerability analysis phase of RST. Like RST, strategic management tools have a dedicated business model focus – they are designed to examine the fundamental assumptions of the business model, how vulnerable these assumptions are to stress and to capture business model uncertainties and strategic risks. Using the example of FinTech banks, the chapter demonstrated how SWOT and PESTLE analysis can help to derive plausible and relevant storyboards. Beyond the common focus on business models, the chapter outlines further considerations about how strategic management tools can support the advancement RST, including the materiality of strategic risks, the structured thought process supported by the tools and the wide range of available tools. Their integration may also be seen as a step to move RST from a one-sided, downside-only perspective towards a view of how a bank can profit from uncertainty.

In **Chapter 13**, Lodha/Eichhorn challenge the common notion that RST would by design be restricted to "Armageddon scenarios" (while steering a bank by such high-impact, low-probability tail events would be inadequate). Under the term Mild reverse stress testing (MRST), the chapter demonstrated that RST can consider adverse but less severe outcomes (e.g. a loss of $100m). For this, the chapter introduced a spectrum of approaches, including iterative expert interviews as a way to address cognitive biases. The results of another method, a historic analysis of risk factor movements, could feed a "cheat-sheet" allowing executives to instantly pinpoint which business lines are exceeding the loss threshold given the recent risk factors moves. The chapter illustrates how MRST can be used to facilitate board discussions on risk appetite and mitigation measures.

---

1 See Peter Grundke (2012): Qualitative inverse Stresstests mit Fehlerbäumen? Zeitschrift für das gesamte Kreditwesen, 65, 3, pp. 131–135.

27.5 Application of Artificial Intelligence, Quantum Computing and Technology (Part IV)

Key takeaways:
- Developments in artificial intelligence, particularly in Natural Language Processing, enrich an analysis of historical stress information through economic and social contexts, providing a broader and unbiased choice of themes that may trigger distress at firm-level or any other scope.
- All RST applications place high computational demands on banks' infrastructure to estimate prices, risk, capital and liquidity. Artificial intelligence applications and Quantum Computing methods provide an acceleration of computing from a factor of 35 to several orders of magnitude, equating to exponential benefits. This allows for a richer set of risk factors and a more exhaustive search of scenarios.
- Further relief from computational demands is given in the form of optimal hardware choice. A configuration suitable for the portfolio and calculation engines achieves accelerations by a factor of 100.
- In a detrimental stress scenario, the interplay between capital and liquidity comes to the fore and wrong-way risks materialise, an interdependency so far only qualitatively described in practice. A holistic framework shows how to rigorously model this interdependency and carry out data mining analyses.
- RST is often seen to deal with areas where internal models do not perform. At the same time, RST requires close model governance as the model risk is elevated.
- Robust model frameworks rooted in both conceptual soundness and flexible implementation enable efficient RST and withstand real-world stress scenarios.
- Artificial intelligence may well risk-manage banks and regulate the entire financial system. This will avoid failures similar to those in the past and be cost-efficient. However, regulatory AI may not consider potential causes that never materialised and might, in a fully transparent setup, enable gaming of the system.

The selection of suitable themes for RST is often limited by decision-making biases and lack of comprehensive information. Mayenberger shows in **Chapter 14** how Natural Language Processing (NLP) technology can be used to detect a bank's specific vulnerabilities and identify suitable topics for an RST narrative and scenario. The NLP methodologies detect sentiments in alternative data sources and thus identify vulnerabilities of specific banks – banks with certain business models or the financial system as a whole. Apart from using well-established search engine methods such as TF-IDF to determine salient themes in past loss events, the word embedding technology takes more context into account to understand the meaning of text information, thus boosting accuracy in the detection of relevant themes. Accuracy is improved further by fine-tuning the word embedding to coincident economic indicators of stress. The next leap will be the natural language *generation* of whole storylines based on such relevant stress topics.

RST can demand substantial computing power, particularly for revaluation of trading portfolios or for risk calculations that for each scenario require the computation of hundreds of prices, multiplying with the number of scenarios explored. In **Chapter 15**, Cotoi and Stamicar demonstrate efficiency gains by a factor of 35–40 by training Gaussian Process Regression, an AI method, for pricing a portfolio of nonlinear derivatives for a popular stochastic volatility model, the Heston model. Cotoi and Stamicar envisage further developments in the form of the extension to other option pricing models or even to the valuation of positions in the banking book whose dependence on risk factors is non-linear.

Portfolio valuation adjustments account for counterparty defaults and the ensuing funding, regulatory capital and liquidity effects, known under the collective term XVA not only present another computational challenge but also make clear the connection between capital and funding. In **Chapter 16**, Albanese, Iabichino, Mammola and Nawani introduce the new concept of funding sets in a fundamentally new approach to XVA that combines exposure, collateral and defaults into a single paradigm to assess the funding implications for the bank's obligors in a stress scenario with rising credit spreads. In **Chapter 17**, Albanese, Crepey and Iabichino present the specific implementation of this fundamentally new approach. They derive the mathematical framework that incorporates counterparty risk (CVA), funding risk (FVA), the regulatory capital effects (KVA) and even wrong-way risk through dynamic market-credit and credit-credit correlations.

All XVA methodologies share the common challenge of requiring considerable computing power. In **Chapter 18**, Bouayoun investigates the possibility of inferring the worst-case combination of scenarios, maximising the loss at a particular time horizon using quantum annealing. Bouayoun demonstrates the utilisation of Quantum Annealing to deliver the acceleration of several orders of magnitude as computational time grows linearly with the number of risk factors and not exponentially as with conventional optimisation techniques. He showcases the new methodology on specific XVA calculations. Further research for other applications of Quantum computing techniques may provide similar speed gains, particularly when the related hardware and software become more widely available.[2]

---

2 The chapter complements earlier contributions that develop proposals to deal with the relationship among the concepts of likelihood, plausibility, and representativeness and in particular multiplicity, i.e. where it is not obvious how to select the most meaningful scenarios to get reasonable coverage of the space of stressful possibilities or even to focus on those that are most probable. For example, Kopeliovich et al. begin with a specified level of loss, use principal components to construct a set of

To accelerate computations and make them more effective, in addition to the innovative methods from Artificial Intelligence and Quantum Computing, the optimal hardware choice is paramount to performance and can make a difference of up to a factor of 100. Dash provides a map to solve this challenge in the form of leveraging technology in **Chapter 19**. The appropriate choice of hardware or software is highly dependent on the specifics of the portfolio to reach the required acceleration. **Chapter 19** shows precisely how to make this optimal choice.

Further elaborating on optimal infrastructure, Mayenberger outlines a future-proof modelling framework in **Chapter 20**. During the Covid-19 crisis, market dislocations such as negative oil prices and unreliable unemployment rates have limited models' predictive power or even rendered models dysfunctional. The chapter walks the reader through changes in the model development, from assumptions to testing to infrastructure design and setup to create models that efficiently handle stress testing and RST as well as actual stress scenarios.

Chapter 21 gives a glimpse into the future: Danielsson, Macrae and Uthemann investigate the use of artificial intelligence in risk management and financial supervision. While this may be a revolutionary innovation and bring efficiency gains, there is a clear possibility that AI may destabilise markets, increase systemic risk and may invite market actors to game the system. In the application to financial regulation, AI can be well trained to prevent scenarios similar to past failures but will not recognise new dangers. Future research may investigate how a regulatory machine can learn to look outside historical scenarios for systemic risks.

27.6 RST and its Link to Recovery and Resolution Planning (Part V)

> Key takeaways:
> - The integration of all scenario-based frameworks in the bank's infrastructure enables the running of ad-hoc scenarios for executive decision-making.
> - To implement such an integration, strengthen the cross-linkage of RST with other risk and crisis management frameworks, conceptually and implementation-wise, particularly recovery and resolution planning (RRP).

---

alternative scenarios that produce the same level of loss but in (maximally) different ways and choose the most likely scenario that generates that loss. (See Yaacov Kopeliovich, Arcady Novosyolov, Daniel Satchkov and Barry Schachter (2013): "Robust Risk Estimation and Hedging: A reverse stress testing Approach".)

In **Chapter 22**, Ahmad highlights the similarities between the recovery and resolution planning process and the RST process, both from a framework and an implementation perspective. He also shows how these two processes can mutually leverage and enrich each other, especially once RST has been properly extended and generalised. The synergies cover identification of vulnerabilities, selection of scenarios, choice of metrics and corresponding thresholds, reinforcement of the control framework, scope and impact of management actions, and the creation of a firm-wide database of standardised scenario case studies.

Chapter 23 further emphasises that bridging RST, RRP and other contingency frameworks offers the chance to develop one overall more coherent framework. The UK PRA already requires firms to integrate ILAAP into the ICAAP, thereby acknowledging the intrinsic dependency of capital and liquidity. Similarly, the FRB requires that banks include the recovery and resolution planning into the capital planning (CCAR) submission. Consequently, the determination of which path – recovery or resolution – each bank takes provides supervisory authorities with salient information for contingency plans in case of severe stress.

27.7 Governance (Part VI)

Key takeaways:
- The financial system cannot be governed in the same way that may be appropriate for other complex systems in natural science disciplines such as geology or meteorology. In the absence of a far more comprehensive understanding of risk, the importance of having experienced non-executive directors on the boards of financial institutions is vital to the better governance of financial institutions, including a better understanding of the tail risks they run both individually and collectively.
- Irrespective of the sparse literature, relevant sources exist to inform challenges and reviews of RST work by governance bodies. Besides analyses of past failures (see also Part II and Part III of this book), recent research can be a helpful source.
- RST users must search for ways to make RST much more useful for decision-makers. This should include the transition to dynamic stress simulations.

In **Chapter 24**, Davies highlights the challenges of governing RST from a non-executive director perspective. His starting contention was that economics and finance are different and are, in many ways, far more difficult to govern than other complex systems. What we have today with stress testing, of which reverse stress testing is a key part, would be an intuitive and easy to understand basis for setting a "state of the world" against which we can establish the regulatory capital requirements of banks. It would be, however, a process that is increasingly far removed from our growing understanding of the extremely complex nature of risk in financial institutions and markets and indeed how financial risk can propagate through the economy to produce systemic risk. The challenge we faced would be to incorporate the results of new research into system dynamics and how sentiment affects these dynamics into our construction of scenarios and thus the capital and liquidity requirements resulting from stress tests of individual banks and of the banking system as a whole. This chapter concludes by proposing that against this background the importance of experience is vital to a good understanding of risk and that the board's non-executive directors play a vital role in creating a better understanding of risk at both the institutional and systemic level.

Chapter 25 presents a portfolio of selected contributions co-authored by Danielsson. Topics covered include the short-term bias in Risk Measurement, Cyber Risk, Political Risk, Model Risk, Systemic Risk and the endogenous nature of the latter. The chapter demonstrates how recent research can help RST users to identify 'white spaces' and inform new scenario narratives. Section 25.1 argues that the type of risk we would most care about is long-term – what happens over years or decades. However, we would tend to manage that risk over short periods. To mitigate this dissonance of the short and long term, the chapter proposes the following steps: focus on resilience; avoid inferring long-run risk from the short run; and use scenario planning. Section 25.2 considers low risk as a predictor of financial crises. It argues that while most indicators consider an observation of high volatility a warning signal, such an alarm would come too late, arriving only once a crisis is already underway. A better warning would be provided by low volatility, which represented a reliable indication of an increased likelihood of a future crisis. Section 25.3 argues that both the integrity and the legitimacy of macroprudential policy would depend on political risk being included. Yet it would be usually excluded from macropru, which could be a fatal flaw. Section 25.4 challenges the common claim that the threat to the financial system posed by cyber risk would be systemic. It argues that almost all cyber risk would be microprudential. Moreover, the discussion seemed to be too focused on IT considerations and not enough on economic consequences. Section 25.5 analyses how the models failed in crises and questions their prominent use in the post-crisis reform process. It argues that over-relying on market data and statistical forecasting models would have the potential to further destabilise the financial system. Section 25.6, on modelling financial turmoil through endogenous risk, argues that actions that an individual institution takes to enhance its soundness may undermine the soundness of others. If the purposes of financial regulation were to shield the financial system from collapse, it would be a deeply flawed practice to base financial regulation on the best practice of individually optimal risk management policies. Risk would be endogenous, and individually optimal risk management would make systemic financial crises sharper, larger and more costly.

In **Chapter 26**, Ivantsov analyses why RST's potential remains underused and offers some changes that should make RST much more useful for decision-makers.

His analysis suggests that there are four areas of the RST process that banks need to improve if they want to open up the full potential of RST as an effective risk management tool. The main weaknesses with a use of RST can be divided into the following groups: weaknesses in the scenario development and scenario selection process, overreliance on stress impact quantification, oversimplification of RST methodology (e.g. ignoring the stress dynamics, interconnectedness and sequencing of events when modelling scenarios), underestimation of the importance of the development of a mitigating action plan which leads to the relegation of the contingency planning to an ancillary element of RST. In this chapter, Ivantsov focuses on these four weaknesses and suggests improvements based on the industry's best practices. The most important improvements that were suggested include an enrichment of the RST scenarios, focusing on the RST process and senior management's dialogue, a transition to dynamic stress simulation and a development of credible and actionable contingency planning.

27.8 Summary

> Key takeaways:
> - Overall, RST can be a rather potent tool to deliver actionable information to executives on the most relevant risks of their business model and the related planning options for rapid response. As such, RST deserves further investments of time and efforts to increase bank stability and risk-adjusted profitability.
> - RST can be a relevant tool in the future as it supports the agenda of Chief Risk Officers as well as important shifts that will underpin innovative risk management practices going forward.

On balance, the book demonstrates that various challenges discussed in **Chapter 1** and throughout other chapters can be addressed (e.g. lack of regulatory guidance and absence on standard practices, challenges related to focus on high-severity, low-probability events, downside-only measure, cognitive biases in scenario narratives, complexity challenges).

The book also derives various proposals for the further development of RST. In fact, the main limitation of RST may not be the limitations of RST itself (which will also differ between configuration sets and test designs), but our own thinking. Systematically applied and further developed, RST promises to be one of the methods that has the potential to deliver on the expectations and meet the criteria for tools of the future.

For example, the Chief Risk Officer of a G-SIB bank reportedly tasked the function with the following practices:
- Coverage of firm risks and "white spaces"
- Elevate management of new risks
- Provide cross-bank strategic insights
- Monitor and challenge known risks while also illuminating unknown risks
- Allow pre-emptive and dynamic management of risks by better connecting the dots
- Being forward-looking and externally aware
- Support the firm strategy by ensuring that risk-based returns are appropriate

The Deputy Governor of the Bank Negara Malaysia identified three shifts in her opening speech at the Malaysian Association of Risk and Insurance Management (MARIM) Conference in 2018 "Innovative Risk Management: GO BOLA! (Go Beyond, Go Original, Go Agile, Go Ahead)":

> There is no question that risk and insurance managers today face significant uncertainty. ... This in turn calls for new ways of managing and thinking about risk. ... For many organisations, current approaches to risk management are likely to be already severely deficient in this new environment. ... Three important shifts ... will underpin innovative risk management practices going forward. ... First is the changing role and focus of risk managers in supporting business decision-making. Second is a shift from risk measures to risk narratives. And third is an increasing emphasis on building resilience alongside the prevailing focus on averting risks.

RST seems to support the aforementioned practices and shifts. Thereby it can equally incorporate lessons learned from past failures (e.g. causes, event chains, interdependencies) and insights from recent research (e.g. potential "white spaces"). As exemplified throughout this book (e.g. **Chapter 9** and **Chapter 11**), RST can also be a vehicle for banks and regulators to take new themes forward. This includes emerging risk stripes, for example:
- Catastrophic risks
- Sustainability risks, including climate risk (e.g. "green swans")
- Novel risks

RST can (potentially better than most traditional stress tests) incorporate these and other risks. Most importantly, it can link them directly to the business model whereby the flexibility allows for bespoke test designs and configuration sets.

At the same time, the future of RST may be dependent on how well it masters this integration and evolves itself – a point illustrated in the context of systemic risk by Davies, author of **Chapter 24**:

> What we have today with stress testing and scenario analysis, of which reverse stress testing is a key part, is an intuitive and easy to understand basis for setting a "state of the world" against which we can establish the regulatory capital requirements of banks. It is, however, a process

that is increasingly far removed from our growing understanding of the extremely complex nature of risk in financial institutions and markets and indeed how financial risk can propagate through the economy to produce systemic risk. The challenge we face is to incorporate the results of research into system dynamics and how sentiment affects these dynamics into our construction of scenarios and thus the capital and liquidity requirements resulting from stress tests of individual banks will impact the banking system as a whole.

In summary, RST users should further complement sensitivity analysis and scenario analysis with RST. Thereby, they should experiment with different RST test designs, work on the cross-linkage of RST with other risk and crisis management frameworks (including recovery and resolution planning) and relentlessly incorporate relevant new (research) insights to evolve and remain relevant.

We hope the book provided inspiration and helped readers to build and expand their own RST toolbox and to further develop their current practices in the future!

List of Abbreviations

a.o.	among others
App	application
BBA	British Banker's Association
CFB	Corporate Finance biz
CET1	Common Equity Tier 1
DC	District of Columbia
EBA	European Banking Authority
EEA	European Economic Area
EU	European Union
EY	Ernst & Young
e.g.	exempli gratia
etc.	et cetera
f.	following
FCA	Financial Conduct Authority
GBP	Great Britain Pound
GDPR	General Data Protection Regulation
HQLA	high-quality liquid asset
IMF	International Monetary Fund
NMD	non-maturing deposits
No	numero
PESTLE	political, economical, social, technological, legal, environmental
PTI	pre-tax income
RST	reverse stress testing
RWA	risk weighted assets
SEC	Securities and Exchange Commission
SS	supervisory statement
SWOT	strengths, weaknesses, opportunities, threats
UK	United Kingdom
US	United States
USD	United States Dollar
USP	unique selling proposition

https://doi.org/10.1515/9783110647907-028

List of Figures

https://doi.org/10.1515/9783110647907-029

List of Tables

https://doi.org/10.1515/9783110647907-030

About the Editors

Michael Eichhorn is an honorary professor at Hochschule Harz, University of Applied Sciences, Germany and a faculty member of Bank Treasury Risk Management, London. He received his PhD degree in Business Administration from the University of Luneburg. Michael works as a Managing Director in the Global Head of Treasury and Liquidity Risk function at Credit Suisse Group. Prior to this, he worked for eight years at the Royal Bank of Scotland Group in different roles, including Head of Market Risk, Wealth Management Division and Group Treasury Chief Risk Officer. Michael has (co)authored 60+ publications, mainly on Treasury, Risk and Audit topics, in German and international journals, including articles on reverse stress testing in the *International Journal for Banking Law and Regulation* (2015) and the *Handbook of ALM in Banking* (2017). Michael has given numerous training courses, seminars and conference presentations on risk management and qualitative methods in Europe and Asia.

Tiziano Bellini is Director at BlackRock Financial Market Advisory (FMA) in London. Previously he worked at Barclays Investment Bank, EY Financial Advisory Services in London, HSBCs headquarters, Prometeia in Bologna, and other leading Italian companies. He is a guest lecturer at Imperial College in London and at the London School of Economics and Political Science. Formerly, he served as a lecturer at the University of Bologna and the University of Parma. Tiziano is author of *Stress Testing and Risk Integration in Banks: A Statistical Framework and Practical Software* Guide (in Matlab and R), and *IFRS 9 and CECL Credit Risk Modelling and Validation: A Practical Guide with Examples Worked in R and SAS*, both edited by Academic Press. He has published in the *European Journal of Operational Research*, *Computational Statistics and Data Analysis*, and other top-reviewed journals. He has given numerous training courses, seminars, and conference presentations on statistics, risk management, and quantitative methods in Europe, Asia, and Africa. Tiziano received his PhD in Statistics from the University of Milan after being a visiting PhD student at the London School of Economics and Political Science. He is a Qualified Chartered Accountant and Registered Auditor.

Daniel Mayenberger has in-depth quantitative expertise across asset class and is an experienced leader of large global teams. He has held a variety of positions in modelling and risk management at Barclays, Credit Suisse, Bank of America, Deutsche Bank and KPMG. At Barclays, he covered model applications such as ICAAP, firm-wide stress testing, IFRS9, VaR, pricing models, counterparty credit, economic capital, treasury/liquidity and artificial intelligence/machine learning, defining the framework standards for these model applications to ensure their effective integration into the firm's business and the consistency of modelling standards globally. Before joining Barclays, Daniel worked at Credit Suisse as Global Head of Portfolio Model Risk Management, leading a global team for CCAR, firm-wide stress testing, ICAAP, economic capital, liquidity and treasury models. He developed the model framework for stress testing models and covered the public 2018 CCAR submission which the bank passed for the first time. Prior to that, he was Head

https://doi.org/10.1515/9783110647907-031

of Enterprise Model Risk Methodology at Bank of America, devising top-level business strategies for models used to underwrite $1.1tn in credits, manage $900bn of mortgage servicing rights and price a $1.8tn derivatives portfolio. Before that, Daniel held positions in Portfolio Risk Management at Deutsche Bank and Financial Risk Management at KPMG. He frequently speaks at high-profile international conferences on the latest methodologies such as artificial intelligence and machine learning. Daniel holds a doctorate in Pure Mathematics from the University of Trier and an executive MBA with distinction from the London Business School.

List of Contributors

Nasir M. Ahmad is the Managing Partner at Basinghall Analytics, a specialist risk consultancy focused on risk management. He leads the strategy of the firm as well as business and solution development. In addition, he focuses on the provision of strategic advice across all areas of prudential regulation, quantitative analytics, risk management, and compliance. Nasir has around 25 years of experience working for leading financial institutions (Royal Bank of Canada, Toronto Dominion Bank, BlackRock) and advisory firms (EY, Arthur Andersen and Parker Fitzgerald). His recent assignments include stress testing, funding in resolution, quantitative models, capital and liquidity management, and implementation of financial regulation. He frequently engages with regulatory authorities on key issues relating to approval of internal models, design of frameworks and other prudential matters. Nasir holds an MSc in Theoretical Physics and a PhD in Mathematics from the Swiss Federal Institute of Technology in Lausanne (EPFL).

Claudio Albanese holds a PhD in Physics from ETH Zurich and gained post-doctoral experience at New York University and Princeton. As an Associate Professor of Mathematics, he founded the master's programme in Mathematical Finance at the University of Toronto and was then appointed Chair of Mathematical Finance at Imperial College London. In 2006, he left academia to pursue software development based on his prior research and founded Global Valuation in London. He contributed the software to the TriOptima XVA service which recently received several industry awards. Claudio published extensively on FVA, KVA, reverse stress testing, initial margin, derivatives pricing and model risk.

Daniel Almehed is a Senior Business Advisor at BearingPoint and a senior expert in the risk management consultancy team within their Banking and Capital Markets practice. Daniel has a specific focus on Treasury risk controlling and management, covering IRRBB & liquidity risk. His projects cover governance aspects (e.g. 3 lines of defence concept), development of risk measurement methodologies and ALM & Risk software implementation. Daniel is a treasury risk expert with more than 10 years' experience in a variety of different roles in consultancy projects for international acting banking groups. He is a regular trainer and author for IRRBB and liquidity risk topics. Daniel holds a doctorate in Theoretical Physics from the Technical University of Dresden.

Assad Bouayoun has over 15 years of quantitative analysis experience in investment banking. He is a quantitative finance specialist focusing on total valuation including funding and capital cost, xVA, risk, stress and reverse stress testing. He was responsible for designing industry standard hedging and pricing systems in equity derivatives during his time in Commerzbank and had the same responsibility in credit derivatives while working for Credit Agricole, and also in xVA in institutions like Lloyds, RBS and Scotiabank. He led the modelling team responsible for the research and development of the simulation engines used for exposure computation within HSBC in London. Now he is XVA and Credit Derivative quantitative analyst at Daiwa. During the different projects Assad has undertaken in quantitative finance, he integrated or evaluated new technologies such as Cloud, GPU and QPU; new design (parallelisation using graphs) as well as new numerical methods such as AAD. He also participated in the firmwide data standardisation and integration that are essential aspects of the success of these projects. He is also leading an effort to leverage quantum annealing for financial quantitative reverse stress testing. He holds a MSc in Mathematical Trading and Finance from Cass Business School and an MSc in Applied Mathematics and Computer Science from University of Technology of Compiegne, France (UTC).

https://doi.org/10.1515/9783110647907-032

Fabio Caccioli is a lecturer in the Department of Computer Science at University College London. He was previously a research associate in the Centre for Risk Studies, University of Cambridge, and a postdoctoral fellow at the Santa Fe Institute (Santa Fe, US). Fabio holds a PhD in Statistical Physics from the International School for Advanced Studies (Trieste, Italy).

Jean-Pierre Charmaille is a Risk professional with in-depth knowledge of financial risk management, Asset-Liability management of pension funds and insurance companies, scenario analysis, stress testing and reverse stress testing. He acquired this expertise mainly at the Pension Protection Fund, which he joined at its creation in 2005. There, among other achievements, he led the development of the PPF stochastic model, developed the PPF financial risk management framework and the PPF scenario and stress testing framework. He also devised an innovative approach to reverse stress testing and has become an expert in the field. Before joining the PPF, Jean-Pierre lived in France and was responsible for asset-liability management at the ACM (Assurances du Credit Mutuel) and prior to that, as a bond portfolio manager at the MAIF (Mutuel d'Assurance des Instituteurs de France). Jean-Pierre graduated at the ENSAE-PARIS TECH, the French national school of economics and statistics. He is a CFA charter-holder and holds a PRM certificate (professional risk management certificate from PRMIA). Jean-Pierre created his consultancy business, Risk Modelling Consulting Ltd, to support small- and medium-sized organisations in the development and implementation of risk models.

Iulian Cotoi is Managing Director and Head of Quantitative Analytics at Qontigo (formerly Axioma). He heads the global Analytics department, which comprises Quantitative Analytics, Risk Analytics, Data Analytics, and Core Analytics. Quantitative Analytics creates and maintains valuation models for equity, FX, interest-rate, commodity, and hybrid derivatives. Risk Analytics produces stress tests, measures of value at risk, and risk-decomposition analytics. Data Analytics develops data-derivation and machine-learning processes. Core Analytics is responsible for software architecture. Before joining Axioma, Cotoi was Executive Director at AIG, where he led a team that produced and calibrated economic scenarios for all business lines, evaluated and proposed risk methodologies and factor models, oversaw CCAR review, and conducted stress testing research and development. Earlier, he was with Barclays, where as Vice President in Market Analytics, he focused on value-at-risk add-ons, risk allocation, and missing-data imputation. Before working at Barclays, he was a quantitative analyst at RiskMetrics, where he developed valuation models for multi-asset class derivatives.

Cotoi holds a Bachelor of Science in Mathematics from the University of Bucharest, a Diplôme d'Etudes Approfondies and PhD in Applied Mathematics from the University Blaise Pascal II, where he specialised in homogenisation of partial differential equations. He also holds a master of science in Financial Mathematics and Computation Finance from the University of Montreal. He pursued postdoctoral studies at École de Technologie Supérieure, Ecole Polytechnique, and Institut de Mathématiques Appliquées de Grenoble on grants from NASA, Bombardier, and Agfa.

Jon Danielsson is one of the two Directors of The Systemic Risk Centre. The Centre was set up to study the risks that may trigger the next financial crisis and to develop tools to help policymakers and financial institutions become better prepared. Jon holds a PhD in Economics from Duke University and is currently Associate Professor of Finance at the London School of Economics and Political Science (LSE). His research interests cover systemic risk, financial risk, econometrics, economic theory and financial crisis. Jon has written two books (*Financial Risk Forecasting*, and *Global Financial Systems: Stability and Risk*) and has published articles in leading academic journals.

Sidhartha Dash is a Research Director at Chartis research with more than 20 years of experience in the financial, energy and commodities markets in various functions across the trade and software development lifecycles. He has held various roles in product development, trading, risk management, software development and consulting in banks, hedge funds, and risk advisory and software firms, including Standard Chartered Bank, TCG Group, HCL and Cognizant. Sid's specific areas of interest and research include risk data, model risk management, quantitative models in illiquid markets, high-performance analytics, energy and commodity trading risk, market structure design, new computational models, and the use of innovative mathematical methods in various emerging areas of risk management.

Heike Dengler is Head of Market Conformity Control at UBS Europe SE with over 20 years of experience in capital markets. She has worked on the sell side in trading and research as well as on the buy side, managing fixed income and balanced funds. Prior to the current role, at the time of making of this article, she has worked for EY in consulting and auditing in the field of market and liquidity risk. She also teaches at the Frankfurt School of Finance and Management. Heike holds a PhD in Mathematics from Cornell University.

Philipp Gann is Professor for Finance with a major focus on Risk Management and Treasury at Munich University of Applied Sciences (MUAS). Prior to joining MUAS in spring 2020, Philipp spent over ten years in different risk management functions of BayernLB Munich and was - among others - responsible for the group-wide conventional and reverse stress testing, Recovery Planning and the consistency of BayernLB's overall ICAAP.

Jérôme Henry is Principal Adviser in the ECB Macroprudential policy and financial stability area. His responsibilities cover financial stability assessments, including via stress testing, and related infrastructure requirements. He led ECB teams for the Quality Assurance of SSM stress tests and was involved in country crisis management. He also worked at the BIS as an FSI fellow. Jérôme was beforehand a long-standing Eurosystem forecast coordinator. He started at the ECB leading the macromodelling team. He arrived in Frankfurt 25 years ago, to prepare Monetary Union, after being a macroeconomist with Banque de France. Prior to his central bank career, he conducted research at the OFCE and the INSEE. Jérôme has numerous academic publications, such as in the Review of Economics and Statistics and with Cambridge University Press, with contributions on stress testing such as the ECB STAMP€ e-book. He is a founding member of the CEPR Euro-Area Business Cycle Network. An ENSAE graduate, Jérôme holds a PhD in Economics and a BA in History from Paris Sorbonne.

Stefano Iabichino earned his PhD in Quantitative Finance at the University of Rome Tor Vergata in 2015, and he holds an MSc in Finance from LUISS "Guido Carli" in Rome. Currently, he is a Vice President at JP Morgan Chase in London, where he works in the model risk division, covering Counterparty Credit Risk. Before working for JP Morgan Chase, Stefano worked at Global Valuation Ltd, where, with Claudio Albanese, he developed cutting-edge solutions for XVA computation. Stefano has led workshops, including Global Derivatives Rising Starts, in London and mainland Europe.

Evgueni Ivantsov is the Chairman of the European Risk Management Council and the author of *Heads or Tails: Financial Disaster, Risk Management and Survival Strategy in the World of Extreme Risk*. He is a member of the Advisory Group on Global Risks of the World Economic Forum and an external advisor to European Investment Bank. Evgueni has a more than 20-year career in the banking sector working in global and large banks. His most recent role in banking was the Head of Portfolio Management & Strategy at Lloyds Banking Group. Prior to this role, he worked at HSBC as the Head of Global Analytics and the Head of Portfolio Risk Europe. Evgueni also worked in senior risk management roles at ING Group and Banque Bruxelles Lambert. In his risk management career, he was responsible for various areas like stress testing, risk appetite, capital management, portfolio risk optimisation and risk modelling and analytics. Dr. Ivantsov was also a Visiting Professor of Cass Business School (City University, London), a Visiting Professor of International Economics at Boston University and a Visiting Professor of Money, Banking and Credit at the United Business Institutes in Brussels.

Magdalena Kolev is an MBA student at the University of Leipzig in Germany. She received her bachelor's degree at Harz University of Applied Science (Hochschule Harz) in 2019, specialising in Financial Risk Management and International Accounting. As part of her degree, she completed a full year at the Burgundy School of Business in Lyon, France. Prior to that she gained experience in the field of finance and regulatory affairs during internships at KPMG in Frankfurt, Germany and Dominion Lending Centres in Toronto, Canada. During her studies, her research work focussed on the use of strategic management tools in the reverse stress testing process.

Meha Lodha is the Program Lead for the newly launched Climate Risk Program at UBS, which is setting the bank's course for embedding climate risk into the risk management and control framework. Meha is leading the initiave to develop methodologies to conduct climate risk scenario analysis and build internal capabilities to manage physical and transition risks arising from climate change. Before joining UBS, Meha worked as Senior Manager for Treasury & Liquidity Risk Management at Credit Suisse where she led a portfolio of cross-risk integration workstreams and was instrumental in establishing second line of defence coverage for a strategic liquidity management programme. Meha also introduced RDARR (BCBS 239) regulatory compliance for Treasury Risk. Meha has shared her knowledge on Mild reverse stress testing and BCBS 239 RDARR in international conferences and academic journal articles.

Paolo Mammola is the UK Chief Risk Officer for Citigroup. His position involves risk management responsibility over all type of risks booked onto the UK Legal Entities, including Credit, Counterparty, Market, Liquidity and Operational risks. Citi's UK Legal entities under Mr. Mammola's remit comprise Citigroup Global Markets Limited (of which Mr. Mammola is the CRO) and Citibank NA London Branch, which are two very large risk management hubs for Citi's international corporate and investment banking activity.

Philippe Mangold serves as the Deputy Global Head of Credit Portfolio Management at Credit Suisse. Previously, he held roles in different risk management disciplines. He covered stress testing and scenario analysis, liquidity risks, and banking book market risks in distinct capacities. Philippe graduated with a master's degree in Econometrics & Mathematical Economics from the London School of Economics and holds a PhD in Economics from the University of Basel. He is also a associate professor in finance at the University of Basel and the Federal Institute of Technology (ETH) in Zurich.

Paolo Mammola is the UK Chief Risk Officer for Citigroup. His position involves risk management responsibility over all type of risks booked onto the UK Legal Entities, including Credit, Counterparty, Market, Liquidity and Operational risks. Citi's UK Legal entities under Mr. Mammola's remit comprise Citigroup Global Markets Limited (of which Mr. Mammola is the CRO) and Citibank NA London Branch which are two very large risk management hubs for Citi's international corporate and investment banking activity.

Before Citi, Mr. Mammola held several senior positions in Risk, most notably at Barclays where he was Global Head of Market Risk for the Investment bank, Interim Group Head of Financial Risk and Global Head of Counterparty Risk for the Investment bank. Mr. Mammola's career also includes a period as regulator at the Italian securities and exchange regulator (CONSOB) where he was a senior officer in the Markets division.

Bahram Mirzai is a managing partner at EVMTech. He has over 20 years of experience in banking, quantitative finance, and risk management. In recent years, he has focused on the development of scenario generation applications and has led numerous projects in the areas of stress testing, scenario design, and IFRS 9 with banking institutions primarily in Europe and North America. Bahram has contributed to the Financial Stability Institute's seminars for senior regulators. He has also been frequently invited to speak on risk management topics before the major regulatory authorities, including the Basel Committee on Banking Supervision, the Board of Governors of the Federal Reserve System, Bank of England and FINMA. Bahram studied Physics at ETH Zurich and Cambridge University, England. He holds a PhD in Neural Networks from ETH and is a Certified European Financial Analyst.

Torsten Pfoh is a Senior Consultant at BearingPoint and is an expert in the risk management consultancy team within their Banking and Capital Markets practice. His projects cover development of risk measurement methodologies, ALM & Risk software implementation and specification of data interfaces. Torsten is a treasury risk expert in a variety of different roles in consultancy projects for international acting banking groups. Torsten holds a doctorate in Theoretical Physics from the University of Mainz.

Aaron Romano is a Vice President within Credit Suisse's Liquidity Risk Management function. His expertise lies in the development of liquidity risk frameworks to address organisational and regulatory requirements. He has been instrumental in helping Credit Suisse establish its Second Line of Defence operating model for Liquidity and Treasury Risk. He has experience in developing stress scenarios for funding in resolution and recovery and resolution planning. Aaron previously worked at Ernst & Young and specialised in Treasury and Liquidity Risk initiatives at Global Systemically Important Banks. Aaron holds a Bachelor of Science degree in Finance from Iowa State University and recently completed the Bank Treasury Risk Management Certification, where he was awarded the Wiley Prize for the highest-performing student in his cohort.

Thomas Steiner is a Partner at BearingPoint and is responsible for their Banking and Capital Markets practice with a special focus on the risk management consultancy practice. Thomas and his team are covering a comprehensive service portfolio for financial institution's risk controlling and management functions, such as Banking Book risk controlling and management, covering IRRBB, Liquidity risk and FTP, among other things. Their services cover governance aspects (e.g. set up the 3 lines of defence concept), development of methodology and ALM software implementation. Prior to that, he was Head of Requirement Engineering at MEAG Asset Management, responsible for the business requirements of the Risk Controlling/Management function. Thomas is an ALM expert with more than 15 years' experience in a variety of different roles in consultancy projects for international acting banking groups. He is a member of the Global Association of Risk Professionals (GARP).

Robert Stamicar is Head of Risk Modelling within the Global Multi-Asset Solutions team at QMA. In his capacity, he is responsible for quantitative risk modelling research for multi-asset investments. Prior to joining QMA, Robert was the Head of Multi-Asset Class Research at Axioma, where he was responsible for the design and extension of risk methodologies supporting asset managers and hedge funds. Robert also served as the Head of Risk Research at Lighthouse Partners, a fund of hedge funds that specialises in managed account investments. Previously, he worked at RiskMetrics as Head of Research and as a Risk Manager at the Royal Bank of Canada.

Robert's articles have appeared in *The Journal of Portfolio Management*, *The Journal of Credit Risk*, *RiskMetrics Journal, and Axioma In-Practice Series*. Robert earned a PhD in Applied Mathematics from McMaster University in Canada.

Index

https://doi.org/10.1515/9783110647907-033

The Moorad Choudhry Global Banking Series

Principles of Green Banking: Managing Environmental Risk and Sustainability
by Suborna Barua

Bank Asset Liability Management Best Practice: Yesterday, Today and Tomorrow
by Polina Bardaeva

Reverse Stress Testing in Banking: A Comprehensive Guide
by Michael Eichhorn, Tiziano Bellini, and Daniel Mayenberger (eds.)

Random Walks in Fixed Income and Foreign Exchange: Unexpected Discoveries in Issuance, Investment and Hedging of Yield Curve Instruments
by Jessica James, Michael Leister and Christoph Rieger